Chapter 4

COMPARATIVE LAW

AN OVERVIEW OF THE DISCIPLINE

Mathias Reimann*

* Hessel E. Yntema Professor of Law, The University of Michigan, Ann Arbor, Mich. The author is greatly indebted to the research staff of the University of Michigan Law Library, especially Keith Lacey, Virginia Neisler and Seth Quidacy-Swan, for their superb and untiring assistance.

I. INTRODUCTION AND OVERVIEW

1. *Purpose and scope of this introduction.* – Understanding comparative law first requires coming to grips with the term itself to survey the activities it comprises and to grasp some fundamental issues characterizing the discipline as a whole. This introduction discusses these matters in order to map the terrain, to set the tone, and to provide an overview for the reader who merely wants a general sense of what comparative law is about. It thus addresses the discipline's definition (A.), four major dimensions (B.), and three pervasive questions pertaining to its character (C.). The discussion of these topics remains on a preliminary level. Matters requiring a more in-depth treatment are more extensively analyzed in subsequent parts, especially the discipline's coverage (IV.), its uses and goals (V.), and its orientations, approaches and methods (VI.).

A. COMPARATIVE LAW DEFINED

2. *The basic term and its pitfalls.* – Comparative law is not a kind of law but its comparative study. It is thus the legal branch, so to speak, of "the broader field of the comparative disciplines which explore the similarities and dissimilarities of different cultural or social phenomena",[1] like comparative linguistics or comparative religion. While that seems easy enough, the term "comparative law" is somewhat problematic because it is potentially misleading and has not always been consistently employed.

"Comparative law" is potentially misleading because to the uninitiated it is apt to suggest that there is body of legal rules that apply to comparisons, just like criminal law is a body of legal rules that apply to crimes. Yet, there is no such body of legal rules for the discipline to study. Other languages avoid this pitfall by using more appropriate terms, namely "law compared" (*droit comparé, diritto comparato, derecho comparado,* etc.) or "the comparison of law" (Rechtsvergleichung, rechtsverglijking, etc.). It would be preferable to speak of the "comparative study of law" in English as well. The traditional term, however, is so firmly entrenched that there is no hope of replacing it on a broad scale, and this contribution will use it as well.

The term "comparative law" and its current equivalents in other languages must also be approached with circumspection because jurists have variously employed other terms as well. In the nineteenth century, for example, "comparative legislation" or "comparative jurisprudence" was popular. In a sense, these terms were simply particular variations of comparative law, the former being geared especially towards lawmaking, the latter related to general legal theory. But where the usage of these older terms has survived, as with the French "legislation comparé", they have over time become by and large co-terminous with "comparative law". In addition, authors today often speak of "comparative legal systems", "comparative legal traditions", or just "comparative legal studies"; sometimes such terms describe a specific approach, sometimes they are used simply as alternatives to the more time-worn "comparative law". In light of these terminological variations across time and space, the term "comparative law" does not have a singular, precise, and uniform meaning.

3. *Over- and under-inclusiveness of "comparative".* – In addition to these basic terminological caveats, the term "comparative law" is both over- and under-inclusive. It is too broad because the discipline is not engaged in the comparison of law *tout court.* Lawyers compare law all the time. In order to establish which norms are valid, which norms apply to a concrete case, or which norms produce the better outcome, they compare constitutions with statutes, statutes with judicial decisions, older norms with newer rules, and general provisions with specific ones. By far most of the time, however, lawyers engage in such comparisons within the parameters of one legal system. This is not what is meant by "comparative

[1] *Jansen,* Comparative Law and Comparative Knowledge: *Reimann and Zimmermann* (eds.), The Oxford Handbook of Comparative Law (ed. 2 Oxford 2019) 291–319, 292.

 | DOI: 10.1163/2589-4021_IECO_COM_0204TOC

law". Instead, the discipline is defined by its focus on the comparison between the laws of different systems. It is thus the very essence of comparative law that it looks across borders.

At the same time, the term is under-inclusive because it suggests that the discipline is engaged only in comparison. In practice, however, other activities are comprised by that term as well, especially the study of foreign law. While these other activities are related to comparison in one way or another, they do not necessarily engage in it, at least not in an explicit fashion (see *infra* B.).

4. *Broad meaning of "law".* – In contrast to some earlier contexts where the discipline focused almost exclusively on specific kinds of law, especially on legislation (see *supra* s. 3.), its province today is "law" in an extremely broad sense. To be sure, the discipline's primary object continues to be the official law of one or more nation states; this includes studies of positive law in the form of legislatively or judicially created rules as well as the study of legal institutions and procedures. Yet, comparative law has also begun to address law beyond the nation state; this includes comparisons with or among legal systems on the inter- and supranational level as well as work on private ordering, i.e., non-state law.[2]

Today, it is generally accepted that the discipline should look at law in as broad a context as possible. In particular, it must aim to understand legal rules and institutions in relation to their historical, philosophical, political, social, and economic background. It should also reach beyond law and consider non-legal mechanisms of social control which in one society may perform the function that legal rules perform in another. Of course, these requirements describe ambition more accurately than practice. They set an ideal that real comparative law work never reaches, good work merely approaches, and most work by and large fails.

5. *Summary.* – Comparative law thus consists of the comparative study of law across different legal systems as well as of various other closely related activities, considering law potentially in all its forms and ideally in all its contexts.

B. FOUR DIMENSIONS OF THE DISCIPLINE – DESCRIBING, COMPARING, MAPPING, AND TRACING LAW

6. *A multi-dimensional discipline.* – Comparative law is, like comparative literature or comparative political studies, an umbrella term for a discipline with multiple dimensions. In practice, most comparative lawyers pursue one of four principal activities (which are then employed for a multitude of purposes). If one lists these activities in the order of their prevalence, one can say that comparative lawyers describe and analyze foreign law; compare the laws of different systems, traditions or cultures; map law on a regional or worldwide scale; and trace the development of law by virtue of borrowing between systems.[3] These four basic activities constitute the main branches of the discipline today – not for any logical reason but simply because this is how comparative law has developed. We will briefly survey these activities here and then delve into them more deeply later (*infra* VI.A.).

7. *Describing foreign law.* – Comparative law encompasses the study of law other than one's own, i.e., usually the law of a foreign country. It is of course true that "the mere study of foreign law falls short of being comparative".[4] But it is also true that studying foreign law is part of comparative law as a discipline, and an important one at that. This is so for at least four reasons. The first reason is factual: studying (and describing) foreign law is what most jurists understanding themselves as comparative lawyers actually do most of the time, and this includes authors who deny such study the status of true comparative law.[5] The second reason is logical: the study of foreign law is the indispensable first step of the comparative process because it produces the material that can then be compared with one's

[2] See *infra* V.A.

[3] This already shows that, at least today, the definition given by *Zweigert and Kötz,* Einführung in die Rechtsvergleichung (ed. 3 Tübingen 1996) 2, that "comparative law is the comparison of the different legal systems of the world", is thus much too narrow.

[4] *Zweigert and Kötz* (*supra* n. 3) 6.

[5] *Zweigert and Kötz,* (*supra* n. 3) consists mainly of a description of the law, in the broad sense just mentioned, of the major legal families of the world.

own (or another) law; simply put, comparative law without the study of foreign law is impossible. The third reason is intellectual: the study of foreign law already implies at least some comparison; if a jurist trained in one system looks at the law of another, he or she inevitably compares them – at minimum, the view from one system inevitably colors the view of the other.[6] The final reason is utilitarian: descriptions of foreign law are often the most valuable service comparative lawyers render to the legal community at large.

Describing foreign law in a manner that makes it accessible and understandable to domestic lawyers requires substantial skills in linguistic, terminological, and cultural translation. It can properly be done only by someone sufficiently at home in both legal systems, i.e., by a comparatist. Successful works on foreign law are thus justly acclaimed as important accomplishments of comparative law.[7]

None of this is to deny that the mere study of foreign law falls short of many of the core goals of comparative law (see *infra* V.). It is also lamentable that much work purporting to be comparative barely, if ever, progresses beyond the mere description of foreign law to the point of explicit comparison, not to mention drawing meaningful conclusions from it. Yet, even such work can provide useful information about other legal systems as well as valuable building blocks for more explicit and fruitful comparisons.

8. *Comparing Law.* – Comparing the laws of different legal systems is obviously at the heart of the discipline. The basic idea seems quite simple: one selects an object of study, finds and describes the law on point in two or more legal systems, identifies the similarities and differences, and explains them.

It is generally agreed that such comparison can legitimately be performed in many different ways. In particular, it can proceed on varying levels of generality. It can focus on concrete, rather narrowly defined issues, such as cause and consideration in contracts;[8] this is often called "micro-comparison". It can also look to broader issues characterizing whole legal systems, cultures, or traditions, such as styles of legal reasoning in the civil and common law;[9] in that case, one can speak of "macro-comparison".[10] Of course, there is no sharp division between the two, and much work falls into a grey zone somewhere in between, such as a comparative study of criminal procedure.[11] Comparison can involve either two or multiple legal systems, with increasing numbers leading to increasing complexity of the task. It can look at apparently fairly similar systems, such as those of England and the United States – perhaps to show surprising differences[12] – or at apparently more different ones, such as those of England and Germany – perhaps to show surprising similarities.[13] It can be primarily descriptive or normative,[14] academic or practical, and it can start from rules, functions, or facts.

Yet, in several other regards, the comparison of laws is also plagued by serious problems. To begin with, relatively few so-called comparative studies actually perform all the steps mentioned above. Many of them exhaust themselves in juxtaposing the different laws without clearly identifying the exact similarities and differences. And many of

[6] It is somewhat of an exaggeration, but not altogether wrong, to say that "a clear distinction between the study of foreign law and comparative law cannot be sustained either in theory or in practice", *Twining*, Comparative Law and Legal Theory: The Country and Western Tradition: *Edge* (ed.), Comparative Law in Global Perspective (Ardsley, New York 2000) 21–78, 47.

[7] Some scholars have actually called for comparatists to "immerse" themselves entirely in a foreign legal system in order to understand it, as far as possible, from the inside, *Curran*, Cultural Immersion, Difference and Categories in U.S. Comparative Law: 46 Am.J.Comp.L. 43–92, 43 (1998).

[8] *Markesinis*, Cause and Consideration: A Study in Parallel: 37 Cambridge L.J. 53–75 (1978).

[9] *Lawson*, A Common Lawyer Looks at the Civil Law (University of Michigan, Ann Arbor MI 1953).

[10] *Zweigert and Kötz* (*supra* n. 3) 4–5; see also *infra* VI.A.ii., ss. 323–325.

[11] *Langbein*, Comparative Criminal Procedure: Germany (St. Paul MN 1977).

[12] See, e.g., *Atiyah and Summers*, Form and Substance in Anglo-American Law (Oxford 1987).

[13] See, e.g., *Vogenauer*, Die Auslegung von Gesetzen in England und auf dem Kontinent (2 vol. Tübingen 2001).

[14] Compare *Kaplan, von Mehren and Schaefer*, Phases of German Civil Procedure II: 71 Harv.L.R. 1443–1472 (1958), with *Langbein*, The German Advantage in Civil Procedure: 52 U.Chi.L.R. 823–866 (1985).

the studies that do identify them fail to provide a proper explanation. Furthermore, even if similarities and differences are clearly identified and properly explained, it is not always obvious what to do with the result. This raises the question of the goals and uses of comparative law. There is, in fact, a large variety of such goals and uses, both academic and practical, but surveying them requires a discussion in its own right (*infra* V.). The most vexing problem, however, is that the actual process of comparison of laws is still poorly understood, as is the essence of the knowledge it generates.[15] To make matters worse, there is little agreement about the proper method to be employed. For many decades, comparative law ducked these central issues, often quite intentionally. As a result there is still much uncertainty, if not confusion, about the hard theoretical and methodological problems lying at the core of the comparative enterprise. They also have to be addressed separately and in somewhat greater depth (*infra* VI.).

9. *Mapping law.* – An important branch of the discipline consists of creating a legal map, or rather legal maps, of the world. Just like geography divides the world into continents and linguistics divides it into language groups and regions, comparative lawyers have spent much time and effort to divide the world into a few "grands systèmes", "legal families", "cultures", or, more lately, "traditions". Standard distinctions are those between Western and non-Western legal systems; within the former between the civil and the common law, among the latter between (East) Asian and (traditional) African systems. Alternative distinctions (e.g., socialist or religious systems) and further subcategories (e.g., Latin American or European legal systems) have been created as well.

Mapping law was particularly popular in the second half of the twentieth century. Since many of the current standard works of the discipline were written during that period, a lot of them are still based on such an approach.[16] Like all such categorizations, dividing the world into a few great systems, traditions, or cultures is helpful in some ways: it reduces complexity, facilitates orientation, and allows one to see both dividing lines and connections on a macro scale.

Yet, like all such categorizations, this approach must also be handled with care. It must inevitably simplify to a great extent, and if too much trust is put into it, it can become positively misleading. In particular, it can create the false impression that there are clearly distinct groups, hide the many ways in which legal systems mix and blend, and create a static impression of a world that is, in reality, constantly changing. For these, and other, reasons, the traditional mapping approach has increasingly come under attack in the late twentieth and early twenty-first centuries. It thus also requires more in-depth discussion (*infra* VI.B.ii., ss. 337–344).

10. *Tracing law.* – Finally, comparative legal studies often trace the development of law across two or more legal systems. This adds a temporal dimension. The main focus of this endeavor is the study of "receptions", i.e., the transfer of rules, institutions, or legal ideas from one system to another. Such receptions have been a constant phenomenon in legal history and occur on the wholesale level (e.g., the reception of Roman law in much of medieval and early modern Europe) as well as on the retail level (e.g., the reception of the Scottish "forum non conveniens" doctrine in many common law countries). While the term "reception" suggests a full-scale adoption of a foreign rule or idea, comparatists more often find lesser degrees of influence by one system on another, such as the influence of US-American constitutionalism on legal systems around the globe. Of course, similarity of law is not necessarily caused by influence but can also be the result of parallel development, often in response to similar socio-economic conditions, problems, or trends. The study of "receptions" and "transplants" also deserves a more in-depth discussion (see *infra* VI.B.iii., ss. 345–351).

In detecting and explaining the development of law across legal systems, comparative law obviously overlaps with legal history. Occasionally, the comparative historical study of law also seeks to generate or support broader theories of how law develops. It then overlaps with legal theory and jurisprudence.

11. *Interactions.* – These four major activities cannot be pursued in pure form or in complete

[15] *Jansen* (*supra* n. 1) 292–302.

[16] In addition, several actual maps of the world showing the geographic distribution of the various sytems have been created; see, e.g., <https//www.foundation-droitcontinental.org/en/2015/civillaw:https://www.juriglobe.ca/eng/index.php>.

isolation from each other. Instead, they constantly blend and interact. The description and analysis of foreign law is implicitly comparative, makes explicit comparison possible, and often tacitly presumes the existence of different legal families. Explicit comparison builds on knowledge of foreign law, influences our perception of legal traditions or cultures, and is often a prerequisite for tracing the development of law across boundaries. Mapping law depends on its description and comparison and provides the background for tracing it. Tracing law is impossible without describing and comparing exports and imports and often affirms or challenges the categories on which mapping depends. As a result, whether particular comparative law work can be said primarily to describe, compare, map, or trace law is a matter of emphasis and ambition.

C. THREE PERVASIVE QUESTIONS

12. *The fundamental character of comparative law.* – There are three basic questions pertaining to the fundamental character of comparative law: whether it is a "science" or something less dignified; whether it is merely a method or rather a substantive area of knowledge; and whether it is, or should be, a distinct discipline or rather an integrated perspective on law in general. These questions must be addressed because they have, at times, enjoyed much interest and generated considerable debate among comparatists. Yet, their discussion can be brief because the debates have neither produced clear answers nor exercised much influence on the practice of the discipline.

13. *Scientific character.* – Much ink has been spilt on the question of the "scientific" character of comparative law.[17] The answer depends primarily on what is meant by "science". If the term is taken in the broad sense common in the civil law orbit (especially in continental Europe, Latin America, but also in much of Asia – "scienza", "ciencia", "Wissenschaft", "nauka" etc.), it denotes pretty much any established academic activity or discipline. In that case, the academic study of law is a "science" ("science juridique", "scienze giuridiche", "ciencia del derecho", "Rechtswissenschaft", "pravovedienie" etc.), and that includes comparative law. If the term is taken in the narrow sense prevalent in the Anglo-American orbit, it means the collection and observation of data, the creation of hypotheses, and the testing of their validity. Then, most of the academic study of law is not a "science", and most of the activities pursued under the label "comparative law" (*supra* ss. 7–10) are not either. If one takes "science" to mean something in between and acceptable in most parts of the world, then it denotes the systematic observation and analysis of a phenomenon and the production of generalized insight about it. In that case, comparative law has a better claim to scientific status than most other forms of legal studies. As has been noted, most such studies are limited to one legal system so that they can hardly produce insight about the phenomenon of law in general, while comparative law rises above the national horizon and thus looks at law more broadly.[18] Thus, where it observes law on a sufficiently broad scale, analyzes its similarities, differences or developments, and reaches general conclusions about law as a whole or about specific aspects of it, comparative law can properly be called "scientific" in this, intermediate, sense. It is then, along with legal history, legal sociology, and perhaps legal philosophy, a form of a "science" of law. It must be admitted, however, that most of the works on comparative law do not fulfill these conditions because they do not aim at, and certainly not succeed in, the production of such generalized knowledge.

Comparatists, especially in civil law countries, usually do call their discipline a "science" either out of academic habit or in order to affirm a certain dignity. In both cases, the use of the term does not imply the methodological claims often assumed by lawyers from the Anglo-American world. In light of this potential for misunderstanding, it is a positive development that the emphasis on the scientific status of comparative law has been declining in the last few decades.

[17] Rabel wisely left the question open but predicted that a properly developed comparative law would become a true "Wissenschaft", *Rabel*, Aufgabe und Notwendigkeit: *Zweigert and Puttfarken* (eds.), Rechtsvergleichung (Darmstadt 1978) 85–108, 87.

[18] *Zweigert and Kötz* (*supra* n. 3) 4, 15.

14. *Mere method?* – It has been debated whether comparative law is merely a method or something more. Undoubtedly, it implies a method, i.e., of legal observation and analysis, but that is hardly all there is to it. The claim that comparative law is limited to a method was somewhat defensible when Harold Gutteridge made it before the middle of the twentieth century.[19] Today, however, this claim is based on much too narrow a view of the discipline for two main reasons.[20]

First, as we have seen, comparative law as it is practiced today comprises much more than the mere comparison of legal rules, institutions, or ideas (*supra* ss. 7–10). At a minimum, it also includes the description and analysis of foreign law, the creation of world maps of law, and the detection and explanation of influences between legal systems. All these activities imply comparison on some level, but they do not exhaust themselves in it. Second, and more importantly, at least in the second half of the twentieth century, comparative law has also developed into a field of substantive knowledge.[21] As a look at the standard works in the field, including this Encyclopedia, amply demonstrates, comparative legal studies have generated an enormous body of well-established information. This information pertains to legal systems, their characteristics, similarities, differences, genesis, and connections; to the various regimes of legal education, professions, institutions, and procedures; to legal styles, mentalities, and predilections; to the utility and limits of comparisons and generalizations; and, last but not least, to many areas of positive law in comparative perspective (for an overview, see *infra* III.). Serious comparatists are, or at least should be, expected not only to use the comparative method but also to possess the basics of that knowledge. In addition, it is not impossible to conceive of comparative law as a multifaceted, yet ultimately coherent, discipline in which the various approaches and strands actually complement each other.[22]

15. *Independent discipline?* – Finally, there is the question whether comparative law is an independent discipline or rather intimately connected with legal analysis as a whole. Comparatists have discussed this issue mainly in two contexts.

One context is intellectual. It has been argued that since comparison is integral to all legal reasoning (*supra* s. 3), comparative law is just a variety of it, namely that which takes foreign law into account.[23] The argument is only partially correct. While it is true that the basic process of comparing legal principles or rules is identical at some level, it still makes a significant difference whether the legal material compared is purely domestic or includes foreign matter. Domestic rules are usually binding, foreign rules are not; domestic rules share the same conceptual and linguistic apparatus, foreign rules do not; domestic rules are cut from the same cloth in terms of the political system, culture, and tradition, foreign rules do not share that background, etc. The argument that nonetheless the process of comparison is essentially the same must in large part be understood as a normative claim: legal reasoning ought to transcend the domestic orbit and include foreign material more or less as a matter of course. In that sense, the argument is mainly that comparative law *should not be* regarded as a distinct discipline.

The other context is, so to speak, institutional. It has been argued, now in explicitly normative terms, that in teaching and research, comparative law should not be kept as a distinct discipline.[24]

[19] *Gutteridge*, Comparative Law (Cambridge 1946, ed. 2 1949) ix, 1. See also *Kahn-Freund*, Comparative Law as an Academic Subject: 82 L.Q.R. 44–45, 54 (1966).

[20] It is, apparently, still held by some leading comparatists, see, e.g., *Glendon, Gordon and Carozza*, Comparative Legal Traditions: Texts, Materials and Cases on Western Law (ed. 3 St. Paul MN 2007) 4 (quoting Kahn-Freund), although most such statements are made in passing and probably without giving the matter much thought.

[21] *Reimann*, The Progress and Failure of Comparative Law in the Second Half of the Twentieth Century: 50 Am.J.Comp.L. 671–700, 673–684 (2002).

[22] See *Valcke*, Comparing Law: Comparative Law as Reconstruction of Collective Commitments (Cambridge 2018).

[23] *Gordley*, Is Comparative Law a Distinct Discipline?: 46 Am.J.Comp.L. 607–615 (1998).

[24] *Pound*, The Place of Comparative Law in the American Law School Curriculum: 8 Tul.L.R. 161–170, 168 (1934); *Reimann*, The End of Comparative Law as an Autonomous Subject: 11 Tulane European & Civil Law Forum 49–72 (1996).

Comparative law has by and large been taught as a separate course, and comparative studies have mostly been conducted as distinct endeavors. To the extent the discipline consists of the actual comparison of domestic with foreign legal material, this is not ideal. It would be preferable completely to integrate such comparison with law teaching and legal research at large. In an increasingly globalized environment, foreign legal ideas should be routinely considered along with domestic ones in the classroom as well as in the study. This is, of course, possible only within the – rather narrow – constraints of time, resources, and human brain capacity.

It must be noted that both these arguments conceive of comparative law as the actual comparison of domestic and foreign material. Thus they do not apply to the discipline's other activities. With regard to these activities (*supra* ss. 7–10), the discipline's methods and goals are quite different from routine legal reasoning, teaching, and research. In these regards, comparative law constitutes a field of techniques and knowledge in its own right.

Comparative law is thus both a potentially integral perspective on legal reasoning, teaching, and research, and a separate discipline. It is, or at least should be, an integral part of legal studies where it actually compares domestic and foreign material. It is a distinct discipline where it provides access to foreign law, creates legal maps of the world, or traces cross-boundary influences and developments. The discipline's janus-faced character is nothing special, however, because it is shared by other fields, such as legal history, sociology, and philosophy.

LIST OF PRINCIPAL WORKS

(Comparative Law in General)

Treatises and Introductions

Aberastury (ed.), Estudios de Derecho Comparado (Buenos Aires 2016)

Alpa et al., Diritto comparato privato. Istituti e problemi (ed. 4 Roma 2019)

Arminjon, Nolde and Wolff, Traité de droit comparé (3 vol.) (Paris 1950)

Bogdan, Concise Introduction to Comparative Law (Groningen 2013)

Constantinesco, Traité de droit comparé (3 vol.) (Paris 1972–1983)

idem, Rechtsvergleichung (3 vol.) (Köln, Berlin, Bonn, München 1971–1983)

Cuniberti, Grands Systèmes de Droit Contemporains (ed. 2 Paris 2011)

David, Jauffret-Spinosi and Goré, Les Grands Systèmes de Droit Contemporains (ed. 12 Paris 2016)

David and Brierley, Major Legal Systems in the World Today (London 1985)

deCruz, Comparative Law in a Changing World (1995 and ed. 3 New York 2008)

Eörsi, Comparative Civil (Private) Law (Budapest 1979)

Gambaro and Sacco, Sistemi Giuridici Comparati (ed. 4 Torino 2018)

Gambaro, Sacco and Vogel, Le Droit de l'Occident et d'ailleurs (Paris 2011)

Glenn, Legal Traditions of the World (ed. 5 Oxford 2014)

Großfeld, Kernfragen der Rechtsvergleichung (Tübingen 1999) (transl. by Vivian Curran as: Core Questions of Comparative Law, Durham, NC 2005)

idem, Macht und Ohnmacht der Rechtsvergleichung (Tübingen 1984) (transl. by Tony Weir as: The Strength and Weakness of Comparative Law, Oxford 1990)

Grosswald-Curran, Comparative Law. An Introduction (Durham, NC 2002)

Gutteridge, Comparative Law (Cambridge 1946 and ed. 2 1949)

Husa, A New Introduction to Comparative Law (Oxford, Portland OR 2015)

Hyland, Comparative Law: *Patterson* (ed.), A Companion to Philosophy of Law and Legal Theory (Cambridge, MA, Oxford 1996) 184–199

Kischel, Rechtvergleichung (München 2015)

Kischel, Comparative Law (Hammel transl., Oxford 2019)

Laithier, Droit comparé (Paris 2009)

Legrand, Le Droit Comparé (ed. 5 Paris 2015)

Losano, I Grandi Sistemi Guiridici. Introduzione ai diritti europei ed extraeuropei (Torino 2000)

Markesinis, Comparative Law in the Courtroom and Classroom (Oxford, Portland, OR 2003)

Menski, Comparative Law in a Global Context. The Legal Systems of Asia and Africa (Cambridge 2006)

Müller-Chen, Müller and Widmer Lüchinger, Comparative Private Law (Zürich, St. Gallen 2015)

Rheinstein, Einführung in die Rechtsvergleichung (ed. 2 München 1987)

Sacco and Gambaro, Sistemi Guiridici Comparati (Torino 1996)

Sacco and Rossi, Introduzione al diritto comparato (ed. 6 Torino 2015)

Saidov, Comparative Law (transl. from the Russian original by Butler, London 2003)

Samuel, An Introduction to Comparative Law Theory and Method (Oxford and Portland, OR 2014)

Siems, Comparative Law (ed. 2 Cambridge 2018)

Somma, Introduzione al diritto comparato (Roma and Bari 2016)

Vicente, Direito Comparado (ed. 2 Coimbra 2012)

Zweigert and Kötz, Einführung in die Rechtsvergleichung auf dem Gebiete des Privatrechts (ed. 3 Tübingen 1996)

Zweigert and Kötz, An Introduction to Comparative Law (Weir trans., ed. 3 Oxford 1998)

Zweigert and Puttfarken, Rechtsvergleichung (Darmstadt 1978)

Handbooks and Encyclopedias

Bussani and Mattei (eds.), The Cambridge Companion to Comparative Law (Cambridge 2012)

Clark (ed.), Encyclopedia of Law and Society. American and Global Perspectives (Thousand Oaks CA, 2007)

Örücü and Nelken, Comparative Law: A Handbook (Oxford, Portland, OR 2007)

Reimann and Zimmermann, The Oxford Handbook of Comparative Law (ed. 2 Oxford 2019)

Smits, Elgar Encyclopedia of Comparative Law (ed. 2 Cheltenham, Northampton, MA 2012)

II. THE RELATIONSHIP WITH OTHER DISCIPLINES

16. *Introduction and overview.* – The relationship between comparative law and other disciplines has long been a standard topic in most introductions to the field. Defining this relationship has been part of the comparatists' ongoing effort to define their own subject. This desire to stake out the terrain has, it must be admitted, at times turned into an obsession. Still, looking at comparative law in the broader context of other disciplines does have two benefits: *distinguishing* it from other disciplines clarifies what comparative law is; and *relating* it to other fields shows how it interacts – or should interact – with neighboring subjects.

In this context, comparative law can be viewed from two sides, and its cognate fields can be put into two corresponding groups. On the one hand, comparative law is a discipline that deals with *other legal systems*, i.e., that goes beyond purely domestic law. It shares this characteristic with fields like private international law, public international law, European law, and – nowadays – transnational law. Together with these (and other) disciplines, it is part of the "international" curriculum (*infra* A.), loosely defined. On the other hand, comparative law often looks at law *from a broader perspective*, i.e., from the outside. This it shares with legal history, legal sociology, legal anthropology, economic analysis of law, and, at least arguably, legal philosophy. Together with these subjects, it is part of the "social science" approach to law, broadly understood (*infra* B.).

Before looking at the relationship between comparative law and each of these fields, two brief caveats are in order. First, the list of subjects considered here covers the most widely discussed areas; it is, however, somewhat arbitrary because other subjects could plausibly be added, such as comparative political science or linguistics. Second, like comparative law itself, all these cognate fields are multifaceted, and the interaction between comparative law and a particular cognate area depends largely on which of their respective branches are involved.

A. COMPARATIVE LAW AND OTHER "INTERNATIONAL" SUBJECTS

17. *Comparative law as an "international" subject.* – The most obviously defining characteristic of comparative law is that it deals with legal systems beyond one's own. As mentioned, this is also true for several other disciplines, especially private international law (conflict of laws) (*infra* i.), public international law (the law of nations, *infra* ii.), European law (as a particular regional order, *infra* iii.), and transnational law (an overarching concept, *infra* iv.). As a result, comparative law is often indiscriminately lumped together with these disciplines as one of the "international" branches of legal study.[25] Tell-tale signs of this tendency are the myriad "Centers" or "Institutes", and "Journals" for "International and Comparative Law".[26] Yet, although non-specialists often fail to realize it, there is of course a fundamental difference between comparative law on the one hand and these other, "international" subjects on the other: comparative law is a method of studying law and a field of academic knowledge (*supra* I.C., s. 14), while private and public international law as well as European and transnational law consist of actual legal principles, concepts, and rules; in other words, the former is not a kind of *law* while the latter are. Beyond this fundamental distinction, comparative law relates to these other topics in very different ways.

i. *Private International Law (Conflict of Laws)*

18. *Fundamental differences in orientation.* – Private international law consists of the doctrines, principles, and rules applying in disputes between private parties (e.g.,

[25] Those who consider the study of foreign law as such a discipline separate from comparative law (see *supra* I.B., s. 7) will add it to this list of "international" subjects.

[26] The most notable is the (English) International and Comparative Law Quarterly (since 1952) which publishes articles, notes, and reviews pertaining to public and private international law, comparative law, European Union law, and transnational law.

about contracts, torts, property rights, or family relationships) that involve more than one legal system. At its traditional core are the rules selecting which of the involved systems' laws applies in such cases (choice of law). In addition, there are rules governing various procedural issues, e.g., which court has jurisdiction, when and how to recognize foreign judgments, or how to serve documents or take evidence abroad. As a system of principles and rules, private international law is thus a branch of positive law whereas comparative law is not.

While both disciplines constantly deal with foreign law, they do so by and large for different purposes. Comparative law looks at foreign law to compare it with domestic (or other) law in order to discern (and then to explain or overcome) the similarities and differences; it is thus primarily a scholarly enterprise (its great practical uses notwithstanding, see *infra* V.B.). Private international law needs foreign rules primarily to resolve actual cases; it is thus, at bottom, a practical discipline (although it is surely not lacking in academic theory).

19. *Commonalities regarding skills and instruments.* – Yet, the fact that both disciplines constantly deal with foreign law also creates significant commonalities. Perhaps most importantly, both disciplines require largely similar skills and instruments: a knowledge of other jurisdictions' laws and a sense of how different legal systems relate to each other, foreign language skills and an understanding of the pitfalls of translation, access to foreign legal materials and resourcefulness in maneuvering on alien terrain. More generally, comparatists share with private international lawyers a view of law that necessarily transcends the domestic horizon. It is no surprise therefore that comparative law and private international law are often pursued by the same scholars and practitioners. Sometimes, the two disciplines are even at home under the same institutional roof, e.g., at the *Max Planck Institute for Foreign and International Private Law* in Hamburg, Germany. Such a symbiotic existence is helpful because the disciplines interact very closely in several regards.

20. *Close interaction in two dimensions.* – One dimension is that comparatists have long made the various systems of private international law their objects of study. Here, one must understand that the rules of private international law have traditionally not been "international" by nature but rather part of the domestic law of the various nation states; in other words, these rules were "international" only in the sense of governing transboundary cases. As a result, private international law regimes have often differed substantially, thus providing fertile ground for comparative studies.[27] To be sure, comparatists have studied lots of other fields as well, but private international law is a somewhat special case. Rules on choice of law or foreign jurisdiction specifically govern transboundary issues and thus invite comparison with their foreign counterparts more urgently than rules designed for the domestic context, such as the law of contracts or torts. And the often close working relationship between, if not the identity of, scholars in both camps has also made comparative private international law studies come quite naturally. Recently, however, such studies have somewhat declined, in part because of the increased unification of conflicts rules (see *infra*, s. 22).

The other dimension of interaction is that private international law constantly resorts to comparative law in three main contexts. First, comparative studies are routinely employed in the making of private international law rules, with a view to achieve as much international harmonization as possible. This is true on the domestic level, i.e., when experts or legislators draft national conflicts rules or codifications. It is *de rigueur* on the international level, i.e., in the making of conventions on conflicts law, especially in the *Hague Conference on Private Internaztional Law*. And it is true on the European level, i.e., in the context of EU legislation (in the form of Regulations) on conflict of laws issues. Second, comparative law comes into play when existing choice of law rules call for the application of foreign law: comparative law not only helps to provide these rules, it also makes them intelligible by translating them in both linguistic and conceptual terms. Third,

[27] The most impressive result of such studies is the monumental work by *Rabel*, The Conflict of Laws – A Comparative Study (4 vol.) (Ann Arbor MI 1945–1958 and ed. 2 1958–1964).

private international law often needs comparative law in order to interpret existing conflicts rules. These rules routinely employ technical terms – such as "contract", "property", or "marriage", and these terms often mean different things in domestic and foreign law. Whether a deal made in a foreign country, a right held in land there, or a union entered into by two partners qualifies as a "contract", "property", or "marriage" under one's own conflicts rules thus requires an understanding of their meaning in the legal orders involved.[28] In addition, international conflicts conventions often explicitly require that courts interpreting them consider the law of other jurisdictions in order to maintain a uniform meaning of the text. The overall result is that, as Arthur von Mehren famously put it, "no system of private international law can escape involvement with the discipline of comparative law".[29]

21. *The disciplines as enemies.* – Ironically, comparative law and private international law are, however, not only necessary allies but also potential enemies because the accomplishments of one can put the other out of work. For well over a hundred years, one of the main goals of comparative law has been legal unification (see *infra* V.B.iv, ss. 302–308). Where this ambition succeeds, law becomes internationally uniform. Conflicts accordingly diminish or even disappear, and private international law loses (at least much of) its importance. This has actually happened in several instances, such as in the unification of international sales law in the CISG. In a similar vein, core parts of private international law have recently been unified by EU legislation (*infra* s. 22). To be sure, neither discipline will be able completely to sideline the other. Legal unification will always remain partial so that conflicts will not vanish entirely; and even where conflicts rules are unified, their application still requires help from comparative law to ensure their uniform application.

22. *Changing relationship.* – Around the turn of the twenty-first century, the rise of supra- and international orders began to affect the traditional relationship between comparative law and private international law.[30]

First, the accelerated integration of Europe entailed, inter alia, the increasing codification of private international law through EU regulations, thus creating conflicts uniformity throughout the European Union, at least with regard to the blackletter rules. On the one hand, this has largely deprived comparative law in Europe of a time-honored object of study. To be sure, one can still compare EU private international law with other conflicts regimes in the world, but once the (European) rules are cast in legislative stone, the motivation do so is much diminished. As a result, comparative conflicts law experienced a significant decline in Europe.[31] On the other hand, comparative studies remain relevant, of course, with regard to the *operation* of the now uniform conflicts rules, in particular to ensure that they are uniformly interpreted and applied.

Second, the increasing importance of international legal orders, especially of treaty regimes in areas as diverse as trade and human rights has added to the formerly horizontal interaction among nation states a vertical dimension of interaction between international and domestic legal systems.[32] This has resulted in a multi-dimensional global legal order. To manage it, conflicts law must also function in a multidimensional fashion. Here, the perhaps most important task of comparative law is to assist private international law in handling conflicts within the multi-level plurality of legal regimes.

[28] The classic essay on this topic is *Rabel*, Das Problem der Qualifikation: Zeitschrift für ausländisches und internationales Privatrecht 5 (1931) 241–288. For an account in English, see *Rabel*, The Conflict of Laws: A Comparative Study I (Ann Arbor MI 1945) 47–60.

[29] *von Mehren*, The Contribution of Comparative Law to the Theory and Practice of Private International Law: 26 Am.J.Comp.L. 31–41, 33 (1978).

[30] *Reimann*, Comparative Law and Private International Law: *Reimann and Zimmermann* (eds.), The Oxford Handbook of Comparative Law (ed. 2 Oxford 2019) 1339–1370, 1362–1368; *Fernandez-Arroyo*, Private International Law and Comparative Law: A Relationship Challenged by International and Supranational Law: YB Priv.Int.L 11 (2009) 31–71.

[31] *Rühl*, Who's Afraid of Comparative Law? The (Side) Effects of Unification of Private International Law in Europe: Eur.Rev.Priv.L. 3 (2017) 485–522.

[32] *Basedow*, Droits de l'homme et droit international privé: *Pedone* (ed.), Ann.Inst.dr.int. (Paris 2017) 391–453.

This requires an understanding of how these regimes relate to each other, i.e., where they are similar or different; whether they fulfill the same or different functions; whether they are based on the same or different logics and mentalities. Thus, comparative lawyers must apply their traditional skills and tools to the study of supra- and international orders as well (see also *infra* IV.A.iii., ss. 183–187).

ii. *Public International Law*

23. *Traditionally weak relationship with the classic law of nations.* – Generalizations about the relationship between comparative law and public international law are difficult because much depends on whether one focuses on the classic core of the latter or one of its many more recently developed subcategories (*infra s. 24*).

The classic core of public international law consists of the principles and rules governing the relationship between sovereign states in the world (the law of nations). As such, it is, like private international law, a field of positive law and thus, again, radically different from comparative studies. The most obvious feature shared by comparative law and public international law is that neither is concerned (at least not primarily) with the domestic legal system.

In contrast to private international law, public international has traditionally interacted rather weakly with comparative law, despite the fact that both disciplines have some common origins in mid- to late nineteenth century progressive liberal thought.[33]

For most of their discipline's history, comparatists rarely made public international law an object of their studies. The reason was at least in part the assumption that there is not much to compare within the law of nations itself because (unlike the various national or regional versions of private international law) public international law is supposed to be a globally uniform regime – an assumption that has increasingly been called into question.[34] To be sure, one could compare this global regime as such with other (domestic or regional) legal systems. But while such comparison could generate important insight, it was not much performed in practice. The situation has recently begun to change, however, as some comparative studies have focused more closely on public international law. This may signal a trend that is likely to continue and possibly to expand.[35]

Public international law also has more limited use for comparative law than private international law. Probably the most important context in which comparative studies sometimes play a role is the drafting of multilateral treaties or (non-binding) "principles". Drafting bodies like the United National Commission on International Trade Law (UNCITRAL) or the UN International Law Commission (ILC) often draw on, and actually compare, the laws and experiences of various legal systems in order to facilitate compromise and to reach consensus. In addition, comparatists routinely point to Article 38 sec. 1 of the Statute of the International Court of Justice which lists "general principles of law recognized by civilized nations" as a source of international law. In theory, one could bring such principles to light through the comparative study of the laws of these "civilized nations". In practice, however, such studies are so rare that they play almost no role. This is understandable because a serious comparative inquiry into which general principles of law are shared by the "civilized nations" is a hopelessly complex, time-consuming, and error-prone undertaking – quite aside from the problem of which nations count as "civilized" and which do not. De facto, the "general principles" invoked under Article 38 sec. 1 are usually so broad – like "abus de droit" or "good faith" – that they go unquestioned and require no comparative study. Comparative law is sometimes also said to be useful for treaty interpretation. In practice, however, its role is quite small here as well. While courts construing treaties do sometimes look at how other tribunals have read the text, they are usually not engaged in serious comparison between the various approaches, e.g., in order to select the most convincing one. Instead,

[33] *Koskenniemi* and *Kari*, A More Elevated Patriotism. The Emergence of International and Comparative Law (Nineteenth Century): *Philajamäki, Dubber and Godfrey* (eds.), The Oxford Handbook of European Legal History (Oxford 2018) 974–999.

[34] See *Roberts*, Is International Law International? (New York 2017).

[35] *Roberts, Stephan, Verdier and Versteeg* (eds.), Comparative International Law (New York 2018).

judges usually perform simple fact-gathering in order to define the parties' intention when they formulated the treaty text – which is an altogether different enterprise.

24. *Stronger interaction within special subcategories.* – Over the last few decades, public international law has developed a plethora of subcategories, and in some of them comparative studies have played an increasingly important role. This is most visible in international human rights[36]. The interpretation of human rights treaties, especially by the European Court of Human Rights (ECHR), is frequently based on a comparison of the member states' laws in order either to find a common denominator or at least to discern general trends. Comparisons, and in particular the search for commonalities, have become more difficult as the number, as well as the legal and cultural diversity, of member states of the European Convention on Human Rights has grown. Comprehensive surveys have thus become nearly impossible. In part as a result of these difficulties, the comparative inquiries undertaken by the ECHR have often been lacking in both breadth and rigor. In many instances, the Court did not advance beyond cherry picking to support pre-conceived arguments, while in other contexts, it made broad generalizing assumptions with little or no empirical basis.[37]

Another area for which comparative law is important is European Union law. Since much of that field can no longer be classified as public international law, it must be addressed separately (*infra* iii., ss. 26–28).

25. *Explanation of cultural differences.* – Beyond the current forms of interaction between the two disciplines, there is a more general contribution comparative law can make to public international law. The comparative study of legal systems can highlight and explain the differences between the legal cultures of the world. In particular, it can show that different people in different regions and countries have different legal values, conceptions of law, techniques of dispute resolution, and degrees of trust in the legal process. An understanding of, and tolerance for, these differences is vitally important for the successful pursuit of the larger goals of public international law, i.e., the maintenance of world peace, the fostering of international cooperation, the management of the global commons, and the protection of human rights. Even today, public international lawyers often lack such an adequate understanding of the differences between legal cultures, and comparatists should make a conscious effort to help them overcome that deficit.

iii. *European Law*

26. *Overview.* – European law, i.e., the law of the former European Community (EC), now the European Union (EU), has developed from a mere treaty regime essentially under public international law into a "new legal order"[38] with many sui generis features. In the two generations since its inception, and especially since the 1980s, it has grown a bewildering variety of branches, ranging from constitutional structures to market regulation and from conflicts law to consumer protection, and beyond. Even in the early twenty-first century, it keeps expanding and diversifying at a frightening pace. Comparative law has played a significant role in this process from the early days to the present. Yet, this role has varied enormously depending on the context so that even a moderately thorough evaluation would fill a book. At minimum, two dimensions should be distinguished: comparison among the laws of the member states, i.e., *within* the EU, and comparison of EU law itself with other legal orders or their elements, i.e., with the *outside*.

27. *Comparative law within European law.*[39] – For a long time, the unrivalled powerhouse of

[36] See e.g. *McCrudden*, Judicial Comparativism and Human Rights: *Örücü* and *Nelken* (eds.), Comparative Law. A Handbook (Oxford, Portland, OR 2007) 371–398; *Besson*, Comparative Law and Human Rights: *Reimann* and *Zimmermann* (eds.), The Oxford Handbook of Comparative Law (ed. 2 Oxford 2019), 1222–1249.

[37] For a more detailed discussion, see, e.g., *Helfer*, Consensus, Coherence, and the European Convention on Human Rights: 26 Cornell Int.L.J. 133–165 (1993).

[38] *Van Gend & Loos v. Nederlandse Administratie der Belastingen* [1963] E.C.R 1, 2.

[39] For an analysis, see *Kükeri*, Comparative Legal Reasoning and European Law: (Dordrecht, Boston, MA, London 2001); see also *Van der Mensbrugghe* (ed.), L'utilisation de la méthode comparative en droit Européen (Namur 2001).

comparative work involving the laws of the member states was the European Court of Justice (ECJ). Since the ECJ is staffed by judges from all member states, comparison of these states' laws comes naturally and is thus part of the Court's daily grind. The Court is ably assisted in its work by a highly professional research staff drawn from the members states and equipped with an extensive library. In its deliberations and decisions, the Court has drawn on the member states' laws not only in interpreting primary Union law, i.e., the texts of the successive treaties, especially in order to keep their meaning compatible with the legal orders of the member states. The ECJ has also derived "general principles of European law" from the shared traditions of the member states; these "general principles" have supplemented the written texts and attained essentially constitutional status.[40] The principle of proportionality is perhaps the most widely known example.

From the 1980s to the early 2000s, the ECJ's engagement with comparative law was supplemented, and in part even overshadowed, by the – legislative and academic – project of a common private law for Europe. This project has been pursued by a proliferating variety of study groups, networks, and conferences largely organized by legal academics. They generated a host of non-binding "principles" and studies covering ever more areas of private law, sometimes (but not always) with a view to a codification on the European level. In the second decade of the twenty-first century, the political leadership of the EU gradually lost interest in this project which has subsequently largely petered out. We will consider this unification agenda in greater detail below (IV.C.i.g., ss. 242–245).

Beyond these large-scale enterprises lies a vast mass of individual comparative studies of two or more member states' laws, with or without particular regard to EU law. Over the last fifty years, a veritable cottage industry of academics, research institutes, government ministries, and EU institutions has produced such studies on areas and aspects of law too numerous to mention. Much of this work is of mediocre quality, suffering from a short shelf-life, or so narrowly focused that it is of interest at best to a few specialists. Some of it, however, also provides important building blocks for larger projects as well as valuable information for law reform efforts both in the member states and at the EU level.

28. *Comparison of EU law with other legal orders.* – The law of the European Union, i.e., EU law proper, has increasingly been the object of comparison with other legal orders as well. This is particularly true for its constitutional aspects, especially its federal structure, and with regard to its approach to market regulation.

In the 1980s, scholars, first in the United States, then in Europe, began to realize that the (then) European Community had developed from a treaty regime into a constitutional order[41]. This observation gave rise to two, related, directions of comparative study. First, the process of Europe's coming together, initially as a common market, then as a political system, triggered comparative studies in "Integration through Law".[42] Second, the recognition of the EC's emerging federal structure gave rise to studies in comparative federalism.[43] Both directions have had a strong transatlantic flavor as they have focused mainly on the comparison between the EC/EU and the United States, though other federal systems, such as Germany or Canada, have also been considered. These studies are now part of the larger area of comparative constitutional law (*infra* IV.C.ii.d., ss. 260–266).

Also, since the 1980s scholars have developed an interest in comparing EC/EU market regulation with its counterparts in other areas of the world, again primarily in the United States. This

[40] See *Tridimas*, The General Principles of EU Law (ed. 2 Oxford, New York 2006).

[41] The seminal article is *Stein*, Lawyers, Judges, and the Making of a Transnational Constitution: *idem*, Thoughts from a Bridge (Ann Arbor MI 2000) 15–49, first published in 75 A.J.I.L 1–27 (1981).

[42] *Cappelletti, Seccombe* and *Weiler* (eds.), Integration Through Law: Europe and the American Federal Experience (5 vol.) (Berlin, New York, 1985–1987). The tradition was begun by *Stein* and *Sandalow* (eds.), Courts and Free Markets: Perspectives from the United States and Europe (Oxford, New York 1982); see also the essays in *Stein* (*supra* n. 42) 87–344.

[43] See e.g. *Halberstam*, Comparative Federalism and the Role of the Judiciary: *Caldeira, Keleman and Whittington* (eds.), The Oxford Handbook of Law and Politics (Oxford 2008) 142–164.

interest was a response largely to the growing economic interdependence of the two largest markets in the world – a process which meant that firms now often had to comply with the regulatory systems on both sides of the Atlantic. As a result, comparative work in this context has concentrated mainly on antitrust law, company law, the regulation of securities markets, and, more recently, some areas of consumer protection, such as products liability. Given the continuously rapid growth and persistent importance of EU law, its comparison with other legal orders, especially those of the major competitor markets, will remain a fertile field for some time to come. This is true both with regard to structural aspects, e.g., comparisons between the EU and other regional systems such as ASEAN, MERCOSUR or OHADA, and for particular topics, such as data protection and privacy, intellectual property, and environmental regulation.

iv. *Transnational Law*

29. *No clear definition of the subject.* – The relationship between comparative law and transnational law is difficult to grasp because the latter field is not clearly defined. More than half a century ago, the term "transnational law" was invented as an umbrella concept encompassing "all law which regulates actions or events that transcend national frontiers".[44] This concept comprised not only public and private international law but also all domestic rules dealing with transboundary issues. In other words, transnational law denoted a huge and disparate mass of *positive law*. As such it was, like its component parts, fundamentally different from comparative law as a method and field of knowledge. In the last two decades, however, a somewhat different meaning of the term "transnational law" has emerged. Today, it usually stands for the study of the multifaceted *world legal order* (or chaos, as the case may be) that has emerged from the various globalization processes since the fall of communism. Thus understood, transnational law encompasses comparative law because this world legal order can only be understood by looking at a multitude of legal systems and by analyzing what connects and what divides them.[45]

30. *New challenges to comparative law.* – The more recent understanding of transnational law thus presents significant challenges and opportunities for comparative law. Most importantly, comparative law is needed to describe, explain, and help to coordinate the multiple legal orders coexisting in the world today. This requires at least three modifications of the traditional approach which today are by and large underway (see *infra* IV.A.iii., ss. 183–187). First, the discipline must look beyond the domestic legal systems of the established nation states and embrace the study of inter- and supranational orders on the global and regional levels, such as international trade systems, human rights regimes, or the European Union. Second, in order to create a more realistic picture of the current situation, comparative law must look beyond state-sanctioned norms and include the many non-state regimes that play so significant a role in many transnational contexts today, ranging from non-binding principles of private or commercial law to corporate governance codes and the regulation of international sports. Finally, comparative law must go beyond mere *comparison* of rules, institutions or systems and seek to understand the complex *interaction* of a plurality of overlapping and intersecting legal orders operating on various levels.

B. COMPARATIVE LAW AND "SOCIAL SCIENCE" APPROACHES TO LAW

31. *Comparative law as a "social science" approach.* – Comparative law is not only the study of other legal systems (and in that sense "international"), it also often seeks to provide a broader perspective on law as a historical, social, cultural, economic, and intellectual phenomenon. It shares this latter feature with disciplines that can loosely be termed "social science" approaches to law – legal history (*infra* i.), legal sociology (ii.), legal anthropology (iii.), and the economic

[44] *Jessup*, Transnational Law (New Haven CT 1956) 2.
[45] See e.g. *Steiner, Vagts*, and *Koh* Transnational Legal Problems (Westbury, New York 1994); *Reimann, Hathaway, Dickinson and Samuels* Transnational Law (St. Paul MI 2013).

analysis of law (iv.); it also shares the search for a broader perspective with legal philosophy (v.).

How comparative law relates to these other disciplines depends not only on which of them we focus on; it also depends on how comparative law itself is conceived. In this regard, however, there is no consensus. Comparative law means different things to different people. Today, there is a veritable panoply of avowed approaches, methods, and orientations, and we shall have to look at them in greater detail below (VI.). For the mainstream, the field consists of the comparison between the current legal systems of the world or between particular institutions, concepts or rules, in pursuit of various academic and practical goals. Many comparatists, however, take a more idiosyncratic view. Some see the discipline's principal objective in tracing legal transplants between legal systems over time which turns comparative law into a form of legal history. Some seek to explore the relationship between law and society and thus consider the discipline a version of legal sociology. Others focus on cultural practices, e.g., in pre-modern societies, and thus associate themselves with legal anthropology. Yet others are primarily interested in the comparative efficiency of legal solutions, e.g., in the context of business regulation, and thus draw heavily on the economic analysis of law. And some explore different legal mentalities and varying conceptions of law which affiliate their studies with legal philosophy. Further directions could easily be added to this list.

We will consider the relationship between comparative law and these disciplines primarily from the mainstream perspective. We will, however, also look at more particular affiliations between specific branches of the discipline and particular cognate fields.

i. *Legal History*

32. *Mutual benefits.* – Comparative law and legal history have been called "twin sisters"[46] because both look beyond the current domestic legal system – the former in space, the latter in time. As a result, both disciplines can greatly benefit from each other. Comparative law often needs legal history in order fully to understand the similarities and differences it observes. For example, the different attitudes towards codification in continental Europe on the one hand and in the United Kingdom on the other are truly intelligible only in light of the respective historical experiences in the eighteenth and nineteenth centuries. Likewise, legal history often benefits from a comparative perspective, in particular when developments were not of a purely local nature. Thus the codification movement of the eighteenth and nineteenth centuries must be viewed at least in an all-European, if not a global, context in order fully to understand its causes and effects. Fortunately, the potential benefits of a combined comparative and historical perspective have not escaped the academic community. Especially since the middle of the twentieth century, most of the high-caliber comparative studies have included a historical dimension, and much of the best work in legal history has been comparative.

33. *Overlaps and amalgamations.* – In several instances, the relationship between comparative law and legal history has been so close that they have virtually amalgamated. In the nineteenth century, for example, authors like Henry Sumner Maine in England, Joseph Kohler and Hermann Post in Germany, and others sought to trace the legal development of the leading civilizations from their primitive origins to their modern state. This *legal ethnology* was based on the theory that all societies develop through the same stages, albeit at different times. Of course, trying to prove that theory required both historical and comparative data. Another example of the blending of comparative law and legal history is the approach of Alan Watson who, beginning in the 1970s, conceived of comparative law essentially as the study of legal transplants from one legal system to another throughout history (*infra* VI.B.iii., ss. 345–351). Still more recently, the agenda to utilize the medieval and early modern *ius commune* as a source for a common private law of Europe has merged both disciplines by creating comparative histories of private law doctrines and rules (*infra* s. 34). Last but not least, the concept of a "legal tradition", which has become a core paradigm of comparative law, creates overlap between the two

[46] *Zweigert and Kötz* (*supra* n. 3) 8.

disciplines by portraying the major legal cultures in the world as products of their historical development (*infra* VI.B.ii., s. 343).

34. *Differences and conflict.* – Despite these affinities and amalgamations, however, the relationship between comparative law and legal history is also marked by differences which have at times led to outright conflict.

Differences exist with regard to both methodology and objectives. With regard to methodology, legal history is blessed with a high degree of consensus, professionalism, and rigor; by contrast, comparative law is frequently plagued by confusion, amateurism, and an attitude of methodological *laissez-faire* (*infra* VI.C., s. 366). With regard to objectives, legal history usually seeks merely to understand the past; it rarely claims, or has, much immediate utility for current legal practice; comparative law, however, is pursued not only for the sake of pure knowledge but also for its practical utility (*infra* V.B., ss. 345-369). It is not much of an exaggeration to say that legal history is methodologically solid but practically useless while comparative law is methodologically incoherent but practically important.

These differences can easily lead to conflict between the disciplines. A case in point is the debate in the 1990s involving the creation of a common private law for Europe. When a group of scholars suggested promoting contemporary legal unification by building on the *ius commune*, an animated dispute arose between two camps. One camp consisted primarily of the comparatists; their main interest was to fulfill current practical needs, and they found the use of historical material for that purpose both legitimate and unproblematic. The other camp consisted of (purist) legal historians; they were quite indifferent to current unification agendas but violently objected to the instrumentalization of the *ius commune* because such a use of historical material for modern practical purposes struck them as methodologically irresponsible and epistemologically disastrous.[47]

Such differences and occasional conflicts make a true integration of the two disciplines difficult.[48] Scholars who have mastered and then combined both fields are a rare breed. And more intensive cooperation between comparatists and legal historians must come to grips with their different interests, working styles, and expectations. Still, this cooperation is not impossible, as is demonstrated in several contexts and institutions, such as various research projects pursued at the Max Planck Institute for European Legal History in Frankfurt, Germany.[49]

ii. *Legal Sociology*

35. *Basic differences.* – The relationship between comparative law and legal sociology has been discussed since the famous Paris Congress of 1900 (*infra* III.C.i., ss. 85–87), i.e., for well over a hundred years[50]. The discussion has often proceeded on a highly theoretical level typical for continental legal scholarship. Whether the – at times extensive – debates have generated much practical benefit is often open to doubt.

In several respects, comparative law and legal sociology are rather different enterprises: one compares legal systems (and their elements), the other explores law in its relationship with society. For the former, law is primarily an aspirational order, for the latter is it primarily a social fact. Thus the former often takes a normative direction (e.g., when it supports legal reform), the latter is at bottom a descriptive social science. It is hardly surprising that these disciplines have often existed in separation. In fact, they can at times function

[47] The debate generated a symposium: *Dilcher* and *Caroni* (eds.), Norm und Tradition/Fra norma e tradizione (Köln, Weimar, Wien 1998); for a critical view of the debate, see *Halperin,* L'Approche Historique et la Problematique du *Jus Commune*: Revue Internationale du Droit Comparé 52 (2000) 717–731.

[48] It has even been suggested to merge them into one discipline, *Pihlajamäki,* Merging Comparative Law and Legal History: Towards an Integrated Discipline: 66 Am.J.Comp.L. 733–750 (2018).

[49] See also *Duve* (ed.), Symposium: Legal History and Comparative Law: A Dialogue in Times of the Transnationalization of Law and Legal Scholarship: 66 Am.J.Comp.L. 727–830 (2018); *Moréteau, Masferrer and Modéer* (eds.), Comparative Legal History (Cheltenham, Northampton MA 2019).

[50] For an overview of the earlier phase of this discussion, see *Drobnig,* Rechtsvergleichung und Rechtssoziologie: RabelsZ 18 (1953) 295–305; more recent material is provided by *Friedman, Perez-Perdomo and Gomez (eds.)*, Law in Many Societies (Stanford CA 2011).

quite well without each other: there is good legal sociology that is not comparative[51] as well as good comparative law that is not sociological.[52] To be sure, claims of an intimate relationship between the two fields are common, but they are, as we will discuss below, valid mainly for particular approaches within the disciplines.

36. *Desirability of cooperation.* – It is true, however, that cooperation between comparative law and legal sociology is often highly desirable and sometimes outright indispensable.

Comparative law often needs help from a sociological approach. This is most obvious when the comparison involves legal systems with different nomenclatures and conceptual structures. In such a case, the comparatist cannot simply rely on his or her own terms and concepts, such as contract or tort, because they may not have the same meaning elsewhere. Instead, he or she must find common ground in the social problem to be solved, such as the breach of an agreement or the compensation for a wrong. The comparatist must, in other words, find the *tertium comparationis* by taking a sociological perspective and then seek to compare law that performs the same (problem solving) function. Such a functional approach has been one of the central paradigms of comparative law since the middle of the twentieth century (*infra* VI.C.i., s. 368). More generally, when one looks at the similarities and differences between legal systems, institutions, concepts, or rules, a sociological approach almost invariably adds not only descriptive depth but also great explanatory potential. Such an approach can show, for example, that law is not always the preferred mechanism of social control – one society may rely on law where another invokes customary or religious norms. In addition, a sociological perspective virtually forces the comparatist to consider not only the law in the books but also the law in action, and thus to look at a much richer, as well as often more realistic, picture. Last but not least, sociology lets us see legal rules, institutions, and processes in the light of societal conditions, political systems or market structures, thus opening the comparatist's eyes for the inevitable social contingency of law.

Conversely, where legal sociology explores the relationship between law and society, considering several legal systems is helpful in at least two regards: it vastly expands the observable database and thus the testing-ground for hypotheses, and it introduces additional variables that can be crucial for controlling results. For example, the claim that law usually makes "the haves come out ahead" is much stronger if it is verified not merely in one, but in several, legal systems.[53] In fact, to the extent legal sociology makes claims reaching beyond the realm of just one society, it *must* look to a number of representative legal systems, and thus inevitably become comparative.

The extent to which comparative law benefits from interaction with legal sociology depends largely on the concept of law embraced by comparatists. Where they conceive of law primarily in a positivist and doctrinal fashion, i.e., where they see their discipline as essentially limited to the strictly *legal* elements, the gap between the disciplines is wide, and legal sociology will rarely be consulted. This has been the mainstream tradition in nineteenth and most of twentieth century continental Europe (as well as Latin America and most parts of East Asia). Even today, prestigious and influential comparative law projects can be amazingly uninterested in the sociological dimension of law. Perhaps the most striking, as well as disconcerting, example are the (now largely defunct) efforts to unify European private law on the (quasi-)legislative level.[54] By contrast, where comparatists conceive of law in a pragmatic and sociological manner, i.e., where they see their discipline mainly as a social science or a *Kulturwissenschaft*, the gap between the disciplines is small, and comparative legal studies without legal sociology become almost unthinkable. In Europe, this approach has its roots in the work of Jhering, Gény, Ehrlich, and Nussbaum; in the United States, it has become

[51] A well-known book that provides an example is *Galanter and Palay*, Tournament of Laywers (Chicago 1991).

[52] See e.g. *Graziano*, Comparative Contract Law (Basingstoke, New York 2009).

[53] *Galanter*, Why the "Haves" Come Out Ahead: 9 Law & Soc.Rev. 95–160 (1974).

[54] See Study Group on European Private Law, Principles, Definitions and Model Rules of European Private Law, Draft Common Frame of Reference (München 2009).

dominant in the wake of sociological jurisprudence and legal realism.[55] Since the middle of the twentieth century, comparative law in much of the world has frequently turned in this, latter, direction. It has thus increasingly looked beyond law as a mere system of concepts and rules and has instead focused on its social embeddedness. This has entailed not only a growing interest in the interaction between comparative law and legal sociology[56] but actually an increasing overlap between the two fields.

37. *Examples of cooperation and overlap.* – As a result, a sociological approach has informed comparative law in a broad variety of contexts. Prominent examples include: the study of non-Western legal systems and the comparative investigation of legal cultures; analyses of the role of custom, especially in former colonies; the debates about Law and Development projects, in particular about efforts to export Western notions of Rule of Law to developing countries; the scholarship on legal actors and institutions; the debate about the relative autonomy of law in the context of legal transplants; the legal formants approach; and, most recently, the scholarship on global legal pluralism and on the role of non-state law. These topics will be explored in greater detail below (VI.B. and C.).

In several contexts the interaction between comparative law and legal sociology has been so close that the disciplines are almost indistinguishable. We find the perhaps most striking example of such an intimate relationship between them right at the birth of modern sociology, i.e., in the work of Max Weber.[57] In this regard (as well as in many others, of course), Weber has cast a "long shadow".[58] His approach has notably shaped the scholarship of his erstwhile student Max Rheinstein who claimed that wherever comparative law seeks to explore the social function of law, it "is legal sociology".[59] Weber's ideas are also front and center in the scholarship of Mirjan Damaska, whose descriptions of authority structures as hierarchical or coordinate have been highly influential in the last quarter century.[60] And Weber has had a deep influence on several other legal sociologists, some of whom have also produced important comparative legal studies, such as Richard Abel, Lawrence Friedman, Mark Galanter, and Inga Markovits.

iii. *Legal Anthropology*

38. *Basic similarities and differences.* – On the one hand, comparative law and legal anthropology are kindred subjects.[61] This is true for two reasons: both disciplines compare legal rules, institutions, and practices in order to draw conclusions from the similarities and differences they find;[62] and the legal systems studied by comparatists are of course part of the legal cultures observed by anthropologists. Both disciplines can easily overlap with legal sociology because legal systems are important elements of human cultures as well as of human societies. Thus, it is often hard to tell (and perhaps pointless to ask) where legal anthropology ends and legal sociology begins.

On the other hand, comparative law and legal anthropology differ in orientation: the former looks primarily at the technical and normative aspects of law while the latter studies mostly its cultural features and functions.

[55] See *Rheinstein*, Einführung in die Rechtsvergleichung (ed. 2 München 1987) 63–78.

[56] See *Drobnig and Rehbinder* (eds.), Rechtsvergleichung und Rechtssoziologie (Berlin 1977).

[57] *Weber*, Economy and Society II: *Roth* & *Wittich* (eds., Berkeley CA, Los Angeles CA, London 1978) 641–900. One can make similar claims with regard to the (much earlier) work of Montesqieu or even Rousseau, as well as with regard to Weber's contemporary, the founder of modern legal sociology as a field in its own right, Eugen Ehrlich.

[58] *Riles*, Comparative Law and Socio-Legal Studies: *Reimann* and *Zimmermann* (eds.), The Oxford Handbook of Comparative Law (ed. 2 Oxford 2019) 773–804, 774.

[59] *Rheinstein* (*supra* n. 55) 28.

[60] *Damaska*, The Faces of Law and State Authority (New Haven CT, London 1986).

[61] For a brief introduction to the latter, see *Donovan*, Legal Anthropology: An Introduction (Plymouth 2008). For a summary of the major issues, directions, disputes, successes, and failures as well as future directions, see *Rosen*, Comparative Law and Legal Anthropology: *Bussani and Mattei* (eds.), The Cambridge Companion to Comparative Law (Cambridge 2012) 73–87.

[62] It is a different issue that the stage of actual comparison (not to mention the drawing of meaningful conclusions from it) is often not reached in either discipline.

This divergence in orientation leads to differences regarding objects and methods. In terms of objects, comparative law usually studies contemporary legal systems, i.e., those of technically developed societies, while legal anthropology focuses mainly on traditional laws and customs, especially of indigenous, and sometimes illiterate, groups.[63] Comparatists deal almost exclusively with official law, i.e., rules created and sanctioned by the state in one form or another, while anthropologists are often concerned with customs (however defined) or practices that do not originate in, and are not backed by, state power. In terms of methods, comparatists usually work from desks and libraries (and nowadays computers), while anthropologists go into "the field" to gather ethnographic data; thus, comparative law does not necessarily involve empirical work while legal anthropology is difficult to imagine without it.

These differences notwithstanding, the lines between the disciplines are often blurred, especially where scholars compare legal cultures and their elements. On such occasions, comparative law can essentially become a variety of legal anthropology and vice versa. Thus, leading legal anthropologists have done important comparative work[64] and several comparative law scholars have successfully ventured into legal anthropology.[65]

39. *Cooperation and synergy*. – On the whole, the anthropology of law "has been of very limited import to comparative law"[66] – in part because comparative lawyers have paid scant attention to legal anthropology, but in part also because legal anthropologists have often harbored prejudices against law.[67] The low level of interaction and cooperation is regrettable because legal anthropologists and comparatists have much to learn from each other. Legal anthropology can benefit from the comparative lawyers' more precise comprehension of legal rules and better technical knowledge of legal institutions and processes. Thus, comparatists can help anthropologists to understand the conceptual frameworks, procedural mechanics, and policy goals of law. Conversely, anthropologists can show comparative lawyers how strongly legal systems are inevitably shaped by their respective cultural contexts and, in particular, how these contexts can entail fundamentally different "legal sensibilities", leading to different perceptions of social realities, moral problems, or attitudes towards facts and law.[68] Such a cultural perspective provides an important corrective for the facile functionalism that has dominated comparative law for much of the mid- and late twentieth century. In particular, an anthropological perspective often casts serious doubt on the comparatists' popular assumption that ultimately all societies have to solve the same problems,[69] through law or otherwise, or that in the long run law will be (globally) converging.

An anthropological approach to comparative law becomes indispensable when the discipline studies legal systems with strong traditional and indigenous elements. Here, the cultural aspects of law will often be more significant than the technical ones. Unfortunately, many of these systems, especially in Africa, have been largely neglected by comparative lawyers. Today, the effects of globalization make it increasingly questionable (or at least costly) to ignore these regions. Thus the calls for comparative law to

[63] Some anthropologists, however, have ventured beyond the traditional terrain into modern societies and their professional norms; see e.g. *Riles*, The Anti-Network: Private Global Governance, Legal Knowledge, and the Legitimacy of the State: 56 Am.J. Comp.L. 605–630 (2008).

[64] See e.g. *Nader*, The Life of the Law (Berkeley CA 2002).

[65] A classic is *Llewellyn and Hoebel*, The Cheyenne Way (Norman OK 1941). A more recent example is *Fikentscher*, Law and Anthropology (München 2009). See also *Cooter and Fikentscher*, Indian Common Law: The Role of Custom in American Indian Tribal Courts, 46 Am.J. Comp.L. 287–337 and 509–580 (1998); *Cooter*, American Indian Law Codes, 56 Am.J.Comp.L. 29–74 (2008).

[66] *Rosen* (*supra* n. 61) 84.

[67] *Idem* 79.

[68] *Geertz*, Local Knowledge. Law and Fact in Comparative Perspective: *idem*, Local Knowledge. Further Essays in Interpretive Anthropology (ed. 3 New York 2000) 167–234. The, by now iconic, article should be mandatory reading for every comparatist though it is fair to assume that most have never looked at (and perhaps never even have heard about) it.

[69] See *Zweigert and Kötz* (*supra* n. 3) 34; see the trenchant critique of *Geertz* (*supra* n. 68) 215–225.

include more non-western systems[70] imply a call to adopt (at least in part) a more anthropological perspective.

iv. *Economic Analysis of Law*

40. *The path to cooperation.* – Modern comparative law has consciously interacted with the economic analysis of law (or "law and economics") only since the 1990s. One reason why the relationship between the disciplines is of such recent vintage is simply that, leaving late nineteenth century efforts aside, law and economics as a distinct field is itself barely half a century old. Moreover, when the economic analysis of law rose to prominence in the 1960s through 1980s in the United States, comparative law was in decline and enjoyed scant attention there. An additional reason why the disciplines ignored each other for decades was the highly abstract approach and narrow theoretical focus of the original, i.e., Chicago, model of law and economics which remained essentially closed to considerations beyond the common law orbit. Since the 1990s, however, several legal scholars, especially in the United States, have brought the two disciplines together. They established "comparative law and economics" as a relatively small but thriving subfield. It has its own specialists, workshops (such as the Comparative Law and Economics Forum under the guidance of Robert Cooter), and a rapidly growing literature.

41. *Insights from combination.* – It is now widely accepted that blending comparative and economic analyses can generate important insights. Comparative legal studies can profit greatly from an economic approach, especially from thinking about different laws and legal systems in terms of efficiency, transactions costs, and consumer preference. Today, the use of economic considerations for both explanatory and normative purposes constitutes one of the most important interdisciplinary dimensions of comparative law; it is explored in greater detail below (VI.B.iv., s. 358).

Conversely, comparative perspectives enrich the economic analysis of law in a variety of ways. Comparative legal studies are a potent antidote to the original (and sometimes persistent) parochialism of law and economics. This parochialism created a glaring discrepancy between theory and evidence: it made scholars derive *general* claims about the efficiency of legal rules from looking only at the *particular* rules of the common law, mainly as manifested in the United States. As a result, these scholars usually ignored that the same rules can have different effects in different legal systems, depending on the respective institutions and procedures, as well as on the social and cultural background conditions. This tunnel vision problem can be overcome by looking beyond domestic law to other legal orders. A comparative perspective not only broadens the data base, it also creates a much more solid testing ground for claims about the economic foundations and functions of law. At the same time, comparative law provides law and economics theory with a reality check, so to speak, because it proffers, in Ugo Mattei's words, "a reservoir of institutional alternatives, which are not merely theoretical but actually tested by legal history".[71]

42. *Cross applications.* – It is also possible to apply the two disciplines to each other. One can study the use (or non-use) of economic analysis in different contexts or systems.[72] Conversely, one could analyze comparative law from an economic (especially efficiency) point of view; while such an approach could be interesting in its own right,[73] so far, it has not been pursued in a systematic fashion.

43. *The "legal origins" debate.* – At the beginning of the twenty-first century, tensions arose between law and economics on the one hand and comparative law on the other in the debate about

[70] See e.g. *Menski*, Beyond Europe: *Örücü and Nelken* (eds.), Comparative Law: A Handbook (Oxford, Portland OR 2007) 189–216.

[71] *Mattei*, Comparative Law and Economics (Ann Arbor MI 1997) 28.

[72] See e.g. *Grechenig* and *Gelter*, The Transatlantic Divergence in Legal Thought: American Law and Economics vs. German Doctrinalism: 31 Hastings Int. Comp.L.Rev. 295–360 (2008).

[73] See *Faust*, Comparative Law and Economic Analysis of Law: *Reimann* and *Zimmermann* (eds.), The Oxford Handbook of Comparative Law (ed. 2 Oxford 2019) 826–857, 842-848.

the "legal origins" thesis. When several economists claimed that jurisdictions originating in the common law tradition provided a more favorable business climate (inter alia for investors) than legal systems in the civil law world, comparative lawyers first ignored these claims, then chastized them as naive and misguided. This debate will be discussed in more detail below (VI.B.iv., s. 358).

v. *Legal Philosophy (and Jurisprudence)*

44. *Different orientations.* – Comparatists rarely discuss the relationship between their discipline and legal philosophy. This attests to the fact that there is very little interaction between the fields. And indeed, comparative law and legal philosophy can almost be regarded as opposites. Broadly speaking, the former focuses on the concrete multitude of legal systems in the world, the latter on law as an abstract idea and general phenomenon; the former seeks to understand similarities and differences between existing laws, the latter explores the deeper meaning and ramifications of fundamental notions about law; the former is essentially positivist and perhaps even empirical (though not necessarily in a social-science sense), the latter is concerned with values and moral judgments (though not necessarily in a metaphysical sense). As a result of these differences, the disciplines do not easily connect.[74]

45. *Need for cooperation.* – Still, the relationship between the fields is worth at least brief consideration because there is considerable potential for cooperation and cross-fertilization. Legal philosophy benefits from recognizing the properties uniting the laws of the world versus the features dividing them. Obviously, deriving general philosophical claims from the knowledge of one system alone is a dangerous business, and a comparative perspective can alleviate that risk. Comparative law, in turn, cannot deeply understand legal orders unless it pays attention to their underlying value systems, conceptions of justice, and general perceptions of the world. Comparatists thus have good reason carefully to consider the philosophical underpinnings of the law(s) they focus on;[75] by rarely doing so, they not only miss epistemological opportunities but actually risk fundamental misunderstandings. Comparative law can also be employed in the service of, or even partner with, jurisprudence, e.g., in order to develop deeper insight into the nature and structure of law.[76] Yet, again, the precise relationship between comparative studies and legal theory is rarely explored in any depth and thus for the most part poorly understood by most comparatists.

C. In Conclusion: Between Independence and Interdisciplinarity

46. *Practical utility and academic respectability.* – Comparative law wants to be both practically useful and academically respectable. The desire for practical utility drives its interaction with the other "international" subjects (*supra* I.). In this regard, comparative law is self-confident since its practical utility is not much in doubt under current conditions of globalization. The ambition to be academically respectable shapes its relationship with the "social sciences" (*supra* B. ii.). In this context, comparative law is often plagued by self-doubt because it is torn between two conflicting needs: to define itself as a subject in its own right and to venture into the terrain of its neighboring disciplines. This conflict requires some further comment.

There are essentially two ways to react to the discipline's competing needs of independence and interdisciplinarity. The perhaps more traditional reaction, which appears to be still widespread in continental Europe, is to emphasize the discipline's independent status. In order to define

[74] There was a time when comparative law and philosophy connected on the field of jurisprudence, i.e., the general theory of law (*théorie générale de droit, Rechtstheorie*); see, e.g., *Pound*, Jurisprudence (5 vol.) (St. Paul MN 1959). Unfortunately, this field has long lost what prominence it once had in the nineteenth and earlier twentieth centuries. Today it is largely out of fashion and in recent decades few comparatists have paid serious attention to it.

[75] See *Ewald*, Comparative Jurisprudence(I): What was It Like to Try a Rat: 143 U.Pa.L.Rev. 1891–2149 (1995).

[76] *Samuel*, Comparative Law and Jurisprudence, 47 I.C.L.Q. 817–837 (1998).

"what comparative law really is", this view insists "to distinguish it from other areas of legal science" so that one also recognizes "what comparative law is *not*".[77] This approach is problematic because the distinctions it draws between comparative law and other disciplines like legal history, sociology, or anthropology are often artificial; as even mainstream European comparatists concede, meaningful comparative work must often include methods and perspectives from other "social sciences". The other reaction, prevalent in the United States today and gaining ground in much of the rest of the world, is to regard comparative law as a pervasively interdisciplinary enterprise.[78] This position views distinctions between comparative law and its neighboring disciplines as a matter of emphasis, if not merely an issue of labeling. The problem here is that comparative law tends to blend into other "social sciences", calling into question whether there is anything distinctive about it.

47. *The need for interdisciplinary teamwork.* – Beyond all these issues lies a further, and rather practical, dilemma. On the one hand, comparatists must consider the historical, sociological, anthropological, economic, and philosophical dimensions of law, at least if they want to go beyond the sterile comparison of concepts and rules on the merely dogmatic level. On the other hand, comparatists can normally not be expected to command the expertise required for serious work in any of these other disciplines, not to mention in *all* of them; it is already a tall order to be conversant with several *legal* systems. This dilemma has two possible solutions: amateurism or teamwork. For better or worse, the nineteenth and earlier twentieth centuries tolerated considerable interdisciplinary amateurism, as in the work of Maine, Kohler, Wigmore, and even Weber; and it should be noted that this work has generated important, and in some cases lasting, insight. Yet, as a result of growing academic specialization, these times of tolerance for amateurism have passed, and they will not return any time soon. Given modern academic standards of professionalism, serious interdisciplinary work is usually possible only as a result of teamwork between comparative lawyers and specialists from other fields. With the notable exception of law and economics such teamwork is still largely lacking or at best in its infancy.

LIST OF PRINCIPAL WORKS

Private International Law

Batiffol, Droit comparé, droit international privé et théorie générale du droit: Rev.int.dr.comp. 22 (1970) 661–674

Fernandez-Arroyo, Private International Law and Comparative Law: A Relationship Challenged by International and Supranational Law, YB Priv.Int.L 11 (2009) 30–71

Flessner, Die Bedeutung der Rechtsvergleichung im Kollionsrecht: *Gamber and Verschraegen* (eds.), Rechtsvergleichung als juristische Auslegungsmethode (Vienna 2013) 1–22

Michaels, Comparative Law and Private International Law: *Basedow et al.* (eds.), International Encyclopedia of Private International Law I (Cheltenham, Northampton MA 2017) 417–425

Muir Watt, Private International Law: *Smits* (ed.), Elgar Encyclopedia of Comparative Law (ed. 2 Cheltenham, Northampton MA 2012) 701–715

Rabel, The Conflict of Laws, A Comparative Study (4 vol.) (Ann Arbor MI 1945–1958)

Reimann, Comparative Law and Private International Law: *Reimann* and *Zimmermann* (eds.), The Oxford Handbook of Comparative Law (ed. 2 Oxford 2019) 1339–1370

Rühl, Who's Afraid of Comparative Law? The (Side) Effects of Unification of Private International Law in Europe: Eur.Rev.Priv.L. 3 (2017) 485–522

77 *Zweigert* and *Kötz* (*supra* n. 3) 6 (emphasis in the original).

78 See e.g. *Mattei*, An Opportunity Not to Be Missed: The Future of Comparative Law in the United States: 46 Am.J.Comp.L. 709–718 (1998).

von Mehren, The Contribution of Comparative Law to the Theory and Practice of Private International Law: 26 Am.J.Comp.L. 31–41 (1978)

Public International Law

Bermann, Le droit comparé et le droit international: alliés ou ennemis?: Rev.int.dr.comp. 55 (2003) 519–537

Besson, Comparative Law and Human Rights: *Reimann and Zimmermann* (eds.), The Oxford Handbook of Comparative Law (ed. 2 Oxford 2019) 1222–1249

Bin Cheng, General Principles of Law as Applied by International Courts and Tribunals (London 1953, reprinted Cambridge, New York 2006)

Butler (ed.), International Law in Comparative Perspective (Alphen aan den Rijn 1980)

Claude (ed.), Comparative Human Rights (Baltimore MD 1976)

Flanz and Ludwikowski, Comparative Human Rights and Fundamental Freedoms (Dobbs Ferry NY 2002)

Mamluk and Mattei, Comparative International Law: 36 Brooklyn J.Int.L 385–452 (2011)

Roberts, Is International Law International (New York 2017)

Roberts, Stephan, Verdier and *Milsteeg* (eds.), Comparative International Law (New York 2018)

European Law

Bermann, Comparative Law in the New European Community: Hastings Int.Comp.L.R. 21 865–869 (1998)

Cappelletti, Seccombe and Weiler (eds.), Integration through Law (5 vol.) (Berlin, New York 1985–1987)

Howse and *Nicolaidis* (eds.), The Federal Vision: Legitimacy and Levels of Governance in the United States and the European Union (Oxford, New York 2001)

Van der Mensbrugghe (ed.), L'utilisation de la méthode comparative en droit européen (Namur 2001)

Zimmermann, Comparative Law and the Europeanization of Private Law: *Reimann and Zimmermann* (eds.), The Oxford Handbook of Comparative Law (ed. 2 Oxford 2019) 557–598.

Transnational Law

Bussani, Il Diritto dell' Occidente. Geopolitica delle regole globali (Torino 2010)

Twining, Globalisation and Comparative Law: *idem*, Globalisation and Legal Theory (London 2000) 174–193

Zumbansen, Transnational Law, evolving: *Smits* (ed.), Elgar Encyclopedia of Comparative Law (ed. 2 Cheltenham, Northampton MA 2012) 898–925.

Legal History

Beiträge zum 32. Deutschen Rechtshistorikertag in Regensburg: ZEuP 7 (1999) 494–641

Duve (ed.), Symposium: Legal History and Comparative Law: 66 Am.J.Comp.L. 727–830 (2018)

Gordley, Comparative Law and Legal History: *Reimann* and *Zimmermann* (eds.), The Oxford Handbook of Comparative Law (ed. 2 Oxford 2019) 752–771

Heutger and *Schrage*, Legal History and Comparative Law: *Smits* (ed.), Elgar Encyclopedia of Comparative Law (ed. 2 Cheltenham, Northampton MA 2012) 505–520

Ibbetson, The Challenges of Comparative Legal History: 1 Comparative Legal History 1–11 (2012)

Kötz, Was erwartet die Rechtsvergleichung von der Rechtsgeschichte? JZ 1992 20–22

Moréteau, Masferrer and Modéer (eds.), Comparative Legal History (Cheltenham, Northampton MA 2019)

Schmidt, From Evolutionary Functionalism to Critical Transnationalism. Comparative Legal History, Aristotle to Present: *Dubber* and *Tomlinson* (eds.), The Oxford Handbook of Legal History (Oxford 2018) 263–289.

Legal Sociology

Clark (ed.), Comparative Law and Society (Cheltenham, Northampton MA 2012)

Cotterell, Comparatists and Sociology: *Munday* and *Legrand* (eds.), Comparative Legal Studies: Traditions and Transitions (Cambridge 2003) 131–153

Cotterell, Comparative Law and Legal Culture: *Reimann* and *Zimmermann* (eds.), The Oxford Handbook of Comparative Law (ed. 2 Oxford 2019) 710–733

Drobnig and *Rehbinder* (eds.), Rechtssoziologie und Rechtsvergleichung (Berlin 1977)
Ehrmann, Comparative Legal Cultures (London 1976)
Friedman, Perez-Perdomo and *Gomez* (eds.), Law in Many Societies (Stanford 2011)
Nelken, Comparing Legal Cultures (Aldershot, Brookfield VT 1997)
Nelken, Legal Culture: *Smits* (ed.), Elgar Encyclopedia of Comparative Law (ed. 2 Cheltenham, Northhampton MA 2012) 480–490
Rheinstein, Rechtsvergleichung und Rechtssoziologie: *idem*, Einführung in die Rechtsvergleichung (ed. 2 München 1987) 143–186
Riles, Comparative Law and Socio-Legal Studies: *Reimann* and *Zimmermann* (eds.), The Oxford Handbook of Comparative Law (ed. 2 Oxford 2019) 772–804.

Legal Anthropology

Bennett, Comparative Law and African Customary Law: *Reimann* and *Zimmermann* (eds.), The Oxford Handbook of Comparative Law (ed. 2 Oxford 2019) 652–680
Fikentscher, Law and Anthropology (Tübingen 2009)
Geertz, Local Knowledge: Law and Fact in Comparative Perspective: *idem*, Local Knowledge: Further Essays in Interpretive Anthropology (ed. 3 New York 2000) 167–234
Nader, Comments (on Comparative Law and Anthropology): 46 Am.J.Comp.L. 751–756 (1998)
Rosen, Comparative Law and Anthropology: *Bussani and Mattei* (eds.), The Cambridge Companion to Comparative Law (Cambridge 2012) 73–87
Sacco, Anthropologia guiridica (Bologna 2007).

Economic Analysis of Law

Bernstein and Parisi, Customary Law and Economics (Cheltenham, Northampton MA 2013)
Caterina, Comparative Law and Economics: *Smits* (ed.), Elgar Encyclopedia of Comparative Law (ed. 2 Cheltenham, Northampton MA 2012) 191–207
De Geest and Van den Bergh (eds.), Comparative Law and Economics (Cheltenham, Northampton MA 2004)
De Geest, Economics of Comparative Law (Cheltenham, Northampton MA 2004)
Faust, Comparative Law and Economic Analysis of Law: *Reimann* and *Zimmermann* (eds.), The Oxford Handbook of Comparative Law (ed. 2 Oxford 2019) 826–857
Ginsburg and Garoupa, Economic Analysis and Comparative Law: *Bussani and Mattei* (eds.), The Cambridge Companion to Comparative Law (Cambridge 2012) 57–72
Mattei, Comparative Law and Economics (Ann Arbor MI 1997)
Schäfer and Ott, The Economic Analysis of Civil Law (Cheltenham, Northampton MA 2004).

Legal Philosophy and Jurisprudence

Ewald, Comparative Jurisprudence (I): What Was It Like to Try a Rat?: 143 U.Pa.L.Rev. 1891–2149 (1995)
Husa, Nicht nur als Auslandsforschung: Rechtsvergleichung als Rechtsphilosophie, Rechtstheorie (2009) 1-20
Samuel, Comparative Law and Jurisprudence: 47 I.C.L.Q. 817–837 (1998).

III. THE DEVELOPMENT OF THE DISCIPLINE

48. *Importance of a historical survey.* – A look at the history of comparative legal studies is important not only because it helps to understand the status quo as a result of past developments. More significantly, it demonstrates the historical contingency of all approaches to the subject. Over time, these approaches have constantly changed in reaction to surrounding circumstances. Thus their history alerts us also to the inevitable historical contingency of the discipline's status quo. In addition, it suggests future directions in response to the ongoing reconfiguration of the global legal order (*infra* E.iii., ss. 161–166).

49. *The problem of geographic focus.* – The following outline of the discipline's development focuses largely on the orbit of Western civilizations. This limitation is somewhat justifiable, by and large inevitable, but nonetheless lamentable. It is justifiable because the concepts of law, as well as of a "legal system", prevailing in the developed world today are largely constructs of Western civilization and scholarship; as a result, so are the prevailing approaches to comparing laws and legal systems. In other words, comparative law in its current form is a Western invention presuming a Western perspective; its historical roots thus lie in the West. The limitation to the West is also inevitable because we know very little about similar endeavors in other cultures. It may well be, and is in fact likely, that laws were compared in non-Western legal traditions as well, but these phenomena have yet to be explored through original research.[79] Finally, the limitation to the West is lamentable because understanding whether and how non-Western legal traditions have dealt with the coexistence of different laws and legal systems could provide the discipline with a more encompassing perspective needed in an age of constant global interaction between legal cultures.

50. *The problem of periodization.* – Like most historiography, tracing the development of comparative legal studies faces the dilemma of periodization. On the one hand, breaking the development up into distinct periods provides a sense of orientation and puts major shifts into sharper relief. On the other hand, continuity and change are often a matter of perspective and context. As a result, divisions into distinct periods are both desirable and debatable.

In the history of comparative legal studies, one can draw a very plausible dividing line around the year 1800. Before that time, there was by and large no comparative law in the modern sense, although there were many, and sometimes significant, precursor efforts (*infra* A.). The discipline in its modern form began to develop in the nineteenth century (B.). Eventually a recognized field of study, it solidified in the early decades of the twentieth century but then declined in the age of tyranny and war (C.). In the second half of the twentieth century, it experienced a quick revival in the post-World War II decades when it grew into a solidly established and increasingly diversified field (D.). After the end of the cold war, comparative law was shaped by the forces of globalization (E.). In the early twenty-first century, it has yet to come fully to grips with these forces and, more generally, to develop into an intellectually coherent discipline (F.).

A. COMPARATIVE STUDIES BEFORE 1800

51. *Broad definition for historical purposes.* – Whether there was comparative law before the nineteenth century depends on how we define that term. If we understand it in the modern sense of a methodologically conscious comparison between national legal systems or their elements with the objective to observe similarities and differences in order to explain or learn from them, then we know of little comparative law before 1800, some important exceptions notwithstanding; in that case, a history of the discipline could, perhaps aside from mentioning some precursor efforts, seriously begin with the nineteenth century.[80] But if we look more

[79] There are some exceptions, see e.g. *Mallat*, Comparative Law and the Islamic (Middle Eastern) Culture: *Reimann and Zimmermann* (eds.), The Oxford Handbook of Comparative Law (ed. 2 Oxford 2019) 624–651.

[80] This is the – from his perspective entirely legitimate – approach of *Constantinesco*, Rechtsvergleichung I (Köln, Berlin, Bonn, München 1971) 70-201.

broadly for comparative studies in the sense of an interest in, attention to, or even juxtaposition of different laws, then comparative law is as old as Western civilization, even though its history is marked by great variations and discontinuities.

Here, we take the latter, broader perspective. We survey the period before 1800 not in order to show the venerable old age of the discipline, but because earlier periods vividly demonstrate how even pre-modern forms of comparative studies were a response to the political and intellectual conditions of their time.

i. *Antiquity*

52. *Greece*. – The most famous, as well as most impressive, example of a work based on comparative studies in all of Western antiquity is Aristotle's (384–322 BC) (or, more likely, his school's[81]) *Politics*. The work reflects Aristotle's consideration of more than 150 Greek city state constitutions (of which only one, the Athenian, has survived). Since he is seeking to learn from the variations between these constitutions, the study must count as a serious comparative endeavor, although one may call it a work of political theory rather than of comparative law proper. We can find a similar, though less thorough, comparative approach in Plato's *Laws*. Plato (428/427–348/347 BC) describes and compares the laws of various Greek city states. His main objective is to analyze how they measure up against a constructed constitutional ideal.

Both works reflect the pluralism of constitutional regimes in the ancient Greek world as well as the general interest of philosophers and statesmen in political systems. The emphasis is thus entirely on what we today call public law. There is almost no comparison of private or commercial law,[82] which was probably regarded as a much more mundane matter of scant theoretical or philosophical interest.

The works of Plato and Aristotle prove that the idea of comparing laws with a view to learning and improvement is by no means a modern one, but at least 2500 years old. While there is no direct continuity between these works and subsequent comparative studies, such ancient pedigree was probably of some importance for much later generations of legal scholars, especially in the Renaissance and beyond. Thinkers like Grotius, Leibniz, and Montesquieu (*infra* iii.) were surely familiar with the ancient texts, and although we do not know for sure, it is likely that Plato and Aristotle provided models and encouragement for similar projects.

53. *Rome*. – It is widely assumed that Roman law was indifferent to foreign law and that this was because the Roman jurists were too firmly convinced of the superiority of their own jurisprudence to care for any other. The first part of this statement is a dangerous oversimplification, the second is largely speculation.

It is true that the classical Roman jurists showed little interest in law other than their own.[83] Yet, that does not mean that ancient Roman law as a whole and throughout its almost 1000-year history remained entirely parochial. Especially in its earlier, formative period, foreign influence is undeniable in several contexts. To begin with, it is generally recognized that the XII Tables, the earliest compilation of Roman civil laws (fifth century BC) betray significant Greek influence.[84] More generally, the Roman law of the early Republican period often adopted elements of other Mediterranean, especially Greek-speaking, cultures. And perhaps most importantly, a whole branch of Roman law once drew heavily on comparative observations: Roman jurists distinguished between the *ius proprium* which applied only among Roman citizens, and the *ius gentium* (or *ius commune*) which applied to all people regardless of their citizenship (in practice in particular to disputes involving at

[81] See *Donahue*, Comparative Law Before the *Code Napoleon*: *Reimann and Zimmermann* (eds.), The Oxford Handbook of Comparative Law (2d ed. Oxford 2019) 3–28, 4.

[82] There were apparently some traces of private law comparison in Theophrastus' *On Laws*, see *Zweigert and Kötz* (*supra* n. 3) 49.

[83] There are some comparative remarks in Gaius' *Institutes* (written ca. AD 160) but they do not evince any sustained attention to, and certainly no systematic investigation of, outside sources, see *Donahue* (*supra* n. 81) 5.

[84] See *Hug*, The History of Comparative Law: Harv.L.R. 45 (1932) 1027, 1031 (with further references).

least one non-Roman). As far as we can tell, the latter (consisting largely of private and commercial law) was originally derived inter alia from observing which institutions and rules were widely shared among the various peoples and thus constituted the perceived law of mankind. In other words, at the outset the development of the *ius gentium* was based on comparative observations, although we do not know anything about this process[85] other than that it was complete by the high classical period of Roman jurisprudence. At that time, the *ius gentium* was fully integrated into the Roman legal system, beyond which the classical jurists normally did not care to look.

The claim that the classical jurists' disinterest in comparative perspectives resulted from their contempt for foreign law is apparently based largely on a derisive remark by Cicero (106–43 BC) that Greek law is a mess bordering on the ridiculous.[86] But we do not know whether Cicero expressed a sentiment widely shared among Roman statesmen, orators, and jurists during his time or merely his personal opinion. Moreover, since Cicero died in 43 BC, i.e., before the classical period of Roman law (ca. 30 BC–240 AD), he could not possibly speak for the vast majority of Roman jurists. It is more likely that these jurists gave foreign law virtually no thought at all – just as they scarcely even considered any law or custom prevailing in the provinces. They were probably so intensely busy with developing their own law in the metropolis that paying attention to anything else did not enter their minds. Periods of high legal culture are often parochial, not because of contempt for all things foreign but because all efforts are directed towards building and perfecting a domestic legal system.[87]

54. *A curiosity from late antiquity.* – It is thus perhaps no accident that we find a – somewhat idiosyncratic – comparative work only long after the end of classical Roman jurisprudence: the *Collatio legum mosaicarum et romanorum* (sometimes also called the *Lex Dei*)[88] which was written in the fourth century AD (the period of its creation is a matter of some debate) and has survived only in part. As its title indicates, it contained a comparison of Mosaic, i.e., biblical, and Roman law. Although not always exact and often lacking rigorous analysis, it was an explicitly comparative study of two laws.[89] It is unclear exactly why it was undertaken, but its main purpose may well have been to show that biblical and Roman law were consistent in principle and thus acceptable to the Christian church.

ii. *The Middle Ages*

55. *Introduction.* – If antiquity proffers only occasional bits and pieces of comparative legal studies, the middle ages also yield a very limited crop. For our purposes, this era can thus be reviewed rather quickly. In doing so, the time-worn distinction between early, high, and late middle ages is actually quite helpful because these periods are marked by different conditions, needs, and states of legal learning. This is true with regard both to legal scholarship in general and to the development of comparative studies in particular.

56. *The early middle ages.* – We know of virtually no comparative legal studies in the first five hundred years after the fall of Rome in the European West. The reason was not a lack of opportunity but a lack of scholarly sophistication. After the Germanic invasions of the erstwhile Roman Empire, a multitude of customary laws (sometimes reduced to writing) prevailed in conjunction with lingering Roman law (now in a much more rudimentary form than during the classical period) and the law of the Roman church (gradually gaining sophistication). Yet, at least outside of the Church, there was no cadre of legal scholars, virtually no organized legal teaching, and almost no academic writing about law altogether. There

85 See *Donahue* (*supra* n. 81) 5–6.

86 *Cicero*, De Oratore i.44.197; see *Schulz*, Principles of Roman Law (Oxford 1936) 116.

87 This was true, for example for the work of the (high-medieval) Glossators, the 19th century German Pandectist School, and, to a lesser extent, for late 19th century American law.

88 The full title is *Lex Dei quam praecipit Dominus ad Moysen*, i.e., God's Law which the Lord commanded unto Moses; the standard edition is *Krüger, Studemund and Mommsen* (eds.), Collectio librorum iuris anteiustiniani III (Berlin 1890) 136.

89 An excerpt is provided by *Donahue* (*supra* n. 81) 6–7.

is occasional evidence that some authors and officials were aware of the coexistence of different legal orders, and that sometimes they put different texts side by side (and presumably compared them),[90] but there are no signs of explicit comparative observations or conclusions.

57. *The high middle ages.* – In the eleventh through thirteenth centuries we still find virtually nothing in continental Europe that would qualify as the comparative study of legal systems. Again, opportunity was not lacking because in most regions there was a continuing multitude of coexisting legal orders, ranging from Roman and canon law to feudal and customary regimes. This time, scholarly sophistication was not lacking either. From the eleventh century, legal culture was quickly reviving, first in northern Italy, then in southern France, and finally throughout much of Western Europe; full-time legal scholars appeared on the scene, law teaching was organized in universities, and academic writings proliferated. What stood in the way of comparative studies now was the jurists' belief in a divinely organized universe, and thus in law as an overarching and harmonious order. This belief directed all efforts at creating consistency within law rather than at recognizing (and comparing) differences. With regard to Roman law, the twelfth- and thirteenth-century Glossators worked doggedly to harmonize the mass of Roman sources (mainly in the recently rediscovered Digest as the central part of Justinian's sixth-century compilation) and thus to construct a consistent (private) law. At the same time, the Canonists sought to overcome the apparent contradictions in the panoply of ecclesiastical rules in order to arrive at an internally harmonious (and thus more easily usable) law of the Church. Of course, at the heart of these enterprises lay the careful comparison of individual pronouncements and sources, but this comparison took place within the four corners of one law, not between different systems. Even when scholars eventually strove to integrate Roman law (*ius civile*) with canon law (*ius canonicum*), they did not view these laws as truly separate regimes. Instead, they viewed the civil and canon laws as elements of a comprehensive legal order whose internal unity must be understood and brought to light.

58. *The late middle ages.* – It was only towards the end of the middle ages that learned jurists in continental Europe gradually came to conceive of the legal orders around them as distinct. The Glossators' successors, the so-called Commentators of the fourteenth and fifteenth centuries, began to struggle more consciously with the similarities and differences between the various laws; sometimes, they even openly recognized that Roman law said one thing, customary or local law another.[91] Recognizing such differences, especially between the various local laws (e.g., between the rising Italian city states), created the need to decide which law applied in a certain case, i.e., a need for choice-of-law rules. It is thus no accident that we find the first scholarly treatment of conflicts law in the writings of Bartolus de Sassoferrato (1313/14–1357) who sometimes also compared the potentially applicable laws.[92] In addition, comparative observations can be found in some of the *consilia* of the late middle ages, i.e., the expert opinions on difficult legal issues written by learned jurists for litigants or judges. In resolving such issues, the authors often had to consider various laws and thus to come to grips with their similarities or differences.

59. *The English difference.* – On the other side of the Channel, the situation was somewhat different. Comparative efforts began earlier and soon became more explicit. The reason was probably a greater awareness that there were distinct legal systems in the world which existed side-by-side and often differed. Perhaps this awareness was already triggered by the coexistence of (and sometimes conflict between) the indigenous English and the incoming Norman law after 1066. Quite likely, it was fostered by England's geographic separateness from the continent and by an earlier sense of national unity, statehood, and thus

[90] *Donahue* (*supra* n. 81) 7–8, mentions the case of the two written laws of the Burgundians from the early sixth century, one for the Burgundians themselves (*Lex Burgundionum*), the other for the Roman population in Burgundian lands (*Lex Romana Burgundionum*) which were very different in substance but highly similar in organization.

[91] For an example, see *Donahue* (*supra* n. 81) 11.

[92] See *idem* 11–12.

a territorial (rather than personal) conception of law. In addition, the indigenous development of English law soon made its distinct character quite obvious – a character which English lawyers often noted with pride. To be sure, the high middle ages, especially the time from the late twelfth to the early thirteenth centuries, were the formative period of the common law in which English lawyers were overwhelmingly preoccupied with their own (emerging) system. But they were not therefore entirely insular in their views. In fact, the two most famous and influential books from this era show that their authors paid considerable attention to another legal system, i.e., the Roman. In the *Tractatus de legibus et consuetudinibus regni Angliae*, written in the late twelfth century and associated with Ranulf de Glanvill (d. 1190),[93] this is evident in several regards. The author was clearly familiar with Roman law; he occasionally compared it expressly with English rules; and he borrowed a fair amount of Roman substance.[94] The Roman element is even stronger in Henry de Bracton's (ca. 1210–1268) mid-thirteenth-century treatise, also entitled *De legibus et consuetinibus Angliae*. Roman influence is clear and strong in the book, especially with regard to form and conceptual apparatus. Bracton obviously had one eye on the *Corpus Juris Civilis*, the writings of the glossator Azo of Bologna (ca. 1150–1230), and several other works on Roman and canon law, although he stopped well short of completely Romanizing the English law of his time.[95] While the authors of these two books looked at Roman (and sometimes canon) law primarily in order to borrow from it, their agenda thus implied a comparative perspective. Apparently, they were not as committed to the idea of an overarching unity of all law, as were their Italian contemporaries. Their view from across the Channel enabled them to look at the Roman, and even at the canon, law from a somewhat detached perspective.

Such an outside perspective on continental law is at center stage in John Fortescue's (c. 1394–1476) fifteenth-century tract *De laudibus legum Angliae* (c. 1470). The book presents an explicit and sustained comparison of English and French law. It is true that Fortescue's analysis is not impartial: it takes a decidedly English point of view and seeks to demonstrate the inferiority of French law.[96] That, however, does not disqualify it as a work of comparative law – a myriad comparative studies since then have been undertaken with the (explicit or implicit) purpose of showing how and why one system, institution, or rule is superior to another. One can thus regard Fortescue as the first European author of a comparative law book.

iii. *The Early Modern Period*

60. *New conceptions of law and new possibilities*. – When the middle ages yielded to the renaissance, the prevailing views of law underwent fundamental changes. These changes, in turn, entailed a new perception of the differences between legal systems. They thus created new possibilities for comparing them.

By the sixteenth century, continental jurists had not only abandoned the medieval techniques of the Glossators and Commentators (known as the *mos italicus*) but also overcome the view of Roman law as a timeless *ratio scripta* and as the benchmark of all law. Instead, they came to regard the Roman and canon laws as historical phenomena and thus as legal systems among others. In short, the early modern jurists liberated themselves from the strict authority of the classical and medieval sources. This enabled them to re-think fundamental precepts and thus eventually to develop systems of natural law; it allowed them to take customary and local laws more seriously and thus to make them an object of study and analysis; and it freed them to accept the

[93] Glanvill was chief justiciar of England under Henry II and almost certainly not personally the author, see *Pollock and Maitland*, The History of English Law before the Time of Edward I (ed. 2 Cambridge 1898) 142–143.

[94] *Plucknett*, A Concise History of the Common Law (ed. 5 Boston MA 1956) 298.

[95] *Pollock and Maitland* (*supra* n. 93) 186–187.

[96] Perhaps somewhat ironically, it was written in France, namely in exile. Fortescue also compared England and France with regard to the political systems in his tract on *The Governance of England*. (ca. 1471)

existence of legal diversity and to seek historical and socio-cultural explanations for it. In all these endeavors, the comparative study of legal systems and rules played a role, although that role differed greatly depending on the context.

a. *Natural Law*

61. *The search for a new universalism.* – A hallmark of the early modern period was the search for a new unity of all law which could no longer be found in the Roman tradition, nor in the law of the church, alone. This search manifested itself mainly in the construction of natural law systems which began in the sixteenth, culminated in the seventeenth, and petered off in the eighteenth century. The comparative observation of existing (positive) laws played a significant role in the search for universal commonalities that could be taken as generally valid for all mankind.[97]

In their efforts, natural lawyers frequently resorted to a multitude of legal sources, drawn mainly from biblical, Roman, and canon law, the writings of the ancients as well as medieval philosophy and jurisprudence. In most instances, the reference to these sources served mainly to illustrate the general validity of the abstract maxims and rules proclaimed by the natural law thinkers; this is typically the case, for instance, in the natural law writings of Hugo Grotius (1583–1645).[98] Occasionally, however, the excerpts from these diverse sources were also analyzed in order to ascertain their commonalities from which universal principles could then be derived; examples of this, at least partially bottom-up, approach can be found in the work of Samuel Pufendorf (1632–1694).[99] In the former case, the natural lawyers did not compare the legal sources they cited, in the latter they did, albeit decidedly in a search for a universal law. Thus, the comparison of laws was a fairly common practice in the "age of reason".

In this context two projects are worth mentioning although neither came to fruition. In early seventeenth-century England, Francis Bacon (1561–1626) suggested the compilation of a universal law; and roughly a century later in Germany Gottfried Wilhelm Leibniz (1646–1716) propagated the plan of a *theatrum legale*, essentially a combination of the laws of the world. Both men wanted to base their projects on the comparative study of all existing legal regimes, but neither made a serious effort actually to undertake it. Still, such ambition to create uniform legal regimes was to become a recurring theme in nineteenth- and twentieth-century comparative law (*infra* V.B.iv ss. 176–178) and to return, in a more sober and limited fashion, in form of various comparative law-based global unification projects.

b. *National Law*

62. *The integration of national laws.* – In continental Europe, the early modern period was also marked by persistent efforts to integrate the multitude of laws into more or less uniform national systems. These, less lofty and more practice-oriented, undertakings laid the foundations for the great codifications of the eighteenth and nineteenth centuries. They were often based on the comparison between the coexisting legal regimes at the time.[100]

In the sixteenth century, the French humanist jurists, such as Guy Coquille (1523–1603), turned their attention to the diversity of the regional and local customs existing in the northern half of their country (*droit coutumier*). At the time, these customs were written down and redacted. In written form, they could be studied and systematically compared in order to identify commonalities and to overcome differences. They were also, albeit more occasionally, compared with the *ius commune* prevailing south of

97 See *Mohnhaupt*, Vergleichende Beobachtung von Staat, Gesellschaft und Recht im 18. Jahrhundert als Vorform der modernen Rechtsvergleichung: Comparative Law 14 (1997) 1–24.

98 Mainly *Grotius*, De iure belli ac pacis (Paris 1625); by contrast, *Grotius*, Inleiding tot de Hollandsche rechtsgeleerdheit (Den Haag 1631), i.e., his introduction to the Dutch legal system, is part of the tradition of establishing, or consolidating, national legal systems by drawing on a variety of contemporary sources.

99 For such an example, see *Donahue* (*supra* n. 81) 20–26.

100 See *Mohnhaupt* (*supra* n. 97) 17–23.

the Loire (*droit écrit*).[101] These comparative studies gradually laid the foundations for the eventual unification of French law two centuries later.

In German lands, comparisons between the received Roman and local customary law began in the sixteenth century *differentiae* books listing the differences between these laws.[102] A century later, German jurists, prominently among them Georg Adam Struve (1619–1692) and Samuel Stryk (1640–1710), began to adapt the inherited Roman law to modern practical usage (*usus modernus pandectarum*). This involved constant comparison between the general *ius commune* and the more particular legislative and customary regimes of the various German regions. Their mutual adaptation and reconciliation gave rise to many foundational doctrines and rules of German private law as it then carried over into the later eighteenth and the nineteenth centuries.[103]

Efforts to integrate a variety of sources within the national orbit can be found on the other side of the Channel as well. An early, and somewhat idiosyncratic, example is Christopher St. Germain's (1460–1540) *Doctor and Student* (1531), which compared canon law and common law in the form of a fictitious dialogue between a representative of each. The work became famously influential for the development of the Equity side of English law. A similar work was published by William Fulbecke (1560–1603) three generations later, also in dialogue form; its title aptly describes the work: *A Parellele or Conference of the Civil Law, the Canon Law and the Common Law of this Realme of England* (1601). The book was no more than that: a parallel description of these three laws; it contained no analysis and had no visible influence. A much more impressive example of this genre came from late seventeenth-century Scotland. In his *Institutions of the Law of Scotland* (1683), Lord Stair (James Dalrymple, 1619–1695) laid the foundations of modern Scots law not only by drawing on indigenous material but also by integrating a large variety of continental jurisprudence. His sources ranged from Justinian's *Corpus Iuris* (and especially his *Institutes*) and the canon law to several dozen continental writers mainly of the natural law tradition, Grotius prominently among them; at the same time, Stair excluded English writers and cases. Finally, one must at least briefly mention another Scot, Lord Mansfield (William Murray 1705–1793), who was, as Chief Justice of the King's Bench, the most influential judge in late eighteenth-century England, and who virtually created modern English commercial law by integrating many civil law principles and doctrines.

It is true, of course, that these early modern jurists in France, Germany, England, and elsewhere in Europe compared laws not with a merely scientific interest in recognizing and explaining their similarities and differences. It is also true that the laws they brought together were not foreign to them in the sense of applying merely somewhere else; they were by and large applicable within their own countries.[104] Still, these jurists did compare different laws in a serious fashion, often with considerable sophistication and painstaking care, and sometimes explicitly with the purpose of identifying the best solutions.

A special case was Portugal where the early modern period was marked by an intense, "but sometimes also excessive",[105] use of comparative law. Portuguese jurists tried to modernize the traditional studies of Roman law by looking at the German (and Dutch) *usus modernus pandectarum*, Italian and French law, and even the statutes of German port cities like Hamburg and Lübeck. This passion for comparative studies of foreign laws later extended to Brazil where it has lingered until the present.[106]

[101] For an illustration, see *Donahue* (*supra* n. 81) 13–16.

[102] Their model was the late-medieval comparisons between civil and canon law, see *Wieacker*, Privatrechtsgeschichte der Neuzeit (ed. 2 Göttingen 1967) 171 (with further references).

[103] The French and German scholars were not alone in these endeavors. Similar efforts were undertaken in other European countries, such as Italy and Spain, as well; see *Hug* (*supra* n. 84) 1041.

[104] Constantinesco aptly termed their work "comparaison interne", *Constantinesco*, Rechtsvergleichung: Die rechtsvergleichende Wissenschaft III (Köln 1983) 71.

[105] *Kleinheisterkamp*, Comparative Law in Latin America: *Reimann and Zimmermann* (eds.), The Oxford Handbook of Comparative Law (ed. 2 Oxford 2019) 252–288, 256.

[106] See *idem*, 256–257.

c. *Academic Law*

63. *Selden and Montesquieu.* – In the early modern period, there were also a few scholars who used comparison not as a mere means to an end – to detect a natural law order or create a national legal system – but simply in order to explore and explain similarities and differences. In other words, they compared primarily to understand the historical or socio-cultural contingency of laws.

Two of these scholars – one English, one French – came to have a lasting influence on later generations.

John Selden (1584–1654) became the founder of comparative legal history. Commanding an exceptional breadth of knowledge, his works on the development of English law are replete with comparative references, especially regarding the influence of Roman law. Selden was unusual for his time in that he ventured beyond the orbit of European law and also wrote on the history of the Judaic and middle eastern traditions.[107]

A century later, Charles de Montesquieu (1689–1755) published his *Esprit de lois* (1748) – a book which is often counted as the first true work of comparative law in a modern sense. Reflecting the by then considerable knowledge of the world, especially of overseas areas such as the Americas, India, and the Far East, Montesquieu's perspective was virtually global. His approach was scientific in the sense that he genuinely observed and described laws as historical data, not as abstract ideals. He did not try to synthesize the observed differences in order to create a higher unity but accepted the diversity of laws in the world as part of the human condition. Montesquieu sought to explain the similarities and differences of laws mainly as results of geographic, climatic, cultural, religious, and social factors (thus underemphasizing the intellectual aspect). To be sure, many of the data which he used were unreliable, if not outright false, and many of his explanations lacked a critical perspective and look amateurish, at least from today's point of view. But in its social science approach, in its effort to maintain an objective perspective, and in its genuine search for understanding, the book laid important foundations not only for the comparative study of law but also for sociology, political science, and economics.

B. THE NINETEENTH-CENTURY FOUNDATIONS OF COMPARATIVE LAW

64. *Modern conditions.* – While comparative legal studies were surely not lacking in pre-1800 Europe, the foundations of comparative law as a recognized discipline in its own right were primarily laid in the nineteenth century. Only now did the conditions exist to make comparative law in the modern sense broadly possible. On the side of academia, the most important factors were the rise of an autonomous legal science of positive law, the increased diversification of legal scholarship, and the rapid institutional growth (in continental Europe) or first-time institutional establishment (in the common law orbit) of university law teaching. On the side of the law, the crucial developments were the consolidation of positive law on the national level (often expressed in codifications), the now virtually ubiquitous territorial demarcation of its force, and the emergence of the idea that comparison must involve legal regimes prevailing in different countries. Thus comparative law could now gradually develop into an academic discipline that focused on the similarities and differences between different national legal systems.

65. *Diversity of developments.* – Yet, even in the nineteenth century, the development of comparative law into a distinct discipline was far from monolithic. To begin with, it was driven by a variety of motives which engendered a variety of approaches: interest in learning about foreign law out of sheer curiosity or for purposes of domestic law reform; a search for universal principles of law similar to the quest for such principles in the rising fields of (comparative) anatomy, linguistics, and religion; a belief that legal evolution could be understood only from a broad, i.e., comparative perspective; a desire to bridge the now obvious

[107] Selden was also a prominent writer on issues of international law, especially on contemporary problems of the law of the sea which he approached from a natural law perspective, and he was deeply involved in the stormy politics of seventeenth-century England.

gaps between national legal systems; etc. In addition, the development of the discipline was not consistent over time. Instead, it was marked by continuities as well as discontinuities, changing fashions and false starts, and in particular by waxing and waning popularity. Finally, it also varied depending on the country involved. This was already true within Europe, and it becomes even more visible when we look overseas.

It must suffice here to consider the most salient developments in the most influential countries.[108] In this context, it is useful first to distinguish the discipline's genesis in continental Europe (*infra* i.) from that in the common law orbit (ii.) because the conditions under which the comparative study of law developed differed considerably between these two spheres. In addition, we will take a quick look at nineteenth-century Latin America (iii.).[109]

i. *The Development in Continental Europe*

66. *Overview.* – In the nineteenth century, the most significant developments took place in the two countries with the, at the time, leading universities in continental Europe, i.e., Germany and France, but some lasting contributions also came from Italy. This does not mean that no comparative studies took place anywhere else, only that such studies had little influence on shaping the emerging discipline on a broader scale.

On the level of scholarship, there was something like an early flowering in the first half of the nineteenth century (*infra* a.), followed by a decline around its middle, and, at its end, a resurgence in a variety of forms (b.). In addition, comparative studies played a significant role in the making of legislation throughout the century (c.). Finally, comparative law came into its own by becoming institutionalized in the form of learned societies, academic journals, and university chairs (d.).

a. *Early Nineteenth-Century Beginnings in Germany and France*

67. *The ambivalent impact of the Historical School.* – Legal thought in early nineteenth-century Germany was dominated by the Historical School under the leadership of Friedrich Carl von Savigny (1779–1861). While it has been said that the Historical School "had a particularly repressive effect on the development of comparative law",[110] the story is actually more complicated. On the one hand, it is true that Savigny and his followers showed virtually no serious interest in foreign legal systems. To be sure, this was somewhat ironic. After all, one of the Historical School's two fundamental credos was that the law is an expression of a nation's *Volksgeist* (spirit of the people). The resulting belief in the deeply idiosyncratic character of each people's law could, and arguably should, have been a good starting point for comparative studies, as Montesquieu had shown. But in practice, the Historical School's followers focused either on the Roman law Germany had received in the early modern period or on the indigenous German law, while they cared little for anything else.[111] On the other hand, however, the Historical School fostered the development of comparative law, albeit unwittingly. Its second fundamental credo was that law is a product of history. This entailed a turn away from the abstract speculation of the natural lawyers and, quite in tune with the rise of historical studies generally, towards observation of positive law. Such observation, in turn, is essential for comparative studies.

[108] For more detailed studies of the developments in the major European countries, the United States, East Asia, and Latin America, see the ten essays in Part I of *Reimann and Zimmermann* (eds.), The Oxford Handbook of Comparative Law (ed. 2 Oxford 2019) 29–288.

[109] Since the development of comparative law in East Asia began only in the closing decades of the 19th century and then expanded in the 20th it is considered below III.C.iv.b.

[110] *Zweigert and Kötz* (*supra* n. 3) 50; see also *Hug* (*supra* n. 84) 1053.

[111] It is usually overlooked in this context, however, that, again somewhat ironically, Savigny himself engaged in a lengthy, and to some extent comparative, analysis of foreign law in one of his key publications. His famous "Vom Beruf unserer Zeit für Gesetzgebung und Rechtswissenschaft" (Heidelberg 1814; transl. by Abraham Hayward, "Of the Vocation of Our Age for Legislation and Jurisprudence", London 1831) spends most of chapter 7 (and nearly a third of the whole pamphlet) analyzing the recent codifications of France (the *Code civil* of 1804) and Austria (the *Allgemeines Bürgerliches Gesetzbuch* of 1811).

In other words, the Historical School's insistence on studying positive law as it had actually developed in history helped to lay the foundations on which comparative law could build.

68. *The German flowering in the first half of the century.* – In the first half of the nineteenth century, comparative legal studies in Germany developed into a limited but sophisticated field of scholarship. This development was fueled by the models provided by other disciplines, especially (comparative) religious and linguistic studies, by the desire to create jurisprudential alternatives to the orthodoxies of the Historical School, and by the practical need for law reform. It involved mainly a small but influential group of scholars, especially in the south of the country, three of whom deserve particular mention.

Important foundations were laid by Paul Johann Anselm von Feuerbach (1755–1833). Heavily influenced by Kantian idealism, Feuerbach became one of the most significant criminal law theorists of the nineteenth century. Feuerbach was a vociferous advocate of a comparative approach to legal studies and thus also a decided opponent of the Historical School's parochialism. His comparative approach was driven by two interests. First, he firmly believed that a true legal science was possible only on the basis of comparing different legal systems – a belief he famously expressed by writing: "Why does the anatomist have his comparative anatomy and why does the legal scientist not yet have a comparative legal science? The richest source of all discoveries in every empirical science is comparison and combination".[112] Second, he considered comparative studies essential to effective law reform. Thus, when he drafted the 1813 Criminal Code for Bavaria[113] – the first modern, and hugely influential, criminal code in Germany – he studied especially French and Italian criminal law which was, at the time, considerably more advanced and enlightened than Germany's.

Even more committed to the comparative study of law, as well as more active in the field, was Feuerbach's student Karl Joseph Anton Mittermaier (1787–1867). Mittermaier was the most prominent scholar of criminal law and procedure of his generation, a long-time member of his state's legislature, a liberal politician in turbulent times, an active law reformer, and a (multilingual) correspondent with a host of foreign scholars. He extended the horizon of comparative studies by reaching out beyond continental European countries to England, Scotland, and even the United States. Mittermaier's interest in foreign law was mainly practical, i.e., motivated by his lifelong pursuit of legislative reform, of which especially the German law of criminal procedure was in dire need at the time. Mittermaier also promoted the formation of comparative law as a discipline by founding, in 1829, the first scholarly journal entirely focused on foreign law, the *Kritische Zeitschrift für Rechtswissenschaft und Gesetzgebung des Auslandes*. Thus if one looks for a founding father of comparative law in Germany, Mittermaier is perhaps the most plausible candidate.

The third member of this group of influential scholars in the German south was Mittermaier's colleague at the University of Heidelberg and co-founder of the *Kritische Zeitschrift*, Karl Solomon Zachariae von Lingenthal (1769–1843). Zachariae was a scholar mainly of private law with a focus especially on the French *Code civil*. His *Handbuch des französischen Zivilrechts* (Heidelberg 1808) provided French law with a systematic structure and became hugely influential even in France (in a French translation) throughout the nineteenth century. Zachariae's work was not only practically important at a time when parts of Germany were governed by French law as a result of Napoleonic occupation; it also powerfully demonstrated the benefits of studying foreign legal sources and helped to bridge the gap between German and French private law.

While the contributions of these scholars to the development of comparative law were very significant, one must not overlook the limitations inherent in their approach. Since they were inter-

[112] "Warum hat der Anatom seine vergleichende Anatomie? und warum hat der Rechtsgelehrte noch keine vergleichende Rechtswissenschaft? Die reichste Quelle der Entdeckungen in jeder Erfahrungswissenschaft ist die Vergleichung und Combination." *Feuerbach*, Blick auf die deutsche Rechtswissenschaft: *idem*, Kleine Schriften vermischten Inhalts (Nürnberg 1833) 152–177, 163.

[113] Criminal Code for the Kingdom of Bavaria (*Strafgesetzbuch für das Königreich Bayern*) of 1813.

ested mainly in the knowledge of foreign law, they often did not proceed to the actual comparison of these laws. Since their interests were primarily practical, they did not build any epistemological frameworks for the comparative study of law. And since they by and large focused on contemporary laws, they paid little attention to law as a historical (or even evolutionary) phenomenon.

The work of a fourth German scholar differed in all these regards. As a professor in Berlin as well as a Hegelian, Eduard Gans (1797–1839) stood apart from Feuerbach, Mittermaier, and Zachariae both in space and orientation. Gans' interest was not merely in knowing foreign law but in comparing it; his ambition was not practical but, one might say, philosophical; and he was primarily interested not in contemporary legislation but in the historical evolution of the law. All this is evident in his *magnum opus*, *Das Erbrecht in weltgeschichtlicher Entwicklung* (The Law of Inheritance in Its Global Historical Development) (4 vol.), (Berlin 1824–1835). The book presents a comparative history of the law of inheritance from an evolutionary perspective. In its universalist ambition,[114] it resembles Montesquieu's *Esprit de lois*, a work much admired by Gans. It is also a major contribution to comparative legal history. Although it was much disparaged by various members of the Historical School (to which Gans was vehemently opposed), and although its universalism seems overambitious and unsound today, the book was a milestone in the history of comparative law because of its commitment to deriving fundamental insights from the comparison of laws on a global scale.

Around mid-century, this early flowering of comparative law in Germany came to an end. By 1850, the work of Feuerbach, Mittermaier, and Zachariae was done – and not continued by others; the publication of the *Kritische Zeitschrift* ended in 1856; and German legal science was dominated by the *Pandektenwissenschaft* with its efforts to perfect the systematization of the Roman law – an entirely domestic enterprise without any concern for the law of other countries. In 1866, Rudolf von Jhering (1818–1892) lamented the state of legal science in words famous among comparatists: "The science [of law] has sunk to the level of a national jurisprudence, the scientific boundaries of jurisprudence coincide with the political ones. A degrading, unworthy state for a science!"[115]

69. *Early nineteenth-century France.* – The early nineteenth century was not a propitious time for comparative legal studies in France. The codification of French (civil, commercial, criminal, and procedural) law at the beginning of the century dominated French legal consciousness in both academia and practice so thoroughly that the mainstream showed no interest in the law of other countries. The vast majority of French jurists were too busy expounding the texts of their codes, and perhaps also too happy finally to have a unified law to be receptive to foreign ideas.

Yet, again, there were countervailing trends as well. The consolidation of French law on the national level also allowed, indeed it invited, looking abroad, and there was in fact *some* interest in foreign law by both writers and government institutions. Yet, it was focused on simply collecting (and translating) foreign legislation in order to create a storehouse of ideas for possible domestic use. Scholarly engagement with foreign law was rare.

An exception of sorts was Jean-Jacques Gaspard Foelix (1791–1853) whose claim to fame, however, rests primarily on his contributions to private international law. Foelix had strong connections to Germany and established ties with jurists in many parts of the world. Still, like his contemporary, Mittermaier, Foelix was mainly interested in promoting the knowledge of foreign law for law reform purposes. Following Mittermaier's example, in 1834 Foelix founded a scholarly journal devoted to that purpose, the *Revue étrangère et française de législation*. Its title already indicated its focus on foreign legislation. There was at the time little interest in actual comparison for academic purposes, not to mention in any kind of theory of comparative law.

[114] It bore the subtitle *Eine Abhandlung der Universalgeschichte* (A Treatise on Universal History).

[115] *von Jhering*, Geist des römischen Rechts auf den verschiedenen Stufen seiner Entwicklung (ed. 2 Leipzig 1866) 15; the first edition, published in 1852, did not contain this statement).

As in Germany, however, these early efforts did not last. Around the middle of the century they came to an end for the time being. In 1850, the *Revue étrangère* ceased to appear.

b. Mid- to Late Nineteenth-century Scholarship

70. *In General.* – In continental Europe, comparative law experienced a gradual revival after the middle of the nineteenth century. This revival had various causes, among them an intensification of international economic relations, and, as a result, a generally growing interest in international cooperation, increasing legislative activity, and a concomitant search for best solutions.

In the second half of the century, a considerable number of comparative works covering a wide spectrum of substantive areas of law were published in several countries by various authors. Prominent among them were Levin Goldschmidt, Joseph Kohler, and Franz von Liszt in Germany, Raymond Salleiles in France, and Ernest Lehr in Switzerland.[116] These studies, however, remained by and large individual works which had little influence on the development of the discipline as such. But there were also three broader directions which helped to shape the field in the longer run, in one way or another: comparative legal history, comparative ethnology, and emerging theories of comparative law itself.

71. *Legal history.* – The nineteenth century was the time when history became established as a full-fledged discipline in its own right, and legal history participated in its rise to prominence, especially in the closing decades. Liberating itself from the Historical School's concern with contemporary law as well as from its narrow focus on Roman and indigenous German sources, legal historiography now began to reach beyond national boundaries. Especially in Germany (Andreas Heusler, Konrad von Maurer, Felix Liebermann) but also in France (Adhémar Esmein), this generated scholarship of lasting value, for example on Nordic and Old English legal history. Most of this scholarship was not in and of itself comparative, but it laid invaluable foundations for twentieth-century historiography on a European scale.

72. *Legal ethnology.* – A related, but idiosyncratic, kind of comparative studies focused on the development of law on a global scale. These studies were influenced by Hegelian philosophy of history, Darwinian ideas of evolution, and comparative philology, and they sometimes built on the earlier work of Eduard Gans (*supra* s. 68), Josef Unger (1828–1915),[117] and Johann Jakob Bachofen (1815–1887).[118] Amalgamating these elements, several late nineteenth-century scholars pursued the writing of truly universal legal histories. In seeking to trace the development of fundamental institutions on a broadly comparative basis, they reached way beyond the Western world and looked at the law of ancient as well as so-called primitive cultures, especially in Africa and Asia. These scholars shared the ambition to discover the laws governing the development of all legal cultures from a primitive to a modern state, but their methods, geographic focus, and scope of inquiry varied. The extreme protagonists of this "legal ethnology" were Albert Post (1839–1895) and Josef Kohler (1849–1919)[119] in Germany whose work, however, was soon discredited as uncritical and superficial. Closely related was Henry Sumner Maine (1822–1888)[120] in England whose scholarship has withstood the test of time somewhat better. In earlier decades, Eugéne Lerminier (1803–1857) and Emerico Amari (1810–1870)[121] had published works in a similar spirit in France and Italy, respectively.[122]

On the whole, the endeavor was a failure. It lacked a sound empirical basis, was heavily biased in favor of finding similarities and regularities, and uncritically believed in uniform and linear historical developments.[123] By the end of the nineteenth century, "legal ethnology" had

[116] *Constantinesco* (*supra* n. 104) 127–129.

[117] *Unger,* Die Ehe in ihrer welthistorischen Entwicklung (Wien 1850).

[118] *Bachofen,* Das Mutterrecht (Stuttgart 1861).

[119] See e.g. *Post,* Bausteine für eine allgemeine Rechtswissenschaft auf vergleichend-ethnologischer Basis (Oldenburg 1880–1881); *Kohler,* Einleitung in die vergleichende Rechtswissenschaft (Würzburg 1885).

[120] *Maine,* Ancient Law (London 1861); *idem,* Early History of Institutions (London 1875).

[121] On Amari, see also *infra* s. 73.

[122] *Lerminier,* Introduction générale à l'histoire du droit (Bruxelles 1829); *Amari,* Critica di uns scienza delle legislazioni comparate (Rubbettino 2005 and Genova 1857).

[123] For a more detailed evaluation and critique, see *Constantinesco* (*supra* n. 104) 150–159.

collapsed – one might say: under its own weight. In the long run, this scholarship has had a negative impact on comparative law: its failure has deterred generations of comparatists from seriously looking beyond the "civilized world"; it has thus contributed to the separation of comparative law from ethnology (and anthropology).

73. *Emerging theories of comparative law*. – The second half of the nineteenth century was also the time when scholars first began to develop theoretical foundations for the comparative study of law. The pioneering effort was made by the Sicilian jurist Emerico Amari (1810–1870). As the title of his major work, *Critica di una scienza delle legislazioni comparate* (Genua 1857), indicates, Amari still focused somewhat narrowly on law in the sense of legislation. Importantly, however, he conceived of its comparative study as an autonomous discipline which needed a theoretical framework. Amari advocated the pursuit of two primary goals. First, the discipline had to explore the forces shaping legislation by considering factors like climate, religion, customs, the economy, i.e., in a manner reminiscent of Montesquieu (see *supra* A.iii.c., s. 63). Second, it had to discover the regularities in the development of the laws in time and space, to arrive at a "biology of laws",[124] i.e., in a manner similar to the "legal ethnology" fashionable in subsequent decades. After Amari, Gumersindo de Azarcate (1840–1917) in Spain and Clovis Bevilacqua (1859–1944) in Brazil also sought to provide comparative law with some general foundations.[125] While these scholars' concrete ideas as such have had little or no impact on the modern understanding of comparative law, their work indicates a gradual change of consciousness: jurists engaged in comparative studies began to think of comparative law not merely as an instrument for this or that purpose but as an emerging discipline in its own right.

c. *Comparative Legislation and Legal Unification*

74. *"Legislative comparative law"*. – In nineteenth-century continental Europe, the legislature eventually became the dominant lawmaker, overshadowing both courts and scholars. And if there was a single dominant purpose of comparative legal studies, it was to serve the making of legislation. This "legislative comparative law"[126] was particularly pronounced in Germany (and later in Switzerland) where national law still needed to be unified, but the focus on legislation was noticeable in France and elsewhere as well.

In Germany, the legislative use of comparative law was prominent already during the early period of flowering, noticeably in the work of Feuerbach and Mittermaier who studied and used foreign laws mainly for law reform purposes (*supra* a., s. 68). It rapidly gained momentum around the middle of the century, and the consideration of foreign ideas soon became a staple in the legislative process. This was noticeable first in the unification of commercial law when the legislature drew on comparative studies in drafting the General German Negotiable Instruments Law (*Allgemeine Deutsche Wechselordnung*) of 1848 and the General German Commercial Code (*Allgemeines Deutsches Handelsgesetzbuch*) of 1861. The use of foreign ideas then influenced many major legislative projects towards the end of the century, such as the Code of Civil Procedure (*Zivilprozeßordnung*) of 1879, and it finally also marked the making of the capstone piece of legislation, the German Civil Code (*Bürgerliches Gesetzbuch*) of 1900. The trend continued into the twentieth century, especially with regard to the ongoing reforms of German criminal law. Ever since, it has been virtually *de rigueur*, especially for the staff of the Federal Ministry of Justice, to consider foreign law in the preparation of important legislation.

One can observe similar developments in Switzerland when its private law was being unified at the end of the nineteenth and beginning of the twentieth centuries (*Obligationenrecht* 1881, *Zivilgesetzbuch* 1907/12). To be sure, as in Germany, much comparative work was "internal", i.e., focused on bringing the various legal regimes within the country together, but foreign law was considered as well and had a significant influence in several regards. Again, as in Germany, legislation in Switzerland is almost routinely influenced by comparative considerations.

[124] *Amari* (*supra* n. 122) 216, 428, 487.

[125] *Constantinesco* (*supra* n. 104) 131–132.

[126] *Zweigert and Kötz* (*supra* n. 3) 51.

France found itself in a different situation because it had unified its law at the beginning of the nineteenth century. Yet, the legislative focus of comparative studies was, if anything, even stronger than elsewhere. In large part, this was simply because in nineteenth-century France legislation was the only officially recognized form of law so that comparative law amounted to "législation comparé". This was already evident in the work of Foelix (*supra* a., s. 69). But there was an official, government, aspect of this trend as well: in 1876, the French Ministry of Justice created a *Comité de législation étrangère et de droit international* which was charged with the collection and translation of the most important foreign codes and statutes.

d. *The Institutionalization of Comparative Law*

75. *Learned societies and legal periodicals.* – The recognition of comparative law as a discipline also expressed itself in the founding of various learned societies and specialized legal periodicals. Again, France and Germany led the trend, although some other countries, like Belgium and England (*infra* ii., ss. 77–80), were not far behind. And again the focus was, at least originally, primarily on comparative legislation, i.e., on the exploration, collection, publication, and sometimes translation of foreign statutes, mainly for purposes of domestic law reform.

The first legal periodical specializing in foreign law was founded in Germany, namely, as mentioned, by Mittermaier and Zachariae in 1829 (*Kritische Zeitschrift für Rechtswissenschaft und Gesetzgebung des Auslandes*). Their example was soon followed, five years later, by Foelix in France (*Revue étrangère et française de législation*). With regard to academic associations, it was the other way around. France took the lead with the *Société de législation comparée* in 1869 which continues to be very active today. Germany followed in 1893 with the *Gesellschaft für Vergleichende Rechts- und Staatswissenschaft*, and in 1894 with the *Internationale Vereinigung für vergleichende Rechtswissenschaft und Volkswirtschaftslehre* which lives on as the *Deutsche Gesellschaft für Rechtsvergleichung* today.

In the late nineteenth century, specialized legal periodicals began to proliferate: this began with the French *Revue internationale de droit comparé* (since 1869) and many other countries followed suit: Belgium with the *Revue de droit internationale et de législation comparé* (1869); Germany with the *Zeitschrift für vergleichende Rechtswissenschaft* (1878) and the *Vierteljahresschrift für vergleichende Rechts- und Staatswissenschaft* (1896);[127] Spain with the *Revista de derecho internacional, legislacion y jurisprudencia comparadas* (1884); and Italy with the *Rivista di diritto internazionale e di legislazione comparata* (1898).[128] As a result, by the end of the century, comparative legal studies had a variety of institutional platforms.

76. *Comparative law in the universities.* – In France, the discipline also established itself in the universities, albeit slowly. Already in 1831, a chair for comparative legal history was founded at the Collège de France, followed in 1846 by a chair for comparative criminal law at the University of Paris. But it took almost half a century for other chairs to be created: for comparative maritime and commercial law (1892), comparative constitutional law (1895), and finally for comparative private law (1902). The German universities were slow to follow, and it took well into the twentieth century for chairs in comparative law to be established. The late acceptance of comparative law in the universities – and in the curriculum – shows that despite its gradual recognition as a discipline its own right, the field still played a very marginal role in late nineteenth-century continental European legal academia and practice.

ii. *The Common Law World*

a. *The United Kingdom*[129]

77. *Overview.* – Politically, nineteenth-century England may have existed in "splendid isolation", but jurisprudentially it was amazingly open to

[127] As of 1897, it appeared under the title *Zeitschrift für vergleichende Rechts- und Staatswissenschaft*.

[128] *Constantinesco* (*supra* n. 104) 137.

[129] For a more detailed account, see *Cairns*, Development of Comparative Law in Great Britain: *Reimann* and *Zimmermann* (eds.), The Oxford Handbook of Comparative Law (ed. 2 Oxford 2019) 111–147.

foreign law and comparative perspectives. As on the continent, the English engagement with other legal systems had an academic and a practical side, although they were often closely related. The academic side was driven by the search for a jurisprudence, first in an analytical, later in a historical mode; the practical side resulted from the needs of the British Empire. Towards the end of the century, comparative studies in England became institutionalized in a manner similar to those in Germany and France.

78. *Academic comparative law.* – It is often overlooked that early nineteenth-century English jurisprudence was highly receptive to continental ideas. Jeremy Bentham's (1748–1832) trenchant critique of the English common law and his advocacy for codification betrayed the impact of French law, especially of the Code civil (1804). John Austin (1790–1859), the founder of analytical jurisprudence, introduced enormous amounts of continental learning, especially of modernized Roman law, into English legal theory. And even the late nineteenth-century version of analytical jurisprudence (Thomas Erskine Holland, John Salmond, et al.) built pervasively on continental learning. To be sure, English analytical jurisprudence was not comparative in the sense of explicitly juxtaposing different laws, but it was highly cognizant of foreign scholarship and brought together legal systems by using continental concepts and structures and by trying to impose them upon English substance.

In the second half of the century, English comparative jurisprudence turned mainly historical, but it did so in a variety of different ways. To begin with, the most prominent representative of this historical jurisprudence was Henry Sumner Maine (1822–1888). Maine studied the development of legal institutions of the Aryan and Indo-Germanic peoples from a comparative perspective, especially in his principal work, *Ancient Law* (London 1861). His work was an early version of "legal ethnology" and thus preceded the efforts of Jhering, Post and Kohler in Germany (*supra* i.b., s. 72). Reflecting contemporary beliefs in evolution, Maine espoused the idea of progress in the development of law, most famously *"from Status to Contract"*.[130] Furthermore, under the influence of Maine, several late nineteenth-century scholars, notably James Bryce (1838–1922) and Sir Frederick Pollock (1845–1937), focused on the comparison between (ancient) Roman and (modern) English law – conscious, of course, that they were comparing the laws of the dominant empires then and now. Their work was motivated in part by the assumption that the development of Roman law paralleled the course of English law and thus allowed predictions about the future of the latter. More generally, they were convinced that a true science of law must be both historical and comparative. In fact, for Pollock, historical and comparative studies were so closely intertwined that he claimed: "it makes no great difference whether we speak of historical jurisprudence or of comparative jurisprudence."[131] Finally, one must mention the work of Frederic William Maitland (1850–1906). To be sure, unlike Maine, Bryce or Pollock, Maitland was not interested in comparative jurisprudence, i.e., in broad evolutionary patterns of law in general. Instead, he was devoted to the meticulous study of English legal history in its own right. Yet, Maitland saw the development of English law in a European context, and his publications include numerous references to, and comparisons with, continental (especially French and German) developments with which he was intimately familiar.

79. *Practical comparative studies.* – Nineteenth-century English comparative law also had a practical side which responded to the needs of both the world's dominant empire and its leading trading nation. As the metropolis of an empire, Britain ruled over numerous colonies governed by Dutch-Roman, Spanish, French, as well as Hindu and Muslim law. Some knowledge of these laws was thus a practical necessity. Not only did appeals from these colonies come to the Privy Council as the British Empire's highest tribunal, at times Britain also had to legislate for its possessions. These needs motivated William Burge's (1787–1849) massive, four-volume *Commentaries on Colonial and Foreign Laws* (London 1838). Burge not only provided a comprehensive survey of a large variety of laws prevailing in the

[130] *Maine*, Ancient Law (*supra* n. 120) 100 (italics in the original).

[131] *Pollock*, The History of Comparative Jurisprudence, 5 J.Soc.Comp.Leg. 74–89, 76 (1903).

colonies, He also compared them and suggested how to resolve conflicts between them. As the world's leading trading nation, Britain was connected with overseas countries all over the globe. This also required an understanding of their respective laws. In response to this need, Leone Levi's (1821–1888) *Commercial Laws of the World* (London 1854) compared the mercantile law of England with its counterparts in 58 other countries worldwide. Both Burge's and Levi's works were truly comparative. They also exemplified the understanding widely shared in Britain at the time that comparative studies must first and foremost serve practical needs. After all, even Maine opined that "the chief function of Comparative Jurisprudence is to facilitate legislation and the practical improvement of the law".[132]

80. *The institutionalization of the discipline.* – The "late-Victorian crystallization of comparative law" in England[133] manifested itself in various institutional forms. In 1869, a chair for "Historical and Comparative Jurisprudence" was founded at Oxford with Maine as its first holder. In 1894, University College, London, created a chair of "History of Law and Comparative Law". In the same year, following the French model (*supra* i.d., s. 76), the *Society of Comparative Legislation* was founded in London; it was, however, focused mainly on the British Empire well into the twentieth century. It still exists today. Like several of its continental equivalents, the *Society* published its own periodical, the *Journal of the Society of Comparative Legislation.*

b. The United States[134]

81. *The continental influence during the "formative period of American law".*[135] – The early United States found itself in a situation very different from European countries like Germany, France, or England: it did not have a fully developed legal system, and it lacked an established academic culture. As a result, the American engagement with foreign law in the ca. 80-year period between gaining independence (1776–1783) and the Civil War (1861–1865) was almost exclusively driven by practical needs. In this period, "comparative law was not an organized force, certainly not a discipline" but rather a method of importing foreign ideas.[136]

Of course, most of the law in the original thirteen colonies came from England, but English law was far from perfectly suited for the young American republic. It was built on a different social structure, reflected different geographic conditions, and responded to a different economic situation. It was widely unpopular as a result of two wars with England (1776–1783 and 1812–1815), out of tune with the enlightenment values of the founding generation, and distrusted by the Puritan immigrants. Also, with all its outdated medieval formalism, it was badly in need of reform even at home. In addition, with westward expansion the United States soon acquired huge territories governed by civil, i.e., French and Spanish, law. Thus, when jurists and statesmen began to build an American legal system, the common law had to undergo a serious transformation. In this process, the import of foreign law played a significant role.

The foreign imports hailed mainly from two related areas. First, early American lawyers drew heavily on the continental natural law tradition. Familiarity with this tradition was part of the general education of lawyers and politicians at the time; many among the founding fathers, John Adams and Thomas Jefferson prominently among them, were conversant with the writings of Grotius, Pufendorf, Domat, Vattel, Burlamaqui and others. Second, American jurists looked to the civil law tradition; this included the modernized Roman law as well as French authors and sources, especially writings of Robert Pothier (1699–1772) and the *Code civil.*

The two most prominent and influential importers of such ideas were also the principal founders of nineteenth-century American law. James Kent (1763–1847) laid the foundations in

[132] *Maine*, Village Communities in the East and West (London 1913 orig. 1871) 4.

[133] *Cairns* (*supra* n. 129) 113.

[134] For a more detailed account, see *Clark*, Development of Comparative Law in the United States: *Reimann* and *Zimmermann* (eds.), The Oxford Handbook of Comparative Law (ed. 2 Oxford 2019) 148–180.

[135] The title is taken from *Pound*, The Formative Era of American Law (Boston MA 1938).

[136] *Clark* (*supra* n. 134) 156.

a four-volume treatise entitled *Commentaries on American Law* (New York 1826–1830). Going through numerous editions, it was destined to become one of the most popular law books in nineteenth-century America. His contemporary Joseph Story (1779–1845) added *Commentaries* and other basic works on almost a dozen central areas of law about a decade later (1832–1845). Many of his treatises also became instant classics. Kent and Story were not only prolific authors but also served as highly influential judges for several decades. Both in their books and on the bench, they adapted the common law to contemporary American needs, and in doing so they frequently drew on continental natural and civil law sources and doctrines. In most instances, references to foreign law merely supported the result Kent and Story could have reached on common law grounds alone. In other words, foreign references helped to legitimize the outcome because it was also in accordance with the law or nature of reason, and with the civilian tradition. Such a showing implied comparison between the common law and foreign materials. In some cases, however, the citation of natural or civil law authors amounted to mere window dressing and may just have served to impress the authors' readers or judicial colleagues.[137] Kent and Story were not alone in their interest in, and reliance on, continental legal ideas. Instead, such interest and reliance was widely common in the early to mid-nineteenth-century United States. This is true both with regard to the legal literature and with respect to judicial practice.[138]

Civil law influence was also noticeable in an entirely different context, i.e., the reform and codification of the law of civil procedure. Around the middle of the century, David Dudley Field (1805–1894) drafted a modernized civil procedure code which was adopted in New York in 1849 and subsequently became hugely influential throughout the United States. Field also drafted a full-fledged civil code which, though failing in New York, became the model for codifications in several Western states. Of course, the concept of codification itself was a civilian one, and some of Field's more specific ideas also suggest a continental European origin. In Field's case, foreign influence likely did not come directly from Europe but rather by way of Louisiana as the only enduring civil law jurisdiction in the United States.[139]

By the time of the Civil War, the work to build an American system of law was by and large done. The need to draw on foreign law diminished radically and interest in continental law declined accordingly. At least among practitioners it seems to have disappeared almost entirely. Yet, it was about to be revived among legal scholars, albeit in a different context (*infra* s. 83).

82. *The cultivation of Roman law.* – Beyond Kent's and Story's enterprise to Americanize the common law, several American jurists also maintained a broader interest in Roman and civil law which endured throughout the nineteenth century.[140] In the antebellum South, this interest coincided with the cultivation of a life-style reminiscent of antiquity (including slave-holding, neo-classical architecture, and fashionable Roman and Greek names). After the Civil War, these scholars focused on civilian learning mainly as a model of conceptual clarity and systematic organization. Thus, when they taught Roman law in the rising American law schools, they no longer sought to influence contemporary positive law, but rather to provide their students with a broad, jurisprudential view of law by showing it in the form of a true "science". The group of American Romanists remained small and their overall influence was marginal. Still, they helped to keep some knowledge of the Roman and civil law alive and thus maintained possibilities for comparison with the indigenous material.

83. *The historical turn during closing decades.* – After the Civil War, American law found itself in a

[137] *Watson*, Chancellor Kent's Use of Foreign Law: *Reimann* (ed.), The Reception of Continental Ideas in the Common Law World 1820–1920 (Berlin 1993) 45–62.

[138] *Helmholz*, Use of the Civil Law in Post-Revolutionary American Jurisprudence: 66 Tul.L.Rev. 1649–1684 (1992).

[139] *Clark*, The Civil Law Influence on David Dudley Field's Code of Civil Procedure: *Reimann* (ed.), The Reception of Continental Ideas in the Common Law World 1820–1920 (Berlin 1993) 63–87.

[140] *Hoeflich*, Roman and Civil Law and the Development of Anglo-American Jurisprudence in the Nineteenth Century (Athens, GA 1997).

very different situation. An indigenous legal system was firmly established, legal education was being institutionalized at the university level, and a cadre of full-time academics formed after the German and French models. In this new environment, comparative studies now took place largely in an academic context.

Under the more distant influence of Savigny and the German Historical School and the more direct influence of Maine in England as well as in tune with contemporary ideas of evolution, American legal scholarship took a historical turn. Postbellum legal scholars focused largely on the history of Anglo-American law, but many of their works contained significant comparative elements. A major reason was the ongoing debate whether the roots of the common law were essentially Germanic or Roman – a debate which also raged in England at the time. In pursuit of this question, scholars such as Henry Adams (1838–1918), James Barr Ames (1846–1910), Melville Bigelow (1846–1921), and James Bradley Thayer (1831–1902) studied especially German scholarship on the history of German(ic) law in order to compare its findings with the development on the common law side.[141] The result was a rather sophisticated comparative legal historiography, albeit with an unmistakable ideological touch. The best-known book from this period is Oliver Wendell Holmes' (1841–1935) *The Common Law* (1881). While Holmes' object was "to present a general view of the Common Law",[142] the book is replete with references to other legal systems and foreign sources. They include Roman law, Germanic folk laws, the writings of Kant and Hegel, and nineteenth-century German and French scholarship. These foreign elements are not mere window dressing but an integral part of Holmes' analysis of the origins and nature of the common law.

iii. *Latin America*[143]

84. *The heyday of legislative comparative law.* – While Europe took the lead in comparative legal scholarship, Latin America was unmatched in "legislative comparative law" in the second half of the nineteenth century. In no other region of the world was lawmaking as thoroughly, consistently, and successfully built on comparative studies as in South America. Even *Meiji* Japan (*infra* C.iv.b., s. 104) could not rival that continent when it came to the breadth and diversity of sources considered, and the intensity of comparison among them.

In a sense, Latin America had been governed by foreign laws for centuries because had it lived under Roman and canon law, the thirteenth-century Spanish *Siete Partidas* as well as other laws of the various colonial powers, although the latter were often ineffective in practice. Yet, the process of national lawmaking consciously based on comparative studies really began when Latin American countries gained their independence in the early and mid-nineteenth century.

To begin with, they needed constitutions. In this regard, the impact of European enlightenment ideas coincided with the model of the United States Constitution, then the most modern and liberal in the world. In some cases, as in Argentina and Mexico, Latin American constitution making involved large-scale adoptions especially of the US model; in others it entailed more careful comparison between competing alternatives. In one way or another, most early Latin American constitutions betrayed the influence both of the French Revolution and of the early American Republic.

In the second half of the nineteenth century, the primary agenda was the codification of private and commercial law. Almost invariably, drafting the codes lay in the hands of leading and erudite scholars. They constitute a long list of names, prominent among them Eduardo Acevedo (1815–1865) in Uruguay, Andres Bello (1781–1865) and José Gabriel Ocampo Davila (1799–1882) in Chile, Texeira de Freitas (1816–1883) in Brazil, and Dalmacio Velez Sarsfeld (1800–1875) in Argentina. These scholars were familiar not only with Roman and canon law, the Spanish tradition, and the French Code civil. They also drew on a

[141] *Rabban*, Law's History: American Legal Thought and the Transatlantic Turn to Legal History (Cambridge, New York 2013); *Reimann*, Historische Schule und Common Law (Berlin 1993) 113–114.

[142] *Holmes*, The Common Law (Boston MA 1881) 5.

[143] For a more detailed account, see *Kleinheisterkamp* (*supra* n. 105) 257–273.

large variety of other European sources, such as Prussian and other German, Italian, and in some cases even English law. Rarely has the world seen such breadth of learning in private law and, for better or worse, such eclecticism in codification. The codes of some countries, such as Chile and Argentina, were then often adopted (usually with modifications) by smaller nations, so that at the beginning of the twentieth century, Latin American private (and often also commercial) law was by and large codified in modern form.

C. THE FIRST HALF OF THE TWENTIETH CENTURY

i. *The Paris Congress*

85. *Paris 1900.* – Rarely is the exact turn of a century as famous a milestone in the history of a discipline as the year 1900 is for comparative law. From July 31 through August 4 of that year, the *Société de législation comparée* organized the (first) *Congrès International de droit comparé*. It was held during the 1900 Paris World Exposition and with the official imprimatur of the French government. The core of the participants consisted of continental European law professors: all General Reporters were French, and virtually all reports were authored by French, German, Italian, and Belgian scholars, with the French taking the lion's share. There were some practitioners and government representatives as well, and a few of the participants came from overseas, e.g. from England, Canada, the United States, and Mexico. Organized in six sections, the Congress covered a wide variety of topics, ranging from general methodological questions to international private, commercial, civil, public, and criminal law. The contributions consisted of 76 reports and comments covering hundreds of pages.[144] Typically for its age, the Congress was animated by a strong belief in the progress of mankind in the spirit of modern rationality.

86. *Birthplace of modern comparative law.* – The Paris Congress is widely considered the birthplace (and -hour) of comparative law as a modern discipline in the sense of a "collective, concerted venture, guided by theories, methods, and projects".[145] Indeed, at least four considerations support such a view. To begin with, the Congress occasioned the first systematic and thorough discussion of the fundamental issues of comparative law as a discipline, i.e., its definition, object, function, and method. These issues were addressed mainly by the two most influential participants, Raymond Saleilles (1855–1912), the principal organizer, and Edouard Lambert (1866–1947), the General Reporter for the first section. (*Théorie générale et méthode*). The problems, however, were not resolved in Paris and continue to be debated today (*infra* IV.). Second, the Congress developed a concept of comparative law as an autonomous branch of legal science. As such, the discipline had to be liberated from (legal) history, sociology, ethnology, etc.; it needed to proceed beyond providing mere knowledge of foreign law; and it had to be more than just a tool of legislative reform. At least in the eyes of Saleilles and Lambert, its task was the scientific exploration of legal systems with the principal goal of discovering their commonalities – the "*révélation du droit commun législatif*".[146] Third, as an event, the Congress provided comparative law with the self-image of a distinct field and its players with a professional identity. Tell-tale evidence of this new understanding was the fact that comparatists showed a sense of tradition: Frederick Pollock's contribution addressed the history of comparative law.[147] Finally, the Congress connected the protagonists of the discipline on an international level. It thus not only created a sense of scholarly community but also boosted

[144] The contributions and proceedings were published as *Congrès international de droit comparé, Procès-verbaux de séances et documents* (2 vol.) (Paris 1905/07).

[145] *Frankenberg*, Critical Histories of Comparative Law: *Dubber and Tomlin* (eds.), The Oxford Handbook of Legal History (Oxford 2018) 43–62, 44. As such, the event's 100th anniversary was duly celebrated at a Congress in New Orleans in the year 2000; see *infra* s. 159. On both the Paris Congress and its successor, see *Michaels*, Im Westen nichts Neues?, RabelsZ 66 (2002) 97–115.

[146] *Lambert*, Théorie générale et méthode: Congrès International du Droit Comparè, Procès-Verbaux des Séances (Paris 1905) 26–60, 47.

[147] *Pollock*, Le Droit Comparé, Prolégomènes de son histoire: Procès-Verbaux de Séances 248–261.

the international discourse among the members of the newly constituted guild.

87. *Narrow conception.* – Yet, the view that comparative law as a discipline was born at the Paris Congress implies a rather narrow definition of the field. It assumes that the projects of Aristotle, Fortescue, St. Germain, and Montesquieu, of Mittermaier, Foelix, Maine, and Kohler had not *really* been comparative law but rather something preliminary or akin to it. Indeed, the concept of comparative law arising from the Paris Congress was marked by several distinct limitations, unsurprisingly evincing considerable French path dependency. First, comparative law could deal only with comparable legal systems, i.e., those of civilized nations; that certainly included the European civil law systems and their various offshoots, but the status of common law jurisdictions was already somewhat in doubt as they lacked the systematic organization and legislative formation expected by French jurists. Second, the principal focus of the discipline was on legislation, quite in the tradition of *législation comparée* – again a distinctly continental perspective which found it difficult to accept law made by judges in the common law style. Third, comparative law was clearly biased in favor of commonalities among legal systems; it was not to focus on differences, never mind the explanation, or even celebration, of diversity. While their approaches were not entirely alike, for both Saleilles and Lambert the ultimate goal was to find the law common to the civilized nations,[148] inter alia to promote the international unification of law. Finally, it was tacitly understood that the discipline was concerned with national legal systems. Comparison of laws had to take place among countries, not (as in much of the early modern period) within them; in other words, it had to be external rather than internal. Nor was it concerned with other, more encompassing, legal orders, such as public international law or the *ius commune*. In summary, at its quasi-official founding, the discipline was essentially conceived as the comparison of the national legislation of civilized nations for the purpose of eliciting commonalities. *That* concept was, at least arguably, indeed born in Paris in 1900. It was also bequeathed to or, one might say, imposed upon the new century.

ii. *Continental European Developments*

88. *Overview.* – It is fair to say that the great hopes resulting from the Paris Congress for the future of the discipline were by and large not fulfilled in the first half of the twentieth century, arguably with the exception of France. For the most part, the field of comparative law remained rather narrowly defined, both in its basic approach and its geographic scope (*supra* s. 87), although some European scholars began to pay more attention to the common law world.[149] The first two decades of the new century were still mainly devoted to further theoretical musings and debates about the discipline's nature, functions, and objectives. In the 1920s, a more practical orientation gradually emerged in the context of a broader turn towards international cooperation, itself a reaction to the horrors of World War I. Yet, before these more practical efforts could bear fruit on a significant scale, the rise of totalitarianism in many parts of Europe, and soon the cataclysm of World War II, massively interrupted further progress.

a. *Comparative Law in the Universities*

89. *France.* – At the Paris Congress, the leadership in comparative legal studies passed from Germany to France, where the discipline gradually consolidated itself. The main protagonists in the early twentieth century, Saleilles and Lambert, intended to use comparative studies primarily to free French legal science from the straightjacket of the *école d'exegèse* which had dominated the nineteenth century and whose obsession with the text of the codes had engendered parochialism and loss of touch with legal realities.[150] Under Saleilles' and Lambert's leadership, and that of

[148] The idea of a "global law" ("Weltrecht") had already been floated by the German jurist Ernst Zitelmann a dozen years before the Paris Congress, *Zitelmann*, Die Möglichkeit eines Weltrechts (München, Leipzig 1916, orig. 1888).

[149] See e.g. *Lévy-Ullmann*, Le système juridique d'Angleterre (Paris 1928).

[150] *Jamin*, Le vieux rêve de Salleiles et Lambert revisité: Rev.int.dr.comp. 52 (2000) 733–751.

their successor Henri Lévy-Ullmann (1870–1947), the field blossomed in the 1920s and 1930s. Gradually, scholars turned from the methodological and epistemological questions raised during the Paris Congress to more practical concerns mainly of two kinds. First, comparative law was employed to provide guidance for the interpretation and further development of domestic law. Second, it had to serve as an instrument of international legal unification, reflecting Saleilles' and Lambert's ideas of a "*droit commun législatif*" (*supra* S. 86). Still, even in France the results of these efforts remained ultimately modest because they had a limited impact on mainstream scholarship.

Comparative law was taught in many French universities on a regular basis, though usually in close connection with private law, as *Droit civil approfondé et comparé*. This indicated the discipline's primary function as an instrument in the service of (domestic) private law development. On the whole, much of this teaching was rather unsophisticated as well as uncoordinated and thus failed to produce significant results.[151]

90. *Germany.* – With the notable exception of criminal law,[152] comparative legal studies were virtually non-existent in early twentieth-century Germany, and in contrast to France, comparative law was not taught in German universities at all. The interpretation of the newly enacted Civil Code of 1900 (*BGB*), as well as of several other major codifications from the late nineteenth century, apparently absorbed virtually all academic energy and led to an isolation of German scholarship and teaching from most of the rest of the world. In addition, the demoralizing effect of the failure of late nineteenth-century legal ethnology (*supra* B.i.b, s. 72) apparently lingered.

Comparative legal scholarship was revived to some extent in the early 1920s. The motivation to look at foreign law again resulted mainly from practical exigencies: the Treaty of Versailles, written in French and English but directed primarily against Germany, forced German authorities to grapple with the laws of the victors, particularly in the context of the international arbitration tribunals adjudicating claims under the Treaty. In reaction, Ernst Rabel (1874–1955), himself a member of one of the tribunals and at times of the Permanent International Court of Justice at The Hague, called for a turn towards comparative law. In 1924, he published an essay on the "Mission and Necessity of Comparative Law" which became foundational for the discipline in Germany and widely influential beyond.[153] In this essay, Rabel first approached the discipline mainly from a theoretical perspective. The main objective of comparative law, Rabel explained, was pure knowledge and understanding; in particular, the discipline's theoretical uses included overcoming the parochialism of a merely domestic perspective on law, clarification of fundamental concepts, and enrichment of perspectives. Yet, Rabel also emphasized the practical uses of the discipline. In particular, he called for the international unification of law to which he contributed with a major comparative study of the law of sales.[154] Rabel went beyond his French contemporaries in three important respects. First, he portrayed comparative law as a broadly enlightening enterprise with a wide array of theoretical and practical uses. Second, in a manner reminiscent of American legal realism, he demanded that comparative studies go beyond legislative texts and include court decisions as well as commercial practices. Third, he called for a truly global approach, resembling the universalism of the legal ethnologists fifty years earlier, though without their belief in ubiquitous patterns of social and legal development. Rabel was destined eventually to become one of the towering figures in twentieth-century comparative law – in his role as the director of the newly founded *Kaiser-Wilhelm-Institut* in Berlin (*infra* S. 92), as a promoter of international legal unification, and as a defining influence on later generations of comparatists especially in Germany and the United States. Despite the work

151 *Constantinesco* (*supra* n. 104) 163.

152 *Birkmeyer et al.* (eds.), Vergleichende Darstellung des deutschen und ausländischen Strafrechts (10 vol.) (Berlin 1905–1908).

153 *Rabel* (*supra* n. 17); *Rabel*, Aufgabe und Notwendigkeit der Rechtsvergleichung: *idem and Leser* (eds.), Gesammelte Aufsätze III (Tübingen 1967) 1–24, reprinted in *Zweigert and Puttfarken*, Rechtsvergleichung (Darmstadt 1978) 85–108.

154 *Rabel*, Das Recht des Warenkaufs (2 vol.) (Berlin, Leipzig 1936 and Tübingen 1958).

of Rabel and a few others,[155] however, comparative law remained at the margin of German legal scholarship, largely because further growth was interrupted by the devastating impact of the Nazi period on German academic culture.

In a darkly ironic way, however, the Nazi regime had a tremendous influence on the future development of comparative law. This was not because the discipline made any significant progress between 1933 and 1945 – quite to the contrary: to the extent comparative studies were pursued at all, they gradually deteriorated into an instrument of National Socialist propaganda. It was rather because many of the leading scholars had to leave Germany as they were (at least in the eyes of the National Socialists) Jewish, Ernst Rabel prominently among them. Most of these jurists ended up in either Britain or the United States. They carried with them the learning which provided a fresh start for the discipline in the common law world in the 1950s and beyond (*infra* D.iii.b., ss. 132–134).

91. *Other continental countries*. – Comparative law gradually established itself in other parts of the continent as well, but by and large progress remained slow.

Italian scholarship experimented with a variety of approaches. In the work of Giuseppe Mazarella (1868–1958), ethnological jurisprudence experienced a revival. In a somewhat similar vein, Mario Rotondi (1900–1984) saw comparative law as a means to detect deeper social laws underlying the positive legal order. Salvatore Galgano (1887–1965), like Saleilles and Lambert, conceived of comparative law as a means to improve and interpret national legislation. And for Giorgio del Vecchio (1878–1970) the discipline was concerned with universal ideas and thus took a philosophical turn. In addition, a small group of practically minded commercial law scholars – Tullio Ascarelli (1903–1959), Angelo Sraffa (1865–1937), and (again) Mario Rotondi – looked at foreign jurisdictions (including common law countries) with an open mind and in a pragmatic spirit; yet, they remained a separate group of specialists without any influence on the larger academic world in their country. Still, several universities created chairs for comparative law, providing a basis for fairly regular teaching. In Switzerland, comparative legal scholarship had emerged already in the late nineteenth century, especially in Eugen Huber's (1849–1923) *System und Geschichte des schweizerischen Privatrechts* (Basel 1886–1893) – a major comparative study, albeit mainly on an internal level, which became the foundation of the Swiss Civil Code (*ZGB*, 1907, in force 1912). Before and after the turn of the century, Ernest Lehr (1835–1919) published several works on foreign (English, American, Scandinavian, and Russian) law. In the early twentieth century, Ernest Roguin's (1851–1939) unfinished multivolume study of comparative private law deserves mention,[156] and Georges Sauser-Hall (1884–1966) wanted the discipline to reveal the trajectory of legal evolution in yet another return to nineteenth-century ideas.[157] Comparative and foreign law was taught at several Swiss universities and especially developed in the French-speaking parts, i.e., in Geneva, Lausanne, and Neuchatel.

b. *The Further Institutionalization of Comparative Studies*

92. *The national level*. – The institutionalization of comparative law, which had begun in the latter half of the nineteenth century, continued apace in the first decades of the twentieth. In this regard as well France took the lead. In 1921, Lambert founded the *Institut de droit comparé* in Lyon which focused mainly on romanist legal systems and on the common law, especially of the United States. Three years later, Jacques Maury (1889–1981) established the *Institut de droit comparé de pays latins* in Toulouse. Lévy-Ullmann followed suit in 1931 with the *Institut de droit comparé* at the University of Paris. The French institutes maintained many international connections, especially with British scholars, and had a significant impact on scholarship and, in some cases, lawmaking abroad.

[155] Especially Ernst Zitelmann (1853–1923) and Franz Schlegelberger (1876–1970).

[156] *Roguin*, Traité de droit civil comparé (7 vol.) (Paris 1908–1912).

[157] *Sauser-Hall*, Fonction et méthode du droit comparé (Geneva 1913).

In Germany, Ernst Rabel founded the *Institut für Rechtsvergleichung* at the University of Munich in 1924. Two years later, Rabel became the director of the *Kaiser-Wilhelm-Institut für ausländisches und internationales Privatrecht* in Berlin. In the seven years under his leadership (1926–1933), the institute acquired an international reputation as one of the most sophisticated and productive enterprises of its kind,[158] with a library of over 200,000 volumes (including the largest collection of American legal materials outside of the United States). Rabel also launched the *Zeitschrift für ausländisches und internationales Privatrecht* (since 1927) which lives on as the *Rabels Zeitschrift* today. On the public law side, there was the *Institut für ausländisches öffentliches Recht und Völkerrecht* which also became the venue of a hononymous *Zeitschrift* (since 1929). In addition, several German universities had comparative law institutes.

Similar developments took place in other European countries. On the Italian side, the *Istituto di studi legislativi* opened in Rome in 1926 and published the *Annuario di diritto comparato e di studi legislativi*; comparative law institutes were established in several other Italian universities. In Brussels, the *Institut belge de droit comparé* opened in 1908 and began publishing a *Bulletin trimestriel* in 1922.

93. *International institutions.* – Comparative studies now also found homes on the international level. A late nineteenth-century case in point was the Hague Conference on Private International Law (founded in 1893 and continuing to operate today). After World War I, broad support for renewed international cooperation led to the establishment of the *Académie International de Droit Comparé* in Geneva which soon moved to The Hague. It held its first International Congress in The Hague in 1932, beginning a tradition of quadrennial congresses which has been maintained until the present. In 1926, the League of Nations sponsored a similar undertaking when the *Istituto internationale per l'unificazione del diritto*, commonly known as *UNIDROIT*, opened its doors in Rome. All these institutions provided permanent, albeit still limited, venues for cooperation between scholars across national boundaries.

iii. *The Common Law World*

a. *The United Kingdom*[159]

94. *The leading figure.* – On the other side of the Channel, comparative law also led a respectable, but ultimately somewhat marginal existence. The most prominent and influential figure was Harold Gutteridge (1876–1953) who taught at the London School of Economics and later in Cambridge. He emphasized the importance of comparative law for private international law, legal unification, international trade, and domestic law reform. Gutteridge had a lasting influence not only as the director of institutes for comparative law in London and Cambridge, but also as the author of the first English treatise on the subject in its modern form, *Comparative Law: An Introduction to the Study of the Comparative Method of Legal Study and Research* (Cambridge 1946). The book was published in Cambridge in 1946, widely read throughout the common law world in subsequent decades, and became somewhat of a classic.

95. *Major directions of the discipline.* – Pre-World War II comparative law in England was oriented in three major directions. First, considerable work focused on France, not only because it was considered the leader in the field but also because French was more commonly understood among academics and students than other foreign languages. The slender *Introduction to French Law* published in Oxford in 1935 by (Sir) Maurice Amos (1872–1940) and Frederick Walton (1858–1948) best exemplifies this direction. Despite their admiration for French comparative law, however, British scholars mostly rejected the French idea of a *droit commun législatif*, thus demonstrating the time-honored British skepticism vis-à-vis international legal unification. Second, much of English comparative law continued to operate in the context of the – gradually crumbling – British

[158] After World War II, it was continued as the *Max Planck Institut für ausländisches und internationales Privatrecht*, first in Tübingen, then at its present home in Hamburg.

[159] For a more detailed account, see *Cairns* (*supra* n. 129) 120–138.

Empire. It thus focused on the laws of the British colonies and protectorates: Ottoman and Islamic law in the Middle East, Hindu law in India, and Roman Dutch law in South Africa. This branch was represented especially by Amos who, besides obtaining a *licence en droit* in Paris, learned Arabic to work as a judge in Egypt and who published a study on the constitutional history of that country.[160] In the 1920s, there were even plans to establish an "Imperial School of Law" in London in which the various laws of the Empire could be studied, but these plans ultimately came to naught. The third area of interest was the relationship between common law and Roman law, inter alia in Scotland and South Africa. A fruit of this Romanist side is the widely known book by William Buckland (1859–1946) and Arnold McNair (1885–1975), *Roman Law and Common Law – A Comparison in Outline* (Cambridge 1936).

96. *Institutional weakness.* – The institutional foothold of the discipline remained fairly weak. One the one hand, the *Society of Comparative Legislation* continued its work, and there were a few institutes for comparative studies in the universities. On the other hand, there was neither a chair directly devoted to the discipline nor any systematic teaching of it, although there were several courses on various laws of the Empire.

Mainly as a result of these weaknesses, British comparatists were frequently unhappy about their discipline's state of affairs at the time. In particular, they felt that it lagged way behind the developments in France, and in 1941 Gutteridge himself lamented the poor state of comparative law in British legal academia.

97. *Lasting contributions.* – At least from today's perspective, however, such gloominess is not entirely warranted, because several "[s]eeds had been sown that germinated after the war".[161] For example, by studying the influence of European laws on overseas colonies, comparatists in the United Kingdom realized that legal cultures often adopted foreign codes or rules. Amos and others thus began to recognize the phenomenon of legal transplants (*infra* VI.B.iii., ss. 345–346). They also came to reject the (Savignian) idea that law necessarily expresses the spirit of a people – if Japan could adopt a quasi-German civil code, Turkey the Swiss *ZGB*, and Egypt an essentially French-style codification, at least private law was apparently much less dependent on culture than it had seemed. Fifty years later, Alan Watson developed this line of thought into a full-blown theory (VI.B.iii., s. 346). Also, by studying the relationship between common law and Roman law in Scotland, and French and English law in Quebec, Walton and others recognized the phenomenon of "mixed jurisdictions" – a concept that became a staple of comparative law in the post-World War II decades (*infra* IV.A.ii, s. 177).

b. The United States[162]

98. *A period of relative strength.* – In the first half of the twentieth century comparative legal studies enjoyed greater popularity in the United States than in England or Germany, especially among practitioners. In particular, there was a great deal of interest in the study of foreign law, perhaps in part as a result of the country's new status and role as an emerging empire. There was widespread eagerness to learn from continental Europe but also nascent interest in the laws of the Far East and of so-called primitive cultures. The two main strengths of the discipline in the United States at the time were the sizeable number of actors with a diversity of interests, and the energetic institutionalization of comparative and foreign legal studies.

99. *A significant group of comparatists.* – The number of jurists interested in comparative and foreign legal studies was significant, comprising not only law professors but also many practicing lawyers and judges. Still, the most prominent American comparatists were two law professors: Roscoe Pound and John Wigmore. Curiously, neither made comparative studies his main field, and neither produced much comparative work of lasting value.

[160] *Amos*, The Constitutional History of Egypt for the Last Forty Years: 14 Trans.Grot.Soc 131–153 (1929).

[161] *Cairns* (*supra* n. 129) 134.

[162] For a more detailed account, see *Clark* (*supra* n. 134); see also *Clark*, The Modern Development of American Comparative Law 1904–1945: 55 Am.J. Comp.L. 587–615 (2007).

Roscoe Pound (1870–1964), long-time dean of the Harvard Law School, was mainly a legal theorist and reformer pushing for a "sociological jurisprudence" inspired by Rudolf von Jhering (1818–1892), Francois Gény (1861–1959), and the continental "jurisprudence of interests". But Pound also had a lifelong interest in, and one might say passion for, comparative law. Yet, calling him "America's leading comparatist" at the time[163] is justified only in a limited sense. It is true that Pound wrote a lot and talked a lot *about* comparative law. In law review articles and at bar meetings he never tired of praising the role of comparative law in nineteenth-century American history, to emphasize its importance for his own time, and to proclaim its revival.[164] It is also true that he taught Roman and occasionally comparative law and that he published teaching materials for that purpose.[165] But beyond that, Pound actually *did* very little comparative work. He produced almost no comparative legal scholarship nor did he much advance the theory or method of the discipline. His importance for American comparative law was thus principally that of an indefatigable advocate who used his own towering reputation to raise the discipline's profile.

The second big name in American comparative law before World War II is John Henry Wigmore (1863–1943). Wigmore, long-time dean at the Northwestern School of Law in Chicago, was primarily an evidence scholar for whom comparative studies were essentially a hobby. During his early years in Japan, as an advisor to the Japanese government and as a professor of Anglo-American law at Keio University in Tokyo, he became an expert in the law of the Tokugawa period. In contrast to Pound, Wigmore did publish several voluminous comparative studies: the multivolume quasi-casebook *Evolution of Law*,[166] a three-volume *Panorama of the World's Legal Systems*,[167] and *A Kaleidoscope of Justice*.[168] His goal was to show foreign law and legal cultures not in the form of rules but in action and context. Wigmore's approach was strongly reminiscent of nineteenth-century German ethnological jurisprudence (*supra* B.i.b., s. 72.), not only in his broad view of comparative law as encompassing history, jurisprudence and cultural backgrounds, but also in his universalist and evolutionary perspective. Yet, his work was even more amateurish than that of his nineteenth-century forerunners.[169] Especially his *Panorama* and *Kaleidoscope* were largely picture books for tourism in legal history and exotic legal cultures.[170] While these works popularized the discipline temporarily, they had no lasting influence and are entirely forgotten today. Thus Wigmore was not a significant comparative law scholar either. Instead, his importance for the discipline lay mainly in his organizational and institutional efforts. Wigmore participated in organizations devoted to comparative and foreign legal studies, attended international congresses, served on committees, and he constantly goaded his contemporaries to follow suit. Over time, these efforts helped greatly to establish the discipline in American legal academia.

One should also mention a third highly prominent scholar who is usually not regarded as a comparatist but whose actual work was ultimately more significantly and seriously comparative than either Pound's or Wigmore's. Karl Llewellyn (1893–1962) was a leader of legal realism as well as the premier commercial law scholar of the American twentieth century. But Llewellyn also worked in a comparative mode. He not only produced an important book introducing the American case

[163] *Clark* (*supra* n. 134) 169.

[164] See for example, *Pound*, The Revival of Comparative Law: 5 Tul.L.Rev. 1–16 (1930).

[165] *Pound*, Readings in Roman Law and the Civil Law and Modern Codes as Developments Thereof: An Introduction to Comparative Law (ed. 2 Cambridge MA 1914).

[166] *Wigmore and Kocourek*, Evolution of Law (3 vol.) (Boston MA 1915–1918)

[167] *Wigmore*, Panorama of the World's Legal Systems (3 vol.) (St. Paul MN 1928).

[168] *Wigmore*, A Kaleidoscope of Justice (Washington DC 1941).

[169] *Riles*, Encountering Amateurism: John Henry Wigmore and the Uses of American Formalism: *idem* (ed.), Rethinking the Masters of Comparative Law (Oxford, Portland OR 2001) 96–126.

[170] The *Panorama* covered sixteen systems and contained 500 illustrations; the *Kaleidoscope's* subtitle anounced "Authentic Accounts of Trial Scenes from all Times and Climes".

law system to German readers,[171] but his work in commercial law generally and even on the Uniform Commercial Code in particular was quietly influenced by his deep knowledge of German private and commercial law, including the German Civil Code. This is often overlooked because political prudence kept Llewellyn from openly acknowledging this aspect of his work at a time when almost all things German were falling into disfavor in the United States because of the Nazi regime and the war.[172]

Most of the actual comparative law work, however, was done by a large number of scholars who were prominent at the time but are less well-known today. They were men like Simeon Baldwin (1840–1927), Edwin Borchard (1884–1951), Francis Deàk (1898–1972),[173] Ernst Feilchenfeld (1898–1956), Mitchell Franklin (1902–1980), Walter Hug (1898–1980), Munroe Smith (1854–1926), William Smithers (1864–1947), and Ferdinand Stone (1908–1989), as well as many others too numerous to mention. They created a substantial body of translations of foreign codes and scholarship, bibliographical reference works, and actual comparative studies. Beginning in the mid- to late 1930s, they were joined by a growing number of European scholars who had to flee the Nazi regime and who were to become important leaders in comparative law after the war (*infra* D.iii.b., ss. 132–134).

100. *Institutionalization.* – Early twentieth-century American comparatists were busy organizers, and successful ones to boot. Most of their activities took place outside of the universities (i.e., the law schools), and many of the leaders were legal practitioners.

Similar to the European continent (*supra* i, ss. 85–87), the United States rang in modern comparative law with a large congress. In 1904, on the occasion of the Universal Exposition, St. Louis hosted the *Universal Congress of Lawyers and Jurists*. It was organized under the auspices of the still young American Bar Association (ABA) and became the first comparative law congress in the United States.[174] Fourteen countries, the majority of them European, were represented at the three-day event. Almost 500 registered participants attended – a huge number at the time. In contrast to the Paris Congress, most of them were lawyers and judges; law professors constituted a rather small minority, in part because there were still relatively few full-time legal academics in America.

In 1907, the ABA established a section entitled "Comparative Law Bureau". Probably modeled on the French *Société de législation comparée* (*supra* B.i.d., s. 75), its principal goals were the translation and publication of foreign laws as well as comparative studies in aid of domestic law reform. It held annual meetings and published an *Annual Bulletin* from 1908 through 1914, when the war interrupted transatlantic contacts. It sponsored a foreign law book series and published, inter alia, translations of the new German and Swiss civil codes as well as a multivolume collection of the commercial laws of the world.[175] From 1915 through 1929, the Bureau controlled one of four annual issues of the *American Bar Association Journal* (ABAJ) which was read by thousands of lawyers in the United States. Unfortunately, the Bureau could not survive the Great Depression and eventually merged with another part of the ABA to form the *ABA Section on International and Comparative Law*. By 1945, this section had over a thousand members. Its principal organ was the Law Review of the Tulane Law School where an Institute of Comparative Law was eventually founded in 1949.

In 1925, Bureau members had also created the *American Foreign Law Association* (AFLA) in New York. Its primary goals were to promote the

[171] *Llewellyn*, Präjudizienrecht und Rechtsprechung in Amerika (Leipzig 1933) translated as *Gewirtz* (ed.), The Case Law System in America (Chicago IL 1989).

[172] *Riesenfeld*, The Impact of German Legal Ideas and Institutions on Legal Thought and Institutions in the United States: *Reimann* (ed.), The Reception of Continental Ideas in the Common Law World (Berlin 1993) 89–97, 95–96.

[173] Deák put together one of the earliest casebooks on comparative law in the United States, i.e., *Deák*, Cases and Materials on Select Topics in the Law of Torts in the United States, England, France and Germany (New York 1934).

[174] Universal Congress of Lawyers and Jurists. Official Report (Published by the Executive Committee, St. Louis MO 1905)

[175] *Bowstead* (ed.), The Commercial Laws of the World (10 vol.) (Boston MA 1911–1914).

understanding of foreign and comparative law. The *Association* continues to be highly active today.

The American commitment to organized activities also expressed itself in a strong presence at international events. At the first two congresses of the International Academy of Comparative Law in The Hague in 1932 and 1937, the United States provided the strongest contingents. It is quite remarkable that more comparatists came from across the Atlantic than from neighboring France.[176]

101. *Respectable Teaching.* – In the first half of the twentieth century comparative law was taught in the United States with some regularity, although it was far from the norm. In 1930, for example, fourteen law schools offered a course in it, usually at the graduate level. This looks like a critical mass, but the number is fairly small compared to the 180 law schools already existing in the United States at that time. Some schools also had courses in Roman law, which could turn into a form of comparative study. A special place in the teaching of comparative law belonged to the Tulane Law School in New Orleans because of Louisiana's special status as a mixed civil-common law jurisdiction.

iv. *Beyond the North Atlantic Region*

a. Latin America[177]

102. *American influence and its opponents.* – In the first half of the twentieth century, most Latin American countries continued to import foreign laws and legal concepts on a significant scale, a process which implied continuous comparisons between indigenous laws and various foreign alternatives. Gradually, the traditional influence of European law gave way to imports from the common law orbit. Many Latin jurisdictions, for example, adopted the common law trust. Under the doctrine of "Pan-Americanism", the influence of the United States was particularly strong, especially in the area of commercial law. Yet, there was also a counter-movement – in opposition to *Yanqui* influence, promoters of "Ibero-Americanism" pursued the unification of existing Latin American laws in an indigenous fashion and with occasional imports from continental Europe.

103. *Comparative law scholarship.* – At least in part as a result of these practical and political issues, scholarly interest in comparative law also remained significant. Candido Luiz Maria de Oliveira (1845–1918), a highly influential politician and lawyer in late nineteenth-century Brazil, rang in the twentieth century for the discipline with his *Curso de Legislação Comparada*, published in Rio de Janeiro in 1903. A generation later, Enrique Martinez Paz (1882–1952) became an influential figure, both by founding the "Instituto de Cordoba" in Argentina (1920) and as an author of two treatises on comparative law: *Introduccion al estudio del derecho comparado* and *El derecho comparado como dogmatica juridica*, both published in Cordoba in 1934 and 1941, respectively. In these works Martinez Paz analyzed the subject, aim, and method of the discipline in the civilian scholarly tradition. In the later book, he concluded that comparative law was neither a philosophy nor a science but rather a genuinely "juridical discipline".

b. The Far East

104. *Japan.* – In Japan, comparative studies occurred first, and for the time being foremost, in the practical context of legislative reform projects. In order to catch up with the Western powers, beginning in the 1860s, the *Meiji* government pursued a program of rapid and massive Westernization not only with regard to industry, technology, the military, and bureaucratic organization, but also, concomitantly, with regard to legal institutions and legislation. This resulted in a major project of "legislative comparative law" (see *supra* B.i.c., s. 74) because it required evaluating the advantages and downsides of the available legal models and adapting them to domestic use. The primary models were France and Germany as Japan imported especially these jurisdictions'

[176] To be sure, this number has to be seen in the context of a larger population; even in 1900, the United States already had about as many inhabitants as France and Great Britain together, and around 1950 its population exceeded that of these two countries plus Germany.

[177] For a more detailed account, see *Kleinheisterkamp* (*supra* n. 105) 273–287.

legal ideas, institutions, and blueprints for legislation on a broad scale. The Japanese government codified core elements of law following the continental European pattern and sometimes adopted whole parts of foreign codifications (almost) verbatim, most famously in the Japanese Civil Code of 1898 which was modeled on the German *Bürgerliches Gesetzbuch* (*BGB*, then still a draft). This orientation towards Western legal models continued well into the twentieth century, both with regard to legal doctrine (especially German private law) and sometimes legislation (e.g., in the Limited Liability Companies Act of 1938). Over time, however, Japan also began to look to English and US-American law, mainly in the commercial context.[178] Yet, it was only after World War II that Japanese lawmakers and scholars began to engage more heavily with non-European models, especially with the law of the United States.

In contrast to the enormous legislative importation of foreign models, the beginnings of comparative law as an academic enterprise were much more sporadic and modest in late nineteenth- and early twentieth-century Japan. Early steps were taken by Naohiro Sugiyama (1878–1966). Sugiyama sought to reconcile various approaches to the discipline's object, aims, functions, and methods. His agenda was reminiscent of the contemporary French approach in its unification goals and visions of a world law. A generation later, Kotaro Tanaka (1880–1974) pursued similar aims. Yet, despite these efforts, it was only after World War II that Japan really entered its "comparative law era".[179]

105. *China.*[180] – Like Japan, in the late nineteenth century, "China embarked on a century-long journey to 'modernize' its legal system in the image of foreign, and primarily Western, law".[181] Motivated by several stinging military defeats (first by the British in the Opium Wars 1839–1842, 1856–1860, then by the Japanese 1894–1895) and by an increasing sense of inferiority vis-à-vis the Western powers, the Qing dynasty sought to import continental European legal models and to codify central areas of law. Germany provided the leading model here as well, either directly or indirectly via Japanese law. Thus, in China, again like in Japan, first-generation comparative legal research supported urgent practical, especially legislative, ambitions. Unlike in Meiji Japan, however, in Qing China the campaign to Westernize the legal system was only partially successful, in part because the agenda was more contested, in part because the Qing dynasty fell in 1912 (which, inter alia, prevented the draft civil code from entering into effect). During the Republican Period (1912–1949), political strife at first impeded further progress with legal modernization through borrowing from abroad. After stability had been regained in 1928, however, various codification projects finally came to fruition, e.g., in the Civil Code of 1930, and the Westernization of Chinese law continued apace.

Academic engagement with comparative law was weak or non-existent during the Qing period, in part because the urgent practical needs absorbed all attention and left little opportunity for methodological reflection, in part for lack of strong academic institutions. That picture began to change in the early Republican Period, i.e., after 1912, with the emergence of modern universities and the professionalization of legal research. In the 1910s through the 1930s, comparative legal studies came into their own in China (a prominent law school in Shanghai actually named itself the "Comparative Law School of China"[182]). Yet, the vast majority of publications merely described the law of this or that foreign country, largely depending on where the author had studied. It is true that some scholars, such as Zhang Dingchang, eventually also took a broader approach, e.g., by comparing various

178 For more detail, see *Kitagawa,* The Development of Comparative Law in East Asia: *Reimann and Zimmermann* (eds.), The Oxford Handbook of Comparative Law (Oxford 2006) 237–260, 239–245; see also *Nottage,* The Development of Comparative Law in Japan: *Reimann and Zimmermann* (eds.), The Oxford Handbook of Comparative Law (ed 2, Oxford 2019) 201–227, 201–204.

179 *Kitagawa* (*supra* n. 178) 242.

180 For a more in-depth description and analysis of the late 19th and early 20th century comparative legal study in China, see *Zhang,* The Development of Comparative Law in Modern China: *Reimann and Zimmermann* (eds.), The Oxford Handbook of Comparative Law (ed 2, Oxford 2019) 228–251, 221–240.

181 *Idem* 228.

182 *Idem* 237.

legal systems and schools or by delving into theoretical issues. Still, rigorous and methodologically sophisticated *comparative* work was much the exception. In particular, there was scant interest in seriously comparing indigenous and foreign (i.e., Western) law, because urban elite academics largely assumed that inexorable Westernization would soon relegate traditional Chinese laws and customs to the museum of legal history anyway. For these, and other, reasons, "the academic and institutional impact of comparative law remained very low".[183]

The founding of the People's Republic of China in 1949 brought radical change. Legislative reform projects were no longer modeled on Western countries but on Soviet law. And comparative law as an open-minded academic discipline first became politically risky, then, especially during the Cultural Revolution (1966–1976), simply impossible.

D. From World War II to the Fall of the Wall

i. *General Developments*

106. *Overview.* – After comparative studies had been widely interrupted by World War II, especially in Europe, the discipline took a new start in many key countries around 1950. In the subsequent four decades, it experienced unprecedented growth and diversification, but it also suffered from methodological stagnation and a loss of orientation (*infra* b., ss. 110–111). This era came to a close around 1990 when the end of the Cold War, accelerated globalization, the suddenly rapid integration of Europe, and the rise of a younger generation of comparatists once again changed the discipline's focus and directions.

a. *Impressive Growth*

107. *Signs of growth.* – When comparative law regained momentum after World War II, it did so as a firmly established discipline. Its post-war growth manifested itself in various ways. Most importantly, the number of jurists engaged in comparative work, which had still been a fairly small club in the earlier twentieth century, skyrocketed. In addition, international congresses – rare events before the war – now became so numerous that they almost turned into routine. Also, many new national organizations and research institutes were founded. All this led to an outpouring of comparative legal literature that soon turned into a deluge: in 1950, one could have read virtually all the important work produced in the field up to that point over a summer; in 1990, one could barely keep up with current publications. The global number of journals specializing in comparative law alone rose from perhaps a dozen to well over a hundred.

108. *Reasons.* – The discipline's growth had three main reasons. First, the expansion of comparative studies was a response to the new, post-war, world order. This order emphasized international cooperation, be it in global or regional political organizations, like the UN, the OECD, and the EEC, be it in the context of renewed legal unification efforts, as in the revitalized Hague Conference of Private International Law or UNCITRAL. Second, comparative law grew because especially Western societies became affluent and could thus afford more scholars, more universities, and more ambitious legal research projects. Third, the growing ease of travel, communication, and of access to foreign legal materials greatly facilitated international and comparative work.

109. *Diversification.* – This quantitative explosion engendered great diversification of research and entailed the production of impressive scholarship. Comparative studies covered an ever wider array of geographic areas (*infra* IV.A.) and substantive topics (*infra* IV.B. and C.). They soon created a large stockpile of knowledge about the genesis, character, and structure of legal systems. And they generated a broad spectrum of approaches, ranging from "legal traditions" to "legal transplants" and from convergence and divergence of legal systems to studies of their "common core" (*infra* IV.B.). In short, comparative law became much more multifaceted and sophisticated than ever before.

[183] *Idem* 239.

b. Stagnation in Fundamental Questions

110. *No progress regarding methods and directions.* – At the same time, little progress was made in fundamental questions of method and direction. These questions had been central to the debates in the first half of the twentieth century, although scant agreement had been reached. In the second half of the century, the mainstream largely abandoned them. With regard to method, most comparatists subscribed to a crude version of functionalism (see *infra* VI.C.i., ss. 368–373) and considered further discussion rather pointless – if they gave any thought to method at all. With regard to objectives, they tended to accept a multitude of – often disparate – goals as equally valid.[184] The few works in which issues of method and direction were seriously pursued at all seemed strangely exotic and had little impact.[185] The prevailing methodological and epistemological indifference was largely due to the feeling that the fundamental questions underlying the discipline were ultimately unanswerable, although sheer complacency also played a role. The result was a loss of general orientation. Since the mainstream was ready to let a thousand flowers bloom as they pleased, comparative law remained methodologically simplistic and stumbled along without an overall sense of direction.

111. *Disengagement from politics.* – This lack of direction was exacerbated by a turn away from political interests and commitments.[186] The pre-war agendas, such the creation of a common law of mankind or the promotion of world peace through better mutual understanding, were quickly abandoned. Probably as a result of World War II, they now seemed illusory. Replacements were not developed or at least not widely shared, and comparative law by and large stayed away from political programs. Taking a stance of neutrality under the banner of "science", it also remained politically uncritical, if not outright blind to its implications for the distribution of social, economic, and political power.[187]

c. Old and New Trendsetters

112. *Shifts in leadership.*[188] – Before the war, France and Germany had provided the lead in the development of comparative law, with the United Kingdom and the United States also playing an important, though secondary, role – and Italy virtually none. In the post-war decades, three developments entailed a reconfiguration. First, France gradually lost its prominent role, especially since the 1970s, in part because interest in comparative studies declined there. Second, the United States became a, and arguably the, world leader in comparative law, largely thanks to the influx of emigrant scholars who had to flee Europe in the 1930s and 1940s and came to America (*infra* iii.b., ss. 132–134.). Third, Italy joined the club of trendsetting jurisdictions in the discipline, mainly because of a handful of scholars whose work became widely influential (*infra* ii.e., ss. 124–126). Germany remained in a prominent position, thanks in no small part to its research institutions. British scholars continued to play a role but shifted their focus from the needs of an Empire to the study of the common v. civil law dichotomy (*infra* iii.c., ss. 135–138).

113. *Implications for the discipline.* – These changes in leadership had important implications for the discipline at large. To begin with, the decline of French and the rise of US-American comparative studies entailed that English now clearly replaced French as the predominant language in the field – a trend that served the scholars in the UK well, was happily embraced in Europe's German-speaking lands, and even found gradual, though more limited favor, in Italy and other Mediterranean countries. Moreover, the growing influence of US-American

[184] In all these regards, the leading treatise of the era aptly represented the orthodoxy, see *Zweigert and Kötz* (*supra* n. 3) 13–31.

[185] Constantinesco (*supra* n. 104) provides the main example; his three-volume study remained largely ignored by all but a few die-hard specialists.

[186] *Kennedy*, The Methods and the Politics: *Legrand and Munday* (eds.), Comparative Legal Studies: Traditions and Transitions (Cambridge, New York 2003) 345–433.

[187] *Frankenberg* (*supra* n. 145) 47–54.

[188] See generally *Mattei*, Why the Wind Changed: Intellectual Leadership in Western Law: 42 Am.J.Comp.L. 195–218 (1994).

scholarship engendered several shifts in focus. With a stronger dose of legal realism in comparative studies, interest in law in the books declined while attention to the law in action grew – a good fit with Rabel's seminal agenda (*supra* C.ii.a., s. 90) and with the prevalence of the functionalist paradigm (*infra* VI.C.i., ss. 368–373). The study of cases came to equal, and at some point to surpass, the study of legislative texts. And comparatists increasingly looked beyond the time-honored subjects covered by continental civil codes – contract, tort, property, etc. – to the factors constituting legal cultures – such as legal education and profession, courts and procedure, constitutional law and judicial review.

d. Comparative Law in the Cold War Era

114. *The impact of the cold war.* – Finally, comparative law in the post-war decades was shaped by the division of the world into an Eastern and Western bloc (the so-called "third world" was largely ignored by the mainstream).[189] Comparatists in the West became more conscious of their shared "Western legal tradition" by seeing themselves in contrast to the communist East. Thus they looked not only to the differences between the civil and the common law traditions but also to their commonalities, such as the cultural heritage of antiquity, the Judeo-Christian religion, the impact of the enlightenment, and the modern commitments to democracy and the rule of law.[190] The East/West division also entailed the recognition of a new "legal family", i.e., Socialist Law (*infra* IV.A.ii., s. 176). This, in turn, generated not only numerous, and sometimes sophisticated, studies especially of the Soviet legal system. It also fueled a debate whether socialist law was truly sui generis or merely a variation of the civil law tradition. With the fall of the iron curtain, socialist law became largely a matter of legal history, especially since the study of Chinese law focused on that country's transformation and thus took a different turn (*infra* IV.A.ii., s. 179).

ii. *Continental Europe*

a. The Treatise Tradition

115. *The great Introductions.* – In the post-war decades, comparative law scholars in continental Europe produced a series of textbooks aimed by and large at the novice, i.e., primarily the student. Though essentially introductory by nature, some of these books became classics because they decisively shaped the view of comparative law throughout the second half of the twentieth century. During that time, a comparatist could not be taken seriously if he or she was not familiar with these works.

The beginning was made by Gutteridge in England with his *Introduction to the Study of the Comparative Method of Legal Study and Research* (Cambridge 1946), but in the 1950s the center of production lay in France. In 1950, Pierre Arminjon, Boris Nolde and Martin Wolff published their *Traité de droit comparé* (3 vols. Paris 195–51), and René David his *Traité élémentaire de droit civil comparé* (Paris 1950) About a decade later, Adolf Schnitzer's *Vergleichende Rechtslehre* appeared in Switzerland (Basel 1961).

The two most widely read books, however, were Rene David's *Les grands systèmes de droit contemporains* (Paris 1964) and Konrad Zweigert and Hein Kötz's *Einführung in die Rechtsvergleichung auf dem Gebiete des Privatrechts* (2 vols. Tübingen 1969–71). Both were translated into several languages and went through several editions. Especially the treatise by Zweigert and Kötz became the veritable bible of comparative law for the second half of the twentieth century virtually on a global scale.

In the 1980s and 1990s, these works were eventually followed by numerous others penned by a large variety of authors and published in countries all over the world. By the end of the century, they constituted a small library in their own right, though none reached the quasi-iconic status of the earlier treatises.

189 For a critique of the cold war's impact on the discipline, see *Mattei*, The Cold War and Comparative Law: A Reflection on the Politics of Intellectual Discipline, 65 Am.J.Comp.L. 567–607 (2017).

190 *Sawyer*, The Western Conception of Law: *Drobnig and Zweigert* (eds.), International Encyclopedia of Comparative Law II, Ch. I (The Hague, Tübingen 1975) 14–48.

b. Major Debates

116. *Four pervasive themes.* – Despite its increasing diversity, comparative law in post-war continental Europe was largely dominated by at most a handful of recurrent themes. These debates spilled over into other areas of the world, but they all originated in European legal scholarship.

To begin with, there was an ongoing debate whether the discipline was merely a method or rather a field of substantive knowledge in its own right (*supra* I.C., s. 14). Closely connected were discussions of the question whether comparative law was essentially a science whose goal was simply the expansion of knowledge and understanding, or whether it was primarily a practical tool serving international legal unification, adjudication, and transactions. The period also saw much discussion about how to classify the world's legal systems into groups, families, or traditions. Scholars developed various competing models, although most of them overlapped substantially (*infra* VI.B.ii., ss. 337–344). In this context, the main focus remained on the relationship between the civil and the common law. This dichotomy was so deeply engrained in the comparatists' consciousness at the time that much "comparative law" was largely synonymous with the study of the continental versus the Anglo-American legal systems.

c. The Gradual Decline of French Comparative Law

117. *Three caveats.* – While it is justified to speak of a "decline" of French comparative law in the second half of the twentieth century,[191] three caveats are in order lest the statement be misunderstood. To begin with, the decline was not immediate. In the 1950s and 1960s, French comparatists still occupied a prominent position, especially through the work of René David (1906–1990) and in the context of the treatise tradition (*supra* a., s. 115). Furthermore, the decline was neither steep nor complete. Even in the later decades, the were several French comparatists of international stature and global importance, such as André Tunc (1917–1999), Denis Tallon (1924–2013) and, although he was not primarily a comparatist, Jean Carbonnier (1908–2003). Finally, French law itself remained influential in many parts of the world, especially in the country's former colonies.

118. *Signs of decline.* – Still, French comparative law did "decline" in a dual sense. First, after the 1960s, it did not generate any new ideas or directions of any significant influence; instead, it by and large stagnated. Second, as a result, French comparative law gradually lost its internationally prominent position; on a global scale it simply mattered less than it had before. To be sure, the French continued to dominate the *Académie internationale de droit comparé* and thus heavily influenced the organization and agendas of the quadrennial *International Congresses of Comparative Law* as the discipline's largest events. But these congresses gradually lost a substantial part of their scholarly significance as their structural rigidity and their overall lack of focus increasingly hindered the production of innovative work.

119. *Reasons.* – The reasons for the relative decline of French comparative law were largely homemade. There remained a strong nationalist element in legal thinking which was often based on a sense of French superiority. Thus, the French legislator as well as the courts often operated in a rather parochial fashion. Perhaps even more importantly, French law teaching and legal scholarship continued to be "overwhelmingly positivistic and legicentric"[192]; as a result, the status of comparative law in the French universities remained low, since most academics regarded the field as exotic and quite useless. Finally, there was a marked reluctance to embrace English as the emerging global language of legal scholarship. Understandable as that reluctance was, it entailed a gradual marginalization of French comparative scholarship in a world in which failure to publish in English was increasingly punished by being internationally ignored.

d. The Gradual Growth of German Comparative Law

120. *Institutional growth.* – From the 1950s to the 1980s, German comparative law experienced

[191] *Fauvarque-Cosson*, Development of Comparative Law in France: *Reimann and Zimmermann* (eds.), The Oxford Handbook of Comparative Law (ed. 2 Oxford 2019) 29–53, 39.

[192] *Idem* 40.

considerable and steady expansion and consolidation.[193] Much of this process was driven by, and expressed itself in, constant institutional growth. Already in 1950, the *Deutsche Gesellschaft für Rechtsvergleichung* was founded;[194] it has since organized bi-annual conferences of high caliber. The main powerhouses of comparative legal research, however, were the institutes founded by the *Max Planck Gesellschaft*: as successors to the *Kaiser-Wilhelm-Institut* in Berlin, two such institutes were revitalized as early as 1949 – the *Institut für ausländisches und internationales Privatrecht* in Hamburg and the *Institut für ausländisches öffentliches Recht und Völkerrecht* in Heidelberg. Several others followed in short order: the *Institut für europäische Rechtsgeschichte* in Frankfurt (1964), the *Institut für ausländisches und internationales Strafrecht* in Freiburg (1966), and the *Institut für ausländisches und internationales Sozialrecht* in Munich (1980). Even in the East, an *Institut für ausländisches Recht und Rechtsvergleichung* was established at the *Akademie für Staats- und Rechtswissenschaft* of the German Democratic Republic. In addition, comparative law institutes were created at several German universities. This plethora of platforms produced an outpouring of comparative law publications, ranging from ambitious projects like the present *International Encyclopedia of Comparative Law* (initiated in 1971 and at home at the *Max Planck Institut* in Hamburg) to hundreds of monographs and a myriad of dissertations of admittedly varying quality.

121. *Major orientations.* – Despite the great variety of research institutes, the mainstream of German comparative law remained private-law centered. Significant work was produced in the areas of contract law, in particular sales, torts, family law, and, last but not least, private international law.

The functional method, developed before World War II especially by Rabel and now advocated primarily by Zweigert and Kötz, dominated the discourse. From the 1950s through the 1970s, valiant efforts were made to enrich comparative law through sociological studies, in part under US-American influence, but the results were ultimately unimpressive. In the long run, however, the teachings of American legal realism were quite influential, in part through Josef Esser's *Grundsatz und Norm in der richterlichen Fortbildung des Privatrechts* (1956), a seminal and revered but cryptic book which few have read, and even fewer have understood.

The main emphasis was on the study of the civil v. common law dichotomy, but other areas were explored as well. Significant scholarship centered on Eastern legal systems, i.e., socialist law, which was of course close to home, and an *Institut für Ostrecht* was founded in Berlin in 1968. French law was studied in the border regions with France, especially at the University of the Saarland, but also in Munich and elsewhere.

122. *Teaching.* – Comparative law established itself as a regular course in most universities, although it remained, as in France, on the margins of the curriculum. Nowhere was such a course obligatory. Since comparative law was not part of the all-important state examinations, studying it was a luxury that students afforded themselves at their own risk and cost. As a result, the number of takers remained notoriously small.

123. *Comparative law in the legislature.* – At least at the federal level, where most German legislation is produced, considering the laws of other countries quickly became routine. While the German legislator could thus not be charged with parochialism, comparative considerations were often limited to a few well-known legal systems and not necessarily profound or influential.

e. *The Rise of Italian Scholarship*

124. *The great post-war scholars.* – The post-World War II rise of Italian comparative law, both within that country and eventually on

[193] Overviews in *Martinek*, Wissenschaftsgeschichte der Rechtsvergleichung und des Internationalen Privatrechts in der Bundesrepublik Deutschland: *Simon* (ed.), Rechtswissenschaft in der Bonner Republik (Frankfurt 1994) 529–619, 546–580; *Schwenzer*, Development of Comparative Law in Germany, Switzerland and Austria: *Reimann and Zimmermann* (eds.), The Oxford Handbook of Comparative Law (ed. 2 Oxford 2019) 54–86, 70–79.

[194] It succeeded the *Vereinigung für vergleichende Rechtswissenschaft und Volkswirtschaftlehre* which had ceased in 1933.

an international scale, had its origins mainly in the work of a small group of academics who produced scholarship with a worldwide influence. Among them three stand out. Gino Gorla (1906–1992) can perhaps be called the father of modern comparative law in Italy. He laid lasting foundations by breaking away from the traditional (German-influenced) dogmatic and conceptual approach to private law. Evincing the impact of Gorla's experience in the United States in the late 1940s, his principal work, *Il contratto* (Milano 1954), presented a comparative study of Italian, French, English, and American contract law from a factual and case method perspective. The book had a tremendous influence in Italy and became a classic of comparative law in general. It triggered the comparative interests of Rodolfo Sacco (*1923). Sacco is mainly known for his theory of "legal formants" which he began to develop in the 1970s.[195] It became the most influential Italian contribution to the theory of comparative law in the second half of the twentieth century (*infra* VI.B.i., s. 336). Finally, Mauro Cappelletti (1927–2004) was instrumental in connecting Italian comparative law with the larger world. These connections arose both from his multiple institutional affiliations – as professor not only at the University of Florence but also at the European University Institute there and at the Stanford Law School – but also from various large-scale international research projects.[196] In addition, Cappelletti co-authored several books which became part of the comparative law canon.[197] In fact, for a long time Cappelletti was "the only Italian legal scholar with a worldwide reputation".[198] This older generation motivated, recruited, and trained a large cohort of younger Italian comparatists who were destined to become influential on a global level in the 1990s and beyond.

125. *Rapid expansion.* – Since the 1970s, comparative law in Italy experienced a rapid expansion in the universities. In 1971, when the *Associazione Italiana di Diritto Comparato* was founded, there was only one full-time chair for comparative law in all of Italy; within a generation, there were dozens; today, there are over a hundred. To be sure, to a considerable extent this growth resulted from the foundation of many new universities, some of which made comparative studies their hallmark, such as the University of Trento in the 1980s. Yet, comparative law also established itself more widely and firmly in the older institutions. In most law faculties it became a mandatory course. As a result, the number of comparative law scholars in Italy grew exponentially, and the number of scholarly publications in that field skyrocketed as well. In line with the Italian tradition of according private law pride of place in the legal universe, Italian comparative law remained heavily private-law centered. Disagreement, however, soon broke out with regard to the proper goals and directions of the discipline as either a "scientific" endeavor aimed at knowledge and understanding or a more practical enterprise serving law reform and unification. This, in turn, led to the emergence of several competing "schools", associated with particular scholars and universities,[199] who often fought each other with Italian enthusiasm.

126. *Reasons for Italy's growing influence.* – The developments chronicled here already explain much of the growing influence of Italian comparatists on the course of the discipline as a whole: the combination of the highly influential work of a few prominent scholars in the 1950s through the 1970s and the explosive growth of comparative law in the universities in the 1970s generated great momentum, attracted younger talent, and encouraged creativity. But the increasing international influence

[195] *Sacco,* Legal Formants: A Dynamic Approach To Comparative Law: 39 Am.J.Comp.L. 1–34 and 343–401 (1991).

[196] Cappelletti was the main editor of Access to Justice (4 vol.) (Alphen aan den Rijn 1978–1979) and a co-author (with Monica Seccombe and Joseph Weiler) of Integration Through Law (5 vol.) (Berlin, New York 1985–87).

[197] Especially *Cappelletti and Perillo,* Civil Procedure in Italy (The Hague 1965), *Cappelletti, Merryman and Perillo,* The Italian Legal System (Stanford CA 1967) and *Livingston, Monateri and Parisi,* The Italian Legal System (ed. 2 Stanford CA 2015).

[198] *Grande,* Development of Comparative Law in Italy: *Reimann and Zimmermann* (eds.), The Oxford Handbook of Comparative Law (ed. 2 Oxford 2019) 87–110, 91.

[199] See *idem* 96–98.

of Italian comparatists had another reason as well: in contrast to many of their French colleagues, the Italians made strong efforts to reach out beyond their borders. Conscious of the limits of their own language abroad, they became functional not only in French but increasingly in English as well. This connected them with their colleagues especially in the United States but also with other parts of the world. In this regard, again, Gorla and especially Cappelletti were important role models. No longer dependent on French, Italian comparatists thus became full participants in projects and congresses all over the world – a trend that became even stronger with the next generation and arguably also put Italy ahead of the rest of Europe with regard to the teaching of comparative law[200]

f. Other Countries in Continental Europe

127. *Beyond France, Germany, and Italy.* – Focusing on France, Germany, and Italy does not imply that comparative law played no role elsewhere in the continental orbit. In fact, it occupied a significant position particularly in many of the smaller countries, such as Austria and Switzerland, the Netherlands and Belgium, which, due to their size and location, were constantly exposed to influence from abroad, especially from Germany and France. It was also an active discipline in the Scandinavian countries, Spain, and Portugal, as well as in Greece. One must also mention Turkey which, though geographically largely beyond Europe, remained part of its academic (and civil law) tradition.

128. *Eastern Europe.* – In Eastern Europe, comparative law first collapsed after World War II and then experienced a gradual, and fairly modest, comeback. During the Stalinist era, comparative law was "strictly off limits"[201] for political reasons. In the 1960s and 1970s, interest in foreign legal systems slowly reawakened, although for the time being it focused mainly on socialist sister states.[202] Comparison with the capitalist West was often considered impossible, or at least pointless. This attitude followed in large part from the functional approach which was widely embraced in the East as well: if the main purpose of the discipline was to compare rules and institutions fulfilling the same function, then the fundamental differences in the functions of law in socialist and capitalist societies largely foreclosed meaningful comparison. It was only towards the end of Eastern European socialism that scholars were willing seriously to entertain the idea of "intersystemic comparison", i.e., between the socialist East and the capitalist West.[203] The impetus came in part from the growing need to facilitate the interplay with Western law caused by increasing economic exchanges across the iron curtain. Often, comparative law was also employed to demonstrate the superiority of the socialist approach. Still, in some socialist countries, as in Czechoslovakia, Hungary, Romania, and Yugoslavia, comparative law actually flourished to a certain degree under the leadership of several internationally noted scholars like Viktor Knapp (1913–1996), Attila Harmathy (*1937), Imre Szabó (1912–1991) and Csaba Varga (*1941). Also, socialist countries increasingly participated in international unification projects, such as the drafting of the Vienna Sales Convention (1980).[204]

g. The European Level

129. *Comparative law in the European Community.* – In addition to the various national developments, comparative law also played an increasingly important role on the international level. To be sure, this was not entirely new because the work of the *Hague Conference of Private International Law* as well as of *UNIDROIT* had been heavily comparative for generations (*supra* C.ii.b., s. 93). Since the foundation of the *European Economic Community* (EEC) in 1957, however, a gradually growing number of countries became

[200] See *Sacco*, L'Italie en tête (àpropos de l'enseignement du droit comparé): Rev.int.dr.comp. 47 (1995) 131–133.

[201] *Ginsburgs*, A Socialist Approach to Comparative Law: 28 Am.J.Comp.L. 113–117 (1980).

[202] See e.g. *Szabo and Péteri* (eds.), A Socialist Approach to Comparative Law (Leyden, Budapest 1977).

[203] *Seiffert*, Wandlungen in der Auffassung zur intersystemaren Rechtsvergleichung in der DDR und UDSSR: *Gutmann and Mampel* (eds.), Probleme systemvergleichender Betrachtung (Berlin 1986) 188–193.

[204] See *Kühn*, Development of Comparative Law in Central and Eastern Europe: *Reimann and Zimmermann* (eds.), The Oxford Handbook of Comparative Law (ed. 2 Oxford 2019) 181–200, esp. 185–192.

part of a more encompassing supranational organization whose purpose went way beyond legal unification and was aimed at the creation of a common market. In creating such a market, the EEC institutions constantly had to deal with the member states' national legal orders. This inevitably involved their comparison, albeit for political and practical, rather than academic and theoretical, purposes. Comparative perspectives became most relevant, or at least most visible, at the *European Court of Justice* (ECJ), which soon became a veritable powerhouse of practical comparative law. The ECJ established a highly professionalized research service equipped with a substantial library and staffed by jurists from all members states who supplied the Court's members with the requisite background knowledge of member state laws. While the Court's terse and technical style, especially in the 1950s through the 1970s, hid much of the comparative considerations underlying many of its judgments from view, these considerations played a significant, and at times decisive, role. This role became explicit, for example, when the Court openly made EEC law by drawing on the "constitutional traditions common to the member states".[205] From this tradition, i.e., from a comparative search for commonalities, the Court fashioned a plethora of substantive and procedural principles, perhaps most importantly the principle of proportionality.

130. *Comparative law in the European Human Rights system.* – Comparative studies also rose to prominence in the *European Commission* and *Court of Human Rights*, organs of the *Council of Europe* that began to operate in the 1950s under the *European Convention for the Protection of Human Rights and Fundamental Freedoms* (1950).[206] In order to decide whether acts of member states violated the rights guaranteed under the Convention, these organs frequently had to gauge how the acts measured up to broader European conceptions and traditions of fundamental rights of other member states. For example, the decision whether certain restrictions could be justified as "necessary in a democratic society" (Arts. 8 sec. 2, 9 sec. 2, ECHR, etc.) was often informed by looking at the laws of other member states.[207] It is true that the comparative research and reasoning of the *Court* often left much to be desired in terms of breadth and depth.[208] Still, there is no doubt that comparative studies became a routine element in European Human Rights adjudication, i.e., in an eminently practical context with far-reaching consequences for the lives of European citizens.

iii. *The Common Law World*

a. *The Casebook Tradition*

131. *Cases and materials.* – While (introductory) treatises defined much of continental European comparative law in the post-World War II period, Anglo-American scholars produced almost nothing of that sort for the time being.[209] Instead, in the common law orbit, introduction to the discipline increasingly occurred through collections of cases, materials, and other sources.

This is primarily true for the United States. Here, the publication of Rudolf Schlesinger's *Comparative Law* casebook in 1950 rang in a new era; the book has since gone through many editions. It was followed by Arthur von Mehren and James Gordley's seminal *The Civil Law System* in 1967 and, since the late 1970s, by a growing number of other casebooks[210] which have continued to proliferate at a disconcerting rate.

[205] *Nold v. Commission* [1974] ECT 491, 507; see also *Internationale Handelsgesellschaft v. Einfuhr- und Vorratsstelle Getreide* [1970] ECR 1125; *Tridimas* (*supra* n. 40).

[206] Both organs were superseded by the new *European Court of Human Rights* established in 1998.

[207] See, for example, *Dudgeon v. United Kingdom* ECHR 45 (1981) 5 (par. 49, 56, 60).

[208] In *Dudgeon*, for example, the Court just referred summarily, and repeatedly, to the "laws of [the] other member states", *idem.*, leaving it unclear whether it had considered them in any detail or depth.

[209] There were a few exceptions. Harold Gutteridge's Introduction to the Study of Comparative Law has already been mentioned, but it appeared in 1946 and generated no successors. The only other noteworthy exception is the slender book by *Merryman*, The Civil Law Tradition (Stanford CA 1969 and ed. 2 1985).

[210] Two became widely used: *Glendon, Gordon and Osakwe*, Comparative Legal Traditions (St. Paul MN 1985); and *Merryman and Clark*, Comparative Law: Western European and Latin American Legal Systems (Indianapolis IN 1978).

But the picture is also largely true for England. To the extent comparative law books were published there at all, they were either monographs focusing on a specific country or region or collections of sources and materials, such as *Negligence in the Civil Law* (London 1950) by F.H. Lawson (1897–1983), the *Source Book on French Law* by Otto Kahn-Freund, Claudine Levy, and Bernard Rudden (Oxford 1973) and the *Comparative Introduction to the German Law of Tort* by Basil Markesinis (Oxford 1986). Introductory treatises to comparative law as a whole appeared only in the 1990s and beyond.[211]

It is not surprising, of course, that civilian comparatists preferred to introduce rookies to their discipline in broad and general outline, while their common law colleagues, especially in the United States, preferred to expose their students directly to cases and other primary materials. It is noteworthy, however, that these approaches gave comparative law a different flavor. In the continental European environment, the discipline presented itself to the beginner essentially as a science with overarching heuristic objectives; in the common law context it appeared more as a hands-on discipline which justified its existence primarily through its utility for legal practice in one form or another.

b. *The Immigrant Jurists*

132. *Comparative law by immigration.* – Postwar comparative law in the common law orbit was decisively shaped by the immigrant jurists. In the 1930s and 1940s, they arrived overwhelmingly as refugees from continental Europe. A second generation came by choice in the 1950s through the 1980s, also mainly from the continent.

133. *The refugee generation.* – When the Nazis took power in Germany in 1933 and then gradually expanded it throughout much of continental Europe after 1938, jurists of Jewish descent not only lost their jobs but increasingly had to fear for their very lives. Of those who thus fled the continent, most sought refuge either in England or in the United States. Among them were many who (re-)established themselves as legal scholars and sometimes as comparatists.[212] In both countries, this meant the import of deep erudition and high sophistication in matters usually beyond the ken of the common lawyers.

In England, especially Otto Kahn-Freund (1900–1979), Ernst Cohn (1904–1976), Clive Schmitthoff (1903–1990), Martin Wolff (1872–1953), and Kurt Lipstein (1909–2006) became major scholars in comparative (and in some cases, private international) law. Other names can easily be added, depending on how broadly one wishes to define the field of comparative studies.[213]

In the United States, the list was even longer.[214] It has to begin with Ernst Rabel (1874–1955) who spent some of his most productive years at the University of Michigan Law School in the 1940s; Rabel did not, however, directly influence the course of comparative law in the United States because he lived in near obscurity and worked by and large on his own, large-scale projects. Three other German emigrant scholars, however, had such a decisive impact that they largely shaped the discipline in the postwar decades in the United States. Max Rheinstein (1899–1977), a former student of Max Weber as well as an assistant to Rabel at the *Kaiser-Wilhelm-Institut* in Berlin, came to America in 1933 and turned the University of Chicago Law School into a citadel of comparative law after the war. Rudolf Schlesinger (1909–1996) authored the most influential American casebook on comparative law (*supra* a., s. 131), became the father of the *common core* approach (*infra* VI.C.ii., ss. 374–377), and taught and mentored generations of future American comparatists. Finally, Stefan Riesenfeld (1908–1999) was a

[211] It is true, however, that the treatises by René David and by Zweigert and Kötz (*supra* II.A), were sometimes used in English translation.

[212] By looking at the success stories, it is easy to forget, however, that many refugees failed to establish themselves professionally in their new environments.

[213] See *Beatson and Zimmermann* (eds.), Jurists Uprooted: German-Speaking Émigré Lawyers in Twentieth-Century Britain (Oxford 2004).

[214] See *Lutter, Stiefel and Hoeflich* (eds.), Der Einfluss deutscher Emigranten auf die Rechtsentwicklung in den USA und in Deutschland (Tübingen 1993); see also *Stiefel and Mecklenburg*, Deutsche Juristen im amerikanischen Exil (Tübingen 1991) 42–109.

towering figure in American comparative law for almost half a century, during which he helped to make the University of California at Berkeley a major center of comparative studies. To this list, at least another dozen scholars could be added, although they were either less influential on, or less directly engaged in, the discipline.

134. *The continuing influx.* – During the 1950s through the 1980s, foreign legal scholars continued to immigrate to the United States – usually not because they were forced to leave their home countries but because they considered the grass greener on the other side. They still mostly hailed from continental Europe, with only a few coming from other parts of the world. Some of them, such as Mirjan Damaska (*1931) from Serbia, Alan Watson (1933–2018) from Scotland, and A.N. Yiannopoulos (1928–2017) from Greece, became prominent players in the postwar decades not only in the United States but even by global standards. All this is less true for other common law countries, although there were some notable exceptions, such as Basil Markesinis (*1944) in England.

c. *The United Kingdom*

135. *Solid but not leading.* – Comparative law in the United Kingdom in the post-World War II era developed in a solid and productive fashion but, with one exception (*infra* VI.B.iii., ss. 345-346), it produced no fundamental insights and thus exercised no significant leadership on a global scale.

The period opened auspiciously with the International Academy of Comparative Law holding its first post-war congress in London in 1950. New institutes, such as the *Institute for Advanced Legal Studies* at the University of London were founded (1946), and the merger between the venerable *Society of Comparative Legislation* and the *Grotius Society* created the *British Institute of International and Comparative Law* (1946). In part as a result, the *Journal of the Society of Comparative Legislation* merged with the *International Law Quarterly* to constitute the *International and Comparative Law Quarterly* (1952) which has since become one of the globally leading periodicals in the discipline. In addition, the teaching of foreign and comparative law boomed, in part because of the huge increase in student numbers in the whole United Kingdom.

136. *The end of empire.* – With the British Empire largely dismantled, the erstwhile need to teach and understand the laws of its far-flung colonies ended, and interest in Muslim, Hindu, and indigenous laws waned; the growing dissociation from South Africa had a similar effect on the teaching of Roman-Dutch law. It is true that the *School for Oriental and African Studies (SOAS)* in London became one of the world's leading centers in its field,[215] but it diverged from mainstream comparative law and turned into an institution for more broadly conceived area studies. On the whole, comparative law in the United Kingdom lost its distinct imperial flavor and became more like the discipline in other Western countries.

137. *Areas of strength.* – Throughout the postwar period, there were two main areas of strength, both continuing earlier paths. One was the study of French law by scholars like Frederick H. Lawson (1897–1983), Otto Kahn-Freund (1900–1979), Barry Nicholas (1919–2002), and Neville Brown (1923–2008).[216] The other was Roman law which had long had a prominent place in British and Scottish legal academia. Both French and Roman law continued to be studied in part as avenues to the civil law of continental Europe more generally.[217]

In addition, some scholars, such as Albert Kiralfy (1915–2001) and Bernard Rudden (1933–2015), turned to Soviet law. Finally, German law enjoyed some attention, thanks in part to the influence of the German immigrants (*supra* b., ss. 132–134). Towards the end of the postwar period, interest in Germany rose – at the expense of French law – especially when Tony Weir (1936–2011) masterfully translated the treatise by Zweigert and Kötz in 1977[218] and when Basil Markesinis (*1944) began to turn to German

[215] The *School* itself was founded in 1916, but it acquired a Law Department only in 1950.

[216] *Brown and Garner*, French Administrative Law (London 1973); *Kahn-Freund, Levy and Rudden*, A Sourcebook on French Law (Oxford 1973); *Nicholas*, French Law of Contract (London 1982). This tradition is carried on today by John Bell (*1953) and others.

[217] See *Lawson*, Negligence in the Civil Law (Oxford 1950); *Lawson* (*supra* n. 9).

[218] *Zweigert and Kötz* An Introduction to Comparative Law (Weir transl. ed. 2 Oxford 1987), ed. 3 Oxford 1998.

private law in the 1980s.[219] In Scotland, mixed legal systems were studied by scholars like Thomas B. Smith (1915–1988) – a tradition that was revitalized at the beginning of the twenty-first century (*infra* IV.A.ii., s. 177).

138. *Legal transplants.* – It may be true that "Britain has never produced a dominant theorist of comparative law",[220] but at least one comparative lawyer from the United Kingdom made a major and lasting contribution to comparative legal theory: in 1974, Alan Watson, a Scottish expert in Roman law and at the time holder of the chair in civil law at the University of Edinburgh, published *Legal Transplants: An Approach to Comparative Law.* To be sure, the concept of legal transplants had been floated decades before by British scholars (see *supra* C.iii.a., s. 97). Still, it was Watson who expounded and widely disseminated the view that law develops mainly through transplants from one age or system to another. His thesis that legal ideas and rules are in fact quite independent of socio-economic conditions and thus rather easily transferable immediately provoked the criticism of his English colleague Otto Kahn-Freund.[221] In subsequent decades, Watson's approach became a staple of comparative law theory as well as an intellectual battleground, especially in the context of European private law unification.

d. The United States

139. *Comparative law in a superpower context.* – The postwar status of the United States as a superpower affected the development of comparative law in at least three ways – two positive, one negative. First, the US now became the world's leading exporter of law and thus the most prominent object of comparative study in most Western countries (especially in Europe and Japan); this in turn attracted legal scholars and law students from abroad and fostered contacts between American and foreign jurists on an unprecedented scale. Second, US-American law schools experienced a boom period and found themselves endowed with resources that became the envy of universities around the world; even though only a small part of these resources were devoted to the study of foreign and comparative (as well as international) law, they funded opportunities beyond the reach of most comparatists elsewhere. Third, however, the status of the United States as a superpower and leading exporter of law also meant that its lawmakers – legislators as well as judges – saw less reason than ever to look abroad; legislation and adjudication thus remained by and large parochial. In short, comparative law grew in the academic context but languished in the legislative and judicial process. This created a dilemma for American comparatists: it was difficult for them – much more difficult than for their colleagues in the law-importing environments of Europe, Latin America, and East Asia – to prove the practical utility of their discipline. US-American comparatists struggled with that problem throughout the postwar decades, albeit with little success – until the new globalization beginning in the 1990s became widely noticed (*infra* E.i., s. 153).

140. *Institutional progress.* – While the development of postwar American comparative law was jumpstarted by the presence of the immigrant jurists (*supra* b., ss. 132–134), much of it was also the work of indigenous scholars, such as Hessel Yntema (1891–1966), John Hazard (1909–1995), and Arthur von Mehren (1922–2006). Immigrants and natives quickly formed an academic community that laid the institutional and scholarly foundations for the coming decades.

The most important institutional step was the foundation of a new association. While there were two comparative law organizations from before the war, i.e., the *American Foreign Law Association* and the *ABA Section of International and Comparative Law*, there was no platform of a truly academic character. To fill this gap, the *American Association for the Comparative Study of Law* was founded in 1951. It was conceived primarily as an association of institutions, i.e., law schools, rather than individuals, and it started out with ten participants. In 1992, it was renamed *The American Society of Comparative Law* (*ASCL*) which arrived at over 100 institutional members, among them

[219] *Markesinis*, A Comparative Introduction to the German Law of Torts (Oxford, New York, 1986).

[220] *Cairns* (*supra* n. 129) 138.

[221] *Kahn-Freund*, On Uses and Misuses of Comparative Law: 37 M.L.R. 1–27 (1974).

roughly one half of all ABA accredited US law schools as well as several foreign institutions. The *ASCL* holds annual meetings with an academic program and has long been the principal organization for the discipline in the United States.

Perhaps the *ASCL's* most important contribution has been the publication of the *American Journal of Comparative Law* (*AJCL*). It was established in 1952 at the University of Michigan with Hessel Yntema as its editor-in-Chief (until 1966). Roscoe Pound wrote the Introduction to the first volume, and both Ernst Rabel and Max Rheinstein contributed articles. The *AJCL* soon developed into one of the leading comparative law journals in the world.

141. *Teaching*. – In the postwar decades, the number of American law professors who considered themselves (at least part-time) comparatists grew impressively. In 1950, the *AALS Directory of Law Teachers* listed a mere 30; by 1970 there were 124; and by 1990 that number had risen to 335.[222] Most US law schools, and virtually all leading ones, began to offer courses in comparative law. Increasingly, they added special courses on particular countries, regions, or substantive topics. In addition, a growing number of law schools organized special (one-year) master's programs; by the 1970s, every year hundreds of students from all over the world obtained an LL.M. degree in the United States. The presence of these students inevitably injected a comparative element into the American law school environment.

142. *Marginal existence*. – Yet, despite all this growth, comparative law continued to linger on the margins of the American academic universe. There were hundreds of self-professed comparative law teachers (and soon half-a-dozen casebooks), but comparative law teaching was never central to the curriculum, not to mention mandatory. There was an impressive output of comparative legal scholarship[223] as well as a growing number of academic journals,[224] but barely a handful of American scholars succeeded in building a career on comparative studies, and even they were usually better known abroad than at home. On the whole, most American law professors (and practitioners) continued to regard the subject as academically exotic and practically useless – be it out of incurable parochialism, be it because the comparatists themselves did little to prove their importance.

143. *Characteristic features*. – For better or worse, postwar American comparative law developed by and large along German lines. This was the result of three factors. For starters, there was the heavy impact of the German immigrant jurists in the 1950s and 1960s. In addition, since the 1960s, German influence came through second generation immigrants, such as Hans Baade and Herbert Bernstein; through the immigrants' disciples, such as Mary Ann Glendon and John Langbein; and through scholars formed by close contacts with Germany (especially with the *Max Planck Institut* in Hamburg), such as David Clark and Peter Hay. Last but not least, the treatise by Zweigert and Kötz, which was pervaded by Ernst Rabel's conception of comparative law (and of functionalism), became a nearly canonical text in the United States when it appeared in an English translation.[225] Altogether, this German influence had several effects not all of which were positive in the long run.

First, American comparative law inherited the German (and more generally European) obsession with the civil/common dichotomy as well as the concomitant eurocentric perspective. As a result, it dealt mainly with the United States and England versus France and Germany (and sometimes Italy); for the time being, the rest of the world received scant attention, with the exception of some significant studies in socialist law and occasional work on third-world countries.[226]

[222] In 2003, the total number had risen to 557. Of course, one must take these numbers with a large pinch of salt. In particular, much of that growth merely reflects the general increase in the number of law professors in the postwar decades.

[223] In the 1950s, roughly 50 comparative law books were published in the United States; in the 1970s, that number had doubled. An even more rapid growth occurred with regard to law review articles.

[224] The number of law journals specializing in comparative (and often international) law grew from 2 in 1950 to 10 in 1960 and 48 in 1989. It continued to rise in the 1990s and early 2000s.

[225] *Zweigert and Kötz* (*supra* n. 3).

[226] *Barton, Gibbs, Li and Merryman*, Law in Radically Different Cultures (St. Paul MN 1983).

Second, the American approach remained firmly committed to Rabel's functionalism; this fit the domestic realist and pragmatist attitude well, but it also narrowed the focus and entailed the bias that, ultimately, legal systems solve like problems alike. Third, throughout the 1950s, 60s, and 70s, American comparative law remained focused mainly on the core areas of private law, in particular contract and tort as well as on the issue of codification. It thus paid too little attention to the most urgent problem areas in the United States at the time which were constitutional, procedural, and regulatory. This, in turn, contributed to the discipline's reputation as practically irrelevant. When scholars like Mary Ann Glendon, John Langbein, and John Merryman in the 1970s and 1980s turned to family law, procedure, and constitutional issues respectively, comparative studies immediately gained attention. Finally, the influence of Zweigert and Kötz, who were openly critical of methodological reflection,[227] confirmed the common lawyers' general skepticism vis-à-vis legal theory; it thus discouraged comparatists from thinking about issues of basic method and fundamental goals. This entailed indulgence in a happy-go-lucky attitude and the overall lack of clearly defined direction described before (*supra* i.b, ss. 110–111).

As a result, American contributions to comparative law theory and method were scarce before the 1990s. Two exceptions, however, are noteworthy. One is the concept of a "legal tradition" which requires looking at legal systems (or families thereof) from a historical, cultural, and value-system perspective. The concept originated in the work of John Merryman,[228] was expounded by scholars like Mary Ann Glendon, and has since become a standard topos (*infra* VI.B.ii, s. 343). The other exception is Mirjan Damaska's Weberian approach to the deep structures of legal systems and his distinction between "hierarchical" and "coordinate" ideals of power distribution.[229]

144. *The big projects.* – An overview of US-American comparative law in the postwar decades must at least briefly mention two big projects which occupied a significant number of comparatists for significant periods of time. These projects differed radically in nature and orientation, but they were also similar in that neither is considered a great success.

In the 1960s, Rudolf Schlesinger (1909–1996) initiated and led a large-scale research project on *The Formation of Contracts* aimed at "finding and formulating" a multinational *Common Core* "among a major portion of the world's legal systems" (*infra* VI.C.ii., s. 375). The project was funded inter alia by money from the Ford Foundation, involved nine scholars from various countries, ran for a decade, and resulted in a two-volume book.[230] Yet, its substantive focus was extremely narrow and it considered mainly Western legal systems. At the end of the day, despite the organizational energy, scholarly effort, and sums of money invested, the "Cornell Project" (as it became widely known) did not generate significant theoretical insights and had virtually no practical impact. Perhaps its greatest contribution was its somewhat innovative method: in order to avoid terminological bias and confusion, it defined the questions to be answered with regard to the various national laws involved not in legal terms but through carefully designed case hypotheticals. Such a "factual approach" has since been widely accepted in comparative legal studies; in particular, it inspired an even larger *Common Core* project in Europe in the 1990s (*infra* VI.C.ii., s. 376).

Around the same time, especially since the mid-1960s, *Law and Development* began to emerge as a new field of, or at least closely related to, comparative legal scholarship in the United States. Its aim was to support economic and political development in (the then so-called) third-world countries, especially in Latin America and Africa, through the export of American law and legal institutions. Based on ideas of progress, law reform, and in particular of social engineering through law, the program was related to the *Law and Society* movement which constituted itself around the same time. Also funded by Ford Foundation (and other) money, *Law and Development* generated conferences, a significant literature,

[227] *Zweigert and Kötz* (*supra* n. 3) 31-47.
[228] *Merryman* (*supra* n. 209)
[229] *Damaska* (*supra* n. 60).
[230] *Schlesinger* (ed.), The Formation of Contracts: A Study of the Common Core of Legal Systems (2 vol.) (Dobbs Ferry NY 1968).

travel to exotic countries, and a great deal of excitement and optimism for about a decade. By the mid-1970s, however, it had become clear that the plan to export American law and institutions to the developing world had been naïve, and that virtually nothing had been accomplished on the ground. Even among its initiators and supporters, many ultimately considered the movement a failure.[231] Yet, similar to the *Common Core* project, *Law and Development* was destined to have a second life towards the end of the century so that the lessons it taught were not all lost (*infra* VI.B.iii., s. 351).

e. Other Common Law and Mixed Jurisdictions

145. *Scotland, Louisiana, Quebec, Israel.* – The emphasis on the United Kingdom and the United States must not lead one to forget that there were comparative legal studies in other common law jurisdictions as well, such as Australia and Canada, although neither played a leading role. More importantly, perhaps, comparative studies were of course pursued in various mixed jurisdictions around the world. Within the United Kingdom, Scottish scholars had to deal with the amalgamation of the Roman-Dutch and the common law traditions; a similar situation prevailed in South Africa. In the United States, Louisiana remained a significant center of comparative studies at the Tulane and Louisiana State law schools which helped to sustain the civil law tradition in private law. In Canada, Quebec confronted the interplay between French-style civil and English-style common law on a routine basis, and some Canadian universities, McGill in Montreal prominently among them, were the home of several noted comparatists. In Israel, the older Ottoman laws coexisted with the rules from the British mandate, and imported continental learning mixed with increasing US-American influence, so that comparative law was simply part of the daily routine in both academia and practice. It was, however, only in the late twentieth and early twenty-first centuries that the study of mixed legal systems became recognized as specialty in its own right (*infra* iIV.A.ii., s. 177).

iv. *Beyond the North Atlantic Region*

a. Latin America[232]

146. *Unusual continuity.* – Most Latin American countries had remained rather uninvolved in World War II, so that it caused less of a rupture there than in Europe, North America, and East Asia. Comparative studies thus also showed more continuity than change. In line with its pre-war tradition, Latin America presented the perhaps most impressive picture of comparative law in action anywhere in the world. As an outside observer intimately familiar with the situation observed, "comparative legal studies are so familiar to Latin-American lawyers that they are often not even noticed".[233]

147. *Unabated borrowing.* – Borrowing from abroad continued unabated. This was perhaps most evident in the context of legislation. For example, the drafters of a new generation of civil codes (Bolivia 1976, Peru 1984, Paraguay 1985) drew heavily on the Italian *Codice civile* of 1942 but also looked to legislation from many other countries in Europe and beyond; when the Chilean economy was liberalized under Pinochet, American market deregulation was imported under the influence of the "Chicago boys" and shaped securities and corporate laws; Brazil adopted class actions, although it turned them into something rather different from their US model. Foreign law has also enjoyed a high degree of authority in the courts, especially at the highest level where, for example, the Argentine and Brazilian Supreme Courts have consulted foreign sources in numerous cases and in an almost routine fashion.

[231] For a critical assessment, see *Merryman*, Comparative Law and Social Change: On the Origins, Style, Decline & Revival of the Law and Development Movement: 25 Am.J.Comp.L. 457–491 (1977). See also *Trubek and Galanter*, Scholars in Self-Estrangement: Some Reflections on the Crisis in Law and Development Studies in the United States: 4 Wis.L.Rev. 1062–1102 (1974).

[232] For more detailed accounts, see *Kleinheisterkamp* (*supra* n. 105) 273–287; *Eder*, A Comparative Survey of Anglo-American and Latin-American Law (New York 1950); *Karst and Rosenn*, Law and Development in Latin America: A Casebook (Berkeley CA 1975).

[233] *Kleinheisterkamp* (*supra* n. 105) 235, quoting Eugenio Hernandez-Breton.

Among scholars, reference to foreign law had long since been virtually *de rigueur*.

On the whole, the attention continued to shift from continental Europe (especially France) to the common law world (especially the United States). Since the 1970s, this shift caused, and was reinforced by, a noticeable re-orientation in foreign academic studies: fewer and fewer Latin American graduate students went to Europe to obtain a doctorate from a French, German, or Italian university, while more and more traveled to the United States to earn an LL.M. degree from one of the top US law schools. As a result, English replaced French as the most widely used foreign legal language in Latin America as well.

148. *Eclecticism – to a fault.* – Yet, the picture was not quite as rosy as it may seem at first glance. Looking at a wider world, Latin-American comparative law became ever more eclectic, sometimes with unhappy consequences. Especially legislative borrowing from abroad often occurred in a rather careless fashion, i.e., without giving sufficient thought to the compatibility of the transplants with the indigenous environment (or, in fact, with each other). Enthusiastic importation of foreign ideas tended to come at the expense of sober attention to domestic law. And academic studies also frequently suffered from a "wild eclecticism which lack[ed] reflection".[234] In short, in the Latin American comparative law paradise, at times there was, as the English saying goes, "too much of a good thing".

b. East Asia[235]

149. *Continuing importation.* – The East Asian countries that continued to import law from the West, primarily Japan, Korea, and Taiwan, and later in the century increasingly the People's Republic of China, remained rather heavily engaged in comparative law – at least in the sense that they constantly had to choose among competing models, and that they needed to adjust transplants to local circumstances and needs. In the post-war period, attitudes towards foreign models became more critical and discriminating, and their fit with the domestic legal structures was more carefully evaluated. This "legislative comparative law" took place primarily in governments and, at least in Japan, sometimes also in the higher courts.

At the same time, attention gradually shifted from Europe, especially Germany, to the common law orbit, in particular the United States as the leading Western power. To be sure, the European influence remained significant, and in some matters dominant. Still, in areas such as constitutional law and the law of the market, the United States clearly took pride of place, at least for the time being.

150. *Teaching and Scholarship.* – The same trend prevailed in teaching. After 1945, comparative law courses gradually focused less on continental Europe and more on the US-American legal system. Especially in Japan, Anglo-American law came to occupy most of the comparative law curriculum. As in Latin America, this was in part due to the growing contingent of graduate students who went to earn LLM degrees in US law schools and then obtained teaching positions in their home countries. Again, where once French and German were the primary Western languages spoken among comparatists, English now became dominant.

Comparative law scholarship remained alive and, in some areas, well in East Asian countries like Japan and Korea. It by and large followed Western patterns, e.g., in the broad acceptance of the functional method, and it has remained strongly connected to Western scholarship.[236] In Japan, comparative studies tended to interact, and indeed overlap, with legal sociology. Yet, neither Japanese nor other East Asian comparative law scholarship had much of an effect beyond the

[234] *Idem* 282.

[235] For more detail, see *Kitagawa* (*supra* n. 178) 237–260.

[236] See e.g. Institute of Comparative Law, Waseda University (ed.), Law in East and West (Tokyo 1988); Institute of Comparative Law in Japan, Chuo University (ed.), Toward Comparative Law in the 21st Century (Tokyo 1998); Symposium: International Cooperation in the Field of Legal Studies and an Agenda for Comparative Law Studies (Nagoya 2005); *idem*, Future of Comparative Study of Law: The 60th Anniversary of the Institute of Comparative Law in Japan, Chuo University (Tokyo 2011).

region. Before the end of the century, publications in Western languages remained the exception so that indigenous scholarship was rarely accessible to readers in the Western world. And comparatists in Japan, Korea, Taiwan, or China did not produce any books or generate any theories with a significant impact abroad.

E. THE 1990S AND BEYOND

151. *A new era.* – Comparative law entered a new era around 1990 as a result of three significant changes. Most importantly, the configuration of the world changed as the cold war gave way to an age of rapid globalization; this opened previously unimagined possibilities for comparative law. Furthermore, the scholars who had created and maintained the postwar tradition were now retired or dead; a new generation took over, faced new challenges, and asked new questions. Finally, the intellectual leadership shifted from Europe to the United States – not because most valuable comparative work was done there (it was not) but because most (though not all) innovative ideas came from America while Europe by and large continued on more traditional paths.

The development of comparative law since ca. 1990 is perhaps best described and evaluated in three parts: the changes brought by globalization (i.), the resultant crisis of the mainstream (ii.), and the presentation of five (other) themes that played a prominent role around the turn of the millennium (iii.).

i. *Comparative Law in the Age of Globalization*

152. *Nagging doubts.* – Despite the discipline's consolidation, growth, and undeniable successes in the postwar decades, much of comparative law suffered from a "Cinderella complex"[237]: comparatists often felt that in both academia and practice, the true importance of their work was not sufficiently recognized. They continued to trumpet the enormous benefits of comparative studies but considered themselves undervalued, marginalized, "in search of an audience",[238] and "without a constituency".[239] They found it hard to believe, and impossible to accept, that the vast majority of their academic colleagues as well as of the bench and bar still focused on national law and cared little for other legal systems. At times, there was an outright sense of despair among comparative lawyers because all efforts to talk the legal profession at large out of its parochial ways seemed doomed to failure.

153. *Globalization to the rescue.* – Beginning in the late 1980s, comparatists were rescued from their – real or imagined – marginalization, as well as from their self-doubt, by a combination of processes that radically changed the environment in which they operated. Four of these processes deserve particular mention here. First, the fall of the iron curtain in 1989 and the end of the cold war created a huge market for law reform in Eastern Europe and then also in China and elsewhere. This reform was usually modeled on Western (i.e., liberal, capitalist, free-market) law and thus entailed legal transplants on a scale unprecedented in recent history. This in turn created enormous opportunities for comparatists as experts in the interplay between different legal systems. Second, the rapid growth of international economic (and other) relations led to an equally rapid growth of international business transactions, litigation, and arbitration. This development was most vividly illustrated by the explosion of the number and size of global law firms, but it also manifested itself in the formation of judicial networks all around the world; knowledge and comparative evaluation of other law(s) turned from an exotic luxury or merely exceptional need into a routine necessity for business people and their lawyers. Third, the growth of international regimes, ranging from trade to human rights, linked the laws of the world ever more closely together and thus enhanced the need for mutual understanding and adjustment. Finally, the accelerated integration of Europe (beginning with the Single European Act in 1987) created a veritable paradise for

[237] *Frankenberg*, Critical Comparisons: Rethinking Comparative Law: 26 Harv.Int.L.J. 411–455, 419 (1985).

[238] *Markesinis*, Comparative Law – A Subject in Search of an Audience: 53 M.L.R. 1–21 (1990).

[239] *Munday*, Accounting for an Encounter: *idem and Legrand* (eds.), Comparative Legal Studies: Traditions and Transitions (Cambridge 2003) 3–28, 10.

comparative lawyers, especially in the context of European unification efforts in private law. In combination, these processes suddenly bestowed upon comparative law a practical significance and academic legitimacy which it had rarely, if ever, enjoyed before. Almost suddenly, the discipline moved from the margins of legal academia and practice to at least a respectable and, in some contexts, even a prominent place.

154. *The emergence of a global discipline.* – At the same time, and in part as a result of these processes, late twentieth-century comparative law became a global enterprise: comparatists now worked in a predominantly international, rather than national, environment. Of course, comparative law scholars had long transcended the context of their own legal systems *in their work*. But in terms of their *location and affiliation*, the members of the postwar generation had by and large still remained tied to their home countries, even if it was, as in the case of the immigrant jurists, a new nation: the French, German, English, or American comparatists had normally conducted their research, taught, and published in France, Germany, England, and the United States respectively. At the turn of the millennium, however, this had changed. Now, comparatists acted on a world stage not only occasionally but routinely. Almost all of them now constantly traveled internationally to congresses and meetings. Most taught in foreign countries at least at some point or another, spent sabbaticals abroad, and published in foreign journals (mainly in English). Many acquired a foreign law degree and some then settled abroad, especially in the common law world. An increasing number came to hold permanent appointments in different countries and thus split their time between different institutions. The United States became their primary playground with a panoply of Asian, English, French, German, Italian, Israeli, Latin American, and other scholars on US law faculties. In addition, now there were also Greeks teaching in England, Italians in Germany, Germans in Canada, a Canadian in France, etc. This new generation not only *looked at* foreign jurisdictions, it increasingly *felt at home* there. As a result of its many multiple affiliations, the perceived boundaries between "our law" and "their law" began to fade. Comparative law discourse increasingly took place in a global context, i.e., in the form of a global literature with a global audience.

155. *Explosive growth.* – In this new global environment, comparative law experienced an almost explosive growth that soon dwarfed the discipline in its previous shape. To begin with, the number of self-proclaimed inhabitants of the field skyrocketed almost everywhere, especially in the United States.[240] To be sure, most new members were not full-time, hard-core comparative law scholars but rather occasional producers or users of comparative work. But the growing number of these part-timers illustrated how comparative perspectives now pervaded more and more areas of law, producing a "comparativization" of law teaching and legal scholarship on an ever broader scale.[241] In most countries, comparative law was now offered in most universities, and in some, as in Italy, it became widely obligatory. The literature, as well as the number of specialized journals, kept growing exponentially, and the outpouring of books and articles soon exceeded what even full-time comparatists could hope to handle. In addition, the comparative work required, or at least triggered by, European integration stimulated a reinvigoration of the discipline in several jurisdictions, notably in France, but also in Eastern Europe where the majority of countries soon joined the European Union. All this growth also had an impact in the courts: in many jurisdictions, references to foreign law increased and comparative considerations became more common, although in the national courts they usually remained on a fairly modest level.[242]

[240] The number of law teachers listing themselves as (at least part-time) comparatists in the Association of American Law Schools (AALS) Directory grew from 201 in 1980 to 335 in 1990 to 515 in 2000 and to 557 in 2004. Some of this growth merely reflects the growing overall number of law teachers in the United States during that period, i.e., not necessarily a rise in percentage. It still means that within barely one generation, the number of American academics seriously interested in comparative law almost tripled.

[241] *Grande* (*supra* n. 198) 103.

[242] For detailed accounts, see *Drobnig and van Erp* (eds.), The Use of Comparative Law by Courts (The Hague, London, Boston MA 1999); *Canivet, Andenas and Fairgrieve* (eds.), Comparative Law Before the Courts (London 2004).

156. *Commercialization of scholarship production.* – To a considerable extent, the explosive growth of scholarship production has been fueled by its commercialization. Around the turn of the century, a handful of major publishing houses (mainly in England, the United States, and the Netherlands) began to launch numerous series in the form of comparative law "Handbooks", "Companions" or "Introductions" which have covered ever more specific topics and have turned into a veritable avalanche of books. It is important to note that in most instances these publications have *not* been initiated by scholars seeking to disseminate their work; instead, they have been invented by the publishers themselves seeking to make a profit from selling expensive books to libraries around the world. Typically, the respective publisher recruits a well-known scholar as the editor of a volume who in turn recruits colleagues to write various contributions.[243] In short, much of the recent output of comparative law scholarship is a response to the marketing strategies of major economic players. This does not mean that the scholarship is of poor quality, but it does mean that much of it is unoriginal. As a result, one must not mistake the explosive growth of scholarly production as proof of an equally explosive growth of ideas. It is thus open to question whether the sheer mass of recent publications have really advanced the ball.

157. *Continuing diversification.* – Diversification not only continued but accelerated as well in three regards: geographic areas, fields of law, and scholarly perspectives.

To begin with, late twentieth-century comparative law significantly expanded its geographic scope, although the Eurocentrism bequeathed upon the discipline by the continental scholars lingered (see *infra* IV.A.i., ss. 172–175). Asian legal systems (first Japan, then China, and to some extent also India, Korea, and Taiwan) became a major focus and eventually a sub-discipline in their own right. Islamic law enjoyed growing attention, especially with regard to legal modernization. Mixed legal systems became a prominent topic with a literature of their own. And in specific contexts, countries with especially interesting developments were increasingly studied, such as India, Israel, and South Africa with regard to individual rights. At the same time, however, Latin America received less attention than its role in the world demanded, and Sub-Saharan Africa continued to be largely ignored.[244]

In a similar vein, while the centrality of private law often persisted (though much more in Europe than in the United States), other subject matter areas now became serious competitors for attention (*infra* IV.B.). The big winners in this regard were (civil and criminal) procedure and constitutional law; while both had been cultivated before, they now grew into established sub-disciplines of considerable sophistication. Other rising fields included courts and the methods of judging, legal education and the professions, as well as labor law and human rights.

Finally, the new generation of comparatists pushed for methodological innovation. It refused uncritically to accept the functionalism revered by the postwar scholars and questioned the traditional presumption that at least developed societies face largely similar problems and find largely similar solutions. Both traditional functionalism and the *presumptio similitudinis* thus came under attack as biased, simplistic, and methodologically harmful (*infra* VI.C.i., ss. 368–373). Pushing beyond these time-honored paradigms, many comparatists now began to pursue an ever more bewildering array of scholarly directions, often with a special emphasis on critical and interdisciplinary approaches. As a result, the methodological and epistemological boundaries of the field expanded way beyond the postwar dimensions (*infra* VI.).

ii. *The Crisis of the Mainstream*

158. *Indeterminacy and "identity crisis".* – The processes of globalization had an ambiguous

[243] In this fashion, scholars, who need to satisfy the ever-increasing publication requirements of their institutions, provide free labor for the publishers.

[244] There were some exceptions, see e.g. *Edge* (ed.), Comparative Law in a Global Perspective (Ardsley NY 2000). As mentioned, Socialist Law was relegated to the museum of legal history; see e.g. *Markovits*, Justice in Lüritz (Princeton NJ 2010).

impact on comparative law. On the one hand, they provided the discipline with new relevance, prominence, and self-confidence; on the other hand, they caused a deep "identity crisis",[245] at least for the mainstream. It is not difficult to see why: in the brave new world that emerged in the 1990s, the discipline's traditional core, i.e., the functionalist comparison of national legal systems in a *macro* or *micro* fashion, suddenly seemed woefully narrow, old-fashioned, and inadequate. This led to uncomfortable questions that defied easy answers. As ever more – part-time, occasional, if not amateur – "comparatists" joined the bandwagon, what, if any, special skills did comparatists really bring to the table? As looking at other legal systems became routine in ever more contexts, what, if anything, was the ultimate core of the discipline? And with an ever greater variety of perspectives and approaches, what, if anything, marked its boundaries? Or was there really no "comparative law" as a clearly defined and separate discipline at all – but merely a panoply of transboundary approaches to law that were available to anybody, depended on the context, and could thus lead in myriad directions?

In addition, the diversification of the discipline entailed ever more specialization which, again, put the existence of common ground into doubt. The various new subject areas tended to drift apart and communication began to turn inward: comparative constitutional law scholars, Asia specialists, critical comparatists, participants in the European private law unification projects, etc., mainly talked within their field but rarely with members of other groups. They also tended to lose touch with the remaining mainstream comparatists who suddenly found themselves in the minority.

In short, in the age of globalization, comparative law became such a pervasive, diversified, and wide-open enterprise that the discipline threatened to disintegrate. Its core became dubious, its coherence weak, and its boundaries indeterminate.

159. *The "Country and Western Tradition" asleep at the wheel.* – Yet, the crisis not only resulted from the forces of globalization, it was also the consequence of the mainstream's long complacency. The "Country and Western Tradition",[246] i.e., the time-honored approach focusing on countries rather than the global legal order, and on the West rather than on the world as a whole, failed to realize, or refused to accept, that the discipline needed to adjust to radically changed circumstances. This became evident at the *Centennial World Congress of Comparative Law*, held on the 100th anniversary of the Paris Congress (*supra* C.i. ss. 85–87) at the Tulane Law School in 2000. Here, the mainstream celebrated the discipline's apparent health and progress, but upon closer inspection most of the chosen subjects and much of the prevailing discourse turned out to be disconcertingly old-fashioned, if not out of date.[247] Several observers noted striking similarities between the Paris Congress of 1900 and the current event – which raised the question whether much progress had been made in the past century at all. The answer given – not only by Young Turks[248] but also by several representatives of the postwar mainstream[249] – was by and large no. In short, there was a growing impression that while the world had moved on at break-neck speed, the mainstream comparatists had been asleep at the wheel.

160. *A critical movement.* – Reactions against the postwar tradition had already begun in the 1990s, i.e., before the Centennial World Congress. They led to two conferences held in the United States at which the mainstream was subjected to serious critiques. These critiques proceeded essentially on two levels – one fairly conventional, the other more radical, although they substantially overlapped.

The fairly conventional critiques were expressed during a two-stage conference at the University of Michigan in 1996 and at the Hastings College of Law in 1997. Searching for "New Directions in Comparative Law", the participants

245 *Glendon, Gordon and Carozza* (*supra* n. 20) 3.

246 *Twining*, Globalisation and Legal Theory (London 2000) 184.

247 The contributions are published in Centennial World Congress on Comparative Law: 75 Tul.L.Rev. 859–1235 (2001).

248 See especially *Michaels* (*supra* n. 145) 97.

249 *Blanc-Jouvan*, Centennial World Congress on Comparative Law: Opening Remarks: 75 Tul.L.Rev. 859–864, 862 (2001); *Clark*, Nothing New in 2000? Comparative Law in 1900 and Today: 75 Tul.L.Rev. 871–912, 894–896 (2001).

criticized, inter alia, the discipline's frequent failure to go beyond mere description of foreign law, i.e., to advance to real comparison and analysis of results; its lack of solid theoretical foundations; its continued obsession with private law in the age of the regulatory state; its persistent Eurocentrism; its outdated fixation on the civil v. common law dichotomy; its excessive rule-orientation and insufficient attention to historical and philosophical dimensions; and its lack of interdisciplinarity. Participants also emphasized the potential of comparative law as a "subversive discipline" to destabilize traditional assumptions. In sum, the critics saw the postwar tradition shaped by the emigrant generation as a straitjacket from which the discipline must liberate itself. They suggested new directions that better account for the current state of the world and promised broader theoretical insights.[250]

The more radical critiques were voiced during a conference at the University of Utah in 1996. They reflected the spirit of the American critical legal studies movement and took a postmodern turn, especially in their emphasis on complexity, ambiguity, and heterogeneity. In particular, the participants accused comparative law of obsession with uniformity and convergence as well as of insufficient attention to, and respect for, difference and pluralism; they deconstructed traditional functionalism, especially its bias towards like solutions, and pointed to the benefits of diversity; they expressed skepticism toward the comparability of legal cultures and pointed to the limits (if not the impossibility) of legal translation; and they explored the political dimensions of the discipline in a variety of contexts.[251]

The larger discipline's reactions to these two conferences was mixed. On the one hand, a substantial segment followed suit and developed what may be called a critical movement in comparative law (*infra* VI.B.v., ss. 360–365). This movement soon spilled over into Europe and into the twenty-first century. It created a substantial literature which has, despite its varying quality, entailed a broad and healthy re-examination and opening-up of the field.[252] On the other hand, large parts of the mainstream paid scant, if any, attention to the critiques or rejected them as extreme and unhelpful. Despite various early twenty-first-century searches for new directions, most comparatists, especially in continental Europa, continued down the traditional paths. This was most visible in the project of European private law unification. Perhaps hoping that the fundamental challenges would turn out to be merely a passing fashion, many comparatists acted as if nothing had happened. Whether the critical movement will have a broad and long-term impact is thus an open question.

iii. *Five Themes of the Post-*1990. *Era*[253]

161. *Overview.* – Beyond the discipline's globalization, growth and diversification, and beyond the "identity crisis" and critical response, turn-of-the-millennium comparative law has also been shaped by a handful of more particular themes: the unification of European private law; the push for greater interdisciplinarity; the rise of a (second) *Law and Development* movement; the debate about *Legal Origins*; and the growing attention to non-state norms. These themes will be addressed here but briefly, because they will be considered in greater depth when we look at the discipline's major current directions (*infra* VI.).

[250] Symposium: New Directions in Comparative Law: 46 Am.J.Comp.L. 597–783 (1998).

[251] Symposium: New Approaches to Comparative Law: Utah L.Rev 255–657 (1997).

[252] See e.g. *Antoniolli, Benacchio and Toniatti* (eds.), Le Nuove Frontiere della Comparazione (Trento 2012); *Egelbrekt and Nergelius*, New Directions in Comparative Law (Cheltenham, Northampton MA 2009); *Legrand and Munday* (eds.), Comparative Legal Studies: Traditions and Transitions (Cambridge, New York 2003); *van Hoecke* (ed.), Epistemology and Methodology of Comparative Law (Oxford, Portland OR 2004); *Örücü and Nelken* (eds.), Comparative Law: A Handbook (Oxford, Portland OR 2007); see also *Mattei*, Comparative Law and Critical Legal Studies: *Reimann and Zimmermann* (eds.), The Oxford Handbook of Comparative Law (ed. 2 Oxford 2019) 805–825.

[253] For an assessment of the discipline at the turn of the millennium, see also the collection of essays published by the *Société du Droit Comparé*, L'Avenir du Droit Comparé. Un Défi pour les Juristes du Nouveau Millénaire (Paris 2000).

162. *Unifying European private law.*[254] – The most prominent comparative law theme at the turn of the millennium was the unification of private law in Europe. While the international unification of law has long been one of the discipline's main objectives, at least since the Paris Congress of 1900, European integration since the 1990s endowed this agenda with unprecedented academic prominence, practical relevance, and public resources. It diversified into a plethora of individual projects involving hundreds of European (and in some cases overseas) academics. At times, it seemed that every comparatist and most private law scholars in Europe were engaged in the unification of private law in one way or another.

The various projects were encouraged and sometimes financed by the European Union itself, and much of their motivation and resources was the result of support from Brussels. Yet, after about two decades marked by great academic enthusiasm and scholarly production, EU politicians and bureaucrats apparently lost interest in the agenda and support petered out. At the same time, many academic projects had by and large exhausted themselves. As a result, the drive for European private law unification ran out of steam in the second decade of the twenty-first century. While it had generated a huge number of studies, principles, and drafts, it did not generate the legislative action on the European level that had been its ultimate goal. Whether history will eventually regard it as a gigantic failure remains to be seen.

163. *Pushing for interdisciplinarity.* – Since the 1990s, a recurrent theme in comparative law has been the need for greater interdisciplinarity. It is no accident that its pursuit has been strongest in the United States where law in general has increasingly been conceived as a social science, at least by academics.[255] The American impulses have had some spill-over effects in other countries. Still, calls for greater interdisciplinarity have ultimately had limited resonance in Europe and other parts of the world, where law has traditionally been regarded as a more self-contained and systematic science of principles and rules.

On the whole, serious interdisciplinary comparative studies have remained fairly rare. It is true that in the last two decades, scholars have created substantial bodies of work in comparative legal history as well as in comparative law and economics; there is also some scholarship in comparative legal anthropology and sociology as well as in comparative law and language (see *infra* VI.B.iv., ss. 352–359). Still, the hopes of a pervasive and sustained cooperation between comparatists and scholars from other social sciences have largely remained unfulfilled.

164. *The revival of Law and Development.* – On both sides of the Atlantic, comparative law received a boost from the revival of the *Law and Development* movement (see also *infra* VI.B.iii., s. 351) at the end of the twentieth century. The collapse of the Soviet Empire, economic liberalization in China, India, and elsewhere, as well as (at least superficial) democratization in many parts of the world, created a huge need for legal reform in new market economies and developing countries. This need triggered renewed claims that political and economic progress requires an adequate legal infrastructure.[256] Both public and private institutions spent billions of dollars or euros supporting the export of Western law to countries supposedly in need of it. In contrast to the first *Law and Development* movement in the 1960s and 1970s, when the United States had been the unquestioned leader, this time Western Europe (including the EU) fiercely competed for influence. The myriad programs and efforts to export law provided dazzling opportunities for comparative lawyers in the Western world – as consultants to governments and private organizations, drafters of legislation, and advisers to law firms. Most of their work, however, was not based on serious comparative studies; in fact, much of it simply presumed the superiority of their own, or more generally of Western, law.

[254] For a more detailed account, see *Zimmermann*, Comparative Law and the Europeanization of Private Law: *Reimann and Zimmermann* (eds.) *The Oxford Handbook of Comparative Law* (ed. 2 Oxford 2019), 557–598; see also *infra* IV.C.i.g., ss. 242–245.

[255] See e.g. *Mattei* (*supra* n. 78).

[256] See e.g. *Rose*, The "New" Law and Development Movement in the Post-Cold War Era: A Vietnam Case Study: 32 Law &Soc.Rev. 93–140 (1998).

The need for comparative lawyers' services lasted but briefly. Within about a decade, most newly liberalized countries had reformed most of their law and thus had no more use for further imports on a large scale. By the beginning of the new century, the comparative lawyers involved in the various projects had by and large returned to their daily routines. A few of them, however, have remained engaged either in development projects or in scholarship about them. Some comparatists have questioned whether law is really as essential to development as had generally been assumed; notably China's economic success without a highly developed legal infrastructure challenges such an assumption.[257]

At the same time, the new *Law and Development* matured as a field of study with its own journals, institutes, web pages, academic and political networks. It has remained connected to comparative law although it is more closely affiliated with the *Law and Society* movement.

165. *The Legal Origins debate.* – Just as the comparatists' involvement with the new *Law and Development* projects tapered off, there were new reasons for excitement about a related theme which came to be known as the *Legal Origins* thesis. It essentially consists of the claim propagated by a group of American economists that systems originating in the common law provide a better environment for economic development than systems in the civil law tradition.[258] The comparatists' reactions ranged from measured skepticism to violent rejection. The resulting debates became a major topic in early twenty-first-century comparative law and will be considered in greater detail below (VI.B.iv., s. 358).

166. *Non-state norms.* – Finally, in the early twenty-first century, comparative lawyers increasingly turned their attention to the rise of non-state norms, especially in the field of private law. Of course, such norms were far from a novelty; in fact, their role had been a topic especially among commercial lawyers for nearly a century. Yet, in the wake of the privatization and deregulation policies predominant in many countries since the end of the twentieth century, non-state norms took on an importance unprecedented in modern times. It thus became more and more obvious that if comparative law wants to reflect current legal realities, it must look beyond state-created rules and take non-state norms into account.[259] Analyzing their significance, and especially their relationship to state-sanctioned law, also provides opportunities for, and in many cases outright requires, interdisciplinary perspectives, such as considerations of political economy, democratic theory, religion, and legal anthropology.[260]

F. IN CONCLUSION: MAJOR ACCOMPLISHMENTS AND THE LOSS OF A CLEAR DEFINITION

167. *Two centuries of comparative law.* – Comparative law in the sense of a *sustained study of the similarities and differences between national legal systems* began in the early nineteenth century and is thus roughly 200 years old. Comparative law in the sense of an *established discipline in its own right*, i.e., with an identifiable community of scholars, a discourse about its particular goals and methods, and an institutional framework, dates back to the turn of the nineteenth to the twentieth centuries and is thus more than a century old. As juristic sub-disciplines go, this is a fairly respectable age. While some (such as private law or legal philosophy) are much older, others (such as labor law or economic analysis of law) are

[257] See e.g. *Clarke*, Economic Development and the Rights Hypothesis: The China Problem, 51 Am.J. Comp.L. 89–111 (2003); *Peerenboom*, China's Long March Towards the Rule of Law (Cambridge 2002).

[258] *La Porta, Lopez de Silanes, Shleifer* and *Vishny*, Legal Determinants of External Finance: 52 J. Finance (1997) 1131–1150; *La Porta, Lopez de Silanes, Shleifer and Vishny*, Law and Finance: 106 J.Pol.Econ. 1113–1155 (1998).

[259] See *Zimmermann* (ed.), Globalisierung und Entstaatlichung des Rechts, Teilband II – Nichtstaatliches Privatrecht, Geltung und Genese (Tübingen 2008).

[260] See the contributions in *Jansen and Michaels* (eds.) Special Symposium: Beyond the State: Rethinking Private Law: 56 Am.J.Comp.L. 527–842 (2008); also published in *Jansen and Michaels* (eds.), Beyond the State. Rethinking Private Law (Tübingen 2008); *Jansen*, The Making of Legal Authority: Non-Legislative Codifications in Historical and Comparative Perspective (Oxford 2010).

much younger. Looking back at its development, it is thus appropriate to ask what comparative law has accomplished and how its contours have changed.

168. *Major accomplishments.* – In its roughly two centuries of existence, and especially in its more than a century as a discipline in its own right, comparative law has generated an impressive record. Its accomplishments can perhaps be put into three categories. First, comparative studies have produced an enormous wealth of knowledge about most of the world's leading legal systems – from their genesis and culture to their institutions and processes and to their sources and positive rules (*infra* IV.). Second, comparative legal studies have led to a fairly sophisticated understanding of several aspects of the legal systems' relationship amongst each other – the similarities and differences of their rules, processes, and institutions; the affinity and otherness of their mentalities and styles; their influence on, and borrowing from, each other; and their convergence and divergence over time (*infra* V. and VI). Third, comparative law has successfully promoted and assisted legal unification and integration, at times on a global, more often on a regional, basis. In addition to all these accomplishments, comparative law has provided a vitally important antidote to the malaise so rampant among lawyers in the modern nation state, i.e., parochialism. Despite the discipline's often marginal existence, comparative perspectives have now become so pervasive that modern legal thought entirely without them is difficult to imagine.

169. *The erosion of a clear definition.* – At the same time, its development, and especially its rapid expansion since the late twentieth century, has led the discipline to outgrow the parameters which had defined it for generations after the Paris Congress of 1900. It is no longer only, or even mainly, the comparative law of Lambert and Saleiles, Rabel and David, or even of Zweigert and Kötz, i.e., an endeavor to compare the rules and institutions of the legal systems of (mainly Western) nation states for purposes of gaining "knowledge", promoting legal unification, and assisting legal practice. As the subsequent subchapters will show in greater detail, the discipline has come to encompass a much broader array of topics, areas, approaches, and methods, in pursuit of a much larger variety of goals and uses. Thus, after more than a century of development, it has become much harder clearly to define what comparative law really is (and is not), not to mention to chart its future course (*infra* VII.).

LIST OF PRINCIPAL WORKS

Ancel, Les grands étapes de la recherche comparative au XXe siècle, Studi in Memoria di Andrea Torrente I. (Milano 1968) 23–32, reprinted in *Zweigert and Puttfarken*, Rechtsvergleichung (Darmstadt 1978) 350–360

Clark, Nothing New in 2000?: 75 Tul.L.Rev. 871–912 (2001)

Constantinesco, Rechtsvergleichung I (Köln, Berlin, Bonn, München 1971) 70–201

Donahue, Comparative Law Before the *Code Napoleon*: *Reimann and Zimmermann* (eds.), The Oxford Handbook of Comparative Law (ed. 2 Oxford 2019) 3–28

Fauvarque-Cosson, Deux siècles d'evolution du droit compare: Rev.int.dr.comp 63 (2011) 527–540

Ginsburg, Monateri and *Parisi* (eds.), Classics of Comparative Law (4 vol.) (Cheltenham, Northhampton MA 2014)

Hug, The History of Comparative Law: 45 Harv.L.Rev. (1932) 1027–1070

L'Avenir Du Droit Comparé: Rev.int.dr.comp. 51 (1999) 741–1071 (collection of essays on the state and future of comparative law in more than a dozen countries)

Michaels, Im Westen nichts Neues?: RabelsZ 66 (2002) 97–115

Reimann and *Zimmermann* (eds.), The Oxford Handbook of Comparative Law (ed. 2 Oxford 2019) 3–288 (chapters 1–10)

Reimann, The Progress and Failure of Comparative Law in the Second Half of the Twentieth Century: 50 Am.J.Comp.L. 671–700 (2002)

Société de Législation Comparée, L'Avenir du Droit Comparé. Un Défi pour les Juristes du Nouveau Millénaire (Paris 2000).

170. *Overview.* – Comparative law today covers a wide variety of areas. This chapter surveys this coverage in three dimensions: the geographic regions of the world (A.), the elements of legal systems (B.), and the areas of positive law (C.), leaving for later the discipline's uses and goals (V.) as well its orientations, approaches, and methods (VI.). In all of the three dimensions addressed here, comparative legal studies have rapidly expanded and diversified in the last couple of decades. This has entailed an exponential growth of the literature which has become far too vast to be comprehensively surveyed.[261] As a result, this chapter can provide only a sampling of some important works as well as some illustrations of particular kinds of studies.

A. LEGAL SYSTEMS OF THE WORLD[262]

171. *Introduction and Caveat.* – In the early twenty-first century comparative law covers almost all inhabited regions of the world, albeit to varying degrees of depth. This was not always so. When the discipline took its modern shape in and after the Paris Congress of 1900 (*supra* III.C.i., ss. 85–87), its focus was by and large limited to what one may call "the West". Convinced that meaningful comparison is possible only among sufficiently similar systems, comparatists in the first half of the twentieth century focused rather narrowly on the developed nations of Western Europe and then, gradually, the United States. Since the middle of the century, however, there has been a constant expansion of geographic scope which accelerated in response to the globalization processes since the 1990s, and which eventually led to the global coverage marking the field today.

Yet, when hailing this expansion as a form of progress one must not forget that comparative studies looking beyond "the West" have significant precursors – such as Montesquieu's mid-eighteenth-century *Esprit des lois* (1748) (III.A.iii.c., s. 63), the mid-nineteenth-century English books on the laws in the far-flung British Empire (III.B.ii.a., s. 79), and the late-nineteenth-century turn towards *legal ethnology* (III.B.i.b., s. 72). In a sense, then, the recent geographic expansion has not really discovered, but rather re-discovered, the regions beyond the Western orbit of law.

This chapter does not undertake a substantive description of the various legal families of the world; for such a description the reader should turn to Volume II of this Encyclopedia.[263] Instead, it is the purpose of this chapter merely to survey how comparative law has come to cover all major legal traditions and systems and to show the resultant geographic diversification of the discipline.

i. *The West*

172. *The traditional focus.* – Since modern comparative law as a discipline in its own right was conceived by scholars from the Western legal traditions, its primary focus has been on the laws and legal systems of the cultural West. In part, the reasons are simply practical: to a lawyer trained in a Western legal system other such systems are fairly comprehensible; they build on the same underlying (Western) conception of law,[264] are accessible in Western languages (primarily English and French, or at least in German, Italian, or Spanish), and they share basic terminological toolkits and organizational structures which make them rather easily comparable. None of this is true for non-Western systems. In part, the focus on Western law was also a product of the

[261] For a collection of writings that have attained the status of "classics", see *Ginsburg, Monateri and Parisi* (eds.), Classics in Comparative Law (4 vol.) (Cheltenham, Northampton MA 2014).

[262] The study of the world's legal systems is addressed here only with regard to its coverage. Grouping these systems is also a specific method of comparative law which is discussed *infra* VI.B.ii., ss. 337–344.

[263] The reader must bear mind, however, that that volume reflects the situation prevailing almost 50 years ago.

[264] *Sawyer* (*supra*. n. 190); *Bussani*, Il diritto dell'occidente (Torino 2010); for a historical perspective, see *Berman*, Law and Revolution: The Formation of the Western Legal Tradition (Cambridge MA 1985); *Monateri and Somma*, Il Modello del Civil Law (ed. 4 Torino 2016).

discipline's traditional orientation: for most of the twentieth century comparative law searched mainly for similarities (rather than differences) and pursued the goal of legal unification; both agendas are much more promising when limited to legal systems from the same general culture.

173. *Continental Europe.* – It can safely be said that throughout the twentieth century, and into the early twenty-first, continental Europe has been the object of comparative legal study more than any other region of the world. The reasons for this enduring prominence are threefold. Most importantly, continental Europe is the cradle of the civil law family. As such, it is the centerpiece of the most influential legal tradition in human history. The majority of legal systems on the globe either are members of this tradition or at least incorporate significant elements of it. This makes continental Europe a natural ground zero for comparative study. Furthermore, the European continent provides ample opportunity for controlled comparison between its various legal systems because they present an attractive balance of similarities and differences. On the one hand, they share the heritage of Roman, canon, and local customary law, creating considerable common ground. On the other hand, there are significant differences, especially between the two leading countries, i.e., France and Germany, and thus between the many European legal systems modeled primarily after one or the other. Finally, the intense economic, cultural, and social interaction among the continental nations creates particularly strong practical needs for comparative law – as a means to facilitate mutual understanding, as a tool to resolve private international law issues, and, most importantly, as an instrument of legal harmonization and unification. Especially the latter agenda gained huge prominence through the integration of Europe which has boosted intra-European comparative legal studies to an unprecedented degree (*infra* C.i.g., ss. 242–245).

174. *The common law orbit.* – The other main focus of comparative studies over the last century has been the common law orbit.[265] Initially, continental European comparatists, especially in France, looked primarily to England as the mother country of the common law and thus the original representative of the second major legal tradition in the world.[266] Scholars soon realized that comparison across the Channel is more challenging than between continental systems. The peculiar development of English law – especially its earlier centralization, lesser Romanization, and emphasis on judicial, rather than legislative, lawmaking – entailed deep structural, conceptual, and terminological divergences from continental European systems. Around the middle of the twentieth century, the law and legal system of the United States also became an important, and eventually the predominant, object of inquiry on the common law side. In fact, for the last 50 years, the United States has been the most frequently and intensely studied national legal system in the world. It did not take long for comparatists to understand that despite membership of the same legal tradition, the English and the US legal systems differ in very significant respects, especially with regard to constitutional, procedural, and regulatory law. Among the other countries in the common law orbit, two former Commonwealth members have received increasing attention in recent decades: Canada (partially because it provides an alternative to the US-American model) and India (*infra* s. 180). Studies involving Australia, New Zealand, or other former British colonies' law have been more intermittent.

175. *Comparative law as civil law v. common law.* – As a result of looking primarily to continental Europe on the one hand and to the Anglo-American world on the other, much of twentieth-century comparative law consisted of studying the relationship between the civil and the common law.[267] For decades after 1950, it often seemed as if mainstream comparatists could think of little else. Civil lawyers were intrigued by the common law model while common lawyers sought

[265] *Legrand and Samuel*, Introduction au Common Law (Paris 2008); *Mattei, Ariano and Marchisio*, Il modello del common law (ed. 5 Torino 2018); *Verbeke*, Elementen van Anglo-Americaans Recht (Antwerp 1994).

[266] See e.g. *Lévy-Ullmann* (*supra* n. 149).

[267] See e.g. *Schlesinger*, Comparative Law (New York 1950).

to understand the civil law culture.[268] The fascination with these legal traditions is largely due to the fact that their comparison raises fundamental questions about law and legal method: legislative v. judicial lawmaking, deductive v. inductive reasoning, reliance on logic v. trust in intuition, general rules v. justice in the individual case, etc. Still, over time, the near obsession with the civil v. common law dichotomy also became a straitjacket[269] from which comparative law on both sides of the Channel and Atlantic has liberated itself only recently and incompletely.

ii. *Post-World War II Expansions*

176. *The socialist law interlude.* – A major, though temporary, expansion of the discipline's geographic focus occurred between the 1960s and 1980s when comparative lawyers turned to the study of law in the Eastern Bloc. With the sweep of communism throughout Central Europe after World War II, its consolidation in China in 1949, and communist revolutions in many other countries around the globe, vast parts of the world became governed by various forms of socialism. As a result, socialist law became a major theme of comparative study – on both sides of the divide.[270] In the East, lawyers taking the official position claimed that socialist law was sui generis – a new form of law unlike any other before it: not an instrument of (feudal or capitalist) oppression and exploitation but rather a means of liberation for, and eventually of governance by, the working class;[271] jurists in communist countries also searched for a new, socialist, approach to comparative law itself.[272] In the West, comparatists debated whether socialist law was merely a variation of the civil law tradition or whether it was truly a distinct form; the former view pointed to the endurance of civil law sources, structures, and modes of (deductive) reasoning; the latter emphasized especially the openly instrumental and political nature of law under socialism.[273] The comparative study of socialist legality raised fascinating questions about opposite conceptions of law: as a platform of allegedly impartial justice or as an openly acknowledged instrument of partisan power. In addition, Western scholars were interested in understanding socialist forms of dispute settlement through means beyond positive rules and neutral adjudication.[274]

After the fall of communism in Europe in 1989 (and its subsequent decline in most other parts of the world), China was the only remaining major

[268] e.g. *Damaska*, A Continental Lawyer in an American Law School: Trials and Tribulations of Adjustment: 116 U.Pa.L.Rev. 1363–1378 (1968); *Lawson* (*supra* n. 9); *von Mehren*, The Civil Law System (ed. 2 Englewood Cliffs NJ 1957 and Boston MA 1977); *Merryman and Pérez-Perdomo*, The Civil Law Tradition (ed. 4 Stanford CA 2018); *Merryman, Clark and Haley*, The Civil Law Tradition: Europe, Latin America, and East Asia (Charlottesville VI 1994) of which a newer edition is *Merryman, Clark and Haley*, The Contemporary Civil Law Tradition (New Providence NJ 2015); see also *Merryman, Clark and Haley*, Historical Development of the Civil Law Tradition: Europe, Latin America and East Asia (New Providence NJ, San Francisco CA 2010).

[269] The problem was particularly acute in the United States where the discipline was heavily shaped by the European emigrants whose personal and professional situation of course invited focusing on the comparison between the laws of their old and new homes.

[270] The standard introductory texts devoted chapters to Soviet or socialist law beginning in the 1950s; see *Arminjon, Nolde and Wolff*, Traité de droit comparé III (Paris 1951) 227–389; *David*, Les grands systèmes de droit contemporains (Paris 1964) 153–271; *Zweigert and Kötz*, Einführung in die Rechtsvergleichung I (Tübingen 1971) 349–419. See also *Bogdan*, Comparative Law (Deventer, Cambridge MA 1994) 198–209; *Glendon, Gordon and Osakwe* (*supra* n. 210) 672–967.

[271] For an in-depth discussion, see *Szabo* The Socialist Conception of Law: *Drobnig and Zweigert* (eds.), International Encyclopedia of Comparative Law II 49–83.

[272] *Szabo and Péteri* (*supra* n. 202); Seiffert (*supra* n. 203).

[273] See e.g. *David* (*supra* n. 270) 153–310; *Zweigert and Kötz*, Einführung in die Rechtsvergleichung auf dem Gebiete des Privatrechts I (Tübingen 1971) 349–419; *Glendon, Gordon and Osakwe* (*supra* n. 210) 395–436. See also *Meador*, Impressions of Law in East Germany (Charlottesville VI 1986).

[274] *Hazard*, Settling Disputes in Soviet Society (New York 1960); *Markovits*, Justice in Lüritz. Experiencing Socialist Law in East Germany (Princeton NJ 2010).

country under socialism, and even it liberalized its economy. This spelled the end of socialist law as a distinct area of comparative inquiry. Some of its themes have lived on in the particular study of the Chinese legal system (*infra* s. 179). And the transition of Eastern and Central Europe from authoritarian and socialist regimes to liberal democracies and market economies provided comparatists with precious opportunities to observe the difficulties of fundamental systemic changes.[275]

177. *Mixed jurisdictions*. – Comparative law expanded its focus in a more lasting fashion by developing a growing interest in the legal systems that blend elements of the civil and the common law. Such mixed legal systems are scattered all over the world: Scotland on the margins of Europe, Israel in the Middle East, Louisiana, Quebec, and Puerto Rico in America, the Philippines in Asia, and South Africa in the southern hemisphere.[276] Looking at these systems made comparatists aware that many, if not most, other jurisdictions also blend elements of various legal traditions – not only civil and common law, but also Western and indigenous customary rules, secular and religious orders, etc.

A special case is the Scandinavian countries whose legal systems mix strong civil law elements with some common law features and local traditions. Though briefly addressed in some of the standard treatises,[277] comparatists paid this part of Europe rather little attention for many decades. Recently, several studies have been devoted to "Nordic law" and "Nordic legal culture", thus putting Scandinavia somewhat more prominently onto the comparative law map.[278]

178. *Latin America*. – Comparatists outside of Latin America long neglected that region.[279] The standard (European) introductions did not devote separate chapters to it, and in most of the world there was fairly little scholarship dealing with its jurisdictions. The main reason was that Latin American legal systems were generally regarded as parts of the civil law orbit – offshoots mainly of the French and Spanish, and to some extent German, traditions – and thus not much in need of separate study. This began to change in the 1970s, especially in the United States, when comparatists looked to Latin America in connection with the "Law and Development" projects (*infra* VI.B.iii., s. 351). While mainstream comparative lawyers have often continued to see Latin American law as a version of the civil law culture, they have come to consider it as sufficiently distinct from continental Europe to be worth studying in its own right.[280] Finally, since the 1990s, interest in Latin American law has grown fast and on a much broader basis. Among the reasons were the region's rise to economic and political importance, its increasing integration, its democratization processes, and the development of

[275] See, e.g., *Kühn*, The Judiciary in Central and Eastern Europe: Mechanical Jurisprudence in Transformation? (Leiden, Boston MA 2011).

[276] *Farran, Örürü and Donlaw (eds.),* A Study of Mixed Legal Systems: Endangered, Entrechned or Blended (Surrey and Burlington VT 2014); *Palmer (ed.)*, Mixed Jurisdictions Worldwide. The Third Legal Family (Cambridge 2001); *Palmer and Reid* (eds.), Mixed Jurisdictions Compared. Private Law in Louisiana and Scotland (Edinburgh 2009); *Örücü (ed.)*, Mixed Legal Systems at New Frontiers (London 2010); *Örücü, Attwood and Coyle*, Studies in Legal Systems: Mixed and Mixing (The Hague and Boston MA 1996); *Du Plessis*, Comparative Law and the Study of Mixed Legal Systems: *Reimann and Zimmermann* (eds.), The Oxford Handbook of Comparative Law (ed. 2 Oxford 2019) 474–501; *Zimmermann, Visser and Reid* (eds.), Mixed Legal Systems in Comparative Perspective (Oxford 2004). The literature on individual mixed systems is vast.

[277] *Arminjon, Nolde and Wolff* (*supra* n. 270) 437–489; *Zweigert and Kötz*, Einführung in die Rechtsvergleichung I (Tübingen 1971) 339–349.

[278] *Husa*, Nordic Law – Between Tradition and Dynamism (Oxford 2007); *Simone and Valguarnera*, La tradizione guiridica dei paesi Nordici (Torino 2008); *Nylund*, Mixing the Past and Future – the Making of a Nordic Legal Culture: *Sunde and Skodvin* (eds.), Rendezvous of European Legal Culture 1850–2050 (Bergen 2010) 167–181.

[279] *Within* Latin America, there has long been a vibrant tradition of comparative law, see *supra* III.B.iii., s. 84, and III.C.iv.a., ss. 102–103.

[280] John H. Merryman considered Latin American law a more typical representative of the civil law culture than France or Germany, *Merryman*, The Civil Law Tradition, ix-x (ed. 2 Stanford CA 1985); see also *Merryman, Clark and Haley* (*supra* n. 268).

strong constitutionalism in some countries, such as Brazil and Mexico. As a result, there are now several general introductions to Latin American law,[281] many books on individual countries, innumerable studies of particular topics (such as corporate law, individual rights protection, and judicial review mainly through the *amparo* procedure), as well as critical assessments of successes and failures in that region.[282] Today, interest in Latin American law is particularly strong in the United States as a result of strong economic ties (e.g., within NAFTA), massive immigration, and also of the large number of graduate students from that region in American law schools.

179. *East Asia – Japan, China, et al.* – The probably most significant geographic expansion of comparative law in the second half of the twentieth century was the inclusion of the major East Asian countries. Initially, i.e., in the 1950s through the 1970s, mainstream comparative law noted the jurisdictions on the Pacific Rim mainly because of a fascination with a specific "Far Eastern Conception of Law"[283] which seemed strange and exotic.[284]` Beyond that, Japan was mostly viewed as a thoroughly Westernized legal system, while China appeared as an alien culture currently embracing a radical form of communism (with little respect for law altogether).[285] The study of Japan and China rapidly gained importance in comparative law when first the former, then the latter, rose to economic power and thus prominence on the world stage in the closing decades of the last century. Today, East Asian jurisdictions receive virtually as much attention from comparatists as continental Europe.[286]

Some earlier studies notwithstanding,[287] interest in Japan has been strong since the 1980s, especially in the United States,[288] where courses of Japanese law are regularly taught and several casebooks on the topic are in use.[289] Foreign jurists have been fascinated by various aspects of the Japanese legal system. Its rapid adoption of Western models – French and German during the Meiji reform era, mainly American in the post-World War II period – presents striking examples of successful legal transplants (*infra* VI.B.iii., s. 349). Its traditional scarcity of lawyers in private practice and its low litigation rates despite a high degree of economic development suggested that even in a modern market society, conflicts can largely be resolved

[281] *Mirow*, Latin American Law (Austin TX 2004); *Oquendo*, Latin American Law (ed. 2 New York 2006 and 2011); *Lopez-Medina*, The Latin American and Caribbean Legal Tradition: *Bussani and Mattei*, The Cambridge Companion to Comparative Law (Cambridge 2012) 344–367; see also *Helmke and Rios-Figueroa* (eds.), Courts in Latin America (Cambridge 2011).

[282] *Esquirol*, The Failed Law of Latin America: 56 Am.J.Comp.L. 75–124 (2008).

[283] *Noda*, The Far Eastern Conception of Law: Int. Enc.Comp.L II, ch. 1, IV (1971) ss. 193-224.

[284] Such "Orientalism" is a major topic of discussion in comparative law today, *infra* VI.B.v., s. 364.

[285] *David* (supra n. 273) 521–541, *Zweigert and Kötz* (*supra* n. 3) 419–434.

[286] Modern introductions to comparative law almost routinely include chapters on Chinese (and often Japanese) law: see e.g. *Cuniberti*, Grands systèmes de droit contemporains (ed. 2 Paris 2011) 197–326; *Head*, Great Legal Traditions (Durham NC 2011) 455–644; *Kischel*, Rechtsvergleichung (München 2015) 729–855; *Menski*, Comparative Law in a Global Context (ed. 2 New York 2006) 493–593; *Müller-Chen, Müller and Lüchinger* (eds.), Comparative Private Law (Zürich, St. Gallen 2015) 277–348; see also *Ruskola*, The East Asian Legal Tradition: *Bussani and Mattei* (eds.), The Cambridge Companion to Comparative Law (Cambridge 2012) 257–277. US-American casebooks began to include China as early as in the 1980s, see *Barton, Gibbs, Li and Merryman* (*supra* n. 226). Today, the most widely used US-American casebook, *Mattei, Ruskola and Gigi*, Schlesinger's Comparative Law (ed. 7 New York 2009) pervasively considers Chinese and Japanese law.

[287] *Von Mehren* (ed.), Law in Japan: The Legal Order in a Changing Society (Cambridge MA 1963).

[288] See e.g. *Upham*, Law and Social Change in Postwar Japan (Cambridge MA, London 1987); *Haley*, Authority without Power (Oxford 1991); *Haley*, The Spirit of Japanese Law (Athens, GA 1998); *Ramseyer and Nakazato*, Japanese Law: An Economic Approach (Chicago IL, London 1999); *Feldman*, The Ritual of Rights in Japan (Cambridge 2000); *West*, Law in Everyday Japan (Chicago IL, London 2005); *Jones and Ravitch*, The Japanese Legal System (St. Paul MN 2018).

[289] *Milhaupt, Ramseyer and West*, The Japanese Legal System (ed. 2 New York 2012); *Port and McAlinn*, Comparative Law: The Role of Law and the Legal Process in Japan (ed. 2 Durham NC 2003); see also *Dean*, The Japanese Legal System (London 1997); *Pedriza*, Lectures on Japanese Law (Osaka 2017); *Tanaka*, The Japanese Legal System (Tokyo 1984).

without resort to the courts. Its attractively low rate of crime despite a high degree of urbanization indicates amazingly successful mechanisms of social control. And its economic rise triggered intense interest in the make-up of its corporate culture and the structure of its labor relations. For these and other reasons, Western observers often saw Japan as a model – an economic and social system which functions smoothly and successfully with enviably little reliance on lawyers and law. Over time, the comparative study of Japanese law has developed into a specialty with its own journals,[290] conferences, and academic associations, which has gradually separated itself from mainstream comparative law.

After China opened up to the West again, started to liberalize its markets, and began its rise to an economic superpower in the 1980s, comparatists' interest in China soon rivalled and eventually surpassed their interest in Japan. Much of the literature on the Chinese legal system is of the "foreign law" variety (I.B., s. 7); reflecting the need of foreigners to learn about this new economic giant's legal system, publications often focus on the description and analysis of Chinese law itself, rather than attempting a comparison with other legal systems.[291] Yet, as with Japan, there are also several dominant comparative themes pervading the study of Chinese law. One is the observation of the development of a legal system almost from scratch – the enactment of modern codes and statutes, the creation of courts and procedures, and the rise of a trained legal profession; this invites the question whether the popular (Western) assumption is correct that a developed market economy depends on a strong legal system, especially on reliable (judicial) protection of property and contractual rights.[292] Another pervasive topic is the question to what extent China has embraced, or will embrace, the "rule of law"[293]; this entails the issue whether this concept has, or can have, the same (largely constitutional) meaning in China as in the West, which in turn connects to issues of judicial independence[294] and human rights protection. Last but not least, there is the larger question whether modern China can be regarded as a civil law system. On the one hand, it displays many features of a civil law culture, such as primary reliance on legislative texts rather than court decisions, a court system and judiciary organized after the continental European model, a criminal law and procedure along civilian lines, and a style of legal argumentation that is in most contexts more formalist than pragmatic. In addition, the majority of Chinese legal professionals tend to see, and to present, themselves as jurists in the continental European sense rather than lawyers in the Anglo-American style. On the other hand, the many reforms of rules governing market activity in the last few decades have entailed a massive import of Anglo-American, and thus in a sense common law, models and rules, ranging from securities regulation to corporate law.[295] As a result, modern China is best conceived as a mixed legal system in which civil and common law elements combine with traditional background conceptions and the current politics of the communist party.

On the whole, comparative scholarship on Chinese law has also turned into in a form of specialized "area study" with its own academic journals,[296] literature,[297] and academic subcommunity which is but loosely related to the traditional field of comparative law. Finally, it

[290] E.g., *Zeitschrift für japanisches Recht* (since 1996); a variety of research papers are published by The Australian Network for Japanese Law.

[291] See, e.g., *Chen*, An Introduction to the Legal System of the People's Republic of China (ed. 4 Hong Kong 2011); *Clarke* (ed.), China's Legal System: New Developments. New Challenges (New York 2008); *Potter*, China's Legal System (Cambridge 2013).

[292] *Ginsburg*, Does Law Matter for Economic Development? Evidence from East Asia: 34 Law &Soc. Rev. 829–856 (2000).

[293] *Peerenboom* (*supra* n. 257); see also *Ruskola*, Legal Orientalism: China, the United States and modern Law (Cambridge MA, London 2013).

[294] *Peerenboom* (ed.), Judicial Independence in China (Cambridge 2009); see also *Woo and Gallagher*, Chinese Justice. Civil Dispute Resolution in Contemporary China (Cambridge 2013).

[295] For an overview, see *Yu* (ed.), The Development of the Chinese Legal System. Change and Challenges (London, New York 2011).

[296] E.g. Chinese Journal of Comparative Law (since 2013); *Zeitschrift für chinesisches Recht* (since 2004); Columbia Journal of Asian Law (since 1996, begun in 1987 as the Columbia Journal of Chinese Law).

[297] A bibliography is compiled by the Max Planck Institute for Comparative and International Private Law in Hamburg, Germany, and published bi-annually in the *Zeitschrift für chinesisches Recht* (*supra* n. 296).

is worth mentioning that comparative law has developed rapidly not only *about* China but also *within* it. Today, Chinese legal scholars are producing a veritable deluge of publications about their own legal system, written in Western languages (mostly in English) and addressed to foreign readers around the world.

The other two Pacific Rim jurisdictions increasingly studied by comparatists are Taiwan and Korea.[298] In these two instances as well, their economic rise and thus growing political weight has made them attractive objects of inquiry, often with regard to market regulation and reform. Both also combine imported Western civil law features, such as a strong commitment to codification, with more traditional Eastern attitudes towards law more generally. Yet, these two countries are of interest to comparatists also for another reason: in connection with their transformation from authoritarian regimes to respectable democracies, they have developed liberal constitutions and surprisingly strong forms of judicial review.[299] Especially from a European and US-American perspective, they thus represent successful models of democratization, constitutionalization, and rule of law implementation in a part of the world where embracing such essentially Western values cannot be taken for granted.

Further East Asian legal systems such as Vietnam, Indonesia, and Malaysia have been studied on a more occasional basis and from a variety of perspectives.

180. *India.* – While comparatists looked at India already in the post-World War II period, their treatment of its legal system has changed significantly over time. When the early introductions to the discipline considered India in the 1950s through the 1970s, the country was a backwater with fairly little global significance. Accordingly, the chapters then devoted to that jurisdiction were brief, and they focused mainly on its mix of secular (common law) and religious (Hindu) elements.[300] In the last few decades, however, India has become a major economic and political power. As a result, its legal system is now an important field for comparative legal scholarship, and the focus has broadened to include new topics.[301] While the relationship between Hinduism and law is still a significant issue,[302] two other areas have recently received much attention. The first, reflecting India's rise to one of the world's most important economies, is the law of the market; here, the major topics have been corporate governance and consumer protection.[303] The second area, mirroring the development of a vibrant constitutional culture in a multiethnic and tension-ridden polity, is constitutional law; the main subjects are the protection of individual rights (especially free speech, religious freedom, and non-discrimination), judicial review, and the country's system of federalism.[304] In fact, India has become one of the most popular topics in the field of comparative constitutional law.[305]

181. *The Middle East – Arab countries and Israel.* – When writing and talking about the Middle East, comparatists have traditionally had the Arab countries in mind. These countries have mixed legal systems, blending traditional Islamic law bequeathed by long tradition with modern secular regimes mostly imported from former colonial masters. Some, especially more recent, studies have emphasized the interplay between these orders or even their secular aspects.[306] Yet, for the

[298] See, e.g., *Choi*, Law and Justice in Korea. North and South (Seoul 2002); *Lo*, The Legal Culture and System of Taiwan (Alphen aan den Rijn 2006).

[299] *Yeh and Chang*, The Emergence of East Asian Constitutionalism: Features in Comparison: 59 Am.J. Comp.L. 805–840 (2011); see also *Khilnani, Raghavan and Thiruvengadam* (eds.), Comparative Constitutionalism in South East Asia (Oxford 2012).

[300] *Arminjon, Nolde and Wolff* (*supra* n. 270), 535–554; *David* (*supra* n. 270) 485–501; *Losano*, I Grandi Sistemi Guiridici (ed. 2 Torino 2000) 225–242; *Zweigert and Kötz* (*supra* n. 3) 446–453.

[301] See e.g. *Cuniberti* (*supra* n. 286) 381–438; *Gambaro and Sacco*, Sistemi Guiridici Comparati (Torino 1996) 484–504.

[302] See *infra* iii., s. 184.

[303] See e.g. *Howson and Khanna*, The Development of Corporate Governance in China and India: *Sornarajah and Wang* (eds.), China, India and the International Economic Order (Cambridge 2010) 513–576.

[304] See e.g. *Reppy*, The Court and the Constitution of India: Summits and Shallows (New York NY, Oxford 2010).

[305] *Infra* IV.C.ii.d., ss. 260–266.

[306] *Mallat*, Introduction to Middle Eastern Law (Oxford 2007); *Mallat* (*supra* n. 79); *Lombardi*, State Law as Islamic Law in Modern Egypt (Leiden, Boston MA 2006).

most part, comparatists looking at the Middle East today are interested in the *shari'a*, which is better addressed in the context of religious orders (*infra* iii., s. 184).

In recent decades, comparatists have also increasingly studied the law of another country situated in the Middle East, i.e., Israel. That jurisdiction indeed proffers a multitude of highly interesting comparative law topics. To begin with, Israel is an extremely mixed jurisdiction straddling the boundaries between secular and religious as well as traditional and modern legal orders. It is shaped by five major forces: lingering traces of the Islamic tradition (in particular the *Megelle*, a late nineteenth-century private law codification of the Ottoman Empire), Jewish law (which continues to dominate family relations), common law elements (as a heritage of the British mandate for Palestine 1920–1948), civil law features (imported by refugee scholars from continental Europe), and, most recently, American ideas (popularized by Israeli students and scholars returning from US law schools). Furthermore, Israel has long struggled with the issue of codification – itself a perennial topic of comparative study.[307] Last but not least, the rapid development of constitutional law and in particular the rise of judicial review has fascinated legal scholars, especially in the United States and continental Europe. On the whole, the comparative study of Israeli law has been boosted by the fairly strong presence of Israeli scholars within the discipline as well as by the availability of virtually all relevant sources in English.

182. *Africa.* – There was considerable engagement with Africa by some leading members of the post-World War II generation of comparatists, especially René David and Max Rheinstein.[308] With their retirement or death, however, the mainstream of the discipline largely lost interest in the continent.[309] Research about African legal systems mostly became a matter of area studies (conducted by institutions like the School of Oriental and African Studies, SOAS, at the University of London), rather than mainstream comparative law.[310] Yet, since the 1990s, comparatists have revived their interest in Africa – to some extent.[311] They have studied the interplay between the Western law imported by the colonial powers and traditional custom, as well as the evolution and prospects of African customary law in and of itself.[312] Since the establishment of the *Organization pour l'Harmonization en Afrique du Droit des Affaires* (OHADA) 1993, the development of commercial law in Africa became a point of interest.[313] In addition, studies have focused on the (often dire) human rights situation in Africa, a topic in which comparative legal scholarship overlaps with international law.[314] Yet, despite this revival, it is fair to say that even today, of all the world's inhabited regions sub-Saharan

[307] See e.g. *Siehr and Zimmermann* (eds.), The Draft Civil Code for Israel in Comparative Perspective (Tübingen 2008).

[308] *David* (supra n. 273) 545–574; *David*, Commentary on Contracts in Ethopia (Addis Ababa 1973); *Rheinstein*, Law and Social Changes in Africa: Wash.U.L.Q. 443–453 (1962); *Rheinstein* (*supra* n. 55) 104–114. More generally, scholars in the former imperial powers, especially France, were often interested in the law(s) of current or former colonies; see e.g. *Gonidec*, Les Droits Africains (Paris 1968).

[309] *Zweigert and Kötz* (*supra* n. 3) for example, did not address it.

[310] See *Edge* (ed.), Comparative Law in Global Perspective (Ardsley NY 2000), especially 173–240. The SOAS also publishes the *Journal of African Law* (since 1957). An attempt to include Africa in comparative law teaching was *Barton, Gibbs, Li and Merryman* (*supra* n. 226).

[311] *Cuniberti* (*supra* n. 286) 441–484; *Menski* (*supra* n. 286) 380–493; *Sacco*, Il Diritto Africano (Torino 1995); *Sacco*, The sub-Saharan Legal Tradition: *Bussani and Mattei* (eds.), The Cambridge Companion to Comparative Law (Cambridge 2012) 313–343.

[312] *Infra* s. 185.

[313] *Mancuso*, Diritto commerciale africano: OHADA (Napoli 2009).

[314] See e.g. *Zeleza and McConnaughty* (eds.), Human Rights, the Rule of Law and Development in Africa (Philadelphia, PA, 2004); *Viljoen*, International Human Rights in Africa (ed. 2 Oxford 2012); *Nmehielle*, The African Human Rights System (New York, Norwell MA 2001); *Church, Schulze and Strydom*, Human Rights from a Comparative and International Law Perspective (Pretoria 2007).

Africa remains the least studied.[315] This is so mainly for three reasons. First, from a global perspective, the region's political and economic importance has remained limited. Second, for Western comparatists, access to African legal systems remains hindered by the weak local infrastructure which makes it difficult to establish and maintain personal and institutional connections; this is especially true since interest in comparative studies seems to be declining in African law faculties themselves.[316] Third, researching African law is a risky business because the law in the books is often meaningless while the law in action is hard to perceive for outsiders.

A special case, and major exception, is South Africa. Private law comparatists have been keenly interested in its mixed (Roman-Dutch and English common law) legal system[317] to which one must add a component of customary law.[318] Comparative constitutional law scholars have studied the process of constitution-making since the end of apartheid as well as the emergence of a sophisticated constitutional jurisprudence, especially in matters of equal protection and social rights.[319] And personal and institutional connections between South African law faculties and legal scholars in many parts of the Western World are strong and enduring.

iii. *Beyond National Systems*

183. *Introduction.* – The classical model of comparative law – conceived in the late nineteenth century and born at the Paris Congress in 1900 (*supra* III.C.i., ss. 85–87) – was a child of the heyday of the nation state. As a result, the discipline's primary focus throughout the twentieth century was the laws of sovereign countries. Yet, when the idea of "great legal systems" and "legal families" came into vogue in the 1950s and 1960s (*infra* VI.B.ii., s. 337), comparatists began to include non-Western religious laws and sometimes traditional customs in their surveys. For the time being, such non-state "systems" were often just briefly addressed and rarely studied in any depth. This changed towards the close of the twentieth century as globalization processes led comparatists to embrace the idea of legal pluralism. Looking at the coexistence of multiple legal orders, often within the same space, scholars became more broadly conscious of legal systems beyond nation states. As a result, non-state legal orders – religious systems, traditional customs, market regulation through private regimes, and supra-national constructs – have become important areas of study.

184. *Religious laws.*[320] – While not part of the discipline's mainstream, today research and writing on religious systems is an established branch of comparative law. This has produced a large amount of information and a considerable degree of understanding, but the accomplishments should not be overrated. For the most part, religious legal systems are merely described and analyzed on their own terms, i.e., without much comparison either between each other or between religious and secular regimes.[321] Also, comparatists have often insufficiently explored the impact of the various fundamental religious beliefs on legal systems and cultures, though that neglect is more pronounced within the Western tradition than with regard to non-Western religions and laws. And scholars have, for the

[315] Still, some journals pay fairly regular attention to the region, especially the *Revue international de droit comparé*, but also the International and Comparative Law Quarterly. It is probably no accident that these journals are published in countries once at the apex of vast colonial empires comprising most of Africa.

[316] *Fombad*, Comparative Research in Contemporary African Legal Studies: 67 J. Legal Ed. 984–1004 (2018).

[317] *Zimmermann and Visser* (eds.), Southern Cross. Civil Law and Common Law in South Africa (Oxford 1996).

[318] *Du Plessis*, South Africa: *Smits* (ed.), Elgar's Encyclopedia of Comparative Law (ed. 2 Cheltenham, Northhampton MA 2012) 814–819.

[319] *Klug*, The Constitution of South Africa (Oxford 2010); *Roux*, The Politics of Principle: the First South African Constitutional Court, 1995–2005 (Cambridge 2013).

[320] See generally, *Ferrari*, Introduzione al diritto comparato delle religioni (Bologna 2008); *Ferrari* (ed.), Religion, Law and Tradition (London 2002).

[321] That is true for most "comparative" law work, however.

most part, not developed general (never mind verifiable) hypotheses about the relationship between religious and secular laws,[322] although there are some recent exceptions.[323] All these traditional shortcomings notwithstanding, the comparative study of religious laws is, or at least should be, one of the most promising – as well as practically important – dimensions of early twenty-first-century comparative law.[324]

In the comparative study of religious legal systems, pride of place clearly belongs to Islamic law (*shari'a*). Its importance especially in the Middle East was obvious already to the authors of the foundational introductions to the discipline written in the 1950s through the 1970s.[325] More recent surveys cover Islamic law as well, often with special attention to its interplay with the secular law of Arab and other countries,[326] but sometimes also under the distinct aspect of a "legal tradition".[327] Beyond such relatively short introductions, there now is an entire library of works on Islamic law written specifically for Western readers. The literature consists of numerous books providing general overviews[328] and of an ever growing multitude of works on specific topics. Islamic law is fertile soil for comparative study on a number of grounds. It confronts the Western reader with a specific, and largely unfamiliar, conception of law. It provides a highly developed law of the market (property, contracts, business associations, banking, finance, etc.), of the family, and of crimes, punishment, and procedure. And Islamic law is relevant for international relations with countries and communities governed by it, especially since it includes rules on war and peace.[329] Today, the (Western) study of the *shari'a* has developed into a sub-discipline in its own right, overlapping with, but also largely independent from, mainstream comparative law.

While Hindu conceptions of law played a significant role during the British governance of India, they receive much less attention among comparatists today. To be sure, many standard works have devoted chapters to Hindu law (usually in conjunction with the legal system of India more generally),[330] and there are some introductions to it.[331] Still, its study is the domain of a few specialists and lingers on the margins of comparative law. The situation is similar with regard to the Buddhist conception of law, although it is often considered in connection with Asian legal traditions.

More recently, comparatists have also begun to pay attention to Jewish law – not only as an element of the Israeli legal system but rather as a

[322] For a general assessment and critique, see *Berman*, Comparative Law and Religion: *Reimann and Zimmermann* (eds.), The Oxford Handbook of Comparative Law (Oxford 2019) 739–751.

[323] *Whitman*, Comparative Law and Religion: *Reimann and Zimmermann* (eds.), The Oxford Handbook of Comparative Law (ed. 2 Oxford 2019) 734–753.

[324] *Michaels*, Religiöse Rechte und postsäkulare Rechtsvergleichung: *Zimmermann* (ed.), Zukunftsperspektiven der Rechtsvergleichung (Tübingen 2016) 39–102; see also (Symposium) Dieu et mon Droit. Religion, sociétè et Etat. Quelques problèmes d'aujourd'hui: Rev.int.dr.comp. 66 (2014) 663–770.

[325] *Arminjon, Nolde and Wolff* (*supra* n. 270) 399–533; *David*, (supra. N. 273) 455–492; *Losano* (*supra* n. 300) 195–223; *Zweigert and Kötz* (*supra* n. 3) 435–446; in this Encyclopedia, *Afchar*, The Muslim Conception of Law: Int.Enc.Comp.L II ch. 1 IV, ss.119-155.

[326] *Bogdan* (*supra* n. 270) 220–228; *Cuniberti* (*supra* n. 286) 327–379; *Kischel* (*supra* n. 286) 856–928; *Menski* (*supra* n. 286) 279–379; *Müller-Chen, Müller and Lüchinger* (*supra* n. 286) 355–411; *Gambaro and Sacco* (*supra* n. 300) 461–484. See also *El Fadl*, The Islamic Legal Tradition: *Bussani and Mattei* (eds.), The Cambridge Companion to Comparative Law (Cambridge 2012), 295–312; *Mallat* (*supra* n. 79). Even the leading US American casebook, aiming to provide a global introduction to the discipline, includes many aspects of Islamic law, *Mattei, Ruskola and Gidi* (*supra* n. 286).

[327] *Glenn*, Legal Traditions of the World (ed. 5 Oxford, New York 2014) 181–236.

[328] *Bhala*, Understanding Islamic Law (New Providence NJ, San Francisco CA 2011); *Castro*, Il Modello Islamico (ed. 2 Torino 2007); *Hallaq*, An Introduction to Islamic Law (New York 2009); *Hallaq*, Shari'a: Theory, Practice, Transformations (New York 2009); see also *Mallat* (*supra* n. 306)

[329] See e.g. *Bhala* (*supra* n. 328) 1309–1382.

[330] *Arminjon, Nolde and Wolff* (*supra* n. 270) 535–554; *David* (*supra* n. 270) 485–517; *Losano* (*supra* n. 300) 225–241; *Zweigert and Kötz* (*supra* n. 3) 446–453; more recently *Kischel* (*supra* n. 286) 815–839; in this Encyclopedia, *Derrett and Iyer*, The Hindu Conception of Law: Int.Enc.Comp.L II, ch. 1, V (1975) ss. 156-192.

[331] *Davis*, The Boundaries of Hindu Law (Torino 2004); *Davis*, The Spirit of Hindu Law (Cambridge and New York 2010); *Lubin, Davis and Krishnan* (eds.), Hinduism and Law (Cambridge MA, New York 2010); *Glenn* (*supra* n. 327) 288–318; *Menski* (*supra* n. 286) 196–278.

specific religious legal order.[332] Of course, the study of Jewish law, like that of the *shari'a*, is centuries old within that religion. What is new is that outsiders have begun to look at it as one of the legal traditions shaping the world today,[333] sometimes form en explicitly comparative perspective.[334] Even general introductory texts sometimes include chapters on it.[335] The reason for this attention is not only that Jewish law provides a sophisticated system of concepts and rules as well as an example of highly developed legal reasoning; it is also due to the strong intellectual presence of Jewish scholars in the community of comparative lawyers.

Perhaps oddly, modern comparative law pays little attention to the ecclesiastical law of the Christian tradition.[336] For centuries, this law (as *ius canonicum*) was virtually on a par with secular law (especially the Roman-based *ius civile*) throughout most of Europe, and there were occasional comparisons between the two orders (see, e.g., *supra* III.A., s. 54). Eventually, the secularization of Western states, and the subsequent commitment to a secular legal order, pushed ecclesiastical law beyond the horizon of our discipline. Yet, if religious systems such as Islamic, Hindu, and Jewish law are worth studying from a comparative perspective, there is no reason to exclude the law of the Christian church.

185. *Customary law regimes.* – Comparative lawyers have long realized that in many parts of the world customary law plays a huge practical role. In many developing countries, the official law of the state is a distant reality for large segments (and indeed often the majority) of the people. Usually shaped after Western models, state law rarely fits the needs of more traditional lifestyles and economies, and especially rural populations often have little contact with it.

Yet, comparative law engaged with customary law regimes rarely and late. While customary law has received some attention in our field, mainly with regard to Africa,[337] it cannot be said that its study is highly developed among comparative lawyers. Part of the reason is that, typically, comparatists are educated in the West where custom is no longer considered an important source of law. In addition, as lawyers, comparatists are used to working with written texts which are often lacking or at least not fully trustworthy when it comes to customary law; and to ascertain and evaluate customary law on the ground requires the skills of an ethnologist as well as mastery of indigenous languages which comparatists usually lack. As a result, customary law is the domain more of legal anthropology than of comparative law, although there is some overlap between the two disciplines. Scholarship on customary law regimes has often been involved with debates about the impact of colonization on the developing world, especially the question to what extent colonial powers westernized and thus distorted indigenous customs (*infra* VI.B.v., s. 363).

186. *"Private law beyond the state".* – While comparatists have for some decades easily recognized the existence of non-state (i.e., religious and customary) legal orders in Asia or Africa, acknowledging the existence of law neither made nor enforced by the state in Western industrialized nations has been a more recent development. To be sure, scholars had long understood that such law was commonplace in the middle ages and early modern period, for example among the

[332] *Saiman*, Halakhah: The Rabbinic Idea of Law (Princeton NJ 2018); *Kischel* (*supra* n. 286) 815–839; *Müller-Chen, Müller and Lüchinger* (*supra* n. 286) 411–424.

[333] *Glenn* (*supra* n. 327) 99–132.

[334] *Levine*, Jewish Law and American Law: A Comparative Study (Vallejo CA 2018).

[335] *Bleich and Jacobson*, The Jewish Legal Tradition: *Bussani and Mattei* (eds.), The Cambridge Companion to Comparative Law (Cambridge 2012) 278–294.

[336] There are some exceptions. See *Ferrari*, Canon Law as a Religious System: *Huxley* (ed.), Religion, Law and Tradition (London 2002) 49–60; *Kischel* (*supra* n. 286) 938–944.

[337] In this Encyclopedia, *M'Baye*, The African Conception of Law: Int.Enc.Comp.L vol. II, ch. 1, VII (1975) ss. 225-277; see also *Fenrich, Galizzi and Higgins* (eds.), The Future of African Customary Law (Cambridge 2011); *Gonidec* (*supra* n. 308); *Bennett*, Comparative Law and African Customary Law: *Reimann and Zimmermann* (eds.), The Oxford Handbook of Comparative Law (ed. 2 Oxford 2019) 652–680. See also the literature on African law, *supra* n. 308-319; *Allot*, The Hunting of the Snark of the Quest for the Holy Grail: *Edge* (ed.), Comparative Law in Global Perspective (Ardsley NY 2000) 79–100.

merchant class (*lex mercatoria*). But comparatists had also (often unconsciously) presumed that the modern nation state's monopoly of lawmaking and enforcement left no more room for non-state legal rules, although prominent commercial and private international law scholars had challenged that presumption since the 1930s.

When the processes of globalization and privatization at the close of the twentieth century caused a proliferation of non-state law, comparatists and legal theorists finally began to pay attention to it as well.[338] They recognized that multiple, often transnational, private legal orders now pervade whole areas of human activity, especially in the commercial realm – ranging from corporate codes of conduct to regimes governing professional sports, and from rules of credit card organizations to industrial norm-setting. Today, the existence of "private law beyond the state" is widely understood within the discipline. Yet, while there are some theoretical foundations as well as outlines for their comparative study,[339] so far little comparative work has actually been done. It would be intriguing to look at such private orders as "legal systems" in their own right, often complete with lawmaking institutions, sources of law, bodies of substantive and procedural rules, dispute resolution mechanisms, and enforcement methods. In light of their enormous practical significance, comparative law must include these non-state regimes on its world map in its quest to understand how legal systems function in a global context.

187. *Supranational systems.* – When comparative law developed its modern profile more than a hundred years ago, it naturally focused on the legal systems of nation states because, at least in the Western World, there was little else. Yet, the twentieth century saw the establishment of more and more supra-national legal orders, and in the last few decades both their sheer number and their importance have skyrocketed. Comparatists, programmed in their traditional nation-state mode, caught up with this development fairly late, with hesitation, and in small numbers.

In the meantime, the comparative study of supranational legal orders has made some progress. Most noticeably, international human rights are often considered from a comparative perspective (*infra* C.ii.g., s. 275), and some introductions to the discipline rightly consider the European human rights system a legal order worth including in their surveys.[340]

In a similar fashion, European Union law is now often mentioned among the legal systems of the world,[341] though even some recent introductions and handbooks continue to disregard it.[342] For many decades, comparatists all but ignored the established order of public international law (the law of nations), despite its lawmaking (e.g., through multilateral treaties), adjudication system (e.g., in the International Court of Justice), and enforcement mechanism (e.g., through the UN Security Council) activities. Fortunately, this has begun to change in recent years,[343] and there are now some impressive comparative studies involving public international law.[344]

Other supranational systems, however, have received scant attention within the discipline, their enormous practical importance notwithstanding. This is true, for example, for international trade law, although it has developed (especially under the World Trade Organization) into a legal order which makes rules, regulates activities, and decides disputes.

[338] *Teubner* (ed.), Global Law Without the State (Aldershot, Brookfield VT 1997).

[339] *Jansen and Michaels* (*supra* n. 260); *Zimmermann* (ed.) (*supra* n. 259); see also *Kischel* (*supra* n. 286) 971–976.

[340] *Besson* (*supra* n. 36); *Glendon, Carozza and Picker*, Comparative Legal Traditions in a Nutshell 5 (ed. 4 St. Paul MN 2016) 87–90, 324–327, 348-355; *Glendon, Gordon and Carozza* (*supra* n. 20) 746–798.

[341] *Idem* 313–347, 686–745; *De Cruz*, Comparative Law in a Changing World (London 1995) 139–182; *Kischel* (*supra* n. 286) 956–971; *Mattei, Ruskola and Gidi* (*supra* n. 286) reference European Law throughout the casebook. See also *Jacobs*, Comparative Law and European Union Law: *Reimann and Zimmermann* (eds.), The Oxford Handbook of Comparative Law (ed. 2 Oxford 2019) 524–556.

[342] E.g. *Cuniberti* (*supra* n. 286); *Örücü and Nelken* (*supra* n. 70).

[343] See, e.g., *Berman*, Comparative Law and International Organizations: *Bussani and Mattei* (eds.), The Cambridge Companion to Comparative Law (Cambridge 2012) 241–254; *Kischel* (*supra* n. 286) 947–956.

[344] *Roberts* (*supra* n. 43); *idem, Stephan, Verdier and Versteeg* (*supra* n. 35).

The comparative study of supra- and international systems is hindered by the longstanding separation of comparative law (with its traditional private law focus) and international law (with its public law orientation). Even today, most comparative law scholars are shockingly ignorant of, as well as uninterested in, public international law in its various forms; at the same time, most international lawyers are shockingly uninformed about, and indifferent towards, even the most basic techniques and obvious benefits as well as pitfalls of comparative law.

More attention to supra- and international legal systems is necessary for at least three reasons. First, today, a survey of legal systems in the world must include supranational orders, lest it be woefully incomplete – and actually misleading. Second, comparing supranational orders with each other as well as with national systems (i.e., distilling similarities and differences) can help us analyze their interplay and facilitate their coordination – both urgent and important tasks. Third, the study of supranational regimes enhances our general understanding of how legal systems function (or fail to function).

B. ELEMENTS OF LEGAL SYSTEMS

188. *Introduction.* – In studying the various legal families, traditions, and systems of the world, comparative law typically focuses on their constituent elements. Especially in the post-World War II period, the discipline developed a fairly standard list of such elements which can thus be found, in one form or another, in most introductions to the field. In a sense, this list can be applied, *mutatis mutandis*, to virtually all legal systems because it responds to almost universally valid questions: where does law come from? (sources); how is it organized? (structure); how do people think about and apply it? (legal reasoning); which institutions decide disputes and in what fashion? (courts and procedure); and which kinds of people run the system? (actors). Yet, the composition of the list also reflects the Western origins of comparative law: its items are what a lawyer trained in the Western tradition deems characteristic of a legal system; a member of a non-Western, and in particular of an indigenous and custom-based, regime may well consider different elements more relevant. In addition, the list also reflects the discipline's preoccupation throughout the twentieth century with the dichotomy between the civil and the common law: its items flag up the perceived main areas of difference between these two traditions; a dichotomy between, for example, secular and religious legal systems may produce a very different list.

i. *Sources of Law* [345]

189. *Scope of the discussion.* – Sources of law have been a topic of central importance for comparative law since its modern beginnings.[346] A main reason is that comparatists have characterized the major legal families and traditions in the world inter alia by how they deal with the various manifestations of law: the civil law by its emphasis on codes and other statutory rules ("written law"), the common law by its development through judicial decisions ("case law"), religious regimes by the recognition of sacred texts as legal documents, traditional systems by their reliance on custom, etc.

The sources of law are, of course, a field of vast proportions and deep jurisprudential complexity, especially since the term "source" can have a variety of meanings.[347] Fortunately, our task here is simplified by two considerations. First, we will discuss sources of law only in the sense in which comparative law has primarily dealt with that concept over the last century. It is true, of course, that in seeking to understand how the law works in different legal systems, the comparatist must take into account every relevant input, often including non-legal factors. Still, the discipline has by and large understood sources of law to mean the various (mostly written) manifesta-

[345] For a more in-depth description and analysis, see *Vogenauer*, Sources of Law and Legal Method in Comparative Law: *Reimann and Zimmermann* (eds.), The Oxford Handbook of Comparative Law (ed. 2 Oxford 2019) 877–901.

[346] For an early example, see Les diverses sources du droit, leur équilibre et leurs hierarchies dans les divers systèmes juridiques, Actorum Academiae universalis iurisprudentiae comparativae II/2 (Paris 1934).

[347] Vogenauer (*supra* n. 345) 877–880.

tions of positive legal rules, such as legislation, court decisions, or academic scholarship, and we will limit our survey accordingly.[348] Second, the purpose of this sub-chapter is not to describe the actual role and significance of these sources in the world's legal systems in any detail; that is the object of a separate and much longer chapter in this Encyclopedia.[349] This subchapter merely summarizes how comparative law has dealt with legal sources, i.e., what types it has discussed, what questions it has pursued, and what insights it has generated over the last century.

190. *Three general observations.* – In discussing the role and significance of sources, comparative lawyers have made three general observations. To begin with, legal sources are often fungible: a particular rule may be statutory in one legal system while it is contained in a court decision in another, or even left to standard contract practice in a third. As a result, comparison can normally not limit itself to one kind of source but must consider all of them. Furthermore, there is often a divergence between theory and practice: the official rule may be that court decisions are not binding or that academic opinion has no legal authority, while in reality appellate decisions are routinely followed and the writings of professors carry decisive weight. Thus, the significance of legal sources must always be evaluated with an eye to how they are actually employed. Finally, understanding legal sources in a particular system is intimately linked to understanding how people create, interpret, apply them. These are matters of legal method which will be addressed below (ii., ss. 200–203).

191. *Constitutions.* – Today, pride of place among the legal sources belongs to constitutions as the foundational texts of most legal systems in the world. Modern comparative law began to engage with them seriously only in the last 50 years, and for good reason: while (written) constitutions have been around for more than two centuries, in most countries of the world they assumed truly *legal* (as opposed to merely political) significance only when they became justiciable, i.e., with the rise of judicial review in the second half of the twentieth century. Since the 1970s, constitutions have been among the most intensely compared sources of law, at first particularly the constitutions of the United States, Germany, and France, more lately also of Canada, India, South Africa, and other jurisdictions around the world. As a result, comparative constitutional law has lately evolved into a subfield in its own right, and it will be addressed in greater detail below (C.ii.c., ss. 256–259).

192. *Codifications.* – In twentieth-century comparative law, codifications were the most frequently and intensely studied legal documents, and the resulting literature is vast. This is particularly true for their archetype, i.e., codifications of private law. The great continental European civil codes, in particularly the French *Code civil* (1804), the Austrian *Allgemeines Bürgerliches Gesetzbuch* (*ABGB*, 1811); the German *Bürgerliches Gesetzbuch* (*BGB*, 1900), the Swiss *Zivilgesetzbuch* (*ZGB*, 1907/12), and the Italian *Codice civile* (1942) have been at the core of mainstream comparative law discourse for decades. In particular, scholars have traced their influence as models for other jurisdictions throughout the world,[350] i.e., as examples of legal transplants (*infra* VI.B.iii., ss. 345–351).

The primary cause of this immense interest in codifications is the time-honored obsession of mainstream comparatists with the civil v. common law dichotomy: codification, especially civil codes, has long been considered *the* hallmark of the civil law tradition, i.e., one of the major features that distinguishes it from the common law family. Indeed, comprehensive codification of the core areas of private law (contract, tort, domestic relations, succession, etc.) is near ubiquitous in the civil law sphere while it is still largely absent in the common law world.

[348] In the future, other sources of law should receive more attention, especially those of supra- and international legal systems as well as of non-state law, *Vogenauer* (*supra* n. 345) 900–901; see *infra* ss. 109–199.

[349] *David*, Sources of Law: Int.Enc.Comp.L II, ch. 3 (1984). This chapter was published a generation ago and thus does not fully reflect some of the modern changes; see *Glendon*, The Sources of Law in a Changing Legal Order: 17 Creighton L.Rev. 663–698 (1984). But it was written by one of the great masters of comparative law whose erudition and perceptiveness make it worth reading even today, especially since its scope is not limited to Western legal systems. See also *Kourilsky, Racz and Schäfer*, The Sources of Law: A Comparative and Empirical Study (Budapest 1982); *Pegoraro and Rinella*, Le fonti nel diritto comparato (Torino 2000); *Pergoraro and Reposo* (eds.), Le fonti del diritto negli ordinamenti contemporanei (Bologna 1993).

[350] See e.g *Schwartz* (ed.), The Code Napoleon and the Common Law World (New York 1956).

Comparatists have duly emphasized the deep historical roots of the code v. non-code traditions. In the civil law, the notion that the law should be enshrined in a book harkens back to Justinian's *Corpus Juris Civilis* (529–534 A.D.), and the enlightenment ideal that such a law book be systematic, comprehensive, and concise has prevailed for more than two centuries in continental Europe, Latin America, and much of East Asia. In the common law orbit, by contrast, codification was not even seriously considered until the nineteenth century, and projects fully to codify private law were rare and mostly failed, some important exceptions especially in the United States notwithstanding. It is true that today there are many "codes" even in common law countries (as well as in some mixed jurisdictions), covering areas as diverse as commercial transactions, civil procedure, criminal, tax, and bankruptcy law. As comparatists have admitted, this has somewhat blurred the distinction between the civil and common law traditions. Even today, however, codifying law is central to the former in a way that it is not to the latter, and a civil lawyer feels completely at home in a codified system while his common law colleague does not. It is noteworthy that in many parts of the civil law world, (re-)codification is an ongoing project and concern, inter alia in East Asia.[351] The persistent strength of the drive for codification is especially apparent in continental Europe. Since the 1990s, comparative law has been engaged with the project of a European Civil Code which became the object of innumerable studies, conferences, and publications.[352] The idea is directly connected to the ideal of legal unification which is, on the whole, dearer to the civil than to the common law mind.

193. *Statutes.* – Though not quite to the same extent as constitutions (more recently) and codifications (traditionally), statutes have also enjoyed consistent attention among comparatists.

Much writing, however, is limited to broad assertions. Again focusing on their favorite dichotomy, authors used to reiterate routinely that civil law jurisdictions prefer statutory rules while common law systems look primarily to cases. Today, it is broadly accepted that this distinction no longer describes the reality; in most common law countries statutory rules have become as important as court decisions, while in most civil law systems courts have de facto begun to rival legislatures. A similar staple in the literature is the assertion that civil law statutes tend to be more pro-active and comprehensive, while legislation in common law jurisdictions is more often a reaction to cases, and thus piecemeal. Again, the more recent literature has shown that at least in the modern legislative jungle, things are no longer that simple; there are many broad and comprehensive statutes in common law countries and many instances of ad hoc and reactive legislation in the civilian orbit.

Beyond such general assertions, there is a considerable amount of scholarship on more particular topics. Examples are comparative studies of the legislative processes in various countries.[353] Another is the field of statutory interpretation, inter alia the examination of the time-honored view that common lawyers tend to construe statutes strictly while civil lawyers tend to interpret them more liberally.[354]

[351] It was the topic of the Second Intermediate Congress of the International Academy of Comparative Law in Tapei, Taiwan, in 2012; see *Wang* (ed.), Codification in International Perspective (Dordrecht, Heidelberg, New York, London 2014); *Wang* (ed.), Codification in East Asia (Dordrecht, Heidelberg, New York, London 2014).

[352] See *Hartkamp et al.* (eds.), Towards a European Civil Code (ed. 4 Alpen aan den Rijn 2011); *Collins*, The European Civil Code: the Way Forward (Cambridge, New York 2008); for a short overview, see *Jansen and Rademacher*, European Civil Code: *Smits* (ed.), Elgar Encyclopedia of Comparative Law (ed. 2 Cheltenham, Northampton MA 2012) 299–314.

[353] Most importantly, *Pizzorusso* (ed.), Law in the Making. A Comparative Survey (Berlin, New York 1988); *Maxeiner*, Failures of American Methods of Lawmaking in Historical and Comparative Perspectives (Cambridge 2018); (Symposium) Die Entstehung von Gesetzen in rechtsvergleichender Perspektive, RabelsZ 78 (214) 315–428.

[354] *MacCormick and Summers* (eds.), Interpreting Statutes. A Comparative Study (Aldershot 1991); see also *Zimmermann*, Statuta sunt stricte interpretanda. Statutes and the Common Law: A Continental Perspective: 56 Camb.L.J. (1997) 315–328; *Zweigert and Puttfarken*, Statutory Interpretation – Civilian Style: 44 Tul.L.Rev. 704–719 (1970). For an overview, see *Vogenauer*, Statutory Interpretation: *Smits* (ed.), Elgar Encyclopedia of Comparative Law (2 ed. Cheltenham, Northampton MA 2012) 826–838.

Challenging earlier assumptions, an in-depth study has shown surprisingly broad similarities between the interpretative practice of (civil and common law) courts on both sides of the English Channel.[355]

194. *Case law.* – Comparatists have spilt rivers of ink exploring the significance of case law in the world's major legal traditions. This is, again, largely due to their focus on the civil v. common law distinction. Originally, the basic idea was that in the Anglo-American tradition judges made law, while in the civil law systems they did not. It was soon understood, however, that things were not quite so simple; that for most of history, even in continental Europe, courts were major contributors to the creation of law;[356] and that today, throughout the civil law world, judges participate in the lawmaking process, albeit to varying degrees and in different fashions.

Yet, according to the traditional view, there is still a significant difference. In the common law world, judicial decisions are precedent which lower and later courts must follow; high court decisions are truly binding and thus (really) "law". In the civil law, by contrast, judicial decisions are, generally speaking, not binding on other courts – and thus not really "law". In other words, common law judges make and follow precedent, while civil law judges are forbidden to pronounce generally applicable rules[357] and must decide according to statutes, not earlier cases.[358]

Even mainstream comparative law has long acknowledged, however, that this picture is a caricature, originating in the late nineteenth century as the high water mark of legislative positivism in the civil law and the heyday of precedent in the common law. While the picture is not outright wrong, two major qualifications are generally accepted today.

First, even in theory, the separation between the civil and the common law approaches is not strict, and much depends on the individual legal system. In some civil law countries, for example, high court decisions can actually be binding as a matter of law, while in others they are not. In fact, in several jurisdictions, especially under the socialist conception of law and today in China, supreme courts even have the power to issue generally authoritative interpretations of statutes. In some common law countries like England precedent continues to be taken very seriously, in others like the United States, less so.

Second, comparative studies have shown that, in practice, in most legal systems high court judgments have a strong, and often overwhelming, impact on how later cases are decided. Lower judges everywhere tend to follow higher judicial authority; whether they do so as a matter of legal obligation or rather because of general obedience or fear of being reversed matters only in exceptional instances. And in most systems, high court judges also follow their own decisions; again, it rarely makes a difference whether they do so because they must or simply for reasons of predictability or efficiency. In addition, judges in all legal systems have ways to circumvent precedent they do not wish to follow, usually by distinguishing the current case, sometimes by overruling previous decisions.[359]

Still, comparative law has not therefore discarded the distinction between case law-based systems and others as entirely meaningless. One lingering difference is that common law judges will openly acknowledge if they feel bound to follow precedent, while in many civil law countries such an admission is still taboo. Comparatists have also noted persistent differences in the style of judicial opinions. Anglo-American judges, conscious of the need to distinguish cases, emphasize facts, extensively consider the arguments for both sides, and tend openly to state their decisions' underlying reasons, often in a personal fashion. By contrast, civil law judicial opinions are usually short on facts, tend to be more terse and deductive, and avoid a personal

[355] *Vogenauer* (*supra* n. 13); see also *Brenncke*, Judicial Law-Making in English and German Courts. Techniques and Limites of Statutory Interpretation (Cambridge, Antwerp, Chicago IL 2018).

[356] *Dawson*, The Oracles of the Law (Ann Arbor MI 1968).

[357] Expressly in Article 5 of the French *Code civil* (1804).

[358] Hence Justinian's famous maxim that "non exemplibus, sed legibus iudicandum est", C.7.45.13 (529 A.D.).

[359] *MacCormick and Summers* (eds.), Interpreting Precedents. A Comparative Study (Aldershot 1997).

tone. Finally, notions of precedent focus the common lawyers' attention quickly on cases, while for a civil lawyer a case-based rule is still second best.

195. *Administrative regulations.* – Comparative law has rarely explored administrative regulations in their role as sources of law. To be sure, administrative law more generally has recently become a major field of comparative study which will be addressed below (C.ii.e., ss. 267–270). But even in that context, the role of administrative regulations in the overall process of making and using law has scarcely been examined.[360] Their neglect in this regard is obviously not due to a lack of practical relevance – in the modern state, the impact of administrative rules is as enormous as it is ubiquitous. Nor is there a lack of interesting comparative issues, such as the different institutional and professional settings in which regulations are created, the style in which they are drafted, or how bureaucrats and courts enforce them. Yet, the comparative study of administrative rules as sources of law is difficult for at least two reasons. First, it requires more knowledge of the administrative organization and process in at least two legal systems than most comparatists command. Second, the traditional distinctions between civil and common law, statutory and case law, and even between national and supranational rules can easily be more problematic than helpful. In summary, effectively comparing the role of administrative regulations as sources of law requires not only expertise but also the ability to think outside of many boxes.

196. *Academic scholarship.* – The role and impact of legal scholarship has also been a pet topic of comparative law for more than a century.

This is, again, true especially for the discussion of the relationship between the civil and the common law. While Western legal systems today do not consider the opinion of scholars binding on courts or other decision makers, the impact of academic writing has differed significantly between the two major traditions: scholarly opinion has been highly influential, and indeed often formative, in the civil law tradition,[361] while it has long played a more intermittent, and by and large lesser, role in the common law world.[362] Somewhat overstating the case, comparative lawyers sometimes characterize the former as the law of professors and the latter as the law of judges.

It is generally acknowledged today that this difference has often been overrated,[363] and that there has been considerable convergence between the two traditions. One the one hand, comparatists have shown that the impact of legal academics on legislators and even judges in the common law orbit has grown significantly. In the United States, generally speaking a common law jurisdiction, legal academics have enjoyed an increasingly influential role in the development of the law since the late nineteenth century.[364] Even in England, judges today no longer shun academic opinion but often seek to cooperate with scholars in resolving legal issues.[365] On the other hand, judges in continental Europe and other civil law jurisdictions have gained more and more self-

[360] Most comparative scholarship on administrative regulations is concerned with the control of regulatory power and its judicial review.. There are some exceptions; see, e.g., *Reiss*, Administrative Agencies as Creators of Administrative Law Norms: Evidence from the U.K., France and Sweden: *Rose-Ackermann and Lindseth*, Comparative Administrative Law 373–386 (ed. 2 Cheltenham, Northampton MA 2017).

[361] In earlier times, the prevailing opinion could actually be binding on judges. This was clearly true in Roman law; according to a rescript of Hadrian (ca. 130 A.D.), if the jurists vested with the *ius respondendi ex auctoritate principis* agreed, their opinion had the force of law (Gaius, Institutes 1, 7); in 426 A.D., the law of citation of Valentinian III provided that the joint opinion of certain classical jurisconsults must be followed. In a similar vein, the Accursian gloss to the Digest and the joint opinion of leading jurists in the late middle ages (*communis opinio doctorum*) were widely accepted as legally binding in many European courts, *Dawson* (*supra* n. 356) 139–40, as were the decisions of law faculties solicited by judges throughout the early modern period (*Aktenversendung*), *Dawson* (*supra* n. 356) 200–201.

[362] In England, a handful of treatises, written between the twelfth and the eighteenth centuries, were accorded the status of "books of authority" (Glanvill, Bracton, Littleon, Coke, Blackstone) and thus assumed to state the law correctly.

[363] *Duxbury*, Jurists and Judges: An Essay on Influence (Portland OR 2001).

[364] *Rheinstein* (*supra* n. 55) 179–186.

[365] *Braun*, Guidici ed Accademia nell' Esperienza Inglese (Bologna 2006).

confidence and often no longer display the reverence for academic opinion that once prevailed.

Scholarly opinion, in particular the learned interpretation of the Quaran and the Talmud, respectively, has played a highly important role in both the Islamic and the Jewish legal traditions. While the views of scholars are not considered strictly binding, doctrine based on the consensus of the learned is effectively authoritative, since there is no other final authority on the proper interpretation of the sacred texts.

Despite all the attention the discipline has paid to the role of scholarly works in the various legal cultures, however, there are no thorough and truly comparative studies of how academic work is produced and disseminated, and how it influences decision makers. Comparatists have sometimes studied how frequently and for what purpose courts cite legal scholarship.[366] While that illuminates the working mode and style of judges, it cannot provide a reliable assessment of academic impact on courts, because they are often influenced by views they never mention.[367]

197. *Custom.* – Mainstream comparative lawyers have made little effort to explore the significance of custom as a source of law.[368] The explanation is different for Western legal systems on the one hand, and traditional orders on the other.

In the domestic laws of modern Western jurisdictions custom plays a marginal role today. The network of constitutions, statutes, administrative regulations, and court decisions is so dense that resort to custom is rarely necessary.[369] In this regard, comparative law just reacts (properly) to the diminishing practical relevance of that source. It is true that current trade usages are sometimes employed as standards of conduct, especially in commercial and tort disputes, but in the domestic context that occurs in a narrow segment of cases which do not make custom broadly relevant.

In more traditional systems beyond the West, custom continues to play an important role for the majority of the population. While comparatists recognize that role, they have scarcely studied indigenous customary law in any depth. For reasons explained before, they have left that field largely to ethnologists who are better trained and equipped to maneuver it (*supra* A.iii., s. 185).

The traditional neglect of custom constitutes a considerable deficit which is particularly troublesome in the realm of modern commercial law on the transnational level. Since treaties or other international agreements leave significant gaps and often cannot keep up with fast-paced developments, many aspects of transnational commercial transactions and trade relations are governed by custom and usages. Despite their enormous practical importance, comparative law has barely begun to analyze the role of such custom and usages as a source of law, for example in transnational contract practice or international commercial arbitration.

198. *Non-state law sources ("soft law").* – As comparatists began to rediscover law "beyond the state" towards the end of the twentieth century (*supra* A.iii., ss. 183–187), they also began to look at non-official texts, often called "soft law" because of their non-binding nature. The main focus has been on quasi-private collections and codes of private and commercial law. The modern prototype was provided by the US-American *Restatements* whose unofficial yet often highly influential nature earned them much attention, particularly in Europe – in part simply because in form they resemble civil law codifications.[370] Inspired by this model, European scholars and institutions created a variety of equivalents, of which the Lando Commissions's *Principles of European Contract Law* and the *UNIDROIT Principles of International Commercial Contracts* are the best-known examples.[371] Their compilation was

366 *Kötz*, Die Zitierpraxis der Gerichte: Eine vergleichende Studie: RabelsZ 52 (1988) 644–662.

367 The highest courts in France, for example, never cite legal scholarship as a matter of tradition, and Italian courts are forbidden to cite academic authors altogether.

368 There are some exceptions; see, e.g., *David* (*supra* n. 270) 97–110; *Gonidec* (*supra* n. 308); 7–17, 211–276.

369 Usages of a trade occasionally define standards of conduct, especially in commercial and tort disputes, but those are special and, on the whole, relatively rare instances.

370 See *Gordley*, European Codes and American Restatements: Some Difficulties: 81 Colum.L.Rev. 140–157 (1981).

371 *Lando et al.* (eds.), Principles of European Contract Law, 3 parts (Dordrecht, 1995/1999/2002); UNIDROIT Principles of International Commercial Contracts (Rome 1994, 3d ed. 2010).

based on the comparative study of multiple legal systems and driven by a desire for transnational harmonization of law, albeit in unofficial form. These Principles have attained the status of legal sources in the sense that they have influenced national and supranational legislation as well as international dispute resolution, especially in commercial arbitration.

In addition, comparatists now occasionally take other forms of "soft law" into consideration, mainly on the transnational level, such as the International Commercial Terms (INCOTERMS) and the Uniform Customs and Practice for Documentary Credit (UCP), both published by the International Chamber of Commerce (ICC).[372]

Despite these beginnings, however, one cannot say that such non-state regimes have found a secure place in comparative law. They still lie largely beyond the horizon of the discipline's mainstream. As a result, their role and impact as sources of law have rarely been analyzed and are currently understood only by a small number of specialists.

199. *Supra- and international sources.* – With regard to the discipline's exploration of legal sources, a lingering weakness is the frequent neglect of supra- and international law. Despite the (practical as well as theoretical) importance of the transnational sphere, mainstream comparative law has long paid but occasional attention to the sources shaping this area[373] with the notable exception of the UN Convention on the International Sale of Goods.[374]

This situation has somewhat improved with regard to European Union law and the European human rights system. There are some general introductions covering these areas as legal systems (*supra* A.iii., ss. 186–187), and they usually deal with the relevant legal sources at least *en passant*. Specialists in these fields sometimes delve more deeply into the matter. Still, there is no serious study of how the respective sources (regulations, directives, court decisions, etc.) compare to the more traditional categories of national legislation, administrative regulation, or case law. There is one, major, exception: since the close of the twentieth century, European law scholars have extensively related the EU treaties to national constitutions, especially comparing the EU's supranational structure with the architecture of various federal systems (see *infra* C.ii.d., s. 265).

A particular blind spot in the discipline's study of legal sources is its virtual disregard of public international law materials. Comparatists have by and large ignored treaties, customary international law, and the decisions of international tribunals (such as the International Court of Justice). Many modern introductions to comparative law mention them barely, if at all.[375] In a sense, this is understandable: the law of treaties is complex and technical, the concept of customary international law is subtle and changing, and the decisions of international tribunals usually deal with issues far removed from the standard fare of domestic legal systems; as a result, the whole terrain is largely alien to the non-specialist. This is even more true for the more modern forms of transnational law, such as the quasi-legislative resolutions of the UN Security Council or international administrative regimes. Still, these barriers to access cannot justify persistent blindness vis-à-vis essential building blocks of the current global legal order. As long as comparatists neglect international law, their discourse on legal sources is badly behind the times and unacceptably incomplete.[376]

ii. *Legal Method (and the Structure of Legal Systems)*

200. *Two caveats.* – Like the sources of law, similarities and differences in the various jurisdictions' legal methods have been a staple of comparative

[372] *Basedow*, The Law of Open Societies – Private Ordering and Public Regulation of International Relations (Leiden, Boston MA 2013) 135–163.

[373] *David* (*supra* n.349) ss. 302-345, was far ahead of his time in the 1980s, and it is disconcerting to realize that mainstream comparatists have neither updated nor surpassed his description and analysis.

[374] See, e.g., Symposium: The Convention on the International Sale of Goods and Its Application in Comparative Perspective: RabelsZ 68 (2004) 427–540; The Convention on the International Sale of Goods – The 25th Anniversary: Its Impact – Its Role in the Future: RabelsZ 71 (2007) 7–129.

[375] A – very limited – exception is *Kischel* (*supra* n. 286) 951–952.

[376] Some beginnings are made in *Roberts, Stephan, Verdier and Versteeg* (*supra* n. 35)

law for more than half a century. This is in part because legal method has been one of the most significant criteria for the definition of legal families and traditions (*infra* VI.B.ii., s. 339), in part because fostering a mutual understanding of different methods is one of the major benefits the discipline has to offer (*infra* V.A.iii., s. 286, and V.B.i., s. 295). Yet, even more than the field of sources of law, legal method is treacherous terrain, for at least two reasons.

First, as others have noted, it is notoriously difficult to define the concept of (legal) "method".[377] In its broadest sense, legal method refers to the manner in which law is handled by all actors and in all regards in a given system. Comparatists, however, have usually understood the concept in a somewhat narrower, and analytically more useful, sense: as the mode of legal reasoning. Legal method then means the manner in which lawyers find, understand, interpret, and apply concepts and rules in order to resolve legal issues, especially how they go about deciding disputes.[378] Obviously, how lawyers think about and handle their material is intimately related to both the legal sources they work with (*supra* i.) and their view of the law's overall structure (*infra* s. 203).

Second, the very concept of legal method is based on the idea that there is a distinct mode of *legal* reasoning, i.e., a way of thinking about legal issues which can be separated from the mode of thinking about religious, moral, or political questions. This reflects the assumption that law is, or least should be, distinct from religion, morality, and politics (which is of course not to deny that law may be influenced by these fields). Yet, the idea of law as a separate, rational, and especially as a professionalized, enterprise is largely a Western construct which is not universally shared, as legal systems based on religious texts or customary regimes demonstrate. Still, since comparatists have overwhelmingly hailed from the cultural West, they have mostly limited their analyses of legal method to Western styles of reasoning, although there are some exceptions.[379] The emphasis has, once again, been on the civil v. common law dichotomy (and, between the 1950s and 1990s, the capitalist v. socialist law distinction (*supra* A.i., s. 175, and IV.A.ii., s. 176).

201. *Civil v. common law modes of legal reasoning.* – It is almost universally accepted among comparatists that there are significant differences between the legal reasoning of civil and common lawyers. As members of a tradition based on the work of scholars and acts of legislators, jurists in civil law systems tend to emphasize abstract principles and to prefer broad norms from which results in specific cases can then be derived in a deductive fashion. By contrast, as heirs of a tradition long based on judicial lawmaking, common lawyers tend to look to concrete cases, generating narrow rationales which will then suggest how the case at hand should be decided. Thus, civil lawyers reason from a general rule to the particular case, i.e., in a top-down fashion, while common lawyers proceed from one concrete case to the next and then eventually to a rule, i.e., in a bottom-up manner. Moreover, a French, German, or Italian lawyer, regarding law as an overarching system, prizes rigorous organization of rules and logical explanation of results; by contrast, his English, US-American, or Australian colleague, seeing law as a storehouse of practical solutions, strives for consistency with tradition and practically workable outcomes. In sum, to draw on Oliver Wendell Holmes' famous phrase, for the civil lawyer the "life of the law" has been "logic", for the common lawyer, it has been "experience".[380] Of course, it is generally understood in comparative law that these contrasting descriptions of legal reasoning are Weberian ideal types, if not outright caricatures; that they match the reality of how civil and common lawyers think about and apply law only imperfectly; that there are many differences between the various jurisdictions within the civil and the common law traditions; and that, as with regard to the sources of law, there has been considerable convergence over time. Still, to the extent that these dichotomies describe expectations and tendencies, preferences

[377] *Vogenauer* (*supra* n. 345) 885–886.

[378] See (Symposium) Juristische Methodenlehre: RabelsZ 83 (2019) 241–397.

[379] See *Fikentscher*, Methoden des Rechts I (Tübingen 1975).

[380] "The life of the law has not been logic: it has been experience", *Holmes* (*supra* n. 142) 1.

and predilections, they are essentially accepted as valid, albeit to varying degrees.[381]

202. *Particular studies.* – There are a few in-depth comparative studies of legal method, but for various reasons most of them have not had much of an impact on comparative law as a whole.[382]

The early work of Josef Esser, which focused on methodological differences between codified and judge-made law, is revered as a classic by scholars of legal theory.[383] But like many classics it is rarely read and even more rarely understood. Analytically complex, stylistically cryptic, and available only in German, it has been ignored by the vast majority of comparatists.

A similar fate befell Wolfgang Fikentscher's comparative study of legal method.[384] The multi-volume survey focuses mainly on civil and common law jurisdictions but also comprises early and religious legal systems. Though somewhat dated after about half a century, it is still unsurpassed in breadth and depth. Still, it is largely unknown among comparatists today, probably because it is available only in German and because its sheer bulk has deterred all but the most determined readers.

Patrick Atiyah and Robert Summers' comparison of legal reasoning *within* the common law family has attracted more attention.[385] The authors show that English legal reasoning is more "formalist" (mainly in the sense of relying on a more positivistic notion of law and thus on abstract rules), while US-American lawyers think in more "substantive" terms (mainly in the sense of considering underlying policies and practical consequences). And yet, even this – extremely thorough and thoughtful – study is not considered a "must read" among comparatists today, nor has it inspired others to undertake similar studies involving different jurisdictions.

The only real success story in this area is Mirjan Damaska's construction of two contrasting "ideals" of law – one "hierarchical", the other "coordinate".[386] While the book contains many insights into how lawyers think and operate according to these ideals, it is not primarily a study of legal method but rather of the structure of legal systems.

203. *Addendum: the structure of law.* – It should be obvious that legal reasoning is heavily related to the law's organization. Since a separate chapter of this Encyclopedia is devoted to the structure and divisions of the law, some brief remarks can suffice here.[387]

Comparative law has dealt with the topic again mainly in the civil and common law context. Here, these differences are most fundamental with regard to the perception of the law's overall layout. The traditional civil jurist's view of law as a coherent system invites deductive reasoning and emphasis on logical consistency. By contrast, the common lawyer's perception of law as a "seamless web" suggests reasoning by analogy and cares more for practical sense than for logical unity. There are several other structural differences that have an impact on legal method as well. To begin with, civil lawyers assume a fundamental difference between private and public law, a distinction which common lawyers consider either useless or at best a matter of basic (and fairly vague) orientation. While the dividing line between these two spheres has recently become blurrier in civil law systems as well, a continental European or Latin American lawyer would still recognize important differences between reasoning about private and public law (e.g., with regard to the extent and nature of property rights). On the other hand, common lawyers have traditionally divided their material into the two great masses of law and

[381] For an argument, that styles of reasoning in these two legal traditiona are more similar than has often been assumed, see *McGrath and Koziol*, Is Style of Reasoning a Fundamental Difference Between the Common Law and the Civil Law?: RabelsZ 78 (2014) 709–749.

[382] In addition to the monographs discussed below, see also the collection of essays in RabelsZ 83 (2019) 241–397.

[383] *Esser*, Grundsatz und Norm in der richterlichen Fortbildung des Privatrechts (Tübingen 1956 and ed. 4 1990).

[384] *Fikentscher*, Methoden des Rechts in vergleichender Darstellung (5 vol.) (Tübingen 1975–1977).

[385] *Atiyah and Summers* (*supra* n. 12).

[386] *Damaska* (*supra* n. 60).

[387] *David et al.*, Structure and Divisions of Law: Int. Enc.Comp.L. II ch. 2 (1974); the chapter covers not only civil and common law systems but also socialist, Islamic, Hindu, and African law.

equity, a distinction not shared by civilian jurists (though lurking beneath the surface of their law as well). While the distinction between law and equity has receded into the background even in Anglo-American law, it can still make a significant difference whether a lawyer relies on one or the other (e.g., whether he or she invokes a court's legal or equitable powers). Finally, civil lawyers tend to focus primarily on substantive law, while common lawyers approach law from the procedural side: the former want to know who is right (often in the abstract), while the latter ask who will win (a concrete dispute). All these structural differences between civil and common law have long been known in the discipline.

In addition, and cutting across the traditional divide, there are important structural differences between unitary jurisdictions with one set of laws, such as France or New Zealand, and federal systems with the coexistence of a federal regime and (multiple) subunit laws, such as Brazil or Canada. It stands to reason that lawyers in the former tend to expect, and to think in terms of, legal uniformity and consistency, while their colleagues in the latter have to maneuver, and are thus more comfortable with, diversity and potential conflicts between legal orders.

A new and more theoretical perspective was added by Mirjan Damaska on the patterns of distribution of state authority.[388] It obviously draws on fundamental characteristics of the civil and common law systems, but it also transcends them by providing a much broader approach. It explores how the organization of state authority in either a "hierarchical" (i.e., top-down) or a "coordinate" (i.e., horizontal) fashion, and the character of the state as either "reactive" or "activist", shape fundamental features of legal systems. This is pertinent to the nature of the legal process, but in that context it also has an impact on how legal actors work and how institutions function, i.e., on legal method.

Unfortunately, such theoretical work is scarce. To make matters worse, while there is no lack of descriptions of how law is organized in this system or that, there is little actual comparison between structural patterns and rarely any effort to draw broader conclusions from the observations made. As a result, comparative law has largely failed to develop a general framework for the study of legal structures and their influence on modes of reasoning.

iii. *Courts*

204. *The organization of courts.* – As core elements of legal systems, courts and the judicial process have enjoyed constant attention from both comparative lawyers and political scientists for several decades.[389] A major topic has been the organization of the judiciary. Most introductions to comparative law cover it in a general fashion, and there is a substantial literature devoted specifically to this subject.

In the world's jurisdictions, court systems are organized in diverse ways and according to a variety of (sometimes overlapping) criteria: by political structure into federal, state, sometimes also local and tribal fora; by subject matter into civil, criminal, administrative, constitutional, and various other courts; by degrees of specialization into courts of general jurisdiction and tribunals for particular kinds of disputes, including those arising under customary or religious law, etc.

Once again focusing on civil and common law systems, comparatists have observed different tendencies in court organization. Civil law jurisdictions tend towards specialization. To begin with, they typically have developed separate and independent court systems for different kinds of law. One particularly frequently finds different courts for civil and criminal cases on the one hand ("ordinary courts") and for litigation between citizens and the state on the other ("administrative tribunals"). German courts even have three additional branches (for labor, tax, and social welfare cases), each with its own (federal) supreme court. In addition, constitutional jurisdiction is often vested in a special institution designed to deal with questions involving a heavy dose of politics. Moreover, civil law systems tend to organize courts internally along subject matter lines, not

388 *Damaska* (*supra* n. 60).

389 E.g., *Abraham*, The Judicial Process (ed. 7 New York, Oxford 1998); *Helmke and Rios-Figuero* (*supra* n. 281); *Shapiro*, Courts (Chicago IL, London 1981); *Cappelletti*, The Judicial Process in Comparative Perspective (Oxford 1989).

only at the entry level but also at the appellate stage.[390] Supreme courts are often large institutions with over a hundred members divided into different panels (or senates or chambers) dealing with different areas of law. Judges thus specialize in their areas and soon know them inside out. As a result, they need to conduct fairly little ad hoc research and often know more about the law than the attorneys who appear before them.

By contrast, since the institutional merger of law and equity in the nineteenth century, common law jurisdictions tend not to divide their courts into separate branches along subject matter lines. Of course, even in the Anglo-American tradition, there are some special courts and internal divisions dealing with particular areas of law. On the whole, however, a more generalist approach to judging prevails. This is most visible on the appellate level where courts are usually staffed by a fairly small number of non-specialized judges who decide an extremely broad spectrum of cases. Often, these courts also handle constitutional cases along with everything else. Judges thus cannot specialize in narrow areas and frequently cannot know the law in question off the tops of their heads; instead, they have to educate themselves more ad hoc, with the help of their clerks or of the litigants.

While it is something of a caricature, one can thus say that in civil law systems "the court knows the law" (*iura novit curia*), while in common law (general) courts, judges tend to be "jacks of all trades and masters of none".[391] As comparatists have often noted, the civilian approach has the advantage that judges acquire greater technical mastery of the law and thus hit the ground running when faced with a case, but their specialization also narrows their perspective. The common law tradition is perhaps less efficient in that regard, but it also discourages strictly technical judging and fosters a broader vision of the issues.

205. *Opinion style and decisionmaking process.* – A standard observation in comparative law is that civil law courts write in a terse, syllogistic, and impersonal style, whereas common law opinions are more expansive, policy-oriented, and personal. There is some truth in this distinction, but it is generally recognized as a broad and dangerous generalization. It is true that many civil law judgments, especially in the French tradition, are minimalist and deductive, but others, as in Germany or Austria, are much more narrative and often not very different from an English or American opinion.[392] It has also been shown that even if civilian tribunals hide the underlying reasons behind a formalist facade, their internal decisionmaking process is not necessarily all that different from that of a common law court which more openly displays its struggle in the written opinion.[393]

206. *Access to justice.* – During the closing decades of the twentieth century there was a growing awareness that in many, if not most, legal systems the majority of the population has very limited access to the courts (except as a criminal defendant). A major research project explored the issue from a multidisciplinary perspective and demonstrated the magnitude of the problem.[394] Among comparatists, however, interest in the topic has recently waned. In most countries, little effort was made to improve access to the courts, and the emphasis has shifted towards promoting methods of alternative dispute resolution. The problem of access to justice is largely (though not exclusively) financial, of course, and thus a function of how litigation is paid for and by whom (*infra* IV.C.ii.a., s. 247).

207. *Political role and independence.* – In reaction to the perceived increase in the politization of the judiciary since the middle of the twentieth century, several comparative studies have focused on the political role of courts. Of course, this is

[390] *Meador*, Appellate Subject Matter Jurisdiction: The German Design from an American Perspective: 5 Hastings Int.Comp.L.Rev. 27–72 (1981).

[391] *Landis*, The Administrative Process (New Haven CT, London 1938) 31.

[392] *Gorla*, Lo stile delle sentenze, Testi commentati de Quaderni: Foro it. 1968 475–544.

[393] *Lasser*, Judicial (Self-)Protraits: Judicial Discourse in the French Legal System: 104 Yale L.J. (1995) 1325–1410. Broader studies of judicial reasoning styles are *Lasser*, Judicial Deliberations: A Comparative Analysis of Judicial Transparency and Legitimacy (Oxford 2004); *Garapon and Papadopoulos*, Juger en Amérique et en France (Paris 2003).

[394] *Cappelletti et al.* (*supra* n. 196); *Cappelletti* (ed.), Access to Justice and the Welfare State (Alphen aan den Rijn 1981).

a major issue with regard to constitutional adjudication (*infra* C.ii.d., s. 263), but the phenomenon has been studied from a variety of broader perspectives as well.[395] In this context, scholars have also tried to gauge the independence and accountability of the judiciary across jurisdictions. The results show that judges are controlled by a multitude of external and internal, official and informal, mechanisms the strength and combination of which vary greatly among legal systems.[396]

208. *Supra- and international tribunals.* – As comparative law has largely failed to include supra- and international material in its study of legal sources, so it has also largely neglected supra- and international tribunals in its studies of courts, with occasional exceptions for the European Court of Justice.[397] Such blindness to the transnational sphere was understandable in the mid-twentieth century when permanent international tribunals were few and far between and when they played a fairly marginal role for populations and economies. Today, neglecting them creates a major lacuna because these tribunals have proliferated and become hugely influential in many areas: the maintenance of international relations, human rights, international criminal law, regional integration, world trade, transnational dispute resolution among business parties, etc. Thus, the comparative study of courts without attention to the International Court of Justice, the European, Latin American, and African human rights tribunals, the European Court of Justice, the WTO Dispute Resolution Bodies, as well as international commercial arbitration, presents a seriously incomplete picture of judicial institutions in the world. It also misses the opportunity to observe what these tribunals have in common with national courts, where they differ from them, and what we can learn from the similarities and differences about adjudicative bodies more generally, including their successes and failures.

iv. *The Legal Professions*

209. *General remarks.* – While legal systems can be defined by the prevailing sources, methods, and court structures, they are ultimately shaped by the people who run them. In modern, and especially in Westernized, systems, these people are professional lawyers. Mainstream comparative law has focused on this group while it has dealt with those in charge of religious or traditional regimes only at the margin.[398]

In all Western systems, lawyers are primarily formed by their legal education. They then take on four major roles: to decide cases (judges), to engage in private practice (attorneys), to work in government (public officials, including prosecutors), and to train future lawyers and conduct academic research (professors); in addition, in the civil law tradition, some specialize in vesting private legal acts with a certain public force (notaries).

The particular character of their education, professional function, social standing, and self-image depends on a combination of historical background, political environment, and modern needs. As a result, comparative legal studies have found significant differences among legal systems, although the globalization of the economy and thus of many legal services has entailed considerable convergence. Before turning to the various groups, three general observations made by comparatists should be mentioned.

First, the importance of lawyers generally, i.e., their power, influence, and public recognition,

[395] See *Shapiro* (*supra* n. 389); *Waltmann and Holland*, The Political Role of Courts in Modern Democracies (New York 1988); *Jacob et al.* (eds.), Courts, Law and Politics in Comparative Perspective (New Haven CT, London 1996).

[396] *Canivet, Andenas and Fairgrieve* (eds.), Independence, Accountability and the Judiciary (London 2006); *Ramseyer and Rasmusen*, Measuring Judicial Independence (Chicago IL, London 2003).

[397] See especially *Lasser* (*supra* n. 393). By contrast, international lawyers of course pay massive attention to what international tribunals do – and sometimes even to the role of national courts; an example is *Nollkaemper*, National Courts and the International Rule of Law (Oxford 2011).

[398] For an extensive, albeit by now somewhat dated, comparative study of the civil and common law orbit, see *Abel and Lewis* (eds.), Lawyers in Society (3 vol.) (Berkeley CA, Los Angeles CA, London 1988); a more recent study is *Uzelac and van Rhee*, The Landscape of the Legal Profession in Europe and the USA: Continuity and Change (Cambridge, Portland OR 2011).

varies greatly across jurisdictions. This variation is but loosely related to the civil v. common law dichotomy. For example, in the United States lawyers have long played a highly important role, while in Ireland that is much less true; in Germany lawyers have considerable influence in the public sphere, while in Japan their profile is fairly low. The importance of lawyers also varies over time – in China, they played virtually no role thirty years ago; since then, they have consistently acquired influence and status. On the whole, the increasing role of law in many societies as well as in the international sphere has boosted the global importance of lawyers over the last few decades.

Second, as has often been observed in comparative law, the mobility of lawyers between the branches of the legal profession varies greatly as well. In some countries, such as the United States, lawyers move easily and frequently from private practice to public employment or vice versa, from the bar to the bench or into academia, or from prosecuting to defending individuals. In other systems, as in France or even in England, lawyers tend stick to their early choice of a career path. As a result, in some countries like the United States, lawyers see themselves primarily as members of an all-encompassing profession the members of which are doing different jobs, while in other jurisdictions, as in France, lawyers see themselves primarily as judges, advocates, government officials, etc. who merely share a common background.

Third, in some legal cultures lawyers identify more directly with the state than in others. Lawyers feel close to state authority, for example, in continental Europe, where until recently all legal education took place in public universities; where lawyers played an enormous role in the formation of the modern nation state; where even judges are widely regarded as (somewhat privileged) civil servants (*infra* s. 211); where the private bar has traditionally been closely regulated by the state; and where, as notaries, lawyers engaged in private practice can exercise public functions. By contrast, lawyers in common law jurisdictions tend to identify less with public authority; they have more often been educated in private institutions; were less involved with the modern rise of public administration; often acquire judicial office by election; and are usually regulated by (quasi-private) bar associations. While these are not categorical distinctions but merely overall tendencies, they do entail differences in how lawyers view themselves, think, and work.

210. *Legal education.* – In the closing decades of the twentieth century, numerous comparative studies dealt with the nature and structure of legal education in various legal systems. These studies were limited, once again, largely to the cultural West.[399] Even here, most studies looked at a small number of jurisdictions considered representative of the civil and common law world, such as France, Germany, England, and especially the United States.[400] While the heyday of the topic seems to be over, articles describing foreign models keep being published.

The discipline's interest in legal education has several causes. Comparatists seeking to understand what characterizes (and thus distinguishes) legal traditions realize that they must understand how the minds and working styles of legal professionals are being formed. In addition, the popularity of legal studies abroad, especially of a graduate year in a United States law school or other common law jurisdiction university, as well as the growing opportunities for foreign visiting professorships have exposed large numbers of students and teachers from one system to the legal education of another. Finally, the challenges caused by the internationalization of legal services have created pressure to reform legal education and thus interest in learning from other countries.

From the myriad observations made about particular systems, one can, by way of broad generalization, distill three basic differences. They concern the nature and orientation, funding and access, and structure and phases of legal education. These differences are related to the civil v. common law dichotomy to varying degrees. All three have lately diminished although they have not entirely disappeared.

The basic difference regarding the nature and orientation of legal education is strongly related to the civil and common law traditions, respectively.

399 Symposium: Legal Education: Comp.L.YB 5 (1983) 3–177.

400 E.g., *Merryman*, Legal Education Here and There: A Comparison: 27 Stan.L.Rev. 859–878 (1975).

In the civil law world, legal education has been academic at least since the late middle ages. Thus it has gone without saying for centuries that legal professionals must be trained in a university and through a course of academic study. This explains the civil lawyer's theoretical bent and his or her view of law as a (logical) "science".[401] In the common law world, lawyers were traditionally trained in practice, i.e., in apprenticeships; for the majority university training is but a century old. Even now, legal education has maintained a more professional orientation; this, in turn, entails a more practical mindset and a view of law as a craft. This difference in orientation has recently eroded to some extent. Today, virtually all common law jurisdictions also train their lawyers originally in universities. And under the influence of the leading US law schools, Anglo-American legal education has become much more academic and theoretical than it used to be.

The second major dividing line pertains to the funding of, and access to, legal education. It is more loosely related to the two great legal traditions. In the civil law world, universities used to be overwhelming public. At least since the twentieth century, the legal education they offered was largely tax-funded so that tuition was low or non-existent. Pursuant to an egalitarian vision of higher education, these universities also offered broad access to many high-school graduates. As a result, legal education under this model has traditionally been cheap but also resource-starved. By contrast, in much of the Anglo-American world, mainly in the United States but also in Canada and elsewhere, there has been a mix of public and private law schools, with the private ones by and large leading. The resultant system of legal education is largely tuition-funded. It also tends to be more elitist, because the best law schools carefully select a relatively small number of students from a large applicant pool. Under this model, legal education can become extremely expensive, but it also benefits from comparatively ample resources. The difference between these two approaches has diminished over the last few decades as well. Private, i.e., tuition-funded, law schools have sprung up in many countries in Europe, East Asia, and Latin America, mainly in response to the underfunding of public institutions.

Finally, there are differences regarding the structure and sequence of legal education. These differences are largely independent of the two great legal traditions. In most countries, legal education combines undergraduate university study with subsequent mandatory practical training. Students typically go straight from high school (or the equivalent) to the law faculties for about four years; after obtaining their law degree, they then enter a mandatory practical training stage lasting from one to several years. At its end, they become fully licensed to practice. This is still the basic approach in the civil law world as well as the predominant tradition in England and the British Commonwealth orbit. A different model has prevailed in the United States and Canada. Here, students first obtain an undergraduate degree in another field and then enter law school, i.e., on the graduate level. At least in North America, further practical training is not formally required. Instead, passing the bar exam directly after law school entails admission to practice. Even this distinction between undergraduate and graduate legal training has recently somewhat decreased. In many countries as diverse as France and China, Italy and India, students now often proceed from their first (undergraduate) law degree to a year or two of advanced and more specialized (graduate) legal study. And some jurisdictions, notably Japan and Australia, have experimented with a graduate approach modeled on US law schools.[402]

On the whole, it is fair to say that the US model has been the predominant reference point for comparative studies of legal education. Observers in other countries have often been intrigued by the American approach – some because of their own positive experience in the resource-rich environment of an elite US law school, others because of the overall success of American-trained lawyers in the global marketplace, and some because they admire the multidisciplinarity of American

[401] See the, by now classic, article by *Damaska* (*supra* n. 268).

[402] See *Fujikura*, Reform of Legal Education in Japan: The Creation of Law Schools without a Professional Sense of Mission: 75 Tul.L.Rev. 941–947 (2001); *Foote*, The Trials and Tribulations of Japan's Legal Education Reforms: 36 Hastings Int.Comp.L.Rev. 369–442 (2013).

legal education at the top level. Yet, the experiments just mentioned notwithstanding, the actual global influence of the American (graduate) model has been very limited, mainly because its cost is too high to be broadly acceptable in most environments.

211. *Judges.* – As modern comparative law has been fascinated with the organization and role of courts (*supra* iii.), it has been captivated by the professionals sitting on them. The main reason is that for many decades the discipline distinguished the two great Western legal traditions in large part through the different status and role of judges: law makers and heroes in the common law, appliers of statutes and faceless bureaucrats in the civil law. Today, it is generally accepted that these distinctions were exaggerated, and that they have diminished over time. Common law judges apply statutes all the time (albeit sometimes reluctantly), and their growth in numbers has often reduced their exalted status, while civil law judges create law all the time (albeit sometimes secretly) and their increasingly political role has entailed a more prominent profile. This is especially true in the context of constitutional adjudication (*infra* C.ii.d., s. 263). In addition, the position of judges varies considerably within these two traditions and even among the various courts.[403]

Still, significant differences between the civil and common law traditions remain, and comparative studies have brought them into sharp relief. To begin with, observers from one tradition have been intrigued by how differently judges are recruited in the other. Scholars in the civil law world have noted how common law judges are usually appointed (or even elected) after a successful career at the bar or in government (or sometimes in academia), i.e., typically past midlife. A judgeship is thus a sign of distinction, or at least of political connections and success, and common law judges are often well-known public figures. By contrast, comparatists in the common law orbit have noted the model of a career judiciary in the continental tradition and beyond. There, judges enter the court system often right at the beginning of their professional lives and at the lowest level; they are then promoted to the higher courts based on a combination of seniority and merit. Being a judge is thus not very different from being a senior bureaucrat, and civil law judges are usually unknown to the public, sometimes with the exception of some constitutional court members. Comparatists have also recognized that the different recruitment modes reflect different attitudes towards special expertise. To the amazement of especially continental European observers, being on a common law bench does not require any specialized training for the job. And to the surprise of Anglo-American observers, in most civil law countries judges are officially trained for their particular position, sometimes even in a special school, as in France. Finally, much has been written about the advantages and disadvantages of these two approaches. On the whole, the common law tradition can be expected to produce more professionally seasoned, personally mature, and self-confident judges; the civil law approach promotes legal expertise, technical dexterity, and political reliability. Broadly generalizing, one can say that common law judges are more independent in the sense of subject to fewer formal controls by peers or superiors, although they are more exposed to public scrutiny and may have to run for re-election. By contrast, their civilian colleagues are more independent in the sense of being sheltered from public view although, as long as they seek promotion, they have to please those controlling their advancement, i.e., members of the higher courts or state ministries.[404]

In addition, individual studies have explored the organization, role, and career patterns of judges in a variety of contexts, sometimes from a sociological and cultural perspective, especially in Europe.[405] This reflects recognition of the increasing importance of judges even in continental legal systems.

[403] *Garoupa and Ginsburg*, Judicial Reputation: A Comparative Theory (Chicago IL 2015).

[404] *Clark*, The Selection and Accountability of Judges in West Germany: 61 So.Cal.L.Rev 1795–1848 (1988).

[405] See, e.g., *Bell* (ed.), Judiciaries within Europe: A Comparative Review (Cambridge 2006).

While mainstream comparatists have, again, paid fairly little attention to judges on supra- and international tribunals,[406] international lawyers and political scientists have studied transnational judiciaries from a variety of angles, including their interaction with national courts.[407] They have also discussed the growth of transnational judicial networks which today often connect (especially appellate and constitutional) judges from many jurisdictions and diverse traditions in multiple ways. While these networks foster convergence of self-images, working styles, and viewpoints, the claim that they construct "a global legal system" is exaggerated.[408]

212. *Private practice.* – The comparative study of lawyers in private practice was a fertile field in the post-World War II decades because, with regard to the bar, there was a plethora of interesting differences between legal systems to observe and explain. (By contrast, comparatists have paid next to no attention to corporate counsel, probably because there is little reason to expect sufficiently interesting differences between legal systems.)

In some systems, most visibly in the United States, the private bar was huge (both in absolute and in per capita terms), while in others, most notably Japan (and in virtually all socialist countries), it was tiny; why did some systems need so many lawyers while others got by with so few? Another observation was that in some common law jurisdictions lawyers soon tended to work in (fast-growing) law firms, while in most civil countries, solo and small-group practice continued to predominate well into the late twentieth century; what did that tell us about the respective legal cultures? Also, in some countries lawyering was understood and organized essentially as a business, while in others it was still conceived of as a quasi-public calling; how should one reconcile the role of lawyers as private entrepreneurs with their duty as officers of the court? The former understanding often went hand in glove with a broad definition of the lawyer's professional role that included giving business advice and handling political issues; the latter conception entailed a narrower view, limiting private practice to strictly legal work and representation in court. Furthermore, one could observe that in a number of countries the bar was loosely regulated so that it could freely set its own fees (including contingency fees), advertise for clients, and use traditional employment relationships to hire manpower; elsewhere, the profession was tightly regulated by the state, operated under mandatory fee schedules (outlawing contingency arrangements), was forbidden to advertise, and lawyers in private practice were regarded as independent professionals who could not work in an employment relationship; what levels and kinds of regulation were desirable? In some jurisdictions there was a single, unified type of private practitioner, such as the German *Rechtsanwalt* or the Brazilian *advocado*; in others there were several types distinguished by their activity, such as the French *avocat* and *avoué* or the British barrister and solicitor; should specialization be required by law or left to the market?

Today, many of these differences are either obsolete or much diminished. In many, if not most, developed countries the number of lawyers in private practice has grown hugely; law firms have become ubiquitous and often very large; legal practice has turned into a business almost everywhere and lawyers in many countries are now routinely involved in their clients' business activities; most countries have liberalized the regulation of the bar, allow advertising, contingency fees, and employment relationships among lawyers; many have gradually unified their legal profession, and while the distinction between solicitors and barristers persists in the commonwealth tradition, even this distinction has lost some of its importance. None of this is to say that there are no differences left regarding the organization, nature, and style of private legal practice in different countries. But over the last couple of decades, the trend towards convergence (driven largely by market forces) has been fast and strong. It has made private practice, especially in developed countries, more and

[406] An exception is the study by *Lasser* (*supra* n. 393) which focuses, inter alia, on the European Court of Justice.

[407] See, e.g., *Cottier, Mavroidis and Blatter* (eds.), The Role of the Judge in International Trade Regulation (Ann Arbor MI 2003).

[408] *Slaughter*, A New World Order (Princeton NJ, Oxford 2003) 65–103.

more similar, leaving fewer and fewer differences to explore and explain.

Legal scholarship has thus shifted its emphasis to topics that lie beyond the traditional field of comparative studies: the rise of lawyers in several fast developing countries, most notably in China;[409] the importance of lawyers for the rule of law, both in particular jurisdictions and on the international level;[410] the role of the private bar in public interest litigation; and the worldwide internationalization of legal practice.[411]

213. *Government lawyers (including prosecutors).* – Very little comparative work has been done on government lawyers. That is not surprising because lawyers in public administration are usually less visible than judges and even private practitioners. But it is infelicitous because as operators of the regulatory apparatus, government lawyers are highly important actors in their respective legal systems. One could learn a lot about the similarities and differences of public administration in modern states by looking at how government lawyers are trained and recruited; by whom and how they are controlled; to whom they respond in making decisions; how much discretion they have and how they exercise it; etc. All this is still largely unexplored comparative law terrain.

There is one exception: comparatists have paid considerable attention to public prosecutors because there are many interesting differences regarding their selection, power, and function. In some jurisdictions, such as the United States, prosecutors are selected through a political process and thus hold quasi-political (and on the state level usually electoral) office; in others, as in Germany, prosecutors are public servants appointed by the government on the basis of their academic performance and pursuing a (usually lifelong and essentially bureaucratic) career. In some countries, especially in the French tradition, prosecutors are closely associated with, and indeed organized as part of, the judiciary: they undergo the same training and often share career patterns with judges; in other systems, as in Switzerland, such a close association would be considered an unacceptable threat to judicial independence, and prosecutors are clearly separated from the bench. In several systems, prosecutors have enormous, and sometimes virtually unbridled, discretion whether to charge a defendant or not, whether to plea-bargain and how, etc.; in other systems, they are forced to prosecute every serious crime and to bring an indictment whenever they have sufficient evidence to expect a conviction. All these differences have invited examination of the underlying causes and of their effects on the nature of the criminal process.

In addition, in the closing decades of the twentieth century, comparative studies explored the extremely powerful and multifaceted role played by prosecutors (*prokuratura*) in socialist legal systems.[412] Observing that role brought the political function of prosecutors into particularly sharp relief. It thus invited reflection upon the tension inherent in that office between the rule of law and political mission.

214. *Academics.* – Comparative law interest in academics has been driven not only by their role in shaping the minds of the professionals who run legal systems but also by the penchant of legal scholars to write about themselves.[413] Thus, comparatists in civil law systems never tire of stressing that in their academically oriented tradition the law has been formed by professors rather than judges, while in the common law orbit the opposite is true. Yet, when continental refugee jurists obtained academic posts in their new homes overseas (*supra* III.D.iii.b., ss. 132–133), they began to emphasize that in twentieth-century American law professors have actually become very influential as well.[414] While these claims are far from false, they illustrate that descriptions of academic roles are often skewed by self-interest.

[409] See, e.g., *Liu, Liang and Michelson*, Migration and Social Structure: The Spatial Mobility of Chinese Lawyers, 36 L.& Policy 165–194 (2014).

[410] *Dezelay and Garth* (eds.), Lawyers and the Rule of Law in an Era of Globalization (Abingdon, New York 2011).

[411] *Drolshammer and Pfeifer* (eds.), The Internationalization of the Practice of Law (The Hague, London, Boston MA 2001).

[412] See, e.g., *Glenn*, Soviet Administrative Legality: The Role of the Attorney General's Office (Stanford CA 1962); *Smith*, The Soviet Procuracy and the Supervision of Administration (Alphen aan den Rijn 1978).

[413] See, for example, Selecting Minds Symposium, 41 Am.J.Comp..L 351–499 (1993); Symposium: Akademische Karrierewege für Juristen, RabelsZ 84 (2020) 264-398.

[414] Rheinstein(supra n. 55)179–186(Einf. 2.A).

Today it is widely recognized that the contrast between law-shaping professors in the civil law tradition and law-making judges in the Anglo-American world was always somewhat overstated, and in any event has much diminished over time. Civilian judges are important lawmakers and common law academics often heavily influence the direction of legal developments. Yet, significant differences remain.

To begin with, academics continue to play a particularly important role in civil law countries – not only as teachers, but as organizers of the law. To an extent still uncommon in the Anglo-American context, they are the creators of coherence, the builders of doctrinal structures, and thus the keepers of order. Also, in a culture typically eschewing dissenting judicial opinions, civilian academics are the crucial commentators and critics of what legislatures and courts produce.

Furthermore, on the whole, academics in civil law countries continue to enjoy greater prestige than their colleagues in common law jurisdictions. It is true that this difference has diminished as well, because Anglo-American legal academics at the most prestigious law faculties are quite highly regarded. Still, while the social standing of an Austrian or Italian law professor is normally considered superior to that of a judge even on the appellate level, this is not true in England or the United States. Special status, however, is widely accorded to constitutional judges. Even in the civil law, members of constitutional tribunals are considered to be at the very top of the legal profession and thus at least equal, or even superior, to the majority of academics. All this is generally known.

Comparatists have not, however, sufficiently explored another difference which has become stark in the closing decades of the twentieth century. In the Anglo-American orbit, especially in the United States, it became at first tolerable, then fashionable, and finally expected that law professors take political positions. By contrast, academics in civil law countries continue to feel a professional obligation to remain politically neutral or at least moderate, and they rarely take openly partisan stances; their reputation is based on technical expertise, not on political activism. This reflects different attitudes vis-à-vis the relationship between law and politics. Academics in many common law countries, and particularly in North America, consider a strict separation between these spheres not only illusory but often undesirable as well. Legal academics in the civil law tradition, by contrast, by and large prefer to keep openly political considerations out of the law.

215. *The special case of notaries*. – Notaries, in the sense of lawyers in private practice vested with certain public authority, have long had a special place in the comparatists' hearts for three major reasons.[415]

First, notaries are the legal profession that most clearly distinguishes the civil from the common law tradition. While judges, a private bar, government officials, prosecutors, and academics exist in all modern legal systems, notaries as understood in the civil law orbit do not: while they can be found in most (though not in all) civil law countries they typically do not exist in common law jurisdictions (though there are some exceptions). Their (limited) public authority also exemplifies the close affinity between lawyers and state power in the civil law culture.

Second, the term "notary" is perhaps the most famous example of the linguistic pitfalls inherent in the comparative law enterprise. As has been pointed out countless times, similar legal terms can have very different meanings depending on the legal systems involved (*infra* s. 357). An English "contract" is not exactly the same as a Spanish (or Mexican) "*contrato*"; "cause" means one thing in Australia, "*causa*" quite another in Italy; and an American "notary public" is very different from a French "*notaire*". The former is not a legal professional, does not draft important legal documents, merely performs certifications of signatures and other essentially clerical functions, and enjoys no particular social prestige. The latter is a fully (and actually specially) trained lawyer, offers particular expertise in drafting important legal instruments, can provide private documents with certain, and sometimes incontrovertible, evidentiary force

[415] For a collection of essays on the history of notaries in various European (and the US-American) jurisdictions, see *Schmoeckel and Schubert* (eds.), Handbuch zur Geschichte des Notariats der europäischen Traditionen (Baden-Baden 2009).

(*publica fides*), and enjoys the status of a highly respected and trusted professional.[416]

Third, more recently, observers have noted that civil law notaries perform a preventive kind of lawyering that is largely missing in most common law jurisdictions.[417] Some have alleged, or at least speculated about, the potential benefits of notarial services. The notary's impartial counseling of the parties in the context of a major transaction discloses risks and thus minimizes misunderstandings; vesting important documents with public force makes them largely immune to later attack; and both measures can help to prevent subsequent disputes and eventual litigation.

C. AREAS OF LAW

216. *Introduction.* – Modern (i.e., twentieth- and early twenty-first-century) comparative law has dealt not only with whole legal traditions or legal systems (*supra* A.) and with their characteristic elements (*supra* B.), but also with multiple different areas of (substantive and procedural) law. In this regard as well, the discipline's coverage has become increasingly broad and diversified. During the first half of the twentieth century it was primarily preoccupied with issues of private law (*infra* i.); after World War II it expanded (ii.) and eventually came to encompass an ever growing array of subject matters, although some fields are just beginning to be addressed. This development reflects the general rise of new legal areas, such as constitutional law and human rights, to prestige and prominence.

As with the legal systems of the world, it is not the purpose of this subchapter to provide an actual comparative analysis of the various areas. That is the purpose of volumes III-XVI of this Encyclopedia. Instead, the object of this subchapter is merely to provide an overview of what comparative law has covered and accomplished – or missed.

i. *The Traditional Pre-eminence of Private Law*

217. *Introduction.* – Throughout the twentieth century, comparative law focused primarily on private law, especially on contracts and torts; in the closing decades increasingly on family law, and more sporadically on property rights, succession, labor law, and other topics. In part, this simply reflected the centuries-long prominence of private law in both the civil and the common traditions. In part, it was driven by the great practical importance of private law in general and of conflict of laws in particular.

Until about the 1950s, when comparative law scholarship was mainly at home in continental Europe, the predominance of private law was nearly overwhelming. On the continent, it has largely lingered even after World War II,[418] albeit in reduced form. When Konrad Zweigert and Hein Kötz published their magisterial treatise in 1969, it seemed almost natural that it provided an "Introduction to Comparative Law in the Field of Private Law".[419] In fact, towards the century's end, the engagement especially with that field was vigorously reaffirmed in the project of a common private law for Europe (*infra* g.).

The situation was somewhat different on the other side of the Atlantic. When the discipline established itself in the United States after World War II, private law remained important[420] but it soon acquired powerful competition as scholars increasingly engaged with other areas. They now tended to focus especially on procedure, the law of the economy, and, eventually, constitutional law.

[416] *Brown*, The Office of the Notary in France, 2 I.C.L.Q. 60–71 (1953).

[417] *Mattei*, Regole Sicure: Analisi Economico-guiridica Comparata per il Notariato (Milan 2006); *Murray*, The Civil Law Notary: Neutral Lawyer for the Situation (München 2010); see also *Malavet*, Counsel for the Situation: The Latin Notary, a Historical and Comparative Model: 19 Hastings Int.Comp.L.Rev. 389–488 (1996).

[418] See, e.g., *David*, Droit Civil Comparé (Paris 1950).

[419] *Zweigert and Kötz, Einführung in die Rechtsvergleichung auf dem Gebiete des Privatrechts* (2 vol.) (Tübingen 1969–1971). Other contemporary introductions also often continue the traditional focus on private law, see, e.g., *Laithier*, Droit Comparé (Paris 2009); *Müller-Chen, Müller and Lüchinger* (*supra* n. 286); *Candian and Gambaro* (eds.), Casiet materiali per un corso di diritto privato comparato (Torino 2016).

[420] See e.g. *Von Mehren* (*supra* n. 268); *Gordley and Von Mehren*, An Introduction to the Comparative Study of Private Law (Cambridge 2006).

This American addition of topics, in turn, induced a similar broadening of the discipline's coverage in many other parts of the world, including Europe. As a result, on a global scale comparative lawyers nowadays probably still pay the majority of their attention to private law issues, but it is no longer the absolute majority of a century ago.[421]

a. Obligations (Contract, Tort and Unjust Enrichment)

218. *Contracts (including sales)*. – Just as private law has been modern comparative law's most popular area, so contracts have been the discipline's most favored topic within private law. This Encyclopedia devotes two entire volumes to contracts;[422] Zweigert and Kötz allocated more than half of their second volume to them;[423] the drive for a common private law of Europe in the 1990s and early 2000s centered around contract law; and the comparative literature on the topic is vast and rapidly growing.[424] In short, for comparatists, contract law has long been something of a "classical subject",[425] and introductions to the discipline often continue to consider it a quasi-natural primary focus.[426]

The centrality of contract law is mainly due to four reasons. One is tradition: contracts have been at the core of the civil lawyer's universe since Roman times and all the way to the modern civil codes, which usually devote more space to that topic than to any other; on the common law side, contract law has been a central concern as well, albeit only since the later nineteenth century, when freedom of contract became a fundamental credo of the liberal state and of the market economy. The second reason is practical utility: the enormous number and importance of transnational transactions (especially between businesses) demand an understanding of contract law in other systems; comparative studies have often met that demand. The third reason is related to the second and also eminently practical: cross-border transactions can be hindered by a diversity of regimes; in response, comparatists have long been instrumental in the international harmonization and even unification of contract law (see *infra* V.B.iv., ss. 302–308). The last reason is academic suitability: mainly for historical reasons, contract rules in the civil and common law are both similar enough to make comparison fairly easy and different enough to make it rewarding; in other words, contracts are an almost ideal topic for manageable and yet interesting work.

Comparative studies in contract law have pursued three major directions. The first is essentially academic: scholars have repeatedly searched for internationally shared features of contract law, i.e., for a "common core", first in Rudolf Schlesinger's large-scale research project in the 1960s (*infra* VI.C.ii., s. 375),[427] later within the framework of the "Common Core of European Private Law" led

[421] Several modern introductions continue this tradition: see *Laithier* (*supra* n. 419); *Müller-Chen, Müller and Lüchinger* (*supra* n. 286).

[422] *Von Mehren* (ed.), Contracts in General: Int.Enc. Comp.L. VII (2008); *Zweigert and Lorenz* (eds.), Specific Contracts: Int.Enc.Comp.L. VIII (1973, 1980, 1983, 1999, 2012: 5 ch.). In addition, there is *Ziegel* (ed.), Commercial Transactions and Institutions: Int.Enc. Comp.L. IX (1979, 1991, 1996, 2000: 4 ch.).

[423] *Zweigert and Kötz* (*supra* n. 419) II 1–245.

[424] The classical study is *Gorla*, Il contratto (Milano 1954). Recent additions to the list of works on comparative contract law in general include *Beale et al.*, Cases and Materials on Contract Law (ed. 2 Oxford 2010); *Bussani and Infantino*, Diritto europeo dei contratti (Milano 2012); *Cabrillac*, Droit européen comparé des contrats (Paris 2012); *Chen-Wishart* (ed.), Studies in the Contract Laws of Asia: Remedies for Breach of Contract (Oxford 2016); *Graziano* (*supra* n. 52); *Kosolchyk*, Comparative Commercial Contracts: Law, Culture and Economic Development (ed. 2 St. Paul MN 2019); *Kovac*, Comparative Contract Law and Economics (Northampton MA 2011); *Levasseur*, Comparative Law of Contracts (Durham, NC 2008); *Markesinis, Lorenz and Dannemann*, The German Law of Obligations I: The Law of Contracts and Restitution (Oxford 1997); *Marsh*, Comparative Contract Law: England, France, Germany (Aldershot, Brookfield VT 1994); *Smits*, Contract Law: A Comparative Introduction (Cheltenham, Northampton MA 2014). In addition, there is a large number of books, and a veritable deluge of law review articles, on particular issues of contract law.

[425] *Farnsworth*, Comparative Contract Law: *Reimann and Zimmermann* (eds.), The Oxford Handbook of Comparative Law (Oxford 2006) 899–935, 900.

[426] See, e.g., *Laithier* (*supra* n. 419) 89–162; *Schwenzer and Müller-Chen*, Rechtsvergleichung (Tübingen 1996) 1–185.

[427] *Schlesinger* (*supra* n. 230).

by Ugo Mattei and Mauro Bussani (*infra* VI.C.ii., s. 376).[428] The second major direction is more practical: for many decades comparatists have pursued the international harmonization or even unification of contract law; this pursuit has taken place both on the global level as in the *UNIDROIT Principles of International Commercial Contracts*[429] and in the European context as in the *Principles of European Contract Law*.[430] The third direction consists of tracing the transboundary influence of contract law, especially of borrowing by one system from another; it is well documented that contract law has been a particularly fertile field for legal transplants.[431] In addition to these major branches, there are myriad studies dealing with a large variety of topics ranging from different conceptions of contract to the intricacies of contract formation, and from principles of performance to sanctions for breach.[432] Some studies have also focused on the distinction between civil and commercial contracts which can be found in many systems but not in all;[433] others have described and variously explained traditional discrepancies in drafting style and contract length.[434]

The enormous wealth of studies notwithstanding, comparative contract law has often been limited in three important regards. First, its focus has been, again, overwhelmingly on the law of developed countries, especially on the differences between the civil and common law, although in the latter half of the twentieth century socialist contract law was studied as well. Other regions, and especially non-Western legal cultures, have received scant attention.[435] Second, most studies deal with general contract issues, not with particular types of agreements. The big exception to that rule is the law of sales,[436] especially with regard to the creation of internationally uniform rules.[437] Unification efforts in sales law go back to the 1930s, continued after World War II, and eventually resulted in the UN Convention on the International Sale of Goods (CISG) of 1980. The law of sales is also at the center of the recent drive for a uniform European contract law.[438] Yet, there is little comparative work on other types of contracts,[439] despite the enormous economic importance of, e.g., licensing agreements, commercial service contracts, or all sorts of consumer deals. Last but not least, the vast majority of comparative studies remain on the level of blackletter law. While they typically include not only statutes but also court decisions, empirical work is exceedingly rare. As a result, we know a lot about contract rules in the major systems but very little about similarities and differences in actual contract practice.

219. *Torts (including products liability)*. – Like contracts, torts have been a major area of comparative research, especially since the middle of the twentieth century. This Encyclopedia devotes

[428] The project has generated a small library of studies on contract law, including *Gordley* (ed.), The Enforceability of Promises in European Contract Law (Cambridge 2001); *Cartwright and Hesselink* (eds.), Precontractual Liability in European Private Law (Cambridge 2009); *Hondius and Grigoleit* (eds.), Unexpected Circumstances in European Contract Law (Cambridge 2011); *Sefton-Green* (ed.), Mistake, Fraud and Duties to Inform in European Contract Law (Cambridge 2005); *Zimmermann and Whittaker* (eds.), Good Faith in European Contract Law (Cambridge 2000).

[429] *Lando et al.* (*supra* n. 371).

[430] *Lando et al.* (*supra* n. 371); see also *Kötz*, Europäisches Vertragsrecht (Tübingen 1996 and ed. 2 2015).

[431] See, e.g., *Riesenfeld* (*supra* n. 172); *Simpson*, Innovation in Nineteenth Century Contract Law: 91 L.Q.R. 247–278 (1975).

[432] See, e.g., Symposium: Contract Law in a Changing World: 40 Am.J.Comp.L. 541–728 (1992).

[433] *Tallon*, Civil Law and Commercial Law: Int.Enc. Comp.L. VIII ch. 2 (1983).

[434] *Langbein*, Comparative Civil Procedure and the Style of Complex Contracts: 35 Am.J.Comp.L. 381–394 (1987).

[435] Vol. VII of this Encyclopedia is an exception in that it includes chapters on the Far East (ch. 6) and the Middle East, including Islamic law (ch. 7). Another exception is the study by *Kosolchyk* (*supra* n. 424).

[436] *Davies and Snyder*, International Transactions in Goods: Global Sales in Comparative Context (Oxford 2014); *Schwenzer, Hachem and Kee*, Global Sales and Contract Law (Oxford 2012).

[437] *Huber*, Comparative Law of Sales: *Reimann and Zimmermann* (eds.), The Oxford Handbook of Comparative Law (ed. 2 Oxford 2019) 933–960.

[438] See, e.g., *Dannemann and Vogenauer* (eds.), The Common European Sales Law in Context (Oxford 2013).

[439] Again, this Encyclopedia is an exception, see *Zweigert and Lorenz* (*supra* n. 422).

its own massive volume to the topic;[440] standard introductions usually cover torts;[441] entire casebooks deal with their comparison;[442] the literature on specific issues or countries is already extensive, and it keeps accumulating at a frightening pace.[443] Unsurprisingly, the original focus was on the major differences between the classic civil and common law jurisdictions.[444] More recently, however, other areas of the world have gradually been included,[445] especially with regard to product liability law (*infra*)

The reason for the topic's popularity is similar to those underlying the comparative study of contracts. To begin with, non-contractual liability has been a central concern in the civil law tradition since the *lex acquilia* (probably 286 B.C.) as well as in the common law since the medieval writs for (various forms of) trespass.[446] Furthermore, compensation especially for accidents is a problem in all legal systems, and since in today's mobile society and economy accidents often involve foreign parties or countries, an understanding of how other legal systems handle them is a practical necessity for many courts, business enterprises as well their insurance companies and lawyers. In addition, there are efforts to harmonize or even unify tort law as well (though only on the European level, see *infra*), which requires its comparative study. Finally, torts, again like contracts, are fertile terrain for comparison because, at least in developed societies, accident fact patterns are often highly similar, and the principles and rules governing delictual liability are a curious mix of similarities and differences. Beyond all that, comparative tort law is particularly intriguing because it invites reflection upon social policies pertaining, inter alia, to risk management (private or public?), insurance (individual or collective?), the role of courts (expansive or restrained?), economic efficiency (ex ante accident avoidance or ex post compensation?), and the relationship between tort and criminal liability (connected or strictly separate?).

Comparative tort law has analyzed a list of major differences between legal systems, many of which again coincide with the civil v. common law divide, although more careful differentiations are often in order. The most obvious difference is that civil law systems tend to base their regimes of delictual liability on general clauses (famously in Articles 1382 and 1383, now Art. 1240 (revised version) of the French *Code civil*), while common law jurisdictions embrace a pluralistic catalog of individualized torts (derived from the older forms of action). This difference, however, is easily overrated since even civil law countries also often distinguish different kinds of wrongs (see, e.g., §§ 823–853 of the German *BGB*), while in the common law the modern action for negligence now broadly dominates the field (having swallowed up several of the more specific torts). Legal systems also vary in their commitment to fault-based or strict liability – and in the construction and application of these concepts.[447] Moreover, there are significant differences regarding the scope of protected interests. Many tort regimes compensate only for damage resulting from the infringement of particular rights, often disagreeing whether certain rights lying beyond the traditional hard core

[440] *Tunc* (ed.), Torts: Int.Enc.Comp.L. XI (1983: part XI/1, 1986: part XI/2).

[441] See, e.g., *Zweigert and Kötz* (*supra* n. 419) II, 313–430; *Laithier* (*supra* n. 419) 163–221; *Gordley and von Mehren* (*supra* n. 420) 234–412; *Schwenzer and Müller-Chen* (*supra* n. 426) 187–302.

[442] See, e.g., *Van Gerven, Lever and Larouche*, Cases, Materials and Text on National, Supranational and International Tort Law (Oxford, Portland OR 2000).

[443] A good overview of the major themes is provided by *Wagner*, Comparative Tort Law: *Reimann and Zimmermann* (eds.), The Oxford Handbook of Comparative Law (ed. 2 Oxford 2019) 994–1030; see also *Magnus*, Tort Law in General: *Smits* (ed.), Elgar Encyclopedia of Comparative Law (ed. 2 Cheltenham, Northampton MA 2012) 873–885.

[444] See, e.g., *Lawson and Markesinis*, Tortious Liability for Unintentional Harm in the Common and the Civil Law (2 vol.) (Cambridge, New York 1982); *Markesinis et al.*, Compensation for Personal Injury in English, German, and Italian Law (Cambridge 2005); *Markesinis, Lorenz and Dannemann,* The German Law of Obligations II: The Law of Torts (Oxford 1997).

[445] See, e.g., *Bussani and Sebok* (eds.), Comparative Tort Law, Part III – Nonwestern Perspectives (Cheltenham, Northampton MA 2015).

[446] On the development of tort law in Europe, see *Bell and Ibbetson*, European Legal Development: The Case of Tort (Cambridge, New York 2012).

[447] *Werro and Palmer* (eds.), The Boundaries of Strict Liability in European Tort Law (Durham NC 2004).

(life, physical integrity, property), such as personality rights, are included;[448] other tort regimes also cover damage not resulting from the violation of a protected right, i.e., "pure economic loss".[449] Considerable variations also exist with regard to the kinds and amounts of damages allowed. For example, most common law regimes permit punitive damages (though they are rarely imposed in practice, even in the United States), while most civil law systems do not (though there are various other means to punish a wrongdoer through tort law), and some systems are more willing than others to compensate for non-pecuniary loss.[450] Finally, the size of actual awards varies greatly across jurisdictions, with the United States being notorious for its large tort judgments, even though much of the information about them is misleading.

To overcome these, and other, differences, comparatists have made significant efforts at harmonization or even unification of tort law as well. In contrast to sales, however, these efforts have been largely intra-European,[451] and even here the practical need for unification remains much more contested than with regard to contracts. In the closing decades of the last century, harmonization in one important area was accomplished under the 1985 EC Directive on products liability.[452] Since then, however, little progress has been made on the political and legislative level. As a result, the momentum shifted to the academic side. Two actors have been particularly involved. One is the European Group on Tort Law (established in 1992, also known as the "Tilburg Group"); in 2005, it published its Principles of European Tort Law.[453] The other is the European Centre for Tort and Insurance Law (founded in Vienna in 1999); it has generated an impressive series of studies on the unification of various aspects of torts. In addition, the Common Core of European Private Law project centered in Trento and Torino has produced several volumes on European tort law as well.[454]

Like sales in comparative contract law, products liability has recently developed into a subfield in its own right in comparative tort law.[455] This development was driven by a combination of factors: the field's great practical importance (all modern societies regularly face problems with defective products which often come from abroad, triggering international litigation); the broad global influence of US-American law (both as a model and as a deterrent); and the harmonization of the law in Europe under the 1985 EEC Directive mentioned above. Over the last three decades there has been a global trend towards convergence of the blackletter rules governing liability for defective products, although the differences in their practical effect often remain vast.[456]

448 *Brüggemeier, Colombi Ciacchi and O'Callaghan (eds.)*, Personality Rights in European Tort Law (Cambridge 2010).

449 *Bussani and Palmer* (eds.), Pure Economic Loss in Europe (Cambridge 2003); *Van Boom, Koziol and Witting* (eds.), Pure Economic Loss (Wien, New York 2004).

450 *Rogers* (ed.), Damages for Non-Pecuniary Loss in Comparative Perspective (Wien, New York 2001).

451 *Bussani* (ed.), European Tort Law – Eastern and Western Perspectives (Berne, Brussels, Athens 2007); *Magnus and Spier* (eds.), European Tort Law (Frankfurt, New York 2000); *Oliphant and Steininger* (eds.), European Tort Law: Basic Texts (Wien 2011); *Von Bar*, Gemeineuropäisches Deliktsrecht (2 vol.) (München 1996 and 1999); English translation: The Common European Law of Torts (2 vol.) (Oxford 1998 and 2000); *Van Dam*, European Tort Law (ed. 2 Oxford 2013).

452 EU member states had to harmonize their laws under Directive 85/374/EEC of 25 July 1985 on the approximation of the laws, regulations and administrative provisions of the Member States concerning liability for defective products.

453 *European Group on Tort Law*, Principles of European Tort Law. Text and Commentary (Wien, New York 2005).

454 Supra notes 447-449.

455 See, e.g., *Fairgrieve*, Product Liability in Comparative Perspective (Cambridge, New York 2005); *Howells*, Comparative Product Liability (Aldershot 1993); *Kellam*, Products Liability in the Asia-Pacific (3d ed. Sydney 2009); *Koziol et al.* (eds), Product Liability: Fundamental Questions in Comparative Perspective (Berlin, Boston MA 2017); *Machnikowski* (ed.), European Product Liability: An Analysis of the State of the Art in the Era of New Technologies (Cambridge 2016); *Nottage and Thanitcul* (eds.), ASEAN Product Liability and Consumer Product Safety Law (Bankok 2016); *Stapleton*, Products Liability (London, Boston MA 1994).

456 *Reimann*, Liability for Defective Products and Services: Emergence of a Worldwide Standard?: Convergence of Legal Systems in the 21st Century, General Reports Delivered at the XVIth International Congress of Comparative Law (Brussels 2006) 367–539.

While comparative tort law is thus highly developed, it needs to look more frequently beyond the substantive rules governing civil liability and to investigate more closely how compensation for accidents actually works. Three improvements would be particularly beneficial. First, tort law must be regarded more consistently in the context of other compensation systems. Its practical role and function can only be understood in conjunction especially with private and public insurance schemes. Several more recent studies have already taken such a contextual approach.[457] Second, substantive law must be analyzed within the institutional and procedural framework of a given legal system.[458] How tort law really operates often depends less on its own rules than on a variety of environmental factors, such as the strength of the regulatory apparatus, the structure and posture of the bar, the cost and fee rules applicable in litigation, the availability (or at least threat) of trial by jury, and public attitudes towards risk and responsibility.[459] Depending on these factors, even strict liability rules may not help accident victims much at all in one system, while a fault-based approach may put defendants' feet to the fire in another. Third, as with regard to contracts, there is a great need for more empirical work. To compare how accident compensation functions across legal systems, one must compare who claims (or fails to do so), who wins (or loses), how much money is awarded (and whether it is actually paid), whether victims are undercompensated (and to what degree), etc. In many legal systems, such as Japan, the United States, and several European countries, empirical data are quite readily available; so far, however, comparatists have made far too little use of them.

220. *Unjust enrichment (and negotiorum gestio)*. – For most of the twentieth century the law of unjust enrichment was a comparative law backwater, at least when compared to contracts and torts. In 1969, *Zweigert and Kötz* addressed it at some length, but that was one of the few exceptions to the rule of neglect.[460]

The reason for this neglect was not only that the field was of limited practical importance but also that formidable differences between the civil and common law approaches made meaningful comparison extremely difficult. In the civil law, unjust enrichment has long been recognized as a cause of action in its own right, whereas in the common law it was often conceived merely as the underlying reason for various causes of action based on quasi-contract, constructive trust, equitable liens, etc., and for providing restitution remedies. Civil lawyers have seen unjust enrichment as a more or less coherent area of the law, while common lawyers often did not regard it as a distinct field at all. Civil law jurisdictions (especially in the German tradition) developed highly refined conceptual frameworks, while in common law systems doctrinal and terminological confusion reigned supreme. In continental Europe the field was constantly refined, but in England and especially in the United States it gradually fell into disregard – and disrepair. As a result, civil lawyers and common lawyers eventually found it hard even to communicate about the topic.

Yet, since the last decade of the twentieth century, unjust enrichment has become a widely discussed subject in comparative law. Its rise to prominence was as sudden as it was surprising. It was mainly the result of two developments.

The first development was an awakening in the common law world. In the United Kingdom, the House of Lords, inspired by recent scholarship, recognized unjust enrichment as a cause of action in its own right; in the United States, the

[457] *Wagner* (*supra* n. 443) 1023–1028; see also *Faure*, Accident Compensation: *Smits* (ed.), Elgar Encyclopedia of Comparative Law (ed. 2 Cheltenham, Northampton, MA 2012) 1–20; *Magnus* (ed.), The Impact of Social Security on Tort Law (Wien, New York 2003); *Ebert*, Tort Law and Insurance: *Bussani and Sebok* (eds.), Comparative Tort Law, Part III – Nonwestern Perspectives (Cheltenham, Northampton MA 2015) 144–150; *Jutras*, Alternative Compensation Schemes as Comparative Law: *Bussani and Sebok* (eds.), Comparative Tort Law, Part III – Nonwestern Perspectives (Cheltenham, Northampton MA 2015) 151–170.

[458] See *Fleming*, The Torts Process (Oxford 1988).

[459] A commendable and impressive effort in that direction is *McClurg, Koyuncu and Sprovieri*, Practical Global Tort Litigation (Durham NC 2007).

[460] *Zweigert and Kötz* (*supra* n. 419) II 246–312; the analysis has been updated, *Zweigert and Kötz* (*supra* n. 3) 538–596. Another, earlier, exception was *Dawson*, Unjust Enrichment: A Comparative Analysis (Boston MA 1951).

project of a new Restatement of Restitution and Unjust Enrichment (Third) was launched; and especially in England (as well as in several mixed jurisdictions) scholars began to write about the topic with renewed vigor and sometimes from a comparative perspective.[461] As a result, there was new and interesting material on the common law side for comparative lawyers to work with. Scholars seized the opportunity, and in just about two decades they produced a wealth of studies, including volume X of this Encyclopedia.[462] Most of these studies focus on comparing the doctrine and decisions in civil law, common law and mixed jurisdictions,[463] but some also deal with historical developments and underlying theory.[464]

The second development boosting comparative scholarship on unjust enrichment was the push for a common private law of Europe. The resulting search for common denominators spawned a variety of impressive studies.[465] To be sure, the doctrinal differences not only between the common law and the civil law approaches but also among several continental legal systems are still formidable, and it remains to be seen whether they can be overcome.[466] Still, even if unification remains elusive, it is generally recognized today that unjust enrichment is an area in which legal systems have a lot to learn from each other and in which much needs to be done.

Negotiorum gestio is often closely associated with unjust enrichment[467] but it has not been frequently studied from a comparative perspective; the major exception is its discussion in this Encyclopedia.[468] Yet, *negotiorum gestio* is often mentioned by comparatists, namely as one of the few instances of private law where a concept firmly established in the continental tradition has no direct counterpart on the Anglo-American side. What is more, this difference actually reflects a fundamental disagreement about principle: while the civil law provides the good Samaritan with a claim for expenses, the common law considers him or her an "officious intermeddler" and thus refuses to compensate. It is true that once all the special rules and exceptions are taken into account the practical results are often similar, but the core disagreement remains, and it is difficult to explain.

b. *Property*

221. *In general.* – Like unjust enrichment, property law used to enjoy fairly limited attention throughout most of the twentieth century. To be sure, particularly towards its end, there was some comparative work in property law, volume VI of this Encyclopedia prominently among it.[469] Also, during the post-World War II decades,

[461] Most importantly *Birks*, Unjust Enrichment (ed 2. Oxford 2005).

[462] *Von Caemmerer and Schlechtriem* (eds.), Restitution/Unjust Enrichment and Negotiorum Gestio: Int. Enc.Comp.L X (2007).

[463] See, e.g., *Johnston and Zimmermann* (eds.), Unjust Enrichment: Key Issues in Comparative Perspective (Cambridge, New York 2002); *Markesinis, Lorenz and Dannemann* (*supra* n. 424); *Gallo*, Unjust Enrichment: A Comparative Analysis: 40 Am.J.Comp.L. 431–465 (1992). This is also true for the casebook by *Beatson and Schrage* (eds.), Cases, Materials and Texts on Unjustified Enrichment (Oxford, Portland OR 2003).

[464] *Schrage*, Unjust Enrichment: The Comparative Legal History of the Law of Restitution (ed. 2 Berlin 1999); *Dagan*, Unjust Enrichment: A Study of Private Law and Public Values (Cambridge, New York 1997); *Dagan*, The Law and Ethics of Restitution (Cambridge, New York 2004).

[465] *Schlechtriem*, Restitution und Bereicherungsausgleich in Europa. Eine rechtsvergleichende Darstellung (2 vols) (Tübingen 2000 and 2001); *Zimmermann* (ed.), Grundstrukturen eines europäischen Bereicherungsrechts (Baden-Baden 2003); see also *Schäfer*, Das Bereicherungsrecht in Europa: Einheits- und Trennungslehren im gemeinen, deutschen und englischen Recht (Tübingen 2001).

[466] While the analysis by *Zweigert and Kötz* (*supra* n. 460) remains relevant, it does not reflect the developments since 1996; a more up-to-date overview is provided by *Visser*, Unjust Enrichment in Comparative Perspective: *Reimann and Zimmermann* (eds.), The Oxford Handbook of Comparative Law (2d ed. Oxford 2019) 961–993.

[467] See *Visser* (*supra* n. 466) 977–978.

[468] *Stoljar*, Negotiorum Gestio: Int.Enc.Comp.L. X ch. 17 (2007); see also *Dawson*, *Negotiorum Gestio*: The Altruistic Intermeddler: 74 Harv.L.Rev. 817–865 (1961); *Whitty and Van Zyl*, Unauthorized Management of Affairs (*Negotiorum Gestio*): *Zimmermann, Visser and Reid.* (eds.), Mixed Legal Systems in Comparative Perspective (Oxford, New York 2004), 366–398.

[469] *Lawson and Yiannopoulos* (eds.), Property and Trust (Tübingen 1971 ss.).

considerable interest arose in socialist conceptions of property, although that interest waned after the fall of socialism in Europe. It may thus be too strong to say that comparatists "seem to have avoided property law".[470] Still, attention to the field long lagged behind the law of obligations.[471]

This relatively low popularity had three major reasons. To begin with, in most countries property law is highly technical. Comparative work thus requires mastery of (at least two jurisdictions') usually very complex and mechanical rule systems. This makes for high barriers to entry which few comparatists have overcome. Perhaps more importantly, for historical reasons, property law in the two major legal families is structured so differently that meaningful comparison is much more difficult than in contracts or torts. On the civil law side, the field is characterized by a categorical distinction of real (absolute) from personal (relative) rights, by the (originally Roman) absolute concept of ownership, and by the principle of a *numerus clausus* of real rights. In the common law, the subject has traditionally been organized as a system of tenures and estates which is hard to grasp for the civilian mind; property rights are in principle all relative (i.e., about who has superior title); and there is a basic division between rights in law and rights in equity which has no direct counterpart in the continental legal culture. A third reason for the relatively weak attention to the field throughout most of the twentieth century is that until recently there were almost no efforts to harmonize or unify property law on an international or even European scale. Thus, there was little need for comparative work for that purpose. All this made the field look rather technical, static, and uninspiring.

Yet, again as with unjust enrichment, comparative property law has become much more popular since the end of the last century. In part this was simply due to the general expansion of comparative legal studies which brought property law more consistently within view of the discipline.[472] In large part, however, new interest in the field was also triggered by a variety of more distinct factors. The integration of global markets created an increasing need to understand, and to harmonize, the multitude of property systems, although that mainly concerned aspects of particular commercial importance, such as trusts (*infra* s. 222) and security rights (*infra* s. 223). The growing interest in mixed legal systems[473] and especially in European private law extended to property issues well.[474] And the rise of law and economics raised interesting questions about property rights that invited comparative analysis.[475] As a result, comparative property law is now a fully active field, although not on the level of contracts and torts.

[470] *Van Erp*, Comparative Property Law: *Reimann and Zimmermann* (eds.), The Oxford Handbook of Comparative Law (ed. 2 Oxford 2019) 1031–1057, 1032.

[471] Note that, for example, neither *Zweigert and Kötz* (*supra* n. 3) in Germany, nor *Von Mehren and Gordley*, The Civil Law System (Bston 1977) paid it much attention, although *Arminjon, Nolde and Wolff* (*supra* n. 270) in France and *Sacco*, Introduzione al Diritto Comparato (ed. 5 Torino 1991) in Italy included it.

[472] See, e.g., *Gordley and Von Mehren* (*supra* n. 420) 157–213; *Van Vliet*, Transfer of Movables in German, French, English and Dutch Law (Nijmegen 2000); *Micheler*, Property in Securities: A Comparative Study (Cambridge 2007). For a short overview, see *Milo*, Property and Real Rights: *Smits* (ed.), Elgar Encyclopedia of Comparative Law (ed. 2 Cheltenham, Northampton MA 2012) 726–743. See also *Van Maanen and Van der Walt* (eds.), Property Law on the Threshold of the 21st Century (Antwerp 2006), esp. 213–414; *Kieninger*, Sachenrechtliche Prinzipien und Grundbegriffe als Gegenstände der Rechtsvergleichung: *Zimmermann* (ed.), Zukunftsperspektiven der Rechtsgleichung (Tübingen 2016) 139–166; *Graziadei and Smith* (eds.), Comparative Property Law: Global Perspectives (Cheltenham, Northampton MA 2017). For studies focusing primarily on former socialist countries in Europe as well as on China, see (Colloque) Actualités de la Propriété D'Europe Centrale et Orientale et en Chine: Rev.int.dr.comp. 49 (1997) 527–625

[473] *Zimmermann, Visser and Reid* (*supra* n. 276) 637–848.

[474] *Von Bar*, Gemeineuropäisches Sachenrecht (2 vol.) (München 2019); *Von Bar and Drobnig*, The Interaction of Contract Law and Property Law in Europe: A Comparative Study (München 2004); *Drobnig*, Transfer of Property: *Hartkamp* (ed.), Towards a European Civil Code (ed. 4 Alphen aan den Rijn 2011) 1003–1024; *Drobnig*, Security Rights in Moveables: *idem* 1024–1042; *Sagaert*, Harmonization of Security Rights in Immovables: An Ongoing Story: *idem* 1042–1063; *Salomons*, Good Faith Acquisition in Movables: *idem* 1065–1082.

[475] *Mattei*, Basic Principles of Property Law: A Comparative Legal and Economic Analysis (Westport CT, London 2000).

222. *Trusts.* – No other element of property law has fascinated comparatists more than the trust.[476] They have dealt with it in two main contexts, one academic, the other practical.

In the academic context, the trust has been a comparative law classic as a characteristic feature of Anglo-American law.[477] As such, it brings the dichotomy as well as the complementarity of law and equity into particularly sharp relief; and it illustrates the ability of the common law to respond to practical needs with great ingenuity and flexibility. At the same time, the trust is a paradigmatic example of an institution that initially looks unique to a particular legal tradition but that soon turns out to have relatives in many other parts of the world. In several mixed jurisdictions, and even in some civil law systems, there are similar institutions, often based on the Roman *fiducia*;[478] and in many other traditions (including Islamic law) we find at least functional equivalents of trusts for particular purposes.[479]

In the more practical context, comparatists have recognized that the trust has recently gained prominence as a result of financial globalization. Historically designed as a means for estate planning and charitable purposes, in the last few decades the trust has also become a hugely important instrument for securitization and international investment. This has motivated comparative research on commercial trusts, especially in connection with the study of European private law.[480]

223. *Security rights.* – Credit transactions usually require collateral, and since such transactions are often transboundary today, there is an increasing need to understand (personal and real) security rights in foreign jurisdictions. Comparatists have begun to respond to that need by creating a growing literature on secured transactions law, both in the European context and on the more global level.[481] In addition, since the great diversity of national laws governing this area creates serious uncertainties and other transaction costs for international business, efforts have been made to harmonize these laws or even to create uniform regimes, as in the UNIDROIT (Cape Town) Convention on International Interests in Mobile Equipment of 2001 (in force 2004).

c. *Family Law*

224. *Difficulty and Necessity.* – In the comparative study of private law family law has a somewhat special status because it constantly operates between inherent difficulty and practical necessity.

The difficulty results mainly from the fact that family law is much more (directly and visibly) contingent on culture, religion, social policy, and in some contexts also on ethnicity and race, than the more "neutral" law of the market, i.e., contract, tort, and even property. While the latter can plausibly be dealt with on a fairly technical level, one cannot ignore that, at its core, "[f]amily law is a political discourse".[482] As a result, it has often been doubted whether it is fit for comparative study at all.[483] Such doubts were particularly strong in the first half of the twentieth century,

[476] See *Fratcher*, Trust: Int.Enc.Comp.L VI, ch. 11 (1973); other studies include *Lupoi*, Trusts: A Comparative Study (Cambridge, New York 2000); *Kötz*, Trust und Treuhand (Göttingen 1963). For a shorter account, see *De Waal*, Trust Law: *Smits* (ed.), Elgar Encyclopedia of Comparative Law (ed. 2 Cheltenham, Northampton MA 2012) 926–939.

[477] "Stiltypisches Element des anglo-amerikanischen Rechtskreises", *Zweigert and Kötz* (*supra* n. 277) 328.

[478] *Helmholz and Zimmermann* (eds.), Itinera Fiduciae: Trust and Treuhand in Historical Perspective (Berlin 1998).

[479] *Fratcher* (*supra* n. 476) Part V, 84–115; *Lupoi* (*supra* n. 476) 287–300.

[480] *Graziadei, Mattei and Smith* (eds.), Commercial Trusts in European Private Law (Cambridge 2005); *Hayden, Kortmann and Verhagen*, Principles of European Trust Law (The Hague, Deventer 1999).

[481] *Kieninger* (ed.), Security Rights in Moveable Property in European Private Law (Cambridge 2005); *Tajti*, Comparative Secured Transactions Law (Budapest 2002); *Veneziano*, Le garanzie mobiliari non-possesorie: profili di diritto comparato e di diritto del commercio internazionale (Milano 2000); *Wood*, Comparative Law of Security and Guarantees (London 1999). For a brief overview, see *Van Erp*, Personal and Real Security: *Smits* (ed.), Elgar Encyclopedia of Comparative Law (ed. 2 Cheltenham, Northampton MA 2012) 647–660.

[482] *Bradley*, Family Law: *Smits* (ed.), Elgar Encyclopedia of Comparative Law (ed. 2 Cheltenham, Northampton MA 2012) 314–338.

[483] *Idem* 314–325.

when comparative law was largely conceived as a tool to build a "droit commun legislatif", i.e., when legal unification was the discipline's most prominent goal. Indeed, comprehensive unification is particularly difficult – and perhaps unachievable – in a field so closely tied to national sentiments and current politics. But even beyond unification, family law poses unusual challenges for comparative law. Its cultural contingency and overtly socio-political nature hinder convergence among jurisdictions and complicate transplants from one system to another. They also render inapplicable the orthodox expectation that legal systems solve identical problems pretty much alike, albeit often by different means (*praesumptio similitudinis*, *infra* VI.C.i., s. 372.).[484] To make matters worse, in recent decades family law has been subject to faster and more radical changes than any other core area of private law; this forces comparatists to deal with a constantly moving target.

The necessity of comparative family law results mainly from the increased mobility of people and the now constant interaction between cultures in the world. In such an environment, family law cannot limit itself to a purely national viewpoint, and comparative study is the best way to overcome that. It fosters an understanding of different family laws which is a practical necessity, inter alia for courts dealing with transboundary cases. More generally, it promotes the much-needed tolerance for diversity which is particularly important in this area.

225. *Current status.* – Today, comparative family law still lies outside the core of the discipline and constitutes a distinct specialty not meant for general consumption; the standard introductions do not include it, and it is rarely taught in the classroom. Yet, in the last few decades it has nonetheless developed into a flourishing field, as volume IV of this Encyclopedia demonstrates.[485] A cadre of specialists has produced a rich literature, even including some casebooks;[486] its study is being promoted by the International Society of Family Law (founded in 1973) which holds regular congresses; and comparative family lawyers engage with cutting edge issues from around the world.[487]

Unlike their colleagues dealing with most other areas of private law, comparative family lawyers have not focused primarily on the similarities and differences between the civil and the common law. Instead, their agenda has been shaped by the – often fundamental – changes that have occurred in virtually all Western societies during the last half-century.

226. *Major issues.* – These changes have confronted comparative family law with five main clusters of issues.[488] The first major upheaval concerned the law of marriage and divorce, which was keenly observed and incisively analyzed by eminent comparatists.[489] The main result of this upheaval was a downgrading of marriage, especially through the widespread introduction of no-fault divorce; this now often allows termination of the marriage by little more than the unilateral action of one spouse. The second significant change was the rise of alternative forms of cohabitation arrangements; they have ranged from unions that require a formal commitment as well as an ordered dissolution ("domestic" or "registered partnerships") to informal relationships to which some states attach legal consequences while others do not. A third, and closely related, development was the gradual recognition of same-sex unions by the state, be it in the form of an alternative arrangement or, increasingly,

[484] *Zweigert and Kötz* (*supra* n. 277) 36.

[485] *Chloros, Rheinstein and Glendon* (eds.), Persons and Family: Int.Enc.Comp.L IV (2007).

[486] *Blair et al.*, Family Law in the World Community (ed. 2 Durham NC 2009).

[487] See, e.g., *Boele-Woelki* (ed.), Debates in Family Law Around the Globe at the Dawn of the 21st Century (Antwerp, Portland OR 2009).

[488] For an overview, see *Scherpe*, Comparative Family Law: *Reimann and Zimmermann* (eds.), The Oxford Handbook of Comparative Law (ed. 2 Oxford 2019) 1088–1109; see also *Antonkolskaia*, Comparative Family Law: Moving with the Times?: *Örücü and Nelken* (eds.), Comparative Law: A Handbook (Oxford, Portland OR 2007) 241–262.

[489] *Rheinstein*, Marriage Stability, Divorce and the Law (Chicago IL 1972); *Glendon*, Abortion and Divorce in Western Law (Cambridge MA 1987); *Glendon*, The Transformation of Family Law: State, Law and Family in the United States and Western Europe (Chicago IL 1989); see also *Glendon*, State, Law, and Family – Family Transition in the United States and Western Europe (Amsterdam 1977); *Glendon*, The New Family and the New Property (Toronto 1981).

in full-fledged marriage; this recognition by an increasing number of legal system has stood in sharp contrast to the continued rejection in others.[490] Major changes also affected the status of children; offspring born out of wedlock were gradually granted the same rights as those born in a marriage, and custody determinations were increasingly based on a "best interest of the child" standard. A final cluster of issues concerns reproduction, especially the legal regulation of non-traditional forms; they run the gamut from artificial insemination and in vitro fertilization to embryo transfers and surrogate motherhood.

A related issue is the regulation of abortion. While it clearly has consequences in family law (e.g., regarding the rights of the father), it is usually conceived primarily as a matter of individual liberty and thus of constitutional rights. Here, as well as in many other regards, constitutional law, and in Europe also international human rights law, has had a significant, and often unifying, effect on family regulation.

227. *Recent developments.* – Comparative family law has recently been a particularly active field in Western Europe,[491] especially in the work of the (unofficial) Commission on European Family Law (CEFL). While efforts to create a common private law for Europe have been strongest in the areas of contract and tort, they have spilled over into domestic relations law as well.[492] Yet, the inclusion of family in this agenda remains contested. On the one hand, the law's cultural and political contingency suggests caution; on the other hand, the principle of freedom of movement, which is guaranteed under EU law, creates a need for harmonization of family law as well.

The massive changes in the family law of most developed countries since World War II, especially the liberalization of marriage and divorce, the concomitant implementation of equal rights for women, but also the frequent (though far from ubiquitous) recognition of same-sex unions, have created a growing rift between the West and the Rest. This is especially obvious when one looks at the jurisdictions in which family relations are governed by Islamic or other religious law. The resulting tensions have increased the need for mutual understanding and tolerance and thus for future comparative studies providing careful analysis and explanation.

d. Succession

228. *Specialty status.* – Like the comparative study of family law, that of succession regimes is a narrow specialty that most comparatists never engage with. In part this is because succession law has, largely because of its close connection with the family, sometimes also been considered so culturally contingent that its suitability for comparative study (and even more for international harmonization and unification) has been doubted. The argument is questionable because, at least in the Western world, much of succession law rests on broadly shared Roman, feudal, and especially canon law foundations. Three other reasons for the subject's status as a narrow specialty are more convincing. First, unlike contracts and torts, succession law is a field that most lawyers never enter even in the domestic context; this keeps the pool of potential comparatists small to begin with. Second, like property law, the field is complex and the devil is often in the detail; these details are hard to master, especially in more than one legal system. And, third, the intricate and sometimes arcane terminology creates further barriers to entry; this is particularly true on the common law side where the person taking property on the death of another is (strictly speaking) an "heir" in intestate succession but a "beneficiary" under a will, and where the "personal representative" of the decedent is

[490] See, e.g., *Boele-Woelki and Fuchs* (eds.), Legal Recognition of Same-Sex Couples in Europe (Antwerp, New York 2003).

[491] *Boele-Woelki and Svendrup*, European Challenges in Contemporary Family Law (Antwerp, New York 2008); *Pintens and Vanwinckelen*, Casebook: European Family Law (Leuven 2001).

[492] *Boele-Woelki, Braat and Curry-Summers*, Perspectives for the Unification and Harmonization of Family Law in Europe (Antwerp 2003); *Boele-Woelki, Braat and Curry-Summers* (eds.), Principles of European Family Law Regarding Divorce and Maintenance Between Former Spouses (Antwerp 2004); *Boele-Woelki, Braat and Curry-Summers* (eds.), Principles of European Family Law Regarding Parental Responsibility (Antwerp etc. 2007).

an "executor" if designated by will but an "administrator" if appointed by a court, etc.

229. *Status quo.* – Again like the comparative study of family law, that of succession has become increasingly relevant, especially for practical reasons. The growing mobility of people and assets entails a mass of transboundary issues and thus a need to understand (and often to coordinate) the succession laws of two or more jurisdictions. This is most obvious in the many instances raising the question which law applies in case of a dispute, but it is no less true with regard to international estate planning.

Yet, unlike the comparative study of family law, succession has not recently become a prominent topic among comparatists. The field did not experience similarly radical rule changes, did not raise high-profile policy issues, did not touch on emotional nerves, and thus remained a largely technical and passionless subject. Thus, it seems condemned to lead a "precarious existence at the outpost of the comparative law landscape".[493] Many well-known publications mainly collect material on foreign succession laws and do not engage in any in-depth comparison, although they contain a wealth of material for it.[494] Nonetheless, there are a few impressive academic studies in this field,[495] including Volume V of this Encyclopedia,[496] especially if one takes the scholarship on trusts into account (*supra* b., s. 222).

230. *Civil v. common law differences.* – Unlike the comparative study of family law, that of succession does often focus on basic differences between the civil and the common law. The former embraces the principle of universal succession, while latter allows the division of estates. In the civil law, the rule is direct devolution of the estate to the heir(s) (sometimes mandating a formal acceptance) while the common law has traditionally required a special procedure under which an intermediary (personal representative) first takes control of the estate, pays all outstanding debts, and then hands the remaining assets over to the ultimate recipient(s). Also, civil law jurisdictions restrict a testator's freedom by requiring that a "forced share" go to certain family members, while the common law has traditionally endorsed unbridled freedom of testation, although there are some (especially modern, legislative) exceptions. And jurisdictions in the continental European tradition consider wills ipso facto effective unless challenged, while the Anglo-American rule has been that they must first be "probated" (scrutinized) by a court before they are given effect, although today many exceptions are allowed in this regard as well. Last but not least, the civil law has by and large operated without the trust (again, with some exceptions), while that instrument is central to the common law of succession.

231. *Modern forms of intergenerational wealth transfer.* – Interesting as these time-honored systemic differences are for pedagogical or even practical purposes, they are increasingly overshadowed by issues arising from new forms of wealth and wealth transfer from one generation to the next.[497] Today, such wealth often consists of insurance benefits and pension rights which are passed on outside the law of succession altogether. And, at least in common law countries, the transfer of other types of assets, ranging from real estate to investments in the stock market, is often handled through trusts established during the owner's lifetime rather than through the law of succession after his or her death, thus bypassing costly and lengthy probate proceedings and formal estate administration. These developments create a dire need for a more broadly conceived comparative succession law as a field on which work has barely begun.

e. *Labor Law*

232. *Definition.* – "Labor law" is an illustration of the general phenomenon that the same term

[493] *De Waal*, Comparative Succession Law: *Reimann and Zimmermann* (eds.), The Oxford Handbook of Comparative Law (ed. 2 Oxford 2019) 1058–1087, 1086.

[494] *Ferid et al.* (eds.), Internationales Erbrecht (9 vol.) (München 1955-, looseleaf); *Gard and Wood* (eds.), International Succession (ed. 3 Oxford, New York 2010); *Hayton*, European Succession Laws (ed. 2 Bristol 2002).

[495] *De Waal* (*supra* n. 493); *Reid, De Waal and Zimmermann* (eds.), Comparative Succession Law (2 vol.) (Oxford 2011 and 2015).

[496] *Neumayer and Drobnig* (eds.), Succession (Tübingen 2018)

[497] *Langbein*, The Twentieth-Century Revolution in Family Wealth Transmission: 86 Mich.L.Rev. 722–751 (1988).

can have different meanings in different legal systems. In the vast majority of today's systems, it comprises both the law governing the individual labor relationship (between employee and employer) and the law of collective bargaining (between employers or their associations and unions); where such structures exist, it also encompasses the regulation of employee representation in the workplace. By contrast, in the United States, "labor law" has come to denote only the collective dimension, i.e., the law governing unions and their relationship with employers (including strikes, boycotts, lock-outs, and related topics); the individual side is treated as a largely separate matter, usually under the heading of employment law. For our present purposes, the term labor law is used in the more encompassing fashion embraced by the majority of the world's legal systems.

233. *Development.* – While legislation addressing labor issues dates back to the middle ages, labor law in the modern sense is a child of industrialization, and especially of the late nineteenth-century factory system. It is notable that the emergence of the field was quickly followed by its comparative study so that labor law was part of modern comparative law from the very beginning. Early comparative studies were motivated by the (then particularly urgent) need of industrialized nations to cope with newly arising labor issues and the concomitant desire to learn from other legal systems. The comparatists' early attention to labor law was facilitated by the idea that the subject still fit (at least roughly) the private law paradigm dominating the discipline around and after 1900: at its core, labor law could be regarded as a variation of contract law, albeit one increasingly subject to public regulation. As a result, there were numerous comparative labor law studies even in the early decades of the twentieth century, focusing, as was then common, on the pertinent legislation of select countries.[498] After World War II, comparative labor law continued to develop, strengthened by the foundation (in 1958) of the International Society for Labor Law and Social Security, which has held regular World Congresses for more than half a century. Today, labor law is a firmly established sub-field of comparative law[499] with its own volume in this Encyclopedia,[500] a core of almost classic treatises,[501] several specialized journals,[502] and a large number of monographs. In addition, the International Labor Organization in Geneva (ILO, founded in 1919) has published numerous reports on a variety of issues, often based on the comparative study of national systems.

234. *Functions and directions.* – The dominant agenda of comparative labor studies has been practical: the effort to learn from other legal systems how best to solve concrete problems. This is in part a cause, and in part a result, of the fact that legal systems have frequently borrowed laws and ideas in this area for well over a century. Colonies adopted the law of their metropolis; developing Asian countries imported Western labor rules; and industrialized nations have accepted transplants from each other on numerous occasions. Beyond instigating or facilitating concrete borrowing, comparative studies have also played a broader, and arguably even more important, role: they have legitimated agendas to regulate certain labor problems by showing that these problems were already regulated elsewhere[503], such as social insurance for workers (with Germany and

[498] See, e.g., *Pic*, Traité Elémentaire de Législation Industrielle (Paris 1930); *Molitor, Nipperdey and Schott*, Europäisches Arbeitsvertragsrecht (2 parts, Marburg 1928–29).

[499] *Finkin and Mundlak* (eds.), Comparative Labor Law (Cheltenham, Northampton MA 2015). For an overview, see *Finkin*, Comparative Labour Law: *Reimann and Zimmermann* (eds.), The Oxford Handbook of Comparative Law (ed. 2 Oxford 2019) 1110–1136.

[500] *Kahn-Freund* (ed.), Labour Law: Int.Enc.Comp.L XV (2014).

[501] See, e.g., *Blanpain and Engels* (eds.), Comparative Labour Law and Industrial Relations in Industrialized Market Economies (The Hague 1998); see also *Berkowitz, Reitz and Müller-Bonanni* (eds.), International Labor Employment Law (2 vol.) (Chicago IL 2008).

[502] Comparative Labor Law & Policy Journal (since 1976); International Journal of Comparative Labour Law and Industrial Relations (since 1984); Zeitschrift für ausländisches und internationales Arbeits- und Sozialrecht (since 1987); Bulletin (now Revue) de Droit Comparé du Travail et de la Sécurité Sociale (since 1981).

[503] *Finkin* (*supra* n. 499) 1134–1135.

England providing the models), gender discrimination in the workplace (following the lead of the United States), or privacy protection for employees (along European lines). In addition, comparative labor law scholars have studied a broad range of individual topics, ranging from job protection to work-time regulation and from union rights to labor dispute settlement.

Two dimensions which have played a major role in several other fields are weakly developed. Theoretical efforts are few and far between (with the exception of economic analyses of labor issues). And there has been relatively little push towards international unification of labor law (with the exception of a growing emphasis on universal human rights standards and on European Union law).

235. *The impact of European labor law.* – The original Treaty of Rome (1957, in force 1958), founding the (then) European Economic Community, already contained a mandate for the (EEC) Commission "to promote close cooperation between Member States with regard to various areas of labour law" (Art. 118), and it announced the principle of equal pay for men and women (Art. 119). Beginning in the 1970s, some Directives, addressed to the Member States, were issued in this area. Yet, European labor law really came into its own after the Maastricht Treaty (1992, in force 1993) when the European authorities began to regulate the field on an increasingly broad scale. It is true that European labor regulation is far from comprehensive because it remains limited to particular topics. Still, over time, it has affected so many important areas – ranging from working hours and part-time work to parental leave and data protection – that European labor law has become a special field of study,[504] as is illustrated by the publication of a specialized periodical, the European Labour Law Journal (since 2010).

To be sure, European labor law is not in and of itself a comparative enterprise. The respective EC (now EU) Directives are not the result of unification efforts based on the study of the Member States' laws, but rather reform projects intended to change those laws and imposed top-down. Still, the Europeanization of the field has generated a variety of comparative studies some of which were solicited by the EU authorities themselves.[505] In addition, the development of European labor law has promoted comparative perspectives by de-nationalizing, so to speak, large parts of labor law, forcing practitioners and scholars to look beyond their own legal systems. Of course, in another sense, European labor law has stifled comparative work because, where uniformity is imposed from above, it extinguishes differences between national systems, leaving little – or nothing – to compare.

236. *Twenty-first-century challenges.* – In the early twenty-first century, labor law – and thus its comparative study – has been faced with several new challenges.[506] Suffice it here to mention just four particularly important ones. First, the significant changes in labor relations caused in part by the market pressures of globalization, in part by the widespread retreat from the social state, have affected the structure of employment relationships. In particular, there has been a move away from the traditional industrial model or full-time, long-term, and relatively secure employment with generous benefits and towards part-time, short-term jobs that can be more easily terminated and carry few if any benefits. Labor law thus faces new issues, such as how to avoid evasion of protective laws through outsourcing or contracting out, and, more generally, the question whether and how to protect those in ad hoc jobs. Second, the declining degree of unionization in many countries (perhaps most dramatically in the United States) has changed the landscape of collective bargaining. Where only a small percentage of the workforce is effectively unionized, its representation in the firm (as well as on the political level) must either suffer or be organized in other ways. Third, the law of individual employment relationships has come under the increasing influence of fundamental rights, particularly those against discrimination

[504] See, e.g., *Blanpain*, European Labour Law (ed. 14 Alphen aan den Rijn 2014).

[505] See, e.g., *Supiot*, Au-delà de L'Emploi: Transformations du travail et devenir du droit du travail en Europe (Paris 1999); the English version is Beyond Employment: Changes at Work and the Future of Employment Law in Europe (Oxford, New York 2001).

[506] For an overview, see *Bronstein*, International and Comparative Labour Law. Current Challenges (Geneva 2009).

on grounds of gender, race, and nationality. This has also brought supra- and international human rights into play, especially in Europe. Finally, since the 1990s, there has been much discussion about the interrelationship between the international trade regime (especially under the WTO) on the one hand and national labor conditions and their regulation on the other. In all these regards, comparative studies can point national decision makers to solutions tried in other countries, help to bridge gaps between legal systems (including inter- and supranational regimes), and even point out avenues for harmonization.

f. The Special Case of Private International Law

237. *Symbiotic relationship with comparative law.* – Private international law (conflict of laws) is a special case because it is tied to comparative law in a quasi-symbiotic relationship. One major aspect of this relationship is that comparative law renders important services to private international law by helping it to understand the foreign law it must deal with; this helping function is not our concern here.[507] Instead, this section focuses on the other major aspect of the relationship between the two disciplines, i.e., on the comparative study of private international law principles and rules. Even in this regard, private international law is a special case because no other area of positive law has been subjected to comparative study as consistently, intensely, and productively – a mere summary of the accumulated knowledge fills more than a thousand pages constituting Volume III of this Encyclopedia.[508]

The traditional intensity of the comparative study of conflicts law is largely due to three factors. The first is that both fields deal with foreign law and thus presume similar interests and skills; as mentioned (*supra* II.A.i., s. 19), many private international lawyers have also (in part simply by necessity) been comparatists. Second, in private international law there has long been an almost globally shared set of basic doctrines and principles that have greatly facilitated the comparison of individual variations and deviations. Finally, the need for international harmonization and unification is particularly strong in private international law: where substantive laws differ among jurisdictions, we urgently need internationally uniform rules deciding which of these laws to apply in a transboundary dispute so that the same rules govern no matter where a case is brought.

238. *A proud tradition.* – Comparative elements were pervasive in private international law scholarship already in the work of early and mid-nineteenth-century theorists (e.g., Foelix, Schaeffner, and Savigny in continental Europe; Livermore, Story, and Wharton in the United States). Yet, the comparative study of the field really came into its own in the late nineteenth and early twentieth centuries. At that point, private international law was integrated into the various national laws, in particular in the civil law orbit through codification. As a result, there were now many national versions of conflicts law which cried out for comparison. The Paris Congress of 1900 (*supra* III.C.i., ss. 85–87) saw several presentations on private international law, and in the mid- and late twentieth century, a number of thorough comparative studies were published. Among them, Ernst Rabel's *The Conflict of Laws. A Comparative Study*, stands out.[509] It presents a functional analysis of the private international law norms of ca. 100 jurisdictions, organized by subject matter. While time has rendered much of this study obsolete, as an achievement it is timeless. Also, the Hague Academy of International Law has since 1923 organized courses on private international law, most of which were given by prominent scholars in the field and then published in the Academy's *Recueil des cours* (and sometimes also as separate books); these lectures constitute a very substantial, and constantly growing, library of comparative studies in conflicts law. In addition, there is a vast number of law review articles, often published in

[507] See *supra* II.A.i., s. 20. For further discussion of this dimension, see also *Muir-Watt*, Private International Law: *Smits* (ed.), Elgar Encyclopedia of Comparative Law (ed. 2 Cheltenham, Northampton MA 2012) 701–715; *Reimann*, Comparative Law and Private International Law: *idem* and *Zimmermann* (eds.), The Oxford Handbook of Comparative Law (ed. 2 Oxford 2019) 1339–1370, 1355–1362.

[508] *Lipstein* (ed.), Private International Law: Int.Enc. Comp.L III (2011).

[509] *Rabel* (*supra* n. 27).

specialized journals such as the *Revue critique de droit international privé* (since 1905), the *Rabels Zeitschrift für ausländisches und internationales Privatrecht* (since 1927), and, more recently, the *Journal of Private International Law* (since 2005).

239. *Boost: the impact of the American conflicts revolution.* – In the 1960s through the 1980s, American conflicts law underwent dramatic changes (affecting especially transboundary torts and contracts) when first scholars, then courts, embraced (in part radically) new approaches and methods. Seeking to abandon the time-honored territorialism and private rights orientation, they increasingly based choice-of-law decisions on the analysis of underlying governmental interests.[510] This American "conflicts revolution" posed a challenge to the traditional assumptions continuing to prevail elsewhere in the world and thus boosted the comparative study of conflicts law. Especially scholars in continental Europe were intrigued by the new American approaches and compared the respective methods, goals, and outcomes on both sides of the Atlantic. While some academics toyed with the idea of a similar revolution in European conflicts law,[511] others rejected the new American ideas.[512] The resulting debates entailed a general re-evaluation of the fundamental orientations of conflicts law (selectivism v. substantivism, conflicts justice v. material justice, jurisdiction v. law selecting approaches) and of the desirable character of conflicts norms (multilateral v. unilateral, rules or approaches, hard and fast v. soft and broad criteria, etc.).[513] The scholarly excitement lasted for several decades but eventually died down towards the turn of the century. At the end of the day, the long-term impact of the American conflicts revolution abroad was very limited.

240. *Damper: The Europeanization of private international law.* – While US-American developments in the 1960s through 1980s provided a boost for the comparative study of conflicts law, European developments since then have put somewhat of a damper on it. This is true in three specific regards. Most importantly, during the last three decades choice-of-law as well as jurisdictional rules have been increasingly "Europeanized", i.e., codified in the form of EU Regulations. Since these Regulations are directly applicable law in the member states, they have largely displaced the variety of national rules with a uniform regime imposed from above. Such uniformity, however, is the death of comparison. Furthermore, the building of a European private international law system has entailed an inward turn among many continental conflicts scholars. This has resulted in a concomitant reduction of interest in other parts of the world, especially in US-American developments. Third, once conflicts rules are legislated, especially on the supranational level, they are, so to speak, cast in stone. This renders efforts to look at, and in particular to learn from, other systems largely futile, at least from a practical point of view. To be sure, comparative conflicts law is not dead in Europe today,[514] but there is no gainsaying that it is not nearly as much in vogue as it was a generation ago.

241. *Assisting codification.* – While the heyday of the comparative study of conflicts law may be over on the academic level, comparative law continues to contribute heavily to the development of private international law in practice. In particular, comparative studies routinely undergird the drafting of (quasi-)legislative conflicts regimes. Such "codifications" occur in a variety of forms. Most traditionally, national legislatures have enacted conflicts rules, either as integral parts of classic civil codes or in freestanding statutes. This tradition has been going very strong: since the late twentieth century an increasing number of countries around the world have

[510] *Symeonides*, The American Choice-of-Law Revolution in the Courts: Today and Tomorrow (Leiden and Boston MA) 2003 (offprint from Rec.des Cours 298 (2002)). See also *Ehrenzweig and Jayme*, Private International Law. A Comparative Treatise on American Conflicts Law including the Law of Admiralty (3 vols.) (Leiden, Dobbs Ferry NY 1967–1977).

[511] *Joerges*, Zum Funktionswandel des Kollisionsrechts (Berlin, Tübingen 1971).

[512] *Kegel*, The Crisis of Conflict of Laws: Rec.des Cours 112 (1964-II), 89; *Kegel*, Paternal Home and Dream Home: 27 Am.J.Comp.L. 615–633 (1979).

[513] *Symeonides*, Private International Law at the End of the 20th Century: Progress or Regress (The Hague, Boston MA 2000): see also *Juenger*, General Course on Private International Law: Rec.des Cours 193 (1984-IV) 123–387.

[514] See e.g. *Cuniberti*, Conflict of Laws: A Comparative Approach (Cheltenham, Northampton MA 2017).

codified, or re-codified, their conflicts rules – a development that has itself been studied from a comparative perspective.[515] In addition, during the last hundred years, the Hague Conference on Private International Law has drafted dozens of international conventions based on the comparative study of national conflicts law. And even the supranational enactment of conflicts rules in the EU regulations mentioned above drew on (more or less thorough) comparative analyses of the members states' laws. Of course, looking at foreign systems often informs the codification of many areas of law; but in drafting conflicts rules comparative background studies are virtually *de rigueur*.

g. *Europeanization and the Reaffirmation of Private Law Dominance*

242. *The emergence of the Europeanization movement.* – The traditional private law focus of the discipline was vigorously affirmed in late twentieth- and early twenty-first-century Europe when comparatists and other scholars pursued the unification of private law on that side of the Atlantic.[516]

The Europeanization movement was a response to a perceived need and to the official EU institutions' incapability of meeting it. When European integration gathered steam in the 1980s, it became a standard (and mostly unquestioned) assumption that the emerging integrated market required a unified private law, at least of contract, perhaps also of tort, property, and other areas, such as corporate law. It soon became clear that the European institutions would not, on their own, fulfill that requirement. To be sure, the European legislator produced a substantial amount of EU private law in the form of Directives, especially for consumer protection in areas such as products liability (1985), doorstep sales (1985), unfair contract terms (1993), and, more broadly, consumer sales (1999); yet, these Directives ultimately constituted merely a poorly integrated patchwork, not a uniform European private law in any general sense. The European Court of Justice did not provide much help either; while the Court made some contributions towards a unified private law, it lacked the jurisdictional mandate to create such a law on a broader scale. When first the European Parliament and then the European Commission proclaimed the ambitious idea of a European Civil Code in the 1990s, it became clear that a common private law for Europe would require thorough preparation on the academic level in an all-European context.[517]

243. *The ius commune debate.* – In the early years of the movement, there was a lively discussion about the question whether a common private law of Europe could (and, if so, should) be built on the foundations of the (Roman and Canon) *ius commune* as it prevailed in most of late medieval and early modern Europe.[518] Going in that direction would have given the Europeanization project a largely historical turn. It would have required a distillation of the common elements from the *ius commune* sources, a determination of their continued viability, and their adaptation to present needs. Of course, this would have involved some comparison among the existing sources and ideas, but such comparison would have occurred in a historical context and perspective. At the end of the day, however, the idea of a renewed *ius commune* faded into the background, and the Europeanization movement did not evolve into a neo-historical school. As a result, the Europeanization of private law focused overwhelmingly on the law of the present and thus turned into a more standard comparative law exercise.

244. *Types of comparative projects.* – In the academic efforts to create a common private law of Europe, comparative law played a central and crucial role. Since the 1990s, a veritable cot-

[515] *Symeonides*, Codifying Choice of Law around the World: An International Comparative Analysis (New York 2014).

[516] *Zimmermann* (*supra* n. 254). For a discussion of the movement in the historical context, see also *supra* III.E.iii., s. 162.

[517] *Hartkamp et al.* (*supra* n. 352); *Jansen* and *Rademacher* (*supra* n. 352) 299–313. Hein Kötz had pointed in that direction already in the early 1980s, *Kötz*, Gemeineuropäisches Zivilrecht: *Bernstein, Drobnig and Kötz* (ed.), Festschrift für Konrad Zweigert (Tübingen 1981) 481–500; reprinted in *Kötz*, Undogmatisches (Tübingen 2005) 20–38.

[518] *Caroni and Dilcher* (eds.), Norm und Tradition, Fra Norma e Tradizione (Köln 1998).

tage industry of projects based on, or pursuing, the comparative study of the various national laws emerged all over Europe. Most, but not all, of these projects aimed at the harmonization or even unification of private law. One can distinguish at least five major types, each comprising various sub-categories.

To begin with, several projects pursued the preparation of (quasi-)legislative texts. When the idea of a European Civil Code was first floated, two groups began to pursue that goal: the Study Group on a European Civil Code[519] and the *Avant-projet* of a European Contract Code.[520] As the wholesale codification of European private law began to look increasingly unrealistic, scholars narrowed their focus and lowered their ambition. Jointly, the Study Group on the European Civil Code and the Research Group on EC Private Law (Acquis Group) eventually published a preparatory Common Frame of Reference covering the law of obligations and some elements or property law.[521]

Second, a considerable number of groups drafted (non-binding) "Principles" of European law in the tradition of the US-American Restatements. The lead was taken, and the model provided, by the so-called Lando Commission, which published Principles of European Contract Law (PECL) in three parts between 1995 and 2003. In its wake, other study groups presented Principles on European Trust Law (1999), Insolvency Law (2003), Tort Law (2004) and even Family Law (Regarding Divorce and Maintenance between Former Spouses, 2004, regarding Property Relations Between Spouses, 2013, etc.). These Principles were drawn from the comparative study of the EU member states' laws and offer guidance for legislators, courts and arbitrators, as well as private parties.

Third, various academic enterprises sought to understand the extent, as well as the limits, of the common ground shared by European private law systems without drafting quasi-legislative texts or principles. The most prominent of these endeavors is the Italian-led Common Core of European Private Law project founded in Trento in 1994 (hence often called Trento Project), later at home in Torino.[522] It consists of a vast network of European private law scholars who, over the years, have published a series of studies showing where European domestic laws agree and where they differ with regard to a variety of topics in the areas of contract, tort, and property. Similar, though more limited, comparative studies have resulted in major treatises on European law of contract, tort, unjust enrichment, and property law.[523] In 2012, a group of German scholars even published an entire encyclopedia on European private law.[524]

Fourth, groups of scholars created several casebooks on European private law. Their goal is to transcend the national horizon in the classroom and to introduce the students to the material in a European – and thus intrinsically comparative – context.[525]

Finally, beginning in the 1990s, a growing number of academic journals have specialized in European private law: the *Zeitschrift für Europäisches Privatrecht* (since 1993), the European Review of Private Law (also since 1993), *Europa e diritto privato* (since 1998), the Maastricht Journal for European and Comparative Law (since 2000), and the European Review of Contract Law (since 2005). Since 2011, there has also been a European Law Institute (ELI), modeled

519 *Von Bar*, The Study Group on a European Civil Code: *Gottwald, Jayme and Schwab*, Festschrift für Dieter Henrich (Bielefeld 2000) 1–13.

520 *Académie des Privatistes Européens*, Code Européen des Contrats: Avant-projet (Milano 2000).

521 *Von Bar, Clive and Schulte-Nölke* (eds.), Principles, Definitions and Model Rules of European Private Law. Draft Common Frame of Reference (München 2009).

522 *Bussani and Mattei* (eds.), The Common Core of European Private Law (The Hague, New York 2003)

523 *Kötz* (*supra* n 430) (transl. by Weir as European Contract Law (Oxford, New York 1997); *Von Bar* (*supra* n. 451); *Schlechtriem* (*supra* n. 465); *Von Bar* (*supra* n. 474);

524 *Basedow, Hopt, Zimmermann and Stier* (eds.), The Max Planck Encyclopedia of European Private Law (2 vol.) (Oxford 2012). See also the collection of essays in *Twigg-Flesner* (ed.), The Cambridge Companion to European Union Private Law (Cambridge 2010).

525 See *Beale et al.*, Cases, Materials and Text on Contract Law (ed. 1 Oxford 2002); *Beatson and Schrage* (*supra* n. 463). *Ranieri*, Europäisches Obligationenrecht (ed. 3 Wien 2009); *Van Erp and Akkermans* (eds.), Cases, Materials and Text on Property Law (Oxford 2012), *Van Gerven, Lever and Larouche* (*supra* n. 442).

after the American Law Institute (ALI). While its primary mission is not the Europeanization of private law, the ELI is a platform not only for the promotion of EU law proper and for general legal integration, but also for the comparative study of the member states' legal systems.

245. *Boon and bane.* – The impact of private law Europeanization on comparative law has been ambivalent.

On the one hand, the movement to Europeanize private law was a boon for the discipline in several crucial regards. To begin with, almost overnight the search for a common private law for Europe provided comparative studies with a (practical) legitimacy that relieved the discipline of its chronic need to fight for recognition. At the same time, the political salience of the Europeanization movement vested comparative law with a prominence that moved the discipline from the margins of the academic universe to a place close to center stage. As a result, the comparative study of private law became more broadly accepted and highly valued in Europe than at any other time in recent history. Furthermore, the various endeavors generated Europe-wide networks of scholars which have provided platforms for cooperation in a truly comparative spirit. Last but not least, the participants in the various Europeanization projects produced a significant number of impressive studies which soon began to constitute a small library in their own right, much of it showing what unites, and what divides, European private law systems.

On the other hand, the Europeanization movement closely resembled early twentieth-century comparative law and reinforced some of the discipline's traditional limitations, biases, and weaknesses. To begin with, comparative law in the context of this movement was essentially a means to the end of legal unification (or at least harmonization), very much in the spirit of Salleilles' and Lambert's *droit commun legislatif* a century before (*supra* III.C.i., ss. 86–87). To be sure, there is nothing wrong with that in principle. Yet, with few exceptions, comparative studies in the Europeanization context accepted both the desirability and the feasibility of legal unification quite blindly; critical reflection was rare.[526] The mainstream's uncritical stance, in turn, both expressed and strengthened the discipline's longstanding bias in favor of legal uniformity at the expense of diversity; an appreciation of pluralism was largely absent, or at least late in coming.[527] Moreover, at its core, comparison for Europeanization purposes was mostly limited to substantive private law, often in blackletter form. Some notable exceptions notwithstanding,[528] the blackletter rules were compared virtually without regard to the institutional, procedural, and professional context – despite the fact that such an isolationist approach has been discredited since Ernst Rabel. In a similar vein, the mainstream projects ignored the lessons of legal realism: they showed little interest in how law works on the ground, e.g., whether the rules compared are routinely obeyed or frequently breached, blindly accepted or bargained around, actually enforced or quietly ignored. Finally, there was also a distinct absence of interdisciplinary perspectives: the Europeanization movement paid scant attention to the political ramifications of legal unification, the economic rationalities underlying the various rules, and the social and distributional consequences of its agenda. As an overall result, much of the comparative law employed in the Europeanization enterprise appears strangely old-fashioned, amazingly context-blind, dangerously divorced from reality, and disconcertingly uncritical.

ii. *The Post-World War II Expansion*

246. *Introduction and Overview.* – Like its geographic scope, the substantive coverage of comparative law has constantly expanded since the middle of the last century. Some subjects, like civil procedure, criminal law and procedure, constitutional law, and administrative law (*infra* a.–e.), had occasionally been addressed before but now rose to much greater prominence. Others began to be first explored in the postwar decades,

[526] An exception is *Brownsworth et al.* (eds.), The Foundations of European Private Law (Oxford, Portland OR 2011).

[527] An exception is *Niglia* (ed.), Pluralism and European Private Law (Oxford, Portland OR 2013).

[528] The most notable exception was the Common Core (Trento) Project, *infra* VI.C.ii., s. 376.

especially topics dealing with market activity, such as competition law (f.). And, finally, there were some more recent additions to the mix, e.g., human rights, tax, and data protection law (g.). A complete catalog is not possible here because new specialties constantly emerge.

a. *Civil Procedure*

247. *A late arrival.* – Although drafting procedural legislation, especially codes of civil procedure, was often informed by looking at foreign law as early as in the nineteenth century, procedure came to comparative law as an academic discipline only in the second half of the twentieth century. For the first couple of decades after the Paris Congress, comparatists focused overwhelmingly on substantive law, perhaps because they perceived procedure as dry, technical, and ultimately boring. The beginning of comparative procedural studies lies in the 1950s when the International Association of Procedural Law (*Association Internationale de Droit Processuel*) began to hold regular conferences. Still, while a few comparatists began to write about civil procedure in the 1950s and 1960s,[529] for the time being the field remained on the margins of the comparative law universe.

Civil procedure finally gained prominence in the closing decades of the twentieth century. Its rise was largely due to two major developments. First, there was a significant increase in high-profile international civil litigation involving antitrust, securities, product liability, and other cases. This created a practical need to understand the procedural system(s) of other countries, and in particular to seek solutions for the clashes that kept occurring in litigation between parties in the United States and Western Europe ("justice conflict"[530]). Second, in several Western countries there was growing discontent with the domestic procedural systems, mainly because of mounting costs and growing delays.[531] Scholars thus began to look to other systems for reform ideas; this triggered an especially lively debate in the United States (*infra* s. 249). In both these contexts, comparatists discovered that (civil) procedure posed extremely interesting academic and practical challenges, and that the truly fundamental differences between the grand legal traditions, especially the civil and the common law, may actual be procedural rather than substantive.

Today, comparative civil procedure is a firmly established field.[532] It is intimately connected, and thus often studied jointly, with judicial institutions and the legal professions (*supra* B.iii., ss. 204–208, and iv., ss. 209–215.). This Encyclopedia devotes a hefty volume to the subject, satisfying the interest of a reader looking for more detail and deeper analysis.[533] Since 2012, comparative procedure has even had an institutional home at the Max Planck Institute for International, European and Regulatory Procedural Law in Luxembourg.

[529] See, e.g. *Kaplan, Von Mehren and Schaefer*, Phases of German Civil Procedure I: 71 Harv.L.Rev. 1193–1268 (1958), *Kaplan, Von Mehren and Schaefer* (*supra* n. 14); *Kaplan*, Civil Procedure – Reflections on the Comparison of Systems: 9 Buffalo L.Rev. 409–432, 414–421 (1960). Scholars also published several treatises on foreign procedural systems, see *Bader-Ginsburg and Bruzelius*, Civil Procedure in Sweden (The Hague 1965); *Cappelletti and Perillo* (*supra* n. 197); *Herzog*, Civil Procedure in France (The Hague 1967).

[530] *Schlosser*, Der Justizkonflikt zwischen den USA und Europa (Berlin, New York 1985); *Stürner, Lange and Taniguchi*, Der Justizkonflikt mit den Vereinigten Staaten von Amerika (Bielefeld 1986); for a more recent assessment, see *Bonomi and Schefer* (eds.), US Litigation Today: Still a Threat for European Businesses or Just a Paper Tiger? (Genève, Zurich, Bâle 2018)

[531] *Zuckerman* (ed.), Civil Justice in Crisis-Comparative Perspectives on Civil Procedure (Oxford 1999).

[532] For an overview, see *Zekoll*, Comparative Civil Procedure: *Reimann and Zimmermann* (eds.), The Oxford Handbook of Comparative Law (ed. 2 Oxford 2019) 1306–1338; shorter accounts in *Chase and Varano*, Comparative Civil Justice: *Bussani and Mattei* (eds.), The Cambridge Companion to Comparative Law (Cambridge 2012) 210–240;*Van Rhee and Verkerk*, Civil Procedure: *Smits* (ed.), Elgar Encyclopedia of Comparative Law (ed. 2 Cheltenham, Northampton MA 2012) 140–156; see also *Chase et al.*, Civil Litigation in Comparative Context (ed. 2 St. Paul MN 2017); *Gilles*, Prozeßrechtsvergleichung (Köln 1996). For a discussion of the specific challenges of comparative civil procedure and an overview of more recent developments, see *Huber*, Prozessrechtsvergleichung heute: *Hess* (ed.), Europäisches Insolvenzrecht. Grundsätzliche Fragestellungen der Prozessrechtsvergleichung (Bielefeld 2019) 77–109.

[533] *Cappelletti* (ed.), Civil Procedure: Int.Enc. Comp.L. XVI (2014).

Comparatists have pursued a large variety of directions. Many have grappled with the basic models and structures in the civil v. common law context (*infra* s. 248). Some looked at civil procedure from an academic perspective, e.g., as an expression of legal cultures and traditions,[534] while others took a practitioner's view, e.g., by comparing how a particular dispute would actually be resolved in several jurisdictions.[535] Some focused on comparing reforms in various countries,[536] while others compiled casebooks for teaching purposes.[537] Several more narrowly focused studies have compared rules of evidence[538] or focused on issues concerning access to justice, such as the allocation of litigation costs (including third party financing and litigation insurance),[539] the handling of mass claims (especially through class actions and their alternatives),[540] and, more recently, the emergence of various forms of alternative dispute resolution (such as arbitration, mediation, and various other non-state mechanisms[541]). In recent years, empirical (numerical) approaches (*infra* VI.C.iii., ss. 378–381) have gained prominence, focusing on the comparison, and sometimes on the evaluation, of procedural systems according to hard data.[542] Overall, four themes have been particularly pervasive, succeeding each other as foci of attention: the problem of classifying procedural systems (*infra* s. 248.); the American system and its critics (s. 249); international harmonization (s. 250), and the Europeanization of civil procedure (s. 251).

248. *Classification of procedural approaches.* – The two predominant legal traditions in the world have long been associated with two fundamentally different approaches to civil dispute resolution. In the civil law orbit, procedure descended from the medieval and early modern Romano-canonical procedure which was largely written, dominated by professional judges, and often termed "inquisitorial". By contrast, in the common law civil litigation was shaped by the writ system, the central role of the jury, and the dichotomy between proceedings in law and equity. On both sides of the divide, nineteenth- (and to some extent twentieth-) century reforms significantly changed the picture. Continental-style civil procedure is no longer "inquisitorial", either in the pejorative (*ancien régime*) sense or in the sense of being entirely controlled by the judge (rather than the parties). Common law-style procedure is no longer based on the writ system, has largely (though not completely) merged law and equity, and in most jurisdictions jury trials are rarely available. Thus it is generally accepted today that the old dichotomies have become largely obsolete – or at least in need of serious modification.[543]

There is less agreement whether classifications based on other features continue to make sense. One such feature is the centrality (vel non) of a (single-event) trial. In the civil law, there has traditionally not been such an event. Procedure has been centered around the professional judge as factfinder and decision maker; this allows a case to proceed through a series of meetings until

[534] *Gilles and Pfeiffer* (eds.), Prozeßrecht und Rechtskulturen (Baden-Baden 2003); *Van Rhee*, European Traditions in Civil Procedure (Antwerp, Oxford, New York 2005); *Maleshin* (ed.), Civil Procedure in Cross-Cultural Dialogue: Eurasia Context (Moscow 2012).

[535] *McClurg, Koyuncu and Sprovieri* (*supra* n. 459).

[536] *Trocker and Varano*, The Reforms of Civil Procedure in Comparative Perspective (Torino 2005).

[537] *Chase et al.* (eds.), Civil Litigation in Comparative Perspective (St. Paul MN 2007). There are also several casebooks on International (Civil) Litigation, which has developed into a sub-field in its own right, especially in the United States. These casebooks usually compare American approaches to litigation with various foreign (especially continental European) counterparts.

[538] *Van Rhee and Uzelac* (eds.), Evidence in Contemporary Civil Procedure: Fundamental Issues in Comparative Perspective (Mortsel, Cambridge 2015).

[539] *Hodges, Vogenauer and Tulibacka*, The Costs and Funding of Civil Litigation: A Comparative Perspective (Oxford, Portland OR 2010); *Reimann* (ed.), Cost and Fee Allocation in Civil Procedure: A Comparative Study (Dordrecht 2012).

[540] *Wrbka, von Uytsel and Siems* (eds.), Collective Actions: Enhancing Access to Justice and Reconciling Multilayer Interests? (Cambridge 2012).

[541] See, e.g., *Collin* (ed.), Justice without the State: Judicial Self-Regulation in the Past and Present (Frankfurt 2016).

[542] For an overview and critique, see *Huber* (*supra* n. 532) 92–94.

[543] *Jolowicz*, Adversarial and Inquisitorial Models of Civil Procesure: 52 I.C.L.Q. 281–295 (2003).

it is ready for decision. There is thus no sharp distinction between a pre-trial and a trial phase – and certainly nothing like (especially US-style, pre-trial) discovery. The common law procedure has been characterized by the decision of the dispute in a concentrated and continuous trial; this was originally necessitated by the impossibility repeatedly to reconvene a jury but has persisted even without lay participation. Since such a trial is a one-shot affair, it must be carefully prepared during a pre-trial phase, especially by evidence gathering (discovery). Another, related, criterion for classification is the role of the judge. In the civil law tradition the judge is, to so speak, in the driver's seat. While the parties control the grand outlines of the dispute (initiation, scope, settlement, etc.), the judge is in charge of organizing and running the proceedings. In particular, the judge determines the sequence of evidence-taking, orders the production of documents, appoints experts, and interrogates the witnesses; and the judge decides the case whenever he or she is ready. In the common law tradition the first-instance judge has played a much more passive role and has left the gathering and presentation of evidence largely to the parties. A third way of classifying approaches is by looking at the institutional and professional context. Common law courts tend to be more generalist, and their judges are usually appointed without specialized training after a successful career at the bar (or perhaps in politics); this presents them with a broader menu of cases which makes it more difficult for them to orchestrate the proceedings. Civil law courts tend to be more specialized and thus deal with a narrower docket, and they are staffed by a career judiciary whose members are trained, and see themselves, as active case managers. If one puts these three differences, concerning phases, judicial roles, and institutional and professional environments, together, distinguishing a basic civil law model from a common law approach still makes considerable sense.

Yet, comparatists have pointed out that there are at least three counterarguments. To begin with, there are significant differences *within* the civil and the common law orbits; for example, some civil law systems have elected judges, others do not, and some common law jurisdiction court structures are largely uniform, while others are fairly specialized. In addition, more recent reforms have led to a gradual convergence between the two traditions in important regards: many civil law jurisdictions now provide for more concentrated proceedings, while in many common law systems pre-trial conferences between the parties and the judge have taken on a central role; several civil law systems have strengthened the parties' power with regard to evidence-taking, while some common law countries (especially England under the Civil Procedure Rules of 1998) have turned judges largely into case-managers. Finally, all developed countries' civil procedure systems share fundamental values and principles, such as the parties' right to proper notice, to assistance by counsel, to active participation in the proceedings, to an impartial judge, and, at least in major cases, to an appeal. And in most systems small claims are now handled in special, fast track proceedings without much discovery, in one hearing, and before a single judge. In sum, many procedural systems today display mixed features and share considerable common ground. This makes it fairly debatable whether dividing them into the traditional categories does more harm than good.

A different approach suggests looking at procedural systems from the perspective of two sets of opposite "ideals" (i.e., ideal types in the Weberian sense). The first set is concerned with the organization of the judicial machinery: it can be structured according to a "hierarchical" ideal, i.e., in a top-down (and professionalized) fashion or a "coordinate" ideal, i.e., in a more horizontal manner (with strong lay participation).[544] The civil law tradition is closer to the former, the common law to the latter, model. The second set addresses the degree and kind of involvement by the state: procedural systems can be shaped by an "activist" state seeking to promote its own policies (through controlling the course of the proceedings), or by a "reactive" state providing just the framework for a fair fight (and otherwise staying out of the fray). High state involvement is associated with civil law predilections, laissez faire with preferences in common law countries. Viewing procedural

[544] *Damaska* (*supra* n. 60).

systems through these prisms opens our eyes to differences in their underlying logic and values. It also shows that in practice all systems are ultimately hybrids of one sort or another. They are perhaps best organized along a spectrum with the line-up depending on the criteria employed.

249. *American exceptionalism and its critics.* – For several decades the US-American form of civil procedure has been the primary reference point of discussion and comparison. The reason is not so much the position of the United States as a superpower, nor even mainly its position as the primary exporter of legal ideas in the second half of the twentieth century. Instead, the American system stands out because it brings the defining features of the common law approach to civil procedure into particularly sharp relief: it remains the only civil litigation system centered around trial by jury (even though the jury is rarely used in practice); it thus continues to adhere to a strict separation between pre-trial and trial phase; it leaves judges in a more passive, and the litigants in a more active, role than almost anywhere else in the world; and it generally shapes civil procedure in an unabashedly adversarial fashion.[545] In addition, American civil litigation has been feared by foreign parties because of several idiosyncrasies: its extensive discovery regime that can impose severe burdens and high costs on the litigants; its strong endorsement of contingency fees combined with its refusal to shift litigation costs to the losing party ("American rule") is said to encourage plaintiffs to pursue non-meritorious claims; its class action procedures that can threaten defendants with crushing liability, etc.[546] The combination of all these features indeed puts American civil procedure in an exceptional position, even in the common law orbit.

At the same time, comparatists have criticized American civil procedure more severely than any other regime in the world. In particular, they have criticized it as overly expensive and destructive of access to justice; as inefficient and poorly designed to find the truth; and as often plagued by delay, incompetence, and unpredictability. According to the leading critics, civil law systems, especially the German, avoid most of these weaknesses and thus perform much better.[547] In the closing decades of the twentieth century, these critiques triggered an intensive discussion about the vices and virtues of the US litigation system in comparison with other regimes, particularly in Western Europe and East Asia. It did not, however, result in any major civil justice reforms in the United States.

250. *International harmonization and unification.* – In line with the general agenda of twentieth-century comparative law, there have been many efforts to harmonize or even unify civil procedure on an international level. On the one hand, these efforts have been driven by undeniable practical needs. In the fast-growing field of international civil litigation, procedural differences among legal systems create serious obstacles, uncertainties, and inefficiencies that could be diminished or even avoided by a uniform set of rules. On the other hand, these efforts have been hindered by the fact that procedural law is notoriously hard to harmonize, not to mention unify. It is so closely tied to institutional designs and professional roles that it has proven much more resistant to unification than most substantive law. As a result, the overall record of unification efforts has been decidedly modest on the global level.

Some important elements of civil procedure have been coordinated among a significant number of countries through international conventions, especially those drafted by the Hague Conference on Private International Law, most importantly the Convention on the Service Abroad of Judicial and Extrajudicial Documents (1965) and the Convention on the Taking of Evidence

[545] *Kagan*, Adversarial Legalism: The American Way of Law (Cambridge MA, London 2001), esp. 99–155.

[546] During the second half of the twentieth century, broad rules on personal jurisdiction also created extensive and, in the view of many foreign observers, excessive forum shopping opportunities. This, however, is no longer the case since the United States Supreme Court dramatically curtailed personal jurisdiction in the early twenty-first century, especially with regard to corporate defendants; see especially *McIntyre Machinery v. Nicastro*, 564 U.S. 873 (2011); *Goodyear Dunlop v. Brown*, 564 U.S. 915 (2011); and *Daimler AG v. Bauman*, 571 U.S. ___ (2014).

[547] The debate was initiated by the now classic article by *Langbein* (*supra* n. 14). See also *Maxeiner*, Failures of American Civil Justice in International Perspective (Cambridge 2011).

Abroad (1970). By contrast, the ambitious project of an international convention on the recognition of judgments failed in the 1990s after many years of negotiations, showing some hard limits of the involved states' willingness to compromise in procedural matters. The negotiations ultimately produced the much more modest Convention on Choice of Forum Agreements (2005, in force 2015) which is slowly gaining acceptance among states. In 2011, the Hague Conference initiated a new "Judgments Project" which resulted in the Convention on the Recognition and Enforcement of Foreign Judgments (2019).

A different approach was taken in a joint project of the American Law Institute (ALI) and UNIDROIT. Reflecting the exemplary comparative work by an international group of prominent civil procedure scholars, these high-profile non-governmental organizations adopted a set of Principles and Rules of Transnational Civil Procedure in 2004.[548] The Principles seek to bridge the gap between the civil and the common law procedural traditions. Not vested with any direct legal force, they were designed as a model that could be adopted by national legislatures, serve as a blueprint for international organizations, or constitute a suggestion for parties seeking to agree on the rules of engagement for litigation or arbitration. So far, however, their influence appears to have been very limited. More recently, UNIDROIT has joined forces with the *European Law Institute* to pursue the regional harmonization of procedural rules. In Latin America, a *Codigo Procesal Civil Modelo para Iberoamerica* was published in 1988 and has served as a model for various national codes. Unification efforts have been fairly successful in the field of international commercial arbitration. The New York Convention on the Recognition and Enforcement of Foreign Arbitral Awards (1958) and various UNCITRAL model laws have been so widely adopted that they have created a global framework in this area.

It is worth noting that some comparative and international lawyers remain critical of international unification, in part because it eliminates cherished local traditions based on local preferences, in part because it destroys valuable diversity. In addition, the creation of (uniform) law specifically for international disputes adds another layer of rules and thus increases the overall complexity of procedural systems.

251. *Europeanization.* – Unification of law is most important among closely interacting countries, especially in a common market, such as that between the members states of the European Union. Accordingly, civil procedure has recently become, and will increasingly continue to be, Europeanized. This has not, however, occurred in any comprehensive manner, but rather in the piecemeal fashion typical for most European law. The European Union (and its predecessor, the European Community) has unified a growing number of select elements of civil procedure, usually by enacting regulations, i.e., supranational legislation directly applicable in the member states. Their topics range from the fundamental issues (such as jurisdiction and judgments recognition) to technical matters (like service of process or taking of evidence), and from commercial fields (like special bankruptcy proceedings) to personal affairs (like family law disputes), and from creating a European order for payment to establishing a procedure for small claims.[549] All this has made the interplay between general national civil procedure and special European rules extraordinarily complex.

Comparative law has not played much of a role in this development. In the early phases, there were some broad comparative studies (in part on behalf of the European Commission) which, however, did not have a lasting impact.[550] Pretty soon, legal unification was taken over by European bureaucrats in cooperation with national government delegates. Government officials, however, are rarely comfortable in developing law bottom-up and much more inclined to impose it top-down. As a result, the various EU regulations are not based on serious comparative studies of the

548 *American Law Institute and UNIDROIT*, Principles and Rules of Transnational Civil Procedure (Cambridge 2006).

549 See *Storme, Meijknecht and van Rhee* (eds.), Civil Procedure in Europe (multivol.) (The Hague, Leiden, New York (1997–).

550 *Storme*, Rapprochement du Droit Judiciare de l'Union Européenne (Dordrecht 1994); see also *Storme*, Procedural Laws in Europe: Towards Harmonization (Antwerp, Apeldoorn 2003).

member states' systems but rather shaped by an agenda of centralization and, in some instances, consumer protection.

Comparative considerations have, however, played a considerable role in the European Court of Justice when it has interpreted the unified procedural rules. This is most obvious with regard to the EU Regulation on jurisdiction and judgments recognition in civil and commercial matters,[551] as well as its predecessor, the Brussels Convention of 1968.

b. *Criminal Law*

252. *Criminal law and "criminal justice".* – Comparatists often look at substantive criminal law together with criminal procedure on the one hand, and the execution of punishments on the other, thus studying (systems of) "criminal justice".[552] There is much to be said for such a comprehensive approach because procedure determines what criminal law (proper) means in the courtroom, and studying punishments shows what it means for offenders. We nonetheless address (substantive) criminal law and criminal procedure separately here because their comparative study has taken different courses and focused on different issues. Comparative work on punishment and penal policy is too sporadic to be treated under a separate entry, although there are some notable publications illuminating major divergencies, especially between Europe and the United States.[553]

253. *Development.* – Leaving aside occasional eighteenth-century forages into the field, such as by Cesare Beccaria (1738–1794),[554] the origins of comparative criminal law lie in the early nineteenth century. Johann Paul Anselm Feuerbach (1775–1833) is usually regarded as the founding father, and much credit also goes to his successor, Anton Mittermaier (1787–1867) (*supra* III.B.i.a., s. 68). At the same time, scholars in other European countries developed an interest in the field as well.[555] At the close of the nineteenth century, the Austrian criminal law scholar and law reformer Franz von Liszt edited a volume on the criminal laws of Europe. It was meant as a first step towards a common (European) criminal law, similar to the contemporaneous program of a *droit commun legislatif* in private law (*supra* III.C.i., ss. 86–87);[556] further steps in that direction, however, were never taken.

More generally, the promise inherent in these nineteenth-century beginnings was scarcely fulfilled in the twentieth. For many decades, criminal law played a distinctly minor role in comparative jurisprudence. It is not hard to see why. At least traditionally, criminal law has been closely tied to notions of state sovereignty and, perhaps more importantly, to national preferences

[551] Regulation 44/2001 of the European Parliament and of the Council on jurisdiction and the recognition and enforcement of judgments in civil and commercial matters; now revised as Regulation (EU) 1215/2012 of the European Parliament and of the Council on jurisdiction and the recognition and enforcement of judgments in civil and commercial matters (recast).

[552] *Grande*, Comparative Criminal Justice: *Bussani and Mattei* (eds.), The Cambridge Companion to Comparative Law (Cambridge 2012), 191–209; *Aromaa and Heiskanen*, Crime and Criminal Justice Systems in Europe and North America 1995–2004 (Helsinki 2008); *Cavadino and Dignan*, Penal Systems: A Comparative Approach (New York 2006); *Cole, Frankowsky and Gertz*, Major Criminal Justice Systems (Newbury Park CA 1987); *Dammer and Albanese*, Comparative Criminal Justice Systems (ed. 5 Belmont CA 2014); *International Institute of Higher Studies in Criminal Law*, Les systèmes comparées de justice pénale (Toulouse 1998); *Fennell et al.* (eds.), Criminal Justice in Europe: A Comparative Study (Oxford 1995); *Pakes*, Comparative Criminal Justice (Cullompton 2004); *Reichel*, Comparative Criminal Justice Systems (Upper Saddle River NY 2008); *Terrill*, World Criminal Justice Systems (ed. 6 Cincinnati OH 2009); *Vogler*, A Worldview of Criminal Justice (Aldershot, Burlington VT 2005); see also *Weigend*, Criminal Law and Criminal Procedure: *Smits* (ed.), Elgar Encyclopedia of Comparative Law (ed. 2 Cheltenham and Northampton MA 2012) 261–278.

[553] *Tonry and Frase* (eds.), Sentencing and Sanctions in Western Countries (Oxford, New York 2001); *Tonry* (ed.), Crime, Punishment, and Politics in Comparative Perspective (Chicago IL 2007); *Whitman*, Harsh Justice: Criminal Punishment and the Widening Divide Between America and Europe (Oxford 2003).

[554] *Beccaria*, Dei Delitti e delle Pene (Livorno 1764).

[555] *Ortolan*, Cours de Législation Pénale Comparée (2 vol.) (Paris 1839–41); *Rossi*, Traité de Droit Pénal (Brussels 1829).

[556] *Von Liszt* (ed.), Le Droit Criminel des Etats Européens (Berlin, Paris 1894).

and politics. The practical need for comparative work also remained small because courts usually apply only their domestic penal provisions and thus have little interest in foreign rules. Nor was comparative criminal law useful to powerful economic actors. As a result, there were few efforts at international unification. It is no surprise then that the standard introductions to comparative law have almost uniformly ignored the criminal side. Nor did the editors of this Encyclopedia see a need to devote a volume to it; half a century ago, it was doubtful indeed whether there was enough worthwhile material to fill one.

It must also be admitted that most twentieth-century work in the field was not very inspiring. Much of it consisted simply of the collection of foreign criminal laws[557] and the translation of penal codes. Much was limited to mere references to foreign (blackletter) rules involving little or no actual comparison. And even after World War II, most of it dealt with criminal law provisions in the abstract, especially in isolation from their procedural and institutional, not to mention their historical and social, context. This prevalence of a doctrinal approach was strongly connected with the geographic center of the field. Especially since the middle of the twentieth century, the leading exporter of substantive criminal law and theory has been Germany, where the subject continues to be treated in an academic and doctrinal fashion. The German influence has been particularly noticeable in regions where jurists think in similar ways and also have a relatively strong interest in comparative criminal law, especially the Spanish-speaking countries (including Latin America)[558] and on the Pacific Rim (in particular Japan and Korea). Even in the United States, criminal law scholars have, if they were interested in comparative perspectives at all, primarily looked to German doctrine.[559]

Since the end of the last century, however, comparative studies in criminal law have taken a new turn in two regards. First, they have experienced a dramatic rise in popularity and prominence.[560] To some extent, this was simply part and parcel of the broadening of comparative law in general. In part, the increase of transnational criminal activity triggered a growing interest in other systems. And in large part the rise of the field was due to the new practical needs for comparative studies by various international criminal tribunals (*infra* s. 259). Second, much of the work has become more seriously comparative and sophisticated. More attention has been paid to the broader context, underlying policies, and in some instances even to interdisciplinary perspectives. In this fashion, studies in criminal law have largely caught up with comparative law in general.

254. *Main directions and objectives.* – Today, there is a very substantial literature in both English and other languages on comparative criminal law.[561] Much of it still consists of global or regional surveys. But some studies are truly comparative and pursue the – largely academic – purpose better to understand particular aspects or doctrines.[562] Some scholars have also sought to group criminal law systems; this ties into the tradition of distinguishing legal families but has produced its own approaches and outcomes.[563] Others have tried to detect common elements, i.e., a basic "grammar", of criminal law.[564] In addition, comparative studies have sometimes served law reform purposes or triggered the transplantation of concepts and ideas from one legal system to another; a well-known example is the adoption

557 An impressive example is *Birkmeyer et al.* (*supra* n. 152)

558 *Ramirez and Bejas*, Derecho Penal Latinamericano Comparado (Buenos Aires 1981).

559 E.g, *Fletcher*, Basic Concepts of Criminal Law (New York 1998).

560 For an overview, see *Dubber*, Comparative Criminal Law: *Reimann and Zimmermann* (eds.), The Oxford Handbook of Comparative Law (ed. 2 Oxford 2019) 1276–1305.

561 See, e.g., *Heller and Dubber* (eds.), Handbook of Comparative Criminal Law (Oxford 2007 and Stanford CA 2011); *Dubber and Hörnle*, Criminal Law: A Comparative Approach (Oxford, New York 2014); *Cadoppi*, Introduzione allo studio del diritto penale comparato (ed. 2 Padova 2004); *Palazzo and Papa*, Lezioni di Diritto Penale Comparato (ed. 3 Torino 2013); *Pradel*, Droit Pénal Comparé (ed. 2 Paris 2002).

562 *Eser and Fletcher* (eds.), Justification and Excuses: Comparative Perspectives (Huntington NY 1987)

563 *Delmas-Marty*, Les Grands Systèmes de Politique Criminelle (Paris 1992).

564 *Fletcher*, The Grammar of Criminal Law: American, Comparative, and International (Oxford, New York 2007).

of the Scandinavian day-fine system in a growing number of (especially European) countries.

255. *Internationalization and Europeanization.* – In the twenty-first century criminal law has acquired an important international, and to some extent also European, dimension. This has created a great practical need for comparative studies.[565]

Since the end of the 1990s, international criminal law (as well as procedure, *infra* ss. 256-259) has developed into a field of its own.[566] It is mainly concerned with a limited number of (massive) offenses against international humanitarian law, such as crimes of aggression, war crimes, genocide, torture, or enslavement. Its most prominent manifestation is the Rome Statute of the International Criminal Court (1998, in force 2002); in Article 21 that document provides that gaps in international criminal law be filled by "general principles of law derived by the Court from national laws of legal systems of the world". In response, and in reaction to broader practical needs, criminal law scholars have been working to construct a more consistent framework of general doctrines needed for adjudicating international offenses, especially by comparing national rules on central concepts such as intent or *mens rea*, aiding and abetting, attempt, and defenses. In addition, the judges sitting on the various international criminal tribunals and drawn from a variety of legal systems have often had to work with the criminal law material provided by domestic systems.

Since the close of the last century a sub-field of European criminal law has emerged as well.[567] It has been fueled by the European Union's legislative activity, especially in the form of various (binding) framework decisions concerning areas such as international drug trafficking, corruption, terrorism, and other forms of organized crime. At some point this even included the ambitious, though ultimately abandoned, project of a quasi-codification ("Corpus Juris") of rules pertaining to European Union fraud.[568] EU criminal law became an even more important topic after the EU acquired further, and more explicit, competences in this area in the Lisbon Treaty (2010).

c. *Criminal Procedure*

256. *The emergence of the field.* – The emergence of comparative studies in criminal procedure roughly paralleled that of comparative criminal law, although its rise was even more sudden and pronounced.

Until about the 1970s, comparatists by and large neglected criminal procedure (like procedural topics generally) even more than substantive criminal law. Introductions to comparative law all but ignored criminal procedure, and at the time the editors of this Encyclopedia had no reason to include it either. This lack of interest was partially due to the absence of a useful analytical framework. To be sure, scholars had long distinguished between an "inquisitorial" and an "accusatorial" version and linked these to the civil and the common law, respectively (*infra* s. 257). Yet, for a long time this picture was so simplistic, ideological, and often distorted that it had little analytical purchase.[569]

The field awakened when a few scholars, mainly in the United States, introduced more useful perspectives, especially in two regards. First, the development of new theoretical models helped to overcome the time-worn stereotypes; these models triggered more precise questions about the involved actors' roles, the procedural phases and goals, and the underlying conceptions of truth (*infra* 257).[570] Second, scholars undertook

565 *Dubber* (*supra* n. 560) 1293–1294; *Roberts*, Comparative Criminal Law for International Criminal Justice: Örücü and Nelken (eds.), Comparative Law: A Handbook (Oxford, Portland OR 2007) 339–370.

566 *Cassese et al.*, Cassese's International Criminal Law (ed. 3 Oxford 2013); *Wehrle*, Principles of International Criminal Law (The Hague, West Nyack NY 2005).

567 *Baum*, Europäische Strafgesetzlichkeit (Frankfurt 2003); *Pradel and Corstens*, Droit Pénal Européen (Paris 1999) (translated as European Criminal Law (The Hague, New York 2002)); *Klipp*, European Criminal Law: An Integrative Approach (Antwerp 2009); *Satzger*, Internationales und Europäisches Strafrecht (Baden-Baden 2005); *Scotis*, Il Diritto Senza Codice. Uno Studio sul Sistema Penale Europeo Vigente (Milano 2007).

568 *Delmas-Marty and Vervaele* (eds.), The Implementation of the Corpus Juris in the Member States (Utrecht 2000).

569 A widely read journalistic book provided wonderfully lively portraits of courtroom scenes in several European countries, but it could also be read in a fashion that fortified the existing stereotypes, especially on the civil law side; *Bedford*, The Faces of Justice: A Traveller's Report (New York 1961).

570 *Damaska*, Structures of Authority and Comparative Criminal Procedure 84 Yale L.J. 480–544 (1975).

more detailed descriptions and realistic assessments of criminal procedure on both sides of the Atlantic; in particular, they showed that in most European countries criminal proceedings were in fact much fairer to, and more protective of, defendants than common lawyers had usually assumed.[571] In addition, two other factors helped to strengthen interest in the subject. Comparatists increasingly woke up to the idea that the most fundamental differences between civil and common law systems may actually be procedural, rather than substantive. And a beginning wave of criminal justice reforms in many European countries provided practical reasons for looking at foreign models – mainly at the adversarial approach in the common law orbit in general, and at the strengthening of defendants' rights by the US Supreme Court since the 1960s in particular.

As a result, comparative criminal procedure experienced an almost meteoric rise in the last quarter of the twentieth century. Since the 1990s, this development has been further boosted by the practical needs of various newly emerging international criminal tribunals. By the turn of the century criminal procedure had matured into an established sub-field of comparative studies. Today, there is an abundance of literature on the subject.[572] Some of it consists of – essentially descriptive – multi-country surveys of criminal procedure systems.[573] But there are also innumerable studies of more concrete topics, such as the basic procedural models and structures (*infra* s. 257) and a host of other issues (*infra* s. 258),[574] as well as some casebooks for classroom use.[575]

257. *Two basic models.* – For decades, the central theme of comparative criminal procedure has been the contrast between two basic forms: an "inquisitorial" and an "adversarial" model. Properly understood, the essence of the "inquisitorial" process is the search for the objective truth by a non-partisan magistrate. At its heart, criminal procedure is thus an official investigation (based on a master-file or dossier). Trials are actively conducted by the (presiding) judge, who orders the production of evidence, employs – non-partisan – experts when needed, and questions the witnesses. He or she ultimately finds the facts and then either acquits or convicts and sentences the defendant. The prosecutor and the accused (with or without counsel) participate in the proceedings but play subordinate roles. By contrast, the essence of the "adversarial" process is a battle between two (theoretically) equal contestants – the state, represented by the prosecutor, and the defendant, usually represented by a lawyer – before a neutral umpire. The contestants run and control the proceedings (including the decision whether to go to trial at all, *infra* s. 258); the judge merely ensures that they comply with the rules of the game (especially the rules of evidence). In the end, a neutral fact finder (judge or jury) declares the winner of the contest by deciding whether the prosecutor has proven the defendant's guilt.

It is generally understood today that these features describe (Weberian) ideal types; that no system is purely "inquisitorial" or "adversarial" (although some come pretty close); and that these terms are somewhat misleading because they can easily imply that an "inquisitorial" procedure pits an all-powerful magistrate against a largely helpless defendant, and that in an "adversarial" system the contestants are truly equal. Yet it is also widely accepted that, carefully employed, these two models are valuable heuristic devices. They enable us better to analyze actual criminal procedure systems by measuring them against these ideal types. And they help us understand the respective roles and structures, internal consistency or contradiction, as well as the underlying expectations and values more clearly.[576]

571 *Langbein* (*supra* n. 11).

572 This includes the "criminal justice" literature, *supra* n. 552.

573 *Bradley*, Criminal Procedure: A Worldwide Study (Durham NC 1999 and ed. 2 2007); *Hatchard, Huber and Vogler*, Comparative Criminal Procedure (London 1996); see also *infra* n. 282.

574 See, e.g., *Jackson, Langer and Tillers* (eds.), Crime, Procedure and Evidence in a Comparative and International Context (Oxford and Portland OR 2008).

575 *Langbein* (*supra* n. 11); *Thaman*, Comparative Criminal Procedure: A Casebook Approach (Durham NC 2002).

576 See, e.g., *Ingraham*, The Structure of Criminal Procedure (Westport CT 1987).

As mentioned (*supra* B.ii., s. 203), a slightly different model has linked types of procedure to different conceptions of state authority, distinguishing a "hierarchical" and a "coordinate" approach. This has turned out to be very helpful in understanding procedural features in the broader context of political structures and conceptions of truth.[577]

258. *Other prominent topics.* – Of the many more specific themes studied in comparative criminal procedure, five clusters of topics have been particularly popular.[578]

To begin with, systems differ substantially in their conceptions of the official in charge of initiating criminal proceedings. Some jurisdictions regard the prosecutor as an essentially political (perhaps even elected) figure, while others conceive of him or her as a civil servant (usually appointed for life). Some vest prosecutors with much (perhaps even unbridled) discretion whether and how to pursue a case; others require prosecution to the full extent of the law whenever the evidence makes a conviction likely (minor offenses perhaps excepted).

A closely related topic is plea bargaining.[579] In systems marked by prosecutorial discretion, prosecutors can make deals with defendants (and their counsel): they can offer a lower charge or a reduced sentence in exchange for a guilty plea or other forms of cooperation; in adversarial systems, such a plea avoids a trial altogether. In inquisitorial regimes, trials are usually mandatory but can be much simplified and shortened. Comparatists have observed that in recent decades plea bargaining has become increasingly popular in many legal systems, mainly for reasons of cost and efficiency. On the extreme end, it now clearly dominates the criminal process, as is the case in the United States where only a very small minority of criminal cases actually go to trial. But even where plea bargaining was once considered unthinkable and full trials were mandatory, it has now made major inroads, as is true in Germany.

Major differences have also been noted with regard to the kind and extent of lay participation. Some systems provide criminal defendants with a right to trial by jury; this has been a longstanding tradition in the common law orbit but also, with regard to major crimes, in France and legal systems modeled after it. In other jurisdictions, laypersons sit with professional judges to form a mixed bench, as in Germany and Italy. In many countries, however, criminal courts are staffed exclusively by professional judges. Since the later twentieth century there has been a marked trend to introduce criminal juries even in civil law jurisdictions, such as in Japan, Korea, Russia, and Spain.

Many studies have compared rules of evidence. Such rules play a muted role where only professional judges sit in criminal cases, but they become highly important before a lay jury which must be protected against prejudicial and misleading evidence. There is an extensive literature especially about exclusionary rules,[580] such as the "fruit of the poisonous tree" doctrine excluding evidence obtained (perhaps even indirectly) through police or prosecutorial misconduct. Exclusionary rules were much enlarged by the Warren (United States Supreme) Court in the 1960s and 1970s. Since then, so many legal systems have introduced them in one form or another that they have become an almost worldwide phenomenon.

Last but not least, comparatists have studied the criminal process from the perspective of legal transplants. Since the 1970s criminal procedure has been among the areas where many legal systems have imported ideas from others. Interestingly however, this is mainly true in the sense that "inquisitorial" systems have borrowed, often massively, from "adversarial" regimes, but not much the other way around. In some countries, especially in Italy, the formerly inquisitorial approach

[577] *Damaska* (*supra* 60).

[578] Other topics include different conceptions of double jeopardy, pretrial detention, possibilities of appeal, and regulation of sentencing.

[579] The topic became popular especially in the wake of the article by *Langbein*, Land Without Plea Bargaining: How the Germans Do It: 78 Mich.L.Rev. 204–225 (1979).

[580] *Thaman*, Exclusionary Rules in Comparative Law (Dordrecht, New York 2013).

has been largely revamped in an adversarial style. In many others, more particular changes have been inspired by ideas from common law jurisdictions, especially the United States. Prominent among these changes are, as mentioned, greater prosecutorial discretion and thus increased room for plea bargaining, jury trials, and exclusionary rules, but also a stronger role for defense counsel. As a result, criminal procedure has often become a hybrid in which inquisitorial and adversarial elements coexist, perhaps uneasily and sometimes in outright tension. Many comparatists have justly regarded this as a convergence of the principles and rules governing criminal procedure. Yet, convergence is much less clear with regard to the realities of the criminal process. Here, huge discrepancies often remain. This is obvious, for example, when one compares the extreme harshness, if not outright vindictiveness, of the criminal process in the United States with the more tempered and human rights-oriented approach in Europe.

259. *International and European dimensions.* – The new international criminal courts founded at the close of the twentieth century needed a workable set of procedural rules even more urgently than international rules on criminal liability. The tribunals vested with regional jurisdiction (for the former Yugoslavia, for Rwanda, Sierra Leone, etc.) had to create these procedures by and large ad hoc, while the Statute for the International Criminal Court (ICC) provides a codified framework which, however, still needs to be fleshed out with regard to many details. The respective procedures developed by and large as hybrids, mixing inquisitorial and adversarial elements as well as principles common to both. Here, comparative studies made important contributions to the development of an international criminal procedure.[581]

Scholars have also studied comparative criminal procedure in a specifically European context.[582] While there is no European criminal tribunal, the European Court of Human Rights has rendered numerous decisions protecting the procedural rights of defendants under the European Convention, often on the basis of comparing the member states' systems. It has thus shaped these systems under a quasi-constitutional framework, creating what some scholars have termed a "European consciousness" or even a "European tradition" of criminal procedure.[583]

d. Constitutional Law

260. *Development.* – In a sense, comparative constitutional law has a longer tradition than private law comparison, reaching back to classics such as Aristotle's *Laws* in the fourth century BC (*supra* III.A.i., s. 52) and, in the early modern period, to Montesquieu's *Esprit des lois* (1748) (*supra* II.A.iii.c., s. 63). A few decades later, the American founding fathers, especially John Adams (1735–1826) and James Madison (1751–1836), drew on their observations of foreign government structures in drafting the United States Constitution (1787). When written constitutions became more common at the end of the eighteenth and then throughout the nineteenth century, comparison was much facilitated, and upon attaining independence former colonies often drew lessons from their mother – or other – countries. In the twentieth century, the United States' constitutional experience became the most popular point of reference. This is especially true with regard to American-style judicial review which foreign observers watched with both fascination and concern, as in Edouard Lambert's (1866–1947) famous warning against a "government by judges"[584] and in Hans Kelsen's (1881–1973) development of an alternative model for the Austrian Constitution of 1920.[585]

[581] *La Rosa*, Juridictions Pénales Internationales: La Procédure et la Preuve (Paris 2003); *Sufferling*, Towards an International Criminal Procedure (Oxford 2001).

[582] Delmas-Marty and Spencer (eds.), European Criminal Procedures (Cambridge, New York 2002); Van den Wyngaert (ed.), Criminal Procedure Systems in the European Community (London 1994); Vogler and Huber (eds.), Criminal Procedure in Europe (Berlin, Freiburg 2008).

[583] *Delmas-Marty* (ed.), The Criminal Process and Human Rights: Towards a European Consciousness (Wien, New York 1995); *Summers*, Fair Trials: The European Procedural Tradition and the European Court of Human Rights (Oxford, Portland OR 2007).

[584] *Lambert*, Le gouvernement de juges et la lutte contre la législation sociale aux États-Units (Paris 1921).

[585] *Wenzel*, Judicial Review and Constitutional Maintenance: John Marshall, Hans Kelsen, and the Popular Will: 46 Political Science 591–598 (2013).

Yet, the beginnings of comparative constitutional law as we know it today lie in the post-World War II period. Now the newly founded constitutional courts in Western Europe began to develop their own jurisprudence that invited comparison with the American case law. At the same time, constitutional law gained importance – and was recognized as a subject in its own right – in more and more countries in the world even on the domestic level. This entailed a slowly growing cohort of specialists and a slowly growing interest in a comparative approach which even led to the publication of some casebooks on the subject beginning in the 1970s.[586]

For several decades, however, constitutional topics still remained on the margins of the discipline, which continued to be private law-centered at its core. This is still visible in the layout of this Encyclopedia: at its beginnings in 1971 constitutional law was not yet sufficiently developed to warrant a volume of its own.

Comparative constitutional law really took off towards the end of the twentieth century as a result of several overlapping developments.

Most importantly, the amount of material inviting comparison increased hugely. In part, this was due to a wave of new, sometimes innovative, constitutions, especially the Canadian Constitution Act with its Charter of Rights and Freedoms (1982), the South African interim (1993) and final (1997) Constitutions, and the transition to many newly democratic constitutions in Eastern and Central Europe in the 1990s. In part, new material also resulted from the worldwide rise of judicial review (*infra* s. 263) which entailed a growing output of constitutional case law. Working with all this material was greatly facilitated by the fact that all relevant constitutional texts and large amounts of case law were now available in English, either in the original or in translation.[587] Another factor boosting the field was the intense discussion about the constitutionalization of the European Community, eventually including the ambitious, though ultimately abortive, project of a constitution for the European Union (2005). Last but not least, the rise of comparative constitutional law was supported by the immense popularity of all matters constitutional in the United States as the country which was becoming the most influential trendsetter in comparative law as a whole.

Today, comparative constitutional law is one of the most popular, vibrant, and highly developed areas of comparative study. It is covered by a vast literature that continues to grow fast,[588] and most, but not all, of it is published in English.[589] It

[586] *Cappelletti and Cohen*, Comparative Constitutional Law (Indianapolis IN 1979); *Murphy and Tanenhaus*, Comparative Constitutional Law (New York 1977).

[587] Translations were originally published in book form, e.g., *Blaustein and Flanz* (ed.), Constitutions of the Countries of the World (Dobbs Ferry NY 1971 ss.); *Maddex*, Constitutions of the World (ed. 3 Washington DC 2008); *Finer, Bogdan and Rudden*, Comparing Constitutions (Oxford 1995); *Kommers and Miller*, The Constitutional Jurisprudence of the Federal Republic of Germany (Durham NC 1989 and ed. 3 2012); *Rogoff*, French Constitutional Law: Cases and Materials (Durham NC 2011). Increasingly, English translations have become available on the Internet, often published by the respective governments or courts themselves.

[588] See, e.g., *Carozza, Giovine and Ferrari* (eds.), Diritto Costituzionale Comparato (2 vol.) (Roma-Bari 2017); *Jakab, Dyevre and Itzcovich* (eds.), Comparative Constitutional Reasoning (Cambridge 2017); *De Vergottini*, Diritto Costituzionale Comparato (ed. 9 Padova 2014); *Ginsburg and Dixon* (eds.), Comparative Constitutional Law (Cheltenham, Northampton MA 2011); *Heringa*, Constitutions Compared (ed. 4 Maastricht 2016); *Pegoraro and Rinella*, Sistemi Costituzionali Comparati (Torino 2017); *Rosenfeld and Sajo* (eds.), The Oxford Handbook of Comparative Constitutional Law (Oxford 2012); *Sajo and Uitz*, The Constitution of Freedom (Oxford 2017); *Tushnet*, Advanced Introduction to Comparative Constitutional Law (Cheltenham and Northampton MA 2014); *Woolman and Bishop* (eds.), Constitutional Conversations (Pretoria 2008). For an overview of the field, see *Tushnet*, Comparative Constitutional Law: *Reimann and Zimmermann* (eds.), The Oxford Handbook of Comparative Law (ed. 2 Oxford 2019) 1193–1221. For a refreshingly unorthodox and critical view of the field, see *Frankenberg*, Comparative Constitutional Law: *Bussani and Mattei*, The Cambridge Companion to Comparative Law (Cambridge 2012) 171–191. For a decidedly critical perspective see *Frankenberg*, Comparative Constitutional Studies: Between Magic and Deceit (Cheltenham UK, Northampton MA 2018).

[589] But cf., *Troper (ed.)*, Traité International de Droit Constitutionnel (Paris 2011); *Scarciglia*, Introducción al Derecho Constitucional Comparado (Madrid 2011).

is often taught in separate courses.[590] And it even has its own legal periodical, the International Journal of Constitutional Law (since 2003).

For some time, comparatists focused primarily on a relatively small number of countries whose constitutional law was seen as particularly developed, interesting, or influential – above all the United States and, since the 1950s, Germany. Yet, like comparative law as a whole, the study of constitutional law has also expanded geographically – in Europe especially to France, Italy, Spain, and, more recently, Russia; in the English-speaking world mainly to Canada, South Africa, and India; in Asia, to Japan, Korea, and Taiwan;[591] and, to a lesser extent, to Latin America,[592] in particular Brazil and Mexico.[593]

261. *Difficulties*. – Constitutional law presents several intrinsic difficulties which are either not present or at least not as salient in other branches of comparative law. Most importantly, it constantly operates in the borderland between law and political science; since the actual functioning of a constitutional regime often depends on non-legal factors (such as the party system or the degree of social diversity), political scientists are often better positioned than lawyers to understand it. Comparative constitutional law also ties directly into the question whether a system has merely a constitution (i.e., normally a written document) or also a live culture of "constitutionalism", in particular real respect for the rule of law.[594] Today, many constitutional issues, especially in the area of individual rights, have an important international dimension which adds a layer of complexity as well (*infra* s. 266).

262. *Principal Purposes*. – The purposes of comparative constitutional law are both practical and academic.

On the practical side, drafters of constitutions have usually, and often intensely, studied existing models in other countries. This became perhaps most visible and well-known in the making of the South African Constitution in the 1990s. Also, constitutional courts often seek guidance from their foreign counterparts' jurisprudence, although that practice is much more common in some countries (such as Canada, Israel, and South Africa) and regions (e.g., Europe[595]) than in others. In the United States, it has been frequently, and at times acrimoniously, debated among members of the Supreme Court whether foreign law should be taken into account in constitutional interpretation.

From an academic point of view, the comparative study of constitutional law promises insights into a broad spectrum of issues. Some of these insights pertain to comparative law as a whole. For example, comparative constitutional law is a fertile field for the exploration of legal transplants[596] (*infra* VI.B.iii., ss. 345–350). It contributes important observations about the convergence (or divergence) of legal systems (*infra* VI.A.iii., s. 333). And it starkly presents the question why systems can be so similar in some regards, e.g., in their private law, and yet so different in others, e.g., in constitutional matters – witness the United States on the one hand (written constitution, strong judicial review) and the United Kingdom on the other (no single constitutional document, weak judicial review) or Germany (full-fledged constitutional court with extensive jurisdiction) and France (semi-political constitutional council with much more limited powers). Other topics are more intrinsic to constitutional law itself. Comparison can shed light on the role of constitutions in different types of regimes[597] and on different

[590] The two leading casebooks are *Dorsen et al.*, Comparative Constitutionalism: Cases and Materials (ed. 2 St. Paul MN 2010); and *Jackson and Tushnet*, Comparative Constitutional Law (ed. 3 St. Paul MN 2014).

[591] *Dixon and Ginsburg* (eds.); Comparative Constitutional Law in Asia (Cheltenham, Northampton MA 2014).

[592] See, e.g., *Brewer-Carias*, Constitutional Protection of Human Rights in Latin America (Cambridge, New York 2009).

[593] Some studies go beyond even that list: see, e.g., *McHugh*, Comparative Constitutional Traditions (New York 2002) (covering, inter alia, China, Nigeria, and Saudi Arabia).

[594] *Sellers and Tomaszewski* (eds.), The Rule of Law in Comparative Perspective (Dordrecht, New York 2010).

[595] Symposium: Foreign Law in Constitutional Courts: 64 Am.J.Comp.L. 797–889 (2016).

[596] See, e.g. *Henkin and Rosenthal* (eds.), The Influence of the United States Constitution Abroad (Washington DC 1986).

[597] See, e.g., *Ginsburg and Simpser* (eds.), Constitutions in Authoritarian Regimes (New York 2014).

models of constitutional design.[598] It illuminates processes of constitution making (by special constitutional assembly or existing parliaments?); adoption (by popular vote or elected legislatures?); interpretation (originalist, restrained, activist?[599]); structures of political systems (presidential or parliamentary?); separation of powers (strict or more limited?); constitutional amendment (easy, difficult, or impossible with regard to basic features?);[600] degrees of constitutional norm entrenchment (change by referendum or, perhaps qualified, legislative vote?); access to constitutional adjudication (only by state actors or also by individuals?), etc.

Three clusters of topics, however, have been studied with particular intensity and thus warrant a somewhat closer look: judicial review, individual rights, and federalism.

263. *Judicial review.* – Since the middle of the twentieth century, judicial review (in the sense of court power to declare legislation unconstitutional) has spread to ever more parts of the world – at first slowly after World War II and mainly in Western Europe, then rapidly since the end of the last century and on a global scale. This spread resulted from the combination of two simultaneous trends: the world-wide wave of constitution-making and the amazing rise of judicial power.[601] Since the late twentieth century judicial review has become the most frequently and intensely studied topic in comparative constitutional law.[602]

Comparatists have distinguished between different versions of judicial review along two major lines: its design and its strength. In terms of design, the de-centralized and non-specialized form of judicial review best exemplified by the United States (where all courts may declare all types of legislation unconstitutional and where the Supreme Court also decides questions of sub-constitutional law) stands in contrast to the (Kelsian) model of concentrated and specialized review first instituted in Austria and later in Germany and other countries (only a special constitutional court has full review power, and this court decides only constitutional questions). In terms of strength, there is a spectrum ranging from systems in which court(s) can declare legislation unconstitutional with universally binding and final effect (as in the United States, Germany, or South Africa) to systems in which court decisions are subject to legislative override (as in Canada) or not even binding on the legislature (as under the United Kingdom Human Rights Act of 1998). Comparatists have asserted that some models of judicial review are characteristic for certain legal traditions (such as the former British Commonwealth[603]) or geographic regions (such as Scandinavia[604] and East Asia[605]). Scholars have also studied several systems side-by-side to find explanations for the rise of judicial review.[606]

264. *Individual rights.* – Virtually all modern constitutions contain individual rights catalogs. Often reflecting both past experiences (e.g., with previous, perhaps totalitarian, regimes) and current needs (e.g., for particular protections or forms of social justice), these catalogs vary substantially

[598] *Ginsburg* (ed.), Comparative Constitutional Design (New York 2012).

[599] *Goldsworthy* (ed.), Interpreting Constitutions: A Comparative Study (New York 2007).

[600] *Albert*, Constitutional Amendments: Making, Breaking, and Changing Constitutions (Oxford 2019).

[601] *Tate and Vallinder*, The Global Expansion of Judicial Power (New York, London 1995).

[602] A precursor of the contemporary literature on the topic was *Cappelletti*, Judicial Review in the Contemporary World (Indianapolis IN, Kansas City KA, New York 1971); see also *Brewer-Carias*, Judicial Review in Comparative Law (Cambridge, New York 1989); *Delaney and Dixon* (eds.), Comparative Constitutional Review (Cheltenham 2018); *Van der Schyff*, Judicial Review of Legislation: A Comparative Study of the United Kingdom, the Netherlands and South Africa (Dordrecht, New York 2010).

[603] *Gardbaum*, The New Commonwealth Model of Constitutionalism (Cambridge, New York 2013).

[604] *Rogvi*, West-Nordic Constitutional Judicial Review (Copenhagen 2013).

[605] *Ginsburg*, Judicial Review in New Democracies: Constitutional Courts in East Asia (Cambridge, New York 2003); *Yeh and Chang* (*supra* n. 299); see also *Khilnani, Raghavan and Thiruvengadam* (*supra* n. 299); on Africa, see *Ngenge*, International Influence on the Design of Judicial Review in Francophone Africa: 61 Am.J. Comp.L. 433–460 (2013).

[606] *Hirschl*, Towards Juristocracy (Cambridge MA, London 2004).

in form and substance. This is fertile ground for comparative studies, and the literature is extensive.

One important angle is the comparison between different categories of rights. All constitutions contain significant classic, i.e., liberal and defensive, rights against state authority; but only some, especially more recent, documents also provide for social and economic rights (often termed "second generation rights");[607] and some even contain cultural and environmental rights belonging to certain groups. Another topic is the various modes of limiting constitutional rights. Some systems rely heavily on the categorical exclusion of certain activities from protection (e.g., by denying pornography the status of "speech"); others usually balance one person's right against that of another (e.g., the right to freedom of expression against the right to privacy) or against more or less clearly defined public interests (e.g., the right publicly to demonstrate against the unobstructed flow of traffic); an increasing number of regimes invoke a more refined proportionality analysis. Most constitutional courts combine these, and sometimes other, methods in a variety of ways.

Four individual rights have enjoyed special attention. In the 1980s and 1990s, the most prominent topic was the right to privacy, in particular whether it entailed the right of women to choose an abortion. Constitutional tribunals in several countries had come to various, sometimes contradictory, conclusions which invited comparison of constitutional texts, underlying values, and judicial attitudes.[608] At the same time, many comparatists began to focus on free speech and expression. In particular, they have discussed the difference between the US-American stance, which is strongly protective of free speech even at the expense of other rights and interests, and the approach prevailing in most of Western Europe, India, and elsewhere, which often limits freedom of expression in order to protect publicly endorsed values or the feelings of certain communities. This is most visible in the respective responses to so-called "hate speech". Many other studies have dealt with issues of equality. Some constitutions protect it in general terms, others are more specific; some take a more rigid approach, others allow broad exceptions; and some embrace a formal concept focused on equality of treatment, while others take a more substantive view and seek to ensure equality of outcomes. These attitudes entail varying ways of dealing with (racial, gender, or other) discrimination[609] and, in particular, significantly different positions towards affirmative action in favor of certain disadvantaged groups. Finally, many studies have discussed the importance and impact of the right to human dignity. Here, especially the strongly protective approach of the German *Grundgesetz* as interpreted by the German Constitutional Court has been contrasted with orders in which that value is less central and influential, as in the United States.[610]

265. *Federalism.* – While the definition of federalism is contested, a defining feature of every constitutional system is whether it is unitary or federal. Of course, the concentration of governmental power at the center or its distribution between the center and various subunits is a matter of degree. Still, some systems are clearly federal, like the United States or Switzerland, while others are essentially unitary, like Israel or Japan; many lie somewhere between these extremes, like Austria or Italy, and one can fairly debate whether these are federal or not.

Since the end of the last century, the comparative study of federal systems has become a major topic, not only among constitutional lawyers but also among political scientists. In part their interest was triggered by the evolution of Europe into

[607] *Tushnet*, Weak Courts, Strong Rights: Judicial Review and Social Welfare Rights in Comparative Perspective (Princeton NJ 2007).

[608] *Glendon* (*supra* n. 489); *Frankowski* (ed.), Abortion and Protection of the Human Fetus: Legal Problems in Cross-Cultural Perspective (Dordrecht, Boston MA, Hingham MA 1987).

[609] *De Búrca* (ed.), Evolutions in Antidiscrimination Law in Europe and North America, 60 Am.J.Comp.L. 1–287 (2012).

[610] E.g., *Eberle*, Dignity and Liberty. Constitutional Visions in Germany and the United States (Westport CT, London 2002). *Whitman* (*supra* n. 553) explores the impact of different attitudes towards personal dignity on the criminal justice system.

a federal system, which invited comparison especially with the United States;[611] in part, it was a response to an almost global trend towards federalism, affecting many formerly centralized countries like China, the United Kingdom, and even, albeit only on the margins, France.[612] Scholars have compared versions of federalism for a variety of purposes, e.g., better to understand divided power systems[613] (including their origins and trajectories, benefits and costs, stability and sustainability[614]), to explore their impact on legal unification,[615] or to develop normative theories of federalism.[616]

266. *Supra- and international dimensions.* – Today, constitutional issues arise no longer only in domestic law but frequently on a supra- or international level as well. This is largely due to the growing number, advancing integration, and increasing power of supra- or international organizations.

The phenomenon is most pronounced in Europe. After much debate at the end of the twentieth century,[617] it is generally recognized today that the treaties constituting the European Union have quasi-constitutional character, and that the EU has a constitutional law of its own.[618] The European Court of Justice de facto exercises a form of judicial review; the EU has its own catalog of individual rights (the Charter of Fundamental Rights of 2000, in force 2009); and it constitutes its own kind of federalism. In addition, the Council of Europe's human rights regime (under the European Convention of 1953) is a quasi-constitutional system of individual rights, enforced by a specialized tribunal (the European Court of Human Rights) which can find national legislation incompatible with the member states' obligations under the Convention.

Even beyond Europe there is, at least arguably, quasi-constitutional law on the international level. The Charter of the United Nations, and perhaps the founding documents of other international organizations, can be regarded as constitutions. There are various international human rights regimes, both on the global level (especially the UN system) and in the regional context (such as the well-established Inter-American, and the emerging African, human rights systems), which are more or less effectively enforced by a variety of committees and courts.

As a result, comparing constitutional systems often has an inevitable international dimension. Especially in the area of individual rights and freedoms, comparative constitutional law has become "continuous with the study of international human rights law".[619] A comparative exploration of constitutional norms governing the death penalty, for example, would be incomplete, and potentially misleading, without a look at Protocol No. 6 to the (European) Convention on Human Rights, the provisions of the Inter-American human rights documents, and the case law of the European and Inter-American human rights tribunals.

[611] *Nicolaides and Howse* (eds.), The Federal Vision: Legitimacy and Levels of Government in the United States and the European Union (Oxford, New York 2001); *Menon and Schain*, Comparative Federalism: the European Union and the United States in Comparative Perspective (Oxford, New York 2006).

[612] *Halberstam*, Federalism: Theory, Policy, Law: *Rosenfeld and Sajo* (eds.), The Oxford Handbook of Comparative Constitutional Law (Oxford 2014) 577–608; see also *Burgess*, Comparative Federalism: Theory and Practice (London, New York 2006).

[613] *Basu*, Comparative Federalism (New Delhi 1987).

[614] A foundational study (from a political science perspective) is *Riker*, Federalism: *Greenstein and Polsby* (eds.) Handbook of Political Science V: Government Institutions and Processes (Reading MA 1975) 93–172.

[615] *Halberstam and Reimann*, Federalism and Legal Unification: A Comparative and Empirical Investigation of Twenty Systems (Dordrecht, Heidelberg, New York, London 2014); *Stein*, Uniformity and Diversity in a Divided-Power System: The United States Experience: 61 Wash.L.Rev. 1081–1102 (1986).

[616] *Halberstam* (*supra* n. 612).

[617] *Stein*, Lawyers, Judges, and the Making of a Transnational Constitution: 75 A.J.I.L. 1–27 (1981); *Weiler*, The Constitution of Europe (Cambridge, New York 1999).

[618] *Lenaerts, van Nuffel and Bray*, Constitutional Law of the European Union (ed 3 London 2011); for brief overviews, see *Claes*, Constitutional Law: *Smits* (ed.), Elgar Encyclopedia of Comparative Law (ed. 2 Cheltenham, Northampton MA 2012) 223–236, 232–234; *Arnold*, European Constitutional Law: Its Notion, Scope and Finalities: *Engelbrekt* and *Nergelius* (eds.), New Directions in Comparative Law (Cheltenham, Northampton MA 2009) 99–107.

[619] *Tushnet* (*supra* n. 588) 1200.

e. *Administrative Law*

267. *Definitional issues.* – At first glance, defining administrative law is easy enough: it consists of the distinctive set of principles and rules that govern the activities of the executive branch of government (below the constitutional level) as well as the judicial review of administrative decisions. Yet, different legal systems have understood the concept in different ways. In the continental European tradition, administrative law (*droit administratif, Verwaltungsrecht*) mainly means the (primary) rules governing the organization, powers, and procedure of the administrative apparatus itself as well as the substantive rules governing its actions. In the common law orbit, the term (administrative law) usually refers to the (secondary) rules pertaining to judicial review of, and remedies against, administrative decisions (*contentieux administrative* in French, *Verwaltungsgerichtsbarkeit* in German).[620]

In this sense, the different understandings of administrative law map onto the time-honored civil v. common law dichotomy: the former concept is in line with the civil law tradition's emphasis on substantive justice, the latter reflects the common law's procedural orientation. The civil law perspective spread throughout much of the world as a result of the influence of the French and Prussian models; the common law understanding is rooted in the English approach, which was exported to the Commonwealth countries, and in part also to the United States.

Beyond that, however, the traditional civil v. common law dichotomy is of limited utility in the context of administrative law. This is not only because the differences between the basic orientations have recently diminished. Perhaps more importantly, there are significant variations within these families (e.g., between the German and the French, or the English and the US-American systems of administrative law). Also, many similarities and differences regarding particular features of administrative law cut across the traditional categories altogether.

In addition, systems often differ about the boundaries of administrative law, i.e., about the issue of who and what is governed by it. Especially in the civil law orbit, this issue is related to the question of how and where to draw the line between private and public law. For example, in the French tradition, the realm of public law is mainly defined by the purpose of an activity (to serve the common good); under the German approach, it is usually defined by the nature of the actor (public authority or private person).

Administrative law is closely connected to, and often overlaps with, the study of public administration, i.e., of the organization, legitimate goals, efficiency, etc., of state bureaucracies.[621]

This invites interdisciplinary study and cooperation between lawyers, political scientists, sociologists, and economists. Today, administrative law is also subdivided into many special branches, ranging from environmental law and zoning to professional licensing and immigration. There are many comparative studies of these specialized branches, but they must be left aside in this general survey.

268. *Development.* – It is debatable whether administrative law should be considered a post-World War II addition to comparative law. After all, a few significant studies were published already at the dawn of modern comparative law around 1900.[622] Still, in the first half of the twentieth century, these studies did not establish comparative administrative law as a recognized and coherent field. In fact, at the time, it was usually doubted whether the subject was even fit for comparison. In striking contrast to the (at least assumed) universality of private law, administrative law was closely tied to the divergent features of states, i.e., their governmental systems, constitutional traditions, public policies, and social values. Administrative law thus seemed

[620] See *Lepsius*, Verwaltungsrecht unter dem Common Law (Tübingen 1997); see also *Morbidelli, Pegoraro, Rinella and Volpi*, Diritto Pubblico Comparato (Torino 2016).

[621] *Heady*, Public Administration: A Comparative Perspective (Englewood Cliffs NJ 1966 and ed. 6 New York 2001).

[622] *Gneist*, Das englische Verwaltungsrecht der Gegenwart (Berlin 1884); *Mayer*, Theorie des französischen Verwaltungsrechts (Strasbourg 1886); *Goodnow*, Comparative Administrative Law (New York 1893); *Koellreutter*, Verwaltungsrecht und Verwaltungsrechtsprechung im modernen England: Eine rechtsvergleichende Studie (Tübingen 1912).

so idiosyncratic and contingent that its comparative study was at minimum extremely difficult and widely perceived as rather pointless. This is understandable in light of the major goals pursued by comparative law at the time, i.e., the detection of universalities, the unification of law, and the facilitation of legal transplants. Two additional obstacles hindered the development of the field. First, comparatists began to focus increasingly on the differences between the civil and the common law, but in the first half of the twentieth century in England (and to some extent also in the United States) administrative law was not yet recognized as a distinct subject. As long as common lawyers adhered to Albert Venn Dicey's famous claim that in England there was no administrative law,[623] it seemed that there was nothing beyond the Channel that could be compared. Second, in the 1930s and 1940s the rise of totalitarian governments in Europe and the cataclysm of World War II derailed the ordinary course of administrative business on a broad scale and made its comparative study largely pointless for the time being.

Thus it was only after World War II and the return to normalcy that comparative administrative law gradually developed into an established topic, with the French side taking the lead.[624] Like many other areas of comparative study, administrative law has finally become a broadly popular topic since the 1990s, as evinced by a steady growth in literary production.[625] Today, comparative administrative law is highly developed, diversified, and increasingly global in scope.[626]

It is also increasingly important. The widening and intensification of transnational regulatory problems, perhaps most visible in the environmental field, demands ever more cooperation between governments. The indispensable coordination and harmonization (or even unification) of administrative regimes and laws requires a thorough understanding of their commonalities and differences – which only comparative study can generate.

269. *Main topics and directions.* – Scholars have compared a large variety of particular elements of administrative law. Most of the published studies can be grouped into two clusters corresponding to the two basic understandings of the subject outlined above (*supra* s. 267). The first cluster concerns features of the administrative authorities themselves: their institutional design (e.g., general bureaucracies or specialized agencies), organization (e.g., centralized hierarchies or federal and local subdivisions), and power (e.g., inherent or only as granted by legislation). This also includes similarities and differences in the procedures before the administrative bodies[627] (e.g., the greatly varying participation rights of interest groups and individuals, the transparency of decisionmaking, and access to government documents). The second cluster contains issues of judicial review. There are significant differences in institutional design: in some systems review is exercised by the general judiciary (as in most common law countries), in others by separate administrative courts (as in Germany), special judicial branches of the administration (as in France), or sector-specific adjudicators (often

[623] *Dicey*, Lectures Introductory to the Study of the Law of the Constitution (London 1885).

[624] *Rivero*, Droit Administratif Comparé (2 vol.) (Paris 1954–58); *Braibant*, Institutions Administratives Comparées (Paris 1975); see also *Schwartz*, French Administrative Law and the Common-law World (New York 1954).

[625] See, e.g., *D'Alberti*, Diritto Amministrativo Comparato: Trasformazioni dei sistemi ammistrativi in Francia, Gran Bretagna, Stati Uniti, Italia (Bologna 1995); *Jacobini*, An Introduction to Comparative Administrative Law (New York 1991); *Napoletano* (ed.), Diritto Amministrativo Comparato (Milano 2007); *Rose-Ackerman and Lindseth* (eds.), Comparative Administrative Law (ed. 2 Cheltenham, Northampton MA 2017).

[626] Overwiews in *Bell*, Comparative Administrative Law: *Reimann* and *Zimmermann* (eds.), The Oxford Handbook of Comparative Law (ed. 2 Oxford 2019) 1250–1275; *Bignami*, Comparative Administrative Law: *Bussani and Mattei* (eds.), The Cambridge Companion to Comparative Law (Cambridge 2012) 145–170; *Nehl*, Administrative Law: *Smits* (ed.), Elgar Encyclopedia of Comparative Law (ed. 2 Cheltenham, Northampton MA 2012) 21–36.

[627] See, e.g., *Torchia* (ed.), Il Procedimento Amministrativo: Profili Comparati (Padova 1993); *Gattigan*, Due Process and Fair Procedure: A Study of Administrative Procedures (Oxford 1996).

in combination with quasi-appellate review by the judiciary, as in England and the federal system in the United States). There are also differences regarding the primary purpose of judicial review: in some jurisdictions its object is mainly to ensure the legality of the administration, in others it is primarily the protection of individual interests against overreaching state power. And while most systems recognize a fairly standard list of grounds for judicial review – illegality (e.g., lack of competence or procedural errors), violation of fundamental rights (e.g., to dignity, privacy, or property), and irrationality or abuse of discretion – there are substantial variations in how these grounds are handled and especially in how closely judges scrutinize administrative decisions.[628] Scholars have paid particular attention to the principle of proportionality which has become a crucial instrument of judicial review.[629] In addition, studies have compared informal dispute settlement mechanisms, especially the institution of the ombudsman.[630]

A separate set of issues concerns state liability for administrative acts.[631] Some jurisdictions follow essentially private law rules (of tort), while others hold administrative bodies to special standards which include unique privileges but also particular obligations. Systems also differ with regard to the grounds for administrative liability, which range from fault and risk to compensation for special sacrifices (*Sonderopfer*) and considerations of social solidarity.

270. *Europeanization – and Globalization?* – Like most other areas, since the 1990s administrative law has increasingly come under the influence of European integration. The core of this phenomenon has been the European Court of Justice's development of administrative law principles for the European Community, now the European Union. Since the Court drew on the administrative laws (and constitutional traditions) of the member states, this has been an inherently comparative enterprise, and one of enormous practical importance. The development of European principles and rules in turn has exercised an influence on the administrative laws of the member states, causing significant, albeit partial, convergence.[632] In addition, the European Court of Human Rights has repeatedly forced the member states of the Council of Europe to bring their administrative laws into compliance with the European Convention on Human Rights and Fundamental Freedoms, especially with Article 6 (Right to a Fair Trial). As a result, European administrative law – arguably grounded in a set of common principles[633] – has almost developed into a field of study in its own right, with its own literature and specialized journals.[634]

Beyond the effects of regional integration, administrative law has also acquired a global dimension, especially through the activities of international organizations and regulatory bodies.[635] There are now many global administrative law regimes governing transboundary activities ranging from aviation to maritime commerce and from public health to industrial standard-setting. The comparative study of these global regimes is particularly challenging because of their disparate

[628] *Frowein* (ed.), Die Kontrolldichte bei der gerichtlichen Überprüfung von Handlungen der Verwaltung (Berlin 1993).

[629] *Sandulli*, La Proporzionalità dell'Azione Amministrativa (Padova 1998); *Ellis* (ed.), The Principle of Proportionality in the Laws of Europe (Oxford 1999).

[630] *Stacey*, Ombudsmen Compared (Oxford, New York 1978).

[631] *Fairgrieve, Andenas and Bell*, Tort Liability of Public Authorities in Comparative Perspective (London 2002).

[632] *Ladeur* (ed.), The Europeanisation of Administrative Law (Aldershot, Burlington VT 2002); *Schwarze* (ed.), Administrative Law under European Influence (London 1996); see also *Fromont*, Droit Administratif des États Européens (Paris 2006).

[633] *Birkinshaw*, European Public Law (London 2003).

[634] *Schwarze*, European Administrative Law (Luxemburg and London 1992); *Nehl*, Principles of Administrative Procedure in EC Law (Oxford 1999); see also *Seerden and Stroink* (eds.), Administrative Law of the European Union, Its Member States and the United States: A Comparative Analysis (Antwerp 2002 and ed. 2 2007). Specialized journals are the *Revue européenne de droit public* (since 1989) and *European Public Law* (since 1995).

[635] *Bignami and Zaring* (eds.), Comparative Law and Regulation: Understanding the Global Regulatory Process (Cheltenham, Northampton MA 2016); *Kingsbury, Krisch and Stewart*, The Emergence of Global Administrative Law: 68 Law &Contemp.Prob. 15–61 (2005).

origin and nature, and because of the various ways in which they interact with domestic administrative institutions and rules. Yet, their comparative study is also of prime importance to ensure better coherence and coordination between the respective regimes. It is particularly crucial to find the right balance between regulatory cooperation reducing conflict on the one hand, and regulatory competition promoting innovation on the other.

f. The Law of the Economy

271. *Boosted by globalization.* – Since the closing decades of the twentieth century, the law of the economy has become a prominent area of comparative studies, especially with regard to commercial transactions, corporations, and competition. The main driver of this increasing importance has been the globalization of economic activity caused by several, mutually reinforcing developments, particularly the nearly worldwide trend towards deregulation, the transformation of formerly planned (socialist) economies into free (capitalist) markets,[636] the global lowering of trade barriers, and the revolution in information technology. The result has been an intensification in transboundary commercial transactions, a growth of globally competing banks and corporations, and an increase of internationally mobile workforces and consumers. This has entailed a multiplication of contacts and conflicts between national legal orders and thus an urgent need for mutual understanding, cross-border adjustment, as well as international harmonization and unification. These needs explain not only the rise of global law firms but also the much increased interest in comparative studies of economic law. Interest in such studies has been particularly strong in three quarters: among scholars in Western – developed and capitalist – countries seeking to export their market laws to the rest of the world; among politicians, policymakers, and scholars in less developed – especially formerly socialist – countries seeking to import sophisticated market law regimes; and among advocates and architects of international legal unification.

272. *Commercial transactions (and regulation).* – Comparatists have long pointed out that legal systems differ in their respective conceptions of commercial transactions in two basic respects.[637] One difference concerns the relationship between (general) private and (specific) commercial law. Some systems (mainly in the civil law tradition) have regarded commercial law as a distinct field with its own courts, codes, and principles, as is the case in France and Germany. Others (mainly in the common law orbit) have not made such a distinction and thus handled commercial disputes by and large in the regular courts and under the usual, albeit occasionally modified, rules of private law, e.g. in the United Kingdom and the United States (notably under the Uniform Commercial Code). The other difference pertains to how commercial transactions are defined. Some systems look to the participants, i.e., whether the involved parties are "merchants" (*commerçants, Kaufleute*, etc.) or not. Others look to the nature of the transaction, i.e., whether it involves business or private (including consumer) affairs. Some systems also blend both criteria in various ways. Such differences in approach and definition are obviously important in practice, e.g., in order to decide which court has jurisdiction or which set of rules applies. But they are also frequently invoked to illustrate a phenomenon of general significance to comparative law, i.e., that identical terms can have very different meanings in various legal systems (*infra* VI.B.iv., s. 357).

Since the final decades of the twentieth century, comparative studies have dealt more closely with particular areas of commercial transactions, such as negotiable instruments, letters of credit, insurance, and banking, which are covered in a special volume of this Encyclopedia.[638] Beyond that, scholars have discussed various broader issues which can be brought under four headings. They all imply questions of general importance to the discipline.[639]

[636] *Madl*, State and Economy in Transformation: Revolution by Law in the Central and Eastern European Countries: Int.Enc.Comp.L XVII, ch. 2 (2000); *Ajani*, Law and Economic Reform in Eastern Europe – The Transformation from Plan to Market During the Formative Years of 1989–1994: Int.Enc.Comp.L XVII, ch. 3 (2006).

[637] See *Tallon* (*supra* n. 433).

[638] *Ziegel* (*supra* n. 422).

[639] See *Kosolchyk* (*supra* n. 424).

A threshold issue is to what extent commercial laws can be compared in separation from their social and cultural context. This is a version of the general question to what degree law leads an existence independent of its environment (*infra* VI.B.iii., s. 350). On the one hand, one can argue that commercial law is relatively independent of social context because, unlike family law, for example, it is not closely tied to people's personal lives and concerns; instead, it reflects the logic of the market which is more uniform across cultures. Commercial law can thus be studied as a set of technical rules which are, or should be, designed to promote efficiency. On the other hand, even commercial law is often embedded in its surrounding culture, reflecting social (and perhaps religious) preferences. From that point of view, comparing it in the abstract is misguided, because it blinds the observer to how rules are shaped by cultural values.[640] There is broad agreement today that the cultural contingency of law, including commercial law, is a matter of degree and that it varies from one area to the next. With regard to business-to-business contracts, for example, the rules governing their formation are less subject to cultural variation than the norms concerning good faith obligations during the negotiation phase.

A related theme has been the transplantation of commercial law from developed to developing markets (which is obviously easier if legal rules have weak cultural roots). Legal transplants have been a general theme in comparative law for several decades (*infra* VI.B.iii., ss. 345–351). Since the export and import of law has recently been particularly intense in the commercial law arena, this area has provided much food for debate about the causes and effects, feasibility and risks of legal transplants. An example from the 1990s is the push (by government agencies and programs as well as by Anglo-American law firms) to export US-American and English commercial law to Central and Eastern Europe, China, and other parts of the world. While this law is widely regarded as particularly developed, its inherent preferences for party autonomy and against restrictive public policies do not sit well with the protection of consumer or labor interests. It is therefore not necessarily fit for legal cultures emphasizing such protection – at least not without substantial modification.

A third theme has been the expansion of comparative commercial law beyond the West. It comes as no surprise that studies have increasingly focused on the economically emerging regions, especially China and Latin America (also in the MERCOSUR context).[641] But they have also included developments of commercial law in traditionally neglected parts of the world, such as sub-Saharan Africa (especially within OHADA, *infra*) and the Middle East (in particular with regard to the Islamic law of finance).[642]

Last but certainly not least, comparative law has played a major role in the surge of efforts to harmonize or even unify commercial law. Some of these efforts, notably in the law of sales, pre-date the latest wave of globalization by half a century; most, however, have gathered steam since the 1990s. The main institutional driver has been the United Nations Commission on International Trade Law (UNICTRAL). The Commission operates largely through working groups consisting of state representatives from all regions and legal traditions of the world. UNCITRAL has produced unified model rules for commercial areas as diverse as insolvency, international payments, security interests in property, transport, and e-commerce. Its greatest success to date is the Convention on the International Sale of Goods (CISG) of 1980 (in force 1988). It has been adopted by over 90 countries, including all major economic players with the notable exceptions of India and the United Kingdom. Yet, even outside of UNCITRAL, international unification efforts have borne important fruit, such as in the (Cape Town) Convention on International Interests in Mobile Equipment 2001 (in force 2006). An important project on the regional level is the *Organisation pour l'Harmonisation en Afrique du Droit des Affaires* (OHADA). It is an international organization founded by treaty in 1993 with its own

[640] *Foster*, Comparative Commercial Law: Rules or Context?: *Örücü and Nelken* (eds.), Comparative Law: A Handbook (Oxford, Portland OR 2007) 263–285.

[641] See, e.g., *Ruskola*, Conceptualizing Corporations and Kinship: Comparative Law and Development Theory in a Chinese Perspective: 52 Stan.L.Rev. 1599–1729 (2000); *Clarke* (*supra* n. 257).

[642] See, e.g., *Malkawi*, Shari'ah Board in the Governance Structure of Islamic Financial Institutions, 61 Am.J.Comp.L. 539–577 (2013).

organs, including a Court of Justice and Arbitration, and a considerable list of uniform acts. On the level of "soft law" there are the UNIDROIT Principles of International Commercial Contracts (orig. 2004, new edition 2010). They provide (non-binding) uniform rules available as a model to legislators, courts, contracting parties, and especially arbitrators in international business disputes. Perhaps needless to say, in all these unification projects the comparative study of national commercial laws has laid indispensable foundations.

In addition, comparative studies have focused on the *regulation* of commercial activity.[643] Such regulation is frequently still produced by national governments, but international organizations have come to play an important, and in some areas primary, role. There is also much self-regulation through business principles and codes of conduct, providing a fertile field for comparative study.

273. *Company (corporate) law (and capital market law)*. – For most of the twentieth century, comparative law scholars largely neglected company law. Beginning in the 1960s, efforts to harmonize the field in Europe kindled some interest, but for the time being the matter was by and large left to policymakers and practitioners. Yet, since the late twentieth century, the law governing business organizations and their activities has become one of the most prominent, challenging, and practically relevant subjects of comparative law.[644] The field rose to prominence not mainly because comparatists discovered company law; more often, it was the other way around: company lawyers began to approach their topic from a comparative (and international) perspective.[645] As a result, much of the literature is written by scholars with deep knowledge of company law but limited understanding of comparative law frameworks, methodology – and pitfalls.

Growing attention to comparative company law was mainly a reaction to the rapid internationalization of business activities in the 1990s and beyond. In addition, the field was fertilized by the rise of the law and economics movement. While company law had of course always been influenced by economic considerations, since the 1980s leading US-American scholars have made economic analysis the predominant paradigm in this field. This approach has had considerable spillover effects in other countries, although in most of them economic analysis has not come to dictate legal discourse as strongly as in the United States. Comparative interest in company law was further stimulated by a series of disastrous business failures in various countries at the beginning of the twenty-first century; these failures triggered a search for preventive solutions, inter alia, by looking abroad.[646]

Substantively, scholars have dealt almost exclusively with the law pertaining to public corporations (stock companies), often in conjunction with capital market law, especially securities regulation. Geographically, they have looked mainly to the world's highly developed market economies. Originally, the focus was on the Anglo-American orbit, continental Europe, and Japan; more recently it has also included China and India as well as various other countries, such as Indonesia, Korea, and Taiwan.

This Encyclopedia thoroughly covers the field in a double volume.[647] The academic literature is rich, diverse, and constantly growing. There are also various specialized journals, e.g., the Journal of Corporate Law Studies (since 2001), the European Business Organizations Law Review (2000),

[643] *Nottage*, Commercial Regulation: *Smits* (ed.), Elgar Encyclopedia of Comparative Law (ed. 2 Cheltenham, Northampton MA 2012) 157–168; *Braithwaite and Drahos*, Global Business Regulation (Cambridge, Melbourne 2000); *Daintith*, Regulation (in relation to private law): Int.Enc.Comp.L XVII, ch. 10 (1997). See also *Basedow et al.* (eds.), Economic Regulation and Competition: Regulation of Services in the E.U., Germany and Japan (The Hague 2002).

[644] *Hopt*, Comparative Company Law: *Reimann* and *Zimmermann* (eds.), The Oxford Handbook of Comparative Law (ed. 2 Oxford 2019) 1137–1167; see also *Siems and Cabrelli* (ed.), Comparative Company Law. A Case-Based Approach (Oxford 2018).

[645] E.g., *Kraakman et al.* (eds.), The Anatomy of Corporate Law: A Comparative and Functional Approach (Oxford 2003 and ed. 2 2009).

[646] *Armour and McCaherty* (eds.), After Enron: Improving Corporate Law and Modernizing Securities Regulation in Europe and the United States (Oxford 2006).

[647] *Conard and Vagts* (eds.), Business and Private Organizations: Int.Enc.Comp.L XIII (2006: 2 parts).

the European Company and Financial Law Review (2004), and the European Company Law journal (also since 2004).

Scholars have mainly discussed the similarities and differences in dealing with the perennial problems resulting from the separation of corporate ownership and control, in particular how to reconcile the interests and goals of management with the protection of investors (stockholders and creditors). Differences among systems arise, inter alia, from the respective structures of stock ownership (concentrated or dispersed, dominated by institutional or private investors, etc.), control (e.g., one- v. two-tier boards of directors), and scope of protected interests (e.g., only investors or also other stakeholders, such as labor).

Since the 1990s the clearly predominant theme has been corporate governance in its various forms, i.e., through the design of corporate law itself, external legislative control, or self-regulation (*infra*). The whole subject has been treated as "essentially international and interdisciplinary";[648] it has thus been studied from both an inherently comparative and an economic, sociological, as well as psychological perspective. Major contributions have come mainly from the United States and Europe.[649]

Comparatists have also looked at the massive amount of inter-system borrowing that has characterized the development of corporate law for a long time. Already in the nineteenth and early twentieth centuries, legislation in Europe was often based on copying foreign ideas, usually those from other European countries. Since World War II the United States has been the globally dominant model.[650] Even today, US-American law is the standard reference point with regard to corporate finance, mergers and acquisitions, takeover regulation, and insider trading prevention. A major point of debate has been the extent to which corporate law and financial regulation transplants, as well as the dictates of a globalized market, have led to a convergence in these areas.[651]

A related issue is the harmonization of company and capital market law. This has been an especially hot topic within Europe.[652] After original plans of full harmonization had failed there, many particular aspects have been harmonized through European directives (and sometimes regulations and recommendations). In addition, two genuinely European types of business organizations have been developed and now exist next to the various national forms: the European Company (*Societas Europaea*) and the European Economic Interest Group. Comparative work has played a major role in the European harmonization efforts, especially through expert groups, e.g., the Forum (on) European Group Law (*Forum Europaeum Konzernrecht*) and in preparation of the Company Law Action Plan of the European Commission (2003).[653] Over time, European company law has developed into a subject in its own right, with its own academic literature,[654] casebook,[655] and a rich case law from the European Court of Justice, mainly regarding the freedom of movement of corporations within the European Union.

Finally, since the 1990s self-regulation has come to play an important role in company law.

[648] *Hopt* (*supra* n. 644) 1139.

[649] *Hopt et al.* (*eds.*), Corporate Governance in Context: Corporations, State and Markets in Europe, Japan and the US (Oxford 2005); *Hopt et al.* (*eds.*), Comparative Corporate Governance. The State of the Art and Emerging Research (Oxford 1998); *Milhaupt* (ed.), Global Markets, Domestic Institutions, Corporate Law and Governance in a New Era of Cross Border Deals (New York, Chichester 2003).

[650] See, e.g., *Von Hein*, Die Rezeption des US-amerikanischen Gesellschaftsrechts in Deutschland (Tübingen 2008).

[651] E.g., *Gordon and Roe* (eds.), Convergence and Persistence in Corporate Governance (Cambridge 2004); *McCaherty et al.* (eds.), Corporate Governance Regimes. Convergence and Diversity (Oxford 2002).

[652] *Buxbaum and Hopt*, Legal Harmonization and the Business Enterprise in Europe and the USA (Berlin, New York 1988).

[653] *High Level Group of Company Law Experts*, Report on a Modern Regulatory Framework for Company Law in Europe (Brussels 2002).

[654] *Barca and Brecht* (eds.), The Control of Corporate Europe (Oxford 2001); *Ferrarini et al.* (eds.), Reforming Company and Takeover Law in Europe (Oxford 2004).

[655] *Hopt and Wymeersch* (eds.), European Company and Financial Law: Texts and Leading Cases (ed. 4 Oxford 2007).

In many countries, there are now myriad so-called corporate codes dealing with issues of corporate governance. They are created by the industry itself, contain non-binding principles and rules, and are enforced through various means and to varying degrees. They provide interesting material for comparative study, not only in order better to understand the reasons for their similarities and differences but also with a view to possible harmonization.

274. *Competition law (antitrust)*. – One must be aware that the term can have different meanings. Here we use competition law synonymously with antitrust law – the former term being common in Europe, the latter in the United States. Sometimes, competition law is also employed in a broader sense, e.g., as encompassing rules about unfair business practices, but that is not the case here. We are thus looking at the comparative study of the law purporting to ensure proper competition among market actors, mainly by prohibiting monopolization, agreements in restraint of trade, and abuse of dominant positions.[656]

Despite some precursor efforts in late nineteenth- and early twentieth-century Germany, comparative competition law is a post-World War II phenomenon. It has two major dimensions: a transatlantic side whose origins lie in the 1950s, and a global dimension which opened up in the 1990s. In both, US-American antitrust law has served as the standard, and almost inevitable, reference point.

Transatlantic comparison began when US-American antitrust law acquired a modern counterpart in Europe. The crucial year was 1957 when Germany enacted modern antitrust legislation (*Gesetz gegen Wettbewerbsbeschränkungen*) and when the Treaty of Rome, founding the (then) European Economic Community, outlawed anticompetitive conduct (in Article 85); in both documents, the American influence was unmistakable.[657] Ever since, continental policymakers and scholars have looked across the Atlantic to gauge whether, and how far, they should follow the American model. For European observers, this model has played two principal and intertwined, roles. One has been empirical: the long American experience has provided rich data from which the Europeans have sought to learn. The other role has been normative: United States antitrust law has served as guidance for European policy- and rule-making. In both regards, European competition lawyers have been engaged in a quasi-permanent comparative enterprise for more than half a century. Towards the end of the twentieth century, American antitrust lawyers also began to look at European competition law. Their reasons were mainly practical. American firms operating overseas were increasingly faced with antitrust issues in Europe, and the American efforts to enforce US antitrust laws against European companies ("extraterritorially") met with increasing resistance from European courts and governments. As a result, European competition law could no longer be ignored.[658] Yet, the predominant American attitude has been different from the European: US antitrust lawyers have rarely tried to learn from Europe; instead they have mostly sought to persuade their overseas colleagues to follow the American model. This attitude is the result of three factors. To begin with, US antitrust lawyers by and large take the superiority of their own approach for granted; in particular, most of their intellectual leaders have been adherents to an (often *exclusively*) economic approach which has dominated US antitrust law for decades and which they have sought to bring to European competition law as well. Furthermore, the Americans looking at Europe have been committed antitrust lawyers with a vested

[656] For a thoughtful and critical review of the field, see *Gerber*, Comparative Competition Law: *Reimann and Zimmermann* (eds.), The Oxford Handbook of Comparative Law (ed. 2 Oxford 2019) 1168–1192. See also *Duns, Duke and Sweeney* (eds.), Comparative Competition Law (Cheltenham, Northampton MA 2016); for a shorter account, see *Geradin*, Competition Law, in *Smits* (ed.), Elgar Encyclopedia of Comparative Law (2d ed. Cheltenham, Northampton MA 2012) 208–215.

[657] On the development of European competition law, see *Gerber*, Law and Competition in Twentieth Century Europe – Protecting Prometheus (Oxford 1998).

[658] *Hawk*, United States, Common Market, and International Antitrust: A Comparative Guide (New York 1996); most American casebooks now contain references to European competition law: see, e.g., *Fox et al.*, U.S. Antitrust in Global Context: Cases and Materials (ed. 3 St. Paul MN 2012).

interest in their own system, rather than trained comparatists with an open mind towards other approaches. Finally, American practitioners have a strong interest in shaping foreign antitrust laws in ways familiar to themselves and their clients.

Comparative competition law eventually expanded its scope beyond the transatlantic context. Beginning in the 1990s, it has included other regions and become an almost worldwide phenomenon. In part, this was of course due to economic globalization, which entailed increased transnational business activities and thus greater friction between a larger set of legal systems. In part, however, it was also due to the fact that many countries now first began to develop antitrust law – often under pressure from the United States or from global financial institutions. Some, like Japan, began to take existing law more seriously; others, like India, enacted new legislation; and yet others at least developed policies in preparation for it. All this provided the opportunity, and indeed the need, for comparative studies dealing especially with Asia (first Japan, then increasingly Korea and Taiwan, finally also China) but also Latin America and other parts of the world.[659]

As a result, the discussion of competition law now takes place among a developing "global epistemic community".[660] This has created an enormous and fast-growing literature consisting not only of books and (innumerable) articles but also of institutional studies (e.g., by the OECD and UNCITRAL) which describe, and sometimes compare, competition law systems. There are also several specialized journals, such as the World Competition Law and Economic Review (since 1987), Concurrences (since 2004), the Journal of Competition Law and Policy (since 1999), and the Journal of Competition Law and Economics (since 2005).

Some of this literature is explicitly comparative in the sense of analyzing the similarities and differences between competition law regimes. Much, if not most of it, however, consists mainly of describing foreign law and perhaps advocating changes in this or that direction. The main reason for this descriptive approach is that only some of the authors are scholars who have the time and interest to take a broad view of the field and to probe deeply into the matter. Most are practitioners in global law firms or government officials who tend to write on narrow topics in order to provide information for their audience or to promote specific positions reflecting particular interests. As a result, there is a plethora of publications which are informative and professionally useful, but a paucity of broad and deep analytical work producing fundamental comparative insight or original ideas. In particular, there is a need for more comparative scholarship that is realistic in the sense of looking at how law actually functions on the ground in the respective jurisdictions, conscious of the often very different conditions prevailing there, and cognizant of social values beyond economic efficiency. Such scholarship can be crucial in bridging gaps and avoiding misunderstandings between legal systems, especially for practitioners dealing with transnational transactions or disputes and for officials negotiating with foreign colleagues.

There are three more particular topics that have generated discussion in comparative competition law in the last few decades: convergence, unification, and enforcement. The first and second are variations on classic themes in comparative law; the third is a special issue in competition law.

Competition law is among the areas in which there has been considerable international convergence. This is undeniable in the sense that during the last half century competition law turned from an American idiosyncrasy first into a transatlantic phenomenon and then into an almost global enterprise embraced by the majority of developed countries in the world in one form or another (at least on paper). While much of this convergence can be ascribed to global American influence, one

[659] *Rosenthal and Green* (eds.), Competition Regulation in the Pacific Rim (New York 1996); *Haley*, Antitrust in Germany and Japan: The First Fifty Years 1947–1998 (Seattle 2001); *De León*, Latin American Competition Law and Policy: A Policy in Search of Identity (The Hague 2001); *Gerardin*, Competition Law and Regional Economic Integration: An Analysis of the Southern Mediterranean Countries (Washington DC 2004); see also *Chao et al.* (eds.), International and Comparative Competition Law and Policies (The Hague 2001).

[660] *Gerber* (*supra* n. 656) 1172.

must be careful not to overemphasize the role of US antitrust law in this development. It is true, of course, that American antitrust law was the original model; that in the post-World War II decades it had a strong impact in Europe; and that it has continued to be highly influential both there and in other regions of the world. But it is also true that since the later twentieth century European antitrust law has provided a competitor model with a significant global influence. As the economic power of the United States has declined relative to that of Europe and China, its antitrust law has also lost its function as the one model that overshadows all others. More recently, global convergence has also been promoted by transnational cooperation among government officials, e.g., in the International Competition Network (founded 2004). One must also be careful not to overrate the degree of convergence. It is undeniable that the basic contours of competition law, such as the illegality of price fixing or of market share cartels, a balancing approach to other forms of potentially anticompetitive product, and the institution of ex ante merger control above a certain economic threshold have become similar among jurisdictions. But one must not overlook that significant differences remain, for example regarding the response to abuse of an economically dominant position or concerning the degree to which economic, and in particular consumer welfare, considerations dominate the law at the expense other values.

The convergence of competition law is related to the question of its international harmonization and unification. In a globalized economy the need for both is strong. Obviously, pursuing these goals is an inherently comparative enterprise. Since the late twentieth century the harmonization of competition law has been promoted by both governments and the private sector with considerable success. Yet, the ambition to create a uniform international competition law regime (e.g., in form of a treaty) has essentially failed.[661]

The final, and particularly salient, topic has been the mode of enforcement.[662] To be sure, enforcement by government agencies is relatively uncontroversial in principle because it is common in almost all competition law regimes. Instead, the main question is whether, and to what extent, there should also be enforcement by private action. As foreign observers have long noted with a mix of fascination and horror, American antitrust laws endow competitors and other victims of violations with powerful weapons against wrongdoers: especially an action for treble damages and the option to band together in order to bring a class action, resulting in potentially crushing liability. The harshness of this regime is officially based on the idea that plaintiffs represent not only their own, but also the public interest, thus acting as "private attorneys general". Other jurisdictions have considered whether also to allow private actions, possibly for multiple damages, and especially whether to permit class or group actions of some kind. Especially the European Union has recently pushed for more private enforcement of competition law, again using the American model as guidance.[663] A sound approach to the issue requires careful comparison of the broader legal environments in the United States and the respective other jurisdictions. In particular, private enforcement must be compatible with existing judicial structures and procedural frameworks, the style and organization of private legal practice, the general approach to cost and fee shifting, and traditional conceptions of the proper domains of public and private authority.

g. *More Recent Additions*

275. *Human rights.* – Modern human rights law is a child of the post-World War II era. Despite the universalism inherent in the very concept of human rights, the field provides fertile ground for comparison because it has developed a variety

[661] *Ullrich* (ed.), Comparative Competition Law – Approaching an International System of Antitrust Law (Baden-Baden 1998); *Drexl* (ed.), The Future of Transnational Antitrust – From Comparative to Common Competition Law (Berne 2003).

[662] See, e.g., *Jones*, Private Enforcement of Antitrust Law in the EU, UK and USA (Oxford 1999).

[663] *Waelbroek et al.* (eds.), Study on the Conditions of Claims for Damages in Case of Infringement of EC Competition Rules. Comparative Report (Brussels 2004).

of largely independent systems – a global (UN) regime and several regional ones in Europe, Latin America, and, much more weakly, Africa; each of these systems has its own basic instruments (mainly in the form of treaties), tribunals (commissions or courts), and body of case decisions (ranging from extensive to fairly minimal). These regimes can be compared not only amongst each other but also with the protection of individual rights under national constitutions; as a result, comparative human studies often overlap with comparative constitutional law.

Since it took several decades for the various international systems to develop and to generate enough material to make comparative study worthwhile, human rights law – like so many other areas – became the object of sustained comparison only towards the end of the twentieth century. Today, there is a substantial specialized literature in this area,[664] and the subject is sometimes taught in special courses, especially in the United States.[665] Most of the literature, however, focuses on Europe, where the world's most robust human rights system developed under the European Convention of Human Rights (1950, in force 1953), and where enforcement through litigation before a powerful and respected tribunal (the European Court of Human Rights) is more effective than anywhere else.[666]

The comparative study of human rights differs from the discipline's mainstream in three regards. It inevitably involves international systems and thus transcends the traditional comparison of national laws. It deals with questions that are much more politically charged than the more common issues of private, criminal, or procedural law. And it is unique in that it is driven mainly by judges rather than by scholars. In most areas of comparative law academic studies trigger judicial reactions, but in the human rights field it has typically been the other way around: the comparative discourse of regional and national tribunals has elicited scholarly comment and critique.[667]

Focusing on human rights law brings several issues pervading the discipline of comparative law as a whole into particularly sharp relief. On the most fundamental level, comparative human rights law starkly presents the tension between universalism and pluralism. On the one hand, there is the comparative lawyer's longstanding pursuit of a "droit commun" or of a "common core" of law (*supra* IV.A.iii., ss. 86–87, and VI.C.ii., ss. 374–377), which aligns easily with the universalist aspirations of human rights advocates. On the other hand, there is the discipline's more recent emphasis on difference (*infra* VI.A.iii., s. 328) which flies in the face of universalist positions, and which suggests a more pluralist approach even to human rights. On the methodological level, comparative human rights studies squarely face the inherent limits of the dominant functionalist approach (*infra* VI.C.i., ss. 368–370). Under such an approach, the goal of comparative studies is to analyze how law in different systems solves (more or less identical) social problems; this can also make good sense for human rights norms. Yet, today comparative law is often regarded primarily as a means to create a dialog between legal systems in order to foster broader understanding and greater tolerance; such a

[664] See, e.g. *Claude* (ed.), Comparative Human Rights (Baltimore MD, London 1976); *Fredman* (ed.), Comparative Human Rights Law (Oxford 2018). For an overview, see *Besson*, Comparative Law and Human Rights: Reimann and Zimmermann (eds.), The Oxford Handbook of Comparative Law (ed 2 Oxford 2019) 1222–1249.

[665] A specialized casebook is *Weisburd*, Comparative Human Rights Law (2 vol.) (Durham NC 2008). Some of the publications for general comparative law teaching also now include chapters on human rights: see *Glendon, Carozza and Picker* (*supra* n. 20) 746–798; see also *Glendon, Carozza and Picker* (*supra* n. 340) 348–358; see also *Reimann, Hathaway, Dickinson and Samuels* (*supra* n. 45) 344–422.

[666] *Gearty* (ed.), European Civil Liberties and the European Convention of Human Rights: A Comparative Study (The Hague, Boston MA 1997); *Blackburn and Polakiewicz*, Fundamental Rights in Europe (Oxford, New York 2001); *Drzemczewski*, European Human Rights Law in Domestic Law: A Comparative Study (Oxford, New York 1983); *Flanz and Ludwiokowski* (eds.), Comparative Human Rights and Fundamental Freedoms (Dobbs Ferry NY 2002).

[667] *Örücü* (ed.), Judicial Comparativism in Human Rights Cases (London 2003); *McCrudden* (*supra* n. 36) 371–397; *McCrudden*, Using Comparative Reasoning in Human Rights Adjudication: The Court of Justice of the European Union and the European Court of Human Rights Compared: 15 The Cambridge Yearbook of European Legal Studies 383–415 (2012–13).

"dialogical" use is particularly important for cooperation, and adjustment, between the various human rights regimes. Finally, on the instrumental level, comparative human rights law raises the fundamental question whether it is legitimate to use foreign law selectively as an argument for a particular position. The mainstream has traditionally regarded comparative law mainly as an academic enterprise and thus as a "science" in search of objective knowledge; in that case, its basic stance must remain as neutral, and thus as circumspect, as possible. But comparative studies can also be regarded from a partisan point of view, i.e., as a means to mine other legal systems for arguments in support of a cause; given its moralist underpinnings, this has been particularly common in the human rights field. From the former (academic) point of view, the selective use of foreign law is improper "cherry picking", from the latter (partisan) perspective it is legitimate advocacy.

276. *Tax law.*[668] – One can justly question whether the comparative study of tax law should be regarded as a recent addition to the discipline because the tax laws of various countries were described, and sometimes even compared, already around the middle of the twentieth century.[669] Yet, the respective publications were mainly aimed at providing information for tax lawyers, and thus remained by and large descriptive. Comparative tax law in the sense of academic research and teaching using the methods and pursuing the goals of comparative law is a much more recent phenomenon which began to develop in the 1990s.

For the most part, comparative tax law studies have been driven by the interests of practice. They have typically catered to the demands of tax practitioners engaged in tax planning for their clients; and they have often responded to the needs of policy makers interested in ideas for tax reform, both on the national level and in international organizations, such as the OECD.[670] These practical needs have also been the focus of the many specialized periodicals as well as of the numerous tax LL.M. programs in universities around the world.

It fits this picture that most authors writing in this area are tax lawyers engaged in comparison, rather than comparatists turning to tax law. This is in no small part due to the highly complex nature and unique terminology of tax law, which create high access barriers for non-specialists. Unsurprisingly, a field driven by practical needs and tilled by specialists has generated a crop consisting mostly of issue-specific and policy-oriented studies rather than comprehensive comparative analyses. As a result of all these factors, comparative tax law has developed largely in separation from mainstream comparative law.

Still, since the turn of the millennium a few truly comparative and fairly comprehensive works have been published.[671] They have begun to connect comparative taxation to the broader discipline. In particular, they have laid the foundations for further studies pursuing established comparative law themes, such as the classification of systems,[672] functional analysis of solutions, the study of legal transplants, or the search for a common core of rules and principles.[673] Yet,

[668] For an overview, see *Thuronyi*, Tax Law: *Smits* (ed.), Elgar Encyclopedia of Comparative Law (ed. 2 Cheltenham, Northampton MA 2012) 862–872.

[669] See especially the Cahiers de Droit Fiscal International, published by the International Fiscal Association since 1939; its by now over 100 volumes contain country reports digested in a general report on a large number of topics. Also, the Harvard Law School International Tax Program published about a dozen country studies in the late 1950s–early 1960s, all of which are now outdated of course.

[670] See, e.g., *OECD*, Taxpayers' Rights and Obligations: A Survey of the Legal Situation in OECD Countries (Paris 1990).

[671] Most importantly *Thuronyi*, Comparative Tax Law (The Hague 2003); see also *Barassi*, La Comparazione nel Diritto Tributario: *Uckman* (ed.), Corso di diritto internazionale (ed. 2 Padova 2002) 1499–1532; *Betrame and Mehl*, Techniques, Politiques et Institutions Fiscals Comparées (ed. 2 Paris 1997); *Ault and Arnold*, Comparative Income Taxation (The Hague, Boston MA 1997 and ed. 3 Alphen aan den Rijn 2010).

[672] *Thuronyi*, Tax Law Design and Drafting (International Monetary Fund 1996–1998).

[673] *Avi-Yonah, Sartori and Marian*, Global Perspectives on Income Taxation (Oxford, New York 2012) 1–16; *Garbarino*, An Evolutionary Approach to Comparative Taxation: Methods and Agenda for Research: 59 Am.J. Comp.L. 677–709 (2009).

much of this work still needs to be done before comparative tax law can be regarded as a firmly established field.

Comparative tax law faces several serious challenges, all of which, however, also entail promising opportunities. The particularly short shelf-life of many tax rules makes their academic study unrewarding and strongly suggests focusing on more enduring fundamental issues; but it also allows the comparatist to observe the circulation of legal models and the effects of transplants in much shorter time frames than in other areas. The close relationship between comparative and international tax law makes it often difficult to tell where one ends and the other begins; but it also highlights the contribution of comparative studies to the design of international tax rules, both in domestic legislation and in tax treaties. The integral role of economics in tax law and policy requires lawyers to understand a neighboring discipline; but it also leads to the kind of interdisciplinary work that is often so sorely lacking in comparative studies elsewhere.

Like many other areas, comparative tax law has begun to acquire a special European dimension. Although the taxation powers of the European Union remain severely limited, since the 1990s, the integration of the European market has created its own, unique set of tax problems that warrant specialized comparative analysis.[674]

277. *Data protection and privacy.* – A major new area for comparative study arising at the close of the second decade of the twenty-first century is the protection of data and privacy in the age of the internet.

In the new millennium, global data flow and gathering have skyrocketed. This has been largely due to the rapid growth of giant corporations operating on the internet (Google, Amazon, e-bay in the United States, Alibaba and Baidu in China, etc.) and the growing popularity of internet-based "social media" (Facebook, Instagram, Snapchat, etc.). At the same time, the public has become increasingly aware of, as well as concerned about, the massive amount of data corporations as well as governments all around the world have been collecting, be it openly or secretly. Both developments have combined to make data protection and privacy one of the top political (as well as social and economic) issues.

In the absence of a global regulatory regime, these issues have largely been left to national and, in Europe, regional legislatures and courts. This has resulted in significant, and sometimes deeply rooted, differences between jurisdictions, especially between the increasingly protective stance of the European Union,[675] a much more laissez-faire regime in the United States, and an increasingly censorship-oriented approach in China. All this has made the comparison of data and privacy protection law not only a fertile field but a growing necessity for international cooperation and harmonization.

At the end of the new millennium's second decade, scholars and practitioners have begun to explore the global situation,[676] but genuinely comparative work is still in its infancy.[677] Given the enormous practical importance and inherent theoretical challenges, data protection and privacy law is, or at least should be, destined to become a major topic of comparative studies in the future.

[674] *Di Malta*, Droit Fiscal Européen Comparé (Paris 1995); *Titard*, Corporate Taxation in EU Countries (ed. 2 London 1994).

[675] Especially in the EU General Data Protection Regulation (GDPR), O.J. L 119, 1–88 (2016, in force 2018).

[676] See, e.g., *Bygrave*, Data Privacy Law (Oxford 2014) 31–116; *Bygrave*, Privacy and Data Protection in an International Perspective: Scand.Stud.L. 56 (2010) 165–200; *Kuner*, Transborder Data Flows and Data Private Law (Oxford 2013); *Mehre*, Creating a 21st Century Personal Data Protection Regime in the United States: Consent, Oversight, and Remedial Reform; Lessons from the German Model: 35 Wis.Int.L.J. 205–235 (2017); *Palmieri*, Data Protection in an Increasingly Globalized World: 94 Ind.L.J. 297–329 (2019).

[677] See, e.g., *German Federal Ministry of Justice and Consumer Protection et al.*, Consumer Data Protection in Brazil, China and Germany: A Comparative Perspective (Göttingen 2016); *Greenleaf*, Asian Data Privacy Laws (Oxford 2014); *Witzleb et al. (eds.)*, Emerging Challenges in Privacy Law: Comparative Perspectives (Cambridge 2014).

D. In Conclusion: Proliferation and Its Price

278. *Rabel's mandate fulfilled.* – In 1924, Ernst Rabel, one of the founding fathers of modern comparative law, published his essay "Aufgabe und Notwendigkeit der Rechtsvergleichung" which has long since become a classic. At the time, Rabel famously demanded that we think about "the law of the whole world" ("das Recht der gesamten Welt") in all its dimensions and all its complexity.[678] In the century that has passed, comparative law has indeed developed in that direction. The discipline's coverage has steadily expanded to encompass ever more regions of the world, ever more legal systems and their constitutive elements, and ever more areas and dimensions of law. In the first half of the twentieth century this expansion was gradual and fairly slow; in the post-World War II decades it accelerated noticeably; finally, in the post-cold war era of the 1990s and beyond the expansion proceeded at a frenetic pace, largely in response to globalization. As a result, the discipline's coverage today is hugely broader than in Rabel's day, in terms both of quantity and of diversity. To a large extent, then, Rabel's mandate has been fulfilled.

279. *The price of proliferation.* – One must not overlook, however, that the discipline's expansion and diversification have come at a cost.

Most obviously, the sheer mass of material has grown so fast that no single scholar can keep up with it. The number of volumes published about comparative law has skyrocketed since the 1990s, though much of the deluge consists of edited volumes; they are, of course, much easier to produce than monographs, but they often contain a fairly haphazard collection of contributions which are more or less loosely related to an overarching theme.[679] Law review articles are written faster than anyone can read them. Even recent overviews of the discipline have significantly grown in size, at times massively.[680] At the same time, the material has become so varied that comparative law is really no longer a single discipline covering a set of subjects that a capable generalist can handle. Instead, like international law, it has largely fragmented into a cluster of full-blown sub-disciplines that only specialists can master. Today, many of the various specialty areas have their own agendas, methodologies, and discourses, as well as their own academic communities operating with little, or no, communication or cooperation with each other. These specialty areas also overlap with other disciplines so that even their boundaries have become blurry. On a field so vast and diversified, the sense of participating in a common enterprise has steadily diminished, often to the vanishing point.

678 *Rabel* (*supra* n. 153) 5.

679 A tell-tale sign of the fragmented state of the discipline is the volume published by the *Société de Législation Comparée*, De Tous Horizons: Mélanges Xavier Blanc-Jouvan (Paris 2005). The more than fifty contributions in honor of a prominent comparatist are so diverse that a common denominator is virtually impossible to find. The same is true for many collected volumes, such as Institute of Comparative Law in Japan, Future of Comparative Study in Law (Tokyo 2011) or, on a smaller scale, *Zimmermann* (ed.), Zukunftsperspektiven der Rechtsvergleichung (Tübingen 2016).

680 Note that the general introduction written by *Zweigert and Kötz* (*supra* n. 3) in ca. 300 pages (1–313), is now covered by *Kischel* (*supra* n. 286) in about 900 pages. The Oxford Handbook of Comparative Law (ed. 2 2019 Oxford) comprises ca. 1400 densely printed pages, and it still does not cover nearly all aspects of the discipline. Still, the volume by *Siems*, Comparative Law (ed. 2 Cambridge 2018) shows that a meaningful introduction remains possible in 400 pp., though only by being carefully, and courageously, selective.

V GOALS AND USES OF COMPARATIVE LAW

280. *Introduction and overview.* – Discussing the goals and uses of the discipline has long been a standard exercise among comparatists, and most treatises address the topic in a separate chapter, sometimes at considerable (and perhaps excessive) length.[681]

There are three principal reasons for this preoccupation with the subject matter. It originally arose mainly from the perception that, in contrast to most other areas of legal study, the utility of comparative law is not immediately obvious so that it needs to be explained to outsiders. This perception was largely justified during much of the 20th century when the discipline often found itself marginalized, especially in legal academia. Since the 1990s, the need to emphasize the utility of comparative studies has diminished as the globalization of law has made it obvious that understanding the relationships among legal orders is essential to modern legal theory and practice. At the same time, however, a new concern arose. As a result of legal globalization, comparative perspectives have increasingly been integrated into legal studies generally. In order to avoid having their discipline lose its specific identity, comparatists have felt the need to emphasize and explain the distinct value added by their various endeavors. Finally, the extensive discussions of the discipline's objectives and benefits also result from its increasingly diverse orientation. Over time, comparative law has come to comprise a growing array of different approaches (*infra* VI.) which, in turn, pursue different objectives and proffer different benefits. The expanding multitude of approaches thus entails an expanding list of goals and uses.

Since the goals and uses of the discipline depend on the particular approach chosen, there is something to be said for treating these aspects together as two sides of the same coin. Yet, this has not been the tradition, and there are good reasons to address goals and uses on the one hand and approaches and methods on the other separately. Most importantly, the correlation between the two sides is far from perfect because some approaches generate multiple benefits and some uses result from a variety of approaches. Also, while the debate about the proper approaches and methods has often been highly contentious, the discussion of the discipline's goals and uses has rarely been divisive. To be sure, comparatists may have different views of their endeavor's primary utility, but there is broad agreement that it can serve multiple purposes, and that these purposes are by and large compatible. Still, addressing these closely related dimensions separately inevitably entails some redundancy. [682]

Scholars have often divided the list into more theoretical (or academic) uses and immediately practical (or utilitarian) benefits. It is generally recognized that there is considerable overlap between these two categories so that the line cannot always be sharply drawn. Still, such a division makes sense because comparative law does envisage two major groups of "clients",[683] i.e., scholars and students with their academic perspective on the one hand (*infra* A.), and hands-on practitioners (including politicians) in making and applying law on the other (B.). We will discuss six traditional objectives and uses in each category for a total of a dozen. This time-honored list is supplemented by some modern additions reflecting early twenty-first century needs and trends (C.).

A. TRADITIONAL ACADEMIC GOALS

i. *Pursuing Knowledge*

281. *The pursuit of knowledge as a sufficient goal?* – It has often been claimed that "the primary aim of comparative law, as of all sciences,

---

[681] This is especially true in German scholarship, see *Constantinesco*, Rechtsvergleichung II: Die rechtsvergleichende Methode (Köln, Berlin, Bonn, München 1972) 331–431; *Kischel* (*supra* n. 286) 47–91.

[682] Addressing these dimensions separately inevitably entails some redundancies because several topics will have to be looked at first from the perspective of uses and goals (this chapter) and then as a matter of orientations, approaches, and methods (infra. VI.).

[683] See *Basedow*, Comparative Law and Its Clients: 62 Am.J.Comp.L. 821–857 (2014).

is knowledge"[684] the pursuit of which is "an end in itself".[685] In a similar vein, the discipline has been called an "*école de verité*",[686] "a means of learning and knowledge",[687] and a platform for "mental training".[688] These claims are noble, but since their generality makes them virtually impossible to deny, they lack analytical purchase. Their main effect is to vest comparative law with intellectual dignity as an academic discipline in its own right.

282. *Knowledge in its own right unsatisfactory.* – Even from a scholarly point of view, the claim that comparative law pursues knowledge for its own sake is dissatisfying for three reasons. First, it is disconcertingly vague because it begs the essential question exactly what kind, or kinds, of knowledge the discipline is supposed to produce – a question comparatists have far too often failed to pursue.[689] Second, the claim simply presumes that all knowledge is valuable without explaining why. Third, while such generalities may satisfy the civil lawyer's mind with its idealistic predilections, they have limited appeal to the common lawyer's reasoning with its more pragmatic and utilitarian bent.

Indeed, even the proponents of the claim recognize – at least implicitly – that the mere pursuit of abstract knowledge is not really enough to justify their enterprise. Consequently, they do not simply rest their case at this point. Instead, they invariably and immediately launch into a discussion of a multitude of more concrete aims and uses.

ii. *Broadening Perspective*

283. *An outside view of one's own law.* – Looking at foreign legal rules or systems means stepping outside of one's own law; almost by necessity, this entails looking back at it from a fresh perspective. The observer recognizes that legal systems often handle legal problems quite differently. He or she will thus realize that alternatives to the familiar rules, procedures, and institutions are usually possible, often plausible, and sometimes even preferable or that different legal systems pursue their (often similar) goals through different techniques (e.g., legislation or judicial lawmaking).[690] A major – mainly educational – benefit resulting from this realization is the insight that the features of one's own legal system are not inevitable manifestations of eternal truths, but just one set of responses to social issues and needs among others. In short, a comparative view of one's own law destroys illusions of its absolute character and reveals it as a product of human will and choice.

284. *Recognition of law's contingency on its environment.* – At the same time, recognition of the existing diversity of rules, procedures, and institutions invites thought about the causes of such variation. It has generally been recognized, at least since Montesquieu, that law is shaped, inter alia, by the prevailing environmental, social, economic, and political conditions. It is also, of course, determined by a variety of other factors, such as historical experiences, philosophical and religious traditions, and cultural predispositions. Showing the variation of law across space, a comparative view is the best way towards the recognition of law's contingency on these, and other, factors (rivalled only by legal history showing change over time). To be sure, comparatists have debated the degree to which law depends on such factors and to which it rather leads an independent (and perhaps path-dependent) life, but this debate is itself based on the comparative study of different legal systems as they have evolved (*infra* VI.B.iii., s. 350).

285. *Varying importance of an outside view.* – The benefits of a broadened perspective are particularly strong in legal education; as a result, comparative perspectives should be routinely introduced into the study of law. Yet, the importance of their inclusion varies depending on the character of the legal system involved.

684 *Zweigert and Kötz* (*supra* n. 3) 14 ("Erkenntnis").

685 *Glendon, Carozza and Picker* Comparative Legal Traditions (*supra* n. 20) 4.

686 *Zweigert and Kötz* (*supra* n. 3) 14 (citing Zitelmann).

687 *Glenn*, Aims of Comparative Law: *Smits* (ed.), Elgar Encyclopedia of Comparative Law (ed 2. Cheltenham, Northampton MA 2006) 65–74, 67.

688 *Kischel* (*supra* n. 286) 48 ("Denkschulung").

689 A major, and important, exception is *Jansen* (*supra* n. 1) 291–319.

690 Kahn-Freund (*supra* n. 19) 40–61.

Inspiring jurists to look beyond their borders is particularly important in systems in which a parochial perspective on law and legal culture prevails, so that existing institutions and rules are uncritically taken for granted. That tends to be true for jurisdictions that are large, consider themselves leading models, and thus revel in a feeling of (global or at least regional) superiority. By contrast, pushing for comparative perspectives is less important in smaller, younger, or less self-confident countries where jurists tend to be more conscious of other legal systems and less likely to assume that these systems are, or should be, all like their own.

In a similar vein, showing the law's diversity and contingency on its environment is particularly important where law is taught, and consequently thought about, in a monolithic, doctrinal, and positivist fashion, as has been the tendency in most civil law jurisdictions; the more law is generally regarded as a uniform and logical system of positive rules based on immutable principles, the greater the wake-up effect of a comparative perspective. Such a perspective is less important where law is already presented as a diversity of approaches and solutions, and where it is looked at from a political and critical point of view, as in the United States since the middle of the 20th century; the more law is regarded as a social phenomenon variously responding to political conditions, societal needs, and economic interests, the less a comparative perspective will change its general perception.

iii. *Fostering Tolerance and Caution*

286. *Tolerance vis-à-vis other legal cultures.* – A comparative perspective fosters tolerance vis-à-vis other legal systems and cultures. It does so in two primary ways. First, the recognition of the law's contingency on tradition and environment makes the comparatist realize that other systems often handle matters differently simply because they respond to different conditions – and that in light of these conditions, their laws, procedures, and institutions make perfectly good sense. Second, even if the underlying conditions cannot plausibly explain the differences, the observer will often have to realize that other systems have different preferences and thus make different choices – and that reasonable people can differ about the best solution for a legal problem. To be sure, these insights do not require complete relativism; a lawyer may very well continue to prefer, and if need be defend, the way matters are handled in his or her own system. But he or she will usually better understand the different ways prevailing elsewhere and thus exercise greater tolerance. Such understanding and tolerance are particularly important under conditions of great, and rapidly growing, interaction and interdependence among legal systems. They are also prerequisites for effective cooperation across legal boundaries (*infra* B.i., ss. 294–295).

287. *Caution vis-à-vis legal imperialism.* – A comparative perspective is also a powerful antidote to legal imperialism. It is tempting for highly developed countries, mainly those in the cultural West, to consider their specific legal systems superior to others. During the age of colonialism, they often imposed their law on other parts of the world; more recently, they have frequently pushed for its adoption by countries that are either less developed, as in much of the so-called Third World, or in transition, as was the case in Central and Eastern Europe in the 1990s. A comparative perspective fosters the necessary degree of restraint in this regard. Showing that law reflects, and is contingent on, the particular historical, social, economic, and political conditions prevailing in a country or region, comparative study teaches why a solution that works well in one tradition and environment may not work well in another. In short, it strongly suggests caution with regard to the export of law.

It is often overlooked that such caution is also necessary with regard to legal imports. History is replete with examples of careless and uncritical adoption of foreign legal rules, models, and ideas. Where such imports did not fit local conditions, they usually caused more harm than good.[691]

iv. *Grouping Legal Systems*

288. *Taxonomies of law.* – Comparative studies have been used to group the world's jurisdictions

[691] Some examples in *Kischel* (*supra* n. 286) 52.

into "systems", "families", or "traditions". By observing that jurisdictions share certain fundamental characteristics regarding, for example, their conception of law, prevalent sources, institutional organization, procedural structures or their style of legal analysis, comparatists have created a variety of competing groupings. Particularly in the immediate post-World War II decades, this endeavor developed into a prominent approach in its own right, and it will be considered in greater detail below (VI.B.ii., ss. 337–344).

289. *Benefits and risks.* – While both the endeavor itself and the various classifications it has produced have been subject to debate, grouping legal systems through comparison generates important benefits. At the most basic level, it organizes the multitude of the world's jurisdictions (counting in the hundreds) into a much smaller, and more manageable, number of operating units. Also, by allowing us to create world maps of law, it aids our spatial orientation because it roughly shows what legal systems to expect in which parts of the world. Finally, by grouping systems according to their fundamental similarities and differences, it brings their allegedly characteristic features into sharp relief and helps us better understand their relationship vis-à-vis each other, e.g., by indicating whether certain legal systems are closely related or not. Yet, such a grouping of systems also entails significant risks. Because it works to reduce complexity, it creates the danger of oversimplification. Since it must, like all classifications, treat some distinctions as important while laying others aside, it invites the charge of arbitrariness. And since it tends to operate with sharply delineated categories, it suggests clearer differences than exist in reality where variance is often a matter of degree.

v. *Understanding Interaction Between Legal Systems*

290. *Patterns of interaction.* – Legal systems rarely exist in isolation; instead, they usually interact in many ways. Studying how they have related to each other over time has revealed several forms of such interaction. Sometimes, legal systems have important roots in a common ancestor but have then developed in various directions; major examples are how civil law systems have evolved in large part from Roman jurisprudence and how common law regimes have emerged from medieval English practice. Sometimes legal systems have converged over time, as is true with regard to constitutional review over the past hundred years; on other occasions they have diverged, as is the case with regard to the death penalty which a century ago was nearly ubiquitous and is now used by some nations but not by others. Sometimes legal systems have imposed their rules on other jurisdictions, as was often done by colonial powers in their overseas possessions; on other occasions legal systems have liberated themselves from outside domination and re-embraced an earlier tradition, as in most Central and Eastern European countries after the end of the cold war. Comparative studies reveal such patterns, instigate a search for the forces driving these developments, and thus contribute to our understanding of how legal systems work and evolve.

291. *Export and import of law.* – Comparative study is particularly useful to detect and understand a specific aspect of interaction between systems: the frequent export and import of legal elements from one regime to another. Throughout history, legal systems have borrowed such elements from outside, be it under pressure or by their own free will, after careful deliberation or without much thought, as a result of a political decision or through gradual assimilation. They have borrowed social policies and doctrinal concepts, substantive rules and procedural devices, institutional designs and decision making techniques. Some of that borrowing has been wholesale, as when foreign codes were adopted almost in their entirety in late 19th century Japan and early 20th century Turkey; some of it has been piecemeal, as when many countries adopted the Scandinavian institution of the ombudsman. Like the classification of legal systems, the study of such "legal transplants" became a distinct subfield of comparative law in the second half of the 20th century, and it will also be addressed in greater depth below (VI.B.iii., ss. 345–351).

vi. *Developing a Transnational Legal Science*

292. *An ambitious agenda.* – An agenda of a very different kind is the use of comparative studies to distill principles, detect structures or even to build systems common to (many or all) legal systems. This pursuit seeks to elevate

legal scholarship above the level of national law. Its goal is nothing less than the establishment of a transnational legal science.[692] To such a science, the positive laws (or, as the case may be, procedures and institutions) of individual jurisdictions are merely particular variations on general themes. In this regard, the endeavor is somewhat reminiscent of the efforts of late 19th century English analytical jurisprudence to create a universally valid systematic exposition of law.

Among comparatists, this agenda is not as widely shared as the ones mentioned before. This is because it presupposes a belief in the existence of pervasive similarities among legal systems which such an approach can bring to light. To be sure, this belief does not have to pertain to commonalities of legal doctrine; instead, under the functional approach which has prevailed for most of the last century, it can also relate to a commonality of social problems to which law then provides varying responses.[693] Yet, even the assumption that all societies share essentially the same problems is not universally accepted among comparatists today, and without it the effort to build a transnational legal science must seem ill-conceived or at least hopeless.

Of course, the assumption of pervasive commonalities is much more easily accepted if the agenda to build a transnational legal science is limited to a particular legal area, such as private law, and a specific geographic or cultural context, such as Europe.

293. *Some examples.* – It is no wonder, therefore, that the project of creating a transnational legal science based on comparative study has been most rigorously pursued, as well as fairly successful, in the context of European private law (for more details, see *supra* IV.C.i.g., ss. 242–245) where most such pursuits have been undertaken with a view to eventual legal unification. Beyond the European context, endeavors to establish universally valid principles or systematic orders have been fairly rare, and their influence on legal theory and practice has remained limited. Prominent examples include the Cornell Project on the "Formation of Contracts: A Study of the Common Core of Legal Systems" from the 1960s (see *infra* VI.C.ii., s. 375) and the "UNIDROIT Principles on International Commercial Contracts", first published in the 1990s. Efforts beyond the realm of private law are rarer still.[694] Thus, on a global level, the establishment of a transnational legal science through comparative study has by and large remained elusive.

B. Traditional Practical Uses

i. *Assistance with International Legal Practice in General*

294. *Facilitating access to foreign law.* – Probably the most common assistance comparatists have provided for practitioners, especially at the bar, is to help them access foreign law.

One form of such facilitation is the publication of foreign legal sources. Obviously, this is not in and of itself a comparative endeavor. Yet, throughout the 20th century and beyond, many noted comparatists have published collections of constitutions, statutes, and, in particular, of select court decisions for lawyers from other jurisdictions. Especially where the authors have provided these texts in translation (often into English) or even with an introduction or commentary, they have rendered an important service to legal practice.[695] It is true, however, that the importance of this service has been reduced since the late 20th century because many foreign legal sources have become available on the internet, often even in translation.

Another form of making foreign law accessible is the writing of introductions and overviews. Again, such work is not strictly speaking comparative, but rather limited to the exposition of

[692] Most decidedly *Zweigert and Kötz* (*supra* n. 3) 42–46.

[693] A transnational systematic order of law could then be organized pursuant to such shared problems, rather than to doctrinal concepts and categories, *Zweigert and Kötz* (*supra* n. 3) 43.

[694] An example is *Fletcher*, General Concepts of Criminal Law (New York, Oxford 1998).

[695] They also provided important textual bases for further comparative study.

foreign law; as a result, many comparatists refuse to count it as part of their discipline (*supra* I.B., s. 7). Yet, again, since the mid-nineteenth century, comparative law scholars have published hundreds of such introductions to foreign legal systems or particular areas of law. Especially when the authors succeed in explaining the material to lawyers from other jurisdictions, they provide valuable assistance to legal practitioners dealing with transboundary issues. The importance of this service has *not* been reduced by the mass of foreign legal sources available on the internet; on the contrary, this mass has made it more important than ever that introductions and overviews explain context, provide coherence, and prevent misconceptions.

295. *Assisting transboundary communication.* – Transnational legal practice is dependent not only on access to, and understanding of, foreign law. It also requires effective communication between lawyers from different systems. Comparative law assists this communication in several ways.

To begin with, a comparative perspective is indispensable for an effective translation of legal texts.[696] The meaning of legal terms is highly dependent on their systems of origin. Literal translations can easily be misleading – the English conception of "property" is not exactly the same as the Mexican conception of "propiedad" – or, outright wrong, a US American "notary public" is very different from a French "notaire publique" (see *infra* VI.B.iv., s. 357). They can also be confusing – a foreign observer can easily mistake a Californian "Superior Court" for an appellate tribunal (rather than a trial court) or a German "Gläubiger" for a religious person (rather than a creditor). Many legal terms come with so much cultural, doctrinal, and political baggage that they are extremely difficult to translate altogether – such as the Anglo-American "rule of law", the German "Verhältnismässigkeit" (roughly: proportionality) or the Chinese "li" (roughly: ritual in the sense of proper behavior). All this often requires that legal terms be not merely translated but rather explained in order to clarify their meaning and implications to a foreign lawyer. While good legal dictionaries are helpful, a fuller explanation of the background, context, and implications of legal terms is often necessary. Such an explanation can be provided only by someone with an understanding of both systems involved, and thus from a comparative perspective.

A special problem of growing importance in a more interconnected world is the multi-lingual nature of international legal instruments, especially of treaties. Of course, writing (and ratifying) treaties in more than one authentic language has a centuries-long tradition. Yet, today the phenomenon is much more prevalent and problematic than ever before. In the last few decades, the number of treaties in the world has skyrocketed; these treaties are increasingly multilateral; and they now often involve well over a hundred states parties. In addition, they are sometimes written in a multitude of languages which are vastly different but equally authentic, such as Arabic, Chinese, English, French, Russian and Spanish in the case of the Convention on the International Sale of Goods (CISG). The inherent translation issues are formidable and can be competently handled only by experts with a solid understanding of all the legal systems involved in a particular case. Managing these translation issues is especially important because the respective texts need to be interpreted as uniformly as possible, as many treaties, such as the CISG in Art. 7, themselves expressly command.

Beyond the linguistic level, effective communication also requires understanding each other's mindsets and predispositions. Lawyers from different legal systems may embrace different conceptions of law (e.g., positivist v. realist, substantive v. procedural, secular v. religious) which in turn shape their professional roles, self-images, and behavior. As a result, they may prefer different approaches and techniques (e.g., analytical and doctrinal v. instrumental and policy-oriented).[697] In addition, they often have different habits and

[696] *De Groot*, Legal Translation: *Smits* (ed.), Elgar Encyclopedia of Comparative Law (ed 2. Cheltenham, Northampton MA 2006) 538–549.

[697] See *David et al.*, The Different Conceptions of Law: Int. Enc.Comp.L II, ch. 1 (1975); for a comparison between England and the United States with regard to legal styles and techniques, see *Atyiah and Summers*, Form and Substance in Anglo-American Law (Oxford, New York 1987).

expectations (e.g., regarding liability for breaking off contractual negotiations[698] or the necessary length of a written contract[699]). And they often differ in their (usually tacit) preferences and predilections (e.g., regarding the modes of dispute settlement or the role of state regulation). In all these, and many other, areas and contexts, the risk of costly miscommunication and unnecessary conflict looms large. In order to avoid, or at least to minimize, that risk, lawyers must seek to understand the mentality of their foreign colleagues as best they can. Comparative studies can foster such an understanding by explaining how legal professionals in other systems think and work, what they believe and assume, and thus what they expect from themselves and others.

ii. *Assistance with Private International Law in Particular*

296. *Deciding disputes.* – Comparative law is an indispensable tool for deciding disputes involving private international law.[700] This is particularly true with regard to choice-of-law issues. When the conflicts rules of one jurisdiction refer to the law of another, comparative law comes into play in three particular ways. First, it provides access to the foreign law in question, especially by making it intelligible to the domestic decision maker.[701] Second, comparative law assists in the application of conflicts norms by helping to relate the concepts and terms used in these (domestic) norms to the concepts and terms used in the (foreign) substantive law. For example, a judge may have to decide whether a (domestic) conflicts rule governing "marriage" applies to a (foreign) same sex "registered partnership"; making that decision requires an understanding of the similarities and differences between the domestic concept of marriage and the foreign institution. Third, a comparative approach is often needed for the interpretation of internationally uniform conflicts law. In order to ensure uniformity not only of the text but also of its application, judges or arbitrators are well-advised, and are indeed often required by law, to consider how other jurisdictions have interpreted the rule in question – i.e., to take a comparative approach.

297. *Planning transactions.* – Comparative law also helps practitioners to plan international transactions.

This is most obvious with regard to negotiating and drafting contractual agreements between parties from different jurisdictions. As a general rule, it is highly advisable to include a choice-of-forum (or arbitration) as well as a choice-of-law clause. Yet, an intelligent choice regarding the mode and place of dispute settlement as well as of the applicable substantive law requires an understanding of the advantages and disadvantages of the available options. Will it be better to litigate here or there? To apply this law or that? Comparative studies can provide the necessary information and analysis.

The help provided by comparative law is less obvious in other contexts, although it can be equally important. For example, a corporation's decision whether to engage in business activities on a foreign market requires an assessment of the legal benefits and risks. The same is true for an insurance company's decision whether to cover events in a foreign country, and even for an enterprise considering an offer from a foreign business.

iii. *Assisting in the Development of Law*

298. *In the legislatures* (*law reform*). – In the modern state, law is regularly developed by legislation. Since this involves a planned effort to improve the law, it is common to speak of law reform. Comparative law has long played a major role in this context.[702] Indeed, at the beginnings of modern comparative law, i.e., in the late 19th and early 20th centuries, comparatists studied foreign

[698] See e.g. *Zimmermann and Whittaker* (*supra* n. 428) 243–257.

[699] *Langbein* (*supra* n. 434); *Hill and King*, How Do German Contracts Do as Much with Fewer Words?: 79 Chicago-Kent L.Rev. 889–926 (2004).

[700] For a more detailed discussion, see *supra* II.A.i., ss. 18–22.

[701] While it is debatable whether this first function is comparative (or, again, merely an exercise in foreign law), the second and third functions surely are.

[702] *Smits*, Comparative Law and Its Influence on National Legal Systems: *Reimann and Zimmermann* (eds.), The Oxford Handbook of Comparative Law (ed. 2 Oxford 2019) 502–523, 504–506.

laws primarily in order to assist with the improvement of domestic legislation. In continental Europe, they often conceived of their discipline as "législation comparé" (*supra* III.B.i.c. s. 74), a term that lives on in France today.[703] The comparative study of law assists domestic law reform in three major ways.

Most obviously, other jurisdictions proffer ideas for how legal problems may be solved. Potential model solutions taken from foreign law have been considered, and often adopted, by legislators throughout history. A well-known early example is provided by the Roman XII Tables (449 A.D.) which drew on Greek (especially Athenian) law. Modern examples are legion. In recent decades, such borrowing has been extended to the inter- and supranational levels. A case in point is that many countries have reformed their domestic sales law in accordance with the UN Convention for the International Sale of Goods (CISG). Another example is how the European Union, in its efforts to strengthen the private enforcement of its antitrust rules, was inspired by US-American law to consider the introduction of class actions.

Moreover, comparative studies furnish information about how a particular legal solution has worked – or not. They provide opportunities to gather empirical data about the success or failure of a legal institution or rule elsewhere, and thus to anticipate and counteract problems. The legislator can then arrive at a better decision whether to adopt the solution at all and, if so, how to fine-tune it. Here, comparative law essentially uses other jurisdictions as laboratories and observes the outcomes of their experiments. For example, looking at the United States' experience with antitrust class actions teaches important lessons about their benefits (e.g., powerful private enforcement and effective deterrence) and risks (e.g., potential abuse and enormous costs). Considering these lessons, a European legislator can decide either to forego class actions altogether or to adopt a modified version that promises to minimize their downsides.

Finally, comparative law must be consulted in gauging whether a legal institution or rule is suitable for adoption. Even if it works well in one jurisdiction, this is no guarantee that it will also be successful in another. Given the contingency of legal institutions and rules on their environment, one must carefully compare the conditions prevailing in the system of origin with those in one's own jurisdiction. Only thus can the legislator avoid importing legal ideas that fail or even wreak havoc.[704] For example, a comparative study of the respective environments should caution a European legislator that introducing a US-style class action may not have the desired effect. Most European jurisdictions lack the aggressive plaintiffs' bar that drives such actions in the United States as well as the resourceful trial courts that can manage them. In addition, European parties will likely hesitate to begin such actions because, unlike in the United States, the losing class representatives would be liable for the winning defendant's (potentially enormous) litigation costs.

Law reform is routinely informed by comparative law in many countries, and in most highly developed legal systems this has become virtually *de rigeur*. Particularly in civil law jurisdictions, (justice) ministries frequently perform comparative studies in connection with the legislative projects proposed by the government, although the depth and sophistication of such studies often leave much to be desired. In several common law jurisdictions, independent law commissions are tasked with taking foreign law and experiences into account, as in England and Scotland. Often, governments will solicit comparative studies from specialized research institutions, such as the Max Planck Institute for Foreign and International Private Law in Hamburg, or from experts in legal academia. An exception of sorts is the United States, where legislative projects rarely include comparative elements. Neither the Congress nor the various state legislatures have shown much interest in considering foreign laws and experiences, some exceptions notwithstanding. In recent years, however, the American Law Institute (ALI) has sometimes looked abroad in several contexts, such as its Global Insolvency Project and in draft-

703 In the *Société de Législation Comparé*, founded in 1869, see *supra* III.B.i.c. s. 74.

704 For a, by now classic, study, see *Kahn-Freund* (*supra* n. 221).

ing the Restatement of International Commercial Arbitration.[705]

While the consultation of foreign law is common practice in many countries' legislative processes, one must be careful not to overrate its actual impact. To be sure, in many cases this impact is strong and clear, for example, when a foreign code or statute itself is adopted (usually with some adjustments). In other instances, however, references to foreign law merely support a result that would have been reached anyway or show alternative paths not chosen. Often, it is difficult to gauge the actual influence of foreign ideas altogether.

Whenever legislative reform projects enlist the help of comparative law, the discipline inevitably faces the question whether it should provide merely (objective) information about foreign law and experience or also proffer a (critical) evaluation of the options involved. On the one hand, there is something to be said for limiting the discipline to the former task. One can, following Rabel, conceive of comparative law as a legal "science" which is concerned with description, analysis, and explanation but not with normative judgments.[706] Of course, normative elements can never be entirely avoided, but comparative study can at least strive for objectivity and renounce judgments on the merits. After all, such a judgment is a legislative business which is the prerogative of political actors. On the other hand, given his or her knowledge, the comparatist is well positioned to assess the options involved. The political actors can greatly benefit from, and perhaps even ask for, his or her evaluation. At the end of the day, law is a normative discipline, and in most legal cultures jurists have long considered a critical evaluation of the law part of their function and thus performed it routinely.[707]

299. *In domestic courts.* – Comparative law can also assist judges in developing law, be it by overruling older decisions or in resolving novel issues.[708] Let us first consider the work of domestic courts and then turn to the special case of international tribunals (*infra* s. 300).

For domestic courts, a comparative perspective may, again, proffer fresh insights found in other jurisdictions, show which solutions work in practice, and provide the context necessary to assess whether a foreign rule would fit the domestic environment. In short, considering foreign ideas is helpful because it shows and clarifies options, even if the court ultimately decides against following a model found abroad.[709]

Yet, while comparative law is useful in all these regards, it is easy to overrate its impact on the development of law by domestic courts. In practice, this impact has by and large remained on a fairly modest level in several regards. To begin with, on the whole, judicial resort to comparative considerations is much less common than in the legislative process. Few national courts in the world routinely consult foreign law. Unlike legislatures, courts normally do not command the resources to engage in comparative studies. Most of the time, they have to rely on the parties to introduce arguments drawn from comparative observations, and even then, normally only appellate judges have the time and space to entertain such arguments. The frequency with which courts look to foreign law also varies widely among jurisdictions.[710] In some, like Israel, South

705 *Bermann*, The American Law Institute Goes Global: The Restatement of International Commercial Arbitration: 16 Willamette Journal of International Law & Dispute Resolution 300–320 (2008).

706 *Rabel* (*supra* n. 153) 3.

707 For a more detailed argument, see *Zweigert and Kötz* (*supra* n. 3) 46–47.

708 There is a rich literature on the use of comparative law by courts; see, e.g., *Adenas and Fairgrieve* (eds.), Courts and Comparative Law (Oxford 2015); *Bobek*, Comparative Reasoning in European Supreme Courts (Oxford 2013); *Drobnig and van Erp* (*supra* n. 242); *Mak* (ed.), Judicial Decision-Making in a Globlized World: A Comparative Analysis of the Changing Practices of Western Highest Courts (Oxford 2013).

709 *Smits* (*supra* n. 702) 506–512. An (English) example is provided and explained by *Markesinis*, Comparative Law in the Courtroom and Classroom (Oxford and Portland OR 2003) 157–183; for various Dutch examples, see *Koopmans*, Comparative Law and the Courts, Intl.& Comp.L.Q. 52 (2003) 545–556, at 550–555. For a vociferous argument that courts should pay more attention to foreign decisions, see *Markesinis* (*supra* n. 238). See also (Symposium) Der verfahrensrechtliche Rahmen richterlicher Rechtsfortbildung, RabelsZ 80 (2016) 237–398.

710 See *Drobnig and van Erp* (*supra* n. 242); *Adenas and Fairgrieve* (*supra* n. 708).

Africa or Switzerland, it occurs with some regularity; in others, like Germany, Italy or the United Kingdom, it is less common;[711] and in the United States, it is notoriously rare, although in the US Supreme Court it has happened repeatedly.[712] These differences in frequency are partially a function of varying need: smaller or younger jurisdictions are more likely to face gaps and novel issues, and thus have more reason to import foreign solutions than bigger or older ones where the domestic sources are usually rich enough for most purposes. In part, however, the differences are also rooted in different attitudes: some judiciaries are outright eager to learn from abroad, some are at least open to it, while others show little interest, be it because of inherent parochialism or because they assume that the rest of the world does not have much to teach them anyway.

Furthermore, even where judges do look abroad, resort to foreign law is rarely comprehensive and often somewhat random. Obviously, judges tend to draw on jurisdictions from their own legal tradition (e.g., within the British Commonwealth or among the Scandinavian countries); on systems they otherwise happen to be familiar with (perhaps through study abroad); and on sources they can access without too much (linguistic or logistical) effort. But they also often draw on whatever foreign law the parties present to them or happens to be referenced in the academic literature. On the one hand, these limitations are understandable because, given the constraints on most courts' time and support structure, it is all one can realistically expect. On the other hand, however, a selective approach risks overlooking important evidence elsewhere, and it allows judges to refer only to the foreign jurisdictions that support their own preferences ("cherry picking").

Finally, the actual impact of looking at foreign ideas on the respective decisions varies a great deal. There are many instances in which foreign institutions, rules, and experiences have truly influenced the outcome of a case. But foreign ideas are also referenced where the same result would have been reached anyway. Sometimes, foreign references merely provide additional support for the conclusion reached, perhaps by invoking the prestige of bigger and more influential jurisdictions; sometimes judges want to demonstrate that their decision is part of a broader, transboundary, consensus; and sometimes references to foreign law may be mere window dressing used by judges to show off their knowledge.[713] It often remains unclear into which of these categories a citation to foreign law falls.

It should be noted, however, that courts refer to foreign law and experience not necessarily because they are genuinely looking for the best solution of a problem. Other motives often play a role as well. Judges may want to follow foreign law for the sake of international uniformity (which saves the parties transaction costs, enhances predictability, and discourages forum shopping); this can be particularly important in interpreting international materials such as multilateral treaties. Courts may adopt a foreign idea in order to save time and information costs (i.e., free-ride on the work done by other tribunals). Or they may be, or feel, compelled by inter- or supranational bodies (such as the IMF, the World Bank, or the European Union) to follow the lead of more developed or more powerful systems.

At least when a court permits an actual impact on the outcome, the legitimacy of looking at foreign law is not beyond cavil. Especially in purely domestic cases, there is a serious question why the decision should be influenced by law that has no force in the respective jurisdiction, and in the making of which domestic actors had no voice. This is particularly true in constitutional matters where politics play an inevitable role and where the stakes tend to be high. As a result, there has been much discussion, and considerable

[711] In some countries, notably in France, court opinions are so terse and stylized that they contain virtually no references to foreign law. This does not necessarily mean that the tribunals did not look abroad for inspiration or guidance. In order to find such influence, one would have to look at the opinions of the advocates general advising the courts or to the judges' internal deliberations; see *Lasser* (*supra* n. 393).

[712] *Breyer*, The Court and the World: American Law and the New Global Realities (New York 2015); *Cleveland*, Our International Constitution: 31 Yale Journal of International Law 1–125 (2006).

[713] For an example drawn from American legal history, see *Watson* (*supra* n. 137).

disagreement, about when it is legitimate for a court to rely on foreign law. This discussion has been particularly intense and visible among the Justices of the US Supreme Court in the last two decades,[714] but it has been pursued in other tribunals as well.[715] The legitimacy of seeking guidance from abroad should depend, inter alia, on the exact reasons why judges look to foreign law. It is relatively easy to defend when they do so simply in order to get a broader sense of orientation, perhaps with a view to fostering international uniformity; to learn whether a rule has worked well somewhere else; and perhaps even when they seek inspiration. It becomes much harder to justify when judges take normative guidance from abroad, i.e., when they claim that a certain result is correct (inter alia) because it has been reached in a foreign jurisdiction as well.[716]

300. *The special case of supra- and international tribunals.* – As a result of their proliferation since the mid- to late 20th century, there are now a considerable number of supra- and international tribunals. Some operate in a global context, like the International Court of Justice, the International Tribunal for the Law of the Sea, or the Appellate Body of the World Trade Organization; others exist on the regional level, like the European Court of Human Rights, the African Court of Human and People's Rights, or the Court of Justice of the Andean Community (*Tribunal de Justicia de la Comunidad Andina,* TJCA). Obviously, these tribunals are in a position very different from that of national courts. Their composition, jurisdiction, and caseload at least invite, and often necessitate, looking at different legal orders. Most of them have more resources than an average national court, often in the form of a research staff. And since they operate on a transnational level to begin with, their resort to a variety of laws raises fewer legitimacy issues.

As a result, in these tribunals comparative perspectives are much more common than in national courts.[717] This is particularly true for the Court of Justice of the European Union (formerly called the European Court of Justice) and the European Court of Human Rights, both of which routinely draw on the laws of their member states (and sometimes beyond) for comparative purposes.[718] In the International Court of Justice this happens more rarely, usually in the context of searching for "general principles" (see *infra* vi., s. 311). While less is known about the practice of many other international tribunals, it stands to reason that they likewise engage with the law of other jurisdictions with some regularity.[719] Yet, again, in many of these tribunals (including the European Court of Human Rights) the use of comparative law can be selective, haphazard, and superficial, and the actual impact of references to other legal orders on the outcome of a case is often far from clear.

301. *In legal scholarship.* – Comparative studies have assisted the development of law not only through legislative projects and in judicial opinions but also through scholarship. Far from being limited to the academic realm, comparative legal scholarship has long had significant practical effects in two regards.

First, in innumerable instances, foreign ideas were originally introduced into the domestic discussion by scholars, prompting legislative bodies and courts to take an interest and sometimes to follow suit. In fact, over time academic writing has probably been the most important means by which foreign ideas have been imported. This is no wonder. It is the job of academics to look around for new ideas and, especially in recent times, they have increasingly looked abroad. After all, academics tend to work with foreign colleagues, operate in foreign countries, and have an opportunity to study foreign legal materials much more frequently than members of the legislature or judges on domestic courts. In addition, academics have more freedom to take intellectual

[714] See *Atkins v. Virginia* 536 U.S. 304 (2002); *Lawrence v. Texas* 539 U.S. 558 (2003); for a discussion, see *Breyer* (*supra* n. 712) 236–246.

[715] Symposium: Foreign Law in Constitutional Courts: 64 Am.J.Comp.L. 797–889 (2016).

[716] For a well-structured analysis, see *Larson*, Importing Constitutional Norms from a "Wider Civilization": 64 Ohio St.L.J. 1283–1327 (2004).

[717] *Peat*, Comparative Law in International Courts and Tribunals (Cambridge 2019).

[718] Symposium (*supra* n. 715); *Kiikeri* (*supra* n. 39).

[719] A vivid example is the Southern African Development Tribunal's decision in *Campbell et al. v. Zimbabwe*, [2008] SADCT 2 (28 November 2008, tribunal ruling).

risks, i.e., to proffer (foreign) ideas merely for the sake of discussion.

Second, quite aside from intended or accidental spill-over effects into the legislatures and courts, comparative studies are practically useful because they sharpen one's understanding of the available options, point to their respective benefits and costs, and thus highlight the choices faced by a legal system. In this sense, comparative law is one instrument in the general toolbox of legal analysis which helps jurists to work through problems and to devise practical solutions.

iv. *International Unification of Law*

302. *Introduction.* – Like the improvement of domestic legislation, the promotion of international legal unification was one of the primary goals and uses of comparative law during its formative stage as a modern discipline. Particularly in the late 19th and early 20th centuries, comparatists pursued the objective of a "droit commun legislatif" with conviction, determination, and zeal. International legal unification has remained an important objective ever since, although in the last few decades the widespread enthusiasm for it had to yield to a more sober attitude. The reason is in part experience: the successes of the various unification efforts have remained much more limited than originally expected and broad international unification of law is no longer considered a realistic goal. In part, the reason is also a change in perspective: comparatists have tempered their erstwhile steadfast belief in the blessings of uniformity with a growing appreciation of diversity. As a result, unification projects today are no longer driven by lofty ideals but by – real or at least alleged – political interests and practical needs. In addition, critics of mainstream comparative law have attacked unification projects as hopeless or fundamentally misguided in a world characterized by legal pluralism (*infra* VI.B.v., s. 362).

For most of the 20th century unification focused almost exclusively on two areas. The first was private law. This was largely in response to the needs of markets for uniform rules governing transboundary transactions; in addition, in private law, state (sovereign) interests are fairly muted, which facilitates international agreement. The second area was private international law. Where uniform substantive rules could not be achieved, as a second best there should at least be uniform rules determining the applicable law in order to promote international harmony of judicial decisions. While both these areas and agendas continue to be important, since the second half of the 20th century unification efforts have increasingly been extended to other subjects as well, notably procedural and regulatory matters. This is particularly true within the European Union where some civil procedure rules and large amounts of administrative law have been unified.

International legal unification is a vast and complex subject which is treated in considerable depth elsewhere in this Encyclopedia by one of the great masters of comparative law.[720] As a result, we can limit the present discussion to a brief review of its major forms and of the various roles comparative law has played in their respective contexts. International unification is most visible, and thus most widely known, in the form of (quasi-)legislative texts (*infra* s. 303). One must not overlook, however, that much of it occurs in several other ways as well, especially through legal scholarship (s. 304), so-called Principles (s. 305), judicial decisions (s. 306), and, increasingly, through private law-making (s. 307). The comparative study of law lies at the core of all these endeavors (s. 308).

303. *In legislative form.* – The international legal unification of positive law relies primarily on legislative instruments. Traditionally, it has proceeded in a coordinate (i.e., international) fashion. Typically, multinational expert groups have drafted treaties (mostly called conventions) containing uniform rules, which have then been presented to the various states for adoption (mainly by implementing legislation). Some conventions have been widely adopted by states, others largely ignored.[721] The drafting process

[720] *David*, The Legal Unification of Private Law: Int. Enc.Comp.L II, ch. 5 (1971).

[721] Among the most successful, as well as practically most important, are the CISG with over 90 member states and the (United Nations) Convention on the Recognition and Enforcement of Foreign Arbitral Awards with over 150 member states.

has long been heavily institutionalized, i.e., conducted by permanent bodies specializing in such work. The most prominent of these bodies on the global level are the Hague Conference on Private International Law (since 1893), the International Institute for the Unification of Private Law (Institut Internationale pour l'Unification du Droit Privé, UNIDROIT, since 1926), and the United Nations Commission on International Trade Law (UNCITRAL, since 1966). Drafting the respective instruments is, of course, based on the comparative study of various national laws in search of a uniform text that is acceptable to as many states as possible. In addition, some international organizations, such as UNICTRAL, have also drafted (uniform) model laws for adoption by states while others, such as the Organisation pour l'Harmonisation en Afrique du Droit des Affairs (OHADA, since 1993) have focused more generally on the harmonization of member state laws.

In the last half-century, legal unification has also occurred in a top-down (supra-national) fashion, namely in the European Union (formerly the European Economic Community, then the European Community). Through thousands of "Regulations", which are directly applicable law in the member states, the EU has created uniform law on a massive scale, mostly of a regulatory nature. In addition, the EU has enacted thousands of "Directives" under which the member states have had to harmonize their laws on a wide variety of topics. All in all, the EU has produced by far the largest body of internationally uniform, or at least harmonized, law in existence today, albeit on a regional level. The role of comparative law in the preparation of this law has not been studied in a comprehensive fashion. This role is difficult to generalize, and even in individual instances it is often hard to gauge. While it is clear that many regulations and directives are based on the comparative study and evaluation of the various (member) state laws, many others show little or no sign of such preparation.

304. *Through legal scholarship*. – For well over a century, legal scholarship has frequently prepared the ground for international legal unification. Scholars have researched and compared national laws, distilled the commonalities from the mass of the material, laid out the differences, and often attempted to reconcile them as far as possible. The perhaps most widely known example of such scholarship is Ernst Rabel's two-volume treatise on sales law[722] which, around the middle of the 20th century, laid the foundation for the subsequent unification efforts in this area, ultimately leading to the adoption of the CISG in 1980.

As explained in greater detail in Chapter IV (C.i.g., ss. 242–245), in the late 20th century, legal scholarship took the lead in the development of a common private law of Europe. Their sheer mass notwithstanding, EU regulations and directives as well as the decisions of the European Court of Justice have remained piecemeal. By necessity, therefore, the pursuit of a more coherent uniform European private law has been almost exclusively the work of legal academics. This work has essentially been an exercise in comparative law in a variety of forms.[723]

305. *Through Principles ("soft law")*. – Inspired by the US-American Restatements of Law, in the last few decades legal scholars have often sought to promote legal unification by drafting non-binding "Principles" of law. On a global level, the most widely known project are the UNIDROIT Principles of International Commercial Contracts which were first published in 1994 and then repeatedly revised. Yet, as explained above (IV.C.i.g., s. 244), far more frequently such Principles have been the result of the academic efforts to create a European private law, resulting in about half a dozen projects. The search for, and drafting of, such Principles is based on painstaking comparative work by experts from a wide variety of EU member states and sometimes beyond.

Yet, despite much enthusiasm, especially among European private law scholars, it must be remembered that, strictly speaking, such Principles are not law in the sense of directly enforceable rules. Thus, how much these efforts have contributed to the unification of actual positive law is a difficult question. At least some legislative projects have referenced them; the UNIDROIT

[722] *Rabel* (*supra* n. 154).

[723] For an overview, see *Zimmermann*, Comparative Law and the Unification of European Private Law: *Reimann and Zimmermann* (eds.), The Oxford Handbook of Comparative Law (ed. 2 Oxford 2019) 557–598.

Principles are often used in international commercial arbitration; and the various texts provide common ground for further discussion.

306. *Through judicial decisions.* – The importance of courts for international legal unification is often underappreciated because courts do not pursue large projects with high visibility but rather work in smaller increments. Yet, courts do play a very important role in this context. Since they are differently situated, we should, again, distinguish between domestic tribunals on the one hand, and inter- and supranational ones on the other.

For domestic courts, the creation or maintenance of international uniformity is not a primary responsibility, but they can contribute to it in two main ways.

Most importantly, where there is a uniform legislative text (based on a treaty or model law), domestic courts are crucial for maintaining the uniformity it provides. All such texts need to be interpreted (and applied), and their interpretation lies mostly in the hands of domestic tribunals. In order to avoid these texts acquiring different meanings in different jurisdictions, it is imperative that judges work comparatively, i.e., consider the text's interpretation by foreign courts. At least when there is agreement among tribunals abroad, judges should decide in line with foreign precedent unless there are powerful countervailing reasons. This is indeed fairly common in domestic tribunals around the world.

Even in the absence of uniform legislation, domestic courts can contribute to international uniformity whenever they face an issue that is open in their jurisdiction but that has already been adjudicated elsewhere. Although this is not imperative, judges may want to consider foreign precedent and decide in line with it unless there are strong reasons against that. In practice, however, considering foreign decisions for the sake of international uniformity in the absence of a uniform legislative text is fairly rare.

For many inter- and supranational tribunals, the pursuit of international uniformity is inherent in their job. These tribunals typically apply, and sometimes develop, a set of rules that is uniform to begin with – often a treaty, sometimes customary international law or a shared regulatory regime. It is true that these courts rarely have the power to interpret or develop such rules with official erga omnes effect, but more often than not their decisions are de facto precedent for all those within their legal system. In this case, such tribunals maintain or create uniformity ipso facto. In doing so, their work is frequently comparative as well. Often, inter- and supranational judges facing novel issues seek inspiration and guidance from the domestic law(s) of nation states; for example, the European Court of Human Rights regularly consults the national courts' interpretation of constitutional guaranties.[724] In other instances, supra- and international courts have fashioned "general principles" from national laws; famously, the European Court of Justice has developed an extensive set of such principles, especially by drawing on the constitutional traditions of EU member states.[725]

307. *Through private lawmaking.* – Today, there is a host of private and semi-private actors creating internationally uniform rules below the level of international law proper or of state legislation (*supra* IV.A.iii., s. 186). Most of these regimes exist in the commercial and regulatory realms. Prime examples are the International Commercial Terms (Incoterms) and the Uniform Customs and Practice for Documentary Credit (UCP), both published by the International Chamber of Commerce (ICC). There are many sets of uniform rules and practices for particular commercial sectors as well as model codes of conduct or of best practices for corporations. Many observers regard this mass of rules as a new (transnational) *lex mercatoria*. In addition, specialized organizations, such as the International Organization for Standardization (ISO), create uniform industrial and technical norms. The degree to which these internationally uniform regimes of non-state law are based on a comparative study of underlying rules has not been explored in a systematic fashion and is likely to vary considerably.

308. *The various roles of comparative law.* – In all these contexts of international unification, comparative law plays four distinct roles. First, it shows where law is already internationally uniform. The comparative study of the various

[724] *McCrudden* (*supra* n. 667).

[725] *Tridimas* (*supra* n. 40).

national rules or cases demonstrates the extent to which legal systems are identical or at least highly similar.[726] For example, virtually all legal systems require a matching offer and acceptance for the formation of a contract. Where legal systems share such common ground, it is relatively easy to draft an internationally uniform rule. Second, comparative studies demonstrate where law is not already uniform. This may sound banal, but it is important because it clearly identifies the differences that need to be overcome in order to advance international uniformity. For example, legal systems vary substantially with regard to form requirements for contracts. Third, comparative law helps to bridge these differences by analyzing and explaining them. For instance, it shows, especially under the functional approach (*infra* VI.C.i., ss. 368–373), which differences (e.g., regarding contract formation) are merely matters of legal technique that may just have to be adjusted, and which embody substantive concerns that require substantive compromise. Last but not least, comparative law helps to define the limits of sensible unification. It shows not only which differences are small enough to be overcome with reasonable effort, but also which are so fundamental that adjustment or compromise is impractical or too costly. Especially where legal differences express deeply rooted cultural or political disagreements, the desire for unification must yield to respect for diversity.

v. *Interpretation of Law*

309. *Comparative perspective as a necessity.* – Beyond its role in the international unification of law, comparative law can also contribute to the interpretation of domestic law, especially by judges but also by scholars.[727] In this context, a comparative perspective may be a necessity or merely an option, depending on the text in question.

It is a necessity with regard to texts that should be construed in an internationally uniform fashion. In order to ensure uniformity of interpretation (especially of the basic terms and concepts), courts must consider how other jurisdictions have handled the issue at stake. The strongest traditional case for such an approach is presented by treaties and the legislation that implements them. More broadly though, a comparative approach is called for whenever a domestic statute is based on a uniform international text, even though that text may not be directly binding, such as the UNICTRAL Model Law on International Commercial Arbitration.

A special case is the interpretation of EU law. On the one hand, the various EU treaties as well as EU regulations are supranational by nature. On the other hand, they must routinely be interpreted by the EU member states' domestic courts because they are directly applicable in, and thus an integral part of, the respective domestic legal orders. In interpreting them, national judges must aim at Union-wide uniformity and should thus take notice of what their colleagues in other member states have done. In practice, however, this obligation is somewhat muted because national judges can (and in some cases must) refer questions of interpretation to the European Court of Justice, which has the final word in this regard.[728] EU directives are a somewhat different matter: as a rule, they are not directly applicable in the member states but merely obligate the national legislatures to bring domestic law into compliance with them. To the extent that member state courts interpret either these directives themselves or national legislation directly derived from them, a uniform interpretation, and thus a comparative approach, is also required. Yet, when the member state legislature has exercised choices left to it by a directive, divergent interpretation is more acceptable.

310. *Comparative considerations as an option.* – With regard to the interpretation of law that is of

[726] This is closely related to the "common core" approach which we will consider in greater detail below (VI.C.ii., ss. 374–377).

[727] *Gamper and Verschraegen*, Rechtsvergleichung als juristische Auslegungsmethode (Wien 2013).

[728] A domestic court may consider a matter so obvious that no reference to the European Court of Justice is required. But it may do so only after it has assured itself that the matter is equally obvious to the courts of the other member states and to the Court of Justice. This implies a duty to conduct the requisite comparative research. *CILFIT v. Ministry of Health*, ECJ Case 283/81, Oct. 6, [1982] ECR 03415, par. 16.

a purely domestic nature (i.e., not derived from international norms), comparative considerations are essentially optional. Convinced of the benefits of their discipline, comparatists tend to call for such considerations on a broad scale. Yet, as mentioned before, limited resources, language skills, and accessibility of foreign material make a comparative approach unrealistic as a matter of routine judicial work. It is, therefore, no surprise that in practice explicitly comparative interpretation of domestic law is rare in most court systems of the world.

Moreover, the strength of the argument for such a comparative approach varies depending on the circumstances. It is strongest where looking abroad is expressly allowed or even encouraged. Perhaps the most famous example is Article 39 sec. 1 (c) of the South African Constitution, which provides that in interpreting the Bill of Rights courts "may consider foreign law". The argument is still fairly strong where domestic law is derived from, or at least heavily influenced by, other legal orders. Where one country has accepted a legal transplant from another, as was the case when Turkey by and large adopted the Swiss Civil Code in 1926, it comes naturally to seek interpretive guidance from the country of origin. And where several jurisdictions share a basic stock of legal ideas, as between the members of the British Commonwealth, looking at each other's interpretations makes obvious sense. The argument for a comparative approach to legal interpretation is also appealing in small or newly established jurisdictions where the scarcity of domestic material may create a particularly strong need for guidance from larger, more established, and perhaps even neighboring legal systems. Thus Austrian and Swiss courts have sometimes looked to Germany, tribunals in Israel have often drawn on continental European and US-American law, and courts in former French colonies have followed the *Cour de cassation* in Paris.

Yet, in the absence of any such particular reasons, it is debatable whether domestic judges interpreting domestic law should seek guidance abroad. There are, in fact, considerable arguments against that: foreign ideas may not fit the domestic environment; judges in one country have no legitimate authority to influence the law in another; they will not have had foreign law in mind at all when they rendered their judgments; and, especially in politically sensitive contexts, such as constitutional interpretation, each jurisdiction must ultimately seek its own path according to its own tradition. Yet, there is also much to recommend a comparative approach: one can often find helpful ideas and general inspiration by looking at foreign interpretations; foreign decisions are obviously not binding in domestic courts in any sense; and in an increasingly interconnected world depending on international cooperation, going solo can be a costly strategy.

vi. *Establishing Sources of Law*

311. *In public international law.* – In some instances, comparative studies are needed to establish directly applicable sources of law. The most widely known example is listed in Article 38 of the Statute of the International Court of Justice (ICJ). S. 1 c of this provision names among the sources of international law "the general principles of law recognized by civilized nations". Strictly speaking, finding these principles requires comparing the laws of such nations. Yet, there is no agreement on what exactly that means. Does a tribunal have to look at the law of all countries in the world (ca. 200)? – this would entail an extraordinarily difficult, time-consuming, and expensive research effort. Or can a tribunal survey just a selection of national laws? – but what would be the criteria of such a selection? May a tribunal trust the written rules it finds or must it also consider how these rules are applied in practice?

Comparatists often argue that by distilling general principles their discipline renders an important service to international adjudication. In practice, however, cases in which such principles are derived from a systematic comparison of national laws are few and far between.[729] Neither the ICJ nor other international tribunals engage in such comparative work with any regularity. More often than not, general principles

[729] For an example, see the separate opinion by Judge Bruno Simma in the Case Concerning Oil Platforms (*Iran v. United States*), [2003] I.C.J. 161.

are accepted on the basis of general assumptions. These assumptions usually remain unchallenged because the principles involved operate on a high level of generality that makes it well-nigh impossible to question them.

312. *In European Union law.* – General principles, and the related concept of common traditions, also play an important role in the European Union. Notably, Article 340 sec. 2 TFEU provides that in cases of non-contractual liability, the Union shall be liable "in accordance with the general principles common to the laws of the Member States". In addition, the European Court of Justice developed a set of fundamental rights based on "the constitutional traditions common to the Member States", a concept eventually codified in Article 6 sec. 2 TFEU.[730] In both instances, however, it is often hard to gauge to what extent such principles or rights are actually derived from in-depth comparative research of the member states' laws. The Court employs a professional research staff which can perform this task but the opinions themselves usually do not reflect all the research conducted. Often, the Court has also sought semi-autonomous European solutions which are informed by the member states' laws but not directly dependent on them.

C. Modern Additions

i. *The "Subversive Function" of Comparative Law*

313. *Comparative law as an instrument of critique.* – Since the 1990s, some comparatists have emphasized the "subversive function" of their discipline.[731] It is not always clear exactly what that means and it can thus be read in various ways. To some extent, it simply denotes that comparative studies are useful as an instrument of critique. They can be a "source of questioning, reflection and opening up new ideas", in particular because they are "capable of freeing legal thought from conceptual constraints by paving the path to new ways of reading the law".[732] While this is an important function, the idea that a comparative perspective creates critical distance from one's own law has, as such, been widely accepted since Ernst Rabel, i.e., for nearly a century.[733] Modern critical approaches to comparative law are discussed in greater detail below (VI.B.v., ss. 360–365).

314. *Destabilizing basic assumptions.* – Yet, the subversive function also has a more radical dimension. Comparative studies allow us better to understand "the factors that make us different, not just on the surface but in our foundations".[734] This goes beyond the well recognized use of comparative law to "dissolve national prejudices".[735] It envisages the discipline as an instrument of "cultural criticism".[736] This requires delving deeply into the political, moral, and especially philosophical underpinnings of legal systems.[737] The goal is to destabilize established assumptions in favor of self-reflection about one's fundamental thought patterns and predilections, including the reasons for "cultural resistance to change".[738]

ii. *The "Coordinating Function" of Comparative Law*

315. *Conflict avoidance and management between multiple legal orders.* – In the age of globalization, an increasingly important function of comparative law is the "coordination" of the multiple legal orders now coexisting in the world.[739]

[730] Today, the primary source in this regard is the Charter of Fundamental Rights of the European Union (2000, in force 2009).

[731] *Fletcher*, Comparative Law as a Subversive Discipline: 46 Am.J.Comp.L. 683–700 (1998); *Muir-Watt*, La fonction subversive du droit comparé: Rev.int.dr.comp. 52 (2000) 503–527.

[732] *Muir-Watt* (*supra* n. 731) 504.

[733] *Rabel*, Aufgabe und Notwendigkeit der Rechtsvergleichung: *Rabel and Leser* (eds.), Gesammelte Aufsätze I (Tübingen 1967) 1–21, 8–9.

[734] *Fletcher* (*supra* n. 731) 700.

[735] *Zweigert and Kötz* (*supra* n. 3) 14.

[736] *Fletcher* (*supra* n. 731) 695.

[737] *Fletcher* (*supra* n. 731) 694; *Ewald* (*supra* n. 75); *Ewald*, The Jurisprudential Approach to Comparative Law: A Field Guide to "Rats": 46 Am.J.Comp.L. 701–707 (1998).

[738] *Fletcher* (*supra* n. 731) 695.

[739] *Buxbaum*, Die Rechtsvergleichung zwischen nationalem Staat und internationaler Wirtschaft, RabelsZ 60 (1996) 201–230; *Kötz*, Alte und neue Aufgaben der Rechtsvergleichung: JZ 2002, 257–264.

Representing "the institutional side of globalization",[740] these orders are not only national but also inter-, and in some cases supranational. With the great volume of transboundary economic activity and the widespread mobility of people, a particular transaction or dispute can easily be subject to the jurisdiction, dispute resolution mechanisms, and substantive rules not only of several nation states but also of inter- or supranational organizations, be they global, such as the UN, the WTO or the World Bank, or regional, like the EU, NAFTA or MERCOSUR. Since these legal orders operate largely independently and often overlap substantially, their relationship is rife with tension and conflict.[741] Avoiding, or at least managing, these problems has thus become a necessity of the first order. Here, comparative law can make important contributions, provided, of course, that it encompasses not only national jurisdictions but also the pluralism of inter- and supranational systems. A comparative approach reveals these legal orders' similarities and differences, especially with regard to their policies and objectives. It thus clarifies their relationships with each other (hierarchical, coordinate, interlaced, etc.). This, in turn, fosters mutual understanding which can open avenues to adjustment and compromise.

Note that such "coordination" is different from both traditional unification agendas and established conflict of laws regimes. Unification means establishing one set of rules for all involved jurisdictions, primarily for the domestic laws of nation states. With regard to the multitude of national and international legal orders, this is impossible because they operate in different domains and pursue different goals, e.g., in one case, the prevention of international terrorism, in the other, the protection of human rights. Traditional conflicts rules are designed to decide clashes between state laws with regard to the same (private law) issue, such as the validity of a contract or the rights in a piece of property. They are ill-suited to handle conflicts between inter- and supranational regimes addressing entirely different aspects of an activity, such as its compliance with rules on international trade and its impact on the environment. By contrast, the purpose of "coordination" is to facilitate the coexistence, and to promote the cooperation, of often highly diverse legal orders to ensure that each can realize its objectives – or at least to minimize conflict as far as possible.[742] This goes beyond the traditional comparative law goal of fostering international understanding in general.[743] It requires the concrete conciliation of institutions, processes, and laws in order to create stable and productive relationships between highly diverse legal orders.

316. *Advice and communication.* – The question of how exactly comparative lawyers can contribute to such an agenda is still somewhat open. Probably their most important function is as advisors to the myriad policy makers, legislators, bureaucrats, and judges involved in the various systems on the domestic and international levels.[744] These professionals usually operate exclusively in their own domain and often know little about others. Comparatists understanding all the legal orders involved can bridge the gaps and assist communication across boundaries. In particular, they can identify the exact nature of tensions between legal orders and explain the underlying reasons. They can thus help not only to seek accommodation, but also, and perhaps even more importantly, to foster tolerance for inevitable differences.

Since most conflicts between legal orders will arise in the regulatory context, getting involved in their avoidance and management will further shift the discipline's emphasis from private to public law. It will also require increasing attention to the political, social, and economic considerations driving the respective legal orders' agendas.[745]

[740] *Basedow* (*supra* n. 683) 855.

[741] A striking illustration is the case of *Kadi and Al Barakaat International Foundation v. Council and Commission of the European Union*, Case C402/05 P and C-415/05 P, [2008] ECR I-6351, which pitted the UN Security Council (and its sanctions regime) against the European Union (and its protection of human rights).

[742] *Fischer-Lescano and Teubner*, Regime-Collisions, The Vain Search for Legal Unity in the Fragmentation of Global Law: 25 Mich.J.Int.L. 999–1046 (2003/2004).

[743] *Zweigert and Kötz* (*supra* n. 3) 14.

[744] *Basedow* (*supra* n. 683) 854–856.

[745] *Buxbaum* (*supra* n. 739) 216.

D. In Conclusion: The Strength and Downside of Goal Pluralism

317. *Strength.* – The long list of objectives and uses of comparative law means that the discipline can create benefits in multiple contexts. These contexts range from the academic to the practical, from the legislative to the judicial, and from the domestic to the international. Reviewing the list can leave the reader with the impression that almost any activity in law can profit from a comparative approach. Of course, in order to make such an approach worthwhile, its pay-off must be substantial, because comparative studies require considerable expertise, time, and effort, and the risk of error is large. Still, with potential rewards on so many levels, there is a strong argument that all legal education should contain a substantial comparative element, and that there is a need for a considerable number of jurists specializing in comparative law.

318. *Downside.* – Yet, this extremely broad range of uses and goals also has a downside: it prevents consensus about an overall purpose that provides an ultimate reference point for comparative studies. Some comparatists want to broaden their audience's perspective and promote understanding and tolerance across jurisdictional boundaries, while others seek to assist legal practitioners in planning international transactions or in resolving transboundary disputes. Some investigate the grouping of legal systems and try to understand their interaction, while others wish to develop domestic law through reform legislation or judicial decisions. Some pursue international unification in a variety of forms while others want to develop a transnational legal science. Some use it for "subversive" purposes, others to "coordinate" national, inter-, and supranational legal orders. Like the discipline's extremely broad coverage in both geographic and substantive terms (*supra* IV.), this goal pluralism fosters a fragmentation into numerous sub-disciplines. To be sure, they all engage in the comparison of laws in one way or another, but the pursuit of such highly diverse agendas means that "a unifying paradigm is lacking".[746]

Without a shared sense of purpose, it is impossible to develop a consistent methodology because the goals comparatists pursue largely determine the methods they employ.

List of Principal Works

Adenas and Fairgrieve (eds.), Courts and Comparative Law (Oxford 2015)

Ancel, Utilité et méthodes du droit comparé (Neuchatel 1971)

Basedow, Comparative Law and Its Clients: Am.J. Comp.L. 62 (2014) 21–857

Buxbaum, Die Rechtsvergleichung zwischen nationalem Staat und internationaler Wirtschaft: RabelsZ 60 (1996) 201–230

Canivet, Adenas and Fairgrieve (eds.), Comparative Law Before the Courts (London 2004)

Constaninesco, Rechtsvergleichung, vol. III (Köln/Berlin/Bonn/München 1972) 331–431

Drobnig and van Erp (eds.), The Use of Comparative Law by Courts (The Hague, London, Boston MA 1998)

Fletcher, Comparative Law as a Subversive Discipline: 46 Am.J.Comp.L. 683–700 (1998)

Glenn, Aims of Comparative Law: *Smits* (ed.), Elgar Encyclopedia of Comparative Law (ed. 2 Cheltenham, Northampton MA 2012) 65–74

Kahn-Freund, On Uses and Misuses of Comparative Law: 37 M.L.R. 1–27 (1974)

Kischel, Rechtsvergleichung (München 2015) 47–91

Kötz, Alte und neue Aufgaben der Rechtsvergleichung: JZ 2002, 257–264, reprinted in *idem.* Undogmatisches (Tübingen 2005) 138–154

Markesinis and Fedke (eds.), Judicial Recourse to Foreign Law: A New Source of Inspiration? (Abingdon, New York 2006)

[746] *Hyland,* Comparative Law: *Patterson* (ed.), A Companion to the Philosophy of Law and Legal Theory (Cambridge 1996) 184–199, 185.

Markesinis, Comparative Law in the Courtroom and Classroom (Oxford, Portland OR 2003)

Markesinis, Comparative Law: A Subject in Search of an Audience: 53 M.L.R. 1–21 (1990)

Muir Watt, La fonction subversive du droit comparé: Rev.int.dr.comp. 2000, 503–527

Örücü, Comparative Law in Practice. The Courts and the Legislator: *Örücü* and *Nelken* (eds.), Comparative Law - a Handbook (Oxford and Portland OR 2007) 411–433

Smits, Comparative Law and Its Influence on National Legal Systems: *Reimann and Zimmermann* (eds.), The Oxford Handbook of Comparative Law (ed. 2 Oxford 2019) 502–523

Stein, Uses, Misuses - and Nonuses of Comparative Law: Nw.U.L.Rev. 72 198–216 (1977)

Van Erp, Comparative Private Law in Practice: The Process of Law Reform, in *Örücü* and *Nelken* (eds.), Comparative Law – A Handbook (Oxford, Portland OR 2007) 399–409.

VI ORIENTATIONS, APPROACHES, AND METHODS

319. *Introduction and Overview.* – Under the general label of their discipline, comparatists have pursued a rich variety of projects and agendas. As a result, "comparative legal studies" come in many forms, shapes, and sizes. There are several plausible ways to present this material, and introductory texts differ widely in that regard. Here, we will divide the material into three clusters.

We will first establish *Three General Orientations* (A.) that, like the general part of a codification, shape everything that follows: the question of the fundamental conception of law – as either a set of rules and institutions or a manifestation of traditions and cultures (i.); the issue of the scope of comparative inquiry – i.e., macro-comparison v. micro-comparison (ii.); and the basic attitude towards similarity v. difference and, as a related matter, towards convergence and divergence (iii.).

Second, we will look at five established *Specific Approaches* (B.), i.e., kinds of projects and pursuits. They range from the comparison of individual rules, concepts, and institutions (i.) to the grouping of legal systems (or families) in the world (ii.); they include the study of legal transplants (iii.), a large variety of interdisciplinary agendas (iv.), and more recent critical approaches (v.).

Third, we will explore the most important *Specific Methods* (C.) employed in these pursuits, especially functionalism (i.), common core research employing the "factual method" (ii.), and the more recent turn to numerical comparative law (iii.).

Organizing the material in this manner makes the categories and their distinctions appear clearer than they are in practice. The lines between them are flexible, and reasonable people can differ on exactly where to draw them. Moreover, orientations, approaches, and methods interact in multiple ways: some basic orientations line up well with certain kinds of projects; some projects call for particular methods; and some methods reflect basic orientations. Still, even though dividing the terrain into distinct orientations, approaches, and methods is inevitably somewhat artificial, it will help the reader grasp these individual elements, recognize them when he or she sees them at work, and understand their potential, problems, and interdependence.

A. BASIC ORIENTATIONS

i. *Rules and Institutions v. Traditions and Cultures*

320. *Two conceptions of "law".* – It is a fundamental question for comparatists what they mean by the "law" they set out to compare. Should they see that "law" as a set (or system) of positive rules, e.g., about contracts, criminal procedure, or fundamental rights, as well as of fundamental institutions, such as marriage, jury trial, and judicial review? Or should they conceive of law primarily as a social and cultural phenomenon and practice consisting of political choices, collective habits, and moral values? The simple answer is that for comparatists today, "law" is both. Yet, the distinction between these two basic conceptions continues to matter. It is, of course, relevant for what comparatists engage with. Yet, as we shall see, it also casts a long shadow affecting the scope of their inquiries (*infra* ii., ss. 323–325) as well as their attitude towards similarities and differences and the convergence of legal systems (*infra* iii., ss. 326–333).

321. *A shift in emphasis.* – Modern comparative law began as the study of positive rules and established institutions. Its continental European origins (especially in the Paris Congress of 1900, *supra* III.C.i., ss. 85–87) entailed a predominantly positivist understanding of law as a set of principles and rules, preferably in a systematic order. It is true that to the extent continental European comparatists began to study (whole) legal systems and families, they departed from their traditional positivism by considering elements beyond rules and principles, such as legal sources, techniques, and styles. Yet, for the time being, this merely modified, but it did not

overthrow, their essentially rule-oriented and positivist conception of law.[747]

This conception acquired powerful competition when American comparatists rose to global prominence in the last third of the twentieth century. As a result of early twentieth-century sociological jurisprudence and legal realism, many of these American comparatists were skeptical of abstract principles and rules and hostile to legal positivism. Building in part on the work of European émigrés (especially Max Rheinstein, 1899–1977), they began to look at law as a historically contingent, social, political, cultural (and eventually also economic) phenomenon. As a result, they pushed comparative law towards the study of "legal traditions" and "legal cultures".[748] Since the 1990s, various European scholars have veered in the same direction.[749] Sometimes drawing especially on French and German social theory and philosophy, they also have compared law from a cultural perspective, either in a sociological or an intellectual sense.[750] For some, the emphasis on law-as-culture entailed a search for the deeply-rooted, unconscious predilections (in the sense of *Vorverständnis*) underlying the legal consciousness prevailing in the respective legal environments.[751]

322. *Remaining differences in orientation.* – While the discipline today embraces the comparison of positive rules and legal institutions as well as the study of legal traditions and cultures, the distinction continues to matter in two main regards.

First, different regions of the world emphasize different orientations. In (especially continental) Europe, where legal positivism is alive and well, rule comparison remains popular, strong, and respected. This is also the case in many other parts of the civil law orbit, such as the Pacific Rim and Latin America. It is true that even in these regions there are comparatists who, often as a result of American influence, pursue a social and cultural approach, but in most jurisdictions they do not constitute the mainstream. In the United States, by contrast, a sociological, cultural, and economic orientation has come to prevail. To be sure, rule comparison is still practiced, but it has been in retreat for the last generation and is no longer widely popular.

Second, for some scholars, the question whether to compare positive rules and institutions or rather legal traditions and cultures is not a matter of neutral choice, driven by considerations of purpose and expediency. Instead, especially for many advocates of a sociological and cultural approach, it has become a question of right or wrong. Some have simply seen little value in rule comparison, considering it a "waste" of "intellectual horsepower".[752] Others, in particular scholars associated with the critical approaches that have emerged since the 1990s (*infra* B.v., ss. 360–365), have attacked rule comparison as "dreary positivism which relegates comparative legal studies to a technical exercise whose output is deeply flawed".[753] At times, these attacks have

[747] Note, for example, that the first two editions of the treatise by Zweigert and Kötz consisted of two volumes. The first characterized and organized the world's legal systems according to their "style", while the second compared the positive rules governing contract, unjust enrichment, and tort; *Zweigert and Kötz* (*supra* n. 419)

[748] The opening volley was the, now classic, volume by *Merryman* (*supra* n. 209); see also *Glendon, Gordon and Osakwe* (*supra* n. 210); *Barton, Gibbs, Li and Merryman* (*supra* n. 226).

[749] See, e.g., *Van Hoecke and Warrington*, Legal Cultures, Legal Paradigms, and Legal Doctrine: Towards a New Model for Comparative Law: 47 I.C.L.Q. 495 (1998).

[750] James Whitman described this shift to a cultural understanding of law as a "neo-Romantic" turn because it drew, inter alia, on major figures of the German Romantic era, such as Johann Gottfried Herder (1744–1803) and Friedrich Carl von Savigny (1779–1861), who had emphasized the intimate relationship between culture and law; *Whitman*, The neo-Romantic Turn: *Legrand and Munday* (eds.), Comparative Legal Studies: Traditions and Transitions (Cambridge, New York 2003) 312–344, 315–319.

[751] *Idem* 324–329; important foundations were laid by *Esser*, Vorverständnis und Methodenwahl in der Rechtsfindung: Rationalitätsgrenzen der richterlichen Entscheidungspraxis (Tübingen 1970), building in part on *Gadamer*, Wahrheit und Methode (Tübingen 1960).

[752] Merryman, quoted in *Legrand*, John Henry Merryman and Comparative Legal Studies: A Dialogue: 47 Am.J.Comp.L. 3–66, 46 (1999).

[753] Legrand, The Same and the Different: idem and Munday (eds.), Comparative Legal Studies: Traditions and Transitions (Cambridge, New York 2003) 240–311, 277.

turned the ongoing debate about the proper orientation of the discipline into a battle between opposing camps.[754] The critics are correct that much traditional rule comparison has remained too context-blind, and that looking at rules and institutions often tells us little about their real meaning, practical use, and impact on outcomes. But the critics also disregard the important contributions that comparisons of positive rules and institutions have made in many contexts, such as the international legal unification of law and our understanding of the law's goals, structures, and directions.

ii. *Macro- and Micro-comparison*

323. *The choice of scale.* – Like scholars in many other disciplines, comparatists have a choice of scale: like economists, for example, they can focus broadly on whole systems or narrowly on particular elements thereof. Operating on a broad scale is commonly known as *macro-comparison;* operating on a narrow scale as *micro-comparison.*

This terminology was first developed by Jean-Leontin Constantinesco in the 1960s,[755] adopted by Zweigert and Kötz in the 1980s,[756] and then broadly popularized through the global dissemination of their treatise, especially in its English translation.[757] As a result, the distinction between macro- and micro-comparison has become a generally acknowledged feature of the discipline.[758]

Even though the terminology is not always entirely uniform, there is broad agreement about what these terms mean. Macro-comparison looks at "legal systems in their entirety" (such as Japanese or Chinese law) or at "entire families of legal systems" (such as Scandinavian or Latin American legal systems);[759] it compares the "large, defining characteristics and the legal systems as such"[760] – "the spirit and style ..., the methods of thought and procedures they use".[761] Thus, macro-comparison lines up easily with a social and cultural conception of law (*supra* i., s. 321), though strictly speaking it does not require that orientation. Micro-comparison, by contrast, looks at the "details",[762] the "elementary particles",[763] especially at particular norms or institutions. It thus lines up easily with rule-comparison, though it is not necessarily limited to that. Many comparative projects can be pursued either on a macro- or a micro-scale. For example, the study of receptions or transplants (*infra* B.iii., ss. 345–349) can look to broad, system-wide imports (e.g. of the Roman law in late medieval and early modern Europe) or focus on particular rules or institutions (e.g., the spread of liability for insider trading from the United States to many parts of the developed world).

324. *Softening the contrast.* – While macro- and micro-comparison are clearly distinct in theory, in practice they often mix and blend. This is true in two regards.

First, the line dividing them is not sharply drawn but rather blurry. In fact, as others have

[754] See the collection of articles in What We Write About When We Write About Comparative Law: Pierre Legrand's Critique in Discussion: 65 Am.J.Comp.L. (Special Issue) (2017).

[755] *Constantinesco*, Les éléments déterminants en tant que critères fondant la science du droit comparé: Mélanges Vallindas (Thessaloniki 1967) 235; Constantinesco then incorporated the terms in his treatise, *Constantinesco* (*supra* n. 104) 79–81. While the terms were first introduced by René David, he applied them in a different manner that has not had any long-term impact: see *idem* 79.

[756] The first edition of *Zweigert and Kötz* (*supra* n. 273) did not contain these terms and made only some, fairly vague, references to the idea, *idem* 5. The terms were introduced in the 2d edition, 4–6, which appeared in 1984, i.e., one year after Constantinesco's treatise, though without attributing the terms to him. Their presentations remained the same in the 3d edition (Tübingen 1996) 4–5.

[757] *Zweigert and Kötz* (*supra* n. 218) 4–5.

[758] See, e.g., *Bogdan*, Concise Introduction to Comparative Law (Groningen 2013) 45–46; *Cuniberti* (*supra* n. 286) 13–14; *Husa*, A New Introduction to Comparative Law (Oxford, Portland OR 2015) 100–104; *Kischel* (*supra* n. 286) 8–9.

[759] *Bogdan* (*supra* n. 758) 45.

[760] *Constantinesco*, Rechtsvergleichung (*supra* n. 681) 80.

[761] *Zweigert* and *Kötz* (*supra* n. 3) 4.

[762] *Bogdan* (*supra* n. 758) 45.

[763] *Constantinesco* (*supra* n. 681) 80.

noted, the two concepts are best conceived as opposite ends of a spectrum with a large middle ground.[764] While a study of the world's mixed jurisdictions (as such) is a pretty clear example of macro-comparison,[765] and a multi-country analysis of the cost-shifting rules in civil litigation can properly be called micro-comparison,[766] a comparative analysis of judging in France and the United States operates on an intermediate level and combines elements of both.[767] Indeed, many comparative studies belong somewhere in the middle of the spectrum, though often closer to one end than the other.

Second, each of the two kinds of comparison will typically employ elements of the other. Macro-comparison needs to resort to detail in order to substantiate its claims and to illustrate the broad outlines it presents. Conversely, micro-comparison must consider the context provided by the respective legal systems, because the meaning and effect of individual rules or institutions depend on their background and environment. As a result, comparative studies are rarely pure macro- or micro-comparison. Instead, most of them are hybrids, and their characterization as one or the other must ultimately turn on which overall orientation prevails.

325. *Implications and consequences.* – If macro- and micro-comparison are largely matters of degree, does the distinction really matter? This is a legitimate question, especially since comparatists have scarcely claimed that it is of great importance. Yet, the dichotomy does have some noteworthy implications and consequences. To begin with, embracing it has a legitimizing function: it implies that both forms of comparison (and the various hybrids) have their proper place within the discipline. Furthermore, the distinction clarifies expectations: it makes the producers of comparative legal scholarship more conscious of what they are, and are not, doing – and their consumers more cognizant of what they are, and are not, getting. The dichotomy also has methodological consequences: some methods of comparative law are more suited for one form than for the other. The prime example is functionalism (*infra* C.i., ss. 368–373). It was developed for the comparison of individual rules and institutions, and it is debatable whether it fits the comparison of whole systems as well.[768] Finally, in certain quarters, the distinction has entailed value judgments about comparative legal scholarship in a manner influenced by, and similar to, the debate about law-as-rules v. law-as-culture (*supra* i., s. 320): micro-comparison has sometimes been equated with narrow-minded analysis of blackletter rules and thus with context-blind positivism, while macro-comparison has been associated with sophisticated understandings of legal traditions and cultures.

iii. *Similarities v. Differences (and the Issue of Convergence)*

326. *Introduction and overview.* – It seems trivial to postulate that comparative legal studies must consider both how legal systems are alike and how they differ – after all, "[t]here is no point in comparing what is identical, and little point in comparing what has nothing in common".[769] Thus, for most comparatists, the exploration of similarities as well as differences is part of the very definition of their discipline. Yet, whether comparative law should focus more on the former or the latter has been a much-debated issue, especially since the 1990s. For most of the twentieth century, comparatists looked primarily to what laws and legal systems have in common. Its closing decade, however, saw an increasingly critical questioning of that tradition and, among a sizeable group of scholars, a rebellious shift towards an emphasis on diversity. As a result, today there are two competing orientations. Yet, like macro- and micro-comparison, they are best understood

[764] *Kischel* (*supra* n. 286) 9.

[765] See, e.g., *Palmer*, Mixed Jurisdictions Worldwide: The Third Legal Family (Cambridge 2001).

[766] *Reimann* (*supra* n. 539)

[767] *Garapon and Papadopoulos* (*supra* n. 393).

[768] While *Constantinesco* (*supra* n. 681) 80 claims that the method for both macro- and micro-comparison is the same, *Kischel* (*supra* n. 286) 8, postulates that functionalism pertains only to micro-comparison. Neither author provides further explanations.

[769] *Dannemann*, Comparative Law: Study of Similarities or Differences?: *Reimann and Zimmermann* (eds.), The Oxford Handbook of Comparative Law (ed. 2 Oxford 2019), 390–422, 391.

as opposite ends of a spectrum with a large middle ground.

327. *Twentieth-century "universalism".* – Modern comparative law as it was established around 1900 was long dominated by what has been called "universalism",[770] i.e., an orientation towards what laws and legal systems broadly share. For the first few decades the focus was primarily on positive (mainly legislative) rules and their unification. At the Paris Congress of 1900, Edouard Lambert announced the search for a *droit commun législatif,* albeit only among countries similarly situated (mainly in continental Europe).[771]. He considered many differences between the various national legislative rules "accidental" and called for them to be overcome.[772] At least in part, this early search for uniformity was a reaction against the loss of the (relative) unity of the erstwhile European *ius commune,* which was abandoned when law was increasingly codified on the national level during the nineteenth century. In part, the comparatists' unification agenda also reflected the belief that international commerce required internationally uniform rules (most importantly in sales law). The period's drive for legal uniformity was evident on the institutional level. Already since 1893 the Hague Conference of Private International law had pursued the unification of conflicts rules through international conventions; in 1926, the *Institut international pour l'unification du droit privé* (UNIDROIT), founded under the auspices of the League of Nations, opened its doors in Rome; and forty years later the United Nations Commission on International Trade Law (UNCITRAL) began to operate in New York and Vienna. All three institutions have continued to play a prominent role in the unification of law ever since.

Around the middle of the twentieth century the focus shifted from the similarity of rules to the similarity of results. When comparatists increasingly compared the civil with the common law, they had to acknowledge significant differences between the respective norms themselves. Adopting the "functional method" first propagated by Ernst Rabel, they now increasingly looked beyond these rules and sought to understand how different societies resolved (presumably) identical problems. They observed that despite often different rules, the outcomes reached in the various jurisdictions were mostly the same, at least in the core areas of private law.[773] In 1971, Konrad Zweigert and Hein Kötz captured this belief in their (in)famous *"praesumptio similitudinis"*[774] (of results) (*infra* C.i., s. 372). The global success of their treatise thus fortified the discipline's basic orientation towards similarity for the remainder of the twentieth century.

One must be careful though not to paint too one-sided a picture of this period. There were always voices calling for attention to the importance of difference, e.g., in the context of transplanting elements from one system to another.[775] In addition, one of the most prominent branches of mid- and late-twentieth-century comparative law thrived on pointing out diversity: scholars dividing the world into legal families have emphasized not only the commonalities that defined these families but also, and perhaps more importantly, what distinguishes them from each other (*infra* B.ii., ss. 337–342). These counterpoints notwithstanding, most twentieth-century comparative law was strongly oriented towards finding similarity. At its end, the drive for uniformity vigorously asserted itself in the various project(s) pursuing a common private law of Europe (*supra* IV.C.i.g., ss. 242–245).

328. *The assertion of "difference".* – Beginning in the 1980s, a slowly growing and increasingly influential group of scholars questioned the discipline's bias in favor of similarity and demanded a shift of focus towards diversity and "difference".

This movement has four, interrelated, components. First, it is part of a broader, left-wing,

770 *Hyland* (*supra* n. 746) 185.

771 *Lambert* (*supra* n. 147) 47.

772 *Idem* 38. Lambert understood that many differences also reflect political, moral, and social conditions, *ibidem.*

773 Thus, the method of "functionalism" and the belief in "universalism" have worked in tandem – a connection much noted by later critics of both.

774 *Zweigert and Kötz* (*supra* n. 3) 39. The authors were careful to point out that this presumption applied only in certain circumstances, *idem* 37, – a limitation often forgotten by their readers.

775 See e.g. *Kahn-Freund* (*supra* n. 221) 1; see also *Gutteridge* (*supra* n. 19) 8–9; *Ancel,* Utilité et méthodes du droit comparé (Neuchatel 1971) 65.

methodological attack on the discipline's mainstream (*infra* B.v., s. 362). The attackers pointed out, inter alia, that as an observer the comparatist will inevitably perceive law from his or her own perspective; as a result, an emphasis on similarity will pick up what is familiar and suppress what is not. Critical self-awareness thus requires particular attention to difference.[776] Second, in some iterations, the attack on the mainstream was rooted in postmodern philosophy and epistemology. Drawing on discourse theory, modern sociology, and (mainly French and German) post-World War II hermeneutics,[777] scholars have rejected the universalism rooted in enlightenment thought and the natural law tradition; instead they have conceived of the (legal) universe in a postmodern fashion, i.e., as fragmented, indeterminate, and diverse (*infra* B.v., s. 362). As a result, they have come to regard pluralism "as a basic condition of the world of law in the twenty-first century".[778] These two strands of criticism have been closely related to a third development: a shift of orientation in some of the discipline from law-as-rules to law-as-culture (*supra* i., s. 321). Where scholars abandoned rule-based comparative law and instead embraced law as "cultural fabric", they quickly came to see it as "inevitably indigenous and, therefore, different in the way something which is unique is different".[779] The fourth element was important as a timely trigger of these critiques: in Europe, much of the turn away from rules and towards culture was a reaction against the large-scale and multi-facetted project of a common private law for Europe which dominated continental comparative law around the turn of the twentieth century. Its critics noted that this project's narrow focus on the unification of law-as-rules risked "impoverishing the life of comparative law in the process".[780] It largely disregarded the cultural and social contingency of law, its symbolic values, its underlying *mentalités*, as well as its political and distributional consequences.[781] In the eyes of the critics, especially the claim of essential commonalities between the civil and the common law[782] and, even more so, the effort to downplay (or even outright deny) the differences between them[783] had all the vices of rule positivism and narrow-minded functionalism.[784]

A convenient label for the cluster of ideas emerging from these four elements is "difference theory".[785] Yet, since the critics of the mainstream's traditional penchant for similarity have embraced these ideas in various forms and combinations, there is really no single, coherent "theory". But there is, among a substantial and influential number of comparative law scholars today, basic agreement that the goal of comparative law should be "to explain legal diversity", rather than "to explain it away".[786] Virtually all these scholars agree that the presumption of similarity – and with it the obsession with the underlying functionalist approach – should be abandoned.[787] Some go further and demand that it be replaced by a "presumption of dissimilarity".[788] As a result, "the other", "otherness", and "difference" became turn-of-the-century buzzwords.

We must not overlook, however, that even beyond the vociferous critics of mainstream "universalism", other scholars also produced notable substantive work with an emphasis on difference. Examples include Mirjan Damaska's distinction between two fundamental models of state authority,[789] Rudolfo Sacco's analysis of the differ-

[776] *Frankenberg* (*supra* n. 237) 424–425, 432–434; *Frankenberg*, Comparative Law as Critique (Cheltenham, Northampton MA 2016); see also *Hyland* (*supra* n. 746) 193–194.

[777] *Frankenberg, ibidem*; *Legrand* (*supra* n. 753) 240.

[778] *Husa* (*supra* n. 758) 182.

[779] *Legrand* (*supra* n. 753) 278. An important stimulus for this line of thought also came from interpretative anthropology: see especially *Geertz* (*supra* n. 68).

[780] *Whitman* (*supra* n. 750) 314.

[781] *Legrand* (*supra* n. 753) 294–295.

[782] See, e.g., *Zimmermann*, Savigny's Legacy: Legal History, Comparative Law and the Emergence of a European Legal Science: 112 L.Q.R. 576–605, 588–595 (1996).

[783] See, e.g., *Gordley*, Common Law und Civil Law: eine überholte Unterscheidung: ZEuP 1 (1993) 498–518.

[784] *Legrand*, European Legal Systems are Not Converging: 45 I.C.L.Q. 52–81 (1996).

[785] The label is *Hyland*'s (*supra* n. 746) 193, although he does not claim that there is a coherent, not to mention uniform, theory.

[786] *Legrand* (*supra* n. 753) 248.

[787] *Legrand* (*supra* n. 753) 292.

[788] *Hyland* (*supra* n. 746) 194; *Legrand* (*supra* n. 753) 279.

[789] *Damaska* (*supra* n. 60).

ences created by the various "formants" of legal reasoning,[790] and Ugo Mattei's display of deeply rooted differences in the character of the world's legal systems.[791]

329. *A critique of "universalism" and "difference theory".* – The growing emphasis on "difference" in the late twentieth and early twenty-first centuries has enriched comparative legal studies by creating a much-needed counterpoint to the previously all-too-dominant search for similarity and drive for unification. It has made comparatists more cognizant of the diversity and significance of cultural values and predilections underlying law and legal systems; it has brought to light that legal diversity (like biodiversity) has significant benefits (such as opportunities for experimentation with different solutions, competition between laws and legal systems, and sheer enjoyment of variety[792]) and that these benefit should not be thoughtlessly sacrificed on the altar of unification; and it has exposed the cognitive bias inherent in much of mainstream universalism: "The desire for sameness breeds the expectation of sameness, which, in turn, begets the finding of sameness".[793]

At the same time, an orientation towards difference can fall prey to exactly the opposite bias: if we prefer difference, we will look for it – and find it. As James Whitman has observed, "scholars who perceive only 'difference' in the world tend get … a little unsteady on their scholarly feet". He thus justly warned against succumbing to a "dizzy Romanticism" which can render discourse "opaque or oracular or simply confused".[794] In addition, even where difference undoubtedly exists, it can, just like similarity, easily be overstated and overrated. Claims of the "irreducibility of difference"[795] or the "incommensurability" of legal cultures[796] exoticize even neighboring legal families (like the civil and common law). They gloss over commonalities and deny the possibility of unification (as well as of convergence, *infra* s. 333). In light of the features undeniably shared by many legal systems and of the numerous successful international unification projects, such an extreme position is difficult to defend.

330. *Political, psychological, and ideological dimensions.* – Both "universalism" and "difference theory" tend to associate themselves with certain political directions – the former towards the conservative, the latter towards the progressive end of the spectrum.[797] Unfortunately, advocates on both sides have sometimes correspondingly divided their fellow comparatists into friends and foes; this impairs communication, hinders cooperation, and clouds critical analysis.

Whether one accords priority to similarity or difference is influenced not only by methodological or political inclinations; it is also a matter of one's psychological, or even emotional, predisposition. It has been pointed out, for example, that the post-World War II generation of comparatists in the United States consisted largely of refugees from totalitarian regimes in Europe who, as a result, had a strong emotional desire for unity.[798] More broadly, fear of, or aversion to, legal chaos can also push a comparatist towards a preference for similarity (and unification). By contrast, enjoyment of cultural diversity, perhaps as a matter of personal background or experience, will often entail an orientation towards difference. So does the concern that massive unification will diminish the importance of comparative studies because, in a world of similar law, there may be little left to compare.

Finally, there is an uneasy relationship between celebrating difference (e.g., between legal cultures) on the one hand, and the contemporary ideology of equality (of groups and their members) on the other. It is true that a focus on difference does not have to "connote nationalism, imperialism, colonialism or isolationism", not to mention "cultural fundamentalism",[799] but it is also true that throughout history "otherness"

[790] *Sacco* (*supra* n. 195).

[791] *Mattei*, Three Patterns of Law: Taxonomy and Change in the World's Legal Systems: 45 Am.J.Comp.L. 5–44 (1997).

[792] Interestingly, the last point was emphasized even by a scholar closely associated with the praesumptio similitudinis, i.e., *Kötz*, Abschied von der Rechtskreislehre?: ZEuP 6 (1998) 493–505, 505.

[793] *Legrand* (*supra* n. 753) 240.

[794] *Whitman* (*supra* n. 750) 314–315.

[795] *Legrand* (*supra* n. 753) 256.

[796] *Idem* 283.

[797] See the graph proffered by Kennedy (*supra* n. 186) 417.

[798] *Curran* (*supra* n. 7) 66–78.

[799] *Legrand* (*supra* n. 753) 298.

has often served to justify discrimination, ranging from the mild to the murderous. Celebrating difference while maintaining equal respect and treatment for all cultures and their members *is* possible but it is a project at which societies have failed more often than they have succeeded.

331. *The surprising lack of a common framework.* – Among comparatists, there is considerable agreement about the factors that may be used to *explain* similarities and differences, such as political situation and economic system, ideology and religion, history and geography, ethnicity and demographics, the availability and strength of non-legal means of social control, as well as historical accident or sheer mood of the moment.[800] Yet, there is virtually no agreement about how to *assess* similarity and difference. Take, for example, the question whether the English rules on the law of contract are similar to, or different from, their French counterparts. Discussing that question in a meaningful way calls for a consensus on at least three points. The first is the relevant frame of reference: if the two bodies of law are compared in the global context (including non-Western legal systems) they look quite similar, but if they are compared in the much narrower context of Western Europe the differences begin to stand out. The second point is the level of generality: if we look just to the grand outlines, English and French contract law appear by and large similar, but the more we focus on the details the more differences come to light. Finally, since no two legal systems are entirely alike nor entirely diverse, similarity and difference are matters of degree, and measuring that degree requires a defined scale. Yet, comparatists have never agreed on such a scale but rather left the assessment of degrees to each observer him- or herself. Without agreements at least on reference point, level of generality, and applicable scale, however, general statements about similarity or difference are not falsifiable: if one comparatist claims that the common and the civil law have become largely alike,[801] another that they remain fundamentally different,[802] neither can be proven right or wrong.

In addition, similarity and difference are not only matters of degree, their assessment also depends "on the comparatist's standpoint, on his epistemological interest, and on his prior expectation". As a result, such assessments are not objective statements of fact but rather "express irreducibly subjective *judgements*".[803]

Recently, some help has come from the growing body of studies in "numerical comparative law" (*infra* C.iii., ss. 378–381). Several of these studies seek to capture similarities and differences in numerical terms and to analyze them by statistical means. Some measure formal features of legal systems, such as the length of statutes or the frequency of citations in judicial opinions; others seek to compare the quality of laws, for example, degrees of shareholder protection.[804] In both cases, legal systems can then be rated as (more or less) similar to, or different from, others, albeit only with regard to specific aspects.

332. *Similarity v. difference and the aims of research.* – Since general preferences are difficult to justify and generalized statements have scant analytical purchase, the debates about them have an air of unreality. It is more rewarding to examine the role of similarity or difference in the concrete context of particular kinds of comparative work.[805]

Some forms of comparative study are driven primarily by the search for similarity. On the practical side, this is most obvious for international unification projects: these projects first have to take stock of what rules are already shared among legal systems. On the academic side, the search for a "common core" of a field of law (*infra* C.ii., ss. 374–377) also tries to capture what is identical, or at least similar, in the laws under investigation. Of course, both kinds of projects must be attentive to differences as well – be it in order to overcome them through legislative compromise and to recognize the limits of possible unification or to demarcate the outer limits of the "common core". Still, the leading consideration is similarity, while attention to difference exercises a control function.

[800] See, e.g., *Bogdan* (*supra* n. 758) 57–62; *Husa* (*supra* n. 758) 157–181.

[801] *Gordley* (*supra* n. 783).

[802] *Legrand* (*supra* n. 784).

[803] *Jansen* (*supra* n. 1) 297–298.

[804] Several examples of such studies are summarized by *Siems* (*supra* n. 680) 180–228.

[805] See the discussion in *Dannemann* (*supra* n. 769) 407–411.

Other comparative law projects look primarily for difference. This is true when law reformers search for foreign models which provide other, and perhaps superior, solutions for a problem at hand. In a similar vein, when businesses make strategic choices about which legal system(s) to associate themselves with, they are looking for particular advantages, such as high investment protection or low litigation risk; thus, they are mainly interested in the variations between jurisdictions. Again, these actors must also keep an eye on what the legal systems under consideration have in common, e.g., to make them workable reform models or preferable business options. Now, however, their primary focus is on what makes laws different, not alike.

In many contexts, researchers must look for both similarities and differences in equal measure. That is true, for example, when comparative law is employed by private international law for purposes of "characterization" (or "classification"): if choice-of-law rules require the application of a foreign law that contains concepts or institutions alien to the judge, he or she must fit them into his own legal environment as best he or she can; this requires a thorough understanding of how these foreign concepts or institutions are similar to, as well as different from, the domestic ones (*supra* II.A.i., s. 20). Also, when a comparatist seeks to understand whether certain social or economic results are caused by particular laws, he or she must identify the crucial variables, which requires careful consideration of both the features that are shared by legal systems and those that are not.

Finally, when comparatists seek to describe and juxtapose several legal systems for introductory purposes, e.g., in a basic course on comparative law, they need to highlight both what these systems have in common and what divides them. If the systems under observation appear similar, like the United States and Canada, it is particularly instructive to point out the differences; if they appear to be radically different, like England and China, it is especially intriguing to look for similarity. Thus whether the search for similarity or a focus on difference is the more valuable heuristic device depends on the objects of comparison.[806]

333. *The convergence (and divergence) of legal systems.* – Similarity or difference are not static but constantly changing. This leads to the question whether, over time, legal systems are becoming more or less alike. Thus the issue of their convergence or divergence has been a major topic in comparative law since the 1970s.[807] While many comparatists have long been predisposed towards convergence, others have more recently pointed to its limits or even emphasized divergence. In canvassing the debates, it is important to keep in mind that they took place mainly in specific contexts: they focused largely on the relationship between the civil and the common law, and they flared up particularly in connection with the drive for a common private law for Europe in the late twentieth and early twenty-first centuries (*supra* IV.C.i.g., ss. 242–245).

Like the discussion of similarity and difference more generally, the debate about convergence (and divergence) has not been free from confusion, and scholars have often talked past each other. In order to gain some clarity, we will distinguish four particular sub-issues: What exactly has been said to be converging or diverging? What forms do these processes take? What underlying forces and motivations drive them? And can we observe a general trend in one direction or another?

First, on the issue of what is converging (or not), scholars have looked at very different aspects of legal systems – often without making that clear. Some have focused merely on the substantive rules of private law – and thus found convergence

[806] For a valuable discussion of the roles similarity and difference can play at the various stages of the comparative process, see *Dannemann* (*supra* n. 769) 406–418.

[807] A convenient starting point is the – by now almost classic – essay by *Merryman*, On the Convergence (and Divergence) of the Civil Law and the Common Law: 17 Stan.J.Int.L. 357–388 (1981). Even more than a generation after its publication, the article is still worth reading for the way in which it maps the terrain. The topic was the overarching theme of the XVIth International Congress of Comparative Law in Brisbane, 2002, although, as usual, the Congress dealt with a broad and disparate variety of topics at best loosely related to that theme; see International Academy of Comparative Law, Convergence of Legal Systems in the 21st Century (Brussels 2006).

between the civil and the common law.[808] Some have considered not only rules and principles but also procedures, sources of law, and institutions – and likewise found growing similarity, at least in the European context, i.e., between English and continental law.[809] Other scholars, however, have protested against these assertions. Looking at legal systems as legal cultures led them to observe that civil and common lawyers have fundamentally different "cognitive structure[s]" (*mentalités*) – and thus to conclude that such deeply rooted and "irreducible" differences prevent a true convergence of European legal systems.[810] Yet others, taking a sociological (and global) point of view, observed a new fragmentation into "functionally differentiated global sectors and a multiplicity of global cultures", which not only prevent convergence but actually cause growing divergence between legal systems.[811] A moment's reflection shows that these views are not incompatible. Legal systems can develop towards similar substantive (and even procedural) rules and yet remain culturally different,[812] as is still largely true within the European Union; or they can be culturally quite homogeneous while developing widely divergent rules, as among the sub-units of the United States.

Second, it is important to distinguish various forms of convergence. Much of it is centralized in the sense of driven by the work of central (mainly supra- or international) institutions. Such convergence can be imposed top down, be it by legislation (e.g, through Regulations and Directives in the European Union) or by adjudication in supra- or international tribunals (e.g., the European Court of Human Rights); it can also result from horizontal coordination (e.g, through the implementation of treaties drafted by bodies like UNCITRAL, UNIDROIT, or the Hague Conference on Private International Law) or it can be due to the global or regional influence of soft law (e.g., in the form of Principles or trade-specific rules and practices). A different, non-centralized, form of convergence occurs when legal systems borrow ideas, rules, or institutions from each other more or less ad hoc, i.e., through legal transplants; particularly in that case, however, similarity may be more apparent than real, because elements often change their meaning and impact when transplanted from one system to another (*infra* B.iii., s. 349). Finally, convergence is often spontaneous in the sense of undirected or even unintentional, e.g., when legal systems react in similar ways to common political, social, and economic problems; while this, "natural", convergence is perhaps the least obvious, it may actually be the most powerful.[813] Just like convergence, divergence can also occur in various ways: legislation in one jurisdiction often departs from that of other systems; many treaties are implemented with reservations and modifications meaning that some members deviate from the common platform; regulators may respond to local circumstances or pressures and thus enact different rules; and courts sometimes interpret even similar rules differently, causing case law to diverge.

Third, comparatists have noted that convergence can have a variety of underlying causes. Two factors, which enjoyed some popularity in past centuries, are largely discredited today: The early modern notion of natural law is no longer considered a common denominator strong enough to ensure that legal systems gravitate towards shared principles, rules, and values;[814]

808 *Gordley*, (*supra* n. 783) 498-518.

809 *Markesinis*, Learning from Europe and Learning in Europe: *idem* (ed.) The Gradual Convergence (Oxford 1994) 1–32, 30–32; *Zimmermann* (*supra* n. 782) 589–590. See also *Glenn*, La civilisation de la common law: Rev.int.dr.comp 45 (1993) 560–575, 559.

810 *Legrand*, European Systems are Not Converging: 45 I.C.L.Q. 52–81, 60, 62 (1996).

811 *Teubner*, Legal Irritants: Good Faith in British Law or How Unifying the Law Ends Up in New Differences: 61 M.L.R. 11–32 (1998).

812 *Merryman* (*supra* n. 807) 379–386.

813 In the words of *Merryman*: "Natural convergence is unquestionably the most effective mode of convergence of law, superior to legal transplantation and to active unification in the depth and permanence of its consequences. Often legal transplantation and unification of laws are merely ways of formalizing a legal consensus already reached by political-cultural *rapprochement*." *Merryman* (*supra* n. 807) 371.

814 An exception is the field of international human rights law, see *supra* s. 275.

and the nineteenth-century belief in the evolution of all legal systems from primitive and crude to similar modern and sophisticated forms has lost its appeal as well. Instead, scholars today see other factors at work, of which four deserve at least brief mention. To begin with, legislators and treaty drafters often purposefully push for convergence in order to eliminate, or at least mitigate, the frictions and uncertainties which legal differences create for cross-boundary transactions and disputes; an important instance is the unification of sales law though the Convention for the International Sale of Goods (CISG). In addition, legal systems converge because they join supra- and international organizations whose common rules they then (have to) adopt; this is most visible in the European Union but also true for other regional or global regimes, such as MERCOSUR and the WTO. Furthermore, legal systems sometimes emulate the same model because it is perceived as particularly powerful and prestigious; the much-discussed "Americanization" of Western law after World War II provides an important example,[815] as does the adoption of European law by many countries far beyond the EU since the 1980s.[816] Finally, to the extent that globalization has created similar economic conditions and personal lifestyles, laws have converged in reaction to that assimilation – in John Merryman's words: "as societies become more like each other, their legal systems will tend to become more alike"[817]; this can be observed in the wake of the rise of liberal democracies and market economies after the end of the cold war. It is widely recognized, however, that the effect of all these (and other) pro-convergence forces must not be overrated. Political and legal systems often display inherent inertia; communities cling to traditional habits and values; and even where legal systems converge on the level of paper rules, this does not necessarily mean convergence in actual practice and results.[818] Moreover, just as some factors drive convergence, others work in the opposite direction. Nationalism, isolationism, and even the desire to be different (and special); the divergent outcomes of political power struggles within jurisdictions;[819] the global and regional influence of various centers of power with different political ambitions and interests (such the United States, the European Union, and China); the trends towards regional autonomy and preservation of cultural heritage; and the rise of religious systems; they all suggest a growing plurality of legal orders. Even globalization itself not only creates similarity, it simultaneously entails fragmentation of existing orders and the emergence of new ones,[820] such as an international regime of commercial arbitration with its own rules and logic.[821]

Fourth, general claims about the prevalence of convergence or divergence are extremely dubious since both processes can affect very different elements of legal systems, occur in a variety of forms, and are driven by multiple factors often pushing in opposite directions. It must thus be acknowledged that both processes are going on all the time, sometimes taking surprising turns.[822] It is true, of course, that where scholars have emphasized convergence, they have done so mostly within Western and Central Europe. Yet, while the unification of large areas of positive law through the European Union is undeniable, and while there is also today a fairly common human rights regime throughout Europe, even in this regional context considerable counterarguments remain.

[815] L'américanisation du droit: Arch.phil.dr. 45 (2001) 7.

[816] An example is the widespread adoption of the European product liability law, see *Reimann*, Product Liability in a Global Context: The Hollow Victory of the European Model: Eur.Rev.Priv.L. 11 (2003) 128–154.

[817] *Merryman* (*supra* n. 807) 369.

[818] See *Reimann* (*supra* n. 816) 145–153. Sometimes, assertions of convergence also turn out to result more from bias and wishful thinking than from solid empirical evidence. See, e.g., the broad convergence claims by *Hansmann and Kraakman*, The End of History in Corporate Law, 89 Geo.L.J. 439–468 (2001), and their refutation by *Cabrelli and Siems*, Convergence, Legal Origins, and Transplants in Comparative Corporate Law: A Case-Based and Quantitative Analysis: 63 Am.J. Comp.L. 109–153 (2015).

[819] See *Kahn-Freund* (*supra* n. 221) 1.

[820] *Teubner* (*supra* n. 811)

[821] See *Garth and Dezelay*, Dealing in Virtue: International Commercial Arbitration and the Construction of a Transnational Legal Order (Chicago IL 1996).

[822] See, e.g, *West*, The Puzzling Divergence of Corporate Law: Evidence and Explanations from Japan and the United States: 149 U.Pa.L.Rev. (2001) 525–601.

It is far from clear, for example, how far convergence in Europe really reaches beyond blackletter rules, i.e., how much it occurs in legal practice and results; nor is it clear how much convergence there has been between the various European legal cultures. In a similar vein, it is true that on a global level transnational legal practice has converged, largely through the prevalence of international law firms. But whether this convergence reaches far beyond the international economic activities of banks and corporations is open to question.

Like the debates about similarity and difference, comparatists' views on convergence and divergence have been intimately connected to recent historical developments, both on the global level and in the specific European context.

On the global level, beginning in the late twentieth century, societies, economies, and even important aspects of culture seemed to converge towards a single dominant model. After the end of the cold war, liberal democracies and free market economies were steeply on the rise; liberalization of international trade and travel continued apace; international human rights regimes gathered momentum; and transboundary communication and mobility increased rapidly. At least from a Western point of view, all this could be understood, if not quite as the "End of History",[823] then at least as "the growth of an international culture"[824] and as the coming of an increasingly homogenous global society. In such an atmosphere, the expectation of a gradual convergence of legal systems made considerable sense. Yet, the second decade of the twenty-first century soon provided many reasons to doubt such a development. Many democracies deteriorated into authoritarian regimes; the liberalization of international trade and travel was hampered by renewed protectionism and nationalism; the global human rights regime was weakened by growing state defiance; and even international communication was becoming more regulated as a result of data protection concerns. In addition, the rise of Islam challenged, often violently, the prevalence of Western models and values; China developed into a massive counterweight to Western political and economic dominance; and a belief in pluralism and cultural diversity became almost *de rigueur* among Western elites. In such an atmosphere, it becomes notable that the convergence of legal systems had slowed down, and in many instances, turned into divergence.

The development was similar in the European context. In the closing decades of the twentieth century European integration seemed unstoppable as the EU grew rapidly in size and forcefully unified ever more areas of law. It seemed only a matter of time until all of Europe would be one big quasi-state with a common currency and open internal borders. During that period, European legal systems were actually converging in many (though not all) regards. Thus, the project of a common private law for Europe seemed both timely and promising. The second decade of the twentieth century, however, brought not only a marked slow-down of European integration, it actually put the whole process in question when, for the first time, the Union lost a member with the (Br)exit of the United Kingdom. In addition, nationalism returned as a major political force in several member states (especially in Central and Eastern Europe); political power was increasingly fragmented by devolution to the regional or local level in many countries; some separatist movements gathered enough strength to threaten national unity (especially in the United Kingdom and Spain); and ethnic and cultural rights became almost universally embraced values. In this changed atmosphere, further convergence of European legal systems quickly became questionable. Note that after twenty years of lavishly funded and highly concerted efforts, the project to create a common private law of Europe ultimately resulted in failure. Suddenly, even divergence became not only a distinct possibility but, with the defection of the United Kingdom, a (partial) reality.

Realizing how contingent expectations of convergence and divergence are on changing political circumstances shows that employing these concepts to *predict* future developments is highly precarious. The main value of these concepts is

[823] *Fukuyama*, The End of History and the Last Man (New York 1992).

[824] *Merryman* (*supra* n. 807) 369.

heuristic: asking questions of convergence and divergence helps us to *observe* more closely, to *recognize* more clearly, and to *understand* more deeply, how legal systems develop in relation to each other.[825]

B. GENERAL APPROACHES

i. *Comparing Rules, Concepts, and Institutions*

334. *As standard practice.* – The comparison of individual rules, concepts, and institutions is not a distinct "approach" in and of itself, but rather the discipline's standard general practice. As a result, it is not specifically discussed in the literature but simply subsumed under the term *micro-comparison* (*supra* A.ii., s. 323). Yet, this practice must be mentioned before we turn to the various specific approaches, lest it be overlooked that it comprises the traditional lion's share of comparative work. In light of all the attention enjoyed by the more particular projects (*infra* ii.–v.), it is easy to forget that for most of the time most comparatists have mostly compared rules, concepts, and institutions. That was certainly true during the twentieth century, and while there are no empirical data to prove it, it is fair to assume that it is true in the twenty-first as well. In short, it is "business as usual" that goes on all the time on a very broad scale, though mostly below the radar screen of those writing about comparative law as a discipline.

The body of comparative work focusing on positive rules is far too large to survey. It mostly comprises studies of rules in constitutions, legislation, and court decisions; in some instances, it has also included international law and non-state norms. Numerous other studies have investigated particular concepts, such as cause and consideration, due process or federalism.[826] Yet others have looked to particular institutions, either of positive law, such as gifts, trusts, or patents,[827] or to particular elements of legal systems, e.g., constitutional courts, judicial councils, or notaries.[828] Sometimes, these studies compare just two jurisdictions; often, they include many more. They vary enormously in their goals and methods, breadth, and quality. A common problem is that they are often limited to a juxtaposition of the data without providing any in-depth comparison and without generating valuable insight.

335. *Rule comparison as a building block and a basic exercise.* – Comparative studies of particular concepts and institutions are by and large considered unproblematic, at least in principle. By contrast, rule comparison has come under fire from scholars advocating a social and cultural approach (*infra* v., ss. 361–362), although it is a continuing practice, especially in the civil law orbit. It must be admitted that the comparison of blackletter rules in and of themselves can easily be disappointingly bland and disconcertingly divorced from legal reality – a critique that has been directed, for example, against the project of creating a body of common private law (rules) for Europe, with considerable justification. It is widely understood today that rules must not be compared in the abstract, i.e., merely in their black-letter form. Instead, they must be understood in the context of their legal systems, in particular in their procedural and institutional environment. Only thus can comparatists pay due regard to the rules' interpretation, impact, and – last but not least – function (*infra* C.i., ss– 368–373).

Still, properly conducted, rule comparison serves two particularly important purposes. First, it provides basic information and essential building blocks for a variety of more specific projects. This is true especially for international legal unification, law reform, choice of law, as well as the

[825] See, for example, the model proffered by *Merryman* (*supra* n. 807) 373–375.

[826] See e.g. *Markesinis* (*supra* n. 8) 53; *Noriho Urabe*, Rule of Law and Due Process: A Comparative View of the United States and Japan: 53 Law &Contemp.Prob. 61–72 (1990); *Halberstam* (*supra* n. 43).

[827] See, e.g., *Hyland*, Gifts (Oxford, New York 2009); *Helmholz and Zimmermann* (*supra* n. 478); *Guntersdorfer*, Software Patent Law: United States and Europe Compared: 2 Duke Law & Technology Rev. 1–12 (2003).

[828] See, e.g., *Rogowski and Gawron*, Constitutional Courts in Comparison (Oxford, New York 2016); *Garoupa and Ginsburg*, Guarding the Guardians: Judicial Councils and Judicial Independence: 57 Am.J. Comp.L. 103–134 (2009); *Schmoeckel and Schubert* (*supra* n. 415).

search for a "common core" of legal systems (*infra* C.ii., ss. 374–377). Rule comparison can even be relevant for the grouping of legal systems (e.g., into those permitting or prohibiting gay marriage) and for our understanding of receptions and transplants (e.g., of the rule of strict liability for injuries caused by animals). Second, rule comparison is a proper training ground for the comparative law novice because its fairly narrow compass makes it more easily controllable than the comparison of principles or institutions, not to mention legal families, tradition, or cultures. Looking at select positive rules, the beginner can learn and exercise the basic steps of the comparative process, from identifying the norms in two or more legal systems to analyzing their similarities and differences and on to drawing conclusions, e.g., in the form of explanations or recommendations. As mentioned, this exercise must of course always consider the rules in their concrete context and practical application.

336. *The multiplicity of rules: "legal formants".* – Yet, even working with positive rules is not as easy as it may seem. For a comparatist it comes naturally to assume that for every issue every legal system has *a* rule. But in a model developed in the 1970s and then widely noted in the 1990s, Italian scholar Rodolfo Sacco demonstrated that things are not nearly so simple.[829] He pointed out two closely related facts: first, in every legal system there are multiple elements, such as constitutions, legislation, judicial decisions, academic writings, even "declamatory" policy statements; second, these elements often contain different rules governing the same problem: the constitution says one thing, a statute another, judicial decisions a third, and so on. Borrowing the term from phonetics, Sacco called these (and other) elements "legal formants".[830] He knew, of course, that jurists are quite aware of this multiplicity. He argued, however, that within their own system they usually either assume that all norms operate in harmony or they ultimately pick one over the rest as the "true" rule through a process of interpretation.

Comparatists, Sacco postulated, must not do that: they must neither assume complete harmony between the various formants nor consider only the "true" rule and leave the others aside. Instead, in order thoroughly to grasp the compared systems' work, scholars must "see the entire law" and thus "recognize all the 'legal formants' of the system and ... identify the scope proper to each".[831] This is no easy job for two main reasons. One is that the number, type, and importance of legal formants varies greatly among legal systems; the other reason is that some formants are not openly stated but operate in a silent or even hidden manner (Sacco thus called them "cryptotypes").[832]

Sacco's approach had enormous influence in Italy, in part due to his towering position among comparatists in that country. While the concept of legal formants also became widely known elsewhere, embracing it is not considered *de rigueur*. It became influential primarily as an element of "common core" research, especially the so-called Trento Project on European private law (*infra* C.ii, s. 376).

Sacco has been criticized for stating the obvious; it has been claimed that nobody seriously contests the multiplicity of sources in each system, the potential contradictions between them, and thus the need to take all of them into account in order truly to understand how the law works.[833] Whether that claim is true depends on where and when one looks. It is entirely true with regard to jurists versed in American legal thought, because Sacco's theory is essentially a form of legal realism imported into comparative law. It is true for the majority of twenty-first-century European lawyers because strict rule-positivism no longer prevails

[829] While Sacco's theory had roots in earlier work, it was fully developed in his treatise on comparative law: see *Sacco*, Introduzione al Diritto Comparato (ed. 2 1979) 27–40. The theory became widely known, however, only through a later English version, i.e., *Sacco* (*supra* n. 195).

[830] At least at times, Sacco seems to count every factor that can influence a legal decision as a "formant", *idem* 30–34.

[831] *Idem* 27.

[832] *Sacco* (*supra* n. 195) 384–386. Working with these "cryptotypes" is part of what constitutes a jurist's specific "mentality", *idem* 386. The idea is much older than Sacco. It was already presented by Rudolf von Jhering in the mid-nineteenth century, *Jhering*, Geist des römischen Rechts auf den verschiedenen Stufen seiner Entwicklung vol. I, 18 (Leipzig 1852).

[833] *Kischel* (*supra* n. 286) 115–117.

in most European legal systems. It is probably not true, however, with regard to the vast majority of Italian jurists who had surrounded Sacco in the 1960s and 1970s. Nor is it true for lawyers in the many systems where, even today, law continues to be regarded as an internally consistent system of (essentially legislative and thus clearly stated) rules.

Sacco's approach is valuable because it asks comparatists to look not only at the law on the books and the law in action but also at the law "in debate"[834] – if they want to obtain a realistic picture of a legal system, they have to consider the competition between various elements of varying strength. Appreciating this competition helps us understand, for example, why two legal systems can share the same legislative rule but still reach different results: the rule may prevail in one system but be sidelined or overpowered by competing elements in the other. It also helps us explain why transplanting a rule from one system into another almost inevitably affects its meaning; in its new environment, the rule becomes part of a new concert of legal formants. In addition, Sacco's approach pushes comparatists to recognize the potential differences between how rules are stated, interpreted, and applied; between how decisions are announced, explained, and actually made; between what policy makers claim, believe, and do; etc. Last, but not least, Sacco shows that and why comparatists cannot simply rely on the rules reported to them by foreign jurists about their respective systems: these jurists may not recognize, or simply not want to admit to, the rules' multiplicity, and they may not be aware of the unarticulated formants that influence their decisions.

ii. *Legal Families and Traditions*

337. *Introduction and overview: classification in comparative law.* – At least in Western culture, the classification of phenomena is a routine exercise in many pursuits of knowledge. In the natural sciences, it has become a defining feature since Carl Linnaeus' taxonomy in 1735.[835] In the social sciences, scholars have grouped languages, religions, political regimes, economic systems, cultures, etc., especially since the nineteenth century. Influenced by these precursors and striving to establish their discipline as a "science", comparative lawyers have grouped the legal systems of the world since the beginning of the twentieth century. Thus, the classification of legal systems has been the most prevalent form of "macro-comparison" (*supra* A.ii., s. 323) for well over a hundred years.

One can perhaps distinguish three main phases. The first coincided roughly with the first half of the twentieth century. Classification projects began at the birth hour of the modern discipline, i.e., the Paris Congress of 1900 (*supra* III.C.i., ss. 85–87), with a brief outline by Adhémar Esmein,[836] were further developed by scholars such as George Sauser-Hall[837] and Adolf Schnitzer[838] in Switzerland as well as John Henry Wigmore[839] in the United States, and culminated in the extensive, three-volume treatise by Pierre Arminjon, Boris Nolde, and Martin Wolff in 1950.[840] These, early, models are no longer much discussed today. The second phase comprised the 1960s and 1970s and saw the publication of the two most influential taxonomies, i.e., David's *Les Grands Systèmes de Droit Contemporains*[841] and Zweigert and Kötz's *Einführung in die Rechtsvergleichung*[842]. In the subsequent decades, both went through several editions, were translated into multiple languages, and became classics. In their wake, enthusiasm for further classificatory efforts waned for a while because it seemed that after these publications there was little left to do. Yet, the end of the twentieth century brought the beginning of a third phase during which interest in classification projects was rekindled. Now,

[834] *Kischel* (*supra* n. 286) 117.

[835] *Linnäus*, Systema naturae (Leiden 1735).

[836] *Esmein*, Le Droit comparé et l'einseignement du Droit", Congrés international de droit comparé, Procés-verbaux des séances et documents I (Paris 1905) 445–454.

[837] *Sauser-Hall* (*supra* n. 157).

[838] *Schnitzer*, Vergleichende Rechtslehre (Basel 1945).

[839] *Wigmore* (*supra* n. 167).

[840] *Arminjon, Nolde and Wolff* (*supra* n. 270).

[841] *David*, Les Grands Systèmes du Droit Contemporains (Paris 1964). A predecessor was *David* (*supra* n. 418) 215–393.

[842] *Zweigert* and *Kötz* (*supra* n. 419); See also *Derrett* (ed.), An Introduction to Legal Systems (London 1968).

comparatists reacted in part to the changes in the world's legal landscape after the end of the cold war, in part to the rising critiques levelled at mainstream comparative law (*infra* v., ss. 360–365). Since then, several scholars, such as Michael Bogdan, Peter deCruz, Diego Fernandez Arroyo, Antonio Gambaro and Rodolfo Sacco, Mario Losano, Werner Menski, Akmal Saidov, Gilles Cuniberti, and Uwe Kischel have expanded or modified established classifications.[843] Others, like Ugo Mattei, Esin Örücü, Mathias Siems, Dario Moura Vicente, and Jacques Vanderlinden, developed or at least suggested new taxonomies.[844] At the same time, in the United States and Canada the emphasis began to shift from defining "legal systems" or "families" to thinking about "legal traditions" – a concept that became the paradigm for John Merryman, Mary Ann Glendon, Patrick Glenn, and others.[845]

On the whole, classification in comparative law has been characterized by a persistent weakness of consensus. This has entailed an often confusing diversity – of terminology (*infra* s. 338), criteria for classification (s. 339), and resultant taxonomies (s. 340). In addition, there has been much discussion of the purposes and benefits of classification on the one hand (s. 341) and of its pitfalls and weaknesses on the other (s. 342). The shift towards "legal traditions" is in part a response to the weaknesses of the older, mainstream, approach (s. 343).

338. *Diversity of terminology: systems, families, etc. – and traditions.* – Comparatists have used a bewildering diversity of terms generically denoting groups of jurisdictions. This diversity is fairly harmless although it can easily confuse the non-specialist.

Following René David, they often speak of "systems" (*systèmes, Systeme, sistemi, sistemas*, etc.), as in "the civil law system"; yet, that term is also often used for the law (etc.) of individual nation states, as in "the French legal system".[846] An equally common expression, at least in English, French, and German, is (legal) "families" (*familles de droit, Rechtsfamilien*, etc.); yet, while this term is borrowed from biology, its use does not necessarily imply a claim that groups of laws are like families of animals or plants. In addition, there are several terms that are common in particular languages, such as *Rechtskreise* (legal orbits) in German or *modelli* (models, or even *esperienze*, i.e., experiences) in Italian. One may justly wonder whether there is a significant difference between systems, families, orbits, models, etc. For the most part, the answer is no – these expressions are by and large used synonymously.[847]

This is not true for the term "legal tradition" which denotes a somewhat different, usually broader, conception than "legal system" or "family". Its use is not completely uniform either, but it mostly includes a historical perspective as well as the modes of thinking about, and the

[843] *Bogdan* (*supra* n. 758); *De Cruz* (*supra* n. 341); *Gambaro and Sacco* (*supra* n. 300); *Saidov*, Comparative Law (London 2003); *Losano* (*supra* n. 300); *Menski* (*supra* n. 286); *Cuniberti* (*supra* n. 286); *Vicente*, Direito Comparado I: Introduçao: Sistemas Juridicos em Geral (ed. 2 Coimbra 2012); *Kischel* (*supra* n. 286). There is also a collection of volumes on particular legal families or topics in *Mirabelli di Lauro* (ed.), Sistemi Giuridici Comparati (5 vol.) (Torino 1996). See also *Arroyo*, Sobre la existencia de una familia juridica Latinoamericana: Annuario juridico y economico escurialense 27 (1994) 73–110.

[844] *Mattei* (*supra* n. 791); *Örücü*, A General View of 'Legal Families' and of 'Mixing Systems': *idem and Nelken* (eds.), Comparative Law: A Handbook (Oxford, Portland OR 2007) 169–187; see also *Örücü*, Family Trees for Legal Systems: Towards a Contemporary Approach: *Van Hoecke* (ed.), Epistemology and Methodology in Comparative Law (Oxford, Portland OR 2004) 359–375; *Siems*, Varieties of Legal Systems: Towards a New Global Taxonomy: 12 Journal of Institutional Economics 579–602 (2016); *Vanderlinden*, Comparer les droits (Diegem, Belgium 1995) 311–389.

[845] *Merryman* (*supra* n. 209); *Merryman, Clark and Haley* Comparative Law: Historical Development of the Civil Law Tradition in Europe, Latin America, and East Asia (*supra* n. 268); *Merryman, Clark and Haley* The Contemporary Civil Law Tradition (*supra* n. 268); *Glendon, Gordon and Osakwe* (*supra* n. 210); *Glendon, Carozza and Picker*, Comparative Legal Traditions: Text, Material and Cases (ed. 3 St. Paul MN 1997); *Glendon, Carozza and Picker* (*supra* n. 340); *Glenn* (*supra* n. 327). See also *Head* (*supra* n. 286).

[846] Frequently, individual (national) systems are also called "legal orders" (*ordres juridiques, Rechtsordnungen*, etc.).

[847] Thus Tony Weir could, for example, translate *Rechtskreise* as "legal families": see *Zweigert* and *Kötz* (*supra* n. 5) 63.

deeply rooted attitudes towards, law. We will consider it in more detail below (s. 343). In addition, the term "legal culture" also has a special, albeit often poorly defined, meaning; in the context of classification it sometimes overlaps with "legal tradition"; it will be addressed in the context of interdisciplinary comparative law (*infra* iv., ss. 354–355).

339. *Diversity of criteria: multitude and arbitrariness.* – Comparatists have also used a bewildering diversity of criteria in their various classification projects. This diversity is *not* harmless because the choice of criteria determines how laws are being grouped.

The problem is not that comparatists have, throughout the decades, employed a large variety of criteria – the list includes, but is not limited to, race and language, culture, technique, substance of law, procedure, sources, style, legal structures, professionalization, politicization, role of custom, as well as varying combinations of these elements.[848] The problem is not even that no consensus has developed about which criteria are more relevant than others – after all, most of them are legitimate in one way or another because they refer to potentially important features of legal systems. The problem is rather that scholars have too often failed convincingly to explain why they picked a particular criterion or criteria and laid the others aside. They have rarely detailed, e.g., why legal technique is more relevant than the substance of rules (or vice versa), why style matters more than the actual enforceability of law, or why structure holds the key while language does not.[849] Without such an explanation, however, the choice of one criterion over others often appears random, if not arbitrary.[850] This is a serious flaw in many classification projects because the randomness of criteria entails a randomness of the resultant grouping.

As in all taxonomies, the choice of criteria must ultimately depend on the goal of the undertaking. If we classify in order to determine which legal systems will resolve similar cases alike, substance and procedure are probably more relevant than technique and language, but if we group in order to determine how well lawyers from different systems can communicate with each other, language and technique may well be more relevant than substance and procedure. Thus, comparatists should clearly determine and state the purpose of their classification projects and then choose and employ their criteria accordingly. Ugo Mattei has shown how that can be done, creating an internally consistent, non-arbitrary, taxonomy.[851]

340. *Diversity of groupings: a plethora of models.* – Since the beginning of the twentieth century, comparatists have presented more than a dozen classificatory schemes. The groupings typically contain around half a dozen legal "systems", "families", etc., with varying degrees of subdivision.[852] In part, this variety of taxonomies follows directly from the variety of the criteria employed. In part, it is a response to changes in the global legal landscape over time which are sometimes also reflected in subsequent editions of the same work.[853] In part, the variety of models simply results from the various authors' perspectives, goals, and inclinations.

As observers have noted, going through all the models that have been developed soon becomes tedious.[854] This is not merely because one can endlessly debate their respective merits and flaws. The main reason is that the reader's learning curve quickly flattens because there are basic patterns that keep repeating themselves. To begin with, scholars have widely shared a fundamental distinction between a civil law and a common law family, the former often being subdivided

[848] *Siems* (*supra* n. 844) for example, uses 15 wide-ranging variables and applies them to over 150 jurisdictions; for an extensive discussion of a long list of criteria, see *Vanderlinden* (*supra* n. 844) 311–337.

[849] *David and Jauffet-Spinosi*, Les grands systèmes de droit contemporains (10th ed. Paris 1992) 15–16, even state that discussions about the proper modes of classification do not make a lot of sense.

[850] This has been pointed out by *Kischel* (*supra* n. 286) 226–227.

[851] *Mattei* (*supra* n. 791) 8–9.

[852] See the table provided by *Siems* (*supra* n. 680) 89.

[853] A particularly notable example of such changes was the rise of a socialist legal family around the middle of the 20th century and its subsequent demise after 1990.

[854] See *Kischel* (*supra* n. 286) 219.

into a French and a German branch (and sometimes a Nordic subgroup), the latter into England and the United States (and sometimes the former commonwealth jurisdictions). Furthermore, authors have typically listed an Asian legal family (consisting mainly of Japan and China), a group of religious systems (Islamic, Hindu, Buddhist, etc.), and sometimes regimes of traditional, especially customary, law, particularly in Africa. Between the 1960s and the 1990s, most authors also included a socialist legal family.[855] Almost all mainstream classifications are variations on these basic themes, though some authors, writing from a particular perspective, proffered alternative categories.[856]

Throughout the twentieth century, and in many cases well into the twenty-first, classifications have heavily focused on the legal systems of nation states. Yet, comparatists designing taxonomies have increasingly opened their eyes to non-state-based systems as well. Since the middle of the last century, religious regimes were usually covered in one way or another, although the standard works have often discussed them in a residual category of "other systems" and in a summary fashion;[857] the same is by and large true for "traditional" (largely: customary) law.[858] Supra- and international legal systems were consistently ignored until the end of the last century,[859] and even in the new millennium their inclusion has been slow in coming.[860] Non-state private law (such as the *lex mercatoria*) has largely remained beyond the scope of the common taxonomies altogether, although it has been on the discipline's radar screen for quite some time (*supra* IV.B.i., s. 198).[861]

Since the end of the twentieth century some scholars have developed alternatives to the traditional state-centered approach. Ugo Mattei proffered a novel tripartite division of legal systems into professional, political, and traditional law, explaining that while all legal systems contain elements of all three categories, most are characterized by the hegemony of one of these types.[862] Mathias Siems presented an "evidence-based quantitative taxonomy" grouping the world's legal systems into five "clusters".[863] In addition, Patrick Glenn presented a worldview of law based on legal traditions largely transcending state-based orders.[864]

341. *Diversity of purposes: the benefits of taxonomies.* – Taxonomic projects can have a diversity of purposes and proffer a variety of benefits. Comparatists have usually claimed these benefits in a general and summary fashion and without any in-depth discussion. One can perhaps divide the advantages of classification into two major and various minor ones.

The first major advantage of creating legal families is didactic: it simplifies the global legal picture and thus facilitates overview. Like looking at continents rather than individual countries, grouping legal systems into half a dozen (or so) categories provides a rough sense of orientation and conveys some basic information. As a general matter, learning about legal systems on the wholesale, rather than the retail, level is an efficient first approach.

855 See, e.g., *David and Jauffret-Spinosi* (*supra* n. 849; *Zweigert and Kötz* (*supra* n. 3).

856 E.g. Felipe De Sola Canizares, addressing a Spanish-speaking audience, included a chapter on Los derechos ibero-americanos: *idem,* Iniciación al derecho comparado (Barcelona 1954) 233–294; Gyula Eörsi, writing from a socialist perspective, divided the world mainly into "Bourgeois" and "Socialist Law Groups", *idem*, Comparative Civil (Private) Law (Budapest 1979).

857 *David and Jauffre-Spinosi* (*supra* n. 849) 367–419; *Zweigert and Kötz* (*supra* n. 13) 296–313. A more thorough discussion is provided by *Menski* (*supra* n. 286) 196–379.

858 See *David and Jauffet-Spinosi* (*supra* n.849); *Zweigert and Kötz* (*supra* n. 3) do not address traditional (customary) legal systems at all. Again, a more serious treatment is provided by *Menski* (*supra* n. 286) 380–492.

859 *Reimann*, Beyond National Systems: A Comparative Law for the International Age: 75 Tul.L.Rev. 1103–1119 (2001).

860 European Union law is covered by *De Cruz* (*supra* n. 341) 139–182; *Glendon, Carozza and Picker* (*supra* n. 20) 686–832. *Kischel* (*supra* n. 286) covers both European Union and public international law, 945–972.

861 A modest but promising beginning is made by *Kischel* (*supra* n. 286) 972–976.

862 *Mattei* (*supra* n. 791).

863 *Siems* (*supra* n. 852).

864 *Glenn* (*supra* n. 327).

Beyond that, some comparatists have also made a more specific efficiency claim which is much more questionable, however. The argument is that the recognition of legal families allows a researcher interested in how legal systems handle an issue to limit his or her comparison to the one or two representative jurisdictions for each legal family, such as France and Germany for the civil law, or England and the United States for the common law group; that can save the researcher from having to look at all the other countries in the respective groups.[865] Yet, even as a mere "rule of thumb",[866] such a limitation strategy is dubious for two reasons. First, there is often no guaranty that the chosen legal orders are truly representative with regard to the particular issue involved:[867] neither is the French *astreinte* (a daily civil fine for non-compliance with a court decision) typical for civil law systems, nor is the American civil jury a typical feature of common law jurisdictions anymore. Second, even fundamental similarities and differences often cut across the boundaries between legal families: in England and Germany the privity requirement has largely prevented contract actions by consumers against manufacturers of defective products, while in the United States and France it has not.

The second major benefit of taxonomic projects is heuristic: they force the comparatist to think about what characterizes legal systems in relation to each other. No matter what criterion is being employed, it must always be applied to the systems under consideration in order to decide whether in that particular regard they are similar (and should therefore be grouped together) or not. Thus, classifying legal systems is itself a comparative exercise of the first order, even though the comparison is more often implicit than explicit. Moreover, since jurisdictions can be grouped according to many different criteria (*supra*, s. 339), the comparatist comes to recognize that legal systems are similar in some regards but not in others. Thus, the coexistence of different taxonomies illustrates that similarity and difference are context-dependent and relative. All this is true not only with regard to the division into the major groups but also for the establishment of subdivisions within each of them. Now, the taxonomist must decide in what respects the members of, e.g., the civil or the common law family are alike or different. And where an author seeks to decide which of these members are most representative of the family as a whole, he or she must, again, compare them to each other according to the chosen criteria.

Beyond these major benefits, grouping legal systems can help to predict the success (or failure) of legal transplants (*infra* iii., s. 345–350). Since members of a legal family share important features as well as a sense of kinship, transplants within a family are more likely to take root than those from outside. Intra-system transplants are, of course, also facilitated if there is a shared family language, as is largely true in the common law world.

Note also that a system's claim to membership of a legal family can serve cultural or political goals. It can, for example, help to strengthen and defend a system's sense of cultural identity. This is true particularly for jurisdictions which identify with one legal family but are exposed to the powerful pull of another. Examples are Louisiana and Quebec with their civil law tradition in the common law environments of the United States and Canada, respectively, or, vice versa, Hong Kong with its common law heritage in the context of China. Identification with a legal family can also support or hinder certain specific agendas: China's often-claimed civil law character supports its codification projects, while England's pride in its common law status hinders the adoption of an international sales law codification (CISG).

342. *Diversity of problems: the weaknesses of classification.* – Its many benefits notwithstanding, the grouping of laws into "major legal systems" or "legal families" is problematic in several regards. We will focus on seven particular critiques. The first three have long been noted and are widely shared, but they can be refuted, or at least softened, quite easily. The second group of four are of more recent vintage and raise more vexing issues.

To begin with, the groupings, and in particular their boundaries, are often imprecise and open to debate. Yet, this is inevitable because, as

865 *Zweigert and Kötz* (*supra* n. 3) 40–42.
866 *Idem* 41.
867 See the critical discussion by *Kischel* (*supra* n. 286) 222–225.

social constructs, legal systems are multifaceted, amorphous, subject to constant change, and thus difficult to categorize with precision. Their classification cannot be an exact science but must often be a matter of perspective and opinion. Thus, even for its advocates, taxonomy is meant merely as a "rough and ready device" which can put "the confusing variety of legal systems into some kind of loose order" – no more, no less.[868]

Moreover, the groupings are often simplistic because they classify legal systems according to a very limited number of criteria. Taxonomies are possible only at the expense of omitting detail – they must focus on select features of their objects and disregard the rest. In addition, simplification through generalization is the very purpose of the enterprise: the virtue of an initial overview and first orientation is that it looks at the forest as a whole, not at all the individual trees. Of course, exactly how much simplification is desirable depends on the purpose of the respective classification. In this regard, the existing taxonomies fortunately cover a broad spectrum, varying widely in length and detail and catering to different audiences and expectations.

The third long-standing criticism is that the traditional classifications are too private-law oriented. It is true that where they focus on substance, they look primarily to contract, tort and property law; where they analyze structures of dispute resolution, they mainly consider civil procedure; and even where they turn to sources, technique, or style of legal thought, they make their observations by and large in the private law context. This orientation still reflects the central role private law has played in the cradle of modern comparative law, especially in early twentieth-century France and Germany (ch. IV.C.i.), as well as the fact that prominent comparatists have, until quite recently, mostly been private law scholars. It is important to note, however, that the private law orientation of the established taxonomies is no argument against the classification of legal systems *tout court*. It is merely an argument against overrating the classic models (especially those by David and by Zweigert and Kötz) as universally valid. Instead, the traditional mainstream taxonomies must be seen and evaluated in their proper light: they present groupings that are plausible and helpful mainly from a private law perspective; again: no more, no less. Today, it is generally recognized that classifications looking to other areas of law are likely to result in different groupings. A standard example is that a taxonomy of constitutional regimes would hardly divide western legal systems into a civil and a common law orbit. Instead, it would perhaps distinguish a group with strong judicial review of legislation (as in the United States, Germany, and Korea) from another where such review is fairly weak (as in England, France, and Japan); or it might distinguish federal systems (such as Canada, Switzerland, and Mexico) from centralized ones (such as England, France and Turkey).

Four more recent critiques hit harder because they point to more deeply rooted flaws. To begin with, the existing classification projects have been shown to lack a sound theoretical foundation as well as a rigorous method. Their exact purpose is mostly unclear; they (often unconsciously) oscillate between different, and at times inconsistent, levels (national, international, transnational, etc.); they put fundamentally different systems side by side (e.g., state-based, religious, and customary regimes); and they tend to operate with oversimplified and reductionist criteria, disregarding that these criteria may play out very differently even within a single "family" (assuming, for example, that all civil or all common lawyers share a certain "legal style").[869] These weaknesses do not seriously impair the function of providing a rough overview for beginners, but they do result "in more of a muddle than a systematic taxonomy" that can withstand serious scrutiny.[870]

A more common critique is that mainstream classifications center too much on the cultural West which, at least in the eyes of critical legal scholars, supports Western global hegemony.[871] It

[868] *Zweigert and Kötz* (*supra* n. 218) 72.

[869] *Twining* (*supra* n. 246) 178–184.

[870] *Idem* 180.

[871] See, e.g., *Frankenberg* (*supra* n. 145) 54. A related critique is that the existing classifications do not, and indeed cannot, adequately reflect "the pluralistic nature of today's situation": *Husa*, Classification of Legal Systems Today: Is It Time for a Memorial Hymn?: Rev.int.dr.comp. 56 (2004) 11–38.

is true that for most of the twentieth century, taxonomies have usually put the civil and the common law at center stage, thus looking primarily at continental Europe on the one hand and England and the United States on the other; at the same time, they have often (though not always) kept the rest of the world, and especially religious and customary regimes, at the margin.[872] This is in large part a consequence of the Western origins of modern comparative law: it was founded and developed by Western scholars who approached it from a Western perspective. The critique of this situation operates on two levels. At the surface level, it essentially accuses the traditional taxonomies of paying too much attention to the West and too little to the rest. To this charge there are three responses. First, more recent taxonomies have taken much greater account of non-Western legal systems, especially those of China, India, and Islamic countries, and some have actually focused on them;[873] as a result, the picture has become considerably more balanced. Second, even where it persists, a Western focus can be defended on the ground that in most instances Western authors write primarily for a Western audience. Western authors can be fairly confident of understanding Western systems, but they may want to tread much more lightly with regard to other parts of the world; and Western audiences may be more interested in Western systems because knowledge about them is practically still more relevant than understanding religious or customary regimes in faraway regions. Third, access to, and understanding of, non-Western systems tends to be linguistically difficult, and problems of translation loom especially large. At a deeper level, however, the critique is more fundamental and much harder to counter: the mainstream's *whole approach* to classification is Western-centric because it is based on the Western conceptions of "legal system" and "law". These conceptions are inextricably linked to the modern nation state, i.e., to a construct which developed in early modern Europe from where it spread all over the globe. Thus, seeing the whole world through the prisms of their Western conceptions, taxonomists tend to regard the Western forms of "legal systems" and of "law" as the norm, while different kinds of legal orders are viewed as peripheral and thus as "other". From here, it is only a small step to regarding non-Western law as exotic and "oriental" (*infra* v., s. 364). It is true, of course, that the world *is* divided into nation states which *do have* legal systems and which *do produce* law in the Western style. Thus, the traditional classifications are neither wrong nor pointless. Yet, in reflecting a Western view of the world, they can easily fail to capture alternative forms of legal systems and laws under which billions of people live.

Another more recent critique is that the mainstream classifications fail to take proper account of the hybrid nature of legal systems. Of course, modern comparative law has long understood that there are several "mixed jurisdictions" with features of both the civil and the common law (*supra* IV.A.ii., s. 177), notably Israel, Louisiana, Quebec, the Philippines, Puerto Rico, South Africa and Scotland; such hybrids have even been claimed as a "the third legal family".[874] Also, comparatists have increasingly noted that many other jurisdictions are "mixed" as well, in one way or another:[875] because they combine Asian and Western features (such as Japan and China), contain elements of secular and religious law (as in the Middle East) or apply modern, written law to some areas while leaving other matters to indigenous custom (as in many African states), etc. If all these hybrids are added together, up to half of the world's legal systems may have to be regarded as "mixed".[876] And from a historical

[872] An exception is *Derrett* (*supra* n. 842) (covering Roman, Jewish, Islamic, Hindu, Chinese, African, as well as English, law).

[873] See e.g. *Kischel* (*supra* n. 286); *Mattei* (*supra* n. 791); *Menski* (*supra* n. 286).

[874] *Palmer* (*supra* n. 765). When the United Kingdom was still a member of the European Union, it was suggested that European private law may develop into such a mixed legal system; *Smits*, The Making of European Private Law: Towards a Ius Commune Europaeum as a Mixed Legal System (Maastricht 2002).

[875] See the typology of hybrids developed by *Siems* (*supra* n. 852) 85–93.

[876] See e.g. *Kischel* (*supra* n. 286) (40% can be classified as mixed); *Siems* (*supra* n. 852) (more than half of the world). In light of modern global communication and interaction, there is every reason to believe that the number of mixed jurisdictions is likely to increase.

perspective, blends are more common still: as Esin Örücü has pointed out, *all* legal systems are the results of many mixed influences.[877] Thus, upon close inspection, hybridity turns out to be normal. The problem with traditional taxonomies is indeed that they have either taken scant account of the mixed nature of legal systems or at least seriously underrated it. Taxonomies that either ignore mixed jurisdictions or present them as fairly rare exceptions paint a seriously misleading picture of the world of law. In addition, the routinely hybrid nature of legal systems raises the question whether they can plausibly be assigned to separate legal families at all. Yet, hybridity does not foreclose taxonomy. It does require, however, that the taxonomist decide which of the several (mixed) elements best defines a jurisdiction's character and profile – and then assign it accordingly.[878] That is, again, a matter of perspective, context, and opinion. Most mainstream classifications have failed to make that clear.

A related critique is that the classification of legal systems leads to systematic overrating of differences between groups and simultaneous underrating of differences within them.[879] At least on the theoretical level, this is true. Classifications make fundamental distinctions and thus emphasize separateness between groups: if a legal system is said to belong to one family (such as the civil law), it is presented as fundamentally different from legal systems in another (such as the common law). At the same time, taxonomies assume essential likeness within families and thus emphasize cohesion: if two legal systems are put into the same group (such as religious systems), they are portrayed as fundamentally alike. One may respond that, in practice, comparatists discussing classifications are aware that both differences between, and similarities within, legal families are often matters of degree – as well as of perception.[880] Yet, this awareness does not really solve the problem because that is wired into the taxonomic enterprise itself: even if we know that there are significant similarities between, say, Spain and Ireland because both countries are subject to the massive influence of European Union law, a taxonomy assigning them to different legal families (civil v. common law) discounts these similarities; and even if we understand that African legal systems vary greatly, inter alia due to their different colonial heritages (French, British, etc.), a taxonomy putting them into one category pushes these variations into the background. In other words, by operating with categories, taxonomies present differences and similarities as categorical. Thus, we must constantly guard against the classification project's inherent risk of overlooking that in reality differences and similarities between legal systems are often *not* categorical but rather matters of degree. Also, as a result of operating in categorical terms, taxonomies have an inherent tendency towards caricature: assigning a legal system to a particular family highlights the features corresponding to that family while downplaying those in conflict with it. China's legal system appears in a different light depending on whether we assign it to the civil law category or group with other Asian countries.

343. *"Legal tradition" as an alternative: abandoning taxonomy?* – Since the late twentieth century, several American scholars have turned away from the continental European concept of a "legal system" (or "family", etc.) and embraced the idea of a "legal tradition". The former, John Merryman explained, "is an operating set of legal institutions, procedures, and rules" largely identified with the modern nation state.[881] The latter, by

[877] *Örücü* (*supra* n. 844) 177. This is true even for the classic representatives of the great families, such as France, Germany, or England which have historically blended Roman, indigenous customary, and ecclesiastical law, and which have more recently also come under the influence of international, European Union, and American law. It is also true for the United States where imported English common law mixed with (Spanish-Mexican) civil law, Roman law concepts with continental European natural law, etc.

[878] "Predominance principle", see, e.g, *De Cruz* (*supra* n. 341) 33.

[879] See *Siems* (*supra* n. 852) 80–85.

[880] For example, they have debated whether there are enough differences left between the civil and the common law to consider them separate categories; see, e.g. *Gordley* (*supra* n. 783); *Legrand* (*supra* n. 784). They have also warned against overlooking differences within a civil law group encompassing both continental Europe and Latin America. See, e.g., *Merryman and Pérez-Perdomo* (*supra* n. 268) Preface to the Original Edition, ix; *Esquirol*, The Fictions of Latin American Law: Utah L.Rev. 425–470 (1997).

[881] *Merryman and Pérez-Perdomo* (*supra* n. 268) 1.

contrast "is a set of deeply rooted, historically conditioned attitudes about the nature of law, about the role of law in the society and the polity, about the proper organization and operation of a legal system, and about the way law is or should be made, applied, studied, perfected, and taught. The legal tradition relates the legal system to the culture of which it is a partial expression. It puts the legal system into cultural perspective".[882] A legal tradition is thus deeply rooted in a past which still shapes the present, in particular with regard to the basic understanding of law and its operation. As such, it is largely independent of individual nation states. "A single legal system can bear the imprint of more than one tradition or belong in meaningful ways to multiple traditions of law".[883]

American comparatists have used the concept of legal tradition in two ways which seem similar at first glance but in fact constitute fundamentally different approaches. One approach essentially *continues taxonomy*, i.e., the originally continental European project of dividing up the world of law, but it now defines the relevant groups along the lines of legal traditions (in particular the civil and the common law, and formerly a socialist law, tradition).[884] This approach is not radically different from many of the European models, such as the taxonomy by Zweigert and Kötz with its emphasis on "legal style", Gambaro's and Sacco's "tradizione" and "esperienza giuridica" or Kischel's "contextual" method.[885] It is true that the American authors tend to put even greater emphasis on historical development, cultural context, and modes of legal thought, but that is a matter of degree.

The other tradition-based approach, taken by Patrick Glenn, is fundamentally different from the European projects: its goal to *abandon taxonomy.* Here, the concept of legal tradition is used to overcome the "epistemology of separation" which underlies "the teaching of legal systems and families".[886] As an alternative, Glenn introduced "The Legal Traditions of the World" (with a special emphasis on their various conceptions of law) not as separate groups with spatial boundaries, but rather as a set of major features which have shaped the world's legal systems.[887] It is true that some of Glenn's traditions track the time-honored ones underlying mainstream taxonomies.[888] Yet, even then, Glenn's point is to help us understand the specific contributions made by these legal traditions to the formation of the world of law today.[889] This approach is meant to overcome many of the problems vexing mainstream classifications, in particular their state-oriented and thus Western-centric perspective, and their emphasis on separation, rather than connection, between legal systems and families. Glenn specifically emphasizes their interconnectedness and hence their inherently pluralistic nature. Since this approach explicitly foregoes taxonomy, it should not be taken as a substitute for the existing classification projects, but rather as a complement to them. Its principal contribution is to make us think about the world's laws from a different perspective: not as separate units but as interrelated mixes of various basic elements – in a sense: from the bottom up, rather than the top down.[890]

344. *An assessment and a question.* – Despite their undeniable problems and weaknesses, classifications in comparative law have stood the test of time: they are part of virtually every comparatist's basic understanding and intellectual toolkit, and they continue to shape many new introductory

[882] *Idem* 2; see also *Glendon, Carozza, and Picker,* Comparative Legal Traditions (*supra* n. 20) 23–49; *Head* (*supra* n. 286). See also *Berman* (*supra* n. 264) 7–10 (on the "principal characteristics of the Western legal tradition").

[883] *Glendon, Carozza and Picker* (*supra* n. 20) 24.

[884] *Merryman, supra* n. 880; *Merryman, Clark and Haley,* The Contemporary Civil Law Tradition (*supra* n. 268); *Glendon, Carozza and Picker* (*supra* n. 20).

[885] *Gambaro and Sacco* (*supra* n. 300); *Kischel* (*supra* n. 286); *Zweigert and Kötz* (*supra* n. 3).

[886] *Glenn,* Comparative Legal Families and Comparative Legal Traditions: *Reimann and Zimmermann* (eds.), The Oxford Handbook of Comparative Law (Oxford 2006) 430.

[887] *Glenn* (*supra* n. 327).

[888] Glenn listed not only a "Chtonic", "Talmudic", "Islamic", and "Hindu", but also a "civil law" and "common law" tradition; the first edition's "Asian legal tradition" was later replaced by a "Confucian legal tradition".

[889] *Ibidem.*

[890] For an extensive discussion and critique of Glenn's work, see *Andersen et al.,* A Fresh Start for Comparative Legal Studies? A Collective Reviewing of Patrick Glenn's Legal Traditions of the World 2nd edition: 1 Journal of Comparative Law 100–199 (2006).

books and treatises.[891] Even many decades after their inception, the discipline's discourse builds on the established taxonomies in so many ways that it seems almost unthinkable without them.

The importance of taxonomies lies mainly in the mapping and orientation they provide. Yet, they can also be, and sometimes are, used as works in progress that force comparatists constantly to reflect upon the ways in which legal systems are similar or different, i.e., what unites or divides them. This is most salient when legal systems change over time and thus call for new assessments – and perhaps assignments.

Thus, most comparatists would agree that, on balance, taxonomies of legal systems are more helpful than harmful, provided they are not overrated but handled with caution.[892] Some of that belief, however, may simply be the result of a century-old force of habit. It is an open question, too little discussed among comparatists, whether the discipline would be better off without assuming that legal systems can be divided into – more or less neatly defined – categories. Perhaps it would be preferable to proceed on the assumption that legal systems constitute an infinite variety of forms with crisscrossing and overlapping characteristics that should be observed and analyzed without any preconceived notions of membership in this group or that. Yet, this would require overcoming the habit of classifying phenomena which is so deeply rooted at least in the modern Western mind.

iii. *Receptions and Transplants*

345. *The phenomenon.* – Just as features of one culture have been taken over by others for millennia (including languages and artistic styles, forms of government and social institutions, technology and eating habits), the development of legal systems has often been affected by the law of others. The strength of the impact has ranged from mere influence by, to outright adoption of, foreign law.[893] In the latter case, one can speak of "transplants" or "receptions", though many other terms have been used as well (*infra* s. 347). Among the most well-known examples are the "reception" of Roman law in late medieval and early modern continental Europe, the spread of English common law throughout the British Empire in the eighteenth and nineteenth centuries, the export of Soviet legal ideas to the communist world in the mid- to late-twentieth century, and the global influence of American law since the end of World War II. Many examples could be added, such as the export of early Chinese law to Japan, the spread of *shari'a* law with the conquests of Islam in the middle ages, and the import of continental European law in Latin America, the Pacific Rim, as well as francophone (and lusophone) Africa. In addition to such large-scale migrations of law, legal systems and cultures have continuously imported more particular elements from others; among the most popular export articles are the English trust, the French codification model, Austrian-style centralized judicial review, US-style antitrust legislation, German proportionality analysis, and European consumer protection rules. Even a roughly complete list of legal elements that have traveled across boundaries between legal systems and cultures would fill an entire book, and a very thick one at that.[894]

Though high to begin with, the volume of such exports and imports has grown dramatically since the late twentieth century as a result of several factors. The contact between legal systems has intensified because of increased global economic and social interaction; lifestyles and consumer habits have become similar in many parts of the world, creating similar problems and thus inviting the copy of legal responses; information about foreign legal systems is more widely and easily available than ever; the democratization of politics and the deregulation of markets in many parts of the world since the 1990s have created an enormous

[891] There are exceptions, such as *Siems* (*supra* n. 852).

[892] But cf. *Siems* (*supra* n. 852) 93–94; *Frankenberg* (*supra* n. 145) 53 also disagrees, calling taxonomy in comparative law "an exercise in futility".

[893] As others have pointed out, the line between influence and adoption is not sharply drawn but often a matter of degree: see *Kischel* (*supra* n. 286) 63.

[894] Further examples are provided, inter alia, by *Graziadei*, Comparative Law as the Study of Transplants and Receptions: *Reimann and Zimmermann* (eds.), The Oxford Handbook of Comparative Law (Oxford ed. 2 2019) 442–473, 444–454, and by *Siems* (*supra* n. 852) 241–255.

need for new rules and regulations; and regimes of "global governance" have exerted a powerful influence, ranging from the impact of international financial institutions to the global rise of human rights regimes. Thus, it is widely accepted today that virtually all legal systems contain elements they imported from somewhere else at one time or another (making all these system, in a sense, "mixed", *supra* s. 342), and that in most parts of the world most major legislative projects are influenced by foreign ideas or models in one way or another. Today more than ever, the export and import of law is not a rare exception but a regular occurrence, incidentally often resulting in convergence between legal systems (*supra* A.iii., s. 333).

How open a legal system is to foreign elements varies greatly depending on a multitude of factors. Younger systems tend to be more open than mature ones; smaller ones more than bigger ones, those in political transition more than politically stable ones, etc. Often, their receptivity has changed over time – for the first hundred years of its existence, the United States was an avid importer of foreign ideas; today, it rarely pays any attention to them.

346. *Comparative law scholarship on transplants and receptions.* – The phenomenon has attracted the attention of legal scholars for a long time. Especially legal historians have discussed receptions, mainly that of the Roman law, for centuries. More recently, it has also been of interest for international law, the sociology of law, and law and economics.

Among comparatists in particular, the discussion is primarily associated with a short book published in 1974, i.e., Alan Watson, *Legal Transplants – an Approach to Comparative Law.*[895] At first glance, this is somewhat surprising because Watson was not at all the first comparative law scholar to turn to legal transplants. Long before him, Jeremy Bentham and Rudolf von Jhering had already reflected upon the topic,[896] and decades before Watson, Frederick Walton and others in the United Kingdom[897] and Roscoe Pound and others in the United States had written about it.[898] Nor was Watson the only one to revive the subject in the post-World War II decades. Imre Zaitay had explored it in the 1950s and 1970s;[899] at the time when Watson's book was being published, Otto Kahn-Freund independently wrote about the phenomenon,[900] and the IX. Congress of the International Academy of Comparative Law in Teheran discussed, inter alia, "The Global Reception of Foreign Law".[901] Yet, it was Watson's *Legal Transplants* that finally became a classic in comparative law. The reason why Watson took all the glory was in part that he put the phenomenon of legal transplants squarely at the heart of comparative legal studies, and that he suggested far-reaching conclusions for legal theory (*infra* s. 350). Perhaps more importantly, Watson's book was short and provocative: He presented his views in a mere 100 pages and in a dramatically exaggerated fashion. It was a book that people could read – and hardly remain indifferent about.

[895] *Watson,* Legal Transplants (Athen GA 1974). A second edition was published in 1993 which contained the original text and added a new Afterword.

[896] *Huxley*, Jeremy Bentham on Legal Transplants: 2 Journal of Comparative Law 177–188 (2007); *Jhering* (supra n. 832) 2.

[897] *Walton*, The Historical School of Jurisprudence and Transplantations of Law: 9 J.Comp.Leg. 183–192 (1927), already laid out many of the ideas later presented by Watson, *ibidem* 189–191. For a history of the scholarship on legal transplants, see *Cairns*, Watson, Walton, and the History of Legal Transplants: 41 Ga.J.Int. Comp.L. 637–696 (2013). While Watson did not mention Walton, a fellow Scot, he did cite Roscoe Pound, *Watson*, Legal Transplants (ed. 2, Athens GA 1993) 22.

[898] A generation before Watson, Albert Kocourek published an article on Factors in the Reception of Law: 10 Tul.L.Rev. 209–230 (1935–36). Two years later, Roscoe Pound stated: "History of a system of law is largely a history of borrowings of legal material from other legal systems and of assimilation of other material from outside of the law", *Pound* (*supra* n. 135) 94.

[899] *Zaitay*, Die Rezeption fremder Rechte und die Rechtsvergleichung: AcP 156 (1957) 361–380, *idem*, Zum Begriff der Gesamtübernahme fremder Rechte: AcP 170 (1970) 251–265.

[900] *Kahn-Freund* (*supra* n. 221). According to the Preface to the first edition, Watson's book was completed in 1973, i.e., before Kahn-Freund's article was published; and when Kahn-Freund wrote his article, he was apparently not aware of Watson's book. They engaged in an exchange of views a few years later, see *infra* n. 940.

[901] See *Sacco*, Le buts et les méthodes de la comparaison du droit: Rapports nationaux italiens au IX Congrès internationale du droit comparé, Teheran 1974 (1974) 113–131.

Reduced to its essentials, *Legal Transplants* made four principal points. First, the proper task of comparative law is to explore the evolving relationships between legal systems with the aim of understanding "the nature of legal development"; thus, comparative law is concerned primarily with legal history and jurisprudence.[902] Second, "most changes in most systems are the results of borrowing".[903] Third, since such borrowing has often occurred between fundamentally different systems (sometimes existing centuries apart), "usually rules are not peculiarly devised for the particular society in which they now operate".[904] Fourth, "the transplantation of legal rules is socially easy".[905] While Watson derived these points from observations made largely in the history of private law in Europe, he did not always limit them to that context but often presented them in a broadly generalized fashion.[906] As a result, especially the claims that there was no necessary connection between law and society,[907] and that transfers were thus easy, became highly contentious (*infra* s. 350).

Watson's book triggered an extensive and ongoing discussion of legal transplants. The International Academy of Comparative Law took up the subject again at its Congresses in Montreal (1990) and Washington D.C. (2010)[908] As transplants became ever more ubiquitous after the 1990s, the number of publications about the topic exploded with dozens of books and hundreds of law review articles discussing every conceivable aspect of the phenomenon, eventually leaving even the specialist reader with a distinct sense of overdose.

Today, the topic is firmly entrenched as a major sub-field of comparative law. Awareness of the importance and virtual ubiquity of legal transplants injects a critically important dynamic element into the comparative study of law. Exploring legal exports and imports shows that legal systems are not hermetically sealed and static but constantly interacting and thus changing.

The study of transplants has developed in multiple directions too numerous and complex to be fully explored here.[909] After a brief foray into the copious terminology (s. 347), we will address the attempts to create a typology of transplants (s. 348), the discussion about successes and failures (s. 349), and the broader implications of legal transplants for the relationship between law and society (s. 350). A related, but still somewhat separate, topic is the experience with Law and Development projects (s. 351).

347. *A panoply of terms.* – Comparatists have discussed the topic under a bewildering variety of labels. Since the phenomenon itself is multifaceted (*infra* s. 348), one could, and probably should, use distinct terms to describe its distinct facets. Yet, this is not what comparatists have done. Instead, terms have often been used indiscriminately. Each has its advantages and downsides.

Due to the influence of Watson's book, the most common label is "legal transplants". Like "export" and "import" of law, it implies that an element has purposefully been taken from one system and brought to another. While that is true in many instances, on many other occasions law has travelled across boundaries in an unplanned or even accidental fashion. In fact, Watson's major illustration, the adoption of Roman law in much of early modern Europe, is a prime example of such an undirected process. That process

[902] *Watson* (*supra* n. 897) 6–7. See also *idem*, The Evolution of Law (Baltimore 1985).

[903] *Watson* (*supra* n. 897) 95

[904] *Idem* 96.

[905] *Idem* 95.

[906] For more nuanced and detailed analyses of Watson's argument, see *Ewald*, Comparative Jurisprudence (II): The Logic of Legal Tranplants: 43 Am.J.Comp.L. 489–510 (1995); *Wise*, The Transplant of Legal Patterns: 38 Supplement Am.J.Comp.L. 1–22 (1990).

[907] Watson made this point more clearly in the Afterword to the second edition, *Watson* (*supra* n. 897) 107–108.

[908] See *Sacco*, La circulation des modèles juridiques, Rapports Généraux XIIIe Congrès International, Montreal 1990 (1992) 1–19; *Sanchez Cordero* (ed.), Legal Culture and Legal Transplants: Reports to the XVIIIth International Congress of Comparative Law, Washington DC: ISAIDAT Law Review 1 (2011, Special Issue) 1–47.

[909] For a useful summary, see *Siems* (*supra* n. 852) 231–261. For a powerful challenge to the traditional assumptions, see *Twining*, Diffusion of Law: A Global Perspective: 49 J.Leg.Plural. &Unoff.L. 1–45 (2004). For a rich and eclectic collection of illustrations with regard to a particular country (Switzerland), see *Drolshammer and Weber*, Wie das Recht auf Reisen geht (Bern 2019).

is much better captured by the other commonly used label, i.e., "reception" (or "appropriation"). This label, however, foregrounds the perspective of the recipient legal culture which risks neglecting the role of the donor system. By contrast, "transfer" shifts the perspective mainly to the donor; but like "transplant", it is dangerously narrow because it implies planned action. In French and Italian, "circulation" (of legal ideas or models) has been popular. This suggests that legal ideas or models travel widely – which may or may not be the case. In a similar vein, "diffusion" implies a broad distribution of legal ideas despite the fact that many transplants are single events between just two or, at any rate, a few systems. "Migration" is more neutral in that regard but intimates that legal elements cross boundaries on their own although many are pushed or dragged across by a variety of legal actors. The term "transplants" has also been rejected in favor of "legal irritants" – a term provocatively coined to indicate that foreign imports have a tendency to upset the recipient system's existing arrangements.[910] Finally, beating a terminological retreat to "influence", "inspiration", or "cross-fertilization" entails utter vagueness. In short, more terminological precision and some kind of general agreement would be helpful, but neither is in sight.

Part of the reason why these terms are often used in a haphazard fashion is the lack of consensus on a single typology of the phenomenon itself.

348. *Typologies.* – Since the transboundary movement of law is highly multifaceted, it is tempting to develop a typology of legal transplants and receptions. Defining different categories may bring some order into a very complex picture and can thus help us better understand the phenomenon in all its ramifications. Yet, developing a typology is a difficult business. A threshold problem is that legal transplants are characterized by a multitude of properties and can thus be categorized according to a multitude of criteria.[911] The process can be formal or informal, planned or unplanned, open or hidden, sudden or gradual, uni- or multidirectional (and even reciprocal); it can involve two or multiple players, happen on a small or broad scale, occur on a regional or global level, succeed or fail (*infra* s. 349), etc. A related problem is that binary groupings cannot fully capture the reality because transplants often straddle the boundaries between categories or belong to several ones at the same time, depending on one's point of view.

Still, some categorizations are worth exploring at least in a summary fashion, in part because they do help to clarify the picture, but in part also because they convey a sense of the phenomenon's complexity. Let us consider three kinds of typologies: according to the transplants' objects (*what* is being transmitted?), modes (*how* do transplants occur?), and underlying reasons (*why* do they happen?). The resultant categories often overlap in various ways.

Considering, first, the *objects* of transplants immediately tells us that the material varies widely in both form and substance. Looking at form, we can distinguish a range of elements. In many well-known instances, transplants have included legal rules in various forms: entire codes (most famously the French Code civil and the German BGB which were adopted, usually in modified form, by numerous countries around the globe), particular legislation (such as the English Sales Act which spread throughout the British Empire), concrete rules (like strict liability for defective products which was embraced by jurisdictions on several continents), but also fundamental legislative principles (e.g., the legal separateness of corporations). At other times, transplants have involved broad ideas and ideals (e.g., of individual constitutional rights), values (such as human dignity), and professional practices (like the contingency fee). Finally, they have also spread style (for example, of judicial opinions), terminology ("rule of law", "precedent", (academic) "tenure"), organizational models (such as the US-style law firm), and even forms of legal consciousness (e.g., understanding law as an instrument of social engineering). Looking at substance, one could distinguish between the legal areas involved. Transplants have affected

[910] *Teubner* (*supra* n. 811).

[911] For a variety of typologies according to a variety of criteria, see *Cohn*, Legal Transplant Chronicles: The Evolution of Unreasonableness and Proportionality Review of the Administration in the United Kingdom: 58 Am.J.Comp.L. 583–629 (2010).

virtually every kind of law. For Watson and many comparatists of his generation, the main examples were still drawn from private law (contract, tort, property, family law, etc.). The liberalization of markets towards the end of the twentieth century brought the broader law of the economy into the picture (corporations, securities regulation, antitrust, etc.). After 1990, constitutional borrowing became very common and received much academic attention.[912] In addition, procedural transplants have often been noted, e.g., in civil litigation, criminal justice, or administrative review.[913]

Second, considering the *mode* of transplants, one can distinguish between the process, the medium, and the direction of transmission. The process has ranged from coercive to voluntary. At one end of this spectrum are the transplants that result from outright imposition, e.g., when the introduction of law follows military conquest or colonization. At the other end, one jurisdiction freely chooses to adopt the law of another. The large middle ground is occupied by transplants that result from more or less powerful external pressure on the receiving jurisdiction to import certain rules, e.g., by global financial institutions, important trading partners, or private investors. It must also be noted that transplants are not necessarily single events but rather complex processes spanning longer periods and involving multiple, interacting players.[914] The media of transmission span a similarly broad range. In the age of the modern nation state, the classic case is the adoption of foreign law through constitution-making or by legislation.[915] Yet, much law has also been received through judicial decisions, and many ideas have first been imported by academic scholarship. In addition, entirely private actors have often driven transplants: professional roles, styles, and practices have spread through the work of global law firms, transnational corporations, and international arbitrators. Law has also traveled directly with the people living under it when migrants have taken it to their new homes, such as the English colonists who brought the common law to America or, more recently, immigrants from Muslim countries who have brought their *shari'a* law to Europe. Transplants occur in different directions. The traditional image, reflecting the Westphalian order of sovereign and co-equal nation states, has been the (so to speak horizontal) transmission from one country to another. Yet, this image is no longer sufficient to understand transplants in today's global legal order in which law is often transmitted in various other directions.[916] It can be imposed in a top-down fashion by supra- or international organizations, such as the EU or the UN, to their members. Transplants also occur when legal systems adopt internationally uniform rules, created, e.g., by UNCITRAL or the Hague Conference on Private International Law. And they can be the result of all sorts of "global governance", especially of transnational regulatory, professional or grass-roots networks which promote their agendas and often work in a bottom-up fashion.[917] In many instances, several modes of transfer occur either successively or simultaneously or both.[918]

Finally, some scholars have established typologies of transplants mainly according to their *reasons*. A plausible approach proffers four main types.[919] "Cost-saving transplants" occur when a legal system copies a foreign model in order to save the resources it would have to spend on creating the law itself. This does not necessarily imply that the foreign model has been thoroughly

[912] *Perju*, Constitutional Transplants, Borrowings, and Migrations: *Rosenfeld and Sajo* (eds.), The Oxford Handbook of Comparative Constitutional Law (Oxford 2012) 1304–1327; *Choudry* (ed.), The Migration of Constitutional Ideas (Cambridge, New York 2006).

[913] See e.g. *Clark* (*supra* 139); *Grande*, Italian Criminal Justice: Borrowing and Resistance: 48 Am.J.Comp.L. 227–259 (2000); Cohn (*supra* n. 911).

[914] *Cohn* (*supra* n. 911).

[915] Before the modern nation state claimed a virtual monopoly of law-making power, legal ideas circulated more easily among legal cultures because their adoption did not require the imprimatur of state authorities: see *Sunde*, The Art of Being Artful – The Complex Reception of Law: *idem and Skodvin* (eds.), Rendezvous of European Legal Cultures (Bergen 2010) 29–43.

[916] See *Twining* (*supra* n. 909) 10–23.

[917] *Graziadei* (*supra* n. 894) 454–456.

[918] See Cohn (*supra* n. 911).

[919] *Miller*, A Typology of Legal Transplants: Using Sociology, Legal History, and Argentine Examples to Explain the Transplant Process: 51 Am.J.Comp.L 839–885 (2003); for an overview, see the table at 885. See also *Graziadei* (*supra* n. 894) 457–463.

investigated, never mind fully understood. In fact, history is full of instances in which the decision to import was based on extremely thin information. "Externally dictated transplants" result when a legal system yields to outside pressure to adopt certain law. This pressure can take the form of outright force (including military violence – such as the export of Soviet law to parts of the former USSR), of unmistakable command (e.g., by an occupying power – such as General McArthur's dictate of the post-World War II Japanese constitution), or of threats to withhold benefits (e.g., of membership of the EU). A third type is the "entrepreneurial transplant" which is driven by the interests of particular groups in the recipient system. These groups (sometimes called "norm entrepreneurs") stand to benefit, economically, professionally, or otherwise, from the adoption of foreign law and thus orchestrate its adoption. This is the case, e.g., when firms lobby for the importation of strong investment protection regimes or when interest groups push for the adoption of foreign models of environmental regulation. Last but not least, there is the "legitimacy-generating transplant" which occurs when the recipient system imports law because of the power or prestige of a foreign donor. For example, new market economies often adopt the law of leading capitalist systems because of the latter's international prestige.[920] Note that this may happen even though the foreign model is not particularly well-suited for the importing system. These four categories are heuristically helpful, but whether they exhaust the list of underlying motivations depends largely on how broadly one construes them. One could, for example, think of an additional category in which systems adopt foreign law because it promises greater economic efficiency, regulatory effectiveness, or social justice, or simply because they want to participate in international legal unification. Note also that such a typology of reasons considers only the interests of the recipient system and thus tells us very little about the donor jurisdictions' motivations. Yet, transplants are often initiated by exporting systems for their own reasons, such as the projection of political or economic power, promotion of professional interests, and perhaps even an altruistic desire to help other systems in developing their law (*infra* s. 351. In some instances, the motivations for adopting a particular foreign law have been quite personal – in 1926 Turkey adopted the Swiss Civil Code in large part because the Turkish minister of justice (Mahmut Esad Boskurt) had studied in Switzerland, and the Egyptian Civil Code of 1949 was modeled on the French Code civil inter alia because its principal author (Abd El-Razzak El-Sanhuri) had obtained his doctorate in France. And in some instances convincing reasons for adopting foreign law are hard, if not impossible, to find.[921]

Any attempt to combine all these types of categories into one, comprehensive, typology must inevitably result in a highly complex picture.[922] Even such a picture, however, could present only a highly simplified reflection of a reality marked by hybrids, combinations, and reciprocal interactions.

349. *Successes and failures*. – Legal "transplant" conjures up the image of a foreign legal element growing into the receiving system, like an organ taken from one body growing into another. Sometimes that works, sometimes it does not, and often it is not clear. Much ink has been spilt on what counts as a success (or failure), how that should be measured, and, most of all, what factors promote or hinder it. The resultant debates have generated many interesting questions but few conclusive answers.

To begin with, it is not clear what exactly constitutes success. If the transplant firmly establishes itself in the recipient system – regardless of its positive or negative impact? If it fulfills the expectations of the receiving or of the donor systems – whatever these expectations may be? If the transplanted law works for the recipient as it

920 *Ajani*, By Chance and Prestige: Legal Transplants in Russia and Eastern Europe: 43 Am.J.Comp.L. 93–117 (1995).

921 Ernst Rabel considered most receptions (at least in the past) "naïve and uncritical", *Rabel* (*supra* n. 153) 9 ("naiv und kritiklos").

922 See the table by *Twining*, Globalisation and Comparative Law: *Örücü and Nelken* (eds.), Comparative Law: A Handbook (2007) 69–90, 86–87.

did for the donor? If it functions at all, albeit in a modified fashion? If it has unplanned but still beneficial effects?

Since success or failure is often a matter of degree, a closely related issue is how to measure it. By the rate of general acceptance, use, and perhaps even popularity? By the degree to which the imported law can be shown to solve a particular problem? To promote certain policies? To increase wealth, be it for certain groups or for society as a whole? Some of the literature has focused on economic efficiency, especially with regard to private law,[923] whereas others have criticized that point of view as too narrow.[924]

While there is no general consensus about any of these questions, there is widespread agreement that there are some pretty clear cases, i.e., that some transplants have worked well while others have not. It is difficult to deny, for example, that, at least in many jurisdictions, the adoption of constitutional review in the second half of the twentieth century has contributed to the control of legislative power and enhanced the protection of individual rights. It is equally difficult to deny that the attempts to export Western capitalist market rules to the developing countries in Latin America and Africa in the 1960s and 1970s have (at least by and large) failed (*infra* s. 351). Many other efforts to import foreign models, however, have been a mixed experience, for example because they have had limited effect on the ground (such as human rights norms imported by authoritarian regimes) or because they have had unintended consequences.[925]

What factors determine success or failure? Certainly, geographic proximity between the systems involved has *not* played much of a role; many transplants have been successful across huge distances between donor and recipient systems, such as the adoption of core parts of the German civil code in 1898 Japan. Nor is linguistic proximity required. Of course, a shared language facilitates transfers, as throughout the British Commonwealth, between Spain and Latin America, or among Germany, Austria, and Switzerland. Yet, transplants have often worked quite satisfactorily although they had to overcome formidable translation hurdles, for example when EU law drafted in English and French had to be translated into the Slavic languages of Central and Eastern Europe. A more powerful argument can be made for the requirement that the transplant must "fit" the recipient culture.[926] Reliance on this criterion calls for two caveats, however. First, it is unclear what exactly that means. Does it require that the involved systems belong to the same "legal family"? While that may help,[927] many transplants have successfully crossed the boundaries between families, such as civil law rules of contract when they were embraced in England or, conversely, the English criminal trial jury when it was adopted in civilian jurisdictions.[928] Does "fit" require cultural, economic, and social similarity between the involved systems? Again, such similarity probably promotes success, but there are countless examples where elements of law have been effectively imported despite the lack of it, such as the Swiss Civil Code into Turkey in 1926 and French-style codification into Egypt in 1949. Probably the most serious "fit" requirement is that the import be compatible with the recipient system's institutional and professional framework. For example, Italy's endeavor to import US-style adversarial criminal procedure in 1988 ran into serious problems because the foreign model was a poor fit with existing system of courts, judicial roles, and professional habits.[929] The second caveat is that even the best "fit" does

[923] See, e.g., *Mattei*, Efficiency in Legal Transplants: An Essay in Comparative Law and Economics: 14 Int. Rev.L.&Econ 3–19 (1994).

[924] *Kischel* (*supra* n. 286) 65.

[925] For an example, see *Grande*, Legal Transplants and the Inoculation Effect: How American Criminal Procedure has Affected Continental Europe: 64 Am.J. Comp.L. 583–618 (2016).

[926] For critical discussion, see *Nelken*, Comparatists and Transferability: *Legrand and Munday* (eds.), Comparative Legal Studies: Traditions and Transitions (Cambridge, New York 2003) 437–466, 446–459.

[927] For an empirically grounded suggestion that it does, see *Spamann*, Contemporary Legal Transplants: Legal Families and the Diffusion of (Corporate) Law: Brigham Young U.L.Rev. 1813–1877 (2009).

[928] See, e.g., *Simpson* (*supra* n. 431); *Padoa-Schioppa* (ed.), The Trial Jury in England, France, Germany 1700–1900 (Berlin 1987).

[929] *Grande*, Italian Criminal Justice: Borrowing and Resistance: 48 Am.J.Comp.L. 227–259 (2000).

not guarantee success. Even if the transplant could rather easily take root in the recipient system, powerful groups may still block its adoption, or at least prevent its success, simply because the imported law would deprive them of advantages. This suggests that a major factor determining a transplant's success or failure is that it be in line with the economic, social, professional, etc., interests prevailing in the recipient system. In addition, the manner in which the transplant was brought to the recipient jurisdiction seems to play a major role.[930]

In any event, it is widely understood that even where a transplant takes root, the imported law is subject to change by the new environment in which it becomes embedded. "Transplanting frequently, perhaps always, involves transformation".[931] This is true even if the wording of a legal rule or the design of an institution is truthfully replicated. Depending on the circumstances, including the need for translation, the change of meaning and effect varies from slight to heavy; a rule that works well in one system may actually become dysfunctional if imposed on another.[932] Thus, even if an element *looks* the same in both the donor and recipient systems, one should never assume that it *works* the same.

350. *Implications for legal theory*. – Comparatists have vigorously debated whether legal transplants are contingent on the social and cultural similarity (or at least compatibility) of the systems involved. Some scholars have claimed such a contingency, while others have denied it. The respective views turn on a fundamental question of legal theory, i.e., the law's relationship with society and culture.

One position is to regard law as reflecting, and thus closely tied to, social conditions and cultural characteristics – a view that has sometimes been called "mirror theory" of law[933] This view has a long pedigree, and it comes in many variations. Its perhaps most famous root is the perspective of Montesquieu, who saw law as so closely tied to the particular conditions prevailing in a country that it would be a great coincidence ("un grand hazard") if law made for one people were to fit another.[934] Nineteenth-century "mirror theories" are associated with a variety of scholars, ranging from Friedrich Carl von Savigny (who saw law as an emanation of a nation's "spirit") to Rudolf von Jhering (who regarded it as the result of the struggle between social interests), and Karl Marx (who considered law part of the "superstructure" of the economy). In the twentieth century, the conception of law as a social construct became dominant, most clearly in the United States. It also became virtually mandatory in post-World War II comparative law more generally.[935] It is easy to see that from the perspective of the various "mirror theories" a successful transplantation of law must depend on a sufficient similarity between the donor and the recipient systems, at least with regard to the context of the transplant.[936] From that point of view, transplants are a precarious business and must thus be handled with great care. An extreme position even finds them impossible: regarding legal rules as entirely defined by their culturally determined meaning, it denies that they can travel across cultural boundaries without losing that meaning – and thus their very identity.[937]

In *Legal Transplants*, Alan Watson developed a very different position. As a legal historian, he observed that law had often been transmitted among vastly different societies and cultures. Watson thus challenged the prevailing view by postulating that law can actually be transplanted regardless of the underlying social and cultural conditions.[938] To be sure, this does not

[930] *Berkowitz, Pistor and Richard*, The Transplant Effect: 51 Am.J.Comp.L. 163–203 (2003).

[931] *Watson* (*supra* n. 903) 116.

[932] See *Teubner* (*supra* n. 811).

[933] See *Ewald* (*supra* n. 906) 492. The expression is taken from *Friedman*, A History of American Law (ed. 2 New York 1985) 595.

[934] *Charles de Secondat, Baron de Montesquieu*, De l'Esprit des Lois (Genève 1748) 8.

[935] A well-known manifestation is *Kahn-Freund* (*supra* n. 221) 1–27.

[936] The connection between law and society is not all-encompassing; instead law is more or less strongly connected to particular segments, groups, interests, etc.; see *Teubner* (*supra* n. 811).

[937] *Legrand*, The Impossibility of Legal Transplants, Maastricht J.Eur.& Comp.L. 4 (1997) 111–124; for a nuanced response, see *Nelken* (*supra* n. 926) 440–446.

[938] For a more nuanced, and highly perceptive, explication of Watson's position, see *Ewald* (*supra* n. 906).

make these conditions irrelevant: the law's original emergence may well be shaped by, and thus reflect, them.[939] Yet, once legal rules have come into existence they take on a life of their own, largely because they become the domain of a specialized elite called lawyers who deal with them as it serves their interests. This is why, according to Watson, transplanting law from one society or culture to another does not depend on any social or cultural similarity between the donor and the recipient systems.

In the 1970s and 1980s, Watson's challenge to the prevailing view triggered a lively debate about the conditions and risks of transplants.[940] The debate was rekindled in the 1990s in reaction to the project of a common private law for Europe. The mainstream of this project paid scant attention to the law's social and cultural contingency and relied, like Watson, heavily on its Roman foundations. Critics thus charged that, like Watson's *Legal Transplants*, the endeavor to Europeanize private law was an exercise in sterile positivism and formalism because it reduced law to its blackletter rules.[941] Thus, the view of law-as-society/culture was once again pitted against an understanding of law-as-rules (*supra* A.i., ss. 320–322).

A major benefit of observing legal transplants throughout history is the insight that neither theory is a complete and accurate description of reality. On the one hand, there are many instances in which the failure of transplants strongly indicates the importance of the law's social and cultural contingency: law developed by a donor system according to its conditions and needs often fell flat when imported to a system in which different social and cultural conditions prevailed (*infra* 351). On the other hand, there are many instances in which the success of transplants strongly suggests the continuing relevance of law as a set (or system) of concepts and rules with a life of their own: such concepts and rules have often traveled between radically different societies and cultures (sometimes centuries apart) and still taken firm hold. The immediate follow-up question is, of course, what explains these different outcomes. Unfortunately, this brings us back to the question of the conditions of success and failure (*supra* s. 349) – a question to which no definite answer has been found.

It is broadly assumed among comparatists, though, that the *kind of law* in question can make a difference: some elements of law are more contingent on society and culture than others. As a result, one can expect technical rules to travel more easily than norms reflecting strong social or cultural values. Yet, traditional assumptions that certain kinds of law are better suited for transplantation than others must be taken with a large grain of salt. For example, the idea that private law is more easily transferable than public law because the former is less tied to the state's interests than the latter is subject to challenge by numerous counter-examples.

Studying legal transplants thus shows that the connection between law on the one hand and society and culture on the other is neither uniform nor straightforward; instead, it varies from one sector and situation to another.[942] More generally, observing the great variety, and the greatly varying fate, of legal transplants throughout history can unsettle time-honored assumptions about law as a rational and coherent response to particular social needs.[943]

351. *The special case of "Law and Development".* – Law and Development has a dual meaning. It primarily denotes the foreign assistance programs provided by international organizations, governments, and sometimes by non-state actors, to developing and transitioning countries with the goal of helping them to update their legal systems. It also stands for the academic scholarship that evolved in connection with these programs.[944] We

[939] Thus Watson did not at all deny the cultural dimension of law, see *Watson* (*supra* n. 903) 107.

[940] See, e.g., the debate between *Kahn-Freund* (*supra* n. 221); *Watson*, Legal Transplants and Law Reform: 92 L.Q.R. 79–84 (1976), and (attempting to reconcile their positions) *Stein*, Uses, Misuses – and Nonuses of Comparative Law: 72 Nw.U.L.Rev. 198–216 (1977); see also the discussion by *Großfeld*, The Strength and Weakness of Comparative Law (1990) 41–49. For a full history of the debate, see *Cairns* (*supra* n. 129).

[941] See, e.g., *Legrand* (*supra* n. 784).

[942] *Teubner* (*supra* n. 811).

[943] See *Graziadei* (*supra* n. 894) 470–472.

[944] For a brief but informative overview, see *Trubek*, Law and Development: *Wright* (ed.), International Encyclopedia of the Social and Behavioral Sciences XIII (ed. 2 Amsterdam 2015) 443–447.

will use the term here mainly in the former sense of actual foreign assistance programs. From the perspective of comparative law, Law and Development is a special case because, despite its obvious relevance for the study of legal transplants, it has largely remained beyond the purview of the discipline's mainstream.

There were two main phases of Law and Development. The first spanned the 1960s and 1970s when global financial institutions, the United States, and some other countries (such as France) invested large amounts of money trying to help developing nations mainly in Latin America and Africa (and to a lesser extent in Asia) to modernize their legal systems. More specifically, target countries were pushed to adopt law modeled on the developed West in order to help them build successful market economies. The endeavor, however, was based neither on a solid theoretical understanding nor on any empirical data,[945] and over time it was increasingly seen as an instance of US-led "legal imperialism".[946] By the mide-1970s, the project was widely considered a failure and by and large aborted. The attendant scholarship also petered out.[947] Mainstream comparative law took very little notice of this first phase. In the 1960s and 1970s, comparatists were still heavily focused on traditional private law, and they were largely unconnected to the Law & Society scholars interested in Law and Development; in addition, legal transplants had yet to be discovered as a hot topic. There were some exceptions, such as John Merryman's suggestion to turn Law and Development studies into a new field entitled "comparative law and social change";[948] at the time, however, the proposal had little impact.[949]

The second phase was triggered by the fall of communism and covered the transition of planned economies to free markets in the 1990s and early 2000s. It was driven in part by the World Bank, in part again by the United States (in particular the United States Agency for International Development, USAID), but this time also by the European Union and its member states which competed with the US for influence, especially in Central and Eastern Europe. It had two main pillars. The first was, once more, a push for legal reforms considered necessary for the building of successful market economies.[950] The second pillar was the promotion of the rule of law, in particular of democratic rule, constitutionalism, and human rights (which could easily conflict with the development of a capitalist economy). To a large extent, the second phase was a repetition of the first, i.e., an attempt to export Western law in the form of statutory (and constitutional) models; yet, it also sought to reform legal education, to professionalize the bar, and to improve the administration of justice. It was similar to the first phase in that it relied heavily on technical assistance provided in a top-down fashion by Western experts who were often "guided more by intuition and hope than by any systematic knowledge or

[945] *Trubek,* Law and Development: International Encyclopedia of the Social and Behavioral Sciences 8443, 8444 (2001)

[946] *Gardner*, Legal Imperialism: American Lawyers and Foreign Aid in Latin America (Madison WI 1980).

[947] The – by now classic – critique of *Trubek and Galanter* (*supra* n. 231) was supposed to revamp the field but actually helped to hasten its demise. See also *Merryman*, Law and Development Memoirs I: The Chile Program: 48 Am.J.Comp.L. 481–499 (2000); *Merryman*, Law and Development Memoirs II: SLADE: 48 Am.J.Comp.L. 713–727 (2000).

[948] *Merryman* (*supra* n. 231) (containing an extensive bibliography of works on law and development as well as a list of law and development projects).

[949] See, however, *Merryman, Clark and Friedman*, Law and Social Change in Mediterranean Europe and Latin America: A Handbook of Legal Social Indicators for Comparative Study (Stanford CA 1979).

[950] This aspect was based largely on the belief that successful economic performance requires proper legal institutions, especially reliable enforcement of property rights and contractual obligations; see *North*, Institutions, Institutional Change and Economic Performance (Cambridge 1990). It is also associated with the package of standard policy prescriptions known as the "Washington consensus", see *Williamson*, What Washington Means by Policy Reform: *idem* (ed.), Latin American Readjustment: How Much Has Happened (Washington DC 1990) 7–20. Yet, the belief that such institutions are indispensable for economic growth is contradicted by several countries' economic development, most notably of course China's; see *Clarke*, Economic Development and the Rights Hypothesis: 51 Am.J.Comp.L. 89–111 (2003); see also *Ang*, How China Escaped the Poverty Trap (Ithaca NY 2016). For a more general, nuanced, assessment, see *Dam*, The Law-Growth Nexus: The Rule of Law and Economic Development (Washington DC 2006).

empirical evidence".[951] To be sure, the second law and development project was not an abject failure, but its success is generally considered quite limited, mainly because the imported law on the books is often not effectively enforced. While this phase was on the comparatists' radar screen, the mainstream was relatively uninvolved in the project itself. As a result, Law and Development did not become a major topic covered by a large comparative law literature.[952]

Since the two phases of Law and Development provide an extremely rich data set about legal transplants (as well as, at least indirectly, about the relationship between law, society, and culture), the mainstream comparatists' low level of engagement is both surprising and indeed a missed opportunity.[953]

A study published in 2003 illustrates how valuable a closer engagement of comparative law with the fate of Law and Development could be. The study analyzes an earlier incidence of transplants, i.e., the reception of European law (mainly English common law as well as the French and German branches of the civil law) by several dozen countries throughout the world in the nineteenth and early twentieth centuries.[954] The study's principal conclusion is that law is most effective when it responds to indigenous demand.[955] While this implies that internally generated law is preferable, legal transplants can still be successful *if* they respond to local need. In addition, success is more likely if transplants are adapted to, and thus compatible with, preexisting social norms, and if the local population is already familiar with the imported law's basic principles.[956] For our understanding of Law and Development the study is valuable in two regards. First, it helps us recognize why the first phase of Law and Development was a virtually complete, and the second still at least a partial, failure: these processes were not driven primarily by local desire to import foreign law but rather by the agenda of Western capitalist nations to impose the features of their legal systems on other countries; the transplants were often poorly adapted to local circumstances, and their underlying principles were largely unknown to the local population. Second, the study has important policy implications: as the authors concluded, "legal reforms simply viewed as technical assistance programs that are implemented by having Western experts design good laws, are unlikely to produce the desired outcome, i.e., an effective legal order and economic growth and development. Instead, attempts must be made to induce an internal process of law development and to generate a self-sustaining demand for legal innovation and change".[957] In sum, the study shows how scholarship on legal transplants can provide guidance for development assistance programs by helping to define conditions for their success.

iv. *Interdisciplinary Comparative Law*

352. *Overview.* – Since the 1980s there have been many calls for more interdisciplinary work in comparative law (*supra* III.E.iii., s. 163), and since the 1990s these calls have increasingly been answered. Today, many scholars undertake comparative studies in combination with other disciplines. This has created a broad-ranging and intellectually rich body of work.[958] Here, we will consider six approaches that have been particularly prominent in the last couple of decades: comparative legal history, comparative legal cultures, socio-legal comparison, comparative law and linguistic studies, comparative law and

[951] *Trubek* (*supra* n. 945) 8445.

[952] When law and development became a prominent topic again in the early 2000s, it was discussed mainly by other legal scholars as well as by political scientists; see the overview and critique by *Davis and Trebilcock*, The Relationship between Law and Development: Optimists versus Skeptics: 56 Am.J.Comp.L. 895–946 (2008).

[953] But cf. the collection of country-specific case studies by *Gillespie and Nicholson*, Law and Development and the Global Discourses of Legal Transfers (Cambridge, New York 2012).

[954] *Berkowitz, Pistor and Richard* (*supra* n. 930).

[955] *Berkowitz, Pistor and Richard* (*supra* n. 930) 189; see also *Gillespie and Nicholson*, (*supra* n. 953).

[956] *Berkowitz, Pistor and Richard* (*supra* n. 930) 189–190.

[957] *Idem* 190.

[958] See, e.g., *Foster, Moscati and Palmer* (eds.), Interdisciplinary Study and Comparative Law (London 2016).

economics, and comparative law and religion. These approaches do not always constitute clearly separate fields of inquiry. Instead, they often overlap or even blend into each other. Thus, while some work can clearly be assigned to one or the other, much scholarship straddles the boundaries and combines elements of two or more approaches.

353. *Comparative legal history*.[959] – The combination of comparative and historical studies has a tradition reaching back to at least the nineteenth century. It is true that the Historical School in Germany showed little interest in foreign legal systems, largely as a result of Savigny's claim that law was an emanation of each people's particular "national spirit" (*Volksgeist*). Yet, in England, nineteenth-century historical jurisprudence often compared legal developments in various legal systems, most famously in Henry Sumner Maine's *Ancient Law* (1861), but also in the work of James Bryce, William Frederic Maitland, Paul Vinogradoff and others. The same can be said for many adherents to historical jurisprudence in the United States, notably Oliver Wendell Holmes and his *magnum opus*, *The Common Law* (1881).[960] In the early twentieth century, historical and comparative elements were impressively combined by Max Weber in his *Sociology of Law* (1922).[961]

Since the middle of the twentieth century, it has been noticeable that, at least in Europe, the lead in this field was taken by scholars who, by training, institutional affiliation, and self-image, were primarily legal historians rather than comparatists. Prominent among them were the scholars of Roman law who almost naturally came to take a European, rather than national, perspective[962] and who sometimes compared their subject to various indigenous law(s).[963]

Since the late twentieth century, continental European legal historians have often more generally written from an all-European perspective.[964] While their writings are rarely explicitly comparative, at minimum they invite observing similarities and differences among the developments in various parts of the continent. In addition, since the mid-1980s, a major focus of European legal history has been the historical relationship between the civil and the common law.[965] It can thus be said that in Europe today there is a firmly established tradition of comparative legal history. It even has an institutional home at the *Max Planck Institut für europäische Rechtsgeschichte* (founded in Frankfurt in 1964),[966] a professional organization, the European Society for Comparative Legal History (founded in The Hague in 2009), as well as its own specialized journal, Comparative Legal History (electronically published since 2013).

The picture is quite different on the other side of the Atlantic. Mainstream legal history in the United States has long pursued a fairly parochial path, occasional studies on foreign countries notwithstanding. Work in comparative legal history

[959] For the relationship between comparative law and legal history, the benefits and risks of their combination, and the conflicts it can create, see *supra* II.B.i., s. 34)

[960] For details, see *Reimann*, Historical Jurisprudence: *Dubber and Tomlin* (eds.), The Oxford Handbook of Legal History (Oxford 2018) 397–417.

[961] *Weber*, Wirtschaft und Gesellschaft (Tübingen 1922) chapter VIII; the standard English translation is *Roth and Wittich* (eds.), Economy and Society (2 vol. Oakland CA 1978).

[962] *Koschaker*, Europa und das römische Recht (Tübingen 1947 and ed. 2 1966); *Wieacker* (*supra* n. 102), *Coing*, Handbuch der Quellen und Literatur der neueren europäischen Privatrechtsgeschichte (3 vol. Berlin 1973); *Stein*, Roman Law in European History (Cambridge, New York 1999); *Zimmermann*, Roman Law, Contemporary Law, European Law: the Civilian Tradition Today (Oxford 2001).

[963] E.g., *Buckland and McNair*, Roman Law and Common Law (Cambridge 1936 and ed. 2 1952).

[964] *Bretone*, Diritto e Tempo Nella Tradizione Europea (1999); *Hattenhauer*, Europäische Rechtsgeschichte (Heidelberg 1992 and ed. 4 2004); *Padoa Schioppa*, Storia del diritto in Europa (Cambridge 2009); *Van Caenegem*, European Law in the Past and Future: Unity and Diversity over Two Millenia (Cambridge 2002); *Wesel*, Geschichte des Rechts in Europa (München 2010).

[965] *Coing and Nör* (eds.), Comparative Studies in Continental and Anglo-American Legal History (more than 30 volumes since 1985); see also the Symposium on Common Law and European Legal History: Z neuere Rechtsgesch. 28 (2006) 2–234.

[966] The Institute has published not only the series *Studien zur europäischen Rechtsgeschichte* (Studies on European Legal History) but since 2014 also *Global Perspectives on Legal History*.

continues to be rare, although there are some noteworthy exceptions. Interestingly, they were published mostly by scholars who would consider themselves more comparative lawyers looking into history than legal historians with comparative interests.[967]

In the last few decades, the general trend in legal scholarship towards global perspectives has presented new challenges to comparative legal history. For a long time, both comparative law and legal history had focused on European, or at best Western, nation states. To many scholars, such a focus now appears too narrow.[968] Indeed, both disciplines have already begun to expand their horizons to include previously neglected regions of the world, such as Latin America and parts of Asia. Operating beyond the West, however, may require adjustments in their frameworks, methods, and modes of cooperation, but it also has the potential of yielding new insights into how law works in particular historical, political, and cultural contexts.

In the early twenty-first century, comparative legal history remains very much in vogue, but it also faces the problem common in modern comparative law more generally: the scholarship increasingly consists of myriad individual studies on myriad individual topics that are at best loosely related but not integrated into a larger, coherent agenda. Tell-tale evidence of this state of affairs is the edited volumes and symposia that collect essays on a broad range of topics under a theme so vague that it is meaningless.[969] As a result, comparative legal history keeps producing much information about particulars but virtually no broader theories or generalizable knowledge.

A special case of combining comparative with historical perspectives is the study of receptions and legal transplants, in particular the work of Alan Watson, which has been discussed separately above (iii., s. 346).

354. *Comparative legal cultures – in general.* – In reaction against the older tradition's often narrow focus on legal principles and rules, scholars have, especially since the 1990s, increasingly approached comparative studies from the much broader perspective of legal culture. This approach has spawned a huge literature which keeps growing apace. Thus, comparative legal cultures have become a vast and difficult terrain which can be surveyed here only in very rough outline. Unfortunately, there has been relatively little cooperation of comparatists with legal anthropologists – a missed opportunity particularly with regard to the study of legal cultures (*supra* II.B.iii., s. 39).

A pervasive problem is that the concept of legal culture is notoriously multi-dimensional. It means different things to different people who use it for different purposes. In addition, it is often poorly defined. As a result, it is difficult to grasp and frequently contested.[970] Sometimes it is used more or less synonymously with "legal traditions".[971] More often, comparatists employ legal culture as a generic term for all aspects of legal systems beyond sheer rules and doctrine, i.e., for the totality of the blackletter law's environment. Striving for somewhat greater precision, one can differentiate the concept in various ways. For example, legal culture can either refer to the world of law itself, i.e., its professionals, institutions, sources, and procedures, or it can refer to the place of law in society at large, e.g., the law's role and impact.[972] Furthermore, the comparatist can look at legal culture in different spacial contexts, i.e., not only on the level of national legal systems (e.g., the French or Australian legal culture) but also on the level of regions (e.g.,

[967] See, e.g., *Dawson* (*supra* n. 356); *Gordley*, The Foundations of Private Law (Oxford, New York 2006); *Langbein,* Torture and the Law of Proof: Europe and England in the Ancien Régime (Chicago IL 1977); *Whitman* (*supra* n. 553). This characterization is less true for *Rabban* (*supra* n. 141).

[968] *Duve,* Global Legal History: Setting Europe in Perspective: *Pihlajamäki, Dubber and Godfrey* (eds.), The Oxford Handbook of European Legal History (Oxford 2018) 115–139.

[969] See e.g. *Moréteau, Masferrer and Modéer* (*supra* n. 49). A similar, though less dramatic, example is *Duve* (*supra* n. 49) 830.

[970] See *Kischel* (*supra* n. 286) 230–234.

[971] *Barton, Gibbs, Li and Merryman* (*supra* n. 226).

[972] This – now fairly common – distinction between "internal" and "external" legal culture was introduced by *Friedman*, The Legal System: A Social Science Perspective (New York 1975).

Europe)[973] or even on the global level;[974] one can also examine the legal culture of particular subject matter areas, such as international commercial arbitration.[975] Finally, culture can be treated as a force that shapes law or is shaped by law; of course, in reality it is often both, and attempts strictly to separate one from the other will often face the chicken-and-egg problem.

Yet, despite these difficulties, comparative law can scarcely avoid engagement with legal culture, at least in the general sense of the historical and social context in which law is embedded. This context crucially shapes the origins, meanings, and effects of law. Thus, even the comparatist who is primarily interested in mere rules and doctrines must take their environment into account, and doing so will produce a much richer, much more realistic, and thus much more useful analysis of similarities and differences. In addition, legal culture is also highly relevant in several particular contexts. It can serve as the criterion for the definition of legal families and traditions, e.g., by distinguishing Western from Asian legal cultures. It alerts comparatists to the limits of comparability across cultural divides, e.g., with regard to the meaning of marriage in secular and religious legal orders. And it shows that cultures may either handle a particular conflict through law or rely on non-legal mechanisms, e.g., when some systems resolve certain disputes between the branches of government through constitutional courts, while others leave the matter to the political process.

Beyond the distinctions mentioned above, there are two fundamentally different, albeit related, ways to understand legal culture. For lack of better terms, they can perhaps be called psychological and sociological. A psychological approach conceives of legal culture as "legal consciousness" or "*mentalité*". Legal culture thus understood comprises the widely shared values, beliefs, and expectations that shape people's attitudes towards, engagement with, and reactions to law. This approach is beholden to the humanities. Seeking to understand the people's "mental software", it works with ideas drawn from intellectual tradition and philosophy,[976] linguistics, and from the comparatist's personal perceptions. Needless to say, these factors are not precisely measurable and/or verifiable. By contrast, a sociological approach conceives of legal culture as the real social environment in which law functions. Legal culture understood as the (quasi-external) environment of law comprises, e.g., professional or institutional structures or the people's de facto use of, or exposure to, law. It is essentially part of the social sciences. Seeking to understand the actual practice of law, it looks primarily to hard data to describe and explain similarities and differences between legal systems. Such data should be verified and used to test concrete hypotheses. In the literature on comparative legal cultures, these two approaches are often mixed together. To some extent, that is justifiable because they are interrelated;[977] after all, the (internal) "cognitive structures" and the (external) environment are connected in multiple ways. Yet, for purposes of further exposition and explanation, it is preferable to consider these approaches separately because they are often pursued by different groups of scholars endowed with different skill sets and engaged in different discourses.[978]

355. *The study of legal "mentalités" – in particular.* Today, many comparatists understand legal culture as the sum of prevalent predilections, preferences, and intellectual habits.

Legal culture in that sense can become the direct object of comparative research. Studies can look either to legal professionals, e.g., compare how a Chinese lawyer and a Swiss jurist perceive legal issues, or focus on populations more generally, e.g., ask how a Japanese or an Iranian citizen perceives law in his or her society. While the

[973] *Gessner, Hoeland and Varga* (eds.), European Legal Cultures (Brookfield WI 1996); *Sunde and Skodvin* (eds.), Rendezvous of European Legal Cultures (Bergen 2010).

[974] See, e.g., *Koch*, Envisioning a Global Legal Culture: Mich.J.Int.L. 25 (2003) 1–76.

[975] *Delazay and Garth* (*supra* n. 821).

[976] E.g. *Ewald* (*supra* n. 75).

[977] *Kischel* (*supra* n. 286) 229–238; *Siems* (*supra* n. 680) 147–179; *Cotterell*, Comparative Law and Legal Culture: *Reimann and Zimmermann* (eds.), The Oxford Handbook of Comparative Law (ed. 2 Oxford 2019) 710–733.

[978] Sometimes, these approaches are skillfully combined, producing subtle descriptions and analyses based on both empirical data and insights into the mentality of legal and non-legal actors in a particular culture: see, e.g, *Markovits* (*supra* n. 244).

results can be very valuable for our understanding of how law functions in the respective cultures, such direct comparisons are relatively rare, in part because of the difficulty of defining epistemological frameworks precisely.

Most of the time, comparatists looking at legal culture in the sense of *mentalité* have employed the concept as an argument in specific contexts of which five are worth mentioning here. First, perceptions of, and in particular attitudes towards, law have been proffered as *explanations for differences in the operation of legal systems.* For example, the fact that litigation rates are much lower in Japan than in comparable Western market economies was often attributed to an Asian predilection for social harmony and a concomitant reluctance to take conflicts to court. Such "cultural" explanations, however, often lack solid empirical grounding, and they have been contested as largely unfounded.[979] Second, comparatists have invoked legal culture *to support claims of both cultural diversity and unity.* Some have emphasized cultural differences, often in reaction against the discipline's older unification agenda (to strive for a common law of all mankind). Here, reference to culture has served, inter alia, to promote an agenda of multiculturalism.[980] Other comparatists, however, have pointed to cultural unity among legal systems, mainly within certain legal families. Such proclaimed unity has been a particularly salient topic on the European level, i.e., in the context of modern Europe's path to integration.[981] Third, comparatists often point to legal culture as a *factor that complicates communication* between legal professionals across boundaries. Cultural differences can lead to costly misunderstandings, e.g., when a lawyer from one country attributes little weight to an informal agreement while her colleague from another jurisdiction considers it (at least morally) binding. In order to avoid, or at least to minimize, such miscommunication, actors must be aware of how differences in legal consciousness shape understandings and expectations. Fourth, legal culture as *mentalité* has played a pivotal role in the *debate about the barriers between legal cultures,* i.e., about whether a lawyer from one legal system can ever truly understand the perspective of a colleague from another. Some scholars have argued that a deep "cultural immersion" in another legal system makes such an understanding by and large possible, some "irreducible differences" notwithstanding.[982] Others have categorically denied that an outsider can ever attain an insider's perspective because the ontological differences in *mentalités* are insurmountable, especially between the civil and the common law[983] – a claim that is widely regarded as exaggerated. Finally, invoking legal culture can be *an antidote to the instrumental conception of law* inherent in the traditional functionalist approach (*infra* C.i., ss. 368–373). Taking a cultural perspective means looking at law not primarily as a problem-solving device but mainly as an expression of traditions, values, and (cultural) preferences.[984]

In all these contexts, arguing from legal culture understood as *mentalité* is subject to several pervasive criticisms. For a start, there is no agreement on exactly what the relevant components are – assumptions, expectations, values, perceptions, thought patterns, etc. In addition, it is very difficult, if not impossible, to determine exactly by whom, how broadly, and how strongly these beliefs, etc., are held, especially since many, if not most, of them may be unarticulated if not subconscious. As a result, claims derived from *mentalités* or "epistemological frameworks" are at best plausible and thought-provoking, but they cannot be reliably verified. A further problem is that these thought patterns, etc., are scarcely uniform even within a certain legal culture, particularly since they can change at different times for different people; thus, arguments from *mentalités* almost invariably involve troublesome generalizations. As a result of all these uncertainties, an observer can often read into a legal culture whatever he or she expects, or wants, to find. Thus, one must constantly guard against the risk that

979 *Haley*, The Myth of the Reluctant Litigant: J.Jap. Stud.4 (1978) 359–390. The article triggered a lively discussion of the topic in the academic literature.

980 *Glenn* (*supra* n. 327).

981 *Hesselink*, The New European Legal Culture (Deventer 2001).

982 *Curran* (*supra* n. 7) 43–92.

983 *Legrand* (*supra* n. 784)

984 *Cotterell* (*supra* n. 977) 730–733.

legal cultures are largely imagined, if not outright invented.

356. *Socio-legal studies.* – If legal culture is understood as the social environment of law, it becomes the subject of socio-legal studies.[985] Such studies focus on the relationship between law and the surrounding society.

The cooperation between comparative lawyers and legal sociologists is a relatively recent phenomenon. The combination of these disciplines in Max Weber's work notwithstanding, for most of the twentieth century comparatists and legal sociologists pursued rather separate paths. The former showed little interest in concrete social data, the latter usually focused on a single legal culture only. Also, comparatists tended to think mainly from inside the law, while sociologists observed it from the outside. Since the late twentieth century, however, there has been a gradual rapprochement, resulting in considerable cooperation and increasing synergy.

The variety of existing socio-legal studies is too large to be summarized here.[986] From the particular perspective of comparative law, it may suffice to outline two basic forms: an essentially empirical and a more theoretical direction.

Empirical socio-legal studies focus on how law actually functions in society. Thus, they look to law in action, rather than in the books. Such studies demand much greater specificity than ruminations about various forms of "legal consciousness". In particular, they require the definition of objectively measurable "cultural indicators". They mostly consist of two steps. The first step is descriptive: empirical socio-legal scholars gather and evaluate data, typically using statistical methods, in order to determine similarities or differences among legal system.[987] These data can show, for example, that despite similar blackletter law, litigation rates vary widely in comparable societies. The second step is explanatory: researchers look for factors that may cause the differences; socio-legal scholars tend to focus on social facts rather than mentalities, e.g., the availability of alternative dispute resolution mechanisms.[988] Today, there is a very substantial body of comparative socio-legal studies using empirical methods. They analyze myriad elements of legal cultures,[989] such as the operation of courts (e.g., how they process their caseloads); the professional practice of lawyers (e.g., styles of contract-drafting); issues of corporate governance (especially the impact of single- v. dual-tier corporate boards); the reality of criminal justice systems (such as conviction and incarceration rates); and access to justice in various legal systems (e.g., barriers created by costs). Such studies are invaluable because they actually show real-world similarities and differences and often proffer explanations in the form of testable hypotheses. This also helps the comparatist to determine the extent to which similarities and differences are caused by the respective legal rules and techniques or are rather attributable to the social environment.

A major difficulty of such studies is the comparability of data. For example, comparing the numbers of "lawyers" in different systems must take varying definitions of that term into account (all holders of a law degree? only members of the bar? only those in private practice?). A comparison between litigation rates has to consider that in some jurisdictions lawsuits get routinely decided by judges, while in others they are routinely settled by the parties with little or no judicial involvement. A comparison of product liability judgments in two or more nations must recognize the different degrees to which legal systems compensate tort victims through alternative mechanisms, especially public or private insurance schemes.

Socio-legal studies of a more theoretical kind have also examined the relationship between law and society in a variety of contexts of which two have gained particular prominence. One is the impact of the globalization of the economy and, as a result, of ever larger parts of law, the

[985] On the relationship between comparative law and legal sociology, see *supra* II.B.ii., ss. 35–37.

[986] For an overview, see *Riles* (*supra* n. 58) 783–793; for a collection of essays, see *Clark* (ed.), Comparative Law and Society (Cheltenham, Northampton MA 2012); see also *Friedman, Perez-Perdomo and Gomez* (*supra* n. 50.)

[987] This approach to studying legal cultures is thus related to "numerical (statistical) comparative law", *infra* VI.C.iii., ss. 378–381.

[988] See, e.g., *Blankenburg*, Civil Litigation Rates as Indicators for Legal Cultures: *Nelken* (ed.), Comparing Legal Cultures (Aldershot 1997) 41–68.

[989] For an overview, see *Siems* (*supra* n. 680) 157–178.

legal profession, and legal practice.[990] One consequence pointed out by socio-legal theorists is the growing importance of legal orders beyond the traditional state-based systems, such as transnational regulatory regimes or specific legal cultures of particular economic sectors. Since these regimes and cultures coexist and overlap in multiple ways, comparative law needs to study legal systems under conditions of global legal pluralism.[991] A second prominent theme in the more theoretical discussion has been the question to what extent law is the result of its social and cultural environment. The traditional assumption has long been that law is crucially shaped by a variety of external factors, be it its overall environment (Montesquieu), the "spirit" of a people (Savigny), social interests and purposes (Jhering), or the economy (Marx, Weber); in addition, one might invoke religion, historical experience, and the political system. Yet, this assumption has been challenged by the claim that law develops largely independently of all these factors, mainly through (internal) professional practice.[992] Law has also been portrayed as a "self-referential" and, in that sense, closed social system.[993] The debates about the law's relative autonomy have a direct impact on comparative law. The more law is conceived as a result of external social and cultural factors the more comparatists must study it in that context; and the more law is regarded as an autonomous practice or system the more their attention must be directed to its specific internal or self-reproducing dynamics. Comparative law, in turn, can also help to test these hypotheses, for example, by investigating whether similar social conditions correlate with similar law, or by observing to what extent various legal systems actually operate in a self-referential mode.

357. *Comparative law and language studies.* – Law and language are closely related not only in the general sense that both are intimately tied to their respective culture and society, but also in the very concrete sense that law is overwhelmingly expressed through, and thus utterly dependent on, language, be it written or oral. Since dealing with different legal systems thus entails dealing with different languages, comparative law almost inevitably operates in a multilingual context. Sometimes, this is even true when countries share the same general language, as between Germany, Austria, and Switzerland or between Canada, England, and the United States, because even among such jurisdictions, the legal terminology often differs.

While this close relationship between law and language was widely known already 200 years ago,[994] it was only in the second half of the twentieth century that comparatists began to think more deeply about the impact of language on their field. We will first address the formidable practical challenges resulting from the discipline's multilingual nature which are generally recognized. We will then turn to the more recent discussion of the rich intellectual benefits of a linguistic approach. Finally, we will look at some truly interdisciplinary work which, however, has been intermittent and rare.

Among the practical challenges the most obvious is that the comparatist must master several languages. The growing dominance of English as the law's global lingua franca has not changed that requirement itself, although it has affected some rules of the game. For non-native English speakers it means that they must acquire mastery of that language in order to participate in the international discourse of comparative law. Native speakers, of course, have a head-start in that regard, but even for them command of English is usually not enough (unless comparison is limited to systems operating in it). To be sure, most prominent legal systems in the world have become more easily accessible because material

[990] *Delazay and Garth*, The Internationalization of Global Palace Wars (Chicago IL 2003); *Drolshammer and Pfeifer* (*supra* n. 411)

[991] *Teubner* (ed.), Global Law without a State (Aldershot, Brookfield WI 1998). A prominent question regarding the multiple legal systems coexisting in the world is the extent to which they have been shaped by the US-American model, and with what results; see, e.g., L'américanisation du droit (*supra* n. 815) 1–267.

[992] *Watson* (*supra* n. 902)

[993] *Teubner*, Law as an Autopoietic System (Oxford, Cambridge MA 1993).

[994] See, e.g., *Savigny* (*supra* 111) 8–12; *Grimm*, Von der Poesie im Recht: ZgeschRW 2 (1816) 25–99. On the many historical connections between law and language, see *Großfeld*, Kernfragen der Rechtsvergleichung (Tübingen 1996) 152–156.

about them is widely available in English. Yet, even if such material is of high quality, working with it cannot fully substitute for access in the vernacular because translated material is still limited and because translations are inevitably imperfect, as will be explained in a moment. In addition, the command of several languages is also important because it has intellectual benefits that are crucial for comparative work (see *infra*). Serious comparatists can certainly read, often also speak, and sometimes even write in, English and at least one, more often two or more, other languages.

The other major practical difficulty is the translation of legal texts. As legal systems with different languages have come to interact ever more frequently and closely, the need for such translations (primarily into English) has massively increased; this is most visible in multilingual organizations, especially the European Union.[995] Comparatists have long been aware of the difficulties of translation. The most obvious problem is that a term in one language rarely has an exact equivalent in another. This is familiar, of course, from translations generally, but for two reasons the problem is exacerbated when it comes to legal texts. First, the meaning of legal terms is derived from, and thus directly connected to, the tradition, doctrine, and structure of their legal system; thus, they cannot be fully grasped without an understanding of a much broader legal context. For example, the exact meaning of the term denoting a person's primary place of abode depends on how the systems involved define it. As a result, an English "domicile" is not exactly the same as a French "domicile" or a German "Wohnsitz", not to mention the term now commonly employed in EU law, i.e., "habitual residence". The lack of exact equivalence is particular salient between cultures with radically different tongues – some terms of Chinese or Japanese law simply have no real counterpart in Western languages. As a result, translation always involves an, at times very strong, element of interpretation. Second, in contrast to literary expressions, legal terms usually have a precise, technical meaning; this makes it dangerous to settle for close equivalents in another language. Legal dictionaries can at best alleviate, but not really solve these problems. There are several ways of approaching them, but all are highly imperfect: simply settling for the closest equivalent is potentially misleading because it falsely suggests complete identity of meaning; leaving legal terms untranslated (i.e., in original) is of little use for the reader who is unfamiliar with them; adding explanations can help, but it may require lengthy detours through the background legal system from which a term is taken. The most important means adequately to handle translation problems is to employ translators with legal training in the systems involved, although such increased qualification requirements will normally entail higher cost. Ideally, the translation of a legal text should also capture the respective legal system's specific style and reflect its immanent values.[996] That, however, requires legal and literary skills beyond the reach of most translators and scholars.

Yet, having to deal with legal materials in foreign languages not only creates problems, it also entails significant benefits. These benefits are crucial both for comparative legal studies and for international legal practice. The main intellectual benefit is that working with foreign languages allows, even forces, the comparatist to overcome cognitive boundaries and to acquire new perspectives. As Umberto Eco pointed out, in a sense a language is a "prison"[997] or, as Wittgenstein put

[995] The EU operates in 24 official languages and employs thousands of (often freelance) interpreters who translate almost two million pages per year. This presents formidable challenges especially for projects of legal unification: see *Pozzo and Jacometti* (eds.), Multilingualism and the Harmonization of European Law (Alphen aan den Rijn 2006); *Sacco and Castellani*, Les multiples langues du droit européen uniforme (Torino 1999).

[996] See *Pozzo*, Comparative Law and Language: *Bussani and Mattei* (eds.), The Cambridge Companion to Comparative Law (Cambridge, New York 2012) 88–113, 102–104.

[997] *Eco*, Interview with Bernard Pivot, quoted by *Grosswald-Curran*, Comparative Law and Language: *Reimann* and *Zimmermann* (eds.), The Oxford Handbook of Comparative Law (ed. 2 Oxford 2019) 681–709, 687.

it, "the limits of your language are the limits of your world".[998] Another language thus opens up new terrain. Vivian Grosswald-Curran aptly wrote of a "crucial entry into another world vision and universe of thought".[999] For a comparatist, looking at foreign law in the original language provides access to the interior, so to speak, of another legal system, its concepts, ideas, and meanings. At a certain level of immersion it even reveals unstated assumptions and underlying beliefs, i.e., the *mentalité* mentioned above (*supra* s. 355). Only thus can comparison drill through the surface of legal texts and take their cultural and social meaning into account.

Providing such access to a foreign legal culture and mentality is also the most important benefit of teaching future practitioners about foreign law in the original language. In most circumstances trying to enable them actually to practice such foreign law in the vernacular is both extremely difficult and unrewarding, since that is usually much better done by their colleagues from the respective jurisdiction. The primary purpose of exposure to another legal system in the original tongue should rather be to provide students with an inside view, and even a feel, for another legal world so that they can ultimately help to bridge the gap between it and their own. Today, it is fairly common in many non-English speaking countries to teach English and US-American law in the original language, though this is often done mainly as a matter of teaching legal English. It is much less common in English-speaking countries to teach foreign law in other (original) tongues. This is understandable since students there already master the prevalent global legal language. It is still regrettable because students are deprived of the opportunity to become sensitive to other legal cultures and mentalities – which would serve them well in international legal practice, quite aside from being educational in its own right.

Truly interdisciplinary work between comparative law and language studies has been rare, however. Two efforts in that direction are particularly noteworthy.

In the 1980s and 1990s, Bernhard Großfeld ruminated extensively about the relationship between language and (comparative) law. He illustrated through many examples how our language generally determines our modes of perception, structures of thought, and even our cultural values. Since law operates largely in the form of language, language also determines how we perceive, think about, and evaluate law. Inevitably, different languages thus shape laws differently, often on a very deep level and in a fundamental fashion. If this is correct, then fully understanding foreign law requires understanding the structural qualities and cultural orientations of the language in which it is cast.[1000] In a similar vein, Vivian Grosswald-Curran explained how the study of language can serve as a "cognitive model for comparative law".[1001] This is most obvious in the sense that the process of translation as an act of bridging the gaps between languages is highly similar to the process of comparing laws as the process of bridging the gaps between legal systems;[1002] for example, both struggle with the limits of translatability of meaning and must accept "irreducible untranslatables".[1003] But there is also a less obvious, but even more fundamental, relationship between language and comparative legal studies: both stand "between the same and the other".[1004] Language operates between listener and speaker, comparative law between the familiar and the foreign legal system. Thus they are both comparative by nature. While comparative law makes that explicit, it is implicit in communication through language: the listener constantly has to compare what he or she hears (or reads) to his or her own experience and understanding. The work

[998] *Wittgenstein,* Tractatus Logico-Philosophicus (London 1933), Proposition 5.6 (1933), quoted by *Grosswald-Curran* (*supra* n. 997977) 693.

[999] *Grosswald-Curran* (*supra* n. 997) 686; see also *Großfeld* (*supra* n. 994) 169–172.

[1000] *Großfeld,* Macht und Ohnmacht der Rechtsvergleichung (Tübingen 1984) 149–186; *Großfeld* (*supra* n. 994) 53–125.

[1001] *Grosswald-Curran* (*supra* n. 997) 683.

[1002] "[C]omparative law is the translator or the law of others and otherness." *Ibidem* 702.

[1003] *Idem* 686.

[1004] *Idem* 683.

of both these scholars is brimming with ideas opening new perspectives for the discipline, and one must wish that eventually others will further develop and test them in the context of concrete projects.[1005]

358. *Comparative law and economics (and "legal origins")*. – Since the 1990s, comparative law and economics has developed into a specialty which has generated a large and growing body of scholarship.[1006] The essentially ancillary relationship between the two disciplines is outlined in subchapter II.iv. (ss. 40–43). Here, we take a closer look at the interdisciplinary use of economics, i.e., how comparatists have employed the economic analysis of law for their own purposes.

It is a truism that in any given jurisdiction the economic and the legal system are closely related. Comparatists have therefore long explained similarities and differences between laws inter alia by reference to underlying economic conditions in a general fashion. Yet, an economic understanding of law can also generate more specific insights, especially when laws and legal systems are compared under the paradigm of efficiency. This expands the more traditional approaches in two particular regards. It can bring "the scientific rigor and explanatory power of modern economics"[1007] to the comparative law table. And it entails a shift of perspective: comparative analysis is no longer based on the conception of law as a means to do justice between specific parties (ex post) but on law conceived as an instrument to generate incentives for more efficient social behavior (ex ante).

At the outset, it is important to recognize that comparatists have by and large refrained from subscribing to the full orthodoxy of mainstream law and economics.[1008] For the most part, they have stayed away from abstract model building and in particular from hegemonic methodological claims. They have rather used law and economics as a toolkit. Keeping an eye on the realities of law, they have usually proceeded in a more circumspect and balanced fashion than the members of the law and economics school.[1009] Comparatists have used the economic analysis of law for two major purposes: mainly better to explain the relationship between laws and legal systems, but sometimes also to support normative claims. We will look at these two purposes in turn.

Looking at law from an efficiency perspective can proffer explanations for several phenomena generally recognized in comparative law. For example, to the extent it is true that, as Zweigert and Kötz famously postulated, legal systems usually solve the same problem in the same, or at least in a similar, fashion (albeit often through different devices),[1010] the reason may be that the common solution is the most efficient one. In a similar vein, the pursuit of efficiency can drive legal transplants (*supra* iii., s. 349), either because legal systems import particular rules or institutions because of their efficiency (such as the common law trust)[1011] or simply because taking law from elsewhere is easier and cheaper than creating it at home from scratch. In addition, an efficiency analysis may shed light on the convergence or divergence of legal systems (*supra* A.iii., s. 333, be it that it helps to understand why they tend towards the same (efficient?) result or why they drift apart (abandoning inefficient solutions?). Economic analysis can elucidate the benefits of legal unification (mainly lower transaction costs) as well as its disadvantages (e.g., loss of competition). It can also generally highlight the obstacles impeding legal change, such as the costs of transitioning from one rule to another: changing legal rules may entail considerable transaction costs because introducing new rules may be effective only with a concomitant change of procedures or even institutions.

[1005] An example of putting linguistic perspectives directly to use for comparative law is Mitchell Lasser's study of the styles of judicial discourse in France and the United States: see e.g., *Lasser*, Comparative Law and Comparative Literature: A Project in Progress: Utah L.Rev. 471–524 (1997).

[1006] See, e.g., the collection of articles in *De Geest and Bergh* (eds.), Comparative Law and Economics (3 vol.) (Cheltenham 2004); in *De Geest* (ed.), Economics of Comparative Law (Cheltenham 2009); and in *Eisenberg and Ramello* (eds.), Comparative Law and Economics (online, Cheltenham 2016).

[1007] *Faust* (*supra* n. 73) 836, quoting *De Geest and Bergh* (*supra* n. 1006).

[1008] See *Kischel* (*supra* n. 286) 139–140.

[1009] See *Mattei* (*supra* n. 71).

[1010] *Zweigert and Kötz* (*supra* n. 3) 38.

[1011] See *Mattei* (*supra* n. 71) 147–177.

Efficiency arguments can also support normative claims. Comparative legal studies are often undertaken in pursuit of law reform, looking at various legal systems in search for the best solution to a problem. Of course, the determination of what is "best" requires a criterion for quality. This could be the fit with tradition and culture, social justice, or general fairness, though all these criteria are by necessity somewhat vague. Measuring the quality of legal solutions by their economic efficiency can promise greater precision. Efficiency then becomes the *tertium comparationis*. Scholars in comparative law and economics usually understand, however, that as a normative consideration efficiency is more important in some areas of law (especially market activities) than in others (such as personal and family affairs), and that it must always be balanced against other concerns. They have also recognized that the efficiency of legal rules is not, as mainstream economic analysis of law has often assumed, absolute but rather dependent on the specific legal environment and socio-cultural context.

The explanatory and the normative use of an economic perspective are combined when comparative law looks at legal systems as participants in a "law market",[1012] in particular, as competitors for acceptance by the users of law.[1013] Especially in an international context, private actors, such as business corporations, banks, or other investors, often determine which country's law shall govern their activities, e.g., by selecting the place of investment or through a choice-of-law, forum selection or arbitration clause. They can thus pick the legal framework that serves them best. Legal systems, in turn, have reason to compete for such clients because winning them can create jobs, generate tax revenue, and bring in fees for legal and other services. Recognizing this competitive relationship between legal systems can help to explain why countries (or international bodies) adopt certain rules, and it can provide normative arguments for change in a particular direction.

Since the late twentieth century, a combination of economic and comparative perspectives has also been common for many scholars of business law and market regulation. This is particularly true in the areas of corporate governance, but also of antitrust regimes, securities laws, foreign investment, and, more recently, tax law. Economic analyses of these fields have frequently looked at rules and institutions beyond the domestic orbit. The traditional focus was on the United States, Western Europe (including the United Kingdom), as well as Japan. More recently, attention has begun to shift to the emerging economies of China, India, and other non-western systems. While the respective scholarship usually does not use that term, it does constitute, so to speak, comparative law and economics in action.

The idea of a competition for business between legal systems is the backdrop of the so-called "legal origins" (or "doing business") debate that took place between comparatists and economists at the end of the twentieth and the beginning of the twenty-first centuries.[1014] In the late 1990s, a group of economists began to claim that the origin of a legal system in either the common law or the civil law tradition determines its friendliness towards economic development. In particular, they argued that legal systems originating in the Anglo-American tradition provide a better environment for economic growth than legal systems with a continental European heritage.[1015] This suggested, of course, that investors would be better off in countries belonging to the common law orbit than in jurisdictions in the civil law world. When the World Bank adopted this view in its *Doing Business* Reports in 2002 and subsequent years, this also implied that in reforming the law governing their economy developing countries are well-advised to borrow from the Anglo-American,

[1012] *Ribstein and O'Hara*, The Law Market (Oxford, New York 2009).

[1013] See, e.g., *Ogus*, The Economic Approach: Competition between Legal Systems: *Nelken and Örücü* (eds.), Comparative Law: A Handbook (Portland OR 2007) 155–167.

[1014] *Nicita and Benedettini*, Towards the Economics of Comparative Law: the *Doing Business* Debate: *Monateri* (ed.), Methods of Comparative Law (Cheltenham, Northampton MA 2012) 291–305.

[1015] *La Porta, Lopez de Silanes, Shleifer and Vishny* (*supra* n. 258) 1131–1150; *La Porta, Lopez de Silanes, Shleifer and Vishny* (*supra* n. 258) 1113–1155; *La Porta, Lopez de Silanes and Shleifer*, The Economic Consequences of Legal Origins: 46 J.Econ.Lit. 285–332 (2008).

rather than the continental European model. These claims of common law economic superiority took the comparative law community by surprise. Many comparatists protested vociferously, especially on the civil law side. They criticized the legal origins thesis (by and large correctly) as in many ways simplistic, blind to a host of essential determinants, unsupported by reliable evidence, and badly biased in favor of a US-centric view of the legal and economic universe.[1016] In their view, the legal origins thesis was not only based on an outdated dichotomy between civil and common law but also outright contrary to common sense – after all many countries belonging to the civil law tradition are among the richest in the world. In reaction, the economists moderated and modulated their position. Comparative lawyers eventually recognized the opportunity to reflect more deeply upon the utility of their own discipline for a better understanding of the dynamics of economic development.[1017] Perhaps the most important lesson to be drawn from the debate is that both sides can, and indeed have to, learn a lot from each other. The debate also raised fundamental methodological issues concerning the comparison of legal systems through coded data and statistical methods (*infra* C.iii., s. 381).

As even this brief summary shows, the label "comparative law and economics" masks a welter of ideas, purposes, directions, and issues. Whether there is sufficient overall coherence between them to think of comparative law and economics as a special (sub)"discipline" in its own right is debatable.[1018] It is perhaps more appropriate to think of comparative law and economics simply as the practice of using the tools of economic analysis for the purposes of comparative legal studies.[1019]

359. *Comparative law and religion.* – Law and religion have been intimately connected for millennia and they remain inextricably intertwined in many parts of the world today, perhaps most obviously in the Islamic sphere. Even in the cultural West, where law has been gradually secularized since the early modern period, much law currently in force has religious origins, and many of its underlying values have Judeo-Christian roots.[1020] The comparative study of law thus invites, and often necessitates, looking at religion. Comparatists have done this in two rather different ways.

One approach is the study of religious systems of law in their own right, especially those beyond the cultural West, such as Islamic law (*shari'a*), Jewish, Hindu, or Buddhist law. The standard books on the world's legal systems, families, or cultures have long included such religious regimes, albeit often as exotic additions to the hard core of Western systems. More specialized publications analyze them in greater detail. There is also is a plethora of book chapters and articles on innumerable particular issues. This literature is surveyed in IV.A.iii., s. 184.

The other approach looks at the connection between law and religion as related normative orders and practices. This approach is interdisciplinary in the sense that it focuses on the similarities and differences between law and religion, their common origins, mutual influence, and the inherent tensions between them. It is part of the trend towards the study of legal pluralism that has gained prominence in comparative law since the 1990s.[1021] Comparative law and religion as an interdisciplinary enterprise is thus largely a child of the early twenty-first century.[1022] It is the topic of this brief entry.

[1016] For a succinct summary, see *Caterina*, Comparative Law and Economics: *Smits* (ed.), Elgar Encyclopedia of Comparative Law (ed. 2 Cheltenham 2012) 191–207, 197–201; see also *Siems* (*supra* n. 852) 208–212.

[1017] See *Michaels* (ed.), Symposium on Legal Origins: 57 Am.J.Comp.L. 765–876 (2009); *Armour, Deakin, Lele and Siems*, How Do Legal Rules Evolve? Evidence from a Cross-Country Comparison of Shareholder, Creditor, and Worker Protection: 57 Am.J.Comp.L. 579–629 (2009).

[1018] For a critical discussion, see *Faust* (*supra* n. 73) 848–850.

[1019] *Idem*; *Kischel* (*supra* n. 286) 140.

[1020] See e.g. *Berman* (*supra* n. 264); *Berman*, Law and Revolution II: The Impact of the Protestant Reformation on the Western Legal Tradition (Cambridge MA 2003).

[1021] See, e.g., *Bottoni et al.* (eds.), Religious Rules, State Law, and Normative Pluralism – A Comparative Overview (Sprűger 2016).

[1022] There is, of course, a rich older literature, dating back to antiquity and the middle ages: see *Whitman* (*supra* n. 323) 736–738. In a sense, Max Weber's *Die protestantische Ethik und der "Geist" des Kapitalismus*: Idem, Gesammelte Aufsätze zut Rechtssoziologie (Tübingen 1920) 1–110, belongs to this genre as well.

At the beginning of the twenty-first century, the comparative study of the relationship between law and religion in the various parts of the world is of prime importance for several reasons. Among these reasons are the increasing influence of religion on law in many regions;[1023] the intensified contacts between different laws and religions which are caused by globalization and which create a dire need for mutual understanding and tolerance; and the fact that the great religions of the world are transnational orders that often command stronger allegiance and exert greater normative pull than nations and their secular laws. Thus comparative law's traditional focus on national legal systems, and the concomitant marginalization of religious laws, is missing a large and crucial part of the normative orders by which people are governed.[1024]

A good starting point for an exploration of the relationship between law and religion in a comparative context is to note their commonalities. Both are bodies of norms that require obedience from the members of their community and sanction transgressions. Both express values not only through rules but also through rituals and traditions. Both are usually based on authoritative texts which are interpreted by specialists. One can even say that both are "universal belief systems" to which people are willing to commit and for which they are ready to make sacrifices. In that sense, law itself can actually be regarded as a "civil religion", especially when it treats some of its texts, such as the Constitution of the United States, as quasi-sacred.[1025] A major difference is, of course, that religious and state-based legal norms often (though not always, see infra) derive their authority from different sources (divine order v. the state) and may be enforced by different authorities through different mechanisms.

A major challenge for comparative law and religion, but also a major source of insight, is the differences between various kinds of religions and the impact these differences can have on conceptions of law. For example, in the cultural West today, religion is in principle considered separate from law (in the sense of rules enforced by state authority); consequently, law is regarded as an essentially secular order. Yet, other religions, such as orthodox Judaism and Islam, make no categorical distinction between sacred and secular norms; the authority of law is always grounded in its divine origins. Thus, for the former religions the separation of church and state makes eminent sense; for the latter it is entirely unacceptable, if not unimaginable. In addition, religions like Judaism, Christianity, and Islam, which are based on the belief in an all-powerful God who created and controls the universe, tend to regard law as an important, often even as the primary, instrument of social conflict resolution. Yet, other religions, such as Buddhism and Hinduism, which focus on inner spirituality and withdrawal from worldly affairs, emphasize conflict resolution though reconciliation and mediation. Thus, for the former religions, law is an ideal, and they encourage its use; for the latter, it is a necessary evil the use of which should be avoided whenever possible. Furthermore, some religions, like Christianity, emphasize "orthodoxy", i.e., require mainly that their members truly *believe* in its dogmas. Others, like Islam, emphasize "orthopraxy", i.e., require mainly that their members *act* in accordance with its dogmas. Under the influence of the former, the law tends to rely heavily on subjective elements, such as intent, fault, and good faith; where the latter have shaped the law, correct performance of external acts, such as prayer, rituals, and compliance with dietary norms, is of prime importance.[1026] Given the close connection between law and religion, understanding these (and other) fundamental differences is obviously crucial for the comparative study of legal orders.

Since the beginning of the twenty-first century, scholars have approached the interdisciplinary study of comparative law and religion in a variety

[1023] Witness, for example, the growing importance of religious courts in many jurisdictions: see *Kischel* (ed.), Religiöses Recht und religiöse Gerichte als Herausforderung des Staates: Rechtspluralismus in vergleichender Perspektive (Tübingen 2016).

[1024] Ralf Michaels even claimed that "how to deal with so-called religious laws" is "[w]ithout doubt, the greatest challenge for comparative law today", *Michaels* (*supra* n. 324) 99.

[1025] *Berman* (*supra* n. 322) 744–746.

[1026] *Whitman* (*supra* n. 323).

of ways. Some have explored the meaning and role of law with regard to each of the world's great religions,[1027] or, conversely, the role of religion (and faith) in law.[1028] Some have advocated that comparative law "explore the common features of the major legal systems of the world in order to determine their source in common features of the major belief systems in world".[1029] This agenda is based on the conviction that the recognition of such shared features can ultimately uncover "a world civil religion",[1030] common to all mankind. Others have argued that working towards mutual toleration requires an understanding of the various religions' deep structures, especially their conception and practice of ritual (which, in turn, influences the role of ritual in law). This necessitates going back to the historical origins of the world's great religions in the so-called "axial age", i.e., the middle of the first millennium B.C. During that era, older forms of religion based mainly on magic were gradually replaced by belief systems incorporating ethical principles, albeit in a variety of ways.[1031] A perhaps even more ambitious plan is the development of a "postsecular comparative law".[1032] Pointing out that defining "law" in a strictly secular fashion is a particular Western view not necessarily shared by other cultures, this agenda seeks to replace the discipline's traditional state-centered approach with the comparison of both secular and religious laws as co-equal and closely intertwined topics. This requires overcoming the common perception of religious laws as less developed than, and fundamentally different from, (state-created) law.

If comparative law actually comes to integrate the study of religious laws into its mainstream activities, comparatists will face the daunting challenge sufficiently to comprehend religions from way beyond their cultural orbit and experience. The familiar problem whether outsiders to a tradition can ever sufficiently understand it will thus present itself in particularly stark fashion. At the minimum, comparatists need close and constant cooperation, not only with scholars of religion but also with members of the respective religious communities.

v. *Critical Approaches*

360. *Introduction and overview.* – Since around 1990, mainstream comparative law has come under growing attack from critics who have challenged the discipline's time-honored assumptions and canon in a more or less radical fashion. The birth-hour of a critical approach to comparative law was the publication of *Critical Comparisons: Re-thinking Comparative Law* by German scholar Günter Frankenberg in 1985, an article which has since become a classic.[1033] Arguing from a post-modern perspective, Frankenberg laid out many of the basic themes which then dominated the discussion for decades to come. He first claimed that established comparative legal studies suffered from various fundamental ills. On the most general level, the discipline lacked "self-critical and methodological guidance"[1034] and displayed a tendency to oversimplify complexity. More specifically, it was "legocentric", i.e., uncritically believing in law "as a given and necessity, as the neutral path to ideal, rational or optimal conflict resolution and ultimately to a social legal order guaranteeing peace and harmony".[1035] To make matters worse, the discipline rested on an unduly narrow, formalist, and positivist conception of law. In addition, comparatists presented themselves as objective and disinterested observers pursuing value-neutral research and writing; this led them to present their culturally biased viewpoints as objective truth, causing hidden ethnocentric assumptions and biases. Their leading model was, of course, Western law; this implied a constant

[1027] *Huxley* (ed.), Religion, Law and Tradition: Comparative Studies in Religious Law (London 2002); see also *Doe*, Comparative Religious Law. Judaism, Christianity, Islam (Cambridge 2018).

[1028] "Comparative Law, Faith, and Religion" was the general theme of the Annual Meeting of the American Society of Comparative Law in Washington D.C. on October 26–28 2017, where more than three dozen papers were presented.

[1029] *Berman* (*supra* n. 322) 746.

[1030] *Idem* 750.

[1031] *Whitman* (*supra* n. 323) Whitman builds in part on the work of *Fikentscher*, Modes of Thought: A Study in the Anthropology of Law and Religion (ed. 2 Tübingen 2004).

[1032] *Michaels* (*supra* n. 324).

[1033] *Frankenberg* (*supra* n. 237).

[1034] *Idem* 421.

[1035] *Idem* 445.

marginalization of "other" legal systems and cultures. Finally, comparatists were seriously biased in favor of similarity, or even uniformity, of law. Frankenberg then advocated a series of changes. Most fundamentally, he urged comparatists to embrace a "political theory of law",[1036] in particular to import the lessons of (US-American) legal realism and critical legal theory. He asked comparative law scholars to recognize and accept that they are not only observers of, but also participants in, global law-making processes and to become aware of their concomitant responsibility; to stop "confusing the present content of (Western) ideas and concepts with the criteria of a universal truth and logic"[1037]; to overcome their ethnocentrism through critical self-reflection; to embrace difference; and to "experience and appreciate ambiguity and heterogeneity".[1038]

Many of these themes were further developed at a large conference held about a decade later at the University of Utah.[1039] Since then, critical approaches to comparative law have blossomed into a broad and diversified body of scholarship which constitutes a small library in its own right. They can be addressed here only in a very summary fashion.

We can distinguish two major branches. One is formed by the work of scholars associated with the "critical legal studies" movement that developed in the United States in the 1970s through the 1990s; it is mainly concerned with the political and ideological character of law. The other branch is rooted in (often postmodern) cultural and literary studies; it looks at law primarily as an expression of culture and as a discourse. In addition, we will briefly consider two more specific dimensions, i.e., studies on post-colonial law and the charge of legal orientalism. To be sure, all these approaches overlap substantially. While presenting them separately is thus somewhat artificial, it helps to attain a modicum of clarity in an area prone to confuse an outside observer.

361. *Critical legal studies: law as politics.* – In the 1970s and 1980s, a loosely affiliated group of younger US-American academics developed radical critiques of existing legal scholarship and practice. Influenced by Marxism, Socialism, and (mainly European) critical philosophy, they challenged primarily the traditional separation of law from politics. Pointing to the inevitably political nature of all law, they emphasized its use as an instrument of power to protect capitalist interests, to perpetuate existing hierarchies, and to justify oppression of the underprivileged.[1040] The original focus of this "critical legal studies" movement was almost purely domestic. Yet, when globalization became a dominant paradigm in the 1990s, some of the most prominent "crits" discovered an interest the international dimensions of law; in part motivated by Günter Frankenberg's article, they eventually turned to comparative law as well. At home mainly at Harvard Law School, they built a network of critical scholars located not only at elite US-American law faculties but also in many foreign countries, especially in Mediterranean Europe, Latin America, and Africa. Thus, this branch of comparative law critique is essentially an internationalized version of the earlier critical legal studies movement. As such, it has been rooted primarily in, and dominated by influence from, scholars and institutions in the United States.[1041]

The core of this critique is that traditional comparative law fails to recognize, or at least to admit to, the political nature of law, the impact of ideology, and thus the inevitably political and ideological implications of comparative legal studies themselves. Since the rise of the discipline in the post-World-War II era, according to the critics, comparative lawyers have usually proclaimed to seek knowledge just for knowledge's

[1036] *Idem* 452.

[1037] *Idem* 414.

[1038] *Idem* 423.

[1039] Symposium: New Approaches to Comparative Law: Utah L.Rev. 254–663 (1997). In an almost simultaneous symposium, comparatists closer to the mainstream voiced their own, though on the whole less radical, critiques, *Mattei and Reimann* (eds.), Symposium: New Directions in Comparative Law: 46 Am.J. Comp.L. 597–756 (1998).

[1040] *Kelman*, A Guide to Critical Legal Studies (Cambridge MA, London 1987).

[1041] As Ugo Mattei has duly noted, these critics are also either at home in, or strongly connected with, American academic institutions of power and privilege, their leftist predilections notwithstanding; see *Mattei* (*supra* n. 252) 821–823.

sake and so styled themselves as politically neutral technicians in a politically neutral enterprise. In fact, they have come to associate professionalization and scholarly credibility with the denial and rejection of any political function. In reality, however, they do play a political role, whether knowingly and willingly or not. "A discipline like comparative law participates in global governance when people practising the discipline do things – decide things, place some and not other knowledge in play, argue in one way and not in another – which have consequences that can be associated either with the ideological positions in the broader society through which political debate happens or with social interests which we understand to be in political contestation."[1042] In short, the mainstream comparatists' "escape from politics…remains a wish".[1043]

A related charge is that traditional comparative law suffers from Western-centrism. It uncritically subscribes to the grand narrative of the great Western tradition rooted mainly in Roman law, thus overlooking and marginalizing the important (multicultural) contributions of other non-Western cultures.[1044] Worse, comparatists often help to maintain Western hegemony, for example when their work is used by global financial institutions, such as the World Bank and the International Monetary Fund, to impose Western models of law on developing countries.[1045] Thus, the "no politics-politics of comparative law"[1046] are ultimately misleading and obscure responsibility. The discipline should acknowledge that "comparatists are people with projects – political, professional, and personal projects of cosmopolitan governance".[1047]

In addition, the critics have accused comparatists of focusing too narrowly on positive law instead of exploring the differences in "legal consciousness" or "mentality" (a central topos of the critical legal studies movement). In particular, traditional comparatists tend to overlook the important role of political ideology as a factor explaining similarities and differences. Accordingly, comparative law should (also) be about "ideological conflict as it translates into the activities of jurists".[1048]

Finally, and most generally, critical scholars have demanded to use comparative law as a "subversive discipline", i.e., to disrupt, de-center, and thus radically challenge established tenets that have gone unquestioned for too long. These tenets include mainstream methodologies, such as functionalism, as well as fundamental conceptions shaping one's own legal system, e.g., notions of constitutionalism or due process.[1049] Such a radical questioning of established constructs also "paves the way for a more political critique: however immemorial their history may appear, these constructs are in fact harnessed to a variety of ideological ends",[1050] including concrete global governance projects.[1051]

As even fellow-travelers of the movement have noted, "[t]he Critical legal scholars' characterization of mainstream comparative law is not beyond challenge, the novelty of their critique is not always free from doubt, and their claims to new discoveries are not always fully convincing".[1052] For example, while the charge that mainstream comparative law is unaware of the law's political implications is by and large warranted with regard to traditional studies of private law, it is hardly sustainable in comparative constitutional law. The critique that the discipline has stuck to a pos-

[1042] *Kennedy* (*supra* n. 186) 408–409.

[1043] *Idem* 353.

[1044] For a provocative challenge to that narrative, see *Monateri*, Black Gaius. A Quest for the Multicultural Origins of the "Western Legal Tradition": 51 Hastings L.J. 479–555 (2000).

[1045] See also *infra* s. 364 (legal orientalism).

[1046] *Idem* 354. David Kennedy ascribed this attitude at least in part to the German refugee scholars' "intellectual and political trauma", *idem* 371.

[1047] *Kennedy*, New Approaches to Comparative Law: Comparativism and International Governance: Utah L.R. 545–637, 551 (1997).

[1048] *Kennedy* (*supra* n. 1047) 553.

[1049] *Muir-Watt* (*supra* n. 731); see also *Fletcher* (*supra* n. 731).

[1050] *Muir-Watt*, Further Terrains for Subversive Comparison: the Field of Global Governance and the Public/Private Divide: *Monateri* (ed.), Methods of Comparative Law (Cheltenham, Northampton MA 2012) 270–282.

[1051] *Idem* 273–274.

[1052] *Mattei* (*supra* n. 252) 807.

itivist notion of law is scarcely justified in light of the many broadly contextualized analyses by even committed functionalists. And the critics' emphasis on legal mentalities as well as on ideology is not truly original because it has long been part of the traditional concept of the various legal systems' "style".[1053] In short, the critique sometimes suffers from caricature, overgeneralization, and an unreflected belief in the novelty of its ideas. At the same time, however, it has also brought to light inherent cognitive biases, serious methodological weaknesses, and, more generally, a disconcerting paucity of self-reflection in the discipline as it stood at the end of the twentieth century.

362. *Postmodern cultural critique: indeterminacy and pluralism.* – Also beginning in the 1990s, several critical comparative law scholars began to draw on mid- to late twentieth-century cultural and literary theory, especially on the post-structuralist and post-modern thought[1054] of Jacques Derrida (1930–2004), such as his notion of "deconstruction". Accepting that our beliefs and perceptions are inevitably shaped by our own dispositions as well as our language, these scholars reject the possibility of a single, objective truth (i.e., the enlightenment idea that human reason can ascertain generally valid knowledge). Instead, they embrace the belief in a virtually endless variety of subjective understandings. Thus texts, including legal texts, are inherently indeterminate – they cannot have a single inherent (objective, true, etc.) meaning but are open to as many interpretations as there are readers. All these understandings and interpretations are culturally contingent. As a result, law must ultimately be understood not as merely a system of rules but rather as a form of culture, specifically as a culturally conditioned discourse. The consequences of these credos for the comparative study of law are of course far-reaching.

To begin with, the traditional discipline's focus on authoritative legal texts looks like an unduly reductive exercise in legal positivism which fails to recognize the law's inherent indeterminacy. Instead of comparing principles or rules, and instead of analyzing them as instruments fulfilling a particular "function", comparative law scholars should look to legal cultures and seek to understand their respective "cognitive structures" and "*mentalités*" (see *supra* iv., s. 355).[1055] According to the critics, without such a cultural perspective attempts to comprehend other legal systems are hopelessly superficial, and attempts to facilitate communication between systems are doomed to failure. To make matters worse, the traditional assumption that a member of one legal system (or family) can truly understand members of another is unwarranted, if not outright naïve. Critical scholars have drawn various conclusions from that skepticism: at minimum, they have demanded that in approaching other systems "the impact of the self, the observer's perspective and experience, [be] scrupulously taken into account;[1056] others have called for a full-scale "cultural immersion";[1057] some have even taken the radical position that a jurist from one legal culture can never attain an insider's understanding of another.[1058] Last, but certainly not least, critics have chastised the mainstream's search for similarity and its drive for legal unification (as well as its assumption that legal systems are converging) as fundamentally misguided.[1059] Since the critics perceive legal cultures as largely unique, they have insisted that comparative studies focus on diversity rather than likeness. Indeed, scholars should celebrate legal pluralism and multiculturalism. At the end of the day, comparative law "has to be an exercise in difference".[1060]

[1053] *Zweigert and Kötz* (*supra* n. 3) 67–71.

[1054] There is no uniform definition of "postmodern", nor an agreement about the meaning of the term among the critics of comparative law; the – by now classic – discourse on postmodern thought is *Lyotard*, La condition postmoderne: rapport sur le savoir (Paris 1979), translated by *Bennington and Massumi*, The Postmodern Condition: A Report on Knowledge (Manchester 1979).

[1055] *Legrand* (*supra* n. 784) 60.

[1056] *Frankenberg* (*supra* n. 237) 414.

[1057] *Curran* (*supra* n. 7) 43–92.

[1058] *Legrand* (*supra* n. 784) 75–78.

[1059] See, e.g., *Fischer-Lescano and Teubner* (*supra* n. 742).

[1060] *Frankenberg* (*supra* n. 237) 414; see also *Curran*, Dealing in Difference: Comparative Law's Potential for Broadening Legal Perspectives: Am.J.Comp.L. 46 (1998) 657–668. For a succinct summary and discussion of what may be termed "difference theory", see *Hyland* (*supra* n. 746) 194–196.

As with the critical legal studies approach, the postmodern cultural critique of the discipline has met with counter-critique.[1061] Some of the iconoclasts' claims are overblown, others not nearly as original as their proponents seem to believe. For example, one can fairly debate the degree to which the critics' charge of positivism was warranted;[1062] and, surely, a cultural approach to comparative law has long been part of the discipline's tradition.[1063] In a similar vein, comparatists recognized for many decades that comprehending foreign legal systems requires overcoming serious barriers.[1064] Finally, the discipline has not been entirely blind towards the sometimes deeply rooted differences between legal systems, occasional (and unfortunate) claims to near-universal similarity notwithstanding.[1065] Still, again as in the case of the political critics, the postmodern cultural critique has "rightly underlined the critical potential of comparative legal studies"[1066] and justly pointed to serious weaknesses of many traditional approaches and methods. It is true, for example, that blackletter comparison and even the functional approach tend to disregard, or at least dangerously to downplay, the cultural aspects of law and the importance of legal mentalities – the traditional literature often failed sufficiently to emphasize how even identical rules can be understood in radically different ways by different legal cultures. Also, the critics' emphasis on difference is a healthy antidote to the discipline's traditional penchant for similarity, even though it remains unclear why a general turn towards the former should be preferable over favoring the latter. Finally, it must be recognized that the approach comparing legal cultures and mentalities has generated important studies which have enriched our knowledge about topics as diverse as, e.g., judicial decision-making, criminal justice, and privacy rights.[1067]

363. *Colonialism: imposed laws as "practices of violence".* – The critical approach to comparative legal studies becomes more narrowly focused where it addresses the imposition of Western law on (former) colonies and its consequences. In part, this approach simply pushes the discipline to look beyond the Western orbit to other, less developed, parts of the world.[1068] Yet, its main thrust is a critique of how comparatists' have traditionally portrayed the role of modern law in the colonial context. As the critics pointed out, comparative legal studies have usually seen the export of the civil or common law to the respective colonies in a positive light: as a project of modernization which helped to emancipate the local populations from more primitive states of existence. Yet, this "master narrative of the progressive Euro-centric legality"[1069] is problematic in at least three regards.

First, it uncritically believes in the superiority of the exported Western law and thus fails to afford "equal discursive dignity to non Euro-American traditions".[1070] In fact, this view assumes that "the masters and makers of the modern law have nothing worthy to learn from the discursive traditions of the Euro-American tradition's

[1061] See especially the thorough and thoughtful analysis by *Peters and Schwenke*, Comparative Law beyond Post-Modernism: 49 I.C.L.Q. 800–834 (2000).

[1062] See, e.g., American Journal of Comparative Law (Special Issue), What We Write about When We Write about Comparative Law: Pierre Legrand's Critique in Discussion: 65 Am.J.Comp.L. 1–255 (2017).

[1063] The studies of comparative legal cultures already capture much of what the critics demand (see *supra* VI.B.iv.ss. 354-355. So does the – by now well-established – concept of "legal traditions" (see *supra* B.ii. s. 343).

[1064] If, as some cultural critics have asserted, legal mentalities were entirely incommensurable, communication across their boundaries would be entirely impossible – which it is not. The phenomenon of legal transplants shows that legal systems interact all the time. Often systems are related also because they are subject to the same inter- or supranational influence.

[1065] *Infra* VI.C.i., s. 370.

[1066] *Peters and Schwenke* (*supra* n. 1061) 830.

[1067] See, e.g., *Lasser* (*supra* n. 393). *Whitman*, The Two Western Cultures of Privacy: Dignity v. Liberty: 114 Yale L.J. (2004) 1151–1221; *Whitman* (*supra* n. 553).

[1068] In that regard, it overlaps with the historical work on the relationship between the imposed and the indigenous (customary and religious) law and the resultant legal pluralism: see, e.g., *Benton*, Law and Colonial Cultures (Cambridge 2002); *Benton*, Legal Pluralism and Empires, 1550–1800 (New York 2013).

[1069] *Baxi*, The Colonial Heritage: *Munday and Legrand*, Comparative Legal Studies: Traditions and Transitions (Cambridge 2003) 46–75, 56.

[1070] *Idem* 50. See also *infra* 364.

Other" because the local populations simply lack "any potential for conceptions of legality, the rule of law, equality and human rights".[1071] These deficiencies were in part due to the fact that the indigenous populations lived according to (unwritten) customs which their European masters either refused to accept as real "law" or turned into law by writing them down, inevitably changing them in the process, e.g., by couching them in Western terms.[1072] Second, the traditional view overlooks (or even hides) that imposing Western legality often amounted to "practices of violence"[1073] – or at least served to justify them. "Contrary to the progress narrative, the gift of law inscribed as a heritage emerges as a repertoire of 'tactics' of repressive governance".[1074] Third, comparatists largely failed to recognize that the imposed Western legality was essentially "predatory",[1075] i.e., that it created the foundations for the economic exploitation of the colonies. "Progress" often meant facilitation of capitalist enterprise, usually to the detriment of the local population. In summary, traditional comparative law has looked at the situation in colonial empires almost entirely from the perspective of the winners (in the metropolis), while disregarding its effects on the losers (on the periphery).

These effects are not just matters of history but often persist in shaping legal structures and ideologies all the way to the present.[1076] For example, they cast a long shadow "in the forms of apparatuses of governance and in the accoutrements which adorn manifestations of supreme executive power".[1077] They are also (at least partially) responsible for the widespread popular distrust in former colonial societies of the legal system, an attitude which is based on the – often painful – historical experience that law serves mainly those in power.

364. *Legal orientalism.* – A closely related critique is that comparatists have tended to "orientalize" non-Western legal systems and cultures. The argument is based on the now classical study of Edward Said (1935–2003).[1078] Said criticized the Western (i.e., occidental) representation of the Eastern (i.e., oriental) cultures as heavily romanticized, largely false, and ultimately discriminatory. It served not only to bolster Western feelings of superiority but also to justify the colonial powers' domination, especially of the Middle East.

Similar biases and effects can be said to underlie much of mainstream comparative law. Comparative studies have traditionally been conducted from a Western perspective. For example, they are based (consciously or unconsciously) on Western conceptions of "law" – which are not necessarily shared everywhere. They also assume (openly or implicitly) that "due process" is indispensable for a proper system of government – again, an assumption not necessarily accepted by other cultures, such as China. These attitudes can lead comparatists to regard legal systems not sharing Western concepts and values as either intrinsically inferior or at least underdeveloped, e.g., because they do not (yet) have "law" or "due process".[1079]

As a result, Western legal scholars often see the need to export their "progressive" Western law (or, more generally, forms of government) to "backward" countries in order to modernize their legal systems. This export can be pursued through voluntary programs or as a condition of economic assistance from the global financial institutions – or even by military force.

To be sure, Western comparatists cannot completely overcome the ways in which they have been programmed. Thus, they will always approach other cultures with certain Western assumptions. But they should at least be keenly aware of their tendency to "orientalize" other legal cultures and strive to approach and evaluate them on their own terms as far as possible.

365. *The effect of the critical approaches.* – The arrival of the iconoclasts in the 1990s soon led to a division of comparative legal studies into the largely traditionalist mainstream on the one hand (best represented by Zweigert and Kötz's treatise[1080]) and the often postmodern critical approaches on the other (best represented by the

[1071] *Idem* 50, 57.

[1072] See *Bennett* (*supra* n. 337) 654–652.

[1073] *Baxi* (*supra* n. 1069) 49.

[1074] *Idem* 55.

[1075] *Idem* 65.

[1076] See, e.g., *Esquirol* (*supra* n. 880).

[1077] *Baxi* (*supra* n. 1069) 53.

[1078] *Said*, Orientalism (New York 1978).

[1079] *Ruskola* (*supra* n. 293).

[1080] *Zweigert and Kötz* (*supra* n. 3)

critical legal scholars and the cultural critics). To be sure, there was considerable overlap between these camps, but for decades many scholars have identified with one or the other.

Communication between these two camps was slow to start. In part, this was due to the often inaccessible and abstract style of the critical contributions. They frequently proceeded on a high level of generality, leaving readers wondering how their ideas should actually be applied in practice and what new results they could really generate. They often borrowed heavily from other disciplines (especially philosophy, language studies, and the social sciences) without providing proper explanations, and they sometimes used jargon annoying to outsiders. In addition, the critiques often suffered from overgeneralizations, sometimes struck a separatist note, and occasionally evinced a condescending attitude. In part, however, the initial lack of communication was also due to the mainstream scholars' reluctance seriously to consider radical critiques of their traditional assumptions and practices.

Since the beginning of the twenty-first century, however, and in part simply due to generational shifts, the critical approaches have gradually become an integral part of the discipline's standard repertoire. This has entailed wide, though not unanimous, recognition that the critics have made many important contributions to the development of the discipline. Their "hermeneutic of suspicion"[1081] has awakened especially younger comparative law scholars to the traditional directions' limitations and weaknesses. Thus, a few decades on, the discipline's mainstream at the end of the last century – aptly caricaturized as "the country and western tradition"[1082] – looks amazingly uncritical vis-à-vis its assumptions, unjustly biased in favor of similarity, overly sanguine about understanding foreign legal cultures, and at times simply self-congratulatory. To the extent that has changed, it is in no small part due to the critical approaches' impact over time. Precisely because of this impact, however, much of the erstwhile radical critique is directed at assumptions, methods, and biases that the majority of comparatists no longer embrace.

C. SPECIFIC METHODS[1083]

366. *From ignorance to pluralism.* – For most of the twentieth century, comparatists showed fairly little interest in the methodology of their discipline.[1084] Until ca. 1970, treatises by and large ignored questions of method. In 1971, Konrad Zweigert and Hein Kötz devoted a chapter of their book to "The Method of Comparative Law", but they immediately disavowed any ambition to delve deeply into the matter and presented little more than a discourse on the virtues of the functionalist approach as well as some practical advice on comparative research.[1085] Since their treatise soon became the globally leading introduction to the discipline, their reluctance to pursue methodological questions set the tone for the closing decades of the twentieth century (*supra* III.E.ii., s. 159). It is true that in 1972 Léontin-Jean Constantinesco published a whole volume on the comparative method,[1086] but his work was largely ignored by the discipline at large even though it was soon translated into French, then still a common working language in the field. Thus, in the post-World War II decades, the dominant functional method remained largely unchallenged, and beyond it comparatists mostly made do with a combination of "sound judgment, common sense, or… intuition".[1087] Perhaps they were also afraid to ask hard methodological questions for fear that

[1081] *Mattei* (*supra* n. 252) 821.

[1082] *Twining* (*supra* n. 6) 21–76; see also *Twining* (*supra* n. 246) 184–189.

[1083] Some of the classic texts on the methods of comparative law are collected in *Zweigert and Puttfarken* (*supra* n. 153). A more recent collection of essays on methods is *Monateri* (ed.) Methods of Comparative Law (Cheltenham, Northampton MA 2012). See also *Samuel*, An Introduction to Comparative Law Theory and Method (Oxford, Portland OR 2014).

[1084] But see the (by now classical) texts collected in *Zweigert and Puttfarken* (*supra* n. 153).

[1085] *Zweigert and Kötz* (*supra* n. 3) 31–47. As an opening volley, they cited Gustav Radbruch's famous bon mot that disciplines engaging in a lot of methodological reflection tend to be "sick disciplines" ("kranke Wissenschaften"), *idem* at 31.

[1086] *Constantinesco* (*supra* n. 681).

[1087] *Zweigert and Kötz* (*supra* n. 3) 33.

there might be no satisfactory answers. Be that as it may, most twentieth-century comparatists remained "weirdly innocent of methodological self-reflection".[1088]

In the early twenty-first century, however, methodology suddenly became a hot topic. The rapid expansion of comparative legal studies (*supra* IV.), the new challenges presented by globalization after the end of the cold war, and the growing influence of postmodern and critical thought combined to trigger an extensive theoretical discussion as well as to instigate the production of a substantial literature.[1089] At times, this methodological discussion has taken on a life of its own, and its pay-off for the practice of comparative law is not always beyond cavil. It has been duly pointed out that many comparative studies have produced excellent work without much methodological head-scratching.[1090]

Still, the discussion of the new century's first two decades produced three important results. It brought to light the inherent limitations and weaknesses of the dominant method, i.e., functionalism (*infra* i., ss. 368–373). It made comparatists more aware of the large variety of methods at their disposal, as well as more conscious of their strengths and weaknesses. And it generated a near consensus that an agreement on a single method, or even on a limited canon of methods, is impossible. In fact, most comparatists today consider such an agreement not even desirable because the discipline's various approaches, uses, and projects call for a broad variety of methods. As a result, early twenty-first-century comparative law has come to embrace largely unbridled methodological pluralism in both theory and practice. As Jürgen Basedow explained, most of the methods are quite compatible, and the choice of a specific method should be determined by the specific kind and object of the study undertaken.[1091] There have been occasional calls for some agreement on at least a common methodological framework[1092] but they have apparently had little impact.

It is not possible here to render a full account of the recent methodological debates. After a brief discussion of the basic process of comparison, we will instead focus on three specific, and particularly prominent, methods: functionalism, which has dominated the discipline since the middle of the twentieth century; common core research, which is connected to past and present unification projects; and numerical comparative law, which has become increasingly popular since the turn of the century.

367. *The basic process of comparison.* – Before we turn to these three particular topics, we must take a brief look at the fundamental operation of comparing (law) because that is common ground for virtually all more specific methods.[1093] Perhaps surprisingly, throughout the twentieth century, the question of what exactly it means to compare was rarely seriously discussed, not to mention conclusively answered.

On the most basic level, the matter is actually quite simple. Comparing essentially means juxtaposing two (or more) objects (such as apples and oranges) in order to understand how they relate to each other and whether (more precisely: to what degree) they are similar or different. Of course, this immediately leads to the question: in regard to *what*? Comparing objects always requires reference to a specific criterion (such as color, taste, nutritional value or price). This criterion is commonly called the *tertium*

[1088] *Whitman* (*supra* n. 750) 325.

[1089] *Van Hoecke* (*supra* n. 252); *Monateri* (ed.), Methods of Comparative Law (Cheltenham 2012); *Samuel* (*supra* n. 1083); *Scarciglia,* Método y Comparación Juridica (Madrid 2018); *Kischel* (*supra* n. 286) 92–216; *Jansen* (*supra* n. 1) 291–319; *Michaels*, The Functional Method of Comparative Law: *Reimann and Zimmermann* (eds.), The Oxford Handbook of Comparative Law (ed. 2 Oxford 2019) 345–389. The volume by *Legrand and Munday* (*supra* n. 252) also deals with methodological issues in a broader sense. A voluminous collection of writing on comparative law methodology (in a fairly broad sense) is the (online) anthology by *Adams, Husa and Oderkerk* (eds.), Comparative Law Methodology (Cheltenham 2017).

[1090] *Kischel* (*supra* n. 286) 92.

[1091] As far as I can see, Basedow was also the first to point out the influence of the demand side of comparative law: *Basedow* (*supra* n. 683) 821–857.

[1092] See, e.g., *Oderkerk*, The Need for a Methodological Framework for Comparative Legal Research, RabelsZ 79 (2015) 589–623.

[1093] For a much more extensive, thorough, and sophisticated analysis, see Jansen (*supra* n. 1).

comparationis: it is the "common comparative denominator"[1094] which determines what we are looking for when juxtaposing the objects in question. For example, if we compare civil procedure in different jurisdictions, we can do so with regard to the proceedings' length, cost, the capability of finding the truth or effectiveness in ending disputes. One can also chose a theoretical model or an ideal type as the crucial reference point and then measure how much the laws compared deviate from that model.[1095]

It is important to note that the *tertium comparationis* is not objectively given. It is chosen by the comparatist. The choice is inevitably normative: it reflects a judgment about what is important – at least to the person undertaking the comparison. It is also shaped by the comparatist's position, predilection, and purpose – an economist interested in efficiency and a philosopher interested in justice will compare civil procedure in two jurisdictions according to different criteria – and thus very differently. To be sure, the choice of the *tertium comparationis* may be unreflected (or even unconscious), though that is likely to entail lack of focus and to confuse the reader.[1096]

Comparison can, and often does, use multiple reference points, i.e., juxtapose laws under multiple perspectives. Obviously, this leads to more complex comparisons, but it can also generate more sophisticated and nuanced results. For example, if certain laws are alike in some regards but different in others, one can try to draw conclusions about the (perhaps causal) relationship between the various criteria employed.

i. *Functionalism*

368. *Introduction*. – Functionalism is a method designed primarily for "micro-comparison" (*supra* A.ii., ss. 323–325), i.e., for the comparison of specific elements of legal systems. It was developed in reaction to the once prevalent "dogmatic method" which compared laws (especially rules and concepts) as such, i.e., in the abstract. The basic idea of the functional method is that these elements must be compared with reference to their function as responses to particular social problems. This function thus becomes the comparisons' crucial reference point, the *tertium comparationis*.

Thus, the process of comparison first needs to identify the problem at hand – a frequently used example is how to determine whether a promise is legally binding (i.e., an enforceable contract). Then the comparatist must analyze how different legal systems solve it – e.g., by requiring indicia of seriousness, such as certain formalities or some kind of mutuality of promises. Finally, he or she should compare the results produced by the respective rules, etc., in order to determine whether the rules are (functionally) alike or different. In this manner, the functional method can recognize, for example, that legal systems often solve similar problems through different mechanisms (e.g., that one imposes strict liability for defective products while another establishes a virtually insurmountable presumption of negligence). It can also show that some systems seek to solve a problem through law (e.g., litigation), while others use non-legal means (e.g., social pressure).

Around the middle of the twentieth century, functionalism became generally prominent in various disciplines, such as sociology and anthropology. Yet, as a method particularly for comparative law it is essentially a product of German legal scholarship. Its deeper roots lie in the late-nineteenth-century turn towards a concept of law as a means to an end (especially in the work of Rudolf von Jhering), i.e., to an instrumental conception of law. The functional method's origins for comparative studies in particular lie mainly in Ernst Rabel's (1874–1955) work in private international law (conflict of laws).[1097] Subsequently, Max Rheinstein postulated that comparatists must generally work in a problem-oriented, i.e. functionalist, manner, though he did not proffer a real theory of functionalism.[1098]

[1094] Őrücü, Methodology of Comparative Law: *Smits* (ed.), Elgar Encyclopedia of Comparative Law (ed. 2 Cheltenham, Northampton MA 2012) 570–576, 561.

[1095] *Jansen* (*supra* n. 1) 300–302.

[1096] *Idem* 299–300.

[1097] See *Graziadei*, The Functionalist Heritage: *Legrand and Munday* (eds), Comparative Legal Studies: Traditions and Transitions (Cambridge, New York 2003) 100–128, 104–106.

[1098] *Rheinstein,* Comparative Law and Conflict of Laws in Germany: 2 U.Chi.L.Rev. (1934) 232–269, 248–250.

The method was widely popularized when Konrad Zweigert and Hein Kötz adopted it in their treatise in the 1970s and beyond. Their elaboration on the functional method has since become the standard text on the topic, in part because it summarizes and illustrates it in just a few pages.[1099] Due to the global influence of their work, their claim that functionality is the "basic methodological principle of all comparative law" put the functionalist approach at front and center for decades to come.[1100] Thus the functional method has often been identified with the traditional approach shaped by Zweigert and Kötz's treatise *tout court*, by both its adherents and its critics.[1101] At least in part, this explains the enormous amounts of ink that have been spilled over the functional method.

Despite its admirable brevity and force, Zweigert and Kötz's text has caused great mischief because it carelessly combined their basic idea of functionalism with two other elements: the claim to functionalism's methodological prominence, if not exclusivity, for *all* of comparative law; and the (in)famous *presumptio similitudinis*, i.e., the postulate that legal systems usually face the same problems and arrive at similar solutions. Neither element is integral to the functional method itself, but both have routinely been associated with it. This, in turn, has caused enormous confusion in the discussion because arguments for or against the method itself have been mixed up with those for or against the other two elements.[1102] Here we will keep these elements separate. We will first focus on the functional method as such, including its promises and pitfalls, and then turn to the other two claims.

369. *The functional method: its principal benefits.* – Zweigert and Kötz's approach was not based on anything like a sophisticated understanding of functionalism. In fact, there are many different varieties of that method,[1103] and there is reason to suspect that comparatists often mix (at times contradictory) elements of these varieties in an undigested and even unconscious fashion, resulting in a "methodological mishmash".[1104] This Encyclopedia entry is not the place to disentangle these elements nor to attempt to cure the resulting indeterminacy. For our purposes, it must suffice to focus on the rather crude version of the functional method that has become orthodox in comparative law: begin by identifying the social problem; then research the respective systems' laws that purport to address it; finally compare both what rules or mechanisms these laws use and what outcomes they produce.[1105]

Despite its crudeness, this kind of functionalism can generate many benefits. They become visible by considering its functions (the "functions of function"[1106]). Of these seven deserve particular mention, although the list is debatable and potentially incomplete.[1107]

The first, and arguably most important, function – and thus benefit – is to provide a meaningful reference point for comparison.[1108] As we have seen (*supra* s. 367), every comparison requires a common denominator which connects the objects to be compared – a *tertium comparationis*. The proponents of comparative law functionalism observed that the legal systems' doctrinal concepts or rules as such are often so different that they lack such a common denominator. Yet, they also observed that these systems often face more or less the same social problem. The shared social problem thus serves as the common denominator that makes comparison of the various responding

[1099] *Zweigert and Kötz*, Einführung in die Rechtsvergleichung I (Tübingen 1971) 29–37.

[1100] It has even been called "probably comparative law's principal gift to twentieth century legal science", *Glendon, Carozza and Picker* (*supra* n. 20) 9–10.

[1101] *Michaels* (*supra* n. 1089) 346.

[1102] An exception is the well-organized discussion of the principal critiques and counter-arguments by *Pick*, Die Kritik an der funktionalen Rechtsvergleichung: ZEuP 21 (2013) 60–88.

[1103] *Michaels* (*supra* n. 1089) 348–365 distinguishes at least eight kinds of functionalism prevailing in various disciplines.

[1104] *Idem* 367.

[1105] Since this is supposed to show what mechanisms are the equivalents in functional terms, this is closest to what Michaels (*supra* n. 1089) 362–365 calls "equivalent functionalism".

[1106] *Michaels* (*supra* n. 1089) 368.

[1107] *Idem* 368–385.

[1108] In line with modern understandings of law, this assumes, of course, that law serves a social function, rather than, e.g., expressing divine will or a natural order of the universe.

rules meaningful. In order to fulfill that function, however, the definition of that denominator must remain uncontaminated by the legal systems involved. It must thus be stated without reference to their respective concepts and structures. Functionalism thus requires a purely factual definition of the social problem – a "factual method".[1109]

A second benefit of functionalism is that it forces the comparatist to look beyond what legal rules *say* (in Roscoe Pound's terms: law in the books) to what they are at least *intended to do* (their purported function), and, if we take sufficient account of their (institutional, procedural, and professional) environment, even to what they *actually do* (law in action). This creates a much more realistic picture of the respective legal systems than mere rule comparison, leading to a more broadly informed analysis and understanding.[1110]

Third, a functionalist analysis shows that legal systems often approach the same, or similar, problems in rather different ways. Some handle a matter as a breach of contract, others provide tort remedies; some resolve issues through substantive law, others employ procedural devices; some resort to private law (and litigation), while others invoke regulatory means (relying on public enforcement). This insight counteracts the parochial belief that there is only one right path toward a solution. It thus breeds tolerance, at least with regard to different techniques, and can illuminate their respective strengths and weaknesses.

Fourth, a functional approach can help to evaluate the compared legal rules and institutions. To be sure, comparatists have disagreed on whether such an evaluation is properly part of their discipline, but in practice, "better law comparison"[1111] is common, especially in the service of law reform. Comparing how legal rules (or procedures or institutions) are used as instruments to solve social problems almost naturally raises the question of their performance: how well do they fulfill their function?[1112] Answering that question, however, is more difficult than it seems at first glance. Since the functional method itself looks only at the relationship between problem and solution, it does not in and of itself provide a standard by which to measure the performance of legal norms. In particular, even finding that the systems compared all employ the same rule does not guaranty its superior quality; at best, it creates a rebuttable presumption in its favor. A standard of evaluation must thus be found elsewhere, e.g., in notions of social justice or economic efficiency. In short, the functional method helps to set up the question, but it is ill-suited to provide a definite answer.

A fifth function of functionalism is the assistance it can render to legal unification. In fact, this was arguably its primary original objective because at the time when the method was brought to the fore international unification of law was widely considered the most important practical goal of comparative legal studies. A functional approach can help to overcome problems created by differences in the conceptual apparatus and positive rules of legal systems because it may show that, one way or another, these systems reach identical, or at least by and large similar, results.[1113] In that case, one can try to formulate and codify rules that reflect this consensus on outcomes. Many unification projects have successfully proceeded in that manner. Yet, a functional approach can also lead to doubts about unification projects: if it turns out that the legal systems involved already reach the same results anyway, the practical need for legal unification is questionable. Of course, there is still something to be said for having uniform concepts and rules as well, but their benefits may not justify the costs incurred by their creation, learning, and maintenance.

[1109] This "factual method" has inspired related approaches, especially the "common core" projects discussed *infra* ii., ss. 374–377.

[1110] This is why functionalism and legal realism can easily go hand-in-glove.

[1111] *Michaels* (*supra* n. 1089) 348.

[1112] See *Gordley*, The Functional Method: *Monateri*, Methods of Comparative Law (Cheltenham, Northampton MA 2012) 107–119, 109.

[1113] Again, such commonality is no guarantee of quality, but the main point of unification projects is to have identical rules, not necessarily optimal ones.

A further benefit is that a functional approach may help to organize a field of law according to shared problems rather than legal concepts and doctrines. This can create a – fairly loose – system that is independent of the various national (doctrinal) systems. Such a problem-based grouping can provide an overarching reference, a common platform for cross-boundary communication, and perhaps even a basis for legal harmonization or unification.[1114]

The last function brings us full circle, i.e., back to the method's origins in Ernst Rabel's work on private international law. Then, as now, a functional approach is often crucial for operating with conflicts rules, especially with regard to issues of characterization, adaptation, and public policy. If a (domestic) choice-of-law rule provides that a marriage is governed by the law of the spouses' common nationality, does that rules apply to a same-sex partnership under foreign law? Answering that question depends largely on whether that partnership fulfills (at least roughly) the same function as a marriage. If the parties establish a trust in a common law country and litigate about rights under it in a civil law country without a law of trusts, the civil law judge must replicate the foreign law as best he or she can in his or her own system; this requires understanding the function of the trust in the concrete case. If a victorious plaintiff seeks to execute a US-American punitive damages judgment in Germany where such damages are not allowed, determining whether their recognition would violate German public policy requires looking behind the doctrinal label and understanding the function of such damages.[1115]

370. *The functional method: its major weaknesses.* – In the last few decades, the functional approach has been subject to widespread and massive criticism.[1116] Some of this criticism expresses the authors' broad disagreement with the more traditional approach to comparative law in general, e.g., from a radical political or postmodern epistemological position (*supra* B.v., ss. 360–362). Yet, critics have also pointed out specific weaknesses of the functional method itself. Again, only the most significant ones can be addressed here.

To begin with, the approach is based on at least two dubious assumptions. First, it assumes that law has "a" function – which is to solve social problems. Yet, law often has many functions some of which are not directly instrumental at all, such as expressing political preferences, symbolizing notions of justice, or simply catering to lobbies. Second, functionalism apparently assumes that law actually solves social problems in a rational way. Yet, law can also be quite irrational, entirely ineffective, and it can create more problems than it solves; in fact, sometimes law entirely fails to address social problems or provides rules for their own sake, i.e., without responding to a social problem at all. It is true that a functional approach is not per se incapable of capturing these aspects, but its traditional assumptions make that difficult.

A related criticism is that the functional method is too rule-centered and thus reductionist. It tends to ignore, or at least to marginalize, the law's broader context, e.g., its history, social background, and cultural embeddedness. While that is largely true, at least with regard to its orthodox version, such an elimination of the context is, in a sense, the point of the approach: it reduces complexity by focusing fairly narrowly on the legal rules, doctrines, or institutions in relation to the underlying social problems. Still, the result is that the functional method has a "positivistic ring"[1117] to it, and that it invites a rule-centered, and thus dangerously narrow, perspective.[1118] Yet, as the treatise by Zweigert and Kötz amply demonstrates, the comparatist is not precluded from bringing the law's broader context back into the picture, although doing so goes beyond the functional method proper.

1114 An example is *Kötz* (*supra* n. 430); English translation of the first edition: *Weir and Kötz* (*supra* n. 523)

1115 See the functional analysis in the Decision of the German Supreme Court (*Bundesgerichtshof*) of 4 June 1992, BGHZ 118, 312.

1116 Among the earliest critiques was the trenchant and hard-hitting attack by *Frankenberg* (*supra* n. 237) 434–440.

1117 *Graziadei* (*supra* n. 1097) 111.

1118 One must not overlook that this was recognized (and openly conceded) by one of the most prominent advocates of the functional principle: see *Kötz* (*supra* n. 792) 504–505.

The functionalist approach is reductionist in another manner as well, however: focusing on the essentially technical question of how elements of law solve social problems (and showing that they often employ different means to reach identical results) tells us nothing about *why* they do so because a functional analysis ignores the underlying interests, policies, and agendas. Nor does it tell us anything about the quality of the *results,* e.g., whether the solution to the social problems is desirable or not, efficient or wasteful, helpful or harmful (and to whom).

The orthodox functional approach has also been blamed for being too Eurocentric, or at least too wedded to the law of the cultural West. That impression is understandable – but only partially correct. The functional method can be applied to radically different cultures as well. In fact, it is particularly suited for that purpose. Since in that context, any comparison of rules or doctrines is often pointless, if not massively misleading, looking at the law's function may be the best hope for finding the common denominator that makes radically different laws comparable.[1119] Still, the comparatist must remain keenly aware that he or she will – inevitably – analyze these laws and their functions from his or her own, usually Western, perspective. A particular problem in this regard is that the traditional functional method presumes a situation in which the state (through legislatures, courts, or agencies) makes laws which are then authoritatively applied to social facts. While this is true in most countries today, it is a thoroughly Western and state-centered viewpoint which is not necessarily shared by all legal cultures. Religious laws, for example, often present a very different picture, and many parts of the international legal order do not work in such a top-down fashion either.

371. *The "basic methodological principle"?* – A major problem with the orthodox version of the functional approach is not the method in and of itself but its alleged dominance over others which was famously claimed by Zweigert and Kötz:

"The basic methodological principle of all comparative law is that of *functionality*. From this basic principle stem all the other rules which determine the choice of laws to compare, the scope of the undertaking, the creation of a system of comparative law, and so on."[1120]

To call functionality *the* basic principle of *all* comparative law from which *all* the other rules, and apparently many other elements of the discipline, are derived was a vast overstatement even when first written in 1971, because by then there was already much more to comparative law than just the functional analysis of legal rules (see *supra* III.D). The statement was even less defensible when it was repeated in the third edition, i.e., as late as 1996, when multiple other approaches had gained acceptance and prominence. It sounds almost absurd in the early twenty-first century as methodological pluralism has become the norm (*supra* s. 366).

Zweigert and Kötz's main justification for this claim seems to have been their belief that the principle of functionality was an indispensable prerequisite for comparability. But the assumption that "in law the only things which are comparable are those which fulfill the same function"[1121] is plainly wrong: law-things can be compared not only according their function but also from many other perspectives, including historical background, cultural meaning, linguistic properties, and professional technique. In fact, they have often been so compared – including by Zweigert and Kötz themselves.

If the functional method is claimed to be *the* only legitimate, or at least the predominant, approach to comparative law, it amply deserves the common criticism. After all, such a claim excludes much, if not most, that is interesting and useful about the discipline – as indeed one of its original champions eventually admitted.[1122] Since such a claim to exclusivity (or at least predominance) is unnecessary, that claim should simply be considered a mistake and henceforth discarded. The functional method can then be employed and assessed as one method in a mutually complementary relationship with many others.

[1119] See *Barton, Gibbs, Li and Merrymann* (*supra* n. 226).

[1120] *Zweigert and Kötz* (*supra* n. 218) 34.

[1121] *Ibidem.*

[1122] *Kötz* (*supra* n. 792) 505.

372. *The presumption of similarity*. – An almost equally infelicitous feature of the functional method as presented by Zweigert and Kötz is its association with the presumption of similarity between legal systems. While this presumption was not at all these authors' original idea,[1123] its inherent universalism remained associated with their approach by subsequent generations, especially of critics.

The presumption is of a dual nature: Zweigert and Kötz claimed, rather apodictically, not only that "the legal system of every society faces essentially the same problems" but also that it "solves these problems ... very often with similar results".[1124] The claimed sameness of problems and similarity of results are often mixed together but should be kept apart. Although both are, as we shall see, unnecessary for the functional method, they raise somewhat different concerns.

The claim that legal systems face essentially the same *problems* is unsupported by any evidence. Closer inspection reveals it as scarcely plausible. Why should the problems of *every society* be the same, despite vast differences in history, culture, racial composition, religion, political constitution, economic system, etc.? In fact, there are kinds of conduct that some societies consider a "problem" worth regulating by law while others do not, such as adultery, blasphemy or suicide. Note also that the very definition of what is a problem for law is shaped by our cultural expectations and legal training: in most Western societies, the enforceability of business agreements is considered a legal problem, while in some Asian cultures it is conceived primarily as a social obligation. As a result, defining problems from one's own point of view inevitably entails bias and risks distortion. Even if a legal problem actually exists in two societies, by what standard do we judge whether it is *essentially* the same? Is the problem of anti-competitive industry agreements identical, or at least sufficiently similar, in a free market economy on the one hand, and a state-controlled economy on the other? At the end of the day, the presumption that problems are essentially the same in all societies is not only untenable, it is also unnecessary. Of course, the functional method works only if there is a common problem. But that does not mean that such commonality can (or even must) be presumed. The presumption should thus be abandoned so that the comparatist can investigate the situation with an open mind. If a common problem is found, the functional method can be applied; otherwise, there is simply nothing for it to do.[1125]

The presumption "that the practical *results* are similar"[1126] is more difficult to assess because it comes in two forms.

At the outset, Zweigert and Kötz presented it as "a basic *rule* of comparative law".[1127] As such, it is stated quite boldly: it applies "even as to detail" and "despite the great differences in the [legal systems'] historical development, conceptual structure, and style of operation".[1128] At the same time, this "rule" is presented in somewhat guarded terms: results are presumed not identical but merely similar, and the presumption applies only to areas of law "not heavily influenced by strong moral and ethical feelings, rooted in the particularities of the prevailing religion, in historical tradition, in cultural development, or in the character of the people".[1129] Still, it is not

[1123] As in the case of functionalism itself, the presumption's main root is the work of Ernst Rabel who assumed a unity of human nature ("Einheit der menschlichen Natur") and of legal thought ("Einheit des rechtlichen Denkens"), thus entertaining the possibility of global law ("Möglichkeit eines Weltrechts"), *Rabel* (*supra* n. 153) 5–6. Another source was probably *Esser*, Grundsatz und Norm in der richterlichen Rechtsfindung (Tübingen 1990, orig. 1956), 30–35, 346–351. Both Rabel and Esser were cited by *Zweigert and Kötz* (*supra* n. 270) 27.

[1124] *Zweigert and Kötz* (*supra* n. 218) 34.

[1125] See *Gordley* (*supra* n. 1112) 119.

[1126] *Zweigert and Kötz* (*supra* n. 218) 40, emphasis added.

[1127] *Idem* 30, emphasis added.

[1128] *Idem* 39. Note that an "unintended side-effect" of presuming the same outcomes everywhere is "legal fatalism", i.e., the notion "that it does not matter how we shape our legal rules and institutions, because the most appropriate results will find their way through those rules and institutions regardless of what they state or what they look like", Dannemann (*supra* n. 769) 419.

[1129] *Zweigert and Kötz* (*supra* n. 218) 39. In addition, although the authors do not make that explicit, the presumption does not necessarily mean that results are similar *in all regards*, just with regard to the particular problem at hand. Consider, for example, how legal systems provide for a surviving spouse. Some employ the law of inheritance, others the rules on marital property. Both ways can result in very similar kinds and levels of support. Yet, there can still be different results with regard to other issues, e.g., the parties' power to modify the default rules (through will or contract).

clear exactly what the basis for such a presumption is;[1130] how it can be justified "as a basic rule" in light of the differences between legal systems admitted by the authors; and how "similarity" is to be measured. Also, if the presumption is limited to law not closely tied to moral, religious, or cultural backgrounds, it applies pretty much only to the market law of Western legal systems and thus excludes much of what comparatists have long been interested in.

Later in their text, Zweigert and Kötz suddenly present the presumption of similar results merely as a "working rule",[1131] i.e., not as statement of actual probabilities but as mere guidance for research and analysis. Yet, it is here that it becomes most problematic: it states a "heuristic principle" that is unabashedly biased in favor of likeness: "It tells us where to look … in order to discover similiarities".[1132] To make matters worse, if the comparatist happens not to find similarity, he or she is advised to suspect that something has gone wrong – and thus to go back and double-check.[1133] A "working rule" that pushes so strongly for the result before the inquiry has even begun is unscientific.

The *praesumptio similitudinis* regarding results should thus be abandoned as well[1134] – not only because it is problematic in so many ways, but also because it is entirely unnecessary for the functionalist enterprise. An inquiry into the results generated by the problem-solving function of law does not need a presumed outcome; in fact, it is much better performed without that.

373. *Overall assessment.* – For the reasons explained, the functional method has long been, and continues to be, a valuable element in the toolkit of comparative legal studies, even in its orthodox and rather crude version. As Jim Gordley put it: "on a pragmatic level, comparative lawyers have found that by using this method, they arrive at results they respect".[1135] In fact, looking beyond the façade of rules and institutions, and understanding them, inter alia, from a functional perspective is justly considered *de rigueur* today. And yet the functional approach is full of pitfalls. Avoiding them requires at least three precautionary measures. First, one must be careful not to overrate the functional approach. Even if it ever was, it can no longer be the exclusive, or even the dominant, method. It can only perform certain functions in certain contexts, no more and no less. Second, it must be liberated from its association with the presumption of similarity, both of problems and solutions. When this presumption was devised around the middle of the twentieth century, it was in line with the discipline's overall preoccupation with similarity and thus struck neither its authors nor their readers as inappropriate. As comparatists have since the 1990s increasingly taken a more neutral stance (and in many instances even shifted their attention towards difference), the *praesumptio's* weaknesses have become glaringly apparent, and it should be relegated to the museum of legal history. Third, even when using the functional method for limited purposes and without presumptions, the comparatist must remain cognizant of its limitations and supplement it by other methods, such as cultural and sociological studies, as needed.

In the new millennium, some scholars have suggested reconceiving the functional method as an "analytical device", a "tool",[1136] a "constructive" or "interpretative approach".[1137] These labels mask

[1130] The examples provided by *Zweigert and Kötz* (*supra* n. 218) 38–39, could easily be countered by examples for different results. Witness, for example, how differently some (fairly comparable) legal systems treat liability for the side-effects of drugs; compare *Brown v. Superior Court*, 751 P.2d 470 (Cal. 1988) and Restatement (Third) of Torts: Products Liability, s. 6 (negligence) with *Arzneimittelgesetz* (Pharmaceutical Products Act, Germany), s. 84 (strict liability).

[1131] *Zweigert and Kötz* (*supra* n. 218) 40.

[1132] *Ibidem.*

[1133] *Ibidem.*

[1134] Note that the author of the treatise's third (and last) edition later himself admitted that outcomes are not always the same – even in contract cases; *Kötz* (*supra* n. 792) 503–504.

[1135] *Gordley* (*supra* n. 1112) 117.

[1136] *Husa*, Farewell to Functionalism or Methodological Tolerance? RabelsZ 67 (2003) 419–447, 432.

[1137] Ralf Michaels first considered turning functionalism into what he termed a "constructive approach": *Michaels,* The Functional Method of Comparative Law: *Reimann and Zimmermann* (eds.), The Oxford Handbook of Comparative Law (Oxford 2006) 339–382, 366. He later further developed the idea into what he called "interpretive functionalism": *Michaels* (*supra* n. 1089) 386–388.

a variety of re-conceptualizations that seek to avoid the well-known weaknesses of the method's traditional version. These new iterations are too complex to be summarized here.[1138] Whether they will eventually take root in comparative law remains to be seen. In any event, they demonstrate that there is more life left in functionalism than its radical critics would like.

ii. *Common Core (and the "Factual Method")*

374. *Objective and method.* – "Common core" is a form of comparative legal research named after a ground-breaking project conducted more than half a century ago. Its objective is to ascertain "the extent to which there exists common ground" among legal systems,[1139] i.e., to show where legal systems are alike, rather than different.

In a manner reminiscent of American legal realism, the focus of "common core" research is *primarily* on actual outcomes rather than on rules, concepts, or doctrines. To determine whether different legal systems actually produce identical (or at least similar) results, researchers construe (hypothetical) test cases (typically based on real court decisions). In order to make these cases workable in all legal systems involved, they need to be stated independently of each jurisdiction's conceptual apparatus and legal terminology. This is accomplished through the "factual method": as far as possible hypotheticals are stated in purely factual terms. Finding out whether outcomes would be identical is left to team-work: the hypotheticals are compiled into a questionnaire; national reporters, i.e., experts from the systems involved, state how their jurisdictions would decide the cases; the answers are synthesized in a general report which determines to what extent the legal systems have a "common core" as a matter of actual results. In a second step, however, the research goes beyond the mere outcomes themselves: it also seeks to understand whether the identical (or different) results are based on identical (or different) rules and doctrines. The national reporters thus also explain how their legal systems reach their decisions, and the general report again summarizes their findings.

Obviously, this, factual, method is closely related to the mainstream's functionalist approach (*supra* i.) in that it also uses a social problem as the *tertium comparationis*. The factual method just couches that problem in terms of a concrete fact pattern (e.g., case involving a party making a gratuitous promise to another) rather than an issue stated in the abstract (how do legal systems distinguish enforceable from non-enforceable promises?).

"Common core" projects are a form of basic research in the sense that their primary goal is simply to produce knowledge. Typically disavowing normative ambitions, they are strictly "focused on what the law is, and not on what the law ought to be".[1140] Of course, their finding can then be used for a variety of purposes, including legal unification, development of inter- or transnational law, the reform of domestic law (e.g., by tuning it to the existing common ground) or professional education.[1141]

Common core research has mainly been performed in two large-scale and widely noted projects: a study on the "Formation of Contracts" in the 1950s and 1960s and a search for "The Common Core of European Private Law" launched in the 1990s.[1142]

375. *Formation of Contracts (the "Cornell Project").* – In the late 1950s, Rudolf Schlesinger (1909–1996), destined to become one of the giants of twentieth-century comparative law, launched an ambitious study seeking to identify the "common core" of the law of contract formation. The project was centered at Schlesinger's academic home institution, the Cornell Law School in Ithaca,

[1138] For a discussion and critique, see De Coninck, The Functional Method of Comparative Law: Quo Vadis?: RabelsZ 74 (2010) 318–350; see also the response by *Michaels*, Explanation and Interpretation in Functionalist Comparative Law – a Response to Julie de Coninck: RabelsZ 74 (2010) 351–359.

[1139] *Schlesinger* (*supra* n. 230 I) 2.

[1140] *Idem* 3.

[1141] *Idem* 7–17, see also *infra* s. 377.

[1142] Other projects have also occasionally searched for a common core of particular areas of law. An important example is the work of the Commission of European Family Law founded 2001. Yet, its work product, the Principles of European Family Law, has a significant normative component; see *Boele-Woelki*, The Principles of European Family Law: Its Aims and Prospects: Utrecht L.Rev. 1 (2005) 160.

New York. It is widely considered path-breaking because it introduced the "factual method" based on a standard list of hypotheticals (then called a "working paper"). The project also impressed contemporaries because it was extremely thorough: the national experts' responses were discussed at three meetings at Cornell University, each lasting several months, and the materials were published in two volumes totaling over 1700 pages.

Still, the project was somewhat underwhelming in two regards. One weakness was that, despite a title suggesting global scope, its geographic range was fairly narrow: it looked at only a very small part of the world's jurisdictions – ten systems were fully covered and another ten taken into broader consideration.[1143] Another disappointment was that its findings specifically about contract formation neither were very surprising nor did they have much of an impact on the work of others.[1144]

Yet, the project did produce important insights in two other respects which ultimately turned out to be more important than the specific topic itself. First, it showed that, at least in the law of contract formation, "the areas of agreement and disagreement cannot be laid out and demarcated in the simple terms used in earlier comparative discussions"; instead "these areas are intertwined in subtler and more complex ways than had been surmised".[1145] It thus indicated that this kind of research revealed far greater complexity of law than more traditional approaches. Second, the project generated important experience with the new, factual, method. It showed not only that the method worked, but also that it required ample resources, committed teamwork, and long time-frames. As Schlesinger himself suspected, in the long run comparatists were much more interested "in common core research as a tool than in the specifics of the law of formation of contracts".[1146]

376. *The Common Core of European Private Law ("Trento Project").* – In 1993, Italian comparatists Mauro Bussani and Ugo Mattei launched a new "common core" endeavor at the newly established University of Trento, Italy; it thus became known as the Trento Project, although its center has since moved to Torino. As the title indicates, the project was designed as a successor to the Cornell study.[1147] It essentially replicates Rudolf Schlesinger's basic goal and method as well as his descriptive (rather than normative) orientation.[1148] Yet, the Trento Project also differs from the Cornell study in two principal regards. First, its scope is merely regional but also more encompassing. It covers all EU member state systems – whose number has more than doubled since the beginning of the project; and it purports to cover three whole areas of private law, i.e., contract, tort, and property (all broadly construed). Of course, this amounts to a vastly more ambitious agenda than the study of just one issue of contract law involving just ten principal jurisdictions. Second, the Trento Project explicitly combines Schlesinger's Common Core research with the "legal formants" approach developed by Italian comparatist Rodolfo Sacco[1149] (*supra* B.i., s. 336). As a result, the Trento research is much more specific in its quest for the rules and other factors that drive the respective case outcomes. In particular, it seeks to understand not only the "operative rules",

[1143] It thoroughly covered the United States, England, France, Germany-Switzerland-Austria, India, Italy, Poland, and South Africa. It took into consideration various jurisdictions from the communist orbit and the British Commonwealth; see *Schlesinger* (*supra* n. 230 I) 189–190. No Spanish- (or Portuguese-) speaking jurisdiction was covered, which of course excluded all of Latin America. The Far East as well as the developing world (with the exception of India) were also left out.

[1144] In part, this was perhaps due to the unwieldy format of their publication: the two volumes contain an enormous amount of detail in which the broad contours get easily lost. One reviewer aptly spoke of the "curiously flat effect which the volumes, as a whole, make on the reader"; *Marsh*, Review of Formation of Contracts: 19 I.C.L.Q. 171–173 (1970), 173.

[1145] *Schlesinger* (supra n. 230 I) 41.

[1146] *Idem* 4.

[1147] One of its leaders, Ugo Mattei, is a former student of Rudolf Schlesinger and became his successor on the chair for comparative law at the University of California Hastings College of Law in San Francisco. When the project was launched, Rudolf Schlesinger served as its Honorary Editor. He passed away in 1996.

[1148] *Bussani and Mattei* (*supra* n. 522) 2.

[1149] Both leaders of the Trento Project are former students of Rodolfo Sacco, and Ugo Mattei has since become his successor on the chair for comparative law at the University of Torino.

i.e., the formants directly invoked to support the results, but also other "descriptive" formants factoring into the decision, and even the "metaformants" lurking in the background, such as policy considerations, social and economic context, and the legal process. Including this, far richer, material leads to a much more differentiated picture of how the various legal systems really operate with regard to the issues covered.

Like the Cornell study's, the Trento Project's record is mixed. On the one hand, after more than twenty years of operation, it remains very far from reaching its originally announced goal "to obtain at least the main lines of one reliable geographical map of the law of Europe".[1150] It is true that the Project has produced about twenty book-length studies, but they each address just one narrowly defined subtopic of contract, tort, and property;[1151] even in the aggregate, they come nowhere near a map of European private law. In fact, for reasons we will address below (s. 377), that goal seems well-nigh unreachable. In addition, like those of the Cornell study, the Trento Project's findings have not had much influence beyond the realm of academic scholarship. In particular, the leaders' hope that these findings will help to guide European private law-making has by and large been disappointed. On the other hand, the Trento Project has played two important roles in the context of European private law since the 1990s. First, it has provided an important counterweight to the various projects in pursuit of unifying European private law in the form of a codification, of legislation, or least of an optional instrument (see *supra* IV.C.i.g., ss. 242–245). In contrast to these essentially legislative agendas, the Trento Project has remained an academic undertaking in search of knowledge and understanding of European private law, without pushing for its unification. As a result of its academic orientation and independence, it has survived the eventual demise of the legislative agendas. Second, the Trento Project has been an important catalyst for a truly all-European discourse on private law. In contrast to the Cornell study, where Schlesinger worked with a small and select group of prominent experts, the Trento Project has been highly inclusive. Over the years, it has brought together literally hundreds of – often junior – scholars, thus creating a platform for discussion, learning, and for establishing personal and professional relationships. This network effect is probably more important for the development of European private law than the published volumes.[1152]

377. *The strengths and weaknesses of common core projects.* – The major strength of the common core research projects has been to produce a picture that is fairly realistic in two senses. First, by looking at how legal systems decide concrete problems (captured in case hypotheticals), they have shown how these systems compare with regard to real outcomes instead of just their principles, rules, and doctrines; that is an important piece of information in and of itself, especially from a practitioner's point of view. Second, and perhaps more important, by looking at what drives these outcomes (in Sacco's terms, the "legal formants"), the common core method alerts us to the complex interplay between the actual results on the one hand, and the underlying principles, rules, and doctrines on the other. In particular, it demonstrates that the relationship between results and rules is anything but straightforward: similar rules can lead to similar or different results, just as different rules can lead to different or similar outcomes.[1153] In short, by combining the comparison of real results with an investigation of what drives them, common core research looks very deeply into the law's operation – and reveals an unsettling complexity.

Yet, such depth inevitably comes at the expense of breadth. Both the Cornell and the Trento Projects demonstrate how difficult common core studies are. They require tremendous

[1150] *Bussani and Mattei* (*supra* n. 522) 1.

[1151] Most of them have been published by Cambridge University Press in a special series; the various titles are listed on the Press's website. One volume was published separately, i.e., *Werro and Palmer* (*supra* n. 447).

[1152] *Reimann*, Of Products and Process. The First Six Trento Volumes and Their Making: *Bussani and Mattei* (eds.), Opening Up European Law (Berne, München, Durham NC 2007) 83–100, 94–95.

[1153] *Reimann* (*supra* n. 1152) 85–90. Of course, even when courts reach the same result on the same facts, they may still use different rules.

planning and resources, teamwork and commitment, perseverance and time. As a result, they are suited for deep sampling but not for covering vast ground. And since their findings are narrowly circumscribed as well as multifaceted, their results are rarely of much immediate use to those engaged in the practical pursuits of law-making or legal unification.

Common core research must also be handled with caution because its reliance on factually described problems suggests more cross-system neutrality than it can offer. It is common knowledge that facts themselves are not just given a priori but rather "socially construed".[1154] As a result, their construction and meaning can differ among (legal) systems; this is especially true if they involve terms with legal implications. In addition, the factual description of situations can never be complete but must inevitably leave out background information – to which some legal system may attach significance while other do not. Thus, as Schlesinger well understood, even resort to factual descriptions cannot completely filter out the diverse preconceptions prevailing in different legal systems.[1155]

Finally, the common core research projects are – at least arguably – vulnerable to the charges of universalism and positivism which have become so popular among critical comparatists since the 1990s (*supra* B.v., ss. 360–362). It is true that the leaders of the Trento studies have sought to avoid the stain of universalism by emphasizing that their project does *not* imply a preference for similarity over difference (or uniformity over diversity); nor do the published volumes directly evince any systematic bias in that direction. Still, searching for a *common* core is by definition oriented towards what systems share, rather than what divides them, and thus, in a sense, is a universalist endeavor. It is also true that the common core projects are of course *not* exercises in positivism in the traditional sense of focusing on blackletter rules; quite to the contrary, their very purpose is to transcend these rules by looking at actual results and at all the legally relevant factors that determine them. Yet, these studies do approach law as a purely professional, and in large part even technical, enterprise, and they can be taken to task (the Cornell project more so than the Trento studies) for giving given social and cultural perspectives very short shrift.[1156]

iii. *Numerical (Statistical) Comparative Law*

378. *The emergence of a new sub-field.* – "Numerical comparative law" is neither a universally accepted term nor does it have a precise meaning. It is simply a convenient label for comparative legal studies that operate with numerical data. Sometimes, such studies have also been called "statistical comparative law".[1157]

While comparatists have referenced numerical data for some time, throughout the twentieth century their use was by and large limited to socio-legal comparative studies (*supra* B.iv., s. 356); beyond that context, reliance on hard data was occasional and rare. This has changed since the turn of the new century. Mainly under the influence of economics, comparative studies relying on statistical data have enjoyed increasing popularity and attention. The trend began in the United States but has since spread to other parts of the world. In the last two decades these studies have both multiplied and diversified. They have developed new forms of comparative research, most prominently projects which code legal rules in order to compare and rank legal systems for a variety of purposes.[1158] The overall result has been the development of a substantial, fast-growing, and highly diverse academic literature as well as of a large number of projects sponsored by international institutions, such as the World Bank, the OECD, and the EU. Today, numerical comparative law can be regarded as a new subfield of the discipline, even though its theoret-

[1154] *Geertz* (*supra* n. 68) 173.

[1155] *Schlesinger* (*supra* n. 230 I) 21.

[1156] For an inspiring, friendly but in part also trenchant, critique of the Trento project, see *Frankenberg*, How to Do Projects with Comparative Law: Notes of an Expedition to the Common Core: *Bussani and Mattei* (eds.), Opening Up European Law (Berne, München, Durham NC 2007) 17–48, 36–47.

[1157] *Siems*, Statistische Rechtsvergleichung, RabelsZ 72 (2008) 355–390; *Kischel* (*supra* n. 286).

[1158] See *infra* s. 379. *Siems* (*supra* n. 1157) focused mainly on this method which he considered, in 2008, "a revolution".

ical and methodological foundations are yet to be fully established. It has become, so to speak, the comparative law branch of the much broader field of empirical legal studies.

In part because of the strong involvement of economists, in part also because of dominant trends in US legal scholarship, numerical comparative research has primarily focused on the law of the market, especially corporate law and investment, but also labor issues.[1159] Increasingly, however, other topics have been subjected to data gathering and statistical analysis as well; examples include institutions (mainly courts), procedures, constitutional law,[1160] and even the rule of law in jurisdictions throughout the world.[1161]

It is neither possible nor desirable here to cover the mass and diversity of these studies in any detail. This is especially true since the field continues to develop rapidly. We will merely take a brief look at the principal methods of data collection, its major benefits, and the widely recognized problems.

379. *Principal methods*. – Researchers typically employ three methods to obtain numerical data. These methods can be used in combination, but that is more the exception than the rule. How these data are then processed and analyzed is a separate question.

First, data can be obtained by simply counting facts or events in the legal systems under scrutiny – the number of judges (to compare judicial populations), of lawsuits filed (to determine litigation rates), of days it takes for a civil case to result in a judgment (to gauge the efficiency of judiciaries), of words in a constitution (to compare their lengths), of citations to foreign sources (to judge the influence of comparative considerations), of provisions adopted from other jurisdictions (to quantify transplants), etc. While this method must struggle with the usual issues of data collection, which are well-known in the social sciences, it is otherwise fairly unproblematic and thus not much debated among the comparatists.

Second, where direct data are unavailable or considered insufficient, comparatists have increasingly conducted surveys through questionnaires or interviews. Depending on the research question, the target audiences may be the actors that operate a legal system (e.g., attorneys or judges), its observers (e.g., legal academics or other experts), or its users (mainly the lay population); they may be insiders or outsiders to the system; involved in the matter under investigation or not; etc. Such surveys can, for example, try to gauge the difficulty of access to justice, the rigor of rights enforcement, or the strength of law in managing social conflict. Leaving aside the well-known generic issues of survey design and execution, this method is problematic because it can only measure people's experiences with, and perceptions of, law. It can thus tell us, e.g., how members of a certain community *view* the difficulty of access to justice, but not, at least not directly, how difficult access to justice *really* is. Obviously, there can be a large gap between perception and reality. This limitation is particularly crucial if authors use their surveys' findings to support claims about the comparative quality of legal systems.

The third method is to code legal norms or institutions numerically in order to compare certain features of legal systems. To take a well-known example,[1162] trying to establish the comparative levels of investor protection, the research can locate the legal provisions pursuing that purpose in each system under investigation. The comparatist can then assign to each legal system a number which depends on whether a pertinent provision is present (1) or not (0). Once all provisions have been checked, the numbers are aggregated, and each system receives a final score. The systems can then be evaluated on that basis: a high score indicates strong, a low score weak investor protection. While this method facilitates cross-system comparability, it entails enormous simplification which is one of the reasons why it is so controversial (*infra* s. 381).

[1159] Examples are cited by *Siems* (*supra* n. 1157) 361.

[1160] See, e.g., *Elkins, Ginsburg and Melton*, Time and Constitutional Efficacy: *Ginsburg and Huq*, Assessing Constitutional Performance (New York 2016) 233–267.

[1161] See the detailed empirical study by the World Justice Project (based on 400 variables), summarized by *Siems* (*supra* n. 680) 221–222.

[1162] The classic case is the study by *Porta et al.* (*supra* n. 258). For a lucid summary, see *Siems* (*supra* n. 1157) 380–382.

Once the data are obtained through one of these methods, they must be processed to allow conclusions about the legal systems involved. That may simply require putting the respective numbers together. The resulting picture can, for example, allow a ranking of legal systems (from most to least judges, from highest to lowest confidence in rights enforcement, or from strongest to weakest investor protection). Or it can support the grouping of legal systems (into those with many v. those with few judges, with high v. low confidence in rights enforcement, and with strong v. weak investor protection rules); obviously, this presents the issue of where to draw the line between the respective groups. Processing the data may also, however, involve running regression analyses in search of causal relationships between the facts as found, the answers as given, or the law as coded on the one hand and certain social or economic effects on the other, perhaps in order to arrive at policy recommendations.

380. *Major benefits.* – After a hundred years with little or no statistical input or methods, modern comparative law is finally joining the established social sciences by increasingly working with hard, numerical, data. To be sure, statistical comparative law is no substitute for other descriptive input or for qualitative analysis. Yet, it generates considerable benefits.

On the most basic level, statistical methods are useful for "developing and testing generalities about legal systems (which have always been part of comparative legal scholarship)".[1163] Traditional comparative law is replete with claims and assumptions largely based on broad impressions and anecdotal evidence, e.g., about legal families, similarities and differences, transplants, and institutions. Hard data and their statistical analysis can, if properly used, make these claims and assumptions at least somewhat measurable.[1164] To be sure, the measurements are often neither precise nor unconditionally reliable, but they can provide some empirical foundation where before there was none.

A major benefit of numerical research is that it encourages the creation of hypotheses that are actually testable through social scientific methods. Note that falsifiable hypotheses are considered crucial in virtually all sciences but have largely been absent from traditional comparative law. Numerical comparative law can, for example, hypothesize that the global influence of the United States Constitution as a model has lost out to competition from other systems – a statement which is verified by hard data.[1165]

In addition, numerical studies often unabashedly challenge time-honored beliefs and thus provoke their re-examination. Take, for example, the common ideology that the United States is a model country for the rule of law – an assumption that statistical evidence puts into serious doubt.[1166] Since hard data are hard to ignore, they trigger discussion and investigation, even if only to refute them. As the debate about the "legal origins" thesis has shown (*supra* B.iv., s. 358), that alone is often a valuable learning process.

Whether numerical methods are also well-suited to assess the quality of legal rules, institutions, or even whole systems is a more difficult question. The answer depends almost entirely on the research design, especially on how the data are generated and analyzed. It is also important that the claims derived from the analysis be limited to those truly supported by the data.

381. *Widely recognized problems.* – Comparative legal scholars have subjected numerical studies to much criticism, some of it harsh.[1167] Yet, closer inspection quickly reveals that this criticism does not pertain to all forms of numerical comparative research but only to specific elements.

The first two methods of data production outlined above (*supra* s. 379), i.e., the mere counting of facts or events and the reliance on surveys, have encountered little or no resistance. Nor has

[1163] *Caterina* (*supra* n. 1016) 202.

[1164] See, e.g., *Siems* (*supra* n. 680) 193–207 (possibilities for measuring similarities and differences).

[1165] See, e.g., *Law and Versteeg*, The Declining Influence of the United States Constitution: 87 N.Y.U.L.Rev. 762–858 (2012).

[1166] The World Justice Program's "Rule of Law Index" ranks the United States considerably below many other (mainly Western) jurisdictions, see the table in *Siems* (*supra* n. 680) 222.

[1167] See e.g. *Kischel* (*supra* n. 286) 147–154.

the use of the resultant data to group systems, gauge influence, or track transfers raised fundamental concerns. Mainstream comparatists wedded to more traditional methods may not be enthusiastic about such numerical projects, but they have not been hostile towards them either. In part this is because these kinds of studies are usually conducted by fellow comparatists who, though empirically minded and often working with social scientists, still operate by and large within the parameters of the craft.

Virtually all the comparatists' trenchant criticism has been directed against the third method mentioned, i.e., data production through coding legal provisions (or institutions) with subsequent regression analyses to draw causal conclusions which then become the basis for policy making. The main targets of criticism have been the studies of economic regulation resulting in the "legal origins" thesis which was accepted, and acted upon, by the World Bank (B.iv., s. 358). Importantly, these, and similar, projects were conducted not by (comparative) lawyers but by economists using their own tools and pursuing their own objectives. Reacting to these trespassers on the terrain of comparative law, legal scholars attacked their method of data production and analysis, their findings, and their policy conclusions.[1168]

The data collection was criticized as woefully narrow and incomplete: it focused on a few, select, provisions only, disregarded functional equivalents (a "capital error" in a comparative study[1169]), took norms out of the (institutional, procedural, etc.) context that shapes their meaning and effect, and coded them in an extremely crude (essentially binary yes/no) manner that disregarded all gradations. Data selection was also biased in two ways: it took the researchers' home jurisdiction as its baseline (a "rookie mistake" in comparative law[1170]) so that the studies really measured how close other systems were to that of the United States; and it gathered just the data that could be easily quantified, leaving out lots of other, potentially important, background factors. When this deeply flawed data-set was run through regression analyses, the errors were compounded, so said the critics, to the point where the results become meaningless at best and misleading at worst.[1171]

The studies' findings have widely been regarded as careless over-claiming. Causal claims – especially that certain legal norms produce certain economic results – were sometimes derived from mere correlation between data, which is a major methodological problem in its own right. Even if there is a causal relationship, it is often unclear in which direction it runs.[1172] In some studies, the conclusions are in and of themselves so bold that they seem outright absurd.[1173]

Finally, where the findings were relied on by international institutions such as the World Bank, the resulting policies reflected the biases inherent in the – largely US-driven – studies themselves, i.e., in favor of Western capitalist economies, neo-liberal values, and market deregulation. This entailed disregarding values other than economic growth and efficiency, such as the protection of weaker parties, preservation of the environment, social peace, and distributive justice.

These criticisms are widely considered justified. Yet, one must not overlook that they were directed against the respective projects in their very early stages. Since then, researchers have made significant adjustments and refinements. Later studies have collected data in a more comprehensive fashion, processed them in a more refined manner, and drawn more circumspect conclusions.

Still, some fundamental differences remain between comparative law on the one hand and econometric studies on the other. Two such differences lie at the root of the problems identified by the critics.

The first major difference pertains to the kinds of knowledge required – which becomes a problem, of course, if it is lacking. The economists conducting the studies so heavily criticized by the comparatists simply did not know enough about

[1168] The critique by *Kischel* (*supra* n. 286) largely targets these studies. For a more balanced assessment, see *Siems* (*supra* n. 1157) 368–378; see also *Siems* (supra n. 680) 207–212.

[1169] *Kischel* (*supra* n. 286) 149.

[1170] *Siems* (*supra* n. 1157) 371 ("Anfängerfehler").

[1171] See e.g. *Kischel* (*supra* n. 286) 151–152.

[1172] Vgl. *Siems* (*supra* n. 1157) 381.

[1173] *Kischel* (*supra* n. 286) 176, describes a striking example.

how to do comparative law. They were ignorant of functional equivalents, the importance of context and underlying values, the enforcement *vel non* of rules, etc. This ignorance caused some glaring errors which were soon widely acknowledged. If economists engage in (numerical) *comparative legal* studies, they must acquire the requisite knowledge or consult comparative law scholars. Of course, the reverse is just as true: if comparatists engage in statistical studies, they need to acquire the requisite skills or to get help from experts.

Second, the two fields follow different logics.[1174] Comparative lawyers tend to emphasize (and sometimes even to exaggerate) the irreducible complexity of law in all its dimensions. By contrast, economists dramatically reduce complexity in order to generate data that can be used to develop or test hypotheses and trace causal relationships. A fundamental problem with the early econometric studies was that they pushed the reduction of complexity too far. Conducting numerical comparative law studies requires a proper balance between reducing and recognizing the complexity of legal systems.

The gap between the two groups of scholars is best handled through cooperation in mutual respect.[1175] Economists (and other social scientists) can teach comparative lawyers how to generate and process data and how to draw at least tentative conclusions from them. Conversely, comparatists can teach economists (and other socials scientists) how to account for the complexity of law and legal systems, and thus how to avoid major errors and distortions. Each group should consider its work not as a substitute for, but as a complement to, that of the other.

D. In Conclusion: A Mixed Methodological Record

382. *Letting a thousand flowers bloom.* – Just as the geographic and substantive coverage of comparative law has hugely expanded throughout the twentieth century, and just as the uses and goals of the discipline have multiplied, so the approaches and methods of comparative law have greatly diversified since World War II. This diversification has massively increased the range and potential of comparative legal studies. Today, they can illuminate not only the rules and institutions of legal systems but also the underlying legal cultures; they not only bring to light similarities but also actively search for, and promote, the appreciation of differences; they go beyond the study of legal families and look at the world from the perspective of great legal traditions; they open a dynamic dimension by analyzing receptions and transplants, including the conditions of their success and failure; they often combine and overlap with other disciplines, such as legal history, cultural, socio-legal, and language studies and, last but not least, the economic analysis of law; they encompass critical approaches, mainly from a (leftist) political or a (post-modern) epistemological perspective; they use more refined forms of functionalism, employ the "factual method" in search of the common core of legal systems, and have recently turned to empirical and numerical studies. As a result, there is no single method of comparative law but rather an impressive diversity of methods. Even the existing line-up is no *numerus clausus* nor are the individual methods always strictly defined. In short, the discipline's approaches and methods are wide-ranging, flexible, and adaptable as needed.

Among comparatists, there is almost universal agreement that this is as it should be. The reason is in part necessity: different projects and objectives call for different approaches and methods. In part, the reason for approval of the status quo is that the various approaches and methods can allegedly be combined to create synergetic effects. And in part, diversity and flexibility are generally considered virtues in their own right, here as elsewhere.

[1174] See *Michaels*, Comparative Law by Numbers? Legal Origins Thesis, *Doing Business* Reports, and the Silence of Traditional Comparative Law: 57 Am.J. Comp.L. 765–795, 794 (2009).

[1175] *Michaels* (*supra* n. 1174) 794; see also *Antoniolli*, The Magic of Numbers – Elucubrazioni sparse in tema di misurazione del diritto: *Mattei, Candian, Pozzo, Monti and Marchetti* (eds.), Studi in Onore di Antonio Gambaro: Un Giurista di Successo (Milano 2017) 37–50; *Spamann*, Large-Sample, Quantitative Research Designs for Comparative Law?: 57 Am.J.Comp.L. 757–810 (2009).

383. *Methodological deficiencies.* – Yet, the methodology of the discipline is also deficient in at least three regards. First, most of its methods, including the basic process of comparison, are still poorly understood; this is in large part the result of the methodological complacency in the second half of the twentieth century (*supra* III.E.ii., s. 159). Of course, several approaches and methods were either broadly popularized (especially functionalism) or newly introduced (such as the "factual approach" used in the "common core" projects), but they were by and large accepted without much reflection. It is true that methodology suddenly became a much-discussed issue in the new millennium, but the literature on the topic has not commanded broad attention and has had a negligible impact on mainstream practice. As a result, even today, most comparatists have but a vague understanding of the methods they (purport to) employ. For example, orthodox functionalism is still very much in vogue despite the fact that its inherent ambiguities and weaknesses have been clearly exposed (*supra* C.i., s. 370). Second, the existing methods are poorly integrated: they exist side-by-side in apparent isolation, and their relationship to each other remains largely unexplored. We have only a vague understanding of when and how they can be combined and when a combination may cause conflict rather than synergy.[1176] For example, it is unclear to what extent the "factual method" and functionalism are mutually exclusive or can rather be meaningfully joined by asking whether the factual scenarios presented by the former really involve the same social problem which is the focus of the latter. Third, despite often claiming the status of a true science of law (*supra* I.C., s. 13), comparative legal studies have rarely proceeded in the manner required by modern science at the most elementary level, i.e., by operating with falsifiable hypotheses. Not only have the vast majority of comparatists shown no interest in developing such hypotheses, they have also remained largely uninterested in empirical data by which to test them. Instead comparatists have often operated with broad assumptions and ad hoc observations about legal systems, i.e., with evidence that any serious social scientist would find gravely deficient. As a result, comparative legal scholarship that even strives for (not to mention actually produces) truly "scientific" knowledge about law in general or in a particular context has been quite rare.[1177] A – welcome – exception is the recent turn of *some* comparatists to empirical and quantitative ("numerical") methods (*supra* C.iii., s. 378–381); yet, it is merely an exception of sorts because these methods are not a product of comparative law but rather borrowed from other disciplines, especially economics. On the whole, it is fair to say that mainstream comparative law is blessed with methodological breadth and diversity but plagued by a lack of methodological sophistication and rigor.

[1176] For a valiant and interesting attempt to integrate the various approaches, see *Valcke* (*supra* n. 22).

[1177] In fact, it has remained largely unclear exactly what the (supposedly scientific) "knowledge" comparative law is supposed to produce is really all about. Notably, *Zweigert and Kötz* (*supra* n. 5) 14 claim that the "primary aim of comparative law, as of all sciences, is knowledge". Yet, the only hint at what such knowledge consists of is that comparative law "can provide a much richer range of model solutions" for social conflict and the "opportunity of finding the 'better solution'" for a particular time and place. It remains unclear exactly how comparative law accomplishes that and, perhaps more importantly, what makes the solutions it can find "better". For a more serious, but also largely ignored, attempt to specify the knowledge comparative law should develop, see *Samuel* (*supra* n. 76).

LIST OF PRINCIPAL WORKS

A. Basic Orientations

Cotterrell, Is It so Bad to Be Different? Comparative Law and the Appreciation of Diversity: Örücü and Nelken (eds.), Comparative Law - A Handbook (Oxford, Portland OR 2007) 133–154

Curran, Cultural Immersion, Difference and Categories in U.S. Comparative Law: 46 Am.J. Comp.L. 43–92 (1998)

Dannemann, Comparative Law: Study of Similarities or Differences?: *Reimann and Zimmermann* (eds.), The Oxford Handbook of Comparative Law (ed. 2 Oxford 2019) 390–422

Frankenberg, Comparative Law as Critique (Cheltenham, Northampton MA 2016)

Frankenberg, Critical Comparisons: Re-thinking Comparative Law: 26 Harv.Int.L.J. 411–455 (1985)

Glenn, Com-paring: Örücü and Nelken (eds.), Comparative Law – A Handbook (Oxford and Portland OR 2007) 92–108

Legrand, European Legal Systems are not Converging: 45 I.C.L.Q. 52–81 (1996)

Legrand, Le Droit Comparé (ed. 5 Paris 2015)

Legrand, The Same and the Different: *Legrand and Munday* (eds.), Comparative Legal Studies: Traditions and Transitions (Cambridge, New York 2003) 240–311

Markesinis, The Coming Together of the Civil and the Common Law (Oxford, Portland OR 2000)

Merryman, On the Convergence (and Divergence) of the Civil Law and the Common Law: 17 Stan.J.Intl.L. 357–388 (1981)

Rheinstein, Comparative Law - Its Functions, Methods and Usages: 22 Arkansas L.Rev. 415–425 (1968)

Smits, Convergence of Private Law in Europe: Örücü and Nelken (eds.), Comparative Law: A Handbook (Portland OR 2007) 219–240

Valcke, Comparing Law: Comparative Law as Reconstruction of Collective Commitments (Cambridge 2018)

Van Hoecke (ed.), Epistemology and Methodology of Comparative Law (Oxford, Portland OR 2004)

Whitman, The Neo-Romantic Turn: *Legrand and Munday* (eds.), Comparative Legal Studies: Traditions and Transitions (Cambridge, New York 2003) 312–344

Zimmermann, Savigny's Legacy: Legal History, Comparative Law, and the Emergence of a European Legal Science: 112 L.Q.R. 576–605 (1996).

B. General Approaches

i. *Comparing Rules, Concepts, and Institutions*

Sacco, Introduzione al Diritto Comparato (ed. 5 Torino 1991) 43–51

Sacco, Legal Formants: A Dynamic Approach to Comparative Law: 39 Am.J.Comp.L. 1–34 and 343–401 (1991).

ii. *Legal Families and Traditions*

Arminjon, Nolde and Wolff, Traité de Droit Comparé (3 vol.) (Paris 1950–51)

Cuniberti, Grands Systèmes de Droit Contemporains (ed. 2 Paris 2011)

David, Les Grands Systèmes de Droit Contemporains (Paris 1964 and ed. 12 by Jauffret-Spinosi, Paris 2016); transl. by Brierley, Major Legal Systems of the World Today (ed. 3 London 1985)

Gambaro and Sacco, Sistemi Giuridici Comparati (Torino 1996)

Garupa and Pargendler, A Law and Economics Perspective on Legal Families: Eur.J.Leg.Stud. 7 (2014) 33–55

Glendon, Carozza and Picker, Comparative Legal Traditions in a Nutshell (ed. 4 St. Paul MN 2016)

Glendon, Carozza and Picker, Comparative Legal Traditions: Texts, Materials and Cases on Western Law (ed. 3 St. Paul MN 2007)

Glenn, Comparative Legal Families and Comparative Legal Traditions: *Reimann and Zimmermann* (eds.), The Oxford Handbook of Comparative Law (ed. 2 Oxford 2019) 423–441

Glenn, Legal Traditions of the World (Oxford 2000 and ed. 5 2014)

Head, Great Legal Traditions: Civil Law, Common Law and Chinese Law in Historical and Other Operational Perspectives (Durham NC 2011)

Husa, A New Introduction to Comparative Law (Oxford, Portland OR 2015) 210–241

Husa, Classification of Legal Families Today: Is it Time for a Memorial Hymn?: Rev.int.dr.comp. 56 (2004) 11–38.

Husa, Legal Families: *Smits* (ed.), Elgar Encyclopedia of Comparative Law (ed. 2 Cheltenham, Northampton MA 2012) 491–504

Kischel, Rechtsvergleichung (München 2015) 217–228

Kötz, Abschied von der Rechtskreislehre?: ZEuP 6 (1998) 493–505

Mattei, Three Patterns of Law: Taxonomy and Change in the World's Legal Systems: 45 Am.J. Comp.L. 5–44 (1997)

Merryman and Pérez-Perdomo, The Civil Law Tradition (ed. 4 Stanford CA 2018)

Merryman, Clark and Haley, The Contemporary Civil Law Tradition (New Providence NJ 2015)

Őrücü, A General View of 'Legal Families' and of 'Mixing Systems': Őrücü and Nelken (eds.), Comparative Law - A Handbook (Oxford, Portland OR 2007) 169–187

Palmer, Mixed Jurisdictions Worldwide: the Third Legal Family (Cambridge, New York 2001)

Pargendler, The Rise and Fall of Legal Families: 60 Am.J.Comp.L. (2012) 1043–1074

Scholler and Tennenbach (eds.), Die Bedeutung der Lehre vom Rechtskreis und der Rechtskultur (Berlin 2001)

Siems, Comparative Law (ed. 2 Cambridge 2018) 84–111

Siems, Varieties of Legal Systems: Towards a New Global Taxonomy: 12 Journal of Institutional Economics 579–602 (2016)

Sistemi Giuridici Comparati (Antonino Procida Mirabelli di Lauro gen. ed., 5 vols., Torino 1996)

Vanderlinden, Comparer les droits (Diegem 1995)

Vicente, Direito Comparado I: Introduçao: Sistemas Juridicos em Geral (ed. 2 Coimbra 2018)

Zweigert and Kötz, Einführung in die Rechtsvergleichung (ed. 3 Tübingen 1996) 62–313 (An Introduction to Comparative Law (3 ed Oxford 1998) 63–319).

iii. *Receptions and Transplants*

Ajani, By Chance and Prestige: Legal Transplants in Russia and Eastern Europe: 43 Am.J.Comp.L. 93–117 (1995)

Berkowitz, Pistor and Richard, The Transplant Effect: 51 Am.J.Comp.L. 163–203 (2003).

Cohn, The Legal Transplant Chronicles: 58 Am.J. Comp.L. 583–629 (2010)

Doucet and Vanderlinden (eds.), La réception des systèmes juridiques: implantation et destin (Bruxelles 1994)

Drolshammer and Weber, Wie das Recht auf Reisen geht (Bern 2019)

Ewald, Comparative Jurisprudence II: The Logic of Legal Transplants, 43 Am.J.Comp.L. (1995) 489–510

Fedtke, Legal Transplants: *Smits* (ed.), Elgar Encyclopedia of Comparative Law (ed. 2 Cheltenham, Northampton MA 2012) 550–554

Gillespie and Nicholson, Law and Development and the Global Discourses of Legal Transfers (Cambridge 2012)

Grande, Imitazioni e Diritto: Ipotesi sulla Circolazione dei Modelli (Torino 2000).

Graziadei, Comparative Law as the Study of Transplants and Receptions: *Reimann and Zimmermann* (eds.), The Oxford Handbook of Comparative Law (ed. 2 Oxford 2019) 442–473

Kahn-Freund, On Uses and Misuses of Comparative Law: 37 M.L.R. (1974) 1–27

L'Americanization du Droit: Arch.phil.dr. 45 (2001) 7–267

Legrand, The Impossibility of 'Legal Transplants,' Maastricht J.Eur.& Comp.L. 4 (1997) 111–124

Linos, The Democratic Foundations of Policy Diffusion: How Health, Family, and Employment Laws Spread Across Countries (Oxford, New York 2013)

Miller, A Typology of Legal Transplants: Am.J. Comp.L. 51 (2003) 839–901

Nelken, Comparatists and Transferability: *Legrand and Munday* (eds.), Comparative Legal Studies: Traditions and Transitions (Cambridge, New York 2003) 437–466.

Rechtstransformation und Rechtsrezeption: RabelsZ 72 (2008) 1–135 (collection of articles)

Sacco, La circulation des modèles juridiques: Rapports généraux au XIII Congrès Internationale de droit comparé - Montreal 1990 (Cowansville PA 1992) 1–19

Sanchez-Cordero (ed.), Legal Culture and Legal Transplants. Culture juridique et l'acculturation du droit vol. II (Paris 2012)

Siems, Comparative Law (ed. 2 Cambridge 2018) 231–261

Symposium: Histories of Legal Transplantations: Theoretical Inquiries in Law 10 (2009) 299–743

Teubner, Legal Irritants: Good Faith in British Law or How Unifying Law Ends Up in New Divergencies: 61 M.L.R. 11–32 (1998)

Trubek, Law and Development: *Wright* (ed.), International Encyclopedia of the Social and Behavioral Sciences XIII (ed 2. Amsterdam 2015) 443–447

Twining, Diffusion of Law: A Global Perspective: 49 J.Leg.Plural. &Unoff.L. 1–46 (2004)

Watson, Legal Transplants: An Approach to Comparative Law (Athens GA, London 1974, and ed. 2, 1993)

Wiegand, The Reception of American Law in Europa: 39 Am.J.Comp.L. 229–248 (1991).

iv. Interdisciplinary Comparative Law

Interdisciplinary Comparative Law Generally

Foster, Moscati and Palmer (eds.), Interdisciplinary Study and Comparative Law (London 2016).

Comparative Legal History

Gordley, Comparative Law and Legal History: *Reimann and Zimmermann* (eds.), The Oxford Handbook of Comparative Law (ed. 2 Oxford 2019) 752–771

Heutger and Schrage, Legal History and Comparative Law: *Smits* (ed.), Elgar Encyclopedia of Comparative Law (ed. 2 Cheltenham, Northampton MA 2010) 505–520

Schmidt, From Evolutionary Functionalism to Critical Transnationalism: Comparative Legal History, Aristotle to Present: *Dubber and Tomlinson* (eds.), The Oxford Handbook of Legal History (Oxford 2018) 263–289

Symposium, Legal History and Comparative Law: 66 Am.J.Comp.L. 727–830 (2018).

Comparative Legal Cultures

Cotterell, Comparative Law and Legal Culture: *Reimann and Zimmermann* (eds.), The Oxford Handbook of Comparative Law (ed. 2 Oxford 2018) 710–733

Cotterell, Law, Culture and Society: Legal Ideas in the Mirror of Social Theory (Aldershot, Bulrington VT 2006)

Grodeland and Miller, European Legal Cultures in Transition (Cambridge 2015)

LeGrand, Fragments on Law as Culture (Deventer 1999)

Nelken and Feest (eds.), Adapting Legal Cultures (Oxford, Portland OR 2001)

Nelken, Comparing Legal Cultures (Aldershot, Brookfield VT 1997)

Nelken, Defining and Using the Concept of Legal Culture: Őrücü and Nelken (eds.), Comparative Law – A Handbook (Oxford, Portland OR 2007) 109–132

Nelken, Legal Culture: *Smits* (ed.), Elgar Encyclopedia of Comparative Law (ed. 2 Cheltenham, Northampton MA 2012) 480–490

Varga (ed.), Comparative Legal Cultures (Budapest 2012).

Socio-legal Studies

Cotterell, Comparative Law and Sociology: *Legrand and Munday* (eds.), Comparative Legal Studies: Traditions and Transitions (Cambridge, New York 2003) 131–153

Dezelay and Garth, Dealing in Virtue: International Commercial Arbitration and the Construction of a Transnational Legal Order (Chicago IL 1996)

Friedman, Perez-Perdomo and Gomez (eds.), Law in Many Societies (Stanford 2011)

Riles, Collateral Knowledge. Legal Reasoning in the Global Financial Markets (Oxford, Portland OR 2011)

Riles, Comparative Law and Socio-Legal Studies: *Reimann and Zimmermann* (eds.), The Oxford Handbook of Comparative Law (ed. 2 Oxford 2019) 772–804

Siems, Comparative Law (ed. 2 Cambridge 2018) 147–179, 332–362

Teubner, Global Law Without the State (Aldershot, Brookfield VT 1997)

Twining, Globalisation and Legal Theory (London 2000)

Weber, Economy and Society (*Roth and Wittich* (eds)., 2 vol., Berkeley CA, Los Angeles CA, London 1968), especially II 641–900.

Comparative Law and Language Studies

Curran, Comparative Law and Language: *Reimann and Zimmermann* (eds.), The Oxford Handbook of Comparative Law (ed. 2 Oxford 2019) 681–709

De Groot, Legal Translation: *Smits* (ed.), The Elgar Encyclopedia of Comparative Law (ed. 2 Cheltenham, Northampton MA 2012) 538–549

Großfeld, Comparatists and Languages: *Legrand and Munday* (eds.), Comparative Legal Studies: Traditions and Transitions (Cambridge 2003) 154–194

Großfeld, Kernfragen der Rechtsvergleichung (Tübingen 1996) (available in English as Core Questions of Comparative Law, transl. by Grosswald Curran (Durham NC 2005)).

Großfeld, Macht und Ohnmacht der Rechtsvergleichung (Tübingen 1984) (available in English as The Strength and Weakness of Comparative Law, transl. by *Weir*, Oxford 1990)

Megale, Teoria della Traduzione Giuridica: fra Diritto Comparato e "Translation Studies" (Napoli 2008)

Olsen et al. (eds.), Translation Issues in Language and Law (Basingstoke, New York 2009)

Pozzo, Comparative Law and Language: *Bussani and Mattei* (eds.), The Cambridge Companion to Comparative Law (Cambridge 2012) 88–112.

Tiersma and Solan (eds.), The Oxford Handbook of Language and Law (Oxford, New York 2012), Part III. Multilingualism and Translation, 159–231.

Comparative Law and Economics

Caterina, Comparative Law and Economics: *Smits* (ed.), Elgar Encyclopedia of Comparative Law (ed. 2 Cheltenham, Northampton MA 2012) 191–207

De Geest (ed.), Economics of Comparative Law (Cheltenham, Northampton MA 2009)

De Geest and Van den Bergh (eds.), Comparative Law and Economics (3 vol.) (Cheltenham, Northampton MA 2004)

Eisenberg and Ramello (eds.), Comparative Law and Economics (online, Cheltenham 2016)

Faust, Comparative Law and Economic Analysis of Law: *Reimann and Zimmermann* (eds.), The Oxford Handbook of Comparative Law (ed. 2 Oxford 2019) 826–857

Garoupa and Ginsburg, Economic Analysis and Comparative Law: *Bussani and Mattei* (eds.), The Cambridge Companion to Comparative Law (Cambridge 2012) 57–72

La Porta, Lopez-de-Silanes and Shleifer, The Economic Consequences of Legal Origins: 46 J.Econ.Lit. 285–332 (2008)

Legrand, Econocentrism: 59 U.Tor.L.J. 215–222 (2009)

Mattei, Comparative Law and Economics (Ann Arbor MI 1997)

Michaels (ed.), Symposium on Legal Origins: 57 Am.J.Comp.L. 765–876 (2009)

Milhaupt and Pistor, Law and Capitalism - What Corporate Crises Reveal about Legal Systems and Economic Development around the World (Chicago IL 2008)

Ogus, The Economic Approach: Competition between Legal Systems: Örücü and Nelken (eds.), Comparative Law: A Handbook (Oxford, Portland OR 2007) 155–167

Parisi and Luppi, Quantitative Methods in Comparative Law: *Monateri* (ed.), Methods of Comparative Law (Cheltenham, Northampton MA 2012) 306–316.

Comparative Law and Religion

Berman, Comparative Law and Religion: *Reimann and Zimmermann* (eds.), The Oxford Handbook of Comparative Law (Oxford 2006) 739–751

Bottoni, Cristofori and Ferrari (eds.), Religious Rules, State Law, and Normative Pluralism - A Comparative Overview (Switzerland 2016)

Caparros and Christians, La religion en droit comparé a l'aube du XXIe siècle (Brussels 2000)

Doe, Comparative Religious Law: Judaism, Christianity, Islam (Cambridge 2018)

Ferrari, Religioni, Diritto, Comparazione: Ferrari and Mori (eds.), Religioni, Diritto, Comparazione (Piacenza 2003) 33–47.

Fikentscher, Modes of Thought: A Study in the Anthropology of Law and Religion (ed. 2 Tübingen 2004)

Huxley, Religion, Law and Tradition (London, New York 2002)

Kischel (ed.), Religiöses Recht und religiöse Gerichte als Herausforderung des Staates; Rechtspluralismus in vergleichender Perspektive (Tübingen 2016)

Mehdi et al. (eds.), Law and Religion in Multicultural Societies (Copenhagen 2008)

Michaels, Religiöse Rechts und postsäkulare Rechtsvergleichung: *Zimmermann* (ed.), Zukunftsperspektiven der Rechtsvergleichung (Tübingen 2016) 39–102

Whitman, Comparative Law and Religion: *Reimann and Zimmermann* (eds.), The Oxford Handbook of Comparative Law (ed. 2 Oxford 2019) 734–753.

v. *Critical Approaches*

American Journal of Comparative Law (Special Issue), What We Write About when We Write About Comparative Law: Pierre Legrand's Critique in Discussion: 65 Am.J.Comp.L. 1–255 (2017)

Antoniolli, Benacchio and Toniatti (eds.), Le nuove frontiere della comparazione (Trento 2012)

Baxi, The Colonialist Heritage: *Legrand and Munday* (eds.), Comparative Legal Studies: Traditions and Transitions (Cambridge, New York 2003) 46–75

Benton, Law and Colonial Cultures (Cambridge 2002)

Engelbrekt and Nergelius (eds.), New Directions in Comparative Law (Cheltenham, Northampton MA 2009)

Frankenberg, Comparative Law as Critique (Cheltenham, Northampton MA 2016)

Frankenberg, Critical Comparisons: Re-thinking Comparative Law: 26 Harv.Int.L.J. 411–455 (1985)

Kennedy, Political Ideology and Comparative Law: *Bussani and Mattei* (eds.), The Cambridge Companion to Comparative Law (Cambridge 2012) 35–56

Kennedy, The Methods and the Politics: *Legrand and Munday* (eds.), Comparative Legal Studies: Traditions and Transitions (Cambridge, New York 2003) 345–433

Legrand and Munday (eds.), Comparative Legal Studies, Traditions and Transitions (Cambridge 2003).

Mattei, Comparative Law and Critical Legal Studies: *Reimann and Zimmermann* (eds.), The Oxford Handbook of Comparative Law (ed. 2 Oxford 2019) 805–825

Muir Watt, La fonction subversive du droit compare: Rev.int.dr.comp. 52 (2000) 503–527

Peters and Schwenke, Comparative Law Beyond Post-Modernism: I.C.L.Q. 49 800–834 (2000)

Riles (ed.), Rethinking the Masters of Comparative Law (Portland OR 2001)

Rosen, Beyond Compare: *Legrand and Munday* (eds.), Comparative Legal Studies: Traditions and Transitions (Cambridge 2003) 493–510

Ruskola, Legal Orientalism: China, the United States, and Modern Law (Cambridge MA, London 2013)

Symposium, New Approaches to Comparative Law: Utah L.Rev. 255–663 (1997)

Symposium: New Directions in Comparative Law: 46 Am.J.Comp.L. 597–756 (1998)

Twining, Globalisation and Legal Theory (London 2000) 174–193.

C. Specific Methods

Methods in General

Adams, Husa and Oderkerk (eds.), Comparative Law Methodology (Cheltenham 2017) (online)

Basedow, Comparative Law and Its Clients: 67 Am.J.Comp.L. 821–857 (2014)

Constantinesco, Rechtsvergleichung II: Die rechtsvergleichende Methode (Köln 1972)

Jansen, Comparative Law and Comparative Knowledge: *Reimann and Zimmermann* (eds.), The Oxford Handbook of Comparative Law (ed. 2 Oxford 2019) 291–319

Monateri (ed.), Methods of Comparative Law (Cheltenham, Northampton MA 2012)

Oderkerk, The Need for a Methodological Framework for Comparative Legal Research: RabelsZ 79 (2015) 589–623

Őrücü, Methodology of Comparative Law: *Smits* (ed.), Elgar Encyclopedia of Comparative Law (ed 2. Cheltenham, Northampton MA 2012) 560–576

Samuel, Introduction to Comparative Law and Method (Oxford, Portland OR 2014)

Scarciglia, Método y Comparación Juridica (Madrid 2018)

Van Hoecke (ed.), Epistemology and Methodology of Comparative Law (Oxford, Portland OR 2004)

Zweigert and Kötz, Einführung in die Rechtsvergleichung (ed. 3 Tübingen 1996)

*Zweigert and Kötz,*Introduction to Comparative Law (*Weir transl.*, ed. 3, Oxford 1998)

Zweigert and Puttfarken (eds.), Rechtsvergleichung (Darmstadt 1978).

i. *Functionalism*

De Coninck, The Functional Method of Comparative Law: Quo Vadis?: RabelsZ 74 (2010) 318–350

Esser, Grundsatz und Norm in der richterlichen Fortbildung des Privatrechts (ed. 4 Tübingen 1990), ch. XVIII, 346–380

Frankenberg, Critical Comparisons: Re-thinking Comparative Law: 26 Harv.Int.L.J. 411–455, 434–440 (1985)

Gordley, The Functional Method: *Monateri* (ed.), Methods of Comparative Law (Cheltenham, Northampton MA 2012) 107–119

Graziadei, The Functionalist Heritage: *Legrand and Munday* (eds.), Comparative Legal Studies. Traditions and Transitions (Cambridge, New York 2003) 100–127

Husa, Farewell to Functionalism or Methodological Tolerance?: RabelsZ 67 (2003) 419–447

Kischel, Rechtsvergleichung (München 2015) 92–108

Michaels, The Functional Method of Comparative Law: *Reimann and Zimmermann* (eds.), The Oxford Handbook of Comparative Law (ed. 2 Oxford 2019) 345–389

Rabel, Aufgabe und Notwendigkeit der Rechtsvergleichung: *Rabel and Leser* (eds.), Gesammelte Aufsätze III (Tübingen 1967)1–24

Zweigert and Kötz, Einführung in die Rechtsvergleichung (ed 3. Tübingen 1996) 33–39 (An Introduction to Comparative Law (ed. 3 Oxford 1998) 34–40).

ii. *Common Core (and "Factual Method")*

Bussani, Current Trends in European Comparative Law: The Common Core Approach: 21 Hastings Intl.Comp.L.Rev. 785–801 (1998)

Bussani and Mattei (eds.), Making European Law: Essays on the Common Core Project (Trento 2000)

Bussani and Mattei (eds.), The Common Core of European Private Law (The Hague 2003)

Bussani and Mattei (eds.), Opening up European Law. The Common Core Project (Berne 2007)

Schlesinger, Formation of Contract: A Study in the Common Core of Legal Systems (2 vol.) (Dobbs Ferry NY, London 1968).

iii. *Numerical (Statistical) Comparative Law*

Antoniolli, The Magic of Numbers - Elucubrazioni Sparse in Tema di Miserazione del Diritto: *Mattei, Candian, Pozzo, Monti and Marchetti* (eds.), Studi in Onore di Antonio Gambaro: Un Guirista di Successo (Milano 2017) 37–50

Gambaro, Misurare il Diritto (Parte Seconda): *Antoniolli, Benacchio and Toniatti* (eds.), Le Nuove Frontiere della Comparazione (Trento 2012) 3–18

Gambaro, Misurare il Diritto: 2 Ann.dir.comp. 17–47 (2012)

Kischel, Rechtsvergleichung (München 2015) 144–154

Michaels, Comparative Law by Numbers? Legal Origins Thesis, Doing Business Reports, and the Silence of Traditional Comparative Law: 57 Am.J.Comp.L. 765–795 (2009)

Parisi and Luppi, Quantitative Methods in Comparative Law: *Monateri* (ed.), Methods of Comparative Law (Cheltenham, Northampton MA 2012) 306–316.

Siems, Comparative Law (ed. 2 Cambridge 2018) 180–228

Siems, Statistische Rechtsvergleichung: RabelsZ 72 (2008) 354–390

Spamann, Empirical Comparative Law: 11 Annual Review of Law and Social Science 131–153 (2015).

VII TWENTY-FIRST-CENTURY CHALLENGES

384. *Introduction and overview.* – Throughout their history, comparative legal studies have responded, with varying success, to the needs of the times. They helped to integrate law on the national level in the early modern period (*supra* III.A.iii, ss. 60–63), to enlarge nineteenth century lawmakers' options (*supra* III.B.i.c., s. 74), to realize twentieth-century projects of international unification (*supra* V.B.iv., ss. 302–308), to increase late twentieth-century appreciation of diversity (VI.A.iii., s. 328), etc. Like earlier periods, the twenty-first century now presents the discipline with its own challenges.

Scholars have regarded these challenges mostly as results of "globalization", and that approach has sometimes provided a helpful framework for discussion.[1178] Yet, "globalization" is also confusingly multifaceted, difficult to define, ideologically charged, and popular as a label for various political, economic, and technological agendas. We will thus refrain from invoking the phenomenon as a whole and rather focus on some of its concrete manifestations. Such a, more specific, approach is also preferable for reasons of modesty and self-restraint: exploring the impact of globalization in an all-encompassing sense on comparative law would require an extensive encyclopedia entry in its own right, especially since this impact is inextricably linked to the effect of globalization on the nature, structure, and function of law as a whole.

Before we turn to some of these more concrete manifestations, we must remind ourselves that comparative law as *an academic enterprise* has itself become globalized in recent decades (see *supra* III.E.i., s. 154). It is true that comparatists have constituted an international guild of sorts at least since the Paris Congress; during the twentieth century their primary transboundary platform was the International Academy of Comparative Law (founded in 1924) with its quadrennial World Congresses. In the twenty-first century, however, this Academy and its Congresses have lost much of their former importance because there is now a much broader community of comparatists with more permanent venues for publication and exchange. Facilitated by efficient electronic communication and benefitting from the rise of a single lingua franca, comparative legal scholarship today is a global enterprise. To be sure, this is only partially true in terms of membership and venues of dissemination: the vast majority of participating scholars are located in the cultural West, especially in Europe and North America, with fewer voices coming from Latin America and Asia and almost none from most of Africa; and the vast majority of the leading publishing houses, periodicals, and websites are at home in half-a-dozen Western countries. Yet, in terms of discourse, the discipline today has a global reach: comparatists routinely discuss, often cooperate, and sometimes compete across national and continental boundaries, largely regardless of their nationality or academic homes.

Of the many new challenges presented to this globalized discipline by its twenty-first century environment three stand out: comparative law must adjust to the "age of information" (A.); it must come to grips with an increasingly pluralistic world order (B.); and it needs to acknowledge its inevitable political implications (C.).[1179]

A. ADJUSTING TO THE "AGE OF INFORMATION"

385. *The decline of the informatory role.* – At least since the nineteenth, and certainly throughout the twentieth, century a major function of comparative legal studies was to provide information about foreign law. This was true not only for sheer descriptions of foreign legal rules, institutions, or systems – which many scholars refuse to count as comparative law (*supra* I.B., s. 7); it was also the case when elements of foreign

[1178] *Muir-Watt*, Globalization and Comparative Law: *Reimann and Zimmermann* (eds.), The Oxford Handbook of Comparative Law (ed. 2 Oxford 2019) 599–623.

[1179] The following discussion is limited to pervasive issues and thus leaves aside particular topics that are arising or have been suggested; for a sample, see Zimmermann (*supra* n. 679). All this is in addition to the challenges presented by the discipline's increasing specialization, fragmentation, and concomitant loss of coherence, see *supra* IV.D., s. 279.

legal systems were juxtaposed to their domestic counterparts.

Providing information about foreign law was an important service, especially to practitioners because for most of the twentieth century such information was difficult to obtain without help. The requisite material was stored in at best a few specialized libraries, hard to identify, and usually available only in the original language. Comparative legal scholarship, particularly by experts in the respective legal systems, described areas of foreign legal systems for a domestic audience, pointed out the relevant sources, and often translated them into the local language.

Since the late twentieth century, however, these functions have increasingly been taken over by the internet. Today, information about foreign law and legal systems is available on myriad websites established by foreign ministries of justice, high courts, research institutes, NGOs, publishers, law firms, and other actors. This includes the texts of constitutions and major legislation, sometimes also of court opinions and regulatory matter. Since much of this information is geared towards a foreign audience, it is often written in, or translated into, English and sometimes even accompanied by introductions or comments. Finding and working with pertinent material is facilitated by powerful search engines and a gradual trend towards open access publication. As a result, the informatory role of comparative legal scholarship has significantly declined. Today, a practitioner looking for information about foreign law will usually turn to the internet, not to the books and articles written by comparatists.

386. *The shift towards an explanatory function.* – While the largesse of electronically (and for the most part gratuitously) accessible information about foreign law has drastically reduced the informatory role of comparative law, it has also drastically increased the need for what one might call the discipline's explanatory function. This is because the electronically available information presents three principal problems, and comparative law is needed in order to solve, or at least alleviate, them.

The first problem is that electronically accessible information about foreign law is largely raw: it is often unprocessed, unstructured, and unexplained. In such raw form, its utility is severely limited. Even if translated, the mere text of, e.g., a foreign constitution, statute, regulation, or court opinion provides very limited help for solving a problem. Making such sources useful requires explaining their rank and relevance, interpretation and application, impact and enforcement, etc. This contextualization must be provided by someone who understands both the foreign legal system *and* the domestic user's intellectual horizon and expectations, i.e., by a comparatist. As a result, in the age of electronic data, the role of comparative law "shifts from getting information to the process of transforming it into useful knowledge – that is, structuring and interpreting information so as to provide answers to the questions posed or problems presented".[1180] This entails a "basic shift of cognitive orientation" from regarding information about foreign law as a product to treating it as a tool.[1181] Some scholars have even called for the development of "a common conceptual language, a comparative legal grammar ... to maximize the benefits of increased information", without, however, specifying exactly what such a language or grammar would look like.[1182]

The second, and closely related, problem is that the internet user can easily be misled to believe that once the pertinent websites have been consulted, he or she has acquired all the knowledge necessary to solve the problem at hand. To be sure, that danger exists whenever a domestic lawyer operates with foreign blackletter rules. Yet, obtaining these rules from the internet makes the problem much more acute. In part, this is because access is deceptively easy, in part because the available information is usually unfiltered and decontextualized. Note that normally nothing alerts the user that, at least in practice, almost everything depends on how rules actually operate. Comparative law can help to mitigate the resultant risk of being misled most effectively if comparative perspectives are an integral part of basic legal education. Students must be taught

[1180] *Gerber*, Globalization and Legal Knowledge: Implications for Comparative Law: 75 Tul.L.Rev. (2000–2001) 949–975, 954.

[1181] *Idem* 960.

[1182] *Muir-Watt* (*supra* n. 1178) 605.

that foreign legal rules always need to be understood in their broader context. Thus, comparative law teaching must also shift its focus from delivering information to providing the skills lawyers need properly to use the foreign law data they can now so easily find. So far little research has been done, and thus little understanding has been reached, about how to teach the requisite information management skills effectively.

The final problem is the ever-increasing mass of information. It results from a combination of three factors: storage space is cheap, legal systems proliferate (*infra* B.), and legal change is accelerating. A century ago, information about foreign law was rare and precious; today it is often massive and sometimes overwhelming. If comparative law is to turn mere information into useful knowledge it also needs to manage the growing overabundance of data, e.g., by developing a system of search capabilities, filters, and sorting mechanisms. Lamentably, at this point almost no efforts have been made in that direction.

387. *The impact of electronic communication.* – Comparative law also needs to develop responses to two special features of communication prevalent in the electronic age. One of these features is simply the much-increased speed of exchange which manifests itself mainly in sharply decreased turn-around times. Thus, information about foreign law must be processed to provide useful knowledge with a view to very short timeframes.[1183] Especially practitioners cannot be expected to consult whole books or even lengthy law review articles. Instead, comparatists must create material that can be accessed electronically and provide help instantaneously. This may require establishing varying levels of information, e.g., brief summaries with electronic links to mid-level explanations and further links to in-depth treatments.

The second feature of modern electronic communication is its "dialogic format".[1184] E-mail and text messages do not lay out the whole problem and solution in a full-size memorandum but typically exchange information seriatim, gradually working through issues in a more or less ad hoc fashion. As a result, there is a growing mismatch between traditional forms of comparative legal scholarship and current forms of communication. If comparative law wants to remain relevant for legal practice in the twenty-first century, it will have to gravitate to forms of knowledge presentation that resonate with lawyers used to constant dialog, short attention spans, and little interest in long-time preservation of messages.

388. *Avoiding linguistic pitfalls.* – The "age of information" is largely the age of the internet, the internet's main operating language is English, and English has become the lingua franca of law. This situation has great advantages: it has given international legal practitioners and scholars access to huge amounts of information since there is so much legal material written in, or translated into, English. Even a generation ago, access to foreign law was severely limited because few people commanded more than one or at best two of the many foreign languages that may have been required; today, whoever reads English can easily (and often gratuitously) obtain significant information about virtually every legal system in the world.

At the same time, this situation has hugely multiplied the notorious translation pitfalls inherent in working with different legal systems: today, most lawyers read about foreign law no longer in the vernacular but in translation – and are thus exposed to the well-known risks of misunderstanding the law and miscommunicating with foreign colleagues or clients. To be sure, helping to control these risks has long been a major objective of comparative legal studies (*supra* VI.B.iv., s. 357). In the age of the internet, however, the task has become not only more important than ever but also more difficult. This is in part because translations available on the internet have often not been made by comparatists, nor have they always been vetted for accuracy. In part, the task is also more difficult because in the age of globalization these translations involve literally dozens of other languages, among them many non-Western tongues which can be extremely difficult to put

[1183] *Gerber* (*supra* n. 1180) 954–955. As Gerber points out, the inherent time pressure increases the temptation to assume that foreign law is essentially like one's own (the "illusion of similarity") and that differences do not really cause any problems (the "illusion of ease"), *idem* 968–969.

[1184] *Gerber* (*supra* n. 1180) 956.

into English. All this has created a somewhat paradoxical, as well as treacherous, situation: on the surface, the available legal information is marked by a great deal of linguistic uniformity; underneath, however, lurks an equally great deal of linguistic diversity. Thus, comparatists must push for more vigilance than ever against the facile assumption that translations can convey a full and accurate meaning of the original text.

B. COMING TO GRIPS WITH GLOBAL LEGAL PLURALISM

389. *The insufficiency of the nation state paradigm.* – Twentieth-century comparative law was solidly based on the paradigm of the modern nation state: it essentially identified legal systems with countries; it regarded law largely as a product of the state; and it conceived of legal families as groups of national legal systems. It is true that twentieth-century comparatists sometimes considered legal systems beyond the nation state, such as religious or customary laws, but these systems were viewed at the margins of the legal universe and received no sustained attention from the mainstream. It must be admitted that from the prevailing Western point of view, the focus on national legal systems was plausible: for most of the twentieth century, the law of nation states indeed played the dominant role in the developed world.

In the twenty-first century, however, the discipline's "nationalist heritage"[1185] has become too narrow. This Encyclopedia is not the place to enter into the debates whether the nation state is in decline (a popular view among political scientists and also among many jurists in the 1990s and early 2000s); nor to what extent it has reasserted itself (especially in response to the global economic crisis of 2008, in the fight against international terrorism, in the growing resistance to migration and immigration and in dealing with the global health crisis excepting in 2020); nor whether we have seen the rise of "a new world order"[1186] (and what such a new order actually looks like). Be all that as it may, it is undeniable that in recent decades national legal systems have acquired powerful competition from other legal orders in at least three regards. First, there are now numerous supra- and international systems, so to speak, above the nation state. On the global level, they range from the United Nations to the World Trade Organization and from the global human rights regime to international investment, criminal, and administrative law in many iterations. On the regional level, they include the European Union, the Council of Europe (with its own human rights system), *Mercosur*, the Association of Southeast Asian Nations (ASEAN), and the African Union. Second, legal systems have increasingly been created, or asserted themselves, below the nation state level. In response to political pressure for greater regional autonomy, many states have devolved significant power to their subunits, which have thus acquired more legislative, executive, and sometimes even judicial competence. Third, non-state legal orders have come to play an increasingly important role. To be sure, such orders have always existed alongside the nation state in various forms (such as the law of the church or the law merchant), but the combination of economic privatization, deregulation, and globalization since the 1990s has made non-state legal orders and dispute resolution mechanisms much more popular and powerful;[1187] witness the spread of global technical standardization, of corporate codes of conduct, and the scope and importance of international commercial arbitration.[1188] In addition, rising Islam has competed with, and in some cases overpowered, state law in some regions of the world. In summary, there has been a proliferation of legal orders above, below, and beyond the nation state, relegating the

[1185] *Glenn*, The Nationalist Heritage: *Legrand and Munday* (eds.), Comparative Legal Studies – Traditions and Transitions (Cambridge 2003) 76–99.

[1186] *Slaughter*, A New World Order (Princeton NJ 2004).

[1187] Whether the nation state remains at least the most powerful of all these legal systems is largely irrelevant for present purposes. Relative state power varies depending on the country in question and the context in which it competes with other orders.

[1188] *Teubner* (ed.), Global Law without a State (Brookfield UK, Dartmouth NH 1997).

latter from its once unchallenged dominance to one competitor for authority among many. As a result, a discipline studying legal systems can no longer limit its attention to the laws of the various nation states, lest it miss much of the current legal universe and create a seriously distorted picture of global legal reality.[1189]

390. *Beyond legal systems?* – In recent decades, comparatists of law have already made occasional efforts to address legal orders not based on the nation state. In particular, they have considered the rise of supranational regimes, looked at the role of non-state law, and rediscovered the importance of religious systems (*supra* IV.A.iii., ss. 183–187). Some have also shifted their attention from the study of "legal families" consisting of national systems to "legal traditions" transcending them (*supra* VI.B.ii., s. 343). As a result, even mainstream comparatists have increasingly recognized that legal orders are not necessarily tied to a specific geographic space. In many instances, there is no link between law and territory because legal orders can be global in scope and primarily defined by subject matter (such as international trade regimes), practices, and objectives (e.g., international commercial arbitration) or even by shared beliefs and values (as with religious systems). Even though these regimes lie beyond the nation state, and even though their law does not necessarily consist of state-created rules, they can still be described as *legal* orders. Thus, they are well within the domain of comparative law, and they will require much sustained attention.

Some comparatists have even proposed to look beyond the concept of legal systems and shift the focus to "epistemic communities".[1190] They may be defined, for example, by personal or professional positions, interests, activities, and even self-perceptions.[1191] In contrast to national legal systems, membership of these communities is not (in principle) exclusive; instead, individuals can belong to multiple ones at the same time in different roles, e.g., as a practitioner in a global network of law firms, a human rights lawyer, a Latino, and a Catholic. Yet, while such communities can constitute "spaces of transnational normativity",[1192] their defining norms are often primarily social and cultural rather than legal. To be sure, comparatists must be cognizant of these normative orders, and their influence on, and interaction with, legal systems is a fertile field of interdisciplinary research. Yet, the study of these communities in and of themselves is better left to other disciplines. Comparative law should remain connected to, but not become synonymous with, the study of normative systems *tout court*.

391. *Pluralism as fact and value.* – In the twenty-first century, comparative law has widely recognized the pluralism of legal orders as a fact which may require a change from a nationalist to pluralist conception of law itself[1193] Yet, pluralism has also increasingly become embraced as a broader value, i.e., as a state of affairs that is positive and desirable. Since the 1990s, many comparatists have thus criticized their discipline's traditional penchant for uniformity and emphasized the importance of difference (*supra* VI.A.iii., s. 328).

To some extent this trend towards an emphasis on "alterity" may also be a result of globalization processes. At first glance this seems counterintuitive, since globalization is usually associated with convergence. Yet, "accelerated contact and juxtaposition with other traditions may mean that all sides develop a sharper sense of identity".[1194] That sense of identity, in turn, entails increased consciousness of "otherness" which can even trigger claims to cultural and political autonomy. Thus, twenty-first-century comparative law must remain keenly aware that globalization processes do not necessarily entail a leveling of legal and cultural differences but can have the opposite effect of increased differentiation.[1195]

To some degree, however, the recent emphasis on difference is also the result of the United States' influence on the development of the

[1189] *Reimann,* Beyond National Legal Systems: A Comparative Law for the International Age: 75 Tul.L.Rev. 1103–1119 (2001).

[1190] *Muir-Watt* (*supra* n. 1178) 603-607.

[1191] For a similar approach to the concept of jurisdiction, see *Berman*, The Globalization of Jurisdiction: 151 U.Pa.L.Rev. 311–545 (2002).

[1192] *Muir-Watt* (*supra* n. 1178) 604.

[1193] *Michaels*, Welche Globalisierung für das Recht? Welches Recht für die Globalisierung?: RabelsZ 69 (2005) 525–544.

[1194] *Muir-Watt* (*supra* n. 1178) 587.

[1195] *Fischer-Lescano and Teubner* (*supra* n. 742); for a jurisprudential perspective, see *Berman*, Global Legal Pluralism: A Jurisprudence of Law beyond Borders (Cambridge 2012).

discipline in the last few decades. Since the last quarter of the twentieth century, American culture has propagated (racial, ethnic, religious, etc.) "diversity" as a social and cultural value, in part as a counterweight to its (older) commitment to equality (before the law). To the extent that the turn to "otherness" in comparative law is a US import, the discipline must guard against blindly following an ideal developed in a very specific context and often without much reflection.

392. *The burdens of global legal pluralism.* – Studying global legal pluralism adds breadth and complexity to a field whose scope has already been hugely expanded over the past century in many other regards (*supra* III.–VI.). It requires the study of ever more, and a growing diversity of, legal orders. This, in turn, entails the consideration of ever more diverse kinds of law, including not only traditional state-created institutions and provisions but also commercial customs, rules of private ordering, and norms of religious communities, etc., as well as many hybrid forms. And it calls for ever more cooperation with other disciplines, such as political science, sociology, economics, religious studies, and anthropology.

This increase of scope and complexity entails inevitable burdens. To begin with, the breadth and diversity of material make an overview of the field more and more difficult. The situation is exacerbated by the acceleration of legal change in many, if not most, legal orders. As a result, comparatists today are "forever condemned to aim at multiple moving targets".[1196] Two generations ago, one could quite easily be on top of the current research concerning the various legal orders of the world; today, nobody can plausibly claim that. As a result, facing global legal pluralism calls for ever greater degrees of every narrower specialization. Yet, even within one's field of specialty, it can be challenging, if not outright exhausting, to keep one's knowledge up to date. In that endeavor, the easy (electronic) availability of information is both a blessing and a curse: it allows twenty-first-century comparatists quick and cheap access to pertinent studies and publications, but it also often confronts them with amounts of information that can be impossibly hard to digest.

C. ACKNOWLEDGING POLITICAL IMPLICATIONS AND RESPONSIBILITY

393. *An apolitical science – tradition and critique.* – In the second half of the twentieth century mainstream comparative law presented itself essentially as an apolitical "legal science" in the tradition of continental European jurisprudence. In contrast to earlier generations who pursued the search for a common law of mankind in the hope of promoting lasting peace, post-World War II comparatists by and large strove to stay clear of political ambitions and contested issues.[1197] Note that for decades their primary focus was on supposedly neutral areas of private law, mainly contract and tort, an orientation that both facilitated and perpetuated that stance,[1198] and that they repeatedly insisted that the goal of their endeavors was simply to create (scientific) "knowledge" (*supra* V.A.i., s. 281).

In the last few decades, the mainstream's political innocence has come under increasing attack. In part, this has been due, again, to the influence of US legal thought, which has long been much

[1196] *Munday* (*supra* n. 239) 26.

[1197] *Kennedy* (*supra* n. 186). Western comparative law maintained its apolitical position by and large even in dealing with socialist legal systems in the 1950s through the 1980s.

[1198] Arguably, the comparatists' involvement in the pursuit of a common private law for Europe around the turn of the twentieth century was an exception (*supra* IV.C.i.g., ss. 242–245). Yet, in important ways, it actually confirmed the discipline's apolitical stance. Witness that the participants did not treat legal unification as a political issue; instead, they considered its desirability beyond cavil in an increasingly integrated market. Some exceptions notwithstanding, they also paid scant attention to the inevitable distributional and other political consequences of the unification agenda; instead, they treated the project as a technical enterprise and limited their involvement by and large to the comparison (and attempted unification) of blackletter rules. Note also that the projects involved only academics from a very limited geographic region (mainly a dozen countries in Western continental Europe) and only from the core areas of private law, leaving more politicized areas, such as employment, consumer protection, or landlord and tenant law largely aside.

more politically charged than traditional European jurisprudence; in part, the attacks have their roots in modern French and German critical philosophy and sociology; in part, they are also derived from political science, especially from studies of colonialism and orientalism (*supra* VI.B.v., ss. 360–365).

It is not difficult to see that comparative legal studies have long had political implications. This has always been noticeable, and indeed their very purpose, when such studies supported law reform agendas. But it has also been true in many other regards. For example, when comparatists developed blueprints for a common private law of Europe, their drafts balanced freedom of contract and protection against abuse of bargaining power; when comparative law has contributed to uniform law projects, it has helped to export western models of law (such as the CISG or human rights agendas based on Western liberalism) to parts of the world with non-western traditions; and when scholars have compared constitutions, they have affected the perception, and perhaps even the recognition, of Western notions of rule of law. Perhaps even more importantly, comparative law has long adopted, and then contributed to the perpetuation of, a view of the world with Western Europe and North America at the center and the other regions on the periphery ("the West and the rest"); this, in turn, has sometimes entailed the exoticization of non-Western legal cultures (*supra* VI.B.v., s. 364). Such political implications are neither novel nor seriously contested, but they have by and large been ignored or marginalized by the mainstream.

394. *Globalization and politicization.* – In the twenty-first century ignoring or marginalizing the political implications of comparative law has become increasingly unsustainable. Globalization, especially of the economy, has dramatically increased the interaction between legal systems, be it through transplants, transactions, in transboundary disputes, or in transnational forms of cooperation. This, in turn, has greatly augmented the political role and impact of comparative law. Suffice it to mention three contexts.

First, comparative law often significantly supports the modernization of legal systems especially in developing countries. Since the discipline was shaped in a pro-western, if not outright pro-American, fashion during the cold war,[1199] more often than not it helps to push developing systems in the direction of free markets, open trade, and general deregulation. Thus, for better or worse, comparative law tends to contribute to the spread of economic neo-liberalism, i.e., to a process which is one of the very hallmarks of globalization.[1200] For example, if scholars compare American and European models of corporate governance, they implicitly promote the idea of a market dominated by corporations and their investors. Second, even where comparative law helps to spread facially neutral rules governing traditional areas of private law all over the world, it causes political effects. Private law norms have significant regulatory functions (such as delimiting the freedom to contract), distributive consequences (e.g., by shifting, or refusing to shift, the costs of accidents), and allocative effects (mainly through the definition and protection of property rights). Third, comparative law plays an important role in helping economic actors exploit what may be called a transnational law market.[1201] The increased mobility of capital and goods often forces states to compete for investment and business; this, in turn, allows powerful economic actors to shop for the legal environment most favorable to them.[1202] Since comparative law is an essential tool in this endeavor (*supra* V.B.ii., s. 297), it can contribute to a "race to the bottom", e.g., towards the lowest levels of labor regulation or environmental protection.

395. *Taking responsibility.* – Thus, comparative law is rife with – more or less open – political dimensions. No matter how neutral comparatists wish to remain, their work often has consequences

[1199] *Mattei* (*supra* n. 189).

[1200] *Muir-Watt* (*supra* n. 1178) 598.

[1201] *O'Hara and Ribstein*, The Law Market (Oxford 2009).

[1202] It is but a slight overstatement to say that, in a sense, this reverses the traditional relationship between the law and the market: no longer does the law determine what the market can do; instead, the market determines what the law can do: see *Muir-Watt* (*supra* n. 1178) 600–601. Ultimately this is because today economic activity is more mobile than state authority.

for the allocation of power and of resources. It is one of the twenty-first century's challenges for the mainstream to acknowledge these implications and consequences more broadly, to explore them more thoroughly, and to take responsibility for them more openly. This is best accomplished in a clear-headed and balanced, rather than an ideological and one-sided, fashion. At the end of the day, comparatists, like all legal scholars, must not duck the question of how their work helps to create winners and losers, and how it serves, or does not serve, the cause of justice.

LIST OF PRINCIPAL WORKS

Gerber, Globalization and Legal Knowledge: Implications for Comparative Law: 75 Tul.L.Rev. (2001) 949

Kennedy, Three Globalizations of Law and Legal Thought: 1850–2000: *Trubek and Santos* (eds.), The New Law and Economics Development: A Critical Appraisal (Cambridge 2006) 19–73

L'Avenir du Droit Comparé: Rev.int.dr.comp. 51 (1999) 747–1071 (collection of essays on the state and future of comparative law in more than a dozen countries)

Legrand and Munday (eds.), Comparative Legal Studies: Traditions and Transitions (Cambridge, New York 2003)

Muir-Watt, Globalization and Comparative Law: *Reimann and Zimmermann* (eds.), The Oxford Handbook of Comparative Law (ed. 2 Oxford 2019) 599–623

Reimann, Beyond National Legal Systems: A Comparative Law for the International Age: 75 Tul.L.Rev. 1103–1119 (2001)

Teubner (ed.), Global Law without a State (Brookfield UK, Dartmouth NH 1997)

Twining, Globalization and Comparative Law: Maastricht J.Eur.Comp.L. 6 (1999) 217, reprinted in *Twining*, Globalization and Legal Theory (London 2000) 174.

VIII. A Summary and Final Critique

396. *Summary: a vast and diverse terrain.* – A hundred, or even fifty years ago, comparative law was a discipline of fairly modest proportions: it pursued mainly the comparison of the positive law(s) of a limited number of Western legal systems, subscribed to a limited number of uses and goals, and engaged a limited number of approaches and methods. There was broad consensus about its parameters, general agreement about its essential literature, and a fairly clear understanding of what it meant to be a comparatist. Since then, the discipline has constantly expanded (since the 1990s at break-neck speed) in three major regards. It has hugely broadened its – geographic as well subject matter – coverage (*supra* IV.); it has embraced various new uses and goals (*supra* V.); and in pursuit of them it has added an array of new approaches and methods, sometimes opening interdisciplinary dimensions (*supra* VI.); most recently, it has engaged with global legal pluralism, further adding breadth and complexity (*supra* VII.B.). As a result, comparative law in the early twenty-first century is a vast and highly diversified terrain, constantly producing a veritable deluge of studies ranging across an extremely broad spectrum of topics. Of course, these studies vary greatly in quality, but on the whole they constitute a rich and multifaceted body of work, often generating insight that is intellectually interesting and sometimes even practically useful.

397. *Critique: a loss of coherence – and identity.* – At the same time, comparative law has lost most of its erstwhile coherence and, at least arguably, a clear identity.

The discipline's massive growth and diversification have come at the expense of unity. Today, comparative legal studies are so broadly scattered over so vast a range of agendas, projects, topics, and issues that they connect, if at all, only within certain specialties. They are not anchored to a common center. A major reason for this lack of overall connection is that there is no consensus anymore about what, if anything, actually constitutes comparative law's ground zero. The fragmentation of the discipline has a personal side as well: scholars engaged in different kinds of comparative work often do not talk to each other; note that many prominent scholars in the field never attend the general (national or international) comparative law congresses.

While comparatists are, by and large, not very concerned about this state of affairs, the lack of a common platform and of communication across specialties impedes the progress of the discipline in an important regard: since individual studies remain largely unconnected, they rarely build on each other, rarely generate synergy, and thus rarely create broader insight. As a result, comparatists have accumulated enormous amounts of information about, and a thorough understanding of, a huge number of individual topics and areas, but disappointingly little generalizable knowledge about law – its unity and diversity, its structure and development, its conditions and impact, etc.

The discipline's enormous diversity has also made it increasingly difficult to define its identity. Today, perhaps the only reliable criterion is that "comparative law" involves the study of more than one legal system – whatever that system, whatever its elements, from whatever perspective, for whatever purpose, and by whatever method. In a sense, such extreme openness is beneficial because it avoids artificial boundaries that hinder creative (and especially interdisciplinary) work. Still, the lack of a more specifically defined identity has at least two pernicious effects. First, it entails the lack of an established canon of knowledge and skill, which, in turn, prevents the establishment of serious graduate study requirements. Thus, comparative law is largely open to the trained and untrained alike. As a result, many, if not most, comparative studies are undertaken by whoever feels like undertaking them – a situation which would seem intolerable in most other disciplines, such as legal history or law and economics. Second, letting scholars pretty much define for themselves what they mean by comparative law makes it difficult to agree upon academic standards. Thus, outside of the few internationally recognized peer-reviewed journals, the discipline has frequently been afflicted by a weakness of quality control which cognate fields like private international law or legal anthropology would scarcely tolerate.

Reasonable people can differ about whether this loss of coherence and identity is an inevitable side-effect of the discipline's enormous expansion – or rather the result of insufficient attention to its theoretical foundations. The fact that public international law has experienced a similar expansion and even fragmentation without an equally pronounced loss of coherence and identity suggests the latter. In any event, if comparative law continues on its current course of growth and diversification without a concomitant establishment of theoretical foundations that define the parameters of the field, it may soon become pointless to speak of comparative law as an identifiable discipline at all, for better or worse.

(Completed February 2020.)

DETAILED TABLE OF CONTENTS

www.ingramcontent.com/pod-product-compliance
Lightning Source LLC
Chambersburg PA
CBHW061205240926
51846CB00006B/1117